Luca Chittaro (Ed.)

Human-Computer Interaction with Mobile Devices and Services

5th International Symposium, Mobile HCI 2003
Udine, Italy, September 8-11, 2003
Proceedings

Springer

Series Editors

Gerhard Goos, Karlsruhe University, Germany
Juris Hartmanis, Cornell University, NY, USA
Jan van Leeuwen, Utrecht University, The Netherlands

Volume Editor

Luca Chittaro
University of Udine
HCI Lab., Dept. of Math. and Computer Science
via delle Scienze 206, 33100 Udine, Italy
E-mail: chittaro@dimi.uniud.it

Cataloging-in-Publication Data applied for

A catalog record for this book is available from the Library of Congress

Bibliographic information published by Die Deutsche Bibliothek
Die Deutsche Bibliothek lists this publication in the Deutsche Nationalbibliografie;
detailed bibliographic data is available in the Internet at <http://dnb.ddb.de>.

CR Subject Classification (1998): H.5.2, H.5.3, H.5, H.4, C.2, I.2.1

ISSN 0302-9743
ISBN 3-540-40821-5 Springer-Verlag Berlin Heidelberg New York

Springer-Verlag Berlin Heidelberg New York
a member of BertelsmannSpringer Science+Business Media GmbH

http://www.springer.de

© Springer-Verlag Berlin Heidelberg 2003
Printed in Germany

Typesetting: Camera-ready by author, data conversion by DA-TeX Gerd Blumenstein
Printed on acid-free paper   SPIN 10931882   06/3142   5 4 3 2 1 0

Preface

Predictions about the booming future of mobile technologies and talk about the mobile revolution abound in every medium, from newspapers to Internet discussions, from TV shows to technical journals. It is given as granted that very soon the most common way to access the Internet will be through mobile devices and that everyone, even those who never wanted to use a computer, will embrace the use of mobile services. However, if human-computer interaction issues of mobile technologies are not properly addressed, the above mentioned scenario is not so likely to come true. Users (especially novice ones) will not enthusiastically adopt mobile computing devices if we are not able to prevent the pains and complexities of interacting through very limited input and output facilities. Mobile services will not be successful if we do not understand mobile users and design for their contexts, those are very different from ones which traditionally studied in HCI.

This volume contains the papers accepted for the Mobile HCI 2003 Symposium on Human-Computer Interaction with Mobile Devices and Services, the premier international conference where academics and practitioners meet to discuss the challenges and potential solutions for effective interaction with mobile devices and services. It covers the design, evaluation and application of HCI techniques and approaches for mobile computing devices and services. This strong focus and specialization on HCI aspects is what makes the symposium truly unique and differentiates it from the other conferences and workshops in Mobile, Ubiquitous and Pervasive computing, that either have a very broad scope or specialize in different aspects.

The 2003 edition of Mobile HCI was the fifth in a series. The first three editions were held as international workshops (in Glasgow in 1998, in Edinburgh at INTERACT 1999, in Lille at IHM-HCI-2001). Then, last year, Mobile HCI successfully expanded into a full symposium (held in Pisa).

In these years, Mobile HCI has kept growing, and this year is no exception. Paper submissions grew significantly with respect to last year (in particular, the number of full paper submissions grew by 60%). This led to a lower acceptance rate and a higher-quality program. In detail, we received 122 paper submissions, of which 63 were full papers and 59 were short papers. Very strict selection rules were applied, and only 21 full papers and 29 short papers were accepted (i.e., a 33% selection rate for full papers and a 49% selection rate for short papers). The Workshops and tutorials proposals also grew: a total of 9 proposals were received, and 6 of them reached the final stage, turning into Mobile HCI 2003 events (5 Workshops and 1 tutorial). The submissions also reflected a truly international spectrum of work, coming from 26 countries.

Many individuals helped in shaping and organizing Mobile HCI 2003, and I thank them all for spending their time, energy, and competence for the symposium. The members of the Program Committee and the additional reviewers carefully read submissions and provided useful suggestions for their improvement. The members of the Local Organizing Committee helped me to carry out a long list of tasks needed to make everything run smoothly during the four symposium days in Udine. The sponsors helped reduce the participants' registration fees, thanks to their donations.

As a whole, this volume shows how the spectrum of HCI methods (ranging from ethnographic studies to automatic interface generation) is being exploited and adapted in a wide range of mobile contexts and applications (ranging from healthcare to gaming), giving a clear picture of today's state of the art in Mobile Human-Computer Interaction. I thus hope that both novices and experts in Mobile HCI will find it a useful source of reference and valuable information regarding the current state of research and practice in the field.

Udine, June 2003

Luca Chittaro
Chair
Mobile HCI 2003

Committees

Chair

Luca Chittaro   *HCI Lab, University of Udine*

Program Committee

Keith Cheverst,	*University of Lancaster*
Luca Chittaro,	*University of Udine*
Joelle Coutaz,	*University of Grenoble*
Boris de Ruyter,	*Philips Research*
Alan Dix,	*vfridge limited*
Mark Dunlop,	*University of Strathclyde*
Tom Gross,	*Fraunhofer FIT*
Ken Hinckley,	*Microsoft Research*
Matt Jones,	*University of Waikato*
Anne Kaikkonen,	*Nokia Research*
Pekka Ketola,	*Nokia Mobile Phones*
Brad Myers,	*Carnegie Mellon University*
Laurence Nigay,	*University of Grenoble*
Reinhardt Opperman,	*Fraunhofer FIT*
Fabio Paternò,	*C.N.R. – ISTI*
Matthias Rauterberg,	*University of Eindhoven*
Jun Rekimoto,	*Sony – CSL*
Daniel Salber,	*IBM – T.J. Watson*
Andrew Sears,	*UMBC*
Chris Schmandt,	*MIT Media Lab*
Albrecht Schmidt,	*University of Munich*
Mathias Schneider-Hufschmidt,	*Siemens*
Constantine Stephanidis,	*Forth*
Manfred Tscheligi,	*CURE*
Bruno von Niman,	*Ericsson*
David Williams,	*Motorola*

Local Organizing Committee

Paolo Coppola,	*University of Udine*
Vincenzo Della Mea,	*University of Udine*
Luca Di Gaspero,	*University of Udine*
Stefano Mizzaro,	*University of Udine*
Roberto Ranon,	*University of Udine*

Additional Reviewers

Ayatsuka, Y.
Bradley, N.
Calvary, G.
Clarkson, B.
Coppola, P.
Della Mea, V.
Eisenhauer, M.
Karefilaki, L.
Klann, M.
Laurillau, Y.
Lorenz, A.
Mohamad, Y.
Nichols, J.
Pachoulakis, Y.
Poupyrev, I.
Protogeros, Z.
Ranon, R.
Rashev, R.
Schmidt-Belz, B.
Tajima, S.
Terrenghi, L.
Zarikas, V.

Sponsors

Gold Level

http://hcilab.uniud.it

Silver Level

http://www.nokia.com

http://www.microsoft.com/italy

Bronze Level

http://www.philips.com

http://web.uniud.it

Fondazione Cassa di Risparmio
di Udine e Pordenone

http://www.fondazionecrup.it

Table of Contents

Location-Aware Guides and Planners

Bringing Mobile Services to Groups in Workplaces

Mobile Gaming

Tools and Frameworks for Mobile Interface Design and Generation

Usability and HCI Research Methods

Short Talks

Posters

People versus Information:
The Evolution of Mobile Technology

Richard Harper

Appliance Studio, Bristol, the Digital World Research Centre
University of Surrey, England

Abstract. This reports research on users' attitudes towards and use of GSM devices and discusses the implications these have for the future evolution of hand-held devices. It argues that current usage patterns suggest that there is unlikely to be a widespread convergence of information accessing devices and person to person communication devices. It also argues that the latter devices and their associated applications could provide much richer opportunities for communication behaviours than is currently available, and that therefore design efforts within the mobile HCI community should focus on this rather than on information use applications.

1   Introduction

1.1   Mobile HCI

If one looks back at the history of mobile HCI, one can see that certain assumptions have underscored the research undertaken within its auspices. Expressed very simply, it has been the case that the research questions have to do with information usage. This in turn has split into two main research topics: access to information when remote and away from an office, and, on the other hand, interaction with information on the hand held devices themselves. The one has to do with the constraints of interaction over distance [e.g. 24], the other with constraints of interaction on small scale devices [e.g., 14,23]. More recently, this basic dichotomy has been supplemented with a concern for how interaction with people (or other users if you will) may be combined with information access. This has taken many forms, ranging from location-based services applications through to how different user groups bring themselves together with the use of distinct types of information, such as provided by games and sports [2, 12].

Throughout the history of mobile HCI there have of course been various tangential research activities that don't fit so easily within these basic assumptions and subsequent strands of research activity. My own early work on location-based services, for example, was one such activity [9]. Here we had neither a clear idea of what information may be interacted with nor how that might augment person to person communications. There are many other curios within the research literature. But these tan-

L. Chittaro (Ed.): Mobile HCI 2003, LNCS 2795, pp. 1-14, 2003.

gents notwithstanding, mobile HCI has remained and is essentially about human-information interaction over devices that are remote and small, in varying degree. In this regard, mobile HCI has been primarily concerned with what goes on inside the head and not, if you like, with what goes on in the heart. It has been concerned what the mind thinks rather than what the body feels.

Without wanting to suggest that this dichotomy between the heart and the mind is the only one of note—though I shall come back to this—what I am wanting to argue is that the information centric assumptions of mobile HCI are not the only ones that one might wish to start with. One could easily start from a different set of assumptions, and this would lead research in different directions. Now it seems to me that one might not want to treat this problem in a *carte blanche* fashion, as if it did not matter which set of assumptions research is built on. After all, a great deal of effort goes into building up the assumptions that underscores any discipline. Nonetheless, it is worth while to occasionally revisit these assumptions and consider whether other disciplines, other paradigms, have something to say about them that may justify their revision.

As a case in point, mobile communications engineering is a discipline that has, until very recently, been quite separate form the HCI community, yet at the current time seems to be moving into a similar space, albeit with a very different set of agendas and research questions. This is because its assumptions are quite distinct. Though the computing power that mobile communications researchers take for granted is equally large to that in mobile HCI, the opportunities that this power is thought to afford, the way that this is leveraged to offer new services and applications, and the model of human needs that underscores examination of these issues, are all different. Instead of interaction with information, it is emotional action with partners, instead of navigation with information on hand held devices, it is navigation to one's friends and family that is investigated; instead of speed of data entry and retrieval, it is the social cost of a communication that is important.

These differences are not merely incidental. They have all sorts of implications for evolution of the research questions that each programme of inquiry—or paradigm if you will—undertakes. They also have implications for certain ideas and beliefs that underscore both. For example, it is commonly believed in both the mobile HCI and mobile communications paradigms that future devices will combine the properties of each: the *converged device*, for want of a more suitable term, will offer both communications power and information access.

But it does not seem unreasonable to ask whether this will happen: after all, can the design solutions of each satisfy both? Or will it be the case that one will win out over the other? In other words, is convergence another name for the dominance of one paradigm over another? Besides, are the two so different anyway that attempts to satisfy what is understood to be the problems that each has to solve will inevitably produce solutions that, in trying to please everyone, please no-one at all, least of all the lowly user?

I want to reflect on the particular differences between mobile communications research and mobile HCI not merely for the sake of it, but because now is an especially opportune time to do so. For one thing, many commentators claim that convergence is imminent; for another, and I think this is more important, there is an increasing amount of data about human behaviour that indicates how the future might be shaped by the user and not by the industry (or even for that matter the research community related to that industry). This is particularly the case in relation to the ways in which people might want to optimize their use of mobile technology. This may force a re-visiting of the idea of convergence.

I want to suggest, and bring a little bit of empirical evidence to show, that the future of mobile devices will be first and foremost about offering users the ability to keep in touch with friends, family and colleagues, and that this will take precedence over technologies and applications that will offer information access and use. This is not to say that the latter will have no role, but it is to say that their role will be of less significance to the user. This will in turn have numerous implications for the kind of devices people will want to carry around with them and, relatedly, the kinds of bundles of services that they want these devices to provide. I will argue that they will want devices that support communication above all else, and other services will be subordinate to this. One consequence of this will be that some services will not find a place in the bundles, and the reasons for this will have to do with what the hierarchy of user preferences imply in terms of the interaction mode(s) that devices support. These modes will constrain what is possible on devices, not in the sense that it might be impossible to design some services and applications for certain of these modes, but because users will find it too hard to do so. Doing so will be, to put it colloquially, too much bother for them. In short, I will argue that to be *in touch* constantly and easily will compromise the design of applications that offer *information use*. To satisfy the former, user needs result in the usability requirements of the latter being cast aside.

This does not mean that the future will be a dull area to research. Just because communications between people will take precedence over interaction with information does not reduce the opportunities for insightful and creative design. The use of information supporting devices will continue, I believe, and thus research will need to continue apace—though these devices might not be so important as some researchers currently think.

On the communications side, even more research is needed than has been undertaken to date. After all, the user of mobile devices would find little different between the devices they currently use and the fixed point telephone user of the 1930s and 40s. The only difference perhaps is the short text messaging service. And yet the possibilities for human contact are inordinately rich and diverse. I am convinced that the future of communication will be as broad as we can design it to be, though as yet no-one has stirred up the mobile communications community to produce any such insights. If the mobile HCI community has been creatively barking up the wrong tree by focusing on information use, the mobile communications community has not even discovered it can bark.

1.2   The Research

I will make this argument on the basis of research I and my colleagues have been undertaking for the mobile industry over a number of years [1,3,24,25,26,27].For those who have been funded by the computer industry, this might hint at the possibility that what I am claiming simply reflects the paradigm of my paymasters. But this is not the case. After all, and this is to restate what I have just mentioned, the idea of convergence—the myth of it if you will—is held equally in the mobile industry as it is in the computer systems world. Both industries have much at stake when it comes to convergence. Neither wants the future to unfold in the way the evidence suggests. Besides, my view is based on evidence from studies of people using technology and these studies have included looking at information use devices just as much as communications devices. This research has been solely motivated by a concern with the user, not with how I or anyone else thinks the future ought to be.

2   From Analogue, to GSM to UMTS

2.1   A Brief History

Mobile telephony is now omnipresent so it may be hard to realise how rapid and recent has been its mergence, especially when compared to the slow pace of adoption for office information systems. In the UK and the rest of Europe, for example, analogue TACS/NMT mobile phone services became available in 1985 and the GSM digital service in 1993 yet by the end of the decade GSM devices were an everyday occurrence.

One also might forget that although people quickly became familiar with the concept of mobile telephony, it was at the outset high priced and targeted at business users. Yet oddly enough, organisational management were unpersuaded of the benefits the technology might provide, and initial take-up of the technology within business was essentially on an individual rather than corporate basis, where individual staff adopted the technology and then gradually demonstrated to their colleagues the benefits they derived. Eventually, business management as a whole began to recognise these benefits and so began to be more willing to pay for and support mobile devices. Despite a regulatory framework designed to reduce price, the products still remained expensive and thus were expected to continue to be primarily for business use. Yet, once businesses made the technology familiar to the public at large, there was an unexpected and rapid growth in non-business, consumer demand. This became so strong that, in less than a handful of years—by the mid to late nineties—a point had been reached where owning a mobile became a social norm, particularly in Western Europe and Japan.

In simple terms, the history of the mobile can then be described as, first of all, a period of individual business people pulling the technology; second, their success leading to a period of business management pull, which resulted in a sufficient level of familiarity with the general public for a third period during which the consumer at large adopted the technology very rapidly; and fourth, this eventually resulted in the situation we have now where having a mobile phone is virtually a social necessity.

In many respects, this path of evolution and in particular, the unexpected uptake of mobile communications as a mass consumer product was a boon for the industry, though the fact that this was a surprise is testament to how ineffective the mobile industry has been at understanding its market place. This is all the more surprising when it is realised that the pattern of adoption of mobile devices is in fact common with the introduction of other technologies, including the fixed line telephone at the start of the last century and the introduction of televisual broadcasting technologies in the middle part of that century [3]. Whether a similar pattern will hold true with UMTS and other so-called 3G standards, is, of course, part of the subject matter of the research reported here.

2.2   The Social Shaping of the Mobile

In any event, if this is the general character of the take up, the actual impact of the mobile phone itself is another matter. Initially the mobile phone did not displace other communications devices, most especially the fixed line. Certainly there was continual change in the technologies in the users' hands, but this had more to do with the cycle of new mobile systems being introduced and replacing antiquated technologies than in what the technology could do [3,27].

Overall however, mobile telephony created an addition to people's lives rather than substitution of previously existing telephony and communications systems. The result was that mobile phones expanded what is called in the literature the 'ecology' of communications technologies, and in so doing became as important to work, family and personal life as the fixed phone and other communications systems [10].

There were nonetheless substantial differences in this ecology, according to culture, social class and the myriad types of relationship consumers could have with providers and manufacturers. This relationship was mediated through not only the devices themselves but also in such mechanisms as billing and payments methods. Differences showed themselves in prepaid being a success in Europe and less so elsewhere, for example, and in the brand acceptance of some terminal manufacturers over others [27].

Research on these and other topics is quite extensive, and without wanting to go into detail about it all, a number of main areas or topics of inquiry can be identified. To begin with, there is a consensus that mobile phones had—and continue—to reinvigorate social relations through providing a voice or text mediated form of face-to-face relations. Some commentators view this 'virtual presence' as counterbalancing the increasing social isolation created by other new digital media, such as interactive digital TV, computer gaming and the Internet [7, 11]. This benefit made mobile communications unlike other digital technologies and unique from the users' perspective.

It is also argued that with mobile communications, person to business relationships could become much more personalised than before, with mobile communications allowing more intimate and frequent contacts. In large part this is because mobile networks provide much more fine grained, 'particularised' information about user behaviours than has been possible hitherto [21], though users did not—and still do not—perceive this as a concern nor has business effectively leverage any opportunities this provides. Much of this data has remained untapped (though new services are likely to latch onto its possibilities – location services, spam text and so on)

Mobile phones also result in more private behaviours in public spaces than ever before, with gradually fewer boundaries to acceptance of where and when people can use their mobile phones. This is a world wide phenomenon, though the extent to which it occurs varies between different countries. This particular aspect of mobile devies is perhaps the one that's been given the most attention, with research reporting the effects of this in Finland [18], France [8], Italy [4,5], the Far East [17] and elsewhere.

Lastly, and this returns us to the main theme of this paper, many commentators argue that the relationship between the user and the device itself has become much more emotional than was hitherto the case with computer technologies. It is argued that this is a function of the social connectivity that mobile phones afford and thus reflects a relationship with the content more so than the device itself [4,16,19,20].

2.3   Explorations in the Emotional Dimension

Clearly, each of these dimensions are deserving of much attention. The one I am exploring here, though, the one about emotion, has I think, a number of important implications. To understand these though requires some careful thought, however.

For example, Fortunanti [4] suggests that mobile devices are treated in an emotionally distinct way because they are, as she puts it, charismatic. This results in users spending more on their mobiles than they would on any other technology, and being covetous of the devices themselves, getting highly distressed when they are lost, and making sure that they are always near them, like a child or a partner. Fortunati makes no suggestions as to what the implications of this might be for future services but it seems not unreasonable to assume that if this is the case, then they should be designed to reflect this charisma, irrespective of how that might be done. Certainly, in human factors and ergonomics and more recently even in HCI, the idea that emotional reactions to an object, what one might call the lust of an aesthetic, has been gaining prominence, whether it be in the work of Jordan in ergonomics [14] or Norman in HCI.

Be that as it may, Fortunati's view suggests that it is simply the object itself that engenders emotional reaction, as if the need for a mobile phone is merely created by marketing. But in contrast, most of the research on mobiles, including my own, takes a different view and this holds that the emotional value is a result of what people do with their phones. In this view, the shape or form of the device—those properties that might reflect its charismatic nature—seem less important than its functions.

Some evidence by a project by Ericsson sums up the issue I and my colleagues have begun to identify (though as it happens the Ericsson researchers do not take the same lesson from it) [22]. Be that as it may, in their research, a young woman from Singapore was presented with all the hand-held and portable devices she currently used or could buy, including her mobile phone, PDA, Blackberry and Walkman, and was then asked which she would like bundled together. Her response was to say that she wanted everything to go into one object *except* the mobile phone. That was special, she explained, and too important to be mixed up with other things. She did not trust that if it were put in with other devices it would be capable of doing what she wanted it to.

Of course, this begs the question of what exactly she did with her phone as well as the question as to what she thought the Ericsson researchers in particular would do to it—given their poor reputation for user friendly devices. That aside, her comments allude to and resonate with the bulk of research into user behaviours that indicates that something about the role of the mobile phone, something about its shape, form and function, when combined, results in users finding that mobiles play an irreplaceable role in their daily lives: not in the sense of bringing charisma to their existence, but in the sense that the phones become key tools in their lives, one of such importance that mobile phones even appear to affect who they are.

2.4   A Methodological Approach to the Issue

Now, as we were gleaning various perspective on emotion in the literature and listening to presentations by Ericsson and others, we were not quite sure where the inkling that something more was afoot might lead to, or even if it would lead us any where at all. But the general swell of evidence recommended us to explore further. We had already been undertaking extensive ethnographic studies, so we opted to compliment these with a research approach that could be more focused. We also wanted to undertake some international comparison. Therefore we decided to undertake focus groups activities with colleagues in Germany (Erfurt) and in the UK (London and South East). We also issued a fairly detailed questionnaire that was completed by 72 individuals in the UK and France. We then presented results from these activities to key players in the mobile industry to test whether our evidence resonated with their insights, and if not, whether it might be revised. The results made it clear that the view of people like Fortunati, though certainly capturing some of the issues in question, did not quite capture the full salience of them. It is to explore what they are that we now turn.

2.5   The Language of Users

Findings from different data sources obviously need to made tractable in various sorts of ways. In our ethnographic research for example, we had discovered that many of the texting activities of the people we studied could be thought of as kinds of gift giving, though many of our subjects would not use that term themselves [25,26]. In contrast, one of the tasks we set ourselves in the focus group endeavour was to address the very issue of language and understanding, and to try and capture users' own ways of formulating and describing their experience.

What we found is that in some of the focus groups, particularly in the UK, few people use the term emotion to describe their relationship with mobiles: *"It's a funny way of putting it"* being a common response to the proposition. Elsewhere, in Germany for example, the term seemed to accurately capture what users though themselves.

Beyond these differences in the initial formulation of language terms, what we did find is that most of our subjects, wherever they were and irrespective of their age, gender or income, use emotional language categories to explain their mobile usage. These categories could be listed and categorized in ways that reflect the complexity of the term emotion. We found that there appeared to be six main types or dimensions of emotional language category used to account for ownership and use.

Strangeness This is perhaps the most interesting term since it is suggestive of how fundamental mobile ownership has become. The term was used to label those who don't have mobile phones. They were viewed as strange not in the sense that "these days everyone has a mobile" and that these people were merely unfashionable. The term strange was used to intimate the idea that those people who do have a mobile phone must live in a world that is quite unlike the world of everyone else. In light of the above account of panic, those who exist without a mobile must be, according to this view, attenuated from society at large. In other words, non-owners could not be normal in a profound sense.

Panic Here the term was used to describe the feelings that absence from the device created. Now, though users of PC's might also feel a sense of panic when their machines break or perhaps are removed from their desktops for one reason or another, the tenor of the panic produced by the loss of the mobile is quite distinct. Here the panic is not for the loss of money or value in the device itself, it is panic for the loss of being in touch that resulted. To put this boldly: what the focus groups suggested is that to loose one's mobile means to loose one's connection to society. T loose one's PC is to not be able to work for a while or undertake some leisure activity.

Irrationality One negative consequence of ownership and use is the fact that people recognize that often they cannot control their behaviour with mobiles. In this sense their actions really are emotional, insofar as it is sometimes the heart that exerts control over the mind, rather than the other way round. The best example of this is when people use their mobile while driving, despite the fact that they 'know' it's dangerous.

Thrill Another obvious manifestations of emotion comes from the excitement that is induced by using mobile devices in particular ways: there is the novelty of use for example, though this pales with familiarity. More permanently, thrill comes from the ability to transcend the borders of public and private behaviours: receiving intimate texts in public places is one such activity.

Anxiety One consequence of having a mobile and knowing that others do too, is the realisation that people might have personal reasons not to be in contact with one another. It is no longer technology that thwarts them. If this is so, then people get anxious because they want to know what are the reasons why some one might not be willing to call. Is it because they are angry? Have they forgotten to? Are they ill? Not knowing the answer to these questions makes people worry. Conversely, if one can always be in touch, when has one been in touch *enough*? How much more could one know? What is the right balance?

2.6   The Actions of Users

So, these are the language categories that people use to explain and account for their relationship with mobile phones. Certainly, these would seem to confirm the idea that there is a distinctly emotional flavour to this experience, and moreover suggest that this is potentially powerful: those who do not own a mobile are viewed as existing in an almost different world to 'normal people', one where being in touch does not matter. According to this, it would appear that having a mobile is not a perk of the 21st century but a prerequisite of living.

Ideas and modes of expression are not sufficient to fully understand what is the character of the mobile in modern society, of course. There is also the question of what people do with their mobiles. Again, from the focus groups, what became clear is that the primary goals relate to achieving emotional ends.

Perhaps the most obvious and most commonly reported has to do with setting up social arrangements: *"I call my friends ...stupid calls...I'm meeting them in half an hour and I'll call them, speak to them... until I meet them"*. Another has to do with avoiding making set appointment times - just arrange to call when you get there: *"meeting in a big park of people"*. And a third (though there are more) has to do with making or breaking relationships: *"You can be silly on texting, you're too embarrassed to phone"*; *"If I want to speak to my girlfriend any time of the day I know that I can & it kind of takes the fun out of it when I'm seeing her."*

In addition to emotional goals, users also behave 'emotionally' in the sense of behave in irrational ways, as alluded to above in the discussion of language terms. They constantly call their partner/spouse, for example, even when they are in the same house: *"I just feel the need to"*. They use the mobile impetuously: *"I just had to call someone"*. And even though they know they should not, they use it in places that creates danger: *"Even when I am driving and I go over those mini roundabouts in 4th [gear]."*

2.7   Interviews with Experts

Before we began trying to explore what these findings meant in terms of the future evolution of services and products, we tested them against what the industry as whole knew about users. The response of various industry experts to these materials, in marketing, in product design and in strategy departments, was generally confirming, though the extent to which the relationship with mobiles could be described as emotional varied according to cultural differences, as we found in our own focus groups. In Israel and Germany, it appeared that there was a widespread recognition of these values, while in the UK this was not so clear. In other countries, Sweden, Italy and Ireland, the view seemed to be somewhere in the middle.

All concurred, however, in believing such things as the personalisation of GSM devices (colour, directories, ring tones) was less a reflection of the normal pattern of the evolution of consumer products (where personalisation to some degree is used to differentiate products) as an indication of the particularly emotional character of users' attitudes toward mobile devices. Some even remarked on the way mobile devices are held and touched to affirm their own understanding that the users relationship with mobiles is indeed different from their relationship with other products, cultural differences of expression notwithstanding.

Looking toward the future, the expert panel commented that, in the first instance, they would be attempting to leverage emotional values to identify and sell new products. Key to this will be using emotional relationships between friends as a route to offer services and products that augment those relationships. In the longer term, the panel explained that they would introduce products and services that would be less and less emotional, thus leading themselves out of the confines of satisfying purely emotional needs. Their view was that they need to start developing 3G services through leveraging person to person emotional needs, and then, step by step, introduce more person to information-like services.

3   Implications

Using emotion in the way described by these industry experts to maximise the potential of products and services would appear to mechallenging not least because it demands a level of understanding of customers—existing and potential—that has kot, historically, at least, been known by the mobile industry. It demands knowledge of the purpose of the user's communications, for example, of how those purposes deliver particular kinds of emotional value, and so forth, that is at a level of granularity that does not seem to fit the typically high level modeling of user needs deployed in the industry.

For instance, the use of SIM card readers by some service providers to collect and store information held on mobiles—phone numbers in particular—is a present day example of a service that responds to users' fear of losing data but goes only a small way to addressing how to do so in a way that reflects the emotional value given to some of the information stored on their phone. Much more needs to be understood about how emotional values are delivered and preserved before designers can identify ways of leveraging opportunities related to emotion. After all, these SIM card readers cannot distinguish between numbers that the users thought they had deleted and those that they 'really want'; between those numbers that link them to people that matter on an emotional level and those that were put in there temporarily for a short trip or such like. The latter can be forgotten; the former are too precious and may even be kept when the relationship in question has finished. SIM card readers treat stored information as much of a muchness (i.e., as all the same). For this to change, of course, not only will the reader technology have to change, since one would imagine that there would also need to be changes in the design of the virtual address book so that application that relied upon in it, like the SIM card reader, would be instructed as to types of information stored on it. One can imagine an address book for temporary numbers for example, the stuff that does not need to be copied over, and a book for personal and permanent numbers, that should be.

This is but one prosaic example illustrating the general point that a failure to understand the emotional aspects of the 'mobile experience' could lead not just to failure to offer everything users might want, but even to undermining their needs. New services could fail if they replace or impinge upon services to which the user ascribes an emotional attachment. For example, the threat of losing text messaging and having it replaced by new technologically better services may create considerable resistance from users. For not only is texting now a key tool in sustaining emotional lives, but storing personal text messages is now a highly valuable element to people's emotional arsenal [1,25,26]. SMS may be thought of as simply a communicative technique from the supplier's point of view, but to the user it has values over and above this [11].

Relatedly, the adoption of new form factors may affect these emotional values. For instance, the current size of GSM devices supports constant carrying around: *"it never leaves you"*, as one of our subjects put it. This means that users are never forced to relinquish contact with those they need to be in contact with. Now, it should be clear that before GSM they would have had to be out of reach for certain times of the day and in certain places. The point is that with GSM they have come to expect this constant access. Future devices must not threaten this. Many information delivering services and products, for example, require larger screens than most current GSM devices do, and this may lead to expanding the form factor to a level that makes constant carrying difficult or at least irritating and burdensome. It does not matter whether these new devices are provided by UMTS providers or the Wire-fee community, each reflecting the two distinct domains of mobile research mentioned earlier, the outcome from the perspective of the user would be the same.

Similarly, one-handed input means that it can be used at almost any time *"even when driving"*. Many 3G devices, particularly those which combine the PDA form factor with soft keyboards for dialing and so forth, require two handed in-put. This inhibits the places in which they can be used. Clearly in some respects this could be advantage: stopping people using the mobile while driving may be viewed by some as a way of increasing safety on the road, for instance. But for many users it is precisely the ability to be in touch at any time that provides the value that has made the GSM phone distinct. Assault these values with new products, even if it is only at the edge, and the overall value may be diminished.

Beyond these specificities of form factor and service change inertia, a further and perhaps more significant implication is that demand for services that sustain emotional lives may be highly inelastic: people may pay "whatever it costs" to have and use a mobile phone (though the cheapest will do). This may drive out other devices simply because the user may have to choose what to spend their disposable income on. Thus, it may be that users will always choose a communications device first, even though this might leave no budget for information access and use devices. This may be despite the fact that the user may recognise that some value would be provided by owning such a device. Their predicament however, relates to the fact that their communications needs, their desire to be in touch and to satisfy their emotional lives, swallows up all the cash they have.

4   Conclusion

What has been argued then has to do with how user needs and patterns of behaviour might shape future demand for services and products. At one level, the argument has been that users place a different value on what one might call information, on the one hand, and words, on the other. The former may be thought of as the kind of content that, let us say, the Web provides, the latter as the kind of content that GSM devices provide (though the latter includes both the spoken and the written word). The claim is that'person to person' connectivity services engender emotion and that in so doing create considerable value. In contrast, 'person to information' connectivity does not achieve the same emotional value. The result is that when it comes to the crunch, when it comes to having to choose between spending on one rather than the other, it would appear that emotion will win out over information.

Now, of course, it may be that in the future the cost of either kind of service will not force a choice between one or the other, though at the current time this looks like being unlikely. But irrespective of economics and the kinds of disposable incomes people may have in the not too distant future, there is also an ergonomic argument that leads to the same conclusion. For the evidence also suggests that the capacity to be 'in touch' any time and place, irrespective of the danger and irrational behaviours that results, is a key added value for the mobile user. The form factor of the current GSM devices, then, may satisfy a need that new form factors more ideally suited to other needs, such as information use, might not satisfy so well.

Underscoring this is what is sometimes called the appliance argument. This holds that interactive devices need to be designed to offer 'radical ease of use' through placing the primary function at the top of the level of functions[13]. In so doing the ideal design for usability is optimized for the application that is most sought after by the user. One byproduct of this is that all other applications have their usability needs compromised. As I said at the outset, though this may result in devices that can be used for a host of applications, in practice, this may lead users to only use one or two applications, primarily the communications ones as I suggest, because the others are too much bother. The users may feel that they just take too long to use, or are simply too difficult. Needless to say, it might be possible to create designs that optimise a multiplicity of applications so that such compromises need not occur. Sadly, if one looks at the efforts of mobile HCI and the mobile communications research community, the likelihood of this occurring is very slim indeed.

But in any case it might be that trying to solve this particularly obdurate problem is not an area that research should focus on. If one thinks about human communication in the general, one will note that exchanges between people are not all the same, as if a hello were the same as a summons, as if a whisper from a lover is the same as a bellow from a boss. Yet if one looks at current communications applications and protocols one will see there are few alternatives made available to the user, and people cannot vary the ways they call their friends, partners, or colleagues, except perhaps through the use of text. Indeed, perhaps this is precisely why texting has been so popular. There are beginning to appear some design ideas that explore this space but as yet these are too few and too limited in imagination. This need not be so. I urge mobile HCI and the communications industry to take up the challenge.

References

[1]   Berg, S. Taylor, A. Harper R. Mobile Phones for the Next Generation: Device Designs for Teenagers, *Proceedings of CHI 2003*: Florida, ACM Press, (2003).

[2]   Borovoy, R. Silverman, B. B. Gorton, T. Klann, J. Notowidigdo, M. Knep, B. Resnick, M Fold. Computing: Revisiting oral traditions as a scaffold for co-present communities, *Proceedings of CH2001*, ACM Press, (2001), pp466 473

[3]   Brown, B., Green, N., & Harper, R. (Eds.), *Wireless World: Social and Inter-actional Aspects of the Mobile Age*. Godalming and Hiedleburg: Springer Verlag (2001).

[4]   Fortunati, L. The Mobile Phone: An Identity on the Move, *Personal and Ubiquitous Computing*, (2001) vol. 5, no. 2, pp. 85-98.

[5]   Fortunati, L., Italy: stereotypes, true and false, *Perpetual Contact. Mobile Communication, Private Talk, Public Performance*, Katz J and Aakhus M, (2002) 42-62.

[6]   Gaver, B. Martin, H. Alternatives: exploring information appliance design through conceptual design proposals, *Proceedings of CHI 000*, An M Press, (2000), pp209-216.

[7]   Gergen, K., The challenge of absent presence, *Perpetual Contact. Mobile Communication, Private Talk, Public Performance*, Katz J and Aakhus M, (2002) pp227-241.

[8]   Gournay, C., Pretense of intimacy in France, *Perpetual Contact. Mobile Communication, Private Talk, Public Performance*, Katz J and Aakhus M, (2002), pp193-205.

[9]   Harper, R. Why People Do and Don't Wear Active Badges: A Case Study, Harper, R.H.R. In *CSCW: An International Journal*, Vol. 4, (1996) pp.297-318.

[10]   Harper, R. The Mobile Interface: Old Technologies and New Arguments, in *Wireless World: Interdisciplinary perspectives on the mobile age*, Brown, B. Green, N. & Harper, Springer Verlag, Hiedleberg and Godalming, UK, (2001) pp207-224.

[11]   Harper, R. Are mobiles good for society? Keynote address for *Mobile Communications: Social and Political Effects*, Institute for Philosophical Research of the Hungarian Academy of Sciences and Westel Communications, (2003) April 24-5th, Budapest.

[12]   Ijas, J Isomurso, M. Isomursu, P. Mustonen, M Still, K. Designing a mobile terminal for horse aficionados, in *Proceedings of CHI 2003*, ACM Press (2003), pp646-647

[13]   Jenson, S. *The Simplicity Shift*, Cambridge University Press, London and New York. (2002).

[14]   Jones. M. Buchanon, G. & Thimbleby, H. Sorting out searching on small screen devices, in Paterno, (Ed), *Human computer interaction with mobile devices*, Springer, (2002) pp81-95.

[15]   Jordan, P. Human factors for pleasure in product use, in Applied ergonomics, Elsevier, Vol 29 (2002), pp25-33.

[16]   Katz J and Aakhus M Perpetual Contact. Mobile Communication, Private Talk, Public Performance, Cambridge.

[17]   Kim, S.D. Korea: personal meanings Perpetual Contact. Mobile Communication, Private Talk, Public Performance, Katz J and Aakhus M,(2002) pp63-79.

[18]   Kopomaat T. The city in your Pocket. Birth of the mobile information society, Helsinki, Gaudeamus (2000).

[19]   Licoppe, C., & Heurtin, J. P. Managing One's Availability to Telephone Communication through Mobile Phones: A French Case Study of the Development Dynamics of Mobile Phone Use. *Personal and Ubiquitous Computing*, vol. 5, no. 2, (2001) pp. 99-108.

[20] Liccoppe C., Heurtin J., France: preserving the image, in *Perpetual Contact. Mobile Communication, Private Talk, Public Performance,* Katz J and Aakhus M, (2002) 94-109.

[21] Lindgren, M. Jedbratt, Svenaaon, E. Beyond Mobile: People, communications and marketing in the mobilised world, Basingstoke: Palgrave, (2002).

[22] Loudon, G. *Design issues in mobile communications*, Ericsson (Singapore) and Light Minds, (2002).

[23] Marcus,A. Ferrante, J. KuutiK, & Sparre, E. Babyfaces: User-interface design for small ispalys, *Proceedings of CHI 98*, ACM Press, (1998), pp96-7;

[24] Perry, M., O'Hara, K., Sellen, A, Brown, B., & Harper, R. "Dealing with Mobility: Understanding access anytime, anywhere," *ACM Transactions in Computer Human Interaction,* Num. 8(4), (2001) p323-347;

[25] Taylor, A. & Harper, R., The gift of the gab: A design oriented sociology of young people's use of mobilZe" in *CSCW: an international journal*, Kluwer, Amsterdam (forthcoming).

[26] Taylor, A & Harper, R. "Age-old practices in the 'New World': A study of gift-giving between teenage mobile phone users", CHI 2002, Minneapolis, ACM Press (2002).

[27] UMTS Forum: *The Social Shaping of UMTS*: http://www.umts-forum.org/servlet/dycon/ztumts/umts/Live/en/umts/Resources_Reports_26_index (2003)

The Zen of Everyday Encounters:
Spontaneous Interaction in Ubiquitous Systems

Tim Kindberg

Hewlett-Packard Laboratories
1501 Page Mill Road, Palo Alto, CA 94304, USA
timothy@hpl.hp.com
http://purl.org/net/TimKindberg

Abstract

The chance encounter with a colleague in the corridor; the discussion around a table or whiteboard in a meeting room; the interactions over sketches on table napkins in a restaurant: those are all examples of spontaneity in the absence of electronic devices. In ubiquitous computing, where there are "hundreds of computers per room" [7]; personal devices carried or worn by the humans; and computational services associated even with non-electronic entities — people places and things [4] — the opportunities for spontaneous sharing of ideas and media *should* multiply [3,5]. In this talk I shall take spontaneity, like mobility, to be a basic human desideratum. While some might prefer the routine, in general we stand to benefit from the serendipitous availability of other people and computational resources as we move around in our everyday lives.

At first sight, there is room for optimism about realising that vision. For example, cash machines are a reasonably successful example of the design of "walk up and use" devices: in a foreign city, we happen upon one and successfully withdraw cash with little chance of error. But spontaneity in ubiquitous computing is far more challenging. First, it encompasses multi-device, multi-human interaction. For example, one user shows the other a document from their mobile personal server [6] on a convenient nearby screen; a group of friends play their media to one another using whatever devices there are between them in a bedroom or living-room [1]. Second, the invisibility of wireless associations can be as much of a hindrance as an aid to spontaneity [2].

I will examine the opportunities and the challenges for spontaneous interaction, using case studies to make a progress report for the research community.

References

[1]   John Barton, Patrick Goddi and Mirjana Spasojevic. Creating and Experiencing Ubimedia. HP Labs tech. report HPL-2003-38.
[2]   W. Keith Edwards, Rebecca E. Grinter. At Home with Ubiquitous Computing: Seven Challenges. In proc. Ubicomp 2001, 256-272.

L. Chittaro (Ed.): Mobile HCI 2003, LNCS 2795, pp. 15-16, 2003.
© Springer-Verlag Berlin Heidelberg 2003

[3]   Tim Kindberg and Armando Fox. System Software for Ubiquitous Computing. *IEEE Pervasive Computing*, vol. 1, no. 1 (2002), 70-81.

[4]   Tim Kindberg et al. People, Places, Things: Web Presence for the Real World. *Mobile Networks and Applications*, vol. 7, no. 5 (2002), 365-376.

[5]   Supporting Spontaneous Interaction in Ubiquitous Computing Settings. Workshop at Ubicomp 2002.
http://www.dcs.gla.ac.uk/~pd/Workshops/spontaneity02.html.

[6]   Roy Want et al. The Personal Server: Changing the Way We Think about Ubiquitous Computing. In proc. Ubicomp 2002, 194-209.

[7]   Marc Weiser. The Computer for the 21st Century. *Scientific American*, vol. 265, no. 3 (September 1991), 94-104.

Understanding Mobile Contexts

Sakari Tamminen[1], Antti Oulasvirta[2], Kalle Toiskallio[1], and Anu Kankainen[2]

[1] Information Ergonomics Research Group (SoberIT)
Helsinki University of Technology
P.O. Box 9600, FIN-02015 HUT, Finland
{sakari.tamminen,kalle.toiskallio}@hut.fi
http://www.soberit.hut.fi/ierg
[2] Helsinki Institute of Information Technology
P.O.Box 9800, FIN-02015 HUT, Finland
{antti.oulasvirta,anu.kankainen}@hiit.fi
http://www.hiit.fi/fuego/between

Abstract. Mobile urban environments present a challenge for context-aware computers, because they differ from static indoor contexts such as offices, meeting rooms, and lecture halls in many important ways. Internal factors such as task goals are different—external factors such as social resources are dynamic and unpredictable. An empirical, user-centered approach is needed to understand mobile contexts. For these ends, we present insights from an ethnomethodologically inspired study. The data consist of travel episodes of 25 adult urbanites (incl. elderly, single mothers, adolescents) in Helsinki. We present how situational and planned acts intermesh in navigation, how people create personal spaces while waiting, and how temporal tensions develop and dissolve. Furthermore, we provide examples of social solutions to navigation problems, examine aspects of multitasking, and consider design implications for context-aware mobile computing.

1   Introduction

Mobile technologies can be seen as new resources for accomplishing various everyday activities that are carried out on the move. People seem to have tremendous capabilities for utilizing mobile devices in innovative ways for social and cognitive activities. For example, mobile phones are nowadays used not only for talking but also for arranging ad hoc face-to-face meetings with friends, finding driving directions, fixing blind dates, and even chatting with unknown people. People seem to have vast resources for mobile lifestyle.

In its complexity, mobile lifestyle presents a challenge for context-aware computing. Context-aware devices are supposed to monitor the changing contexts of the user and to adapt in an appropriate way through interpreters, aggregators, and services [5]. Sensitivity to user's situation is necessary. For this end, mobile computers need

L. Chittaro (Ed.): Mobile HCI 2003, LNCS 2795, pp. 17-31, 2003.

"awareness" of several contextual factors: social, psychological, physical etc. What factors, and how they should be interpreted and acted upon, is the million-dollar question. The majority of the research in context-awareness cannot help us much in addressing this question, because it has concerned mainly what we call *static,* or fixed, indoor contexts—e.g., offices, meeting rooms, and lecture halls. Maybe because of the static nature of such contexts, it has tried to create rigid taxonomies and general "all-embracing" definitions of context—with a negligible success (see e.g. [3]).

Because of having deep social roots and involving dynamically changing environment, mobile context seems to be even tougher concept to be "defined". Therefore, deciding, from an armchair, which attributes are relevant is problematic. We believe that in order to be socially acceptable and useful, context-aware technology must be based on *empirical* knowledge of context, analysed from the perspective of social and human sciences. In this paper we describe such study. We will show how different aspects of mobile contexts are created and maintained by situated actions in everyday life. Furthermore, we will draw implications for the design of context-aware computing.

2   Our Approach

What goes into a context is a widely debated and controversial issue. There is a wide body of literature with a slight philosophical flavor concerning the issue [2, 6, 7, 12, 20, 22]. Attempts to standardize a definition of context have been made (e.g. ISO 13407 [13]). However, some researchers consider these conceptualizations too vague and general to be adapted to any *specific* design processes. The common objection is the following [12, 7]: Because context is tightly intertwined with users' internal and social—continuously changing—interpretations, it seems very difficult to capture context in any general sense that would support practical designers. Consequently, there have been doubts if the concept of context is of any use [21,12]. The demand for new approaches to tackle the problem is imminent.

This demand has been noted. For example, Dourish [7] has distinguished two strands of context-aware computing research. The first is informed by the research on physically based interaction and augmented environments. The second attempts "to develop interactive systems around understandings of the generally operative social processes surrounding everyday interaction" [7, p.231]. The study presented here falls under the second line of research. We hypothesize that situated actions vary richly in mobile contexts. Many actions and routines are performed simultaneously while being on the move. For these reasons, we believe, mobile contexts do not lend themselves to rigid general definitions or static taxonomies. Importantly, however, actions performed while moving and their contexts also have *regularities* that can be captured by context-aware devices. Regularities in mobile contexts presumably differ from those in static contexts.

Our starting point is that important contextual attributes are always determined by the *specific* use situation in loaded with different action resources: motives, plans, other people, mobile computers etc. To understand what is relevant for adaptive interaction, the use situation must be studied with *user-centred* methods. This paper contributes to empirical attempts in trying to understand how context-aware computing might make its place in mobile activities, especially in the rapid change of the contexts in everyday urban navigation. Our aim is to understand important characteristics of mobile contexts. How are different mobile contexts constructed and upheld by people's interactions with other people, available technology and the outer surroundings of action? What kind of resources do present technologies, such as mobile phones or Internet cafés, provide for rendering people's everyday activities contextually accountable and by that way culturally meaningful?

In addition to the user-centered empirical approach, two points are emphasized in this study. First, our interest is confined specifically to context-changes occurring on the move in urban public and semi-public places (typically somewhere between home, leisure activities, and work). In contrast to previous work that has involved restricted areas such as museums, offices or university campuses, we are interested in the interplay between dynamic context-changes, moving people, and their actions. Another point of departure to previous research is that we are specifically interested in the majority of consumers—the elderly, single mothers, and youngsters in this study—instead of, say, businessmen or researchers.

Finally, this study is an analysis of activities taking place in present-day urban environments. We do not try to predict the future on the basis of present-day technology. Instead, we believe that an understanding of present-day activities is necessary for gaining an insight on how future devices and applications could support or even challenge the present interactions in mobile contexts[1].

3   Method and Data

The data was gathered using the principles of ethnographic participant observation and analyzed with an ethomethodological focus (see e.g. [10, 18, 25]). Twenty-five adults (names changed in the following) were observed in moving from one place to another during their normal days in the Helsinki Metropolitan Area. The amount of subjects resulted in a saturated observational data.

The study took place during the summer 2001. However, the data is still valid two years later, in 2003, for two reasons: 1) Obviously, people still do those kinds of everyday activities (commuting, shopping, parenting) we observed and 2) no widely adopted mobile services, that could have changed urbanites' moving patterns, have yet been launched.

Five researchers spent 1 to 3 days with each participant. Video, still camera, and field notes were used as tools of documentation during observations. The focus of our observations was on subjects' everyday activities, especially activities related to their urban everyday journeys. Our method has been *near* participant observation because we have been part of those social settings. However, we have been there as purely researchers, not as participants. A broader description of our data collection method is given in [14].

---

[1] Discussions about the usefulness of this kind of "Technomethodology" can be found in [8].

For the analysis of mobile context, observations were transcribed and represented in a notepad-like format. Photographs were presented on the left side of the notepad, and explanation of pictures and storyline were beside. Storylines were in the form of *thick descriptions*, that is, including all the details we could observe and document. These documents were then divided to *travel episodes*. A travel episode consists of temporally organized (i.e., it has a beginning, middle, and end) action patterns depicting a meaningful journey between two places. "Meaningfulness" here means that actions were performed in sequences in order to fulfil a need. A special emphasis was given to finding *nodal events* (e.g., see [19]), that is, events where an action transformed the present context into another recognizable context. A good example of such nodal event is the space claiming act (see Section 4.2). These nodal events, if they were reoccurring throughout the data and carried out on the move by our subjects, were analysed further. Specifically, we tried to identify means and resources by which these contexts are situationally contructed and upheld.

4   Characteristics of Mobile Contexts

We here describe five characteristics of mobile contexts. The characteristics can be seen as the sum of different resources and actions, by which the mobile contexts are situationally contructed and upheld, and which are utilized to render actions accountable. Characteristics presented here are 1) diagnostic of mobile contexts, but not so much of static contexts, and 2) recurring in many travel episodes. We present the characteristics closely linked to the constituting activities and give illustrating examples. Discussion of design implications is postponed to the last section.

4.1   Situational Acts within Planned Ones

When moving, people usually have a mental plan that represents how to navigate from place A to place B and what actions must be performed on the way in order to fulfill the plan. However, several actions can be performed in a situational, *ad hoc* manner during the journeys. One important aspect of mobile navigation seems to be that unplanned context changes lead to unplanned situational acts. Our participants often dropped or popped in somewhere or to somebody on their way to their primary destination, as our field observations indicated (see Fig. 1 and 2).

Lucy Suchman's [21] notion that plans do not simply determine action but provide resources through which individuals organize their own actions and interpret the actions of others in certain situations seems to be valid also in our observations. People keep their main target in mind while simultaneously acting on "oncoming" opportunities, such as interesting boutiques or cafés. Thus, in that sense the pattern of the modern urban journey can be similar to those of native Polynesian navigators who do not forget their final target although they are constantly reacting to their immediate environment, such as waves and winds of the ocean [11].

Fig. 1. *Semi-planned sidestepping.* Jane was on her way to a café to meet with her friend. She got off her tram in front of another café that provided an Internet access. She dropped in there to read her e-mails and then carried on to meet her friend

Fig. 2. *Popping in to a store.* After missing her bus, Anne was walking from work to home. She noticed nice postcards in the bookstore window and decided to go in the store to have a closer look at the cards. She realized that she needed to buy one, since she was going to a party tomorrow

Certain contexts enable people to perform actions that are significant only at that specific moment. These actions do not necessarily replace the "main" plan; rather they are little *side-steps* on the way to the goal. However, the threshold for doing these side-steps has to be low if they are to be performed while still adhering to the main plan—otherwise the sidestep could become the main plan.

Another point we want to make here is that unplanned acts are often social in nature. From time to time, people may unexpectedly run into acquaintances—for example, people they know but have not seen for a while. Sometimes it takes time for people to recognize each other from a crowd. But since they've done that, they usually stop to chat about latest happenings—it would be impolite to act otherwise (Fig.3).

4.2   Claiming Personal Space

People need space for themselves and for the action they are about to make. According to many psychosocial studies, the upholding of personal space is a universal need—only the dimensions of this space are culturally dependent. Public and semi-public spaces, a café for example, shape the use of space rather strongly. In some mobile situations, for example in the tram, the space must be claimed more actively by certain socially recognized actions.

Transformation to the private space triggers activities characteristic to that context. For example, space claiming in a bus is often followed by reading newspaper, watching out of the window, talking to a mobile phone etc. According to our field observations free newspapers are read when travelling alone. Using the newspaper, the reader claims a personal space [4]—a sphere of privacy in the middle of other passengers.

Another example from our data is a group of friends sitting around a table and sharing a newspaper, turning their backs to other people, and that way isolating from them. The number of people in the group seems to be an important factor affecting how spaces are claimed and actions carried out in the created context. People walk or ride alone, with or among other people. In that situation, a "territorial space", i.e. a socio-spatial space that is slightly larger than a mere personal space, is claimed [4]. The group takes the needed space for example by indicating that it will not yield others while roaming ahead, or by setting objects (e.g. when having picnic in the park) belonging to them around them, widening thus their personal space to territorial one.

Fig. 3. *Ad hoc, unplanned side-stepping triggered by social context.* Jane was riding in a tram in order to visit to her friend. While talking on the phone, she noticed her another friend, Albert, stepping in. Jane finished the phone call and went to Albert. They started to chat. Jane told him about her moving together with her boyfriend, about her new job, and about quitting her old job. Albert told her that he got out the civilian service, that he had moved to Helsinki, and that he was going to get a job

Fig. 4. *Marking a boundary of personal space with newspapers.* Jane was riding alone on a bus. All the passengers were reading a similar free newspaper. So did Jane. There were no discussions among the passengers

Fig. 5. *Gathering in a circle as a sign of claiming group space.* Anne and Maija met Jaana at a metro station. They got together in a circle to talk about the clothes that Jaana had bought. They share a territorial space

What is apparent here is the way spaces are transformed to one's own places by using available situational resources. In trams the free newsletters, and in groups the circling act provide physical resources to socially mark the place.

By these situational actions the actor(s) manifests herself from an outsider to a participant of a certain social activity. Many of the markers of changes in personal/group space, such as picking up the newsletter or forming a circle with friends, could be used as starting points in the recognition of transformation to new contexts.

4.3   Social Solutions to Problems in Navigation

Navigation in urban spaces is difficult for a number of reasons. Maps are complicated and hard to remember, streets and buildings resemble each other, exact addresses are difficult to keep in mind, and complicated bus routes are difficult to envision. These problems are usually solved in interaction with other people. When persons on the move come up against obstacles or are simply feeling unable to estimate their routes correctly, they often seek help via their social channels.

In our data, navigation problems were solved with the help of mobile phone. For example, when people realize that a bus has already gone, mobile phones are quickly picked up from pockets. Telephone connection is invoked mainly for two reasons: for announcing that the schedule has changed, and for negotiating what to do next.

From the point of view of context recognition, phone calls to important persons related to the activity in the middle of moving could be one predictor (i.e., a nodal event) of being lost in navigation.

4.4   Temporal Tensions

Time plays a crucial role in moving through urban areas. It has been argued that mobile devices free people from limitations of time and place. Our data, however, in agreement with previous work [15], firmly disagree with this. In fact, time and place are overemphasized in mobile contexts. Fluctuations of importance of time and space as contextual factors are here called *temporal tensions*. Temporal tensions are (loosely) analyzed to four stages: *acceleration, normal (anticipated) proceeding, slowing down, and stopping*. Some situations get accelerated so that many tasks should be done more or less simultaneously, and some prepared tasks may become impossible at the very moment. They can be carried out only if events unfold as anticipated. Sometimes everyday life gets "slower", or even "stops"; for example because of a suddenly cancelled appointment, misunderstood timetable of a public transport vehicle.

Fig. 6. *Missing a bus triggers social activity.* Kaarina was on her way with her children to meet a friend. They missed the bus they planned to take and she called her friend in order to ask when the next bus is going. She preferred to call even though the timetable was in front of her. In spite of this, she made an assumption that her friend had time to speak with her before her visit

Fig. 7. *Hurrying.* Kaarina needed to run with her children because they needed to catch a bus. Before running they were in a fast-food restaurant, and the children didn't enjoy their meals fast enough

The two temporal tensions emerging from our data are hurrying and waiting. When moving in a hurry, physical and social surroundings change rapidly but attention is directed mainly to space (e.g., shortest route) and time (e.g., monitoring time). In the middle of human and inhuman moving actors, finding the fastest route becomes importantand co-ordinating the hastening requires all the attention of the person. Activities that need constant monitoring involve route selection, checking time schedules, informing related persons, and anticipating changes in the surrounding environment.

Sometimes people simply hurry too much, which results in waiting. Waiting can be then utilized, for example, by calling somebody as in our data (Fig. 8). Physical and social environments restrict what people can do while waiting. Talking on the mobile phone in public places has become socially acceptable during the last five or six years (in the Nordic counties), whereas projecting one's slides onto the wall with a laptop and portable video projector, for example, would be inappropriate in public places. The issues surrounding the problem of "waiting" are central for mobile computing and should be explored more by the future work.

4.5   Multitasking

The fact that navigating through an urban environment requires constantly paying attention to surroundings means that attentional resources available for e.g. interacting with a device are limited. We noticed that moving and waiting pose somewhat different demands on how the environment on the one hand and the task itself on the other are attended.

Navigation *while moving* obviously restricts multitasking. As discussed in Section 4.1, people seem to have a longer-term plan of navigation (e.g., "to go and visit parents") divided into sub-goals (e.g., "turn left in the next corner"). Therefore, monitoring the environment so as to notice if a sub-goal has been reached requires atten-tional resources away from other tasks. The requirement for attention is higher in situations involving more uncertainty, such as when getting more and more closer to a signal that indicates the fulfillment of a sub-goal (e.g., "the corner of the street"). Another attention demanding task is manipulating or creating sub-goals "on the fly" (e.g. inferring the shortest route when coming to a street-crossing). These are likely reasons why our participants tended to have less multitasking while moving than while waiting. However, when the route is familiar and navigation more automatic, more multitasking can be carried out.

While waiting, people tend to engage only in such multitasking that does not hin-der them from noticing the signal in the environment that indicates the end of waiting. This signal constitutes a nodal event that must not go unnoticed. For example, making a call with a mobile phone while waiting for a bus does not interfere with the demand of seeing and waving a hand to the bus coming closer. In contrast, writing an SMS message or email would (since it requires eye gaze and hands) interfere with captur-ing this nodal event.

Fig. 8. *Waiting.* Maikku was swimming with her grandson. She rushed to the bus stop in order to go home in time, but after checking the timetable she noticed that she would need to wait a while. She decided to call her son (the father of the grandson) to let him know that everything went well in the swimming hall

Fig. 9. *Mobile multitasking.* After her work shift, Jane took a tram to visit to her friend. In the tram she received several phone calls. She continued talking while stepping out from the tram, crossing the street, walking to a kiosk, grabbing some money out from her bag, actually buying the tobacco and trying to manipulate malfunctioning door bell buttons

5   Design Implications

Empirical studies of mobile contexts offer a rich source for innovation of new context-aware services and for the design of underlying context recognition mechanisms. We conclude the paper by proposing what kind of context-aware functionality would be useful for devices aiming to cater mobility. These suggestions fall into three broad categories: navigation, social awareness, and user interface. The purpose of these suggestions is not to advocate certain specific technological platform or infrastructure but to direct designers' attention to higher-level issues in mobility. If designers consciously take into consideration viewpoints from social and human science, context-aware devices can be made more useful, meaningful, enjoyable and socially acceptable. To support this point, we provide examples of applications (see also [14]).

5.1   Navigation

1. **Monitoring Side Steps.** The phenomenon of occasional side steps, for example reading one's email in an Internet café on a way to meeting friends (see Fig. 1), creates a challenge for route-guidance systems. Route-guidance systems could monitor and learn information about recurring side-step destinations (and activities performed there). This information could be utilized, for example, in a busy-alerting service that watched person's timetable and warned if the ongoing process might make him or her busy in the next phase. Understanding temporal tensions caused by side-stepping would be the key in creating this kind of service. This is also relevant from the viewpoint of affective computing [13], because temporal tensions are usually accompanied by changes in the emotional moods of the users (e.g. frustration about having missed the bus).
2. **Adapting to Side Steps.** The notion of situational acts within planned acts implies that it is important to allow users to choose or create a route that is not necessarily the most shortest or fastest but is otherwise lucrative. Understanding side-stepping is relevant because travelling should not be just about moving from place A to B. Suggested routes should not be too rigid and optimised based on minimizing distance. Collected information about side steps could be used to support more flexible, customized routes. Ideally, routes would represent possibilities for beneficial side-steps such as stopping to chat for a while with suddenly appeared friends.
3. **Predicting Navigation Problems.** When coming up against an obstacle, for example not finding the way to a meeting place or missing a bus, people tend to find a social solution. In our data, this was achieved by calling to the friend (see Fig. 6). This could implicate a need for a supporting digital or live agent as in route-guide services (direct social navigation), or having available a representation of history of solutions other people have made in the same situation (indirect social navigation). For example, proactive agents are already in use in some car navigating devices that create a direct connection to a live person who advise the driver about the route, or even give advice and mental support in the case of a car accident. It would be important that agents could benefit from observations of common and frequently repeated problems in certain mobile contexts. An example illustrating this kind of service could be a mobile agent available for people that missed their bus triggered by a bus station.
4. **Enhanced Awareness of Navigation-Related Changes in Remote Contexts.** To address the problems of waiting for environmental signals (see Fig. 8) that indicate an important forthcoming context change, we suggest considering devices that "boost" these signals. For example, a vibration of a mobile device could indicate that one's bus is approaching the bus stop. This could work also in two steps. First alert might come about 3 minutes before the vehicle arrives, and the final alert just before it really arrives. This service would free resources for other, potentially more interesting, activities. Our analysis in Section 4.5 implies that it is important that interacting with the device does not interfere with the noticing the signal in the environment that indicates the transformation from one (e.g., waiting) to another context (e.g., going to bus).

5.2   Social Awareness

5. **Communication of Context Information.** At the beginning of mobile phone conversations, it is very common to both ask about and describe one's own contextual situation [4, 16, 24]. During the temporal tensions of hurrying (see Fig. 7), contextual information would be useful to prevent unnecessary waste of time in calling to a person too busy or unavailable for communication. Context-aware technology could provide additional representational tools of the present or remote environment (e.g., what resources are present in the present or remote context or in what availability state other social contacts are or how likely they are to know an answer to the problem).

6. **Recognition of Personal Spaces.** The observation that people need to create one's personal space, or place, or, "bubble" (Figs. 4 and 5) points out that issues of *privacy* are important in mobile context maybe even more central than in work environments where people usually know each other. A somewhat trivial user interface design implication is that on the one hand to services should be provided efficiently to all group members, but on the other hand privacy of the participants of the territorial space should be maintained. For example, the display's visibility angle should be easily changed from single user to a group use. Group spaces also pose challenges for auditory user interface design, because they should adapt to the need of personal space and possibly extending this personal space in the future to a private virtual space as well (compare this idea e.g. to "Geonotes" [9]). It could be fruitful to consider in more detail what the *ad hoc* groups' virtual space claiming would mean in future services and how could it be technically achieved. There already are prototype services that can be used to overlap the physical and virtual worlds and to turn the virtual space into a location-dependent social place. This can be done for example posting interactive virtual post-it notes on a physical place (see e.g. "Geonotes"[9]). It could be fruitful to consider services that would extent the claiming of individual or group space out to the virtual space as well.

    Personal spaces are more, however, than just a user interface issue. Personal spaces are important indicators of user's activity and willingness for different types of services. We propose here that context-aware devices could try recognizing acts of space claiming because they are indicators of these context transformations.

7. **Representation of Nearby Associates.** Ad hoc meetings among persons who know each other (see Fig. 3) might be arranged easily (also in virtual space) if persons on the same route, or on the routes near each other, would be aware of each other's movements.

5.3   User Interfaces

8. **Adapting Interaction Modalities.** Our participants rarely just "walked" or "waited" but instead engaged in multiple activities simultaneously (Fig. 9). Multitasking naturally gives rise to multi-modal interfaces. Traditional PDAs, for example, require both hands and visual attention to operate, which is clearly inappropriate for mobile contexts in which some modalities are preserved for other

tasks. On the other hand, nomadic user interfaces (designed for interaction while walking) might be too clumsy and awkward for situations where all modalities are available such as when waiting for a longer period. Context-aware adaptation in the selection of input/output modalities and interaction styles is thus needed.

We want to point out that all of the five characteristics discussed in the previous section involve some "marker" of context change that context-aware computing might be able to recognize and act upon, and all of these context-transformations lead to contexts that presume different modalities. We propose that recognizing user's temporal tensions (e.g., waiting vs. hurrying), side-stepping off the route, acts of space claiming, and social solutions to navigation problems, might offer valuable indicators of what modalities are needed in monitoring significant signals in the environment (e.g., seeing the bus coming while waiting), because they all mark changes between context where different tasks, modalities, and goals are prominent.

Acknowledgements

We thank all other between project researchers, among others Salla Hari, Sauli Tiitta, Tomi Kankainen and Esko Kurvinen. Moreover, we are grateful for our industrial partners Alma Media, Elisa Communications, Nokia, Sonera, and SWelcom.

References

[1]   Abowd, G.D, Mynatt, E.D., & Rodden, T., The Human Experience. Pervasive Computing, vol. 1 (2002) 48-57
[2]   Bellotti, V. & Edwards, K., Intelligibility and Accountability: Human Considerations in Context-Aware Systems. In Human-Computer Interaction, vol. 16 (2001) 193-212
[3]   Chen, G. & Kotz, K., A Survey of Context-Aware Mobile Computing Research. Darthmouth: Department of Computer Science, Dartmouth College, Technical Report (2000)
[4]   Czarnowski, T.V., The street as a communications artifact. In Anderson, S. (Ed.), On streets. MIT, Cambridgre MA (1978) 207-211
[5]   Dey, A.K, Abowd, G.D., & Salber, D., A conceptual framework and a toolkit for supporting the rapid prototyping of context-aware applications. Human-Computer Interaction, vol. 16, (2001) 97-166
[6]   Dix, A., Rodden, T., Davies, N., Trevor, J., Friday, A. & Palfreyman, K., Exploiting Space and Location as a Design Framework for Interactive Mobile Systems. ACM Transactions on Computer-Human Interaction, vol. 7, (2000), 285-321
[7]   Dourish, P., Seeking a Foundation for Context-Aware Computing. In Human-Computer Interaction, vol. 16, (2001) 229-241

[8]   Dourish, P. & Button, G., On "Technomethodology": Foundational Relation-
       ships between Ethnomethodology and System Design. Human-Computer Inter-
       action, vol. 13, (1998) 395-432
[9]   Espinoza, F., Persson, P., Sandin, A. Nyström, H., Cacciatore, E. & Bylund, M.,
       GeoNotes: Social and Navigational Aspects of Location-Based Information
       Systems, in Abowd, Brumitt & Shafer (eds.) Ubicomp 2001: Ubiquitous Com-
       puting, International Conference, Atlanta, Georgia, September 30 - October 2.
       Springer, Berlin (2001) 2-17
[10]   Garfinkel, H., Studies in Ethnomethodology. Prentice–Hall, New Jersey (1967)
[11]   Gladwin, T., Culture and logical process. In Goodenough, W. H., Explorations
       in cultural anthropology: essays in honor of George Peter Murdock New York:
       McGraw-Hill, cop. (1964)
[12]   Greenberg, S., Context as a Dynamic Construct. In Human-Computer Interac-
       tion, vol. 16, (2001) 257-268
[13]   ISO 13407. Human-centred design processes for interactive systems. Interna-
       tional Standard, The International Organization for Standardization (1999)
[14]   Kankainen, A., & Oulasvirta, A., Design ideas for everyday mobile and ubiq-
       uitous computing based on qualitative user data. The 7th ERCIM Workshop for
       UserInterfaces for All. In press.
[15]   Kopomaa, T., The city in your pocket: birth of the mobile information society.
       Gaudeamus Kirja, Helsinki (2000)
[16]   Laurier, E., Why people say where they are during phone calls. Environment
       and Planning D: Society and Space, vol. 19, (2000)
[17]   Picard, Rosalind W., Toward Agents that Recognize Emotion. Actes Proceed-
       ings IMAGINA, March (1998) 153-165
[18]   Sanjek, R. (ed.), Fieldnotes: the makings of anthropology. Ithaca, N.Y. : Cornell
       University Press (1990)
[19]   Schilit, B. N., Adams, N., & Want, R., Context-aware computing applications.
       In   Proceedings of the IEEE Workshop on Mobile Computing Systems and
       Applications (Santa Cruz, CA). IEEE Press, Piscataway, NJ, (1994) 85-90.
[20]   Schmidt, A., Beigl, M. & Gellersen, H.W., There is more to context than loca-
       tion. Computer & Graphics vol. 23, (1999) 893-901
[21]   Suchman. L.A., Plans and situated actions. The problem of human machine
       communication. Cambridge University Press, Cambridge (1987)
[22]   Svaneas, D., Context-Aware Technology: A Phenomenological Perspective.
       Human-Computer Interaction, vol. 16, (2001) 379-400
[23]   Tolmie, P., Pycock, J., Diggins, T., MacLean, A., & Karsenty, A., Unremark-
       able Computing. In the Proceedings of CHI 2002. ACM Press (2002) 399-406.
[24]   Weilenmann, A., "I can't talk now, I'm in a fitting room": Availability and Lo-
       cation in Mobile Phone Conversations, The Journal of Enviroment and Plan-
       ning, A special issue on Mobile Technologies and Space, forthcoming.
[25]   Wolcott, H., The art of fieldwork. AltaMira press, Walnut Creek (1995)

Motorcyclists Using Hocman – Field Trials on Mobile Interaction

Mattias Esbjörnsson, Oskar Juhlin, and Mattias Östergren

Mobility, Interactive Institute
P.O. Box 24081, SE – 104 50 Stockholm, Sweden
{mattias.esbjornsson,oskar.juhlin,
mattias.ostergren}@tii.se

Abstract. We have performed an ethnographic study that reveals the importance of social interaction, and especially traffic encounters, for the enjoyment of biking. We summarized these findings into a set of design requirements for a service supporting mobile interaction among motorcyclists. The Hocman prototype is designed to meet these requirements. It is an application for handheld devices equipped with wireless ad hoc networking interfaces. It uses a peer-to-peer architecture to accomplish sharing of HTML documents with peers in the immediate proximity. The aim of sharing is to spark social interaction among motorcyclists during brief encounters. We report a field trial on the prototype service in its naturalistic setting. Despite the unmanageable setting, e.g. the vast area, the speed, and unacquainted users, we demonstrate field trials as an effective approach to get feedback on how well a prototype service fulfils the design requirements. The results indicate that the conceptual idea of Hocman was appreciated, which suggest that the focus on interaction in traffic encounters fit with current practice of motorcycling.

1 Introduction

Motorcycling is a popular and highly mobile activity where people spend a considerable amount of time on the roads mostly to enjoy themselves. The activity is highly social seeing that the bikers appreciate riding in the presence of other bikers. There are several forms of social interaction. We argue that encountering bikers briefly and unexpectedly along the vast road network is what bikers appreciate most. This is obvious, for instance, in how they make effort in saluting. They give a quick nod, or wave, as they pass each other. Moreover, they often appreciate looking at modifications on other bikes or even show-off a quick stunt. However, these encounters are too brief and often occur too sparingly. Therefore, to get more out biking, they are eager to organize it, for instance regularly meeting at specific locations, as well as using new technologies, such as intercoms, or even web chats. This suggests

L. Chittaro (Ed.): Mobile HCI 2003, LNCS 2795, pp. 32-44, 2003.

that biking is an interesting activity to consider when innovating new services that exploit the benefits of the mobile life [3].

We performed an ethnographic study on bikers during the summer 2001 [5]. We used the analysis of the fieldwork to inform the design of a prototype service to add value to biking. Hocman [6] is an application for a handheld computer capable of wireless networking. It makes use of ad hoc networking [9] to accomplish automatic sharing of HTML documents, images and audio clips, during brief meetings. It is designed to support encounters in traffic between unacquainted bikers. First, it aims at being useful in situations that are contingent and very brief, i.e. two bikers passing each other in opposite direction. Second, it increases the likeliness of these meetings.

We report on field trials with the prototype. The purpose was to learn about the users' experience of the Hocman prototype. We wanted to know both if the Hocman prototype fulfils the requirements, as well as to get indications whether the requirements are valid i.e. that the analysis of the fieldwork was sensible. However, the general characteristics of bikers' interaction provide a challenge for evaluation. Bikers' meetings are distributed over a vast network of roads, and may occur anytime. How is the use of such service evaluated and observed? What data should be collected? By employing field trials, we were successful in giving the bikers enough experience to give valuable comments on usage. In general, they expressed that Hocman is able to add value to biking as it prolongs and enriches the brief meetings among them. They also gave comments on how to further improve the concept.

In the following section we present an overview of the biking study that informed the design. We continue in section 3 by presenting an outline of the Hocman implementation. We give an overview of the related work in section 4. In section 5 we give a detailed account of the set-up of the field trial. Finally, we present the results of the field trial, and conclude with a summary.

2   Design Requirements

Out of a field study on motorcyclists we generated a set of design requirement for a mobile service, which should increase the pleasure of biking [6]. Bikers take interest in encountering other bikers in traffic. However, these stray meetings are brief and the social interaction is often scant, e.g. a quick nod or wave. In order to get more out of encounters, biking is often organized e.g. they travel in groups, or meet other bikers at specific locations. In turn, these efforts naturally increase the likeliness of actually meeting somebody on the road; however, they can fail to give the same experience as such attempts often concern acquainted people. We argue there is room for some kind of further support for social interaction, seeing that one way of increasing interaction among unacquainted bikers would be to aid setting up future joint rides with bikers which have a history of meetings. This would *include* the stray encounters they cherish. Accordingly, we identified the following set of requirements on such mobile services.

- Enjoyment of driving: Motorcyclists drive their bikes to enjoy themselves. The service should augment the experience of driving or get them to drive even more, rather than rationalizing their movement in order to decrease travel time.

- Enrich traffic encounters: Motorcycling would be more fun if moments of visual interaction between fast moving bikers were enriched.
- Elaborate expression of identity: Currently, bikers express their personality by the way they drive, as well as with the bike itself and their clothes. Biking would be more rewarding if there was better means of acquiring knowledge about other bikers, and if there was more means of expressing personal identity.
- Increase likeliness of interaction: Motorcycling would be more fun if the likeliness of social interaction increased. It would be easier and more interesting to set up physical meetings, through other prevalent electronic media such as the web or mobile phones, if the people invited to negotiate joint biking where selected among those that had a history of previous encounters.
- Simultaneous activities: The ergonomics of the service must accommodate variability in attention, since driving a bike is demanding.

3   The Hocman Prototype

Hocman (Figure 1) is a prototype service designed to meet the previous requirements [6]. It is a HTTP peer-to-peer application for handheld computers capable of wireless ad hoc networking. It works as an automatic HTTP client to be used in the background of the user's attention. Upon detecting a new peer entering the ad hoc network, it plays a sound icon and downloads the index page of the main directory on the newly discovered peer.

HTML is a flexible format that may contain various media formats other than tagged text, such as embedded audio clips, and images. By letting the user be in control of the authoring he or she is in control of both content and format, which allows the service to mediate a personal expression accurately among semi-anonymous users. Users are identified by the content of the title tag of his or her index page.

We designed Hocman to be used as in the following scenario. Before heading out on the roads, the biker activates the device and then tucks it away, e.g. in a pocket. Thus the service is designed to operate and provide added value to biking even when being on the move. However, it will not disturb driving. Whenever encountering another Hocman-user he or she hears the sound icon telling that he is about to meet a biker who will be sharing web pages. This increases the experience of the encounter, which they cherished. The service will automatically download a page through the background downloading mechanism. Later on, for instance, when at home, the biker can browse these pages. Being able to share HTML documents containing embedded sounds, pictures or texts, adds to the short experience during an encounter. For example, when browsing the shared material, a biker may enjoy increasing his knowledge of some other biker. By sharing images, a user may communicate his personal identity with a wide range of representations e.g. acceleration graphs or pictures of modifications. Audio clips, that contain engines roar, ambient sounds, conversations, music, also add value to this experience. Finally, the biker can take contact through other prevalent media to set up future rides with the bikers he or she met. The contents of their pages may provide contact information such as phone numbers, ICQ number, email address, that may be helpful in planning and organizing biking. Thus, this will increase the likeliness of future encounters along the roads.

4   Related Work

There are several research projects that propose badges and devices providing inter-personal awareness or supporting various other aspects of mobile ad hoc collaboration. The principal systems, all relying on personal technologies and wireless communication, are the Hummingbird device [7], GroupWear Tag [2], the MemeTags System [1], and Proxy Lady [4]. Below we will give a brief introduction to each project and summarize how they were tested or evaluated.

The Hummingbird is a device used to monitor presence of other Hummingbirds in the close proximity. The presence of other devices is displayed as a continuous "humming" sound. The Hummingbird device have been studied through a set of usage experience cases [7, 10]. First, the researchers themselves tried their prototype at their lab, at a rock festival and at an academic conference. The Hummingbird device was also evaluated at a larger scope and setting. Six devices were handed out to ski in-structors, who used them during a five-day trip. The researcher observed them using the devices in their daily activities. Two focus groups were arranged after the trip to complement the studies.

The GroupWear is an active badge system that lets user share and compare an-swers to a set of multiple-choice questions. The GroupWear badge was tested during an annual gathering of researchers, students and business people. A badge was given to all participants, and the usage of the tags was then observed.

The MemeTags System provides mechanisms to monitor other user's presence, but at a shorter range than the Hummingbird device. In addition to the awareness mecha-nism, the Meme Tags System also offers a simple way for personal expression, through short sentences. The MemeTags system was tested in a similar fashion as the GroupWear system. Some data on usage, such as who met and which sentences were exchanged was displayed on large screens with the purpose of giving feedback to the participants.

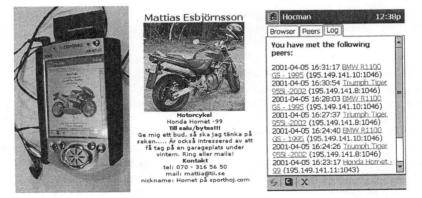

Fig. 1. The hardware used (left). A typical biker's page (middle). Screenshot of the log (right)

Proxy Lady is a system making use of handheld computers, with radio transceivers, to initiate face-to-face communication in workplaces. The design was informed through workshops. At a later stage, a user study was arranged in an office, involving four subjects, during a three-week period.

Summing up, the Hummingbird was evaluated with a limited a group of acquainted people in several different environments. The tests were performed within a well-defined area in order to make meetings probable and observable. The size of the area varied however, from very limited as in the lab case, to large, as in the ski slope case. The GroupWear tags and the MemeTags system are both intended as co-operative tools to be used at conferences. Consequently, they are both tested in such settings. Both tests are characterized by a large implementations, with hundreds of simultaneous users and, since the tests are performed during a conference, a limit in time and area. Proxy Lady is designed to leverage on the many meetings that happen in, hallways, cafeterias etc. of an office. The area of an office is quite small and the test involved four acquainted users.

5   Field Trials

The related prototypes have been developed for a different context of use than Hocman. They support or spur interaction occurring face-to-face and among often acquainted users. Consequently they also differ in their design, most prominently in terms of user interface, but also in networking, software architecture, and hardware platform. Moreover, they are tested in environments where the social interaction is governed by other principles than the interaction happening on the roads. Roads are public places, the people crowding them are usually unacquainted and the time for interaction is brief.

We designed Hocman to be used on the roads among unacquainted bikers. Some of the situations it has to react on are very brief i.e. occurring during chance encounters on the road. Moreover, the encounters may take place anywhere along the road network. Taken together these factors constitute a challenge when studying the user experience. The likeliness for a traffic encounter in a small set of unconstrained users is very low. However, similar to the related work, we can increase it by setting restrictions on when and where the devices are used. We argue it is possible to overcome these challenges with a realistic, although constrained, approach. The study presented here provides early feedback on the user experiences of Hocman as well as the users' ideas for improvement of the service. Both types of user feedback will be beneficial when determining the validity of the design requirements.

We decided to conduct a field trial, where the subjects use the prototype during a limited period of time in its intended setting i.e. on the roads. We argue this approach gives an opportunity to obtain holistic data on usage. However, we found it very difficult to observe the actual meetings as they take place. Instead we settled for a semi-structured interview [8] of each user performed immediately after the trial. The interviews were performed in parallel with different investigators. The investigators had a common list of topics to cover; however each individual investigator also had the opportunity to examine other issues the respondent felt important. We opted out focus groups although we would in such case be able to pose a coherent set of questions. In a focus group we would also gain from participants stimulating each other in the discussion [11]. However, we felt it was more important to keep the bikers apart and stay unacquainted making their comments to the point.

5.1   Participants

We sought subjects to our field trial by posting to mailing lists for employees interested in biking at various companies. We got in contact with twelve people willing to undergo the trial. Out of these, we selected eight participants on a first-come-first-serve basis, with finally six people performing the trial. All subjects were males, about thirty years of age, working in a range of professions, mainly technical as engineers, web designers, etc. They had a solid knowledge in using information technology, e.g. desktop computers, and web browsers. They also had experience of mobile devices, e.g. mobile phones, and pagers. They drove different kinds of bikes such as off-road bikes e.g. Honda Transalp; sports bikes e.g. Suzuki GSX 600; and cruise bikes e.g. Yamaha Virago.

A few days prior to the experiment, we asked the test subjects to fill in a form with information we could use to prepare their respective personal pages. The information we asked for was the make and model of their bike and a picture of it. We asked them if they hade made any modifications to it or whether they used any fancy equipment they would like to tell other bikers. We also asked if they used any special web forums and in that case, which one and what nick name they used. In the form they could also specify the URL to a personal homepage, their e-mail address, mobile phone number etc. Moreover, they could specify if they had something to advertise. We prepared a personal handheld for each user based on this data. A typical page is shown in Figure 1. We selected the name of the biker or the model of their bike as the title of the page. This title labels an item in the log.

5.2   Setting

The trial was situated to a route circulating around a recreational area in downtown Stockholm. The traffic along this route is varied. In the northeast corner is a harbour and occasional heavy trucks appear. In the South and southwest there are a number of museums and embassies and the traffic is sparse. In the west we find the national radio and TV offices and many traffic lights and roundabouts to regulate the inner-city traffic flow happening there. The official speed limit along the route is 50 km/h, and driving a lap at this speed takes about 7 to 8 minutes.

5.3   Procedure

We conducted two separate trials, which engaged three test subjects each time. We set up rendezvous locations along the route at suitable parking lots. The participants should stay unacquainted during the trial, and only meet during traffic encounters to best represent realistic situations. The numbered dots in Figure 2 display each biker's initial position for both trials. The dot labeled with an A shows the position of one researcher, who remained stationary, equipped with a Hocman unit. After some motivations, instructions and rigging the equipment, i.e. tucking away the handheld computer in their pockets and plugging in the earphones, we had them to drive two laps at the speed limit. The arrows of Figure 2 tell in what directions they drove off and the numbers show in what order they left to guarantee some encounters. When the bikers returned, we watched them use the prototype and asked them about their experiences. All interviews were taped and later transcribed.

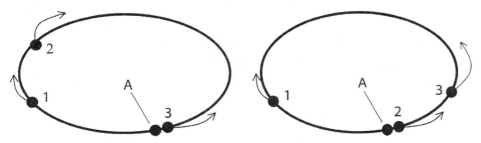

Fig. 2. Schematic view of the first (left) and second trial (right)

6   Results

Most of our questions concerned experiences from the trial. However, we also followed up on their comments on improvements and suggestions for alterative designs. Finally we encouraged them to comment on some of the functionality that was not included in the field trial, e.g. the use of Hocman to organise and plan future rides.

6.1   Hearing the Sound Icon

A central aspect of the Hocman prototype is the sound icon. Besides informing that a meeting is evident, it also signals there is more to the situation, i.e. a page has been downloaded. Three users gave detailed account for where the signal was heard. They used distinct and easily recognised landmarks i.e. the watchtower, museums, but also traffic lights, roundabouts etc. to specify the situations, such as in:

```
at the watchtower. When arriving to the watchtower the
first time. Then I heard the beep down by the museum,
and at the roundabout. On the second lap I was a bit
ahead of him, so I passed the watchtower the second
time
```

All users recognized the situations where the mechanism was activated, and consequently where the encounter took place. They commented upon the timing of the signal, which most often was played in advance of the encounter, i.e. prior to becoming co-located with other bikers. Such as in:

```
then I met a bike, and it was like 50 meter before we
met
```

Five bikers noted that after hearing the signal, they had plenty of time to look for the approaching biker. Three of them found this time intriguing. This is illustrated by the following comment:

> I didn't expect this long time span. In some way it was amusing, seeing that you had time to react and think: Look!

Furthermore, one biker was even a little disappointed when he realised he met a biker without hearing the sound icon, consequently a biker not part of the test. Another biker found it slightly confusing when being alerted and thus expecting meeting someone on the road, when the cause for it was someone equipped with a Hocman-unit standing by the road. Finally, one biker found the sound icon negative and somewhat stressful. He expressed some concern of being interrupted by the sound while being concentrated on driving, as he felt he was compelled to look for the upcoming biker.

Three users said that after having heard the signal, they waved to the approaching biker. They also stated that this is what they would normally do in such situations. However, they felt a tendency to wave even more than usual, as Hocman made them feel more akin to each other.

> you wave even more while hearing this beep, so to speak. Then you realized, you were a bit curious on the others who drove with this thing

Another biker felt extremely strong about the affinity Hocman use introduced, even claiming that hearing the signal would replace the need to wave entirely.

6.2   Sound Icon Design

Seeing that the prototype is used in the background of user attention, the design of the sound icon plays a central role in the user experience. Five out of six found the sound icon being comfortable and having an appropriate design, however two respondents were stunned by the loud volume. Nevertheless, both of them agreed that they would quickly get used to it. At the same time, three users found the high volume justified, since noise from the engine and the headwind easily would have drown the alert otherwise.

> the volume was loud enough for these speeds and circumstances

However, all users had some suggestions on how this awareness signal might be improved or re-designed. The alternatives were divided into three categories. The first concerns improvements on the use of audio. Two users suggested ways of personalizing the sound icon. The first wanted to be able to record voice messages and have them sent over instantly, like an open-invitation audio-conference. The other wanted to be able to select among a variety of signals that the other biker would hear when he met them. The second category of proposals comes from bikers who preferred visual feedback to audio. Two bikers suggested that a lamp on the handlebars should indicate the meetings.

> I preferred a lamp or something similar

One user suggested that the handheld computer should be mounted on the handle-bars and the screen should display the name of the meeting biker in large letters. The last category suggested tactile feedback instead. Two bikers proposed devices that would vibrate rather than sound to indicate an upcoming meeting.

6.3   The Handheld Computer

Apart from the sound icon, our choice on the tangible properties, such as the hardware, influenced the user experience. All users found it acceptable to carry a handheld computer in their pocket. However, some were concerned with the bulkiness of the particular device used in the test. They needed their jackets to wear many other things:

```
the problem is the size, it is a bit big. In this shape
it takes to much place, when having it in the pocket.
Seeing that I use a quite thin leather suite, I can't
have too much in my pockets. I already have my wallet
and my mobile phone, while driving. It becomes too
tight with these clothes
```

Three bikers suggested that instead of carrying the handheld, it should be either mounted on the handlebar or placed in their rucksack or in the top-case. Finally, four bikers expressed some disappointments with the earphones. Wearing earphones was not comfortable, i.e. they would fall out or squeeze the ear. Moreover, two users stated they normally wore other things in their ears, such as intercom earphones or ear defenders, which would make no room for the kind of earphones we provided. On the other hand, the peer discovery signal could easily be integrated with the existing intercom earphones.

6.4   Remembering Encounters

The system is intended to reinforce the encounters with other bikers, but also to sustain them a bit longer. By examining the entries in the log, five out of six users could easily refer back to the meetings they had experienced on the road. By looking at the list they could tell where and when most of the meetings took place and which bike they had seen. For instance:

```
Honda hornet, I suppose that is Mattias own bike, if
I'm not mistaken. GSXR 750 is the sport-bike, and the
Tiger, wasn't it parked by the road the last time I
passed here. It must be that one. Ehhh, or if I caught
up with him by the traffic light, at some occasion? I
heard the beep by the traffic light, but if I caught up
with him, or if I met him, I leave unsaid
```

A single biker expressed that he could not make a connection only by looking at the log. Despite that the meetings took place recently, he could not associate them with the log items.

One encounter involved two bikers that happened to be acquainted: Eric and Patrick. They found it more relevant to think about whom they met, instead of where the encounter took place. However, the actual meeting was to brief for them to recognize each other properly. While looking through the log Eric commented this:

```
was it… do you know who… was it Patrick I met on the
road?
```

Later he was able to confirm that it actually was Patrick he met when locating the corresponding entry. Patrick expressed a similar concern, as he was examining the items in his log, he said:

```
ok, this one, which I suspect is Eric… which it was
```

Four respondents expressed positive attitudes to having a downloaded picture to look at, when recalling a particular meeting. However, further questioning also revealed that some users found that the picture was not helpful when remembering a specific meeting, as it did not resemble the actual situation that they experienced. Some users said, on the road, they notice the colour of the other bikers' suites and helmets rather than the model and colour of the bikes. They also found it hard to distinguish bikes as they often are used in their standard make without any modifications. Finally, one user found the picture of limited value. Most pictures used in the trial portrayed the bike straight from the side, but during the encounters he only saw the front of it.

6.5   Sharing HTML Pages

HTML is a flexible document standard, and may encompass a wide variety of information interesting to bikers. Five bikers found it intriguing to read about other bikers on the downloaded pages we supplied them with. They liked the brief presentations:

```
to get a feeling of who it is. Name, phone number and
something more
```

One user said he did not find general information as presented here very interesting. Some user also followed up their claims on how they perceived the pages and talked about in which situations they would be useful.

One user said that he wanted the information when he engaged in other off-road activities, i.e. visiting web forums where biking is discussed. Being logged on, he wanted to know which other forum users he had met physically. Another user said he would find it very useful when going to places where many bikers got together. He also imagined contact information useful if he saw another biker doing something he wanted to rebuke. On the other end of this spectra, a third biker would like to know more about the people he had engaged in "mischief" with i.e. performing stunts, such as, going on one wheel.

The matter of what they wanted to know about other bikers and what they wanted to tell was divided into two themes. The first concerned the social habits of biking. One biker wanted to know other bikers' where-to-go tips. He also wanted to know other biker groups' hangouts, such as cafés. Another biker even wanted to know whether the biker he met was of the opposite sex, as he was looking for dates. The other theme concerned the motorbikes. The bikers expressed that they wanted to know more if they met someone using the same model or having interesting extra equipment or modifications.

6.6   Distributing the Pages

The response on the matter of with whom the pages should be shared, concerned two extremes: the pages should be distributed to all bikers, or kept within members of a certain group. The fact that they potentially would spread contact information with unacquainted people intimidated one biker. However, two others found that a positive experience of the concept require widespread usage in the general public.

```
to have a reason for using it, the system has to be
widespread
```

At the same time, being able to single out a group as the target of your page appealed to two bikers. Two bikers suggested that the user should specify what he or she wanted to show to whom. Finally, one biker was concerned that some authority, such as police or insurance companies, would use the service to monitor biking activities.

Even if the group that the user is sharing is delimited it might still be very large. Three bikers stated they would like to filter out some log entries on reception.

```
perhaps you could talk about that you want a Honda Hor-
net, or that kind of bike, or say that you want... use it
for advertising. Its easy to use a tag, which it reacts
on... so it will receive everything, but then throwing
the irrelevant stuff. Like when you are going to the
yellow café, you would like a filter
```

Two other bikers also stated a similar idea. They suggested a mechanism to sort entries, however receiving them all.

6.7   Contacting Other Bikers

Finally, would Hocman be useful when contacting other bikers? Four bikers were positive to the idea of using the information on the pages as a starting point to contact other bikers.

```
it you are interested in buying or selling, or if you
formulate that you want a bike like the one I have
```

One of these users elaborated the idea and found many plausible reasons for doing it in order to get company on the roads. For example:

```
or if you looking for company on your rides, or why not
a dating functionality
```

A second user found it more appropriate to supply an URL or email address. He thought that following up a joint meeting through postings to web chats or sending email messages would be an unaffected way of approaching somebody. Finally, one user did not think he would contact somebody on the basis of having a persons' page only.

6.8   Summary

The field trial indicates that Hocman is able to add to the *enjoyment of driving*. It was evident that the bikers did not think that using Hocman would rationalize overly biking; however hearing the sound icon, inspecting logs and browsing contact information etc. would add something positive. Moreover, the feedback we received also indicates that the requirements we derived are complete i.e. there were no other important issues that we overlooked, and valid i.e. they made sense to bikers.

Fundamentally, all bikers recognized that the sound icon alerted co-location of other Hocman users i.e. motor bikers. About half of the subjects could also account for where and when it was heard, which indicates they had plenty of time to react, look around, and let the experience sink in. More importantly, almost all of the bikers enjoyed hearing the sound icon to an extent that was surprising to us. For instance, some bikers changed their driving behaviour, i.e. waving more or less as what is custom when otherwise passing a biker. Besides remembering where they heard the sound icon, most users were also able to associate a particular log entry to it. In one case an entry and the associated web page was helpful when recognizing an acquaintance. The feedback we got on hearing the sound icon and being able to inspect the log, indicates Hocman was able to *enrich traffic encounters*.

The users found it interesting to read the information on the downloaded pages we prepared for them. Collectively they also had many suggestions on what other data the pages could contain, which acknowledges that Hocman provides ways for bikers to *express identity*. On the other hand, there was no consensus on the matter of sharing pages with all users or a limited group. However, all agreed that some sort of user defined filtering or sorting mechanism would improve the concept.

Most bikers we interviewed claimed that they took interest in which bikers they ride together with. They found it plausible that they could contact somebody on the premise of reading a page someone shared. Moreover, a few users recognized that Hocman also could be used for a variety of other purposes, such as ads or dating. This tells us that Hocman may *increase the likeliness of interaction* among bikers.

Finally, we are confident that Hocman meets the requirement of *simultaneous activities*, however some details could be improved. Lowering the volume of the sound icon playback, a less bulky device, and more comfortable earphones perhaps integrated with the helmets, would have been better appreciated.

7   Conclusion

We have demonstrated that field trials are an effective approach to get feedback on how well a prototype service fulfils the design requirements derived from an ethnographically informed study of motor bikers. The field trial was performed in two runs with a total of six bikers. The bikers used Hocman, a HTTP peer-to-peer application for handheld computer capable of wireless ad hoc networking, in a constrained however naturalistic setting. We gathered the feedback through parallel interviews. Our results indicate that we could improve on our choice of hardware. However, Hocman was appreciated, especially hearing the sound icon when encountering another biker.

Acknowledgements

We would like to thank the Swedish Research Institute for Information Technology and the Swedish Agency for Innovation Systems funding this research. Symbol Technologies Sweden provided us with handheld computers. We would also like to thank Daniel Vesterlind for performing an interview, and Professor Kia Höök for valuable comments on a preliminary version of this paper.

References

[1]   Borovoy, R., Martin, F., Vemuri, S., Resnick, M., Silverman, B. and Hancock, C. (1998). Meme Tags and Community Mirrors: Moving from Conferences to Collaboration. In Proceedings of CSCW'98, ACM Press, New York.

[2]   Borovy, R., Martin, F. Resnick, M. and Silverman, B. (1998). GroupWear: Nametags that Tell about Relationships. In Proceedings of CHI'98, ACM Press, New York.

[3]   Chincholle, D. et al (2002), Lost or Found? A Usability Evaluation of a Mobile Navigation and Location-Based Service, In the Proceedings of the 4th International Symposium, Mobile HCI 2002, Pisa Italy

[4]   Dahlberg, P., Ljungberg, F., & Sanneblad, J. (2002). Proxy Lady – Mobile Support for Opportunistic Communication. In Scandianavian Journal of Information Systems, Vol. 14, pp. 3 – 17, The IRIS Association, Sweden.

[5]   Esbjörnsson, M., Juhlin, O. and Östergren, M. (2002). Making Motorbikers Come Together – Fast Moving Users & Mobile Ad Hoc Networks, In proceedings of IRIS'25, Copenhagen, Denmark.

[6]   Esbjörnsson, M., Juhlin, O. & Östergren, M. (2002). The Hocman Prototype: Fast motor bikers and Ad Hoc Networks, In proceedings of MUM, Oulo, Finland.

[7]   Holmquist, L.E., Falk J. and Wigström, J. (1999). Supporting Group Collaboration with Inter-Personal Awareness Devices. In Journal of Personal Technologies, 3 (1-2), Springer Verlag.

[8]   Jordan, P. W. (2000). Designing Pleasurable Products – An Introduction To The New Human Factors. Taylor & Francis, London.

[9]   Mobile Ad-hoc Networks (manet) Charter, http://www.ietf.org/html.charters/manet-charter.html

[10]   Weilenmann, A. (2001). Negotiating Use: Making Sense of Mobile Technology. In Personal and Ubiquitous Computing, Vol. 5, Issue 2, Springer Verlag.

[11]   Patton, M. Q. (1990). Qualitative evaluation and research methods. Sage Publications, London.

Connecting Remote Visits and Design Environment: User Needs and Prototypes for Architecture Design

Giulio Iacucci[1], Antti Juustila[1], Kari Kuutti[1], Pekka Pehkonen[1], and
Arto Ylisaukko-oja[2]

[1] Department of Information Processing Science
P.O. Box 3000 FIN-90014, University of Oulu, Finland
{giulio.iacucci,antti.juustila,kari.kuutti,
pekka.pehkonen}@oulu.fi
[2] VTT Electronics
Kaitoväylä 1, P.O.Box 1100, FIN-90571, Oulu, Finland
arto.ylisaukko-oja@vtt.fi

Abstract. We present a case of mobile and tangible computing prototypes developed for architecture design. We have carried out extensive
observation of how architecture students visit places, collect material
and manipulate it in design projects. The direct implications we inferred analyzing the field work material were the need of *mobile support* to link contextual information and the collected material. Moreover we envisioned the opportunity to create a *tool to navigate and manipulate* material from visits. Finally we identified the need of integrating and linking digital media from visits, with the physical environment in the atelier. We have concretized the user needs in a scenario
and we describe a set of prototypes: a mobile application to create a
media path of the visits, a visualizing tool to navigate and manipulate it,
and an infrastructure in the atelier environment to share and access media objects and links between them. In the discussion we analyze challenges in integrating two design spaces of architects with computational
support: the remote sites and visits on one hand, the atelier environment
with design representations on the other.

1   Introduction

The Atelier project is exploring ways in which pervasive and mobile technologies can
be used in creating "inspirational" learning environments - environments not only for
learning about predefined contents, but environments which would help in activities
where data and other materials is explored and novel connections and new contents
generated. Design is one characteristic form of such activities, and the experiments
presented in this paper come from an attempt to support a particular design activity,
that of architects. One of the testing grounds of the project is a master class in architecture at the Academy of Fine Arts in Vienna, and one of the purposes of the project

L. Chittaro (Ed.): Mobile HCI 2003, LNCS 2795, pp. 45-60, 2003.

is to construct an environment to support the master class students in their project work during the final year. This paper describes an experiment focusing on a "slice" of that environment - using mobility to connect students' two spaces of design. It is characteristic to work in architecture that the work is divided between two places and spaces: between the design office (atelier) and the site to be designed. Architects constantly travel between these two places, and, in a way, try to connect the places by transporting different materials related to design between these places. This slice of design work, the creation of a "virtual design space" by moving between places and transferring materials is the target of our experimental system.

Methodologically our work is based on iterative prototyping based on an extensive fieldwork and participatory sessions [10, 11]. The initial user needs have been collected by means of the fieldwork, and then initial prototype ideas have been experimented with by the users, experiences fed back in the prototype design, and so on.

Even such a relatively narrow slice of a support system presents a number of conceptual, human-computer interaction and technological challenges, some of which are not yet solved properly at this stage of the development of our prototype. We think, however, that some interesting issues found during our work are worth of a broader audience and discussion. In particular the challenge of connecting the atelier with the remote sites has brought us to envision three aspects of computational support: a mobile application to collect material and create a multimedia path of the visits, and a tool to navigate and edit the path, and an infrastructure in the environment to share multimedia objects and related information in other applications.

In the next paragraph we describe the setting of our field study, provide selected episodes to exemplify current practices, and we present what we analyzed as requirements. We then present the concept behind our prototypes by providing a brief scenario and a description of a test with an early prototype, along with detailed description of the technical implementation.

2   Current Practices and Requirements

2.1   The Setting

The case we present is part of a design project to develop a ubiquitous and mixed media environment for inspirational learning. One of the application sites is the architecture department at the Academy of fine Arts in Vienna. We have observed seven student projects in the first half of 2002. In the second half we introduced and observed the use of several tangible computing prototypes [11]. In the projects, groups of students have to work out designs of interventions for remote physical locations. During the project they concretize solutions experimenting with several representation techniques. Visit at sites are frequent and there are weekly feedback meetings with staff and external reviewers. The goal of the students is to be creative in getting ideas and develop them into a convincing solution.

The diversity of material and media is an important characteristic that is exploited in the handicrafts they produce. Students work with and produce text, diagrams, comics, video, sketches, screenshots, virtual models, and prototypes – material of different degrees of abstraction, different scale and materiality.

We used participant observation to study current practices and the use of proto-types. We set out to observe the students not only in topical events as presentations or meetings but also in everyday work. Inspired by interaction analysis we used a digital still camera and a video camera to record audiovisual material to analyze selected episodes. In the next paragraph we provide brief episodes that describe ways in which students currently manipulate materials from visits.

2.2   Selected Episodes

A Diagram, Audio and Pictures of Interviews for the Design of an Inner Court-yard. Built into their work are excursions to the outside world, e.g. the site of a project, where they collect video and audio material, pictures, sketches, and objects, such as in the case of this project, which deals with redesigning an inner courtyard.

In the first phase of the project the student interviewed people living in the area. She represented each person with a list of keywords and symbols around a map. Each list had a pin and a thread connected to another pin in the map showing where the person lives. When presenting the model she used electronic devices to augment her diagram, a digital camera and an audio recorder playing parts of the interview (Figure 1).

Fig. 1. Digital pictures and recorded audio around a diagram

Fig. 2. Photos on the wall and the physical model, showing where they were taken

Fig. 3. a) Some of the photos of the visit to the stadium are arranged during storytelling; b) a diary is used to navigate pictures of the visit with a barcode reader

Photographs and Models from a Visit in the Alps. A group of 8 students is working on one project where the aim is to design an intervention in a valley in the Alps near the Italian-Swiss border. A general concept was developed within the group then individual student chose particular interventions like buildings or paths in the valley. While visiting the valley, a student has taken photographs on top of a small mountain and has built a physical model of it. When telling about his project and about the visit, he shows in which location the pictures were taken and in which direction on the model of the mountain. The pictures where taken from a particular place at specific time of the day for the different light effects. The pictures were attached on the wall near drawings of the mountain (Figure 2).

Visits around Stadiums. During the development of prototypes a visit was organized. This was a very important moment of reflection for envisioning technological support. The visit was carried out thinking that students would have produced a multimedia presentation of the visit. The teaching staff used additional 'constraints' – roles, observational techniques, timing – to facilitate the collecting of material. It was an excursion to excursion London-Lille-Paris where students had the opportunity to visit eleven different stadiums. Different roles had been assigned to the students. Each of them belonged to one of four groups – context, construction, hybrid, and conversion. They also assumed specific roles – from recording all kinds of liquids and machines and focusing on the penalty shooter, to recording guiding systems and colors and looking at seats+smallness. This helped them focus on particular aspects of the stadiums and their environments. Another instruction students got was to use a particular rhythm such as e.g. taking a picture every 30 sec from the moment they stepped out of the underground until they arrived at the stadium.

The tools that were used during the visit where: Different types of cameras, digital, analog, camcorders; MD sound recorders; diaries, note book with records of the journey and to which objects where attached; background material, e.g. maps. Pictures where taken in the part of the city surrounding the stadium. Inside the Stadium, pictures were taken from different points (it was important to have different perspectives, player or observer). Pictures where taken in a particular temporal sequence as approaching the stadium or documenting the stadium filling up (Figure 3a pictures are arranged on the table while they are explained to other group member). Also the recording of sound was tied to particular moments as for example a dedicated "one minute of silent". In presenting the visit in the Atelier environment media was integrated with existing material using computational support: an application with a barcode scanner (*animating bAR code* links barcodes and digital media), a tool to paint objects with a projector (*texture brush* developed at IMAGINATION Computer Services, Vienna).

For example, pictures were projected on existing physical models of stadiums (As in Figure 4). A diary of the visit was used to navigate pictures using a barcode reader. Barcodes were attached to several points in the diary linking the page to pictures. Barcodes were used also to attach pictures to large diagrams and physical models.

Fig. 4. Parts of physical models are painted with projections of the pictures

2.3   Requirements for Computational Support

The analysis of the fieldwork and observations pointed to several requirements for technological support:

Experiencing Places, and Collecting Material. Visiting and Collecting material is a crucial activity in architecture design. Not only pictures are taken, or other objects are carried back to the studio, but places are experienced. Moreover students and architects might visit several sites in one project for comparison or inspiration.

Contextual Information. Important in the manipulation is the place where the media and objects have been collected. Along with the place, other information is important like the direction of the picture, the time of the day. Or in other case information of people that were interviewed etc. More importantly pictures carry a meaning for the person who has taken them. We observed many storytelling around pictures of visits and other objects. The students or architects narrate important impression of the situation and the relevancy for the design project.

Manipulating, Linking, Integrating the visit material with other material. In the studio the material from the visits were linked, integrated with other representations, like diagrams, plans, and physical models.

Sharing of Experience, Multiple Traveling. *The need to share the experience of the visit is an essential part of the group work in the architecture design project we ob-*

served. This facilitates creating a shared understanding of problems and reflections. Moreover the same person that conducted the visits uses the material to travel again to re-experience the situation with its richness.

The direct implications we inferred in our prototyping efforts were the need of *mobile support* to link contextual information and the collected material. Moreover we envisioned the opportunity to create a *tool to navigate and manipulate* material from visits. Finally it became clear there is a need for providing ways to integrate and link digital media from visits, with the environment in the atelier.

2.4   The Concept in a Scenario

After having analyzed the observation material we developed a video-scenario that explained the use of the support for the visit (we reproduce here a shortened version). Danielle is visiting a square for which she is designing a temporary exhibition with tends and stands. She starts her visit by wearing the *Jacket* (a wearable application to collect material from visits) that helps her in recording aspects of the environment (Figure 5,6). The Jacket can take pictures and sounds, is location aware and can record walking paths.

While walking, Danielle takes pictures along the path (Figure 3,4,5) by touching one of the pockets of the Jacket. She takes pictures of the playground and of the city walls from one side of the square. She records soundtracks for pictures and positions. It is important for her to know from which position and in which direction the photograph was taken.

Fig. 5. Danielle wearing the jacket, interviewing and recording sound, taking pictures

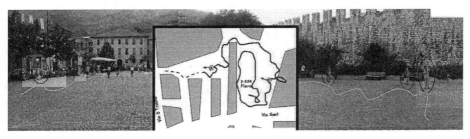

Fig. 6. Danielle creates a media path

The pictures and sounds (for example the meaning of the picture) are stored along with additional information, position, direction, and time. Out of these, the *Jacket* creates a media-path of the visit. When Danielle returns to the Atelier, the documents of the visits are stored in a database in the environment. In the environment Danielle can navigate and re-experience the visit, or can use media objects collected during the visit in different applications, for example linking them to existing material.

The sounds and pictures she collected are organized in a virtual 3D environment showing the path of the visit. Danielle navigates the visit in a group discussion with her colleagues on a wall screen using an Infrared remote control. She can now manipulate the path and link the audiovisual files to physical tags that can she attaches to her physical models of the exhibition. In this way she can navigate through the material interacting with her model.

3   The Current Prototype

3.1   Related Applications

Location based applications have been object of research mostly as touring guides. Davies et al. [4, 5] developed GUIDE, where the systems obtain information through a high-speed wireless network deployed throughout the target city. GPS has also been used for touring guides and other playful applications [9,12,14]. In [16] the 'Shopping Jacket' – uses two positioning devices, GPS and 'Pingers' (used to signal the presence of a shop, and to indicate the type of shop and it's website). The system uses this information "to determine whether the wearer needs to be alerted that they are passing an interesting shop, or to direct the wearer around a shopping mall. The shopping jacket integrates a wearable CardPC; GPS and Pinger receivers; a near-field radio link; hand-held display; GSM data telephone; and a speech interface into a conventional sports blazer." In [15] infrared beacons, radio frequency ID tags, or bar codes are attached to people, places, and things to create a hyperlink between a physical entity and a Web resource, these hyperlinks rely on commonly available wireless mobile devices to help users automatically access services associated with physical objects.

Less frequent are systems like the one we propose to collect multimedia material from visit. In the following we will present a collection of prototypes to collect multimedia media material and information from sensors to create a media path that can be manipulated in an augmented environment.

3.2   The Mobile Support

The Jacket is our vision of a wearable component that supports designers during visits. Our prototype for the iPAQ pocket PC is an application to support visitors in organizing media material created during visits. Users can log the path of a visit through GPS, log position and direction (with SoapBox) for recorded media like photographs and sounds, and create a hyperdocument of the visit that can be used to store the media files and information of the visit in Database. An external stereo microphone can be connected to the iPAQ and users can set the sound quality of the recording in the iPAQ system settings. The application makes use of two accessories: a GPS receiver and SoapBox, which is a sensor box developed at VTT Electronics, Finland.

The Pretec Compact Flash GPS-card is inserted in a Dual-Slot PC Card Expansion Pack with a CF-slot (Compact Flash). The GPS receiver is used to read the current latitude and longitude every 5 seconds. Although it does not provide always the right accuracy it has been selected for being the easiest and cheapest way to implement our concept in early stages.

VTT Electronics has developed a general-purpose SoapBox module (Sensing, Operating and Activating Peripheral Box, [17]). It is a light, matchbox-size device with a processor, a set of sensors, and wireless and wired data communications. It was developed as a research tool as well as to be utilized as a generic prototype for experimenting with product ideas and developing prototypes for them. The basic sensor board of SoapBox includes acceleration sensors (3-axis), illumination sensor, magnetic sensor (2-axis), optical proximity sensor, and as an option, a temperature sensor. The application uses the magnetic sensor as a compass to determine the current direction. The SoapBox is connected to iPAQ by RS-232 serial port.

The user interface (Figure 7) has a simple menu to test the connection to peripherals (the GPS reader and SoapBox) and to save the visit in an XML document. There are four buttons, Start (to start the visit), Stop (to stop the visit), Photo (to be pressed when a photograph has been taken), Voice (to be pressed when audio is recorded). The display shows the information that is stored in the document of the visit. Every five seconds the longitude and latitude are stored along with the time. When the Photo button is pushed, the time of the number and time of the photograph are stored, and the information from sensors is recorded. The direction is inferred from the data received from the SoapBox magnetic sensor (e.g. East 88°). The location is provided by the GPS receiver.

Fig.7. a) the interface of the mobile application, b) the prototype

3.3   The IT Infrastructure in the Environment

The Infrastructure software in the Atelier environment is a platform that enables different kinds of components to be added to the Atelier Inspirational learning space, thus extending and also changing the functionality of the space. The platform is open in a sense that different kinds of input technologies, display systems and, for example, mobile devices (that may themselves contain advanced functionalities) can be brought into the space, as long as the technologies conform to specified (programming and messaging) interfaces of the environment. The architecture of the system is based on the Micro Kernel architecture [2].

The current implementation has been developed using Java 1.4 SE. Components and the Infrastructure and services within communicate with each other using XML messages. Because of the messaging based model of cooperation, it is also possible to create components with other programming languages than Java.

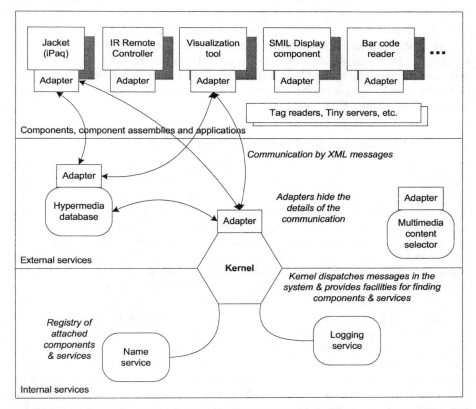

Fig . 8. The Atelier Infrastructure (example instantiation of the components; two lower layers) contains External services, as well as internal services (Kernel services) for managing the elements in a learning environment

The role of the Infrastructure is to act as a mediator between the components that provide the separate functionalities that the components enclose. The main advantage of the Infrastructure is flexibility and configurability; it is possible to replace a positioning (tagging) technology, display or a mobile device with another kind, without losing the interoperability of the Atelier environment. This allows the Atelier project to build more than just one implementation of a specific component or application, that is usable in a specific context, but an environment that is reconfigurable and also extensible in future experiments utilizing different technologies. The Figure 8 illustrates the Atelier Infrastructure in relation to the other system elements in the Atelier learning space. Elements in the two lower layers are included in the Infrastructure, as the elements (components, component assemblies and applications, build by composing components and component assemblies) in the upper part register to the Infrastructure and can use the services in it.

The example instantiation in the Figure 8 shows a situation where the Jacket has registered itself as a component of the atelier environment. The information about Jacket is then stored in the Name service under Kernel's control. Now, Jacket can query the Kernel for the existence of the Hypermedia database (registry information is stored with the Internal service called Name service), and then connect directly to it to store the path with attached multimedia information. Later, the Visualization tool can connect similarly to the Hypermedia database to access and display the stored path information. All interaction between the components happens by sending messages in XML, using TCP/IP sockets.

3.4   The Database and the Visualization Tool

The design processes of architects are based on representation and manipulation of multimedia information that is associatively linked and location-based. Therefore the information management solution of the system must be capable of handling large multimedia objects, relationships between them, and adapt to constantly changing content. We store the recorded multimedia files and the path in a special hypermedia database. It is a major service included in the Atelier Infrastructure that provides various hypermedia services for client applications to use. The main purpose is to enable the associative linking of different kinds of multimedia objects. The Jacket constructs a special hyperdocument during an environment recoding session. It is constructed from different multimedia objects taken during the visit and their meta-information such as GPS location, date and time, and direction of the recorded item (see figure 9). The multimedia objects along with meta-information are called hyperobjects in the hypermedia system and users are later able to link them to other hyperobjects with specific tools. The path of the user's visit is modelled using hypernodes. They are containers for hyperobjects and have the GPS coordinate of the recording spot as their meta-information. The hypernodes are created periodically as the user wanders in the environment and each recorded multimedia element is attached to a hypernode located at the user's location. Several nodes therefore form a model of the user's path wandered in the environment. The nodes are then attached to a hyperdocument that models the whole visit. The hypermedia information recorded during visits must be visualized to users in a way that is effective and inspirational. The two tools provided by the Atelier system are the environment browser and the hyperobject manager.

The purpose of the environment browser is to enable users revisit the environments they have recorded with the Jacket. It displays users the wandered path over a map and the lets users freely navigate in a three dimensional world that models the recorded material of the visit (see figure 10). The hyperobject manager enables users to view various hyperobjects, create associations between them, and edit their meta-information.

The main task of the application is to enable users to view different types of multimedia information and create associations between different parts in the multimedia element. Users might for example find a specific part of an image interesting and add a textual note to it. Also, certain parts of video clips may be linked to still images and textual descriptions. The hypermedia system is able to handle all types of multimedia objects but currently only the most common formats are supported by client applications. Currently, the first running version of the Infrastructure Kernel has been implemented. It is possible to create Atelier components and External services and register them to the Infrastructure Kernel. The Infrastructure supports XML based communication, and includes various supportive elements for easier integration of components and services into the Infrastructure. The visualization components are also functional, as well as the Hypermedia database. In the near future, we will complete the integration of these system services and components into the Infrastructure so that they can be used in the context of the Atelier learning environment. One significant benefit of this integration is the possibility of any Atelier component to use the Hypermedia database for storing and retrieving hyperlinked multimedia data.

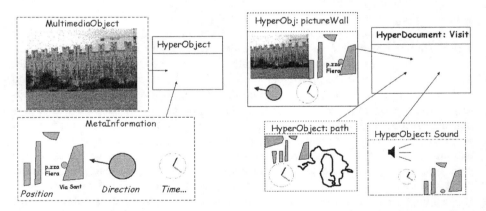

Fig. 9. The Jacket creates a media document out of the visits containing information and media objects that can be reused in the Atelier environment

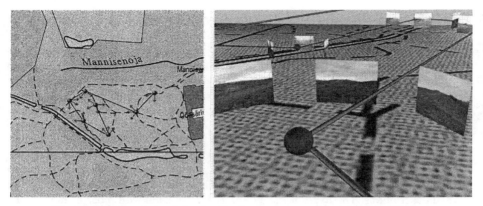

Fig. 10. The recorded path is visualized over a map and in a separate 3D view

3.5   Test with an Early Prototype

Andreas and Dieter (two Architects) used the mobile support application while visiting a small harbour in Sweden. They walked around the harbour taking pictures and recording sound (for example the sound of walking on the sand, two person talking on a small boat, sound of the waves, etc. Figure 11). Every time they took a picture with the digital camera or a sound with the MD recorder they were entering this information through the interface on the iPAQ. In this way the Jacket stored information about the position (from a GPS receiver) in which picture or sound where recorded.

The current version of the mobile application supports the recording of sounds with the iPAQ, and the logging of the files in the document of the visit. As at that time the visualization application was not completed, we developed an interactive picture showing the path on a map (Figure 12). Although we collected GPS information the walked path was corrected manually to have a more precise path and better test the concept behind the prototype. Clicking the red points on the map user could view images or play sounds that were recorded in that position. When using this prototype, users perform a walking path and actions (taking pictures and sounds in particular positions) to create a multimedia track. There are narrative elements that can be created for example, the particular way taken by the users and sequences of actions that are recorded. An architect, after having used the Jacket and navigated the media path, to explain the advantages of the Jacket cited Michel De Certeau [3] with these words: "it's hard to be down when you're up". That explains the problem of architects of designing with this bird-eye view on plan models and drawings, loosing the particularity of the 1:1 life. According to the users the prototype in its simplicity, was able to combine in a new way the two views.

Fig. 11. Two architects testing an early prototype in a harbor

Fig. 12. a) the architects during the visit, b) the interactive picture of the walked path, c) some of pictures taken during the visits

4   Discussion and Conclusions

Using virtual space in design or even combining real and virtual spaces is nothing new in architecture. In Drewe [7] the focus has been in the expansion of CAD-modeling to navigable spaces while maintaining the accuracy and completeness of CAD-models (for example see Bowman [1]) or connecting several design offices together by means of a virtual space (for example see [13], or our own related work [8]). Our approach differs from these in that we explicitly address the mobility aspect of design work, and that instead of accuracy and completeness of models we aim at sufficient material to evoke necessary experience and meanings – use computers as "thinking support" tools [18]. As we have seen in our fieldwork, architects have a well-developed practice to reconstruct the design site in the design office. Material is collected and different representations are created and linked. Conceptually our major challenge has been how to record aspects of the visits (the remote design space) so that the record is meaningful for the purposes of design in the atelier. According to our limited experimentations, we have been successful in providing mobile computational tools that offer new valuable ways for architects to re-travel in their material.

For example, we provide ways of combining the bird-eye perspective of the architect with the 1:1 experience of the visitor. We can consider the technological components individually.

The Mobile Application. The main human-computer interaction challenge is to achieve an artful integration of devices and applications with the social and physical environment. The aim is to provide technologies that integrate seamlessly in the everyday practices of people. The prototype we presented need to be handheld to be operated, while a more wishful solution would be wearable or integrated with operations as taking a picture.

The Navigation Tool. Although we started thinking of a virtual navigation tool, we are recognizing that computation should be integrated with the existing environment (as with the animating bAR code, and the texture brush). We have implemented an infrared remote control component to navigate the visit away from the desktop computer. We are now concentrating on other tangible interfaces as sensors, tags, and barcodes to navigate and manipulate the path. As tangible computing artifacts participate in a radical way in user's social and physical environment, it is harder to design applications compared to desktop software (where designer have a more controllable environment). As Dourish [6] points out "the precise *way* in which the artifact will be used to accomplish the work will be determined by the user, rather than by the designer." So that "the designer's attention is now focused on the resources that a design should provide to users in order for them to appropriate the artifacts and incorporate it into their practice." [6, p 173] We maintain that we (and generally the rest of the HCI field) are still at the beginning in learning how to accomplish this.

The Infrastructure. In heterogeneous technical environments with tagging systems, mobile devices, bar code readers, PC:s, servers, etc., it still should be possible to integrate different kinds of devices to and through the Infrastructure, using as much common implementation base as possible. For example, the software components used to hide the details of the communications and creating and handling XML messages should work as well in iPAQs and other mobile devices as in PCs. Also, the requirement to be able to use any type of physical input device to control virtually any type of functionality in the environment will be challenging to meet. For example, the bar code reader or the tagging devices, or a mobile phone, could be used to control the navigation of the 3D multimedia path, recorded during a visit. Moreover we have until now not addressed group aware feature in the system. For example, we have not addressed solutions to deal with multi-user hyperlinked multimedia data. Should all users see each other's links? What if the user changes a multimedia content? Should this change be reflected in all the other users' view of the data, or should a new, modified multimedia object be created for this user?

Reconsidering the Requirements. The mobile tool with its primitive functionality makes it possible for users to *collect and organized material* of visits while *Experiencing places* (Recording of sounds and paths that can be later combined with pictures). The material is made available in a document, which is stored in a database and can be *navigated* and *shared*. The material of the visit can be *linked* with other objects in the multimedia database. The *integration* with physical artifacts can be achieved using barcodes and scanners, tag-readers, and sensors. We are currently investigating ways to *manipulate* the path (e.g. changing the form of it by dragging nodes), and interact with it using tangible interfaces.

Acknowledgements

We are grateful to our co-researchers in the Atelier project, which is funded by the EU IST Disappearing Computer program. We wish to acknowledge in particular the contributions of Michael Gervautz, Heimo Kramer (Imagination Computer Services), Rüdiger Lainer, Kresimir Matcovic, Thomas Psik, Andreas Rumpfhuber, Dieter Spath, Virtu Halttunen (University of Oulu), and students at the Academy of fine Arts in Vienna. Finally we would like to acknowledge Infotech Oulu for supporting this research at the University of Oulu.

References

[1] Bowman, D., "Conceptual Design Space - Beyond Walk-through to Immersive Design," in Bertol, D., Designing Digital Space, John Wiley & Sons, New York, 1996

[2] Buschmann, F., Meunier, R., Rohnert, H., Sommerlad, P., Stal, M. Pattern-Oriented Software Architecture A System of Patterns. John Wiley and Sons Ltd, Chichester, UK, 1996.

[3] Certeau, M. de, Kunst des Handelns, Merve Verlag Berlin 1988.

[4] Cheverst, K., Mitchell, K., Davies N., The role of adaptive hypermedia in a context-aware tourist GUIDE. CACM 45(5): 47-51 (2002)

[5] Davies, N., Cheverst, K., Mitchell, K., Efrat, K., Using and Determining Location in a Context-Sensitive Tour Guide. IEEE Computer 34(8): 35-41 (2001)

[6] Dourish, P. (2001) Where the action is: the foundations of embodied interaction. MIT Press.

[7] Drewe, P. (2001) Physical and Virtual Space. How to Deal with Their Interaction? The Journal of Design Research, Volume 1, Issue 1, 2001

[8] Durstewitz, M., Kiefner,B., Kueke, R., Putkonen, H., Repo, P., Tuikka, T. (2002) Virtual Collaboration Environment for Aircraft Design, in Proceedings of 6th International Confer-ence ofInformation Visualization, Information Visualisation Society, London.

[9] Gaver, B., Martin, H. 2000. Alternatives Exploring Information Appliances through Conceptual Desing Proposals. ACM CHI 2000 Vol. 2 issue 1.

[10] Iacucci, G., Kuutti, K., Everyday life as a stage in creating and performing scenarios for wireless devices. In: Personal and Ubiquitous Computing Journal Vol 6, Springer Verlag, 2002, pp. 209-306.

[11] Iacucci, G., Wagner, I., Supporting Collaboration Ubiquitously: An augmented learning environment for architecture students, In: the Proceedings of the 8th European Conference of Computer-supported Cooperative Work, 14.-18. September 2003, Helsinki, Finland, in press.

[12] Izadi, S., Fraser, M., Benford, S., Flintham, M., Greenhalgh, C., Rodden, T. and Schnädelbach, H., Citywide: supporting interactive digital experiences across physical space. Journal of Personal and Ubiquitous Computing 6(3): 2002.

[13] Maher, M.L. et al (1996) The potential and current limitations in a virtual design studio, 16 pages http://www.arch.su.edu.au/~mary/VDSjournal/index.html (18-02-03)

[14] Persson, P., Espinoza, F., Fagerberg, P., Sandin, A. & Cöster, R (forthcoming) GeoNotes: A Location-based Information System for Public Spaces, in Kristina Höök, David Benyon and Alan Munro (eds) Readings in Social Navigation of Information Space, Springer.

[15] Pradhan, S., Brignone, C., Cui, J.H., McReynolds, A., Smith T, M., "Websigns: Hyperlinking Physical Locations to the Web", IEEE Computer, August 2001 (Vol. 34, No. 8), pp. 42-48.

[16] Randell C., Muller, H., The Shopping Jacket: Wearable Computing for the Consumer In Personal Technologies vol.4 no.4, pages 241--244. Springer, September 2000.

[17] Tuulari, Esa; Ylisaukko-oja, Arto, SoapBox: A Platform for Ubiquitous Computing Research and Applications. Lecture Notes in Computer Sc. 2414: Pervasive Computing. Zürich, CH, August 26-28, 2002. Mattern, F. Naghshineh,M. (eds.). Springer (2002), pp. 125 – 138.

[18] Watanabe, M.S. (1995) Induction city, in search of a free order: how to guide, not design, the city, InterCommunication, No.12 http://www.ntticc.or.jp/pub/ic_mag/ic012/watanabe/induction_e.html (18-02-03)

Everyday Wearable Computer Use: A Case Study of an Expert User

Kent Lyons

College of Computing and GVU Center, Georgia Institute of Technology
Atlanta, GA 30332-0280 USA
kent@cc.gatech.edu

Abstract. Wearable computers are a unique point in the mobile computing design space. In this paper, we examine the use of a wearable in everyday situations. Specifically, we discuss findings from a case study of an expert wearable computer user in an academic research setting over an interval of five weeks. We examine the use of the computer by collecting periodic screen shots of the wearable's display and utilize these screen shots in interview sessions to create a retrospective account of the machine's use and the user's context. This data reveals that the user employs the computer to augment his memory in various ways. We also found evidence of the wearable's use while engaged in another primary task. Furthermore, we discuss the intricate strategies developed by the participant that enable him to utilize the wearable in these roles.

1 Introduction

A wearable computer is a computer worn on the body as clothing and is highly personal. While the technology is still novel, a few researchers and hobbyists have adopted wearable computers into their everyday lives. These users are often seen wearing their head–up displays or typing on one handed keyboards in a wide variety of situations. Anecdotally, these users report that they often take notes or retrieve information in a large variety of everyday situations. However, we do not have a firm understanding of exactly what tasks the computers are supporting or in what situations. Likewise, we know little about how these users employ the wearable to accomplish those tasks.

We are interested in researching how early adopters take advantage of wearable computing technology. In this paper, we present a formative study designed to uncover wearable user practices. Specifically, we present data collected from a case study of an expert wearable computer user during the course of his normal daily activities over a period of five weeks. Our participant is in an academic research environment where he uses the machine routinely in a large variety of situations and has been doing so for over eight years.

Sample size is an issue when studying wearable computer use especially given our particular interest in everyday use. There are only a handful of people in the world who have adopted wearables into their lives and have continued to use the computers daily. Obviously, with such a small user population one could not

L. Chittaro (Ed.): Mobile HCI 2003, LNCS 2795, pp. 61–75, 2003.
© Springer-Verlag Berlin Heidelberg 2003

hope to span the possible space of wearable computer use. The small number of current users may not be representative; however, they are using their computers while doing typical everyday tasks working with information and managing their daily lives. As a result, instead of attempting to generalize across a very small number of users, we are seeking to understand the practices developed by a single successful wearable computer user. This is an attempt to lay the foundation for future work such as designing explicitly for wearable computers or comparing the wearable computer's unique features and usage to those of other mobile technologies.

In this paper, we detail the findings from our case study. We describe the technology our study participant employs as well as general characteristics of the machine's usage. We discuss our technique for capturing data on the wearable computer and our interview methods used to assist in the qualitative interpretation of that data. Next, we present detailed examples of interaction with the wearable computer in everyday situations from our collected data. Using these examples, we discuss trends in the data showing how the computer is used to augment the user's memory and in situations where the wearable is not the primary focus of the user's attention.

2   The Wearable Computer

The participant in our study has been using a wearable computer daily for over eight years. The computer is a derivative of the Lizzy design [10] and is housed in a bag worn over the shoulder and rests on the user's left side by his hip. This arrangement allows the user to continually wear the machine throughout the day. The Twiddler2, a one handed chording keyboard, is the input device (Figure 1). It serves as a combination of keyboard and mouse; however, the participant only utilized the keyboard functionality during our study. The display is a MicroOptical CO-3 VGA head–up display designed to mount on a pair of eyeglasses (Figure 2). The user modified the mount so he could quickly attach and remove the display as needed. Finally, the wearable is designed for low power consumption so that it can be powered throughout the day. The user reports he typically gets ten to twelve hours of use from a set of batteries and swaps out batteries as needed to get a longer runtime. Together, these design features allow the user to call the machine to action quickly at any time by snapping the display to the user's glasses and grabbing the Twiddler from his side.

Our participant's wearable computer runs Linux and the X Windowing System. Emacs is the primary application used, and the vast majority of interaction with the machine happens within this versatile text editor. For the few occasions where the user did not directly interact through Emacs, an xterm was opened and used temporarily. This occurred when the built–in Emacs shell was not sufficient at displaying the needed application. It is interesting to note that the user did not run any software explicitly designed for wearable use during this study.

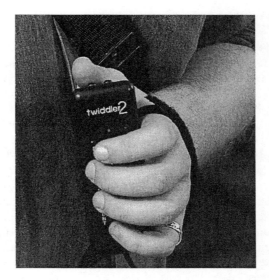

Fig. 1.   The Twiddler2 one handed chording keyboard with mouse

Fig. 2.   An example of the MicroOptical head–up display mounted on eyeglasses

Figures 3 through 6 show typical screen shots of the user interacting with the machine.[1] Emacs fills most of the user's display. Xclock runs in the bottom right corner of the screen but is partially covered by the Emacs window. As a result, only half of the clock is visible. The user indicated that when he recently changed the font for Emacs it covered up the clock, and he had not yet fixed it.

Within Emacs, the line of text at the bottom of the screen in inverse video is the mode line. This line shows various status information such as attributes about the current state of the file (modified, saved or read–only), the name of the file being edited, the time, and the CPU load of the machine. In parentheses, information about the current mode is displayed. The last two items show the current line number and the percentage from the top of the file.

---

[1] The figures have been altered for anonymity and readability.

3 Related Work

While our focus is on general everyday use, other research has been conducted examining the use of wearable computers to support industrial tasks. These applications are designed to aid the user in accomplishing a specific job such as vehicle inspection [5] [9] or oil rig maintenance [4]. The wearables used in these situations tend to be worn only to accomplish a very specific function. Ross and Blasch developed a wearable application to support the specific everyday task of wayfinding for the visually impaired[8]. Despite these efforts, little work has been done on exploring how wearable computers can be used to support more general everyday activities beyond a single task.

The Remembrance Agent (RA) [7] is one program designed for everyday wearable use. This application enables retrieval by performing a continuous search on the user's archive of information stored on the computer. The RA utilizes the text on the user's screen as the key for the search and proactively shows one line summaries of the best few matches. While the participant in our study has used the RA in the past, we did not find any usage during our study.

Want et al. investigated the use of the ParcTab, a mobile palm–sized computing device, in a work setting and characterized its usage after deployment to several users [11]. While both the users in this study and our participant utilizes mobile devices to support their work, there are significant differences in the computational capabilities and the interface. We found much less variety in the number and types of applications used by our participant; however, we found a rich variety of computer usage centered on the user's information practices.

Perry et al. [6] examined mobile workers' management practices of information through documents and mobile technology. Some aspects of this work relate to the availability of infrastructure at remote work sites and the ability of a user to access her information and devices. For instance, they found that laptops might be carried to a remote site but not from meeting to meeting in one location. They noted that "the physical form of these objects does not facilitate 'casual' carrying and prevents them from being ubiquitously available to the mobile worker". The wearable computer our participant uses helps compensate for these aspects. Even though infrastructure in a mobile setting might be questionable, we found that the user always has the support from his wearable. Unlike the laptops in this study, the user wears the machine and tends to always carry it with him.

Kidd explored characteristics of knowledge workers and revealed some of their information practices: "This study suggests that knowledge workers may be uncomfortable with these [mobile] devices as note–takers except for non primary aspects for their work such as noting a telephone number, a diary date or a short message for a colleague" [2]. As we will show, we did find the use of the wearable to store these types of facts; however, the computer was also employed to store information about primary tasks of interest to the user.

4 Method

We developed a method to accommodate the everyday nature of our participant's wearable computer use. Our data consists of screen shots captured on the wearable computer augmented with interviews of the participant. We chose this method because it is difficult to directly observe the interaction between the machine and user. Capture on the wearable enables us to gather information directly about the interaction with the computer [3]. Furthermore, the user operates in a wide range of environments making representative direct observation of wearable use logistically impractical.

Our participant's existing wearable computer was augmented to capture screen shots to the hard drive approximately every five seconds. After some initial experimentation, five seconds was chosen to minimize the impact on the user's machine while still maintaining a high rate of capture. The screen shots were later used in interview sessions to create a retrospective account of the machine's use [1]. During these sessions, we played back the captured log to the user as a movie while often stopping and revisiting portions of an interaction. The user detailed how the machine was being used and the interviewer asked questions about general context such as who was around, his location, and the current activities. We believe the screen shots played an invaluable role during the interview sessions because everyday tasks become tacit. The screen shots serve as a cue to remind the user of what he was doing instead of needing the user to try and recall what happened. The recorded log provides an objective record of what happened and how often.

Because the wearable is a very personal device, potential access of private information in the course of daily use such as passwords, sensitive email, and medical records is an issue. Our solution to censoring this private information was to give the user the ability to control the capture software. The user could pause the logging if he was working on private information for an extended period of time. Additionally, the user could also black out screen shots already logged if he realized sensitive information was recorded.

5 Case Study Findings

During the course of our five week study, we collected 68 hours of interaction with the machine from 15 different days. This was approximately 15,000 screen shots. The wearable was used in a large variety of situations, and after exploring the data, it became clear that the situation influenced how the machine was used. In addition to being used while alone, the wearable was often used while engaged with other people. This could be in the form of one–on–one meetings, small groups, talks, demos, or impromptu gatherings.

Most of the usage of the machine occurred in the user's academic work setting. The machine was used in the user's office, the hallway, the social area near his office, the lab, and conference rooms. The user also spent some time working in another building across campus using the machine in classrooms and around the building. During our study, the user also went on two trips to visit other research institutions, one in a foreign country. The machine was used to prepare for these trips and for support during the trip. In the interviews, the user also indicated that he used the machine while riding on a train, as a passenger in a car, and while walking. The wearable contains a wide variety of information including notes, email, to do lists, contact information, and personal records. It was also used as a scratch pad, and on a few occasions for writing and editing articles.

We next introduce the data collected through examples. Some of these are common activities for this user, while others are more rare but demonstrate the range and richness of the situations in which the wearable is used. These categories of examples emerged upon analysis of the data. They reflect the patterns in his information and in turn the patterns of wearable use in different everyday situations.

5.1 "Today"

Our first example of a typical interaction with the wearable centers on the "today" file. This file acts as a very flexible to do list that is instantiated as a free form text file and contains short term important activities that have little meaning long term. This file is not intended for archiving; items are deleted as they are completed or become irrelevant.

The "today" file is one of the most commonly used files as we captured its usage on 11 of the 15 days that we obtained data. The interactions take place in a wide variety of situations and tend to be brief with intermittent usage throughout the day. In the midst of other tasks, the user will quickly switch to this file to jot down an item or check the list. Likewise, he will occasionally browse the file to review the list more thoroughly and clear out old items.

The contents of this file are terse notes to the user that serve as reminders. These are often simple and can be as short as a one word prompt such as "tax" shown on the second line in Figure 3. The user characterized this file in jest as "everything I should be doing but don't".

5.2 Recurring Meetings

The wearable is also used to support recurring meetings. These meetings tend to be with one to a few people where the user is familiar with the attendees and their work. The topics of discussion include new points of interest as well as revisiting old items. While listening and participating in a discussion, the user takes concise notes on general points of interest or specific details that he wants to remember. The focus of the user's attention is on the discussion, but the user takes notes as a background task.

Terse notes are sufficient because they tend to be accessed only in the context of the meeting, whereas other styles of notes are accessed outside the context in which they were taken. The user's organization of this type of information affords quickly reviewing notes from past meetings. This is a fast interaction because the previous notes are stored adjacent to the new ones, and as the user is often already wearing the display, the only operation needed to peruse the file is paging up or down.

This note taking practice occurs regularly given that meetings are a common work activity for this user. A typical example is shown in Figure 4. This is a screen shot captured during a one–on–one meeting a few minutes after the start of the conversation. Here is a reconstruction of the interaction with the wearable that took place during this meeting:

> The user first opened the file of all notes on student meetings called "students" (see status line on Emacs buffer). He found the proper place to record new notes about the conversation with this individual by searching for his name, "mike". He created a new spot for this meeting by entering a few blank lines between the name and the previous meetings notes which start with the line containing "021302". Next, he typed in a the string "031302" representing March 13th 2002, and a few lines of text that are notes on the current conversation. The user continued to take a few lines of notes for the duration of the meeting.

The area of the file for this person is marked with the line "mike:". The user said that he uses this convention of a name followed by a colon to attribute some information to a person. Here it is being used to attribute the notes in the

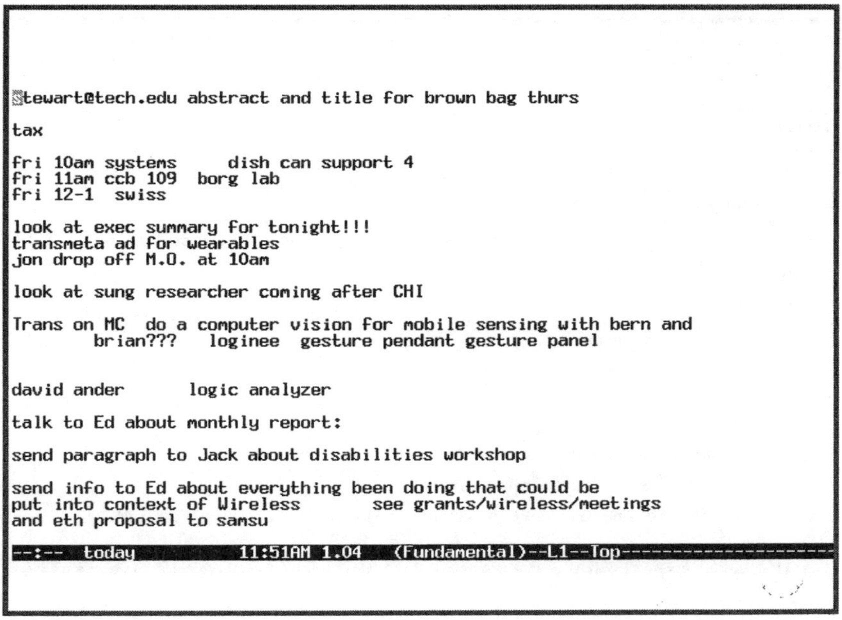

```
Stewart@tech.edu abstract and title for brown bag thurs

tax

fri 10am systems      dish can support 4
fri 11am ccb 109  borg lab
fri 12-1  swiss

look at exec summary for tonight!!!
transmeta ad for wearables
jon drop off M.O. at 10am

look at sung researcher coming after CHI

Trans on MC  do a computer vision for mobile sensing with bern and
          brian???   loginee  gesture pendant gesture panel

david ander       logic analyzer

talk to Ed about monthly report:

send paragraph to Jack about disabilities workshop

send info to Ed about everything been doing that could be
put into context of Wireless       see grants/wireless/meetings
and eth proposal to samsu
--:--  today         11:51AM 1.04    (Fundamental)--L1--Top----------------
```

Fig. 3. The "today" file which contains brief notes on to do items

next part of the file to Mike and is used as the key when searching for this part of the file. Following that line are subsections for meetings from different days with that person. Each of these begins with strings representing the date and is followed by the notes from that meeting. The text before "mike:" is notes taken during a conversation with a different person.

5.3   Talks and Demonstrations

Over the course of our study, our participant attended several events relevant to his interests such as talks and demonstrations. These activities tended to be one–time meetings with a single person disseminating information. The speaker was often from another institution and usually had infrequent contact with the user outside this event. Talks are often given in a class room or meeting room with the wearable user sitting in the audience. When the user is attending a demonstration, there are usually only a few other people listening to the speaker at one time, and often there are many other demonstrations going on. The user will often walk up to one demonstration, listen and take notes for a few minutes, and then go to another demonstration.

In this setting, the user generates more descriptive and complete notes compared to the previous examples. He stated his goal as "want[ing] to refer back to research notes" whenever they might be relevant. For a talk that the user attends, he creates a new file in the "talks" directory and names the file after

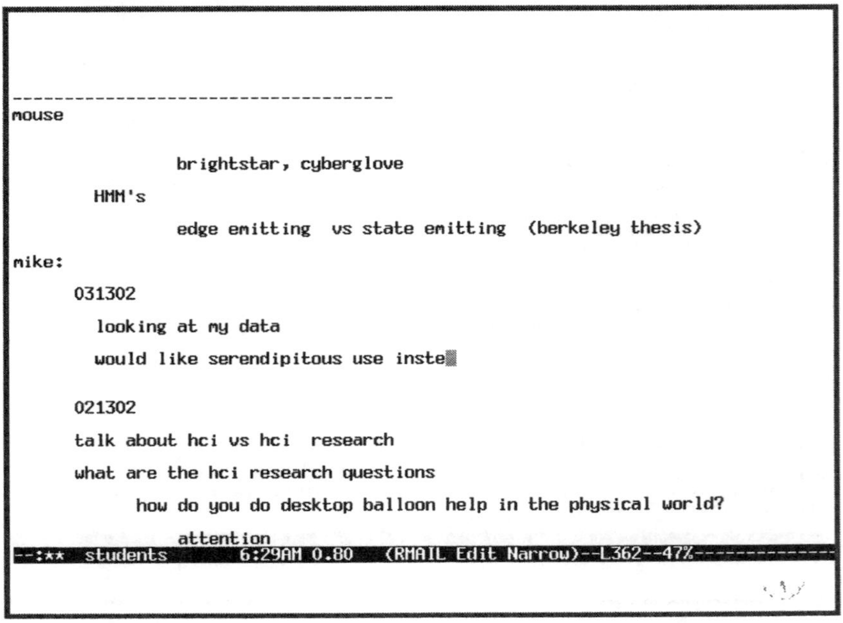

```
------------------------------------
mouse

                brightstar, cyberglove
        HMM's
                edge emitting  vs state emitting  (berkeley thesis)
mike:
        031302
          looking at my data
          would like serendipitous use inste

        021302
        talk about hci vs hci   research
        what are the hci research questions
            how do you do desktop balloon help in the physical world?
            attention
--:**   students       6:29AM 0.80    (RMAIL Edit Narrow)--L362--47%-------------
```

Fig. 4. An example of notes from a recurring meeting

the speaker's last name (for example "Tern" in Figure 5). For a demonstration at a remote site, a new section of an existing file about the place or trip is made, or if needed, a new file is created.

The notes start with some basic context about the situation, usually including the date, person, and location. Tabs and new lines are used to separate and organize the ideas represented in the notes (Figure 5). The user actively structures, restructures, and fills in more details as the talk progresses and his understanding of the content changes.

5.4   Contact Management

The wearable user has a file named "phones" devoted to contacts. He uses this file to help manage information about the people he knows. It contains information such as names, phone numbers, email addresses, titles, and locations or addresses of people. In addition to this traditional contact information, the user includes other reminders about the person which are stored in the same file. He often has a note about when he last met the person and why they met, or a more general description of why that person is included in the file. Directions to locations are not uncommon and sometimes include travel times.

The user indicated that he would write down new information when he met someone. Usually, this new information came from a business card. Our data also

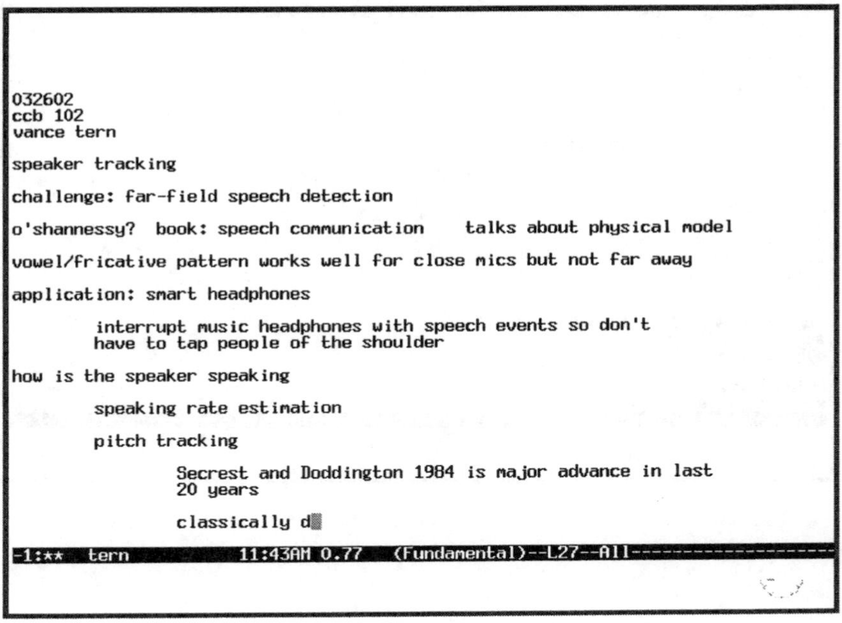

```
032602
ccb 102
vance tern

speaker tracking

challenge: far-field speech detection

o'shannessy?  book: speech communication     talks about physical model

vowel/fricative pattern works well for close mics but not far away

application: smart headphones

            interrupt music headphones with speech events so don't
            have to tap people of the shoulder

how is the speaker speaking

        speaking rate estimation

        pitch tracking

                Secrest and Doddington 1984 is major advance in last
                20 years

                classically d
-1:**   tern              11:43AM 0.77    (Fundamental)--L27--All----------
```

Fig. 5. Research notes taken during a talk

showed that the user also occasionally copied email signatures from messages stored on the machine into the file.

This file is used when the user wants to remember details about a person he just met or to recall information about someone he met previously. When he encounters someone he has met before, the user quickly searches through the file during the conversation to find when they last met and other information about that person's work.

In Figure 6, we see the variety of ways the user records information about his contacts. For example, the first line was entered because the user frequents a local sandwich shop and repeatedly sees the same employee. However, he can never remember his name, Yan. One time, the wearable user asked for the employee's name and wrote it down at the top of this file so he could look it up the next time he was there. The information for Mara Wareall, Mark Tersey and Dakis Yahonce was all entered while the user was organizing a business dinner. He went through the "phones" file ensuring that he knew how to contact all of the people attending. He did not have any information for these people in the file so he added it.

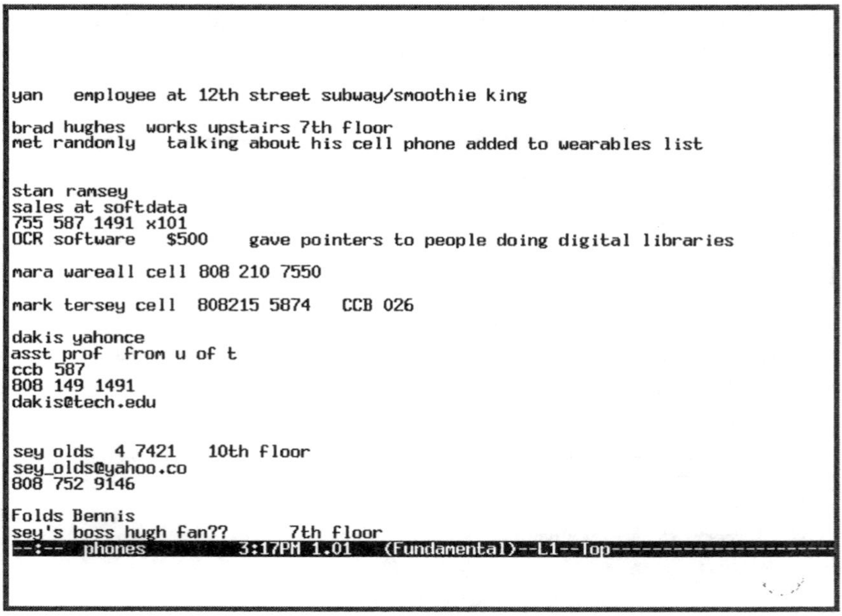

```
yan   employee at 12th street subway/smoothie king

brad hughes  works upstairs 7th floor
met randomly   talking about his cell phone added to wearables list

stan ramsey
sales at softdata
755 587 1491 x101
OCR software   $500    gave pointers to people doing digital libraries

mara wareall cell 808 210 7550

mark tersey cell  808215 5874   CCB 026

dakis yahonce
asst prof  from u of t
ccb 587
808 149 1491
dakis@tech.edu


sey olds  4 7421   10th floor
sey_olds@yahoo.co
808 752 9146

Folds Bennis
sey's boss hugh fan??    7th floor
--:--    phones         3:17PM 1.01   (Fundamental)--L1--Top------------------
```

Fig. 6. The "phones" file which serves as the user's contact list

5.5 Scratch Pad

While the previous examples occurred regularly, there are other interactions that are less typical but demonstrate the versatility of the user and his wearable computer. One instance is the computer's use as a scratch pad:

> After a pause in using the machine of about ten minutes, the user was at a command line prompt in an xterm. He cleared the screen and started entering a string of numbers at a moderate rate: "1 3 2 4.5 3 6.75 4 1...". The input was obviously not a command to be executed. After 43 seconds, a total of 10 numbers were entered. Then there was a pause of 13 minutes after which the user continued use of the machine by first closing the xterm, erasing the numbers.

When queried about the purpose of the numbers in an interview session, the user indicated that he was doing some math in his head and was writing down the intermediate results. He happened to use the xterm that was available on screen. He did not want to worry about opening a file or saving the information and just needed to jot down some numbers.

The user's own working memory or a scratch piece of paper could have sufficed, but the wearable provided adequate support for this type of task. He was able to use the wearable as a scratch pad since there was very little setup time. The machine was most likely more convenient than looking for a piece of paper since his machine is always with him and has been integrated into his way of working.

6 Discussion

These examples of "today", recurring meetings, talks and demonstrations, contact management, and scratch pad show three main trends: the wearable as a device to augment the user's memory, the wearable used as an aid for a primary task, and information organization. These items highlight the versatility of the wearable computer and the strategies adopted by the user to enable effective use in everyday situations.

6.1 Memory Augmentation

A key theme of the wearable's use supported by our data collection and exemplified in the previous section is how the user has adopted the wearable computer as a tool to augment his memory. The machine is employed to aid the user's memory over a spectrum of time frames and in a large variety of situations. There is a low cost associated with machine use because the interaction is quick and the machine is almost always with the user. The user leverages these features to store information in his self–described "other brain".

The majority of interactions with the machine augment the user's long term memory in some way. The user relies on the machine's perfect storage capability to compensate for the fact that his memories can degrade with time. The "today" file is used to remember near term events. The meeting notes serve as reminders in the context of the meeting about past discussions. The "phones" file archives a variety of information about whom the user has met. Lastly, notes such as those from talks and demos comprise a large amount of archived information relevant to the user's work.

On a few occasions, the data revealed the user applying the wearable as a tool for short term memory augmentation. These interactions are characterized by the need to remember a small number of items for no more than a few minutes. The previous scratch pad example demonstrates this technique. The user employed the wearable because it was a convenient place to jot down some numbers while performing calculations in his head. Instead of remembering the temporary values or finding some other support mechanism, the wearable computer interaction was fast enough and the machine flexible enough to aid the user. Like working memory, the items are temporary, and there is no need for long term storage.

While the user employs the wearable computer for augmented memory support, it often does not replace the user's memory. It serves as a repository for details, and the notes provide cues to refresh the user's memory.

6.2   Wearable as Secondary Focus of Attention

While the machine is commonly used to augment the user's memory, most of the interaction occurs under tight attention or time constraints because the user is actively involved in some other primary task. In these situations in which the user is often engaged with other people, the primary use of the wearable is in a support role. In a conversation, the user might take notes on points of interest or retrieve support material from the machine relevant to the discussion. However, the primary focus is still on the conversation at hand, and the user tries to adhere to the social constraints of the situation.

While engaged in another activity, the user must quickly make many decisions that govern his interaction with the machine. First, to use the machine effectively for memory augmentation, the user must be able to know where to store new notes or find old information. The user has developed several strategies that revolve around the organization of his information which enable him to quickly return to the task at hand.

While taking notes, the user also decides how much effort and time to spend on recording the information. For a subject familiar to the user, he may only record details that he might otherwise forget such as during a weekly meeting (Figure 4). For less familiar material of interest, he might spend more time taking richer notes (Figure 5). The process of recording the information with the wearable computer tends to take minimal attention as the user touch types his notes at a rapid pace (approximately 55 words per minute) and the head–up display enables him to check on the notes being written with a quick glance.

Even while primarily engaged in another activity, it is clear from the data that the user does occasionally shift his focus to the machine while recording information. This usually takes the form of editing the content of the notes or restructuring them. On several occasions, the user would go back a few lines and change a line of text or expand on an idea by writing down more details. The user indicated that the changes in the structure of the notes were so that the information would be easier to access when needed. Furthermore, he said that if he did not spend the time to organize the information while taking it he knew he would not go back later to do so.

On some occasions, the user spends time directly interacting with the machine. These interactions usually center around maintenance of his information. There might be other people around, but he is not engaged in activity with them. For example, although the user generally decides where to place information as he is storing it, sometimes he explicitly spends time consolidating and organizing his data. When the user was on a trip and preparing to meet his hosts and attend a demo, he spent part of the morning going through a collection of email he had gathered about that trip. He went through the email copying out contact information, placing it into the "phones" file. He annotated and rearranged the information so he could refer to it later that day when he met his hosts.

6.3   Information Organization

The data show that the user has developed an intricate scheme for organizing his information space. In addition to using traditional file hierarchies, there is often structure within individual files. The notes from a meeting (Figure 4) represent a composite file consisting of several separate entries from meetings with different people on different days. Another example of this technique includes taking notes in a file containing several emails on a subject. In general, tabs, blank lines, dashed lines, or email headers are used to define the structure within a file.

Within a composite file, the user can impose additional structure to keep related information together. In the "phones" file, the user indicated that he often tries to group people from the same organization together (Figure 6). The student notes file is organized by person at the highest level. Each area devoted to an individual is further subdivided into meetings labeled with the date (Figure 4).

There were only a small number of explicit retrievals found in the data; however, the composite file structure might facilitate incidental access. Because the user co-locates related information he can quickly and easily review previous notes as he is about to enter new ones.

It is also worth reiterating that none of the applications our participant used during our study were designed specifically for wearable computers. The current machine and programs are sufficiently flexible to enable this expert user to operate in these conditions with the aid of his strategies. However, there is poor support for a novice user attempting to accomplish similar tasks.

7   Future Work

While we gained insightful data from our user, we are interested in performing a followup study to examine other everyday wearable computer users' practices. Again due to the extremely small user population, we will not be able to characterize the design space fully. However, we believe other users might have their own interesting practices that could be leveraged in future wearable computer designs.

Through the data obtained in our case study we have been able to examine an expert user's practices, and we have identified the computer's role in augmenting his memory. Now that we have begun to characterize the situations in which this expert user employs the wearable, we can explicitly study key themes such as incidental access, augmented memory, and secondary attention. Furthermore, we can use our preliminary findings to begin designing better support for these tasks.

More generally, work needs to be done on reducing the overhead of using the computer. The user has been able to use the wearable's current interface and applications for years, but there is room for improvement. With a large portion of the computer's use happening in a secondary support role, it is critical that the machine minimize its needs for the user's attention so the user's focus can remain on his primary task. While doing so, the wearable should retain its power and the flexibility to be adopted into various everyday situations.

A key aspect of designing new wearable applications will be reducing the need for the expert's strategies of organization. By creating explicit support in the applications for the uses identified in this work, we can begin developing interfaces better suited for novice users. Likewise explicit application support would also hopefully reduce the breakdowns currently experienced in the user's strategies.

8   Conclusion

This case study is a first step in understanding some of the capabilities a wearable computer can provide in supporting everyday life. We found that the wearable computer was used by the expert to aid his memory in a large variety of situations. The wearable was occasionally the primary focus of attention; however, it is also common for the machine to be used in a secondary role supporting another primary task. We found the user developed several strategies that enabled him to use the wearable computer in situations where his attention is limited. This initial understanding of an early adopter's expert work practices will help direct our exploration into the potential of wearable computers. Our findings will also help to enable the design of applications suited to the conditions of everyday use.

Acknowledgements

This work is funded in part by NSF Career Grant #0093291. Thanks to Amanda Lyons, Gregory Abowd and Thad Starner for their contributions.

References

[1] H. Beyer and K. Holtzblat. *Contextual Design: Defining Customer-Centered Systems*, chapter Contextual Inquiry in Practice. Morgan Kaufmann, 1998.

[2] A. Kidd. The marks are on the knowledge worker. In *Conference proceedings on Human factors in computing systems*, pages 186–191. ACM Press, 1994.

[3] K. Lyons and T. Starner. Mobile capture for wearable computer usability testing. In *Proceedings of IEEE International Symposium on Wearable Computing (ISWC 2001)*, Zurich, Switerland, 2001.

[4] J. Moffett, D. Wahila, C. Graefe, J. Siegel, and J. Swart. Enriching the design process: Developing a wearable operator's assistant. In *IEEE Intl. Symp. on Wearable Computers*, pages 35–42, Atlanta, GA, 2000.

[5] J. Ockerman. *Task Guidance and Procedure Context: Aiding Workers in Appropriate Procedure Following*. PhD thesis, Georgia Institute of Technology, Atlanta, GA, April 2000.

[6] M. Perry, K. O'Hara, A. Sellen, B. Brown, and R. Harper. Dealing with mobility: understanding access anytime, anywhere. *ACM Transactions on Computer-Human Interaction (TOCHI)*, 8(4):323–347, 2001.

[7] B. J. Rhodes. *Just-In-Time Information Retrieval*. PhD thesis, MIT Media Laboratory, Cambridge, MA, May 2000.

[8] D. A. Ross and B. B. Blasch. Evaluation of orientation interfaces for wearable computers. In *Proceedings of IEEE International Symposium on Wearable Computing (ISWC 2000)*, pages 51–58, Atlanta, GA, 2000.

[9] J. Siegel and M. Bauer. A field usability evaluation of a wearable system. In *IEEE Intl. Symp. on Wearable Computers*, pages 18–22, Cambridge, MA, 1997.

[10] T. Starner. *Wearable Computing and Context Awareness*. PhD thesis, MIT Media Laboratory, Cambridge, MA, May 1999.

[11] R. Want, B. N. Schilit, N. I. Adams, R. Gold, K. Petersen, D. Goldberg, J. R. Ellis, and M. Weiser. An overview of the PARCTAB ubiquitous computing experiment. *IEEE Personal Communications*, 2(6):28–33, Dec 1995.

Using Mobile Keypads with Limited Visual Feedback: Implications to Handheld and Wearable Devices

Miika Silfverberg

Nokia Research Center
P.O. Box 407, FIN-00045 Nokia Group, Finland
miika.silfverberg@nokia.com

Abstract. Mobile devices are often used in busy contexts, where the operation takes place – at least temporarily – with limited visual information. In such 'blind use', the passive tactile properties of the device become crucial. Two mobile keypads with very different tactile properties were tested in an experiment with twelve experienced mobile phone users. Results highlight the importance of passive tactile feel. Most clear differences were seen in errors: while the keypad with high tactile cues could be used even in total absence of visual information, the performance with low tactility keypad collapsed. This underlines the importance of the industrial design in creating mobile devices that are accessible by anyone, in any context. Wearable keypads may also benefit from indirect visual feedback shown on the display. In this study, simple indirect feedback increased subjective ease, although only moderate effects were found in performance. Also more sophisticated feedback types need to be studied.

1   Introduction

Handheld and wearable devices can be used anytime and anywhere. Our primary sense, vision, is inherently limited since the eyes can be fixated only to one place at a time. Especially in mobile context, the visual domain is often occupied by other simultaneous tasks. For example, when operating a mobile phone while walking on a busy city street, the user has to monitor other people and the surrounding traffic in order to avoid collisions. Some of this activity can be done using the peripheral vision, but from time to time eye-fixation must be moved away from the device, at least temporarily.

Using a device under temporary unavailability of vision is often coined 'blind use'. While some may regard this term as dismissive of the daily problems that the visually impaired people confront, there is also a positive side in the term, highlighting the similarities between so-called 'normal' and 'disabled' people. Another widely used term is 'eyes-free' use, similarly to 'hands-free'. We will use the term blind use in this paper.

L. Chittaro (Ed.): Mobile HCI 2003, LNCS 2795, pp. 76–90, 2003.

When vision is unavailable, the auditory modality is often suggested as a compensatory modality (e.g. [1]). Speech and audio are indeed useful in closed contexts, or when communication is not private (e.g. announcement delivered to a group of people). However, in open, public contexts, the use of auditory information is often limited by factors related to social acceptability and privacy.

In personal devices, tactile information is clearly less problematic than audio, since often only the user her/himself can perceive it. The tactile sense is also always available. While auditory information is often drowned by the roar of the traffic, such masking happens less often with tactile sensations. Whenever the user touches the device in order to operate it, skin contact is made, allowing tactile information be transformed through pressure receptors located in the skin. Put together, when visual information is temporarily unavailable, tactile sense can potentially give us valuable compensatory information in a discreet and personal way, in any environment.

1.1 Mobile Keypads and Keyboards

This study focuses on compensatory use of passive tactile information in mobile keypads. Passive tactile information refers to the natural tactile sensation that is obtained when the finger is moved along any surface, as opposed to active tactile feedback produced by force-feedback devices.

Keypads or keyboards are input devices that consist of several individual keys arranged in an orderly fashion, typically in a grid-like pattern. The term keyboard is used here for input devices that are mainly designed for two-handed operation, while keypads are mainly used with one hand. This study concentrates on mobile use of the latter, although the results are partly applicable also to keyboards. (Keypad is used also when referring to keypads and keyboards together.)

Keypads are potentially efficient input devices. Previous studies show that when visual and tactile senses are fully available, experienced mobile phone users are able to operate the keys with the rate of about 3.3 presses per second, which provides considerable input bandwidth [13]. However, when feedback through either visual or tactile sense is reduced, the situation may be different.

Mobile, physical keypads can be classified in two main categories: handheld and wearable.

Handheld Keypads. Handheld keypads are used in devices that are small enough to be held and operated in hand. Depending on the device form-factor, one or two hands are used. Handheld devices are typically fully integrated, consisting of a single unit; thus the keypad is not separated from the display. In optimal conditions, eyes can be easily moved between display and keypad, allowing almost continuous visual feedback from the keypad area. Therefore, in handheld keypads, tactile information becomes especially critical in contexts where visual information can be fragmentary, as in a city context described above.

The standard 12-key telephone keypad is the most widespread of handheld keypads. With the recent success of mobile phones, this 3 x 4 matrix layout has hundreds of millions users worldwide. Although originally designed for telephone number dialing, the keypad is also used for several other purposes in current mobile phones. Most importantly, with the success of SMS messages, billions of text messages are sent each month [6]. The number keypad can also be used for accessing menu functions or data. Although the keys are often relatively small, the limited number of keys in a simple matrix makes this layout highly potential for blind use. A standard feature is a 'blind dot', a small rise at number key 5 (either in the center of the key, or above/below it), which helps blind use, but other tactile cues are also essential (e.g. key shapes and edges). Phone keypad is most often used with one or two thumbs.

Another common key arrangement is the QWERTY layout, which has been adopted recently also to mobile use. QWERTY has much higher number of keys than the phone layout, forcing the keys to be packed even more tightly. This limits the effectiveness of tactile information. For example touch-typing using all ten fingers – a common form of blind use in full-size computer keyboards – is hardly possible in handheld devices. In contrast, thumbs are often used here also. Most keyboards incorporate blind dots on both sides of the keypad (on keys F and J).

Phone and QWERTY keypads have been studied extensively, but only rarely in relation to mobile devices ([4], [13]). None of these studies cover blind use.

Wearable Keypads. In contrast with handheld devices that consist of 'one box', wearable devices can be distributed over various parts of the user's body and clothing. Also, the keypad and display may be separated, which has special consequences for visual feedback. As Lehikoinen and Röykkee noted [8], wearable devices are often most comfortably used in relaxed, neutral position, where the arm is kept straight. In this position, the keypad and the operating fingers are completely outside the visual field. This further emphasizes the role of tactile information. While handheld keypads suffer only from temporal absence of visual feedback, wearable keypads may have to be used without visual information throughout the task.

Even though direct visual feedback (i.e. looking directly at the keypad) may be unavailable, many wearable solutions rely on a special display that is constantly visible to the user (e.g. a head-worn display). Therefore, it might be possible to provide some indirect visual feedback on the display that helps the user in operating the keys. This study tackles both direct and indirect visual feedback.

Several wearable keypad ideas have been proposed. Of these, the 'Finger-Joint Gesture' (FJG) wearable keypad glove [5] is closest to the phone layout, retaining the 3 x 4 layout: the four fingers from index to little finger form the keyboard rows, while the phalanges (finger bones) of each finger represent the columns. Thumb is used as an operator. While FJG uses the hand itself as the input device, and therefore probably provides good tactile ground for blind use, it is still to our knowledge only on a concept level, and no formal user studies exist.

To the contrary, much more information exists from a related wearable keypad called 'N-fingers' [8]. Prototypes of this keypad have been studied formally, and the results are encouraging, although high error rates were observed. More interestingly, from the viewpoint of the present study, the results showed that N-fingers could be used with no visual feedback at all. However, the keypad consists of only four keys, which simplifies the use of tactile sense. It is still open whether such a high level of blind use can be obtained with keypads with higher key count.

A slightly different wearable idea, also utilizing the phone layout, is called 'Embroided Capacitive Key Pad [11]. This keypad is stitched to the front of a jacket. The keypad faces away from the user. This limits the use of visual sense, and highlights the importance of tactile feel. However, no published studies exist from this keypad.

Another class of wearable keypads are so-called chording keypads, where one or several keys are pressed in combination. They involve delicate movement patterns, and require several hours to learn. This has limited their adoption in commercial products. Some of them also require a firm surface (e.g. [3], [12]), which limits their use in mobile settings. Some are attached to user's clothes, and are thus more interesting from present viewpoint, since they are can be used in any mobile situation and are therefore also susceptible to limitations in visual feedback. One such keyboard is the 'Half-qwerty' by Matias et al. [10]. This keypad was indeed studied in blind use, and the results were relatively positive. However, only completely blind use was studied, and no comparisons between different visual conditions were made.

Other Solutions. Other mobile keyboard solutions exist that are neither handheld nor wearable. These are often variations of the computer keyboard, applied to mobile context. One example is the popular foldable keyboard for palmtop computers, another more exotic variation is provided in [4]. While these keyboards can be easily carried around between different locations, the use itself is much more limited since a table is needed for comfortable operation. These solutions are not thus 'truly mobile', and are therefore out of the scope of this paper.

1.2   Purpose and Scope of this Study

To our knowledge, no systematic studies exist about the combined roles of tactile and visual information in the use of mobile devices. An experiment was designed to study this issue in mobile keypad-operated devices.

Keypad operation consists of a series of key presses. For each key press the finger is first moved to the intended key and then pressed down. While the second phase is probably trivial, the first is definitely not. Although moving one's finger to a certain key is quite easy in optimal conditions, it might be more difficult in conditions with reduced visual information. However, users may be able to compensate some lack of vision with tactile information. This issue will be studied in different combinations of tactile and visual information. Tactile information is varied by using two keypads with very different tactile properties: one with very clear tactile cues, another with very limited tactile cues. Visual information is varied between full feedback and blind use.

In addition, in wearable devices, indirect visual feedback through the display may provide information of the finger location, and thus help in blind use. To study this issue, an intermediate condition of indirect visual feedback is added to the study.

The subjects in this study are experienced mobile phone users with normal vision. Other user groups, e.g. visually-impaired users or users with no mobile phone experience, may obviously have very different needs and skills, so the results may be only partly applicable to these user groups.

2   Method

2.1   Participants

Twelve volunteers (7 male, 5 female) participated in the study. All were employees of the Nokia Research Center in Helsinki. Their age ranged from 25 to 36 years, with an average of 31.8 years. One of the subjects was left-handed, but all choose to use their right hand in the study. All subjects had normal or corrected-to-normal vision.

All participants were highly experienced mobile phone users, writing several SMS messages each day using keypad-based text input methods. The average mobile phone experience of all participants was about 6 years. None were regular users of the two keypads of the present experiment.

2.2   Phone Mockups

Two phone keypads with very different tactile properties were used. The keypads were selected by the author to represent two extremes of contemporary keypads. (Some old phones from mid-1990's or before have even more explicit tactile cues, but this is obtained by using very large key sizes and distances, and is therefore not a realistic solution for contemporary mobile devices.)

A Nokia 5110 acted as the high tactility keypad (Fig. 1). This phone has very protruding keys, with 1.0 −1.3 mm key depth. The keys are also placed quite far apart, with inter-key distances of 2.8 mm (horizontal) and 3.3 mm (vertical). This factor together with the surface material makes the keys potentially easy to separate by tactile feel: the keys are made from soft and somewhat 'sticky' rubber, while the phone chassis that separates the keys is made of more slippery and hard plastic. The keys have also sharp edges, which makes it easier to feel the boundaries. Number key widths are 8.3 − 9.9 mm, key heights 4.6 − 5.9 mm. Two 0.5 mm high blind dots are located in the phone chassis, one above and one below the number key 5.

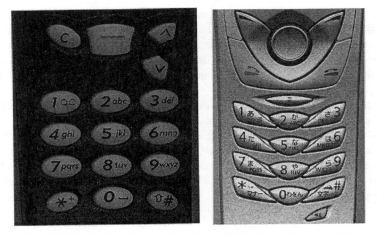

Fig. 1. High (left) and low tactility keypad (right). (Scale = 100 %.)

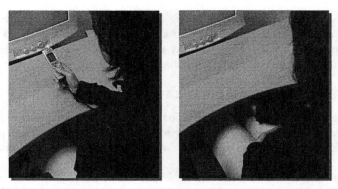

Fig. 2. Participant using phone mockup above the desk (direct visual feedback) and below the desk (indirect and no visual feedback-conditions)

The low tactility keypad was a prototype phone from Japan. The keypad is typical for Japanese market, with very flat keys. The keys are only 0.5 – 0.6 mm deep. In horizontal direction, the keys are totally connected; in vertical direction there is 1.5 – 1.9 mm inter-key distance. The materials of keys and phone chassis are almost identical, and all keys have round corners. The number keys are slightly larger, with 10.2 – 11.8 mm width, and 4.9 – 7.0 mm height, although comparison is not straightforward, because of very different key shapes. In the center of number key 5 there is a 0.2 mm high blind dot.

The phones with the selected keypads were modified to connect with a cable through the keyboard PS/2 port to a desktop PC (Pentium III, Windows NT), running the experimental software (see below). Visual feedback was shown on a 17" computer CRT screen.

2.3   Visual Feedback Conditions

Both phone mockups were tested in *three visual conditions*:

1. *Direct Visual Feedback*: in this condition, users were allowed to keep the phone above the table. They were instructed to try out a position where the phone is kept near the computer screen, since this minimizes the eye movement and accommodation between phone keypad and screen (see Fig. 2, left), but were allowed to choose any position convenient to them. Most subjects chose to hold the phone as instructed; however, one subject held the phone about 40 cm in front of the screen.
2. *Indirect Visual Feedback*: In this condition, subjects held the phone and their hand (up to wrist) below the desk (see Fig. 2, right), removing the possibility of receiving any visual cues from the phone itself or through the subject's hand. Although direct visual feedback was thus eliminated, the experimental computer application gave indirect visual feedback on the display after each trial, informing the subject which key he/she had pressed (see details below).
3. *No Visual Feedback*: This was identical to previous condition, but also the indirect feedback was removed. No visual information was available, so the subjects had to search the keys using tactile information only.

In each condition, only the thumb of one hand was allowed to press the keys. The other hand and fingers could be used to stabilize the phone but not to operate the keys. Before each condition, the subjects were allowed to adjust the desk, monitor and seat to make the position as comfortable as possible.

2.4   Experimental Software and Test Task

The experimental software was developed with Borland's Delphi (version 5). The program presented the stimuli to the participants and logged each key press on the phone mockups to a text file. Each press was time-stamped with 1 millisecond resolution.

The experimental software showed an illustration of the keypad to the subject. The illustration was 42 mm wide and 44 mm high, and was shown in white color in the center of the computer screen on a middle gray background. Stimuli were shown one by one by turning the present target key black (see Fig. 3a). The subject's task was to press the indicated key on the phone mockup keypad. The stimulus remained visible until the subject pressed any of the keys on the phone mockup. This made the stimulus disappear. If subject made an error, an error tone was played.

In the indirect feedback condition, some additional visual feedback was shown immediately after stimulus disappearance. If the key that the subject had pressed was right, the stimulus turned green (Fig. 3b); when pressing a wrong number key, the erroneous key was shown in red (e.g. wrong press on number key 8, Fig. 3c); if the erroneous key was none of the number keys (but one of the function keys), then the border surrounding the keypad illustration turned red (Fig. 3d). This feedback disappeared after 200 ms. Next stimulus was then shown after a 700 ms stimulus interval.

As the number keypad consists of 12 keys, the there are 12 x 11 = 132 possible key pairs (when key repetitions are excluded). To cover all key transitions, a 'key loop' of all 132 key pairs (i.e. 133 stimuli) was designed (the first stimulus was always excluded from the analysis, because there is no transition from a previous key). Each test round consisted of one full key loop started from a random position, run randomly in one of the two possible directions. This arrangement made the stimulus order appear random to the subjects. Each test round lasted between 3 and 7 minutes in total.

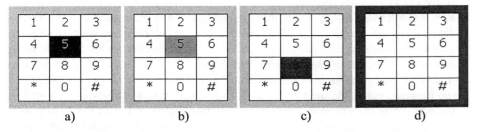

Fig. 3. a) Displaying the stimulus; b, c, d) indirect visual feedbacks forms (see text for details). (Scale = 59 %.)

2.5   Design and Procedure

A 2 x 3 within-subjects design was used:

- 2 tactile conditions: high tactility vs. low tactility keypad
- 3 visual feedback conditions: direct, indirect, none

This makes 6 test conditions in total. For each condition, one test round was run. The order of test conditions was fully counterbalanced using Latin Square design. With 12 subjects and 132 recorded key presses per test round, the total number of key presses was 6 x 12 x 132 = 9504.

Before each test round, the forthcoming test condition was explained to the subject. After that, a short practice round was run. This consisted of 12 trials, one press on each number key. These trials were discarded from all analyses.

Then the actual test round with 133 trials was run, after which the experimental software displayed the number of errors to the subject, both in absolute number and percentage. The subject then filled-in a differential scale on subjective ease: 'How easy was it to find the right key on this keypad in this test condition?' using a scale from 1 ("very difficult") to 7 ("very easy"). We also briefly interviewed the subjects about the strategies they used in locating the keys with the present keypad, and general pros and cons of the keypad designs.

Each subject performed the test in two sessions, one for each phone. The time between the sessions varied between 1 and 24 hours.

3   Results

The dependent variables were key press time and error rate and subjective ease. For each of these we analyzed the following effects:

- overall effect of visual and tactile conditions, and their interaction,
- the difference between no visual feedback and direct visual feedback (the applicability of both keypads for blind use), and,
- the difference between indirect visual feedback and no visual feedback (how much the indirect feedback can compensate blind use).

In addition, qualitative findings were obtained in the post-test interviews. These findings are handled in the discussion.

3.1   Key Press Time

Key press time is the time from the onset of the stimulus to the key-down action.
Key press times increase quite consistently when visual or tactile information is reduced. A two-way analysis of variance on key press time showed clear main effects for visual feedback condition ($F_{2,66} = 4.88$, $p = .01$) and keypad tactility ($F_{1,66} = 4.86$, $p = .03$). The visual x tactile interaction was not significant ($F_{2,66} = 0.24$, $p = .79$).

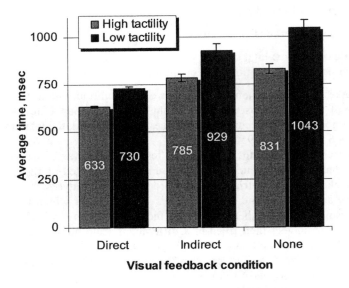

Fig. 4. Average key press times for different visual and tactile conditions with 95% confidence limits

Removing all visual feedback slowed down key presses on both keypads compared with full visual feedback (direct vs. none; high tactility: $t_{11} = -2.80$, $p < .05$; low tactility: $t_{11} = -2.84$, $p < .05$).

When looking at the effect of indirect feedback, the difference between indirect and no visual feedback conditions are quite small. In post-hoc t-tests, the differences between conditions with indirect and no visual feedback were not significant (high tactility: $t_{11} = -1.46$, $p = .17$; low tactility: $t_{11} = -1.93$, $p = .079$), although with low tactility keypad, the result approaches significance.

3.2   Errors

A two-way analysis of variance on error rate showed very clear main effects for visual feedback condition ($F_{2,66} = 18.8$, $p < .001$) and keypad tactility ($F_{1,66} = 57.6$, $p < .001$). The visual x tactile interaction was also highly significant ($F_{2,66} = 11.2$, $p < .001$).

Overall, the differences in error rates are much clearer than those observed in key press times. The interaction between visual and tactile information is also notable. With the high tactility keypad, the error rates are relatively low even in the total absence of visual feedback, although the difference is significant ($t_{11} = -2.77$, $p < .05$). However, with low tactility keypad the error rate remains low only with full visual feedback, but increases dramatically when direct visual feedback is disabled, with a highly significant difference ($t_{11} = -5.12$, $p < .001$).

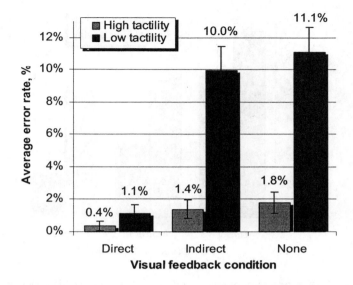

Fig. 5. Average error rates for different visual and tactile conditions with 95% confidence limits

Also notable is the role of indirect visual feedback. It seems that this type of indirect feedback alone does not reduce keying errors very effectively. The differences between conditions with indirect and no visual feedback were far from significant (high tactility: $t_{11} = -0.84$, $p = .42$; low tactility: $t_{11} = -0.68$, $p = .51$).

3.3   Subjective Ease

The subjective rating on the ease of finding the keys gives similar results as key press time and errors. Reducing the visual and/or tactile information has a very consistent effect also on subjective ease. A two-way analysis of variance on subjective ease showed very clear main effects for visual feedback condition ($F_{2,66} = 28.2$, $p < .001$) and keypad tactility ($F_{1,66} = 54.3$, $p < .001$). The visual x tactile interaction was not significant ($F_{2,66} = 1.78$, $p = .18$).

Removing all visual feedback had very clear effects on the subjective ease with both keypads (direct vs. none; high tactility: $t_{11} = 7.10$, $p < .001$; low tactility: $t_{11} = 6.77$, $p < .001$).

When comparing the indirect with no feedback condition, the effects are more distinct than in key press times or errors, reaching statistical significance (high tactility: $t_{11} = 2.57$, $p < .05$; low tactility: $t_{11} = 4.00$, $p < .01$).

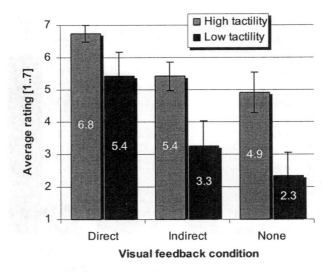

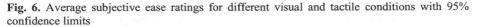

Fig. 6. Average subjective ease ratings for different visual and tactile conditions with 95% confidence limits

4   Discussion

Overall, the results are very consistent: both visual and tactile information had very clear effects on all dependent variables, most clearly on errors.

The performance was obviously best when subjects were allowed to look at the keypad while pressing the keys. However, when visual feedback was prevented, the results were very different for the two keypads. Although statistically significant effects were found for both keypads, the magnitude of the effect of blind use was very different, especially in terms of errors: the high tactility keypad could still be used with few errors, but with low tactility keypad the errors increased dramatically.

Compared with full blind use, indirect visual feedback lead to relatively mild improvement in the actual performance (i.e. key press times and errors); all effects remained insignificant. However, on the subjective ratings, the benefit was clearer, with statistically significant differences observed with both keypads.

The results have important practical implications for the design of mobile keypad-operated devices, both handheld and wearable. These implications are discussed separately.

4.1   Implications to Handheld Keypads

Two physically very different handheld keypads were included in the study. Very clear differences were observed between these two keypads in all dependent measures, although the task was identical. The differences are most clear in errors. Fig. 7 shows selected error data (from Fig. 5) in a new format. This layout shows very clearly the crucial role of passive tactile feel. The first bar on the left shows the 'optimal condition', where a keypad with rich passive tactile cues is used in presence of full visual feedback. Error rate is very close to zero. The second bar shows the same keypad in total blind use situation. Since there are plenty of tactile cues available, users can still operate the keypad with very few errors. However, in the third bar, where the keypad is changed to a one with poor tactile cues, the error rate increases dramatically!

This result highlights the importance of the industrial design of mobile products. The second and third bars of Fig. 7 compare two different designs in an identical task, in identical conditions – and yet the difference in error rate is substantial. What exactly made the difference so clear? The post-test interviews were able to shed some light on this question. One of the most interesting findings was the almost total uselessness of the blind dot. Both phones had quite low blind dots at number key 5, and several subjects spontaneously mentioned that they had no benefit from this feature. Most tried to use it in the beginning but started using other strategies, because failing to locate the blind dot by tactile sense only. Such a small dot may perhaps be useful for visually impaired users who have more experience in relying on their tactile sense, but it is hardly of any use for users with normal eyesight.

Instead, subjects reported other strategies that we classified in five categories. The categories, in rough order of frequency are: key shape, keypad edges, key depth, key distance and key size. Issues related to shape of individual keys were clearly most common. Also keypad edges seemed to be important: many users used e.g. a corner of the keypad as a landmark where the thumb was returned from time to time for 'calibration'. In summary, based on these very informal interviews, the most important feature in blind use seems to be a distinct shape of the individual keys (e.g. sharp enough key edges) and the whole keypad (i.e. keypad edges), but keys also need to be deep enough (1.5 mm in high tactility keypad worked well), placed far enough from each other and be large enough in size.

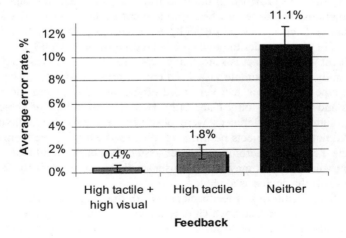

Fig. 7. Average error rates - redrawn

These observations are obviously very preliminary, and there are many independent variables that may affect the overall performance in blind use conditions. More research is needed, with larger variation of keypads, in order to understand what are the critical variables that make a keypad accessible by anyone, in any context.

While this study focused on the telephone keypad, the notion of the importance of industrial design applies equally well also to other layouts, for example the handheld QWERTY keyboards. Even though the usage style is different – i.e. one thumb vs. two thumbs – the problem of blind use remains the same: i.e. locating the intended key with one's thumb(s) without looking at the keys. In QWERTY, the degree of difficulty may only be even higher, because of greater number of keys.

Virtual keypads were also out of our main focus, but certain conclusions can be drawn. These keypads are operated on a touch-screen using a finger or a stylus; however, current touch-screens are completely flat and uniform, providing very limited – if any – tactile information to the user. On contrary, although one of the keypads in the present study was termed low tactility, the keypad was not completely flat, providing at least some tactile information to the subjects. The highest error rate of figure 7 would probably be even higher if both visual and tactile information were *completely* ruled out. This issue is critical to products that use virtual keypads. Certainly there is need for new technologies that can provide passive or active tactile information also with touch-screens, making pen-based appliances usable in all mobile contexts. The 'Active Click' touch panel by Fukumoto and Sugimura provides a good start to this direction [2].

4.2   Implications to Wearable Keypads

Although keypads in this study were not wearable, the results have certain implications to wearable keypads also.

Just like handheld keypads, the wearable keypads are sometimes used blindly. Therefore, tactile cues provided in the industrial design are equally important also in wearable solutions. The issue may be even more critical here, since any visual contact with a wearable keypad may be difficult, either because of a fixed location of the keypad (e.g. [11]), or in order to obtain a natural use position (e.g. [8]).

When direct visual contact is scarce, any type of indirect feedback may be invaluable. This study included simple visual indirect feedback that took place after a key press. This type of feedback had very mild effects on performance, decreasing key press times and error rates only marginally. However, in ratings of subjective ease, statistically significant differences were observed. It seems that although indirect feedback did not make subjects perform significantly better, it gave them confidence in using the keypads. Therefore, indirect visual feedback should be considered, whenever possible, since it may increase user's satisfaction towards the keypad, and, perhaps, towards the device as a whole.

More sophisticated forms of feedback are worth studying also. While we used very simple passive visual feedback, which only informed – after a key press – which key was pressed, also more active forms of feedback exist. Two examples are worth noticing. Firstly, Hinckley and Sinclair [7] studied a touch-sensing mouse and trackball. Using similar technologies, the individual keys on a keypad could be made sensitive to touch. This would allow showing on the display the location of a user's finger in relation to the keypad, even before any key is pressed. This would most probably have a positive effect on accuracy, perhaps also on operation times. Secondly, active feedback could also be given through the tactile sense. Different forms of active tactile feedback has been used in several studies (e.g. [2], [9]), but none of these tackle the specific solutions of mobile keypad-operated products. As a summary, active feedback through various senses, as opposed to passive tactile feel used in this study, need to be studied and applied to keypads-operated products to improve their usability in mobile context.

5   Conclusions

Very few studies exist about keypad use. Keypads are technically very simple input devices, and much of the research attention has focused on more advanced input technologies. However, keypads have strong passive tactile feel, and are thus highly potential for mobile use. This study showed that a properly designed keypad can be used even in total absence of visual feedback. Advanced forms of feedback, e.g. indirect visual feedback or active tactile feedback, could be used to further strengthen the blind use capabilities of keypads, in both handheld and wearable devices.

References

[1]   Brewster, S., Leplâtre, G. and Crease, M., Using Non-Speech Sounds in Mobile Computing Devices. In First Workshop on Human Computer Interaction with Mobile Devices. http://www.dcs.gla.ac.uk/~stephen/papers/mobile98.pdf, Glasgow (1998)

[2]   Fukumoto, M. and Sugimura, T., Active Click: Tactile Feedback for Touch panels. In Extended Abstracts of the CHI 2001 Conference, ACM Press (2001) 121-122

[3]   Fukumoto, M. and Tonomura, Y., "Body Coupled Fingering": Wireless Wearable Keyboard. In Proceedings of the CHI 1997 Conference, ACM Press (1997) 147-154

[4]   Goldstein, M., Book, R., Alsiö, G. and Tessa, S., Non-Keyboard QWERTY Touch Typing: A Portable Input Interface For The Mobile User. In Proceedings of the CHI 1999 Conference, ACM Press (1999) 32-39

[5]   Goldstein, M. and Chincholle, D., The Finger-Joint Gesture Wearable Keypad. In Second Workshop on Human Computer Interaction with Mobile Devices. http://www.dcs.gla.ac.uk/mobile99/, Edinburgh, Scotland (1999)

[6]   GSM association. SMS (Short Message Service), http://www.gsmworld.com/technology/sms/index.shtml

[7]   Hinckley, K. and Sinclair, M., Touch-Sensing Input Devices. In Proceedings of the CHI 1999 Conference, ACM Press (1999) 223-230

[8]   Lehikoinen, J. and Röykkee, M. N-fingers: A Finger-Based Interaction Technique for Wearable Computers. Interacting with Computers, vol. 13 (2001) 601-625

[9]   MacKenzie, I.S. and Oniszczak, A., A comparison of three selection techniques for touchpads. In Proceedings of the CHI 1998 Conference, ACM Press (1998) 336-343

[10]   Matias, E., MacKenzie, I.S. and Buxton, W. One-handed touch typing on a QWERTY keyboard. Human-Computer Interaction, 11 (1996) 1-27

[11]   Orth, M., Post, R. and Cooper, E., Fabric Computing Interfaces. In Summary of the CHI 1998 Conference, ACM Press (1998) 331-332

[12]   Rosenberg, R. Computing without Mice and Keyboards: Text and Graphic Input Devices for Mobile Computing, Doctoral dissertation, Department of Computer Science, University College, London.
       http://www.obscure.org/rosenberg/ (1998)

[13]   Silfverberg, M., MacKenzie, I.S. and Korhonen, P., Predicting Text Entry Speed on Mobile Phones. In Proceedings of the CHI 2000 Conference, ACM Press (2000) 9-16

Time-Out in Mobile Text Input:
The Effects of Learning and Feedback

Juha Marila[1] and Sami Ronkainen[2]

[1] Nokia Research Center, PO Box 407, FIN-00045 Nokia Group, Finland
`juha.marila@nokia.com`
[2] Nokia Mobile Phones, Oulu, Finland
`sami.ronkainen@nokia.com`

Abstract. In many user interfaces with restricted input/output capabilities, a time-out is used to automatically change the UI from one mode into another. In this paper we studied the learning of time-outs and the effect of feedback on it in mobile phone text entry. The effects of three different feedback schemes (auditory/visual/no feedback) on learning of two different time-out lengths were compared. We measured the response time from the time-out occurrence to the time of user's reaction. Error rates and the development of the response times in different schemes were used as measures of learning. We also studied if the users learned to estimate the time-out lengths, or if they just reacted to the available feedback. There were three main findings. Without feedback, response times had great variation. Auditory feedback enabled faster response times than visual. Finally, we found evidence of short-term learning, but not as much of a lasting effect.

1   Introduction

Time-out is used in many mobile phones' text input, as well as other user interfaces. When the user completes an action, for example typing a character, the following user action is interpreted differently if it occurs within the pre-set time-out period or after it. In the case of text entry, two subsequent same-key presses either produce one character or two different characters depending on whether user pressed the key before or after time-out. The user must be able to adapt to this time-out period to be able to use the text entry method.

Some software solutions, best known being T9 from Tegic Inc., overcome this by producing all characters with single key presses, using algorithms to disambiguate the intended word from the key press combinations. Not all users are happy with the disambiguating methods, however, for various reasons. Thus the time-out method is still widely used in mobile phone text entry.

It has been unclear to which extent users can learn the lengths of time-out periods. If they do not learn them, their only available strategy to ensure their action occurs before the time-out, is to perform a selected action very quickly. Consequently, in

L. Chittaro (Ed.): Mobile HCI 2003, LNCS 2795, pp. 91–103, 2003.

cases where they need to ensure that they only act after the time-out has occurred, they need to wait for an undetermined period. This can lead to unappealing and unusable user interfaces.

However, if time-out periods can be learned, it would be possible to make them fairly short and still ensure that people are able to use the system. The time-out lengths could also be adapted according to each user's behavior.

On the other hand, if the learning effect is very strong and long-lasting, it causes problems for automatic adaptation since the previously learned time-out length will disturb them when the time-out length is changed.

In order to find out which viewpoint is more close to truth, we set out to study the users' ability to learn the time-out lengths, and the effect of different feedback schemes on their performance.

2   Time-Out as a Control in User Interfaces

Time-out in user interfaces has been used when either the input or output capabilities of the device are restricted, or when it is more convenient for the user to just wait a while than perform some other action.

For example in Microsoft Windows the user can click on an icon to select it. After the initial click, there is a time-out period during which the next mouse click will be interpreted as double-clicking, which has a special meaning. However, if the second click comes after the time-out period, it will be interpreted as something else. For instance if the user clicked on the filename part of an icon representing a file, the next click will be interpreted so that the user wants to rename the file.

In mobile phones using a standard telephone keypad [1] keys 0-9 all have several characters assigned to them. When a user is entering text using the keypad, in most implementations he needs to press a single key several times, in order to enter the character he wants. At more or less even intervals, two successive characters must be entered from the same key, for instance when typing two 'a' characters in a row, or typing 'a' followed by 'b'. These characters will be referred to as "Subsequent Same-Key Characters" (SSKC, or SSK character) later on in this document. This is the situation where time-out plays a crucial role in typing errors. Pressing a key too quickly to produce next SSK character as well as pressing too slowly to choose the right character both produce errors in the text.

In some implementations it is possible to use a button other than numbers 0-9 to abort the time-out period manually. Even here reacting slowly creates problems in the form of unwanted key presses. For example, in Nokia phones the cursor key is used to abort time-out. Pressed after the time-out period, cursor moves to beginning of the text. Temporal precision is thus still needed from the user's part.

2.1   Human Temporal and Rhythmic Memory

Deutsch [2] has shown that in remembering musical rhythms, the memory works accurately on relative timings between musical notes, but not as accurately on the absolute lengths of notes. This implies that long-term remembering of time-outs might not be very accurate since there the user is dealing with absolute time values.

On the other hand, Levitin has shown [3] that people can remember tempos of musical pieces very accurately, within approximately 8% of the original tempo. This implies that there is some memory mechanism that stores absolute time interval information.

Above-mentioned studies relate to musical timing related to rhythm, though, and may not be applicable to memory for time-out periods. There are some crucial differences between rhythmic tapping, like in music production or listening, and the kind of tapping in interaction with a machine or device – in our case, text input. Firstly, the purpose in tapping in text input is not to produce or follow any rhythm, but to simply produce text on the display. Secondly, there are intervening factors from the task at hand that affect the device user's mental workload, unlike a music listener's rhythm production. User must concentrate on following the feedback from the device, track the progress of his/her task and be prepared to correct errors or perform special actions (like changing adjustments or properties of the device). In comparison, a listener only needs to concentrate on keeping rhythm. Other factors and requirements s/he can just neglect. This being the case, existence of rhythmic memory may not offer clues to whether there is memory for latencies and time-out periods.

Basically it has been shown that people can retain short time intervals in memory. In one such study, people were able to estimate 0.25 sec to 4 sec intervals with 0.03 to 0.125 sec accuracy [4]. Deviation increased with the interval. Once again, though, there were no other requirements or cognitive demands to participants in this experiment. It thus must be tested, whether this memory holds in situations with cognitive load – such as typing in text.

2.2   System Latencies

Studies on people's experience and behavior with latencies and delays show that people switch their strategies depending on the latency of an interactive system. Teal and Rudnicky [9] show that people learn and adapt to system latencies, and choose the best fitting usage strategy to each kind of latency. Teal & Rudnicky's research concerned workstation PC users and included latencies up to 10 seconds. In their study an anticipation error (pressing a key too early, before the system latency period was over) did not have any effect on user performance, whereas in mobile phone text input this causes a wrong character to be inserted - an error that must likely be corrected. This factor is taken into account for by O'Donnell & Draper [5]: based on their replication of Teal & Rudnicky's study they suggest that increased penalty on errors affects user behavior, making them act more careful and thus increasing response times.

The difference that time-out causes to text input speed has been theoretically modeled by Silfverberg, Korhonen & MacKenzie [8]. In their model, waiting for a time-out causes roughly 20% decrease in typing speed compared to aborting the time-out period with a dedicated key press. The model assumes an expert user typing at fastest possible speed without any consideration for errors. Here it is assumed that the user knows perfectly well the time-out length, and always responds exactly at the end of time-out. The model's predictions do not take into account the user's possible poor judgement of the time-out period.

3   Testing the Effect of Learning and Feedback

In an experiment by Ronkainen and Marila [7] the effect of auditory feedback to users' performance on a simple text input task was studied. Theoretically there could have been a major improvement to performance times (typed words-per-minute, or WPM rate) from using auditory feedback on time-out, but no such improvement was found. The authors suggested the hypothesis that people may be able to learn the user interface time-outs quite accurately. That way their performance would not be affected by feedback as much as was originally anticipated.

The purpose of this current experiment was three-fold:

1) to verify if users are capable of learning the relatively short time-out period in text entry
2) to investigate whether the different feedback methods (auditory or visual) have an effect on the rate of that possible learning.
3) to test whether long-term learning of time-outs occurs – do users remember a time-out period's length when no feedback is provided?

3.1   Learning the Time-Out Period Length

The major research question was, are the users able to learn time-out periods during test tasks. If they do, that would show in the test as uniform response times to time-out occurrences. Also the rate of anticipation errors - caused by responding before the time-out has actually occurred - should be low. If that were the case, the response times should stay fairly uniform also in situations where no feedback of the time-out occurrence is available.

3.2   Remembering the Time-Out Period

Another issue was the long-term remembering of time-out lengths. If people do learn the length of a time-out, does that stay in the long-term memory? If yes, it would show as uniform and fast response times to occurrences of a previously learned time-out, in a test case where no feedback of the time-out is provided and where considerable time has elapsed from the previous time the user has been dealing with an user interface utilizing that time-out.

3.3   The Effect of Feedback

If users do learn the lengths of time-outs, the available feedback presumably plays a major role in learning. In that case, feedback provided through different senses can lead to different learning curves and response times.

The effect of feedback through different modalities would probably lead to different performances, independent of temporal learning. It is previously [10] known that at least in simple reaction time tests people on the average react faster to an auditory stimulus than to a visual one.

Obviously, in cases where no direct feedback of the time-out occurrence is available, users still get indirect feedback from the errors they make by reacting before a time-out has actually occurred. If learning occurs, it should be slower with no feedback than with feedback.

3.4   Test Design

We used a within-subjects design, and balanced the order of the test conditions containing either auditory or visual feedback, having one half of the subjects try auditory feedback before visual, and vice versa.

The test consisted of typing short texts – Finnish proverbs - on a Nokia 6210 mobile phone. Proverbs were chosen because their length was convenient, simulating text message length, and their familiarity helped the subjects to memorize them so that they did not need to check the text constantly. All texts were typed using the multi-tap text entry method that utilizes time-out period to differentiate between several characters from same keys.

The test phone keypad is shown in figure 1 below.

Fig. 1. The Nokia 6210 mobile phone keypad, used in the test

Test subjects were instructed to type single-handedly, waiting for the time-out period to pass when necessary. They were instructed not to abort the period by pressing the cursor keys, even if they occasionally did so in their everyday text input.

There were three different feedback schemes to accompany the time-out occurrence: auditory (A), visual (V) and no feedback (N). Auditory feedback consisted of two 4 msec simple pulses at frequency of 1600 Hz. Visual feedback was given as the cursor disappearance when time-out period started, and re-appearance as the time-out period had passed. Two different time-out periods were used, lengths being 1.5 seconds and 2.25 seconds. The 1.5 s time-out is the same as is used in the off-the-shelf version of the phone.

In the first four test conditions, time-out period was the familiar 1.5 s. Subjects first typed 10 proverbs with no feedback. This was done to measure their performance in a situation where they only had their previous learning of the same time-out to lean on. The first 20 SSK characters were dropped later from the analysis, to leave out the possible effects from accommodation to the test situation.

Participants then typed another 7 proverbs with either auditory or visual feedback as the second and third test conditions. Half of the subjects received auditory and another half the visual feedback first. Finally, all subjects again typed 4 proverbs with no feedback as the 4th condition. These schemes were supposed to reveal the short-term learning of time-outs and the effect of different feedback methods.

In the second half of the test, consisting of three conditions, subjects were provided with phones using the 2.25s time-out length. They first performed the typing task with no available feedback, then with visual feedback, and finally with no feedback again (10, 7 and 4 proverbs again, respectively).

3.5   Test Measures

The users' response times to the time-out occurrences were measured to a precision of 1/100th of a second. Only real response times were measured, i.e. only when the user was typing a SSK character and had to wait for the time-out. For the analysis, both the development of the mean and the standard deviation of the response times were calculated during the test.

Also error rates were measured for each feedback condition. Only anticipation errors were taken into account.

3.6   Test Equipment

Modified Nokia 6210 phones were used as test equipment. Modifications were made on feedback of the multitap time-out occurrence, and on the time-out lengths. For the visual feedback condition, cursor blinking in text entry screen was turned off as it interfered with the visual feedback for time-out – the cursor appearing. For the auditory feedback condition, visual cursor was removed altogether and replaced by a short beeping sound of 4 milliseconds duration. For the no-feedback situation both the visual cursor and auditory feedback were removed.

The phones were connected to a PC using a serial cable. On the PC, automatic logging software kept track of the time-out occurrences and the user's key presses, including error correction. The key presses and time-out occurrences were time-stamped for analysis.

3.7   Test Subjects

Participants in the test were experienced 6210 users. This way, the possible effects due to different mechanics in their everyday phones could be eliminated. They were also all familiar with the 1.5s time-out length in the multitap text input. All subjects were Nokia employees. It was supposed that their phone usage is not different from non-employees. The selection could have caused bias in users' opinions, but those were not assessed in this test.

There were six participants, aged from 26 to 31, three male and three female.

3.8   Test Procedure and Tasks

In the test, users watched familiar proverbs on a PC display. Their task was to type these proverbs using the multi-tap text entry. They were not instructed to proceed at any specific speed, and to correct only the typing errors they noticed immediately after doing them. Error correction was allowed since it was not necessary to ensure that every participant typed exactly the same amount of SSK-characters in the test.

After all texts in one condition were typed, the test facilitator switched the phones and next condition was started. The amount of typed texts was limited to avoid user fatigue. Thus, we only used 4 proverbs in the last no-feedback conditions.

The proverbs were deliberately selected so that they would contain as many SSK-characters as possible. Selected proverbs had 6 SSK-characters on average. So, the average SSKC count in each condition was 60 for the first and 5th conditions (no feedback), 42 for the feedback conditions (2,3 and 6) and 24 for the last conditions with each time-out length.

275 SSKC time-out response times were collected from each subject on the average.

4   Results

As data from the test, we received response times (in 1/100ths of a second) for each SSKC and the amount of errors for each condition. As errors, we only count the anticipation errors

Outlier values were removed from response times. Deciding upon the correct maximum response time in the "no feedback" conditions was a tricky decision – variation was so great. Trying different cut points – 1.5 sec, 1.8 sec or 2.5 sec - had only effect on the first condition's mean response times (RTs), and even these differences were not significant (mean RTs 0.56, 0.59 and 0.61 sec, respectively). A Student's t-test for significance of differences between cut points at 1.5 sec vs. 1.8 sec and 1.5 sec vs. 2.5 sec yields $p > 0.25$ and $p > 0.5$, respectively. So, we ended up with the outliers removed at or above 2.5 sec.

4.1   Analysis Methods

Data was analyzed by depicting and comparing moving average and standard deviation diagrams for each condition's response times, and by comparing mean response times and error rates with statistical tests for significant differences.

Moving average was centered, 15 cases wide. So starting from the 7th case in each condition, a mean value for each case was calculated from the case value, the 7 previous cases' values and the 7 following cases' values. This procedure smoothes the mean response time curves enough to give clearer picture of their direction and development than just plain mean RT curves.

For checking the differences between means, we employed the widely used Student's t-test. This method gives indication of whether two samples are representative of two different populations or just one (populations here refer to the hypothetical difference in participants' behavior in the different conditions).

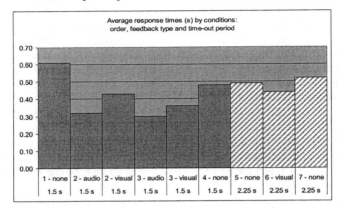

Fig. 2. Mean response times by condition

4.2   Response Time Differences between Conditions

Mean response times differed significantly between several of the conditions, as can be seen from Figure 2 above.

For the conditions with 1.5 s time-out period, response times were slower in no-feedback conditions than in the feedback conditions, and faster in auditory than in visual feedback conditions. The differences between auditory and visual conditions were statistically significant in both 2nd and 3rd conditions (Student t-test $p<0.001$ and $p = 0.024$). Likewise, the differences between no-feedback and feedback conditions are significant, all with $p < 0.001$.

The difference between the first and last no-feedback conditions are significant with $p<0.001$. Also, the difference between visual feedback as 2nd or 3rd condition (0.43 vs. 0.36 sec) was significant with $p<0.001$.

In the conditions with the longer, 2.25 s time-out period (5 to 7) the differences between no feedback and visual feedback are significant with $p = 0.003$.

Differences in all seem real just as in how the figure shows them: auditory feedback enables faster response times than visual, and both feedback types enable faster response times than no feedback. The response times in the first condition, with no feedback, were slower than in the 4th condition without feedback.

4.3   Response Time Development during the Test and the Conditions

Mean response times thus differed between conditions. To find out how response times developed inside conditions, we applied the afore-mentioned centered moving average smoothing technique. Figure 3 below shows the curves thus produced for each condition.

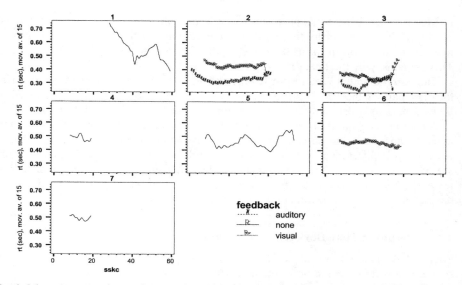

Fig. 3. Mean response times of centered moving average of 15 cases in each condition. X-axis displays the amount of SSK characters, depicting progress in each condition from first to last response time measured

The curves alone seem to hint, that response times went down a lot during the first condition, a little during the second, 4th and 6th condition, and stay about on the same average level in rest of the conditions.

Spearman correlations between response time and SSKC confirm these interpretations. Correlations are given below in table 1 (values significant at p <0.05 are flagged with *), ordered from highest to lowest correlation by time-out period length.

Table 1. Correlation of response times and amount of exercise in different conditions

condition	r (rt, SSKC)
1.5 s time-out period	
2nd auditory	-0.375*
2nd visual	-0.322*
4th no feedback	-0.210*
3rd visual	-0.159
1st no feedback	-0.142*
3rd auditory	-0.086
2.5. s time-out period	
6th visual	-0.130*
7th no feedback	-0.033
5th no feedback	-0.003

Mean response times slope down towards the end, most so in the 2nd and 4th condition. It is noteworthy that while the correlation coefficient for 1st condition is low, the actual drop in mean RT's is steep but has a high rising point near the end. This explains, why the final r remains low.

The correlation between response time and amount of SSK characters typed during the first part of the test, with the familiar 1.5 sec time-out indicates that response times consistently decreased: r combined for conditions 1 to 4 is -0.299 ($p<0.05$).

An interesting question is, whether different feedback conditions affect learning rates. If this were the case, it would show in the correlation figures in Table 1. However, the differences in block 2 between auditory and visual feedback conditions are minimal. Furthermore, in block 3 the differences are even smaller and insignificant. Therefore it can be said that no evidence was found of either feedback having an advantage in learning rates over the other.

4.4   Response Time Deviation in Conditions

Standard deviation from all conditions' mean response times was calculated. This should show the variation in different conditions. However, since mean RT's differed widely between conditions, a more harmonic representation than the plain standard deviation was used: the coefficient of variation (CV), expressed as percentage. CV is calculated by dividing standard deviation by mean ($\times$ 100 for percentage values). Figure 4 depicts CV% for each condition.

This shows that variation in response times was greatest for the 1st, 4th , 5th and 7th condition with no feedback. With auditory feedback in condition 3, there is great variance – but one should bear in mind that the mean RT was very low here.

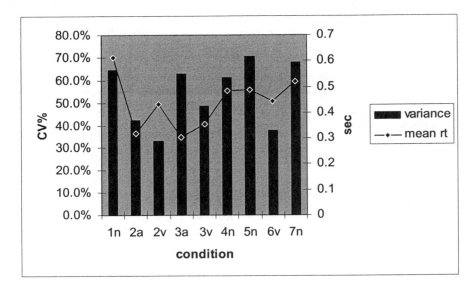

Fig. 4. Coefficient of variation (%) and mean RT for each condition

4.5   Error Rates

Anticipation error rates were calculated for each condition. Figure 5 below depicts the error rates as percentage from SSK characters in each condition.

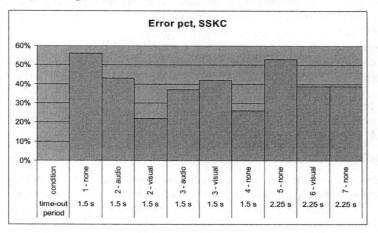

Fig. 5. Mean error rate ratio to typed SSK characters in each condition

As we can see, most errors occurred in initial no feedback conditions (1 and 5). In conditions with feedback, error rates were lower. Likewise, error rates were lower in subsequent no feedback conditions again.

Least errors were made in condition 3 with visual feedback. Coupled with the fact that visual condition 3 also had the highest RTs (of the feedback conditions), a connection can be seen here – less speed, less errors.

4.6   Conclusions

The results from our experiment allow us to confirm some of our initial expectations, to some extent.

4.6.1   Do People Learn Time-Out Period Lengths?

Subjects learned the time-out periods during the test. Participants' response times in no-feedback conditions developed for the faster between subsequent conditions. Likewise, error rates dropped. This implies that users learned to estimate the time-out length more accurately.

Feedback type did not affect learning rates. On the average however, auditory feedback enabled participants to ultimately reach a faster response time level. This is in line with the general finding that people react faster to auditory stimuli than to visual stimuli [10].

4.6.2   Does Feedback Enhance Responding to Time-Out?

Feedback helped participants to faster performance, which comes as no surprise. The difference between later visual feedback conditions (with both time-out periods) and no-feedback conditions is 0.12 sec between means. This implies that people's estimates of time-out length were generally quite accurate. When one considers, that subjects had reason not to underestimate the time-out, to avoid errors, their estimates of the time-out periods can be said to be fairly accurate. Considered in terms of user behavior, this means that the subjects' estimate of the time-out length differed only 0.12 sec more than what they reacted with visual feedback. For 1.5 sec time-out this is only 8% and for 2.25 sec, 5% of over-estimation.

Response time variance is somewhat greater in no-feedback conditions than in feedback conditions. This implies that the learning of the time-out period was not very permanent, but included guessing. The reason for the large variance in 3rd auditory feedback condition is unknown, but could be assumed to partially stem from the low response times in general in that condition. For the low mean response time, the relatively slower responses make up a bigger effect for variance than for a high mean RT.

4.6.3   Is There Long-Term Memory for Time-Out Period?

Long-term memory for time-outs, according to these results, does not seem to exist. In the first condition, participants should have performed roughly as well as in the 4th condition, but instead they made 56% errors – pressing too early, thus estimating the time-out shorter than it was – and also responding 0.61 seconds later than the time-out length, which is 41% over-estimation. Since the error rate and response time with no feedback dropped to comparable levels with feedback conditions in later conditions, this initial under-performance is not due to only lack of feedback. This shows that the accurate memory for the time-out length could be retained for the duration of the test, presumably in working memory. are not remembered for long. Some estimate of the length apparently is retained also in long-term memory, but could be coded as a knowledge structure of type "the time-out is shorter than 10 seconds", instead of a sensorimotor procedural memory.

5   Discussion

The results from the experiment enable us to reason, that an adaptive time-out would work well with users of electronic devices. The adaptation could work by computing the average inter-key press times for the user and then adding a constant overhead to this, yielding a time-out that would be just the right length for each user. If people quickly learn a fairly accurate approximation of the time-out length, a user-specific time-out that adapts itself to user speed of acting with-in time-outs would be learned without any major effort.

The observed differences in response times between auditory and visual feedback conditions (average 0.09 sec) are somewhat greater than what has previously been observed in simple reaction time tests for populations [10]. The difference itself is not great on a single key press. Considered for a text containing 30 SSK characters, the execution time for typing would decrease 3 seconds. For optimal usage conditions, the increase would be meaningless. That, of course, doesn't mean that auditory feedback wouldn't still be more efficient – the difference is just very small. But consider conditions with limitations to visual feedback, such as being mobile – walking on the street or keeping track of commuter train stops. There the auditory channel might be a lot more useful than visual for providing information on such issues as time-out. It is also known that temporal resolution for the ear is much higher than for the eye. Human beings can hear a succession of clicks in a series of hundreds of clicks per second (instead of a continuous tone) [6] whereas more than 20 images per second are perceived as one moving image. This higher temporal resolution might also enable more accurate estimation of time-out with auditory feedback, perceived as the time between key press and the time-out tone. This could explain the greater differences in performance.

Acknowledgements

We like to thank Mr. Miika Silfverberg for providing information on adaptive time-out.

References

[1] ETSI Human Factors (HF): Assignment of alphabetic letters to digits on standard telephone keypad arrays. ETS 300640. European Telecommunications Standards Institute. (1996)

[2] Deutsch, D.: The Processing of Pitch Combinations. In: D. Deutsch (ed.): The Psychology of Music. Academic Press. (1999)

[3] Levitin, D. and Cook, P.R.: Memory for Musical Tempo: Additional evidence that auditory memory is absolute. Perception & Psychophysics, Vol. 58 (1996) 927-935.

[4] Näätänen, R., Muranen, V. and Merisalo, A.: Timing of expectancy peak in simple reaction time situation. Acta Psychologica, Vol. 38. (1974) 461–470.

[5] O'Donnell, P. and Draper, S.W.: Temporal aspects of usability: How machine delays change user strategies. SIGCHI Bulletin, Vol. 28 (1996)

[6] Pierce, J.: Hearing in Time and Space. In Cook, P.R (ed.): Music, Cognition and Computerized Sound. MIT Press (1999)

[7] Ronkainen, S., and Marila, J.: Effects of Auditory Feedback on Multitap Text Input Using Standard Telephone Keypad. In: Proceedings of the 8th International Conference on Auditory Display, Kyoto, Japan, July 2-5 (2002) 125-129

[8] Silfverberg, M., MacKenzie, I.S., & Korhonen, P.: Predicting Text Entry Speed on Mobile Phones. Proceedings of CHI '00, The Hague, Amsterdam. ACM Press (2000) 9-16.

[9] Teal, S.L. and Rudnicky, A.I.: A performance model of system delay and user strategy selection. Proc. CHI '92. ACM Press (1992) 295-305

[10] Woodson, W.E., Tillman, B., and Tillman, P.: Human Factors Design Handbook, 2nd edition, McGraw-Hill Inc. (1992) 630-631

SyncTap: An Interaction Technique
for Mobile Networking

Jun Rekimoto, Yuji Ayatsuka, and Michimune Kohno

Interaction Laboratory, Sony Computer Science Laboratories, Inc.
3-14-13 Higashigotanda, Shinagawa-ku, Tokyo 141-0022 Japan
{rekimoto,aya,mkohno}@csl.sony.co.jp
http://www.csl.sony.co.jp/person/rekimoto.html

Abstract. This paper introduces "SyncTap", a user interface technique
for making a network connection between digital devices. When a user
wants to connect two devices, he or she synchronously presses and releases the "connection" buttons on both devices. Then, multicast packets
that contain press and release timing are sent to the network. By comparing this timing with locally recorded one, both devices correctly identify
each other. This scheme is simple but scalable because it can detect and
handle simultaneous overlapping connection requests. It can also be used
for making secure connections by exchanging public keys. This paper describes the principle, the protocol, and applications of SyncTap.

1   Introduction

When many networked devices – ranging from personal computers to various
digital appliances – are used in combination, to provide an intuitive user interface with which people can easily and correctly establish network connections
becomes important[1]. For example, we may frequently need to create ad-hoc
network connections for multiple purposes:

- Printing a hardcopy of a document contained in your PDA with an available
  printer nearby.
- Showing presentation data on a meeting room screen. Your note-PC transmits data to the presentation computer using wireless networking.
- Your PDA becomes a remote commander for a TV at hand.
- At public wireless LAN hotspot, you transfer files to your colleague's computer, but you would like to make sure this transmission is secure.

These network connections are different from traditional network communication. These connections are frequently made and broken according to users'

---

[1] In this paper, we use the term "connection" to refer a network service association,
and we also assume all the devices already have IP packet access. For example, when
printing a document from the PDA to the printer, these two devices must have an
"association", by knowing each other's addresses, and by optionally sharing a session
key for security.

L. Chittaro (Ed.): Mobile HCI 2003, LNCS 2795, pp. 104–115, 2003.
© Springer-Verlag Berlin Heidelberg 2003

real world activities, and the durations of these connections are generally short. These differences create new user interface challenges.

Traditionally, a device's network addresses, such as IP addresses or machine names, are used to specify devices. However, as network configuration becomes more complex and dynamic, such address-based targeting becomes ineffective. To inspect IP addresses is often a tedious task. In particular, finding IP addresses of digital appliances with limited IO capability is not easy (i.e., getting IP address of a printer often requires unfamiliar maintenance commands). In addition, as dynamic host configuration protocol (DHCP) becomes popular, many devices use dynamically assigned network addresses, and this makes situations even more difficult for users.

To address these situations, more "direct" ways to specify target devices are desirable. For example, an infrared beam that contains an IP address could be used; a user could "beam" a target device with a mobile device, and that triggers a wireless communication between the two [1, 2]. To create a secure connection, infrared beaming might contain a one-time session key. This solution works if all the devices have same sensors, but in reality this assumption is not always valid.

This paper proposes an even simpler way to dealing with such a problem with minimum hardware and sensor requirements. One only assumes that both devices have at least one button, called the "SyncTap" button.

The SyncTap button is used to create a network connection. When a user wants to establish a network connection, he or she synchronously presses and releases SyncTap buttons on both devices (Figure 1). By checking this press-release synchronicity, both side can correctly identify each other and can establish a network connection. As we explain in more detail later, the SyncTap button can be used for other purposes (e.g., a keyboard key such as the "Escape" key can be used as a SyncTap button without neglecting its original key function).

More generally, SyncTap is the simplest instance of synchronous actions. The concept of synchronous actions is that when two networked devices are operated with synchronizied operations, such as button taps, keystrokes, mouse strokes, pen gestures, light changes, device motions, or even voice inputs, these device

Simultaneous button press/release   Network connection

Fig. 1. SyncTap: user synchronously presses and releases the buttons on the devices, then these device establish a network communication

should be able to identify each other by multicasting the received operation information on the network.

2   SyncTap: Synchronous User Actions for Creating Device Association

2.1   Principle

The idea of SyncTap is very simple. Assume that one needs to *connect* two network devices such as a notebook PC and a digital camera. To achieve this, one first synchronously presses and releases SyncTap buttons on both devices. On releasing buttons, both the devices multicast user datagram protocol (UDP) packets that contain:

– Time interval between button press and release,
– Sender's IP address, and
– (Optional) public key information for secure connection.

Since these are multicast packets, all the devices (not limited to devices with which the user is interacting) that listen to a specific UDP port receive them (Figure 2). Both the devices also receive the packets, and checks if this connection request if for them, by comparing:

– the (locally recorded) button release time and the packet arrival time, and
– the (locally recorded) interval between button press-release, and the corresponding time contained in the packet.

Accounting for the fact that the local button release time differs from the packet arrival time due to network delay, and the accuracy of human performance, we set a fixed error limit to C1 and C2. In our current implementation, this is ranging between 100-200ms. When values are within these limits, the device recognizes that the other end is requesting a connection. Note that this check does not directly compare timestamps on the device A and device B, thus synchronized clocks are not necessary.

2.2   Selection of SyncTap Buttons

SyncTap assumes devices have network connectivity and have at least one button (we refer to this as the "SyncTap" button) for operation. The button can be newly installed or an existing one such as a keyboard key of a PC. It can also be implemented as GUI (on screen) buttons.

Our current prototype uses the Escape key or the Shift keys as SyncTap buttons for PCs. These keys also act as normal keyboard keys. For example, when the Escape key is pressed and immediately released (e.g., within 500 ms), the operation is treated as a normal use. When the press-release interval exceeds a predefined time, the operation is handled as a SyncTap operation. The Shift keys are handled similarly. When the Shift key is pressed and released without any other keystroke in-between, the operation is treated as SyncTap; otherwise, it is treated as a normal shift. These techniques greatly reduce the number of unnecessary SyncTap packets and, thus, reduce the probability of collision (described in the next section).

2.3   Collision Detection

When other sets of devices also try to establish another network connection, other SyncTap multicast packets might be transmitted. The system can detect this "collision" situation by collecting all the multicast packets that arrive within a certain time interval around the local button release time. If two or more packets arrive, the device regards it as a collision, and asks a user to press SyncTap button again. The device also records the IP addresses of these multicast sources. In the next trial, the device only accepts multicast packets from these recorded IP addresses (Figure 4).

By using this simple scheme, even though the first SyncTap operation fails because of colliding with other operations, the second try is almost collision free

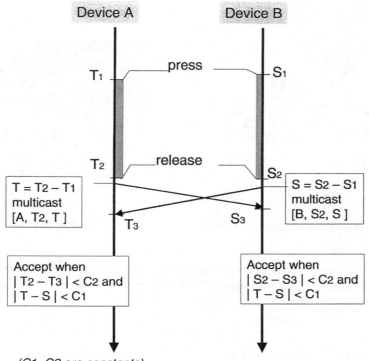

Fig. 2. SyncTap packet exchange protocol

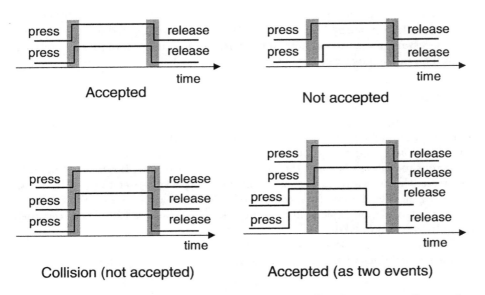

Fig. 3.   Packets timings are used to distinguish SyncTap events from other collisions

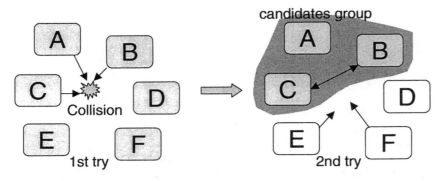

Fig. 4.   Multiple overlapping SyncTap operations can be detected and handled

because the number of connection candidates is greatly reduced (limited to the message senders of the first trial). This feature makes SyncTap scalable, and usable in an environment where many (typically several hundreds) devices are on the same LAN segment.

2.4   Secure Communication

Protecting wireless communication is important, especially when using a public wireless service (i.e., *Hotspot*). SyncTap can also be used for creating a shared session key for secure communication by piggybacking Diffie-Hellman public keys on multicast packets (Figure 5). Each device generates and exchanges public keys (Ya, Yb) by using multicast packets. These public keys are used to calculate a shared secret session key for encrypted communication.

Normally, the Diffie-Hellman algorithm is subject to the "man-in-the-middle" problem and requires an additional method to authenticate the end points. Using SyncTap, however, becoming the "man-in-the-middle" is very difficult because it requires interception of all the multicast packets and transmission of faked packets substituted for them. Since SyncTap is used for connecting nearby devices, devices can easily give immediate connection feedback (e.g., showing a message on a screen, blinking LEDs, etc.); thus, hidden man-in-the-middle hosts can be easily detected. As a result, a simple public key exchange scheme is reliable enough in practical situations.

3   Application Examples

As described in the previous section, the SyncTap is an easy and intuitive way to establish a network connection between various types of digital devices. This section explains how this technique is used in realistic contexts with several examples.

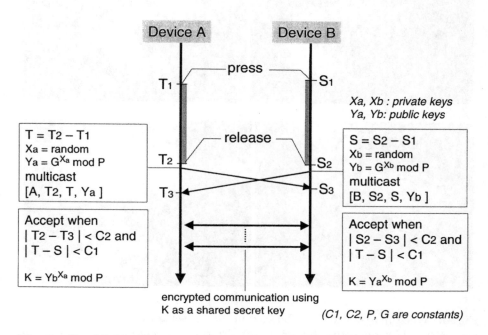

Fig. 5. Establishing secure communication: The Diffie-Hellman key exchange protocol is used to create a shared secret key K

3.1   Instant Connection between PCs and Appliances

Suppose one has a digital camera that is capable of connecting to a wireless network. After taking photographs, one would like to transfer pictures to one's notebook PC. Then, one presses the shutter button and the Shift-key (of the notebook PC) synchronously, and wireless communication between the PC and the camera is established (Figure 6 (a)). Then, a window corresponding to the camera appears on the computer screen and one can drag picture files from this window to one's PC's document folder.

3.2   Ad-Hoc Connection at a Hotspot, or a Meeting Room

Suppose that one is at a public lounge and using a hotspot service. One would like to exchange a file with one's colleague. One can both presses both SyncTab buttons on devices to create a connection (Figure 6 (b)). Then both devices exchange Diffie-Hellman public keys and secure communication starts.

(a)   (b)

(c)   (d)

Fig. 6. SyncTap operations can be used in various settings. (a) A Digital camera and a PC. (b) Connecting two PCs. (c) Printing a document from a PDA to a nearby printer. (d) Presentation using wireless connection between a notebook PC and a presentation screen

3.3 Printing

When one wishes to print a document that is listed on one's PDA to a nearby printer, one presses the PDA's and the printer's SyncTap buttons. Then a printer icon appears on ones PDA screen, and one can drag a document icon to the printer icon (Figure 6 (c)). Note that the contents of the documents might be contained in the PDA's flash memory, or the PDA may only manage links (e.g,, URLs) to documents.

3.4 Presentation

When presenting a slide show in a meeting room, by using a wireless connection, a user transfers slide data from his or her computer to the presentation computer. To do this, one simultaneously presses and releases the remote controller's SyncTap button and the PC's SyncTap button (Figure 6 (d)). The presentation computer receives an IR beam from the remote controller, and a network connection between the two (notebook and presentation computer) is established.

This example demonstrates how SyncTap can be used when two devices are not within an arm's length. A simple intermediate device, such as an IR remote controller, can be used as a remote SyncTap button (Figure 7). In this

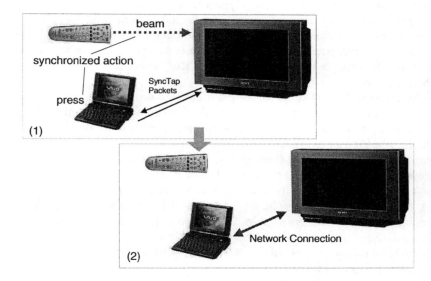

Fig. 7. Combination of infrared beaming and SyncTap. The IR commander is just used as a "remote" SyncTap button. The time of the beaming and button press on the PC are synchronized (1). Then a network connection between TV and note PC is established (2). Note that no previous settings are required for this combination

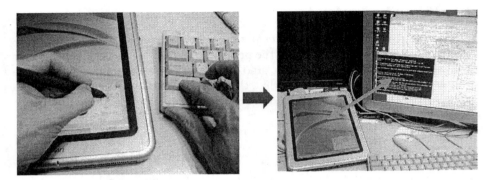

Fig. 8. SyncTap for setting up the HyperCursor connection

case, the controller is only used to transmit press and release timings, and thus, transmitting any complicated data, such as the address of the target device, by using the IR beaming, is unnecessary.

3.5   Using SyncTap for HyperCursor[3] Communication Setup

As a part of our "Augmented Surfaces" system, we previously implemented a migrateable cursor system called HyperCursor [3]. Using HyperCursor, a user can control two computers by using a single mouse and keyboard. When the cursor reaches the edge of one computer, the cursor automatically "jumps" to the next computer. Keyboard inputs are also delivered to the second computer. A user can also drag an object from one computer to another across the boundary of their screens.

The original HyperCurosr relies on a camera sensor that recognizes computer positions. The sensor enables spatially continuous operation because logical mouse movements reflect the physical positional layouts of computers. For example, when a user places the second computer on the first computer's left, the cursor is configured to jump through the left edge of the first computer's screen. However, without such sensors, users had to manually configure the environment. This is cumbersome especially when mobile computers are using DHCP.

A combination of HyperCursor and SyncTap addresses the problem. For example, when a user brings a tablet PC (without keyboard) to his or her office's desk, and wants to manipulate the tablet PC with his or her desktop PC's keyboard and mouse. To set this, a user simply presses the PC's SyncTap button (e.g., Escape key) and synchronously taps the tablet PC's screen[2]. Next, one controls the mouse to hit the screen edge of the desktop computer screen. This operation tells the system about the relative location of the tablet PC, and the cursor automatically jumps to the tablet PC's screen. We are also trying another

---

[2] Some of the tablet PC have physical "hot" buttons, and these buttons are often act as the "Escape" key. In this case, these hot buttons can also be used as a SyncTap button.

method in which a user can specify physical layout by choosing SyncTap buttons. For example, pressing the left Shift key on a device tells the system that the other device is placed on the left.)

4   Discussions

4.1   Related Work

The work described in this paper is inspired by a series of previous systems that tried to connect nearby devices using physical actions [4, 3, 2, 1]. Those systems relied on additional sensors, such as radio frequency identification (RFID) tags, infrared beaming, or barcodes. These systems become ineffective when some of the devices do not have these sensors.

Some recent work on network services try to provide a method for accessing network resources by using understandable names such as "Kate's PC" or "the printer in the copier room" [5]. Users could choose the target device by selecting an item from a menu. However, maintaining the long list of such names still requires considerable effort. Some digital devices, such as wireless headsets, do not have a screen and thus GUI-based selection is not available. SyncTap can coexists with these technologies and act as a "greatest common denominator" because of its minimum hardware requirements.

In the presentation example we showed how a simple intermediate device, such as an infrared controller, could be used as a "remote" SyncTap button. We are also considering other types of intermediate devices, such as similar to the Pick-and-Drop pen[6]. While the pick-and-drop technique mainly handles data, this intermediate device also handles network connection.

Although this paper mainly focuses on network connection, user interfaces *after* the connection is established are equally important. Holland et al. proposed a method called "Dynamic Combination", that effectively chooses available operations based on the combination of selected devices [7]. For example, when selecting two devices, such as a PDA and a Printer, the number of the possible operations would be greatly reduced. Thus, the user interface could be simplified by first connecting two devices, then choosing a command. We consider that similar techniques can be used with SyncTap.

4.2   Human Operation Accuracy

SyncTap relies on humans to perform synchronous operations by using both hands. To effectively distinguish SyncTap events from other coincidental operations, a selected threshold (maximum allowable time lapse as SyncTap event pairs) is important. When this value is too small, some SyncTap actions are not correctly recognized. On the other hand, when this value is too large, the probability of collisions increases.

We actually measured human performance accuracy by providing SyncTap software to several users. The average time lapse between two SyncTap actions is 27ms. Based on this measurement, we currently use +- 50ms as a threshold. Figure 9 shows an actual timing chart when SyncTap pairs are being established.

We also installed a HyperCursor (a remote cursor) system that uses SyncTap on 15 PCs in our laboratory, and five people actively used this system. During the one-month trial, no collisions were detected. This is mainly because the number of simultaneous users was small. We are currently planning to distribute this system throughout the entire laboratory and investigate the probability of collisions and their effects on usability.

4.3   Other Synchronous User Operations Possibilities

Although this paper mainly treats button pressing, mouse clicking, and IR beaming as methods for initiating SyncTap, many other user actions could be used. Two interesting examples are shown in Figure 10. The first one is to use a button of the first device is used to press the button on another. For example, if the tip of the cellular phone antenna was a button, it could be used to "press" other devices' SyncTap buttons. This style might be more natural than using both hands, and offer a metaphor, which is similar to real world actions such as connecting a plug to the socket, or inserting a key into the keyhole.

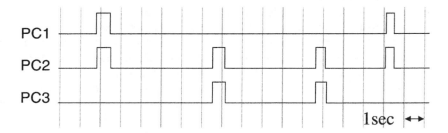

Fig. 9. Timing records when establishing SyncTap pairs

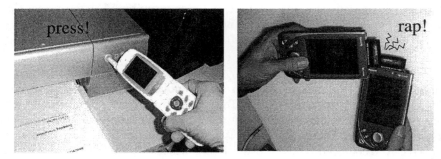

Fig. 10. Variations of SyncTap operations (left: a button of one device is used to "press" the other device's SyncTap button, Right: knocking on the device with the other device, causes synchronously generated sound)

Another possibility is to detect synchronous sensor values, such as sound. Figure 10 right shows how one device is used to "knock" on the other device, the resulting sound captured by the both would be similar and synchronized. By comparing this similarity, creating a SyncTap pair between these two devices should be possible.

5 Conclusion

This paper presents the SyncTap method, a simple user interface for making network connections between digital devices. Unlike previous systems that assume various sensors for device identification, SyncTap only assumes both devices have human-controllable buttons, and uses synchronous timing as an identification method.

References

[1] Rekimoto, J., Ayatsuka, Y., Kohno, M., Oba, H.: Proximal Interactions : A direct manipulation technique for wireless networking. (In: to appear in proc. INTER-ACT 2003)

[2] Swindells, C., Inkpen, K. M., Dill, J. C., Tory, M.: That one there! pointing to establish device identity. In: Symposium on User Interface Software and Technology (UIST'02). (2002) 151–160

[3] Rekimoto, J., Saitoh, M.: Augmented Surfaces: A spatially continuous workspace for hybrid computing environments. In: Proceedings of ACM CHI'99. (1999) 378–385

[4] Want, R., Fishkin, K. P., Gujar, A., Harrison, B. L.: Bridging physical and virtual worlds with electronic tags. In: CHI'99 Proceedings. (1999) 370–377

[5] Zero Configuration Networking: (http://www.zeroconf.org)

[6] Rekimoto, J.: Pick-and-Drop: A Direct Manipulation Technique for Multiple Computer Environments. In: Proceedings of UIST'97. (1997) 31–39

[7] Holland, S., Oppenheim, D.: Direct combination. In: Proceedings of ACM CHI 99 Conference on Human Factors in Computing Systems. (1999) 262–269

Experiments with Multi-modal Interfaces in a Context-Aware City Guide

Christian Bornträger[1,2], Keith Cheverst[2], Nigel Davies[2], Alan Dix[2], Adrian Friday[2], and Jochen Seitz[1]

[1] Technische Universität Ilmenau
Fakultät für Elektrotechnik und Informationstechnik
98693 Ilmenau, Germany
[2] Lancaster University, Computing Department
Bailrigg, Lancaster LA1 4YR, UK

Abstract. In recent years there has been considerable research into the development of mobile context-aware applications. The canonical example of such an application is the context-aware tour-guide that offers city visitors information tailored to their preferences and environment. The nature of the user interface for these applications is critical to their success. Moreover, the user interface and the nature and modality of information presented to the user impacts on many aspects of the system's overall requirements, such as screen size and network provision. Current prototypes have used a range of different interfaces developed in a largely ad-hoc fashion and there has been no systematic exploration of user preferences for information modality in mobile context-aware applications. In this paper we describe a series of experiments with multi-modal interfaces for context-aware city guides. The experiments build on our earlier research into the GUIDE system and include a series of field trials involving members of the general public. We report on the results of these experiments and extract design guidelines for the developers of future mobile context-aware applications.

1 Introduction

In recent years there has been significant research interest in developing mobile context-aware applications. Such applications typically provide information and services that are tailored to the user's context, including their environment, preferences and usage history. Probably the most familiar example of these forms of application is the 'context-aware tour-guide', of which a number of prototype systems have been developed (e.g. [1, 8]). Among these systems, one of the most widely reported is the Lancaster GUIDE system developed by the authors [8, 5].

GUIDE provides users with a comprehensive mobile context-aware tour-guide that can be used to explore the city of Lancaster. The system is based on a tablet PC (the Fujitsu TeamPad) that was made available to the general public from the Lancaster Tourist Information Centre. GUIDE uses a familiar web-browser based user interface to present users with a mixture of hand crafted and generated textual descriptions, pictures and maps about key attractions in the city.

L. Chittaro (Ed.): Mobile HCI 2003, LNCS 2795, pp. 116–130, 2003.

In addition to this information, GUIDE also provides a number of additional features including guided walking tours, group messaging facilities and simple interactive booking services.

The initial GUIDE system, developed and deployed in the late 1990s, used solely static media types that were requested by the user explicitly (i.e. we adopted a PULL-based approach to information dissemination [7]). The decision to restrict ourselves to static media types (i.e. text and images) was taken for two reasons. Firstly, the hardware platform lacked the capability to deal with audio and video playback. Secondly, and more importantly, feedback from users and tourism officers had suggested that audio was not an appropriate media type for use in a city environment. Specifically, there were concerns that users would not wish to use headphones because they would feel isolated from their environment (including other members of their party) and would not wish to use a loudspeaker for fear of attracting attention to themselves (and hence feeling even more conspicuous than a tourist normally does). The decision not to use audio was at odds with the prevailing commercial trend for indoor guide systems, which often employ 'walkman' style cassette players or handheld solid state units – but reflected the more comprehensive visual capabilities of our end-system and the different deployment environment.

In later tests [6] the GUIDE system was extended with additional capabilities including audio. In these tests we compared the PULL-based approach used in the first version of GUIDE with an information PUSH model. Though there are different ways of defining PUSH and PULL, our definition is based on the model of Cheverst et al. [7]: information PULL is characterised by the fact that the user expects the information (i.e. in response to some explicit action) while in information PUSH, the user receives the information unexpectedly (e.g. in response to some contextual trigger).

In early 2002 the decision was taken to begin a total redesign of the GUIDE system allowing us to explore a new set of research challenges in the field of mobile context-aware computing. As part of this redesign process we became interested in understanding which media types are best suited for providing information on city attractions. This is clearly important since the range of media types that needs to be supported impacts all aspects of a system's design, including the choice of end-system, interaction method and required level of network, processor and storage support. Our study of the literature indicated that while different prototype tour-guide systems had used different interfaces, these had largely been developed on an ad-hoc basis. Furthermore, none of the widely deployed systems had implemented multiple user interfaces and attempted to systematically study user preferences with regard to these interfaces. As a result, there are no design guidelines available to indicate which media types and interface modalities are most appropriate for providing information to users of mobile context-aware tour-guides. In this paper we aim to provide such guidelines based on a series of user trials.

In section 2 we describe an experimental mobile context-aware tour-guide application that we developed specifically to research user interface modality

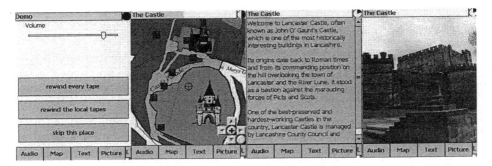

Fig. 1. There are 4 visual interfaces besides the audio

issues. Our experimental methodology is described in section 3 and our results
in section 4. These results include quantitative data we obtained from log files
as well as qualitative results from interviews with users. Section 5 provides an
interpretation of the data and explains why some results met our expectations
and why some did not. The observations of the experimenter are used to round
up the analysis. Section 6 gives an overview of related work and section 7 contains
our concluding remarks.

2   Experimental Application

To support our experiments into multi-modal user interfaces we developed a new
tour-guide application for the city of Lancaster. This prototype is based on
a Compaq iPAQ PocketPC, which compared to the existing GUIDE units, provides support for a wider range of media types, a smaller form factor, an improved
(i.e. colour) display and a more up-to-date image (recent interviews with tourists
indicated that the Fujitsu TeamPad looked somewhat old-fashioned when compared to the new PocketPCs).

Our system allows tourists to receive information about city attractions in the
form of text, pictures or audio commentary, supplemented with a map available
in various styles and resolutions. Figure 1 shows screenshots of all of the visual
interfaces.

These interfaces fill the complete screen, as experiments with combinations
of visual interfaces failed since it was not possible to achieve good readability
(because the resolution and screen size, 240 by 320 pixels, is too small). Reading
from left to right, the interfaces are as follows:

Audio Control This interface provides users with a simple means of controlling
the audio playback of the device.
Map This interface provides users with a scrollable, resizable map of the area,
overlayed with markers indicating tourist attractions and an icon representing the user's current location.

Text A description of the current tourist attraction in textual form. This text is identical to the audio commentary.

Picture A picture of the current tourist attraction.

Users switch between the interfaces using the tabs at the bottom of each screen. While only one visual interface can be shown at a time, the audio is always available with all visual interfaces. The audio can be played through the built-in speaker or via headphones, and can be muted if not required. Because of the limited quality of speech synthesis, the output is constructed from pre-recorded mp3-files that were spoken by a native English speaker. It is hoped that this has avoided any negative feedback associated with speech synthesis that might have influenced the results.

In addition to the variant shown in the screenshot, the map was made available in different resolutions and styles. The map offers two different graphical representations of the available information "hot spots", i.e. areas for which information is available. The first representation uses a translucent blue colour that covers the areas of the map where attractions are located. The second representation of hot spots uses red question marks that turn into green 'X's after the information has been played. Users can switch between these representations by clicking on the appropriate button at the bottom of the screen.

The information flow used in this prototype is PUSH-based. For each attraction we define a surrounding geographic area equivalent to the attraction's nimbus [2] or "hot spot". When a user enters this area we push the information associated with the attraction to the user. The size and shape of these geographical areas were determined by trial and error. We used a standard GPS receiver attached to the iPAQ both to define the hot spot regions and to track the tourists' position during the trials (this represents another departure from the original GUIDE system, which obtained location information from its point of attachment to the network).

The descriptions of attractions are composed in a hierarchy: the logic of the system ensured that the general information about the attraction is always provided before more detailed information is given. For example, before the prototype played information about the "Shire Hall", some general information was first provided about the "Lancaster Castle".

The following example text is an extract (about one third) of a typical description:

"Around the arch of the Shire Hall is perhaps the most famous display of heraldry in the country. This display, numbering over 600 shields, includes those of the monarchs, the High Sheriffs of Lancashire, and the Constables of the Castle. The High Sheriffs date back to the 12th Century. This is an ancient rank with responsibility for organising the administration of justice..."

A key part of the prototype was the logic of replacement [6]: in a PUSH-based system it is always hard to tell when and how to update information since there is a risk of overwriting data that is still being used. Our prototype uses a time based solution. More specifically, if a tourist leaves the nimbus of the currently active attraction but the audio is still playing, the device waits for 10 seconds. If the tourist does not return to the attraction within this period **and** enters the nimbus of another attraction, the current presentation is stopped and the device changes to the new attraction. The device also offers the user a manual override that allows navigation backwards and forwards using the left and right buttons of the iPAQ. This control can be used to rewind, if the prototype replaces information the tourist was still listening to.

Since in this experiment we were principally interested in exploring the use of multi-modal interfaces and not in developing another version of GUIDE, the context stimuli used to tailor information was less than that used in the original system. Specifically, only the usage history and the location was used to tailor the presentation rather than including factors such as user interests and the time of day.

The system was designed to provide comprehensive usage data for later analysis. Every interaction, including interface changes and button presses are logged. This information is recorded with the current time, the current GPS coordinates and the currently active attraction. The data is saved into a log file that can be used to replay the complete test run. The log files are parsed afterwards by a specially designed program to gather statistics.

3   Experimental Methodology

Our tests were conducted during November and December 2002 in an area known as "Castle Hill" in Lancaster, UK. This area covers Lancaster Castle and its immediate surroundings and was chosen because it is close to the city's Tourist Information Centre and rich in tourist attractions. Figure 2 shows a map of the test site. In total there were 16 separate tourist attractions all located within approximately 5 minutes walk of the castle. The area is predominately pedestrianised with a low volume of traffic (on those roads that allow vehicles).

Most of the test subjects were recruited from visitors to the Tourist Information Centre. Basing ourselves within this council-run facility lent a degree of respectability to the test and helped avoid tourists thinking that we were trying to sell them something. In order to convince people to participate in the test we advertised the trial as a free opportunity to learn more about Lancaster. We accepted tourists with no knowledge of Lancaster as well as those that had studied the city before their trip.

After recruiting a tourist or tourist group[1], we started the test with a short introduction to the device. This introduction was designed to last about 3 minutes: our previous experiences have led us to believe that minimising the time necessary to learn how to use a system is critical in the tourism domain, since users perceive this learning process as cutting into their leisure time. To make the introduction as efficient as possible, the prototype offers a tutorial mode,

---

[1] We define a tourist group as being two or more persons co-visiting the city.

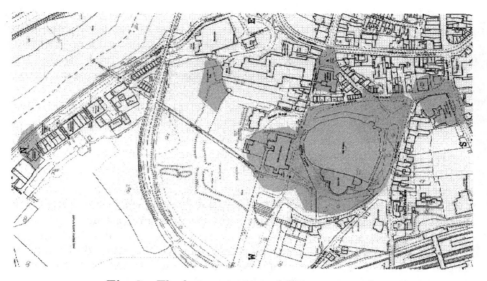

Fig. 2. The hot spots around Lancaster castle

which behaves much like the normal mode and offers all possible interactions. However, instead of giving information about attractions, the tutorial mode has short descriptions of the interfaces. In our tests the experimenter introduced the tourists to each interface, showed the possible interactions, and described the purposes of the various buttons. The tourist could then play with the device and ask questions until they felt comfortable with its operation, at which point the guide unit was changed from tutorial mode into normal mode.

Finally, the general task we set the tourists was to discover and explore the area and use the interfaces to maximise the experience. We did not provide them with any further information on the purpose of the experiment. The unit was left with the tourist to use as they wished. An experimenter followed at a distance of 5 to 10 metres to help in a case of a problem and to observe patterns of behaviour. The intention was not to control the test, rather to observe, though we accept that this process may have affected how some users interacted with the system. We set no time limit for the tourists, they could use the system for as long as they liked.

Once the tourists had finished using the prototype we asked questions in a semi-structured interview. This interview focused on the users preferences for different interfaces. Specifically we asked whether users preferred the audio or textual information and why this was the case. Details were also asked about the map, the picture and the text interfaces. For example, we asked how important these interfaces were to the user and what they were used for. If users indicated that a particular interface was poor or little used, we asked why and described alternative designs to gain an understanding of the factors that affected user reactions. In addition to interface selection, we were also interested to learn how users reacted to the PUSH model used in the prototype. For example, do people have problems if only a PUSH-based interface is available? As tourists normally do not understand the terms PULL and PUSH, the methods were described as "having a list of attractions and choose the appropriate one" and "getting the information without asking for it". Finally, we asked for further comments on what additional features the tourist would like to have and how they would rate the GUIDE system overall. If the participants agreed, the interview was recorded for later analysis.

4 Results

During our field trial we conducted 20 independent tests, 11 with individuals and 9 with groups of two or more tourists. In 4 cases the test runs were particularly short as the participants were in a hurry. As the period of interaction in these cases was extremely short, we chose to disregard this data and focus on the remaining 9 individuals and 7 groups. The groups were composed of 5 sets of couples, one group of 3 and one of 4 persons. The age of the youngest person involved in the trial was 19 and the oldest was 71.

The average time spent using the system was 11 minutes with a maximum of 21 minutes[2]. Most tests ended prematurely as the subjects wished to continue their tour inside a particular attraction. Overall, most test participants were quite enthusiastic about the prototype system.

4.1   User Interaction

All user interactions with the system were logged. We analysed the log data to determine which of the available user interface modalities was preferred. The results show that there is no single user interface preference valid across all of the test subjects. However, it is possible to partition the results into 3 separate groups: the majority of participants – 11 out of 16 – spent most of the time using the map interface. 4 of the 16 preferred the picture view and 1 individual used the textual descriptions most of the time. Table 1 shows a summary of the test data. The result of the modality choice is more obvious: nobody used the volume control to mute the audio and hence these interfaces were always used in conjunction with the audio commentary.

Effect of Group Size. One aspect we were interested in was whether the group size affected the choice of user interface. Though there is a small observable difference in the time spent in a given interface by groups versus individuals, the results are not significant according to a t-test (the error-probability is 20 percent).

Effect of Mobility. Another important aspect in our analysis is the mobility of the user. Figure 3 shows the change in use according to the speed of the tourist (as measured by the GPS compass).

---

[2] The total amount of audio that is available around Lancaster Castle is 13 minutes, if played continuously.

Table 1. Distribution of test persons according to the most used interface

	All Participants	Groups	Individuals
Audiocontrol	0	0	0
Map	11	4	7
Text	1	0	1
Picture	4	3	1

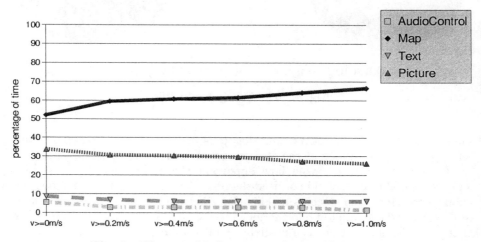

Fig. 3. The speed influence on the interface choice

For most participants there is a correlation between the subject's speed and map usage: the higher the speed the more the map is used. This is valid for both the map-oriented subjects as well as the picture-oriented subjects. The picture appears to be used less while moving. A t-test comparing a slow and a fast speed indicates with less than 5 percent error that the change in the usage of the map and picture is statistically significant.

Effect of Audio. We have observed a difference between the use of the interface modalities depending on whether audio is being used. Figure 4 shows the average time spent in an interface while (a) the prototype is playing and (b) the prototype is not playing audio.

While the audio is being played the usage of the picture view increases significantly. Conversely, the map view is preferred when the audio commentary is not played.

4.2 User Interviews

We found a number of interesting results from the semi-structured interviews. Most of the tourists thought that audio guides were preferable to text based

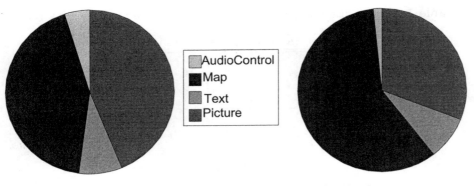

(a) audio is playing   (b) no audio is playing

Fig. 4. The influence of audio

guides. The main reason given was that it is easier to follow the information when you are able to look at the attractions while they are being described.

Importance of Text. Asked how important the additional text was, most subjects stated that they did not need the text. We then suggested some possible changes to the system, such as highlighting the currently spoken text, reducing or increasing the amount of information. The vast majority of the subjects stated that it would not matter. The availability of headlines or keywords instead of whole passages of text was also rejected by the majority of people. About one third thought that keywords might be of some use. During the test a small number of subjects said that the text was useful to replay information they'd heard in the commentary.

Importance of the Map. Asked which interface the users considered to be the most important, most people stated that the map view was essential. Even if precise audio guidance was available, such as "mind the step" or "turn right on the next corner into Church Street", people stated that they would still like to have a map. Typical comments made by the tourists included "I want to see what's available", "people are visual" as well as "I always have to ask twice if I only have spoken guidance". In contrast, one subject stated "I got lost on maps".

We asked people about the design of the maps. We asked whether the subjects believed that the map should use a compass and automatically compensate for the direction of the unit. There was no common answer. All possible opinions from "absolutely necessary" and "I hate it if I have to do it on my own", to "might be useful" and "it would distract me" were given. Most people agreed on the use of the map – it was used to find out "where to go".

Importance of the Picture. In our tests, the picture was mainly used for "seeing if I am right' or "finding the object the device is talking about". The subjects universally agreed that a picture of an attraction was really helpful.

Importance of How Information Is Delivered. Some subjects mentioned that it would be nice to have the ability to request information: they wanted to know if it was worth going somewhere in advance. Although they were quite happy with the prototype itself they missed the level of control of a user initiated (PULL-based) approach.

One tourist complained about the information replacement strategy. Though there was a back button, he was surprised that the device started to talk about a different attraction while he was walking. He suggested that the device should give a warning signal or other hint. *(Design guideline: In a case of replacing information a warning should be included, no matter how clever the replacement logic is.)* Possibilities for such a warning might include a mobile phone like 'reception bar' or reducing the volume of the audio. Alternatively the colour of the current object on the map might be faded out or the title bar could show "Leaving...".

Delivery of Audio Information. We offered all single tourists new headphones and earphones: everyone rejected the offer. One reason given was "headphones look strange". Another was that tourists did not want to look like tourists. Ironically, the use of an audio guide which delivers audio information out loud clearly demarks the user as a tourist. One possible explanation might be that headphones are visible over a long distance, whereas the audio can only be heard over a relatively short distance. Only one person switched to headphones: he was hard of hearing and unable to understand the speech under normal conditions.

5   Analysis

In some cases the lessons learnt from our testing and observations could have been predicted. The increased use of the map while moving is consistent with our expectations, as maps are well known and familiar tools for navigation. Similarly, the text interface is extremely difficult to use while moving due to the level of attention it demands – especially when preoccupied with other cognitive tasks such as avoiding traffic and other pedestrians. Furthermore, a subject is unlikely to want to look at a picture of the last attraction while moving away from it. These factors all help to explain why the map is the dominant form of interaction while on the move.

Audio and Movement. As stated in the results section above, we have observed an influence of the audio on the choice of secondary media type. There may also be a correlation between user mobility and the audio: quite often the user stopped soon after the audio started playing. From the perspective of the experimenter there is a typical set of observable behaviour. As soon as the audio starts to play, the test subject stopped and looked around. If they were not successful in determining the attraction mentioned in the commentary, they interacted with the device and looked around again. Normally the tourist needed some time to locate the unknown attraction, especially if it was not immediately obvious. *(Design guideline: in a PUSH-based audio system the designer should plan to include some time for the user to locate the attraction. Consequently, no important facts should be pushed during the first few seconds of audio.)* This observation of the experimenter is supported by the results of the interviews. The

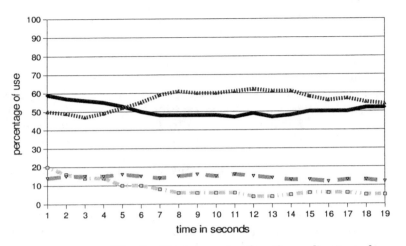

Fig. 5. First seconds after the audio started

test subjects used the map for finding where to go and the picture for identifying the attraction. This behaviour is also clearly common sense.

Control of Audio. Figure 5 shows the percentage that each modality is in use during the first few seconds after the audio begins. From these results we can see that after approximately 5 seconds the principal choice of interface switches from map to picture – further supporting the anecdotal observation of the experimenter. The results also highlight that the audio controls are often used during these first few seconds. Our interpretation of this phenomenon is that the audio control interface allows the subject to restart the audio. A representation of a typical usage cycle is shown in figure 6.

Acceptance of Audio. As we have already mentioned, one of the prime justifications for the success of an audio based guide is the ability of the user to be able to be looking at the sites while simultaneously being presented with accompanying information. Similar results have been identified in indoor guide systems [21]: the attention of the user has to be split between the guide, the

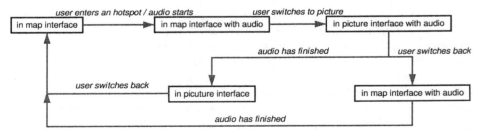

Fig. 6. The typical interaction cycle of a PUSH-based audio guide

attraction and their companions. Text guides are seen to be particularly problematic for groups as they are difficult to use collaboratively – in contrast, with an audio guide it is much easier to share the experience. Such sharing might even promote interaction within the group.

Our experiments also revealed that a guide system definitely should offer more than just the audio commentary: both the map and the picture were considered as necessary in our interviews. *(Design guideline: a guide system should offer an optimised interface for navigation and an optimised interface for identification.)*

Effect of Group Size. We were surprised to find that being part of a group was not statistically significant. Though groups show a small tendency towards using more pictures and less text, the statistical analysis reports this as being within the margin of error. One possible explanation for this outcome might be that most groups had a "leader". This person was the principal user of the device and typically decided where to go – using the device like a single person.

In the small sample set and group sizes we studied, everyone was able to hear the audio acceptably. The audio was found to trigger an interaction with the other group members: when the audio started and the group leader could not find the attraction immediately, the companions were asked for help. In other cases the audio seemed adequate for the other group members as the leader would decide where to go and normally point to the attraction.

In our largest group (with 4 members), the behaviour was different: as the audio began the leader had to call everybody together, he then rewound the audio once they had assembled. Consequently, this group used the audio control the most frequently. Clearly, no definite conclusions can be drawn from a single statistical sample.

Use of Headphones. The most surprising result was the universal avoidance of headphones. One possible explanation was given by the tourists – headphones look strange. Tourists do not want to be easily recognised as tourists. This seems somewhat anomalous given the popularity of personal music players and hands-free kits for mobile phones. Curiously, one of our subjects was already wearing a 'Walkman' with his own set of headphones. He rejected the offer to use his headphones with the iPAQ, insisting that he used the speaker instead. One possible explanation might be the wish to avoid feeling isolated from the environment. The use of open headphones instead of semi-open or closed ones might help to reduce this effect. *(Design guideline: headphones might be unwanted. An alternative audio system should be available.)* Other possible explanations might be the fear of invasion of personal privacy [11] or fear of the unknown. Audio that is pushed to the user without their specific interaction might be deemed as an invasion of personal privacy – this effect might be further enhanced by the intimate form of delivery (through headphones). A user might also fear the lack of control over the spontaneity or volume, given that the audio is played directly into the ear. We suspect that these results are especially interesting as a number of other projects have proposed the use of spatialised audio with headphones for tourist guide applications [9, 10]. A further possibility for future work would be to determine if the reluctance to use headphones is only valid for outdoor guides.

6 Related Work

There have been numerous research projects involving context-aware tourist guide systems. Besides the Lancaster GUIDE the most well known is the Cyberguide project at Georgia Tech [1]. The Cyberguide project was created in the early 1990s and was one of the first context-aware applications. The system was developed using Apple Newtons and relied on a combination of text and images to provide information to visitors.

The Lancaster GUIDE project has previously experimented with audio. An extended version of the GUIDE application running on an Fujitsu TeamPad was used. The test [6] showed that tourists happily accepted a GUIDE version with additional audio-PUSH. Our tests confirmed this result even in the absence of any PULL mechanism, though some users stated that they would have liked to have had the option of requesting additional information.

The HIPS project [3] created a prototype tour-guide system called Hippie [17] designed for use in museums. Hippie can be personalised and the information is web-based. Interestingly, tourists can start interacting with Hippie at home and continue in the museum. Hippie appears to offer most of the functionality of a web based system and hence can include multiple media types.

Other projects dealing with audio interfaces are AudioGPS [10], Guided By Voices [13], Hear & There [20], Audio Aura [16], LISTEN [9], and Nomadic Radio [18]. These projects use audio as the main interface or are audio only. Nomadic Radio, AudioGPS, LISTEN, and Hear & There use spatial audio for transmitting information. As our tests showed a reluctance against headphones at least for outdoor guides, alternative designs should be considered. Apart from Hear & There none of the mentioned projects offer an additional visual interface. This might be a problematic design as tourist in our tests stated that they like to have a visual component as well. Nevertheless, audio only systems have the advantage of being useful for blind people. Projects that deal with guidance in unknown areas are Strider [14, 4, 15], Personal Guidance System [12] and InfraVoice [19]. Strider uses an audio map describing the way and Personal Guidance System use an acoustic display for giving information about distance and angle. InfraVoice is based on cheap receivers and a pre-installed network of infrared-transmitters in a town. These transmitters send directed infrared beams containing information. The user can find these object by pointing the receiver to tune into the information. All of these projects have to live without any possibility of visual interaction, and consequently a lot of effort has had to be made in promoting their usability. The huge effort necessary in supporting navigation in such systems, confirms the results of this test: an appropriate interface for navigation is mandatory. Visual components like maps are a common choice which are also well known to potential users.

7   Conclusion

As mobile context-aware applications begin to proliferate it is important there are design guidelines available to help developers. The canonical example of a mobile context-aware application is a tour-guide system and yet, despite the development of numerous prototype systems, there has to date been no systematic study of user acceptance of different user interface modalities in such systems. In this paper we have presented the results of our efforts to address this shortcoming.

Our experiments have highlighted a number of issues that we believe are generally applicable to mobile context-aware tour-guide systems. Firstly, users clearly benefit from having information available in multiple modalities. Moreover, different users exploit this information in different ways, making it difficult to make a strong case for the inclusion or omission of a specific form of information. Secondly, users were clearly able to make use of different interfaces for navigation and for information access, implying that it might be possible to develop a system with different interfaces optimised for these distinct tasks. Thirdly, we observe that when audio is pushed to users they typically do not give it their full attention for the first few seconds, implying that important information should not be provided at this time. Fourthly, we observe that no matter how clear the replacement logic appears to be for PUSH-based information delivery, confirmation or explanation of this action is almost always desirable. Finally, we note that while audio is becoming a more accepted form of information delivery, users exhibit a remarkable reluctance to wear headphones. This is a surprise to us given the popularity of personal music players and hands-free kits for mobile phones.

In conclusion, we believe that our experiments provide a useful set of guidelines for developers of future mobile context-aware tour-guides. The extent to which these guidelines can be applied to other context-aware application domains is a subject for further study.

References

[1] Gregory Abowd, Christopher Atkeson, Jason Hong, Sue Long, Rob Kooper, and Mike Pinkerton. Cyberguide: A Mobile Context-Aware Tour Guide. *ACM Wireless Networks*, 3:421–433, 1997.

[2] Steve Benford and Lennart E. Fahlen. A Spatial Model of Interaction in Large Virtual Environments. In *Proceedings of The Third European Conference on Computer Supported Cooperative Work*, pages 109–124, 1993.

[3] Jonathan Broadbent and Patrizia Marti. Location Aware Mobile Interactive Guides: Usability Issues. In *Proceedings of The Fourth International Conference on Hypermedia and Interactivity in Museums*, pages 88–98, 1997.

[4] Michael Busboom and Michael May. Mobile Navigation for the Blind. In *Proceedings of The Wearable Computer Conference (ICWC)*, 1999.

[5] Keith Cheverst, Nigel Davies, Keith Mitchell, Adrian Friday, and Christos Efstratiou. Developing a context-aware electronic tourist guide: some issues and experiences. In *Proceedings of CHI'00*, pages 17–24, 2000.

[6] Keith Cheverst, Keith Mitchell, and Nigel Davies. Exploring Context-aware Information Push. *Personal and Ubiquitous Computing*, 6:276–281, 2002.

[7] Keith Cheverst and Gareth Smith. Exploring the notion of information push and pull with respect to the user intention and disruption. In *Proceedings of The International workshop on Distributed and Disappearing User Interfaces in Ubiquitous Computing*, pages 67–72, November 2001.

[8] N. Davies, K. Mitchell, K. Cheverst, and G. Blair. Developing a Context Sensitive Tourist Guide. In *Proceedings of The First Workshop on Human Computer Interaction for Mobile Devices*, 1998.

[9] Gerhard Eckel. Immersive Audio-Augmented Environments. In *Proceedings of the 8th Biennial Symposium on Arts and Technology*, 2001.

[10] Simon Holland and David R. Morse. Audio GPS: spatial audio in a minimal attention interface. In *Proceedings of The Third International Workshop on Human Computer Interaction with Mobile Devices*, 2001.

[11] Marc Langheinrich. Privacy by design – principles of privacy-aware ubiquitous systems. In G.D. Abowd, B. Brumitt, and S. Shafer, editors, *Ubicomp 2001 Proceedings*, volume 2201 of *Lecture Notes in Computer Science*, pages 273–291. Springer, 2001.

[12] Jack M. Loomis, Reginald G. Golledge, and Roberta L. Klatzky. Navigation system for the blind: Auditory display modes and guidance. *Presence: Teleoperators and Virtual Environments*, 7(2):193–203, 1998.

[13] K. Lyons, M. Gandy, and T. Starner. Guided by Voices: An Audio Augmented Reality System. In *Proceedings of The International Conference on Auditory Display*, 2000.

[14] Michael May. Strider: A Presentation. In *Proceedings of The Wearable Computer Conference (ICWC)*, 1998.

[15] Michael May. Accessible GPS Navigation and Digital Map Information for Blind Consumers. In *Proceedings of The Wearable Computer Conference (ICWC)*, 2000.

[16] Elizabeth D. Mynatt, Maribeth Back, Roy Want, Michael Baer, and Jason B. Ellis. Designing Audio Aura. In *Proceedings of The Conference on Human Factors in Computing Systems*, pages 566–573, 1998.

[17] R. Oppermann, M. Specht, and I. Jaceniak. Hippie: A Nomadic Information System. *Lecture Notes in Computer Science*, 1707:330–, 1999.

[18] Reinhard Oppermann and Marcus Specht. A nomadic information system for adaptive exhibition guidance. In *ICHIM*, pages 103–109, 1999.

[19] Royal National Institute for the Blind. InfraVoice.
http://www.rnib.org.uk/jmu/infravoice.htm.

[20] Joseph Rozier, Karrie Karahalios, and Judith Donath. Hear & There: An Augmented Reality System of Linked Audio. In *Proceedings of The International Conference on Auditory Display*, 2000.

[21] Allison Woodruff, Paul M. Aoki, Amy Hurst, and Margaret H. Szymanski. Electronic Guidebooks and Visitor Attention. In *Proceedings of The International Conference on Hypermedia and Interactivity in Museums*, pages 437–454, 2001.

Design Criteria
for Location-Aware, Indoor, PDA Applications

Carmine Ciavarella and Fabio Paternò

ISTI-CNR
Via G.Moruzzi 1, Pisa, Italy
{c.ciavarella,f.paterno}@isti.cnr.it

Abstract. The design of interactive systems has to take into account the context of use. In this paper we discuss the design criteria to use when developing location-aware, indoor, PDA applications. We analyse some of the technologies currently available for this purpose and examine how to provide users with location-dependent information. The discussion of such criteria is based on our experience in the development of an interactive guide for museum visitors.

1   Introduction

Nowadays mobile devices have powerful computing capabilities. This opens up new scenarios where users can interact with them in many environments, so that they can access the information they need anytime, anywhere. Old paradigms in human computer interaction, all addressed by traditional GUI mechanisms, need to be revisited [4] because of new elements such as the mobility of the users and the availability of interaction modalities unfettered by mouse and keyboards: voice, sound, gesture, and user position can also be used to interact with a system. In this paper we want to discuss the criteria for designing location-aware, indoor, PDA applications. This discussion is based on an experience in developing an application that localizes users' positions by interacting with infrared emitters, and adapts the presentation of information to the context of use. This solution can be applied in other context-dependent indoor applications, where the user's position cannot be tracked through GPS. Another advantage is that it provides better results than using wireless LANs [6] or Bluetooth technology for identifying the users' location in indoor environments. We also provide users with audio feedback to help them in interacting with the application.

The museum domain has been considered by a number of researchers (see for example, [2], [6], [10]), and is characterized by mobile users who need context-dependent information, which should be provided without disorienting the user. This need was also highlighted by an empirical study of the first version of the Marble Museum PDA application, which did not include any automatic support for location detection [7]: several visitors complained that sometimes they encountered problems understanding where they were during the visit.

L. Chittaro (Ed.): Mobile HCI 2003, LNCS 2795, pp. 131-144, 2003.

In this paper, after a discussion of related work, we analyse technologies to support location-awareness in indoor environments. Then, we introduce our case study and present a solution to identify user location, describing how we provide our users with audio feedback. After that we analyse the results of the evaluation test and we summarise the lessons learnt from this work.

2   Related Work

To better support users in their daily activities, a system has to provide them with information they need while taking into account the context in which interactions are performed. This problem requires different solutions depending on where the users are, i.e., in an outdoor or indoor environment. Whereas in the former case, the GPS technology helps the developer to find outdoor users' positions, in the latter the researchers have to find different solutions to localize user positions. In our work we focus on indoor environments. The museum domain has been considered by a number of researchers because in such environments the users walk freely in a building, without a fixed path, and need information related to the context (i.e. section) they are. So, museums are an ideal test area for researchers in human-computer interaction with mobile devices.

In IrReal [5], the authors designed a building information and navigation system based on Palm Pilot PDAs and a set of powerful infrared emitters located throughout a building. When the users are walking in the building, the infrared sends them information related to their current position. The information is grouped in a cluster of "pages" connected to each other making an acyclic graph. These pages are broadcast using the infrared beacons. This solution has some problems, the first is that the information provided to the users concerns only nearby objects: this can be a problem in a large room because even if the users are near an object, they may be interested in a different object whose description is contained in another group of pages (i.e., located far away). For each beacon, the pages are broadcast repeatedly: no back button is provided. Another problem concerns the cost of the solution: each beacon is connected with a PC in order to broadcast the pages.

In our solution we want to preserve the possibility for the user to move easily not only in the building, but also through the information in the system. We provide them with a back button that acts like the back button in Web browsers: so, for example, they can easily access the last artwork they visited.

Another approach has been proposed by the Cyberguide project [1]. In this project, the authors provide users with context-aware information about the projects performed at the GVU Center in Atlanta. They installed TV remote controllers throughout the building to detect users' locations and provide them with a map that shows the area neighbouring the user, highlighting corridors and nearby objects, such as project demos. In this way they have divided the building into a series of cells. The information on location (i.e. cell) and objects is provided in textual and graphical modalities. The users were also provided with the possibility of exploring the map of the entire Center. The project authors intended to support the visitors' tasks by taking into account their positions and what they are currently looking at: to detect this information, they assume that the users are looking in the same direction they are walking. So, when the user passes from one cell to another, the system shows the map of the new cell where the user is entering, oriented according to this direction. This approach requires a large number of beacons and a consequently costly system. Moreover, the application provides the users with textual information. A better solution would be to use audio for the project presentations. In our solution, we use MP3 files to give users information about the artworks in the museum. This solution was appreciated by users who, as we will describe in the section about our last test evaluation, liked the possibility of observing the object of the presentation while hearing information about it. Also, in our solution we chose to install infrared emitters on the entrance of each section. In this way, installing only a small number of devices, we have implemented a low cost, easy to install system.

The two projects discussed so far address the problem of locating the user through interactions with infrareds in a generic building. Now let us examine two projects that aim to detect users position specifically in a museum.

The Hippie system developed in the HIPS project [10], locates users via an infrared system composed of beacons installed at the entrance of each section and emitters installed on the artworks. This solution creates a sort of infrared grid through which the system can detect the artworks nearest any given user. Hippie provides the users with the information related to the artwork nearest them, assuming that visitors stop walking only because they are near an artwork they find interesting. However, the design does not consider other potential reasons for stopping, such as a crowd preventing movement. This project also addresses the problem of how to adapt the user interface to the user model. The model can be modified either directly by the user at the beginning of the session or by the system, which takes into account the history of user interactions and the choices performed by the user; in both cases the system highlights proposals for further information to the user through a blinking light-bulb icon. The suggested information can be accessed through links to the descriptions of the works that best correspond to the current user model. When accepted, the suggestions are used to update the user model. The information is provided by taking into account the user model and presentations are modified accordingly.

The limitation of this approach is that often the user's position alone is not enough to indicate interest in the closest work of art. Thus, the risk is that the system erroneously identifies the user interests and determines the corresponding user model. Consequently, the audio presentations will probably be of little interest to the user. In our approach in order to prevent such wrong deductions that can negatively influence the visit, we have chosen to insure users' freedom of movement. Once the system has detected the room the user is in, then the user can freely activate audio comments regarding the artworks of interest.

Another work has been proposed [2] for visiting "Filoli", a Georgian Revival house. In this case the application provides the users with an image of the current room with the works of interest highlighted by red borders. Then, the user can select the object of interest with a pen, which activates an audio comment or a video. It is possible to change the viewpoint of the room's representation by selecting one of the device's buttons; when the users want to enter in a new room, they have to indicate explicitly to the system by selecting the door of the next room in the last photo. In this project, one possible limitation is the use of pictures to represent the room content duplicating the information that the user is already seeing, with the risk of requiring multiple interactions to identify the selectable elements of interest. In addition, this solution is valid only for those museums where the elements of interest are arranged along each wall, while it becomes difficult to follow in cases where they are spread throughout the room. Our system detects automatically the room where the users are and provides them with a sound each time they enter in a new section. This audio feedback assures the users that the system is aware of the change of the context.

3   Support for Location Identification

The identification of a user's position in an in-door environment can be performed at various levels of granularity: for example, one is the identification of the exact user position, thus, in a museum application, the system can identify the closest work of art; another level is when the system is only able to identify the room where the user is located. The first case can be useful to try to identify what works of art are more interesting to the user based on the assumption that the time the user spends near a work of art is proportional to the interest in it [10]. However, this hypothesis may be incorrect because there are many reasons for a user to stop somewhere (it could be because of other visitors or some obstacles). Thus, erroneous deductions may negatively influence the application in determining user interests. This is one of the reasons for our choice of the second criterion. To explicitly localize the users in the museum, we have considered three recent technologies that allow mobile devices to offer some services: WLAN, Bluetooth and Infrared (IR). In the next subsections we analyse advantages and disadvantages of each of them and explain the reasons for our choice.

3.1   WLAN

WLAN technology allows devices to immediately connect to Internet/Intranet in a range of 100 meters (in indoor environments without obstacles) without any cables using an access point and a PCMCIA wireless Card. As in a classic LAN, a group of devices with wireless cards installed creates a wireless Intranet and can theoretically share files at 11Mbps (but real throughput is closer to 4-5Mbps [8]). The connection via WLAN has a high cost in terms of battery power of the devices and this can be a problem for mobile users. It also requires an external PCMCIA card to connect to the network until this technology is available directly on the motherboard of the devices. Moreover, walls and iron objects can interfere with the signal. To locate the position of the users in a building, WLAN is not so simple a solution because the system has to apply triangulation methods [3] to the data coming from the three access points nearest the user. Thus, the developers have to devote a great deal of attention when installing access points to prevent ambiguous situations on the borders of the intersections of the covered areas.

We studied the possibility of adopting the WLAN technology to localize the users during their visit. In our system we only need to know when the users enter a new section. We would need to install an access point for each room and position all of them in such a way that at the entrance of each section three access points overlap their coverage area. Then, on the basis of the intensity of the signal received the server could identify the location of the user. The problem was that we have not been able to find a solution that univocally indicates what section the users are entering because of the issue of the overlapping area, which was in some cases larger than some sections of the Museum. Another motivation was the cost of each access point: we would need 19 of them and consequently the cost of the system would increase.

3.2   Bluetooth

This recent technology has been introduced to avoid the problems we hinted at before. Bluetooth is a de facto standard for very low powered connections. Nowadays, Bluetooth is commercially available for many devices. The interaction between Bluetooth devices starts from a distance of 10 meters. The devices are grouped in *piconet* (i.e. 8 devices). Bluetooth allows users to connect easily to devices such as printer or headphones or to Internet via hot spots [8]. Once the connection is established, two ore more devices maintain the connection in spite of interference of walls or iron objects. The Bluetooth devices can share files at theoretically 1Mbps. Bluetooth communication protocol is composed of a preliminary step called "discovery": during this step the devices have to discover if there are other devices to interact with. This step costs in terms of time (between 5 and 10 seconds) [11] that each user has to wait before starting the communication. Once the discovery step finishes, the communication remains open until one of the two devices goes outside the range of the other. We wanted to develop a system that supports users during their visits in the museum; the interaction with the device has to be immediate because when the users enter in a new section, we want to offer them, immediately, the presentation of the section and the dislocation of the artworks. In this way we prevent the disorientation of the tourists. Using Bluetooth technology, the visitors would have to stop their moving at the entrance of each section, waiting the discovery step of their device. Also, if the museum is crowded, there is the possibility that more than 10 people can visit the same section: there can be problems in finding the piconet to enter in. We thought that this discovery step is not so natural for museum visitors and that can be an obstacle to the full enjoyment of their visit.

3.3   Infrared

IrDA protocol of communication supports high data rates (4Mbps), point-and-shoot style application. It is also characterized by non-interference with other electronics devices. The technology involved is the same of TV remote controller: the cost is not so high like WLAN and Bluetooth solutions. IrDA signals rebound over the surfaces: the developer has to take into account this peculiarity. The communication over IrDA protocol involves only another device at time and requires that sender and receiver are aligned or the interaction occurs within a 30 degree cone angle (which means that sender and receiver should have the corresponding ports tilted at a 30-degree angle each other).

As mentioned before, we intended to provide the visitors with the information regarding the section they are entering, at the instant they enter. Having considered the pros and cons of these three technologies, we chose to adopt the last one because of the immediateness of the connection and the relatively low costs of the manufacture and the installation. In addition, we noticed that we did not need to support communication of data during the user visit because current PDAs can have one gigabyte of additional memory. This information is sufficient to provide users with audios, images and videos on related aspects. In addition, during a museum visit a user is not interested in navigating in the Web because their main goal is to appreciate the artworks that are in exhibition.

4   The Case Study

We have developed and delivered an application for a museum. The application has been developed for the Marble Museum. The managers of the museum decided to provide their visitors with information additional to that contained in traditional labels. While guides are available for large groups, they can be too expensive for single visitors or small groups, an interactive automatic guide is a better solution in these cases. In our approach the design is driven by three main elements: the context of use that includes both the device used for the interaction and the environment where such interaction occurs, the tasks users wish to perform and the objects they need to manipulate in their performance (both interface and domain objects).

4.1   Context of Use

For the context of use, we consider the environment considered for the interactive system, the interaction platforms and the users of the interactive system who wish to achieve their goals through it.

In our case, the users can vary in terms of ability in interacting with computing devices and knowledge of the application domain.

The structure of the museum forces to some extent the order of visit among the rooms. Such rooms contain many types of objects from the ancient Romans to pieces of quarrying technology of the past century. Thus, visitors need support able to interactively select those more interesting for them and receiving related information. The application has been developed on a Compaq Ipaq 3660, with windows CE and additional one Gbytes Flash Memory Card. We decided to use text-to-speech synthesis for supporting audio comments. Unfortunately, the possibility of dynamic text-to-speech generation is not supported in these environments because the necessary libraries are lacking for Windows CE. In addition, the synthesized Italian voice was considered too unpleasant and was replaced with audio-recorded comments.

The mobile system reacts with sounds, context-aware information provided by text or audio channel to better support the users in their activity. The system interacts with users reacting to their change of the section providing them with audio feedback.

Currently, the application contains description of about 150 works of art, each of them with an associated Jpeg picture (dimensions are about 140x140 pixels). The audio files are in MP3 format. For the English version we have used text-to-speech provided by Text Aloud MP3. The application requires about 3 Mbytes of memory, with about 220 Mbytes of multimedia data (videos, images, vocal comments).

4.2   Tasks

In the design of the user interface we considered three main types of tasks that users can perform in the context considered:

- *orientation within the museum*, for this purpose three levels of spatial information are provided: a museum map, a section map, and, for each physical environment composing the section, a map with icons indicating the main pieces of work available in the room and their location. By selecting such icons the picture of the related element is displayed along with some basic information and the corresponding audio description is activated. The purpose of the picture is not to show the details of the work of art (that is supposed to be in front of the user), but to allow users to check that the information they are receiving regards the work that they are viewing.
- *control of the user interface*, for example, to allow changing the volume of the audio comments, to stop and start them, and to move through the various levels of detail of the museum description;
- *access to museum information*, also this is provided at different abstraction levels (museum, section, physical environment, single work).

4.3   Domain Concepts and User Interface

Through an analysis of the behaviour of museum visitors and the information provided them by the human guides we identified three levels of information that are interesting for them:

- Museum, overall introduction and short information regarding its history and peculiar aspects;
- Section, information regarding the main features of the sections, the common aspects of the artworks in them and the motivations for their introductions. Most relevant artworks are highlighted as well.
- Artworks, the description of the artworks and additional information regarding them are provided.

If we follow a Web metaphor we can say that for each instance of a level of information there is a page designed following some criteria. In these pages there is not only information regarding the artworks but also supporting the orientation or the control of the navigation within the application.

Figure 1 shows how a generic presentation is structured. The main area is used to provide information regarding the artworks whereas the lower part provides a command bar with menus to control the various parameters of the application.

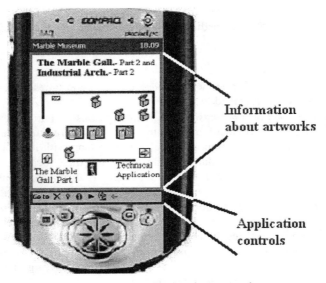

Fig. 1. Structure of a generic presentation

5   Location-Dependent Interaction

In order to determine user position, we have installed infrared emitters at the entrance into each room (see Figure 2). Such emitters have been expressly made for our application. They transmit a unique identifier through the IrDA protocol. When the user enters a new room the emitters send the identifier to the PDA, the application detects it and changes the presentation accordingly. The angle covered by the infrared emitter is 90°. This angle is sufficient to assure a good communication with the PDA assuming that the user keeps the device in vertical manner, even if it is not completely lined up with the infrared beacon. The signal transmitted by the emitter is composed of eight characters. Initially we used only three characters; thus the string sent by the emitters had the following format '001@@@@@'. However, after the first experiments we realized that this solution needed to be improved because infrared waves can be reflected by surfaces.

Consequently, the signal that reaches the infrared port of the PDA may not respect the spectrum of the IrDA protocol, then it can be misinterpreted. In this case, we can obtain three character strings with erroneous content because the identifier detected is different from that associated to the room where the user is entering.

Indeed, when the first version of the application was tested, it happened often that the infrareds signals distorted because of the rebounds, thus the string identifying the room was either completely corrupted or provided a wrong information (the identification of a room different for that of the room were the user was actually entering). Thus, we have extended the string transmitted by the emitters by adding three characters that are used as "parity bits". Each number is associated with an alphabetical character: "0" is associated with "A", "1" is associated with "B", etc. The algorithm is simple: each time a new string is detected, the application checks that the part of the string composed of numerical characters corresponds to that composed of alphabetical characters. For example, a valid string is "001AAB@@". Thus, the application can correctly determine when it detects a correct signal indicating the room where the user has entered. The emitters have been developed adopting stand-alone technology: they are made in such a way as to transmit one eight-character signal per second. This solution was easy to install and with low cost.

Fig. 2. Example of interaction between a visitor and an IR emitter

5.1   Visual Feedback

When the users change the section they are visiting, they want information about the artworks they are looking at. So, the detection of the section where the users are is important data to support them in their visit. In our system, this information is detected automatically through the interaction with infrared beacons: upon entering a new section, the application provides users with a Museum map, where the section is highlighted; after that, an audio presentation of the characteristics of the section and a map indicating the location of the artworks in that section are provided to the users. In other words, we use location information only to furnish the users with context-dependent information that help them to orient themselves in the museum.

5.2   Audio Feedback

The use of audio in the interaction between human and system plays an important role because the system can indicate its internal state: error, alert and information messages are generally displayed coupled with a sound associated to each event; in this case, the sound is used to call users' attention to a system message. In our application, we decided to highlight the automatic detection of the room where users are entering, obtaining two results: the first it to signal this event to the users who might not be looking at the PDA display; the second reason is to assure the visitors that the system is aware that the context has changed and that the information is related to the new section. The choice of the sound to use is important. In this case we have chosen the same sound generated when the PDA is connected to a desktop system. The rationale for the choice lies in the fact that an information link is established: when the application detects a new user position, to some extent it shows that there is a connection between the application and the surrounding environment, just as when the PDA and the application exchange information.

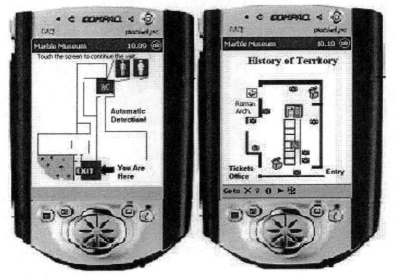

Fig. 3. Visual feedback when entrance in a new room is detected

As we show in the section on the user tests, the association of a sound to the section change help them to get oriented in the museum. To improve the support to the users during the visits, we have also added audio feedback when the users select artworks on the section map to assure users that the system has received their input. We adopted this solution because we noticed that, after selecting an artwork, users often reselected the artworks because they were unaware that the system was processing the request. We want to avoid this kind of double-clicking because it can generate some confusion that can negatively influence the interaction of the users with the system.

6   Design Criteria for the Graphical Part

Designing an application for a PDA should take into account the specific features of this type of device: it provides a broader range of interaction techniques than current mobile phones. The possibilities are similar to those of desktop systems but there are two main differences: the limitation of the screen resolution and the possibility of using it on the go.

We have followed some criteria during the design of the application:

- **Web metaphor,** while not many users have had much experience with PDAs, most have some experience with Web browsers, which are characterised by pages that can be uploaded through links with the possibility of going back and forward through the page history. We have designed our application trying to implement similar features into our application, but also taking into account its specific goals. Thus, the resulting system is composed of a number of graphical presentations that can be navigated through icons. Each page is also associated with a voice comment automatically started the first time it is accessed. Using the back button in the toolbar it is possible to go back to the previous presentations in a way similar to that of Web browsers.

- **Navigation feedback,** in Web browsers, links that have been selected have a different colour from the others. This is a useful feedback for navigators. In our application we adopted the same design: icons associated with artworks already accessed have a different colour (red) from those associated with artworks yet to be visited (grey).

- **Orientation support in the surrounding environment,** in order to help users to orient themselves we provide various information: the map of the museum highlighting the section where the user is, and then a map of the section highlighting the physical elements that identify it (walls, doors, supports for disabled people). Each of these act as a sort of landmark that can be useful for orientation. In addition, the map is displayed with the same orientation that the user has when entering.

- **Minimise graphical interaction,** for this purpose as soon as the user enters a new section or selects an artwork then the application immediately starts a vocal comment.

- **No redundancy in input commands,** in desktop graphical interfaces usually it is possible to interact through both lists of pull-down menus and icon toolbars. So, often the same command can be activated either through an element of a pull-down menu or through an icon. In our case, because the display has a very limited resolution, commands can be activated only through the icon toolbar.

7   Evaluation of the Application

In order to have feedback from real users a first test of the application has been performed. A group of users (35) received a PDA with our application installed at the entrance of the museum. The goal of the test was to understand to what extent the application provides a valid support from various viewpoints: quantity and quality of the information provided, modality of presentation, interaction with infrared devices, capacity to orient themselves in the museum. At the end they had to fill in a questionnaire with many questions structured into various parts regarding:

- Previous experience in museum visits (4 questions);
- Quality of the information provided regarding the artworks in the museum (9 questions);

- Quality of the multimedia techniques used: audio, images, and videos (7 questions);
- Quality of the interactive part of the application: its use, the underlying concepts, the user interface (10 questions);
- Capability to support users' orientation (10 questions);
- Some personal information, such as age, instruction, etc.

The test was composed of various types of questions: some of them required only positive or negative answers, others required a numerical scoring (on a scale from 1 to 7), and open questions aiming to stimulate critics and suggestions were introduced as well.

On average a visit took 73 minutes, 25 users were Italians, 18 were women, the average age was 37. 63% was graduated, 29% had a high-school diploma. Only 15 of them had already used a PDA before the experiment.

The application provides audio information in either Italian or English. The data show that foreign visitors appreciated the quality of the information more than Italians. In particular, the information regarding the museum sections received better ratings (average 5.72 with 1.10 standard deviation for Italian and 6.33 with standard deviation 0.71 for foreign visitors).

From the open questions, we found the need for more information regarding quarrying in ancient time, for example the quarrying methods and the life of quarry men. The answers regarding the multimedia techniques show that the audio presentations were appreciated from both Italians and foreign visitors. Very high ratings were provided to the videos whose utility was highlighted by most visitors. Some problems were raised for the images, some visitors were dubious regarding their dimensions and clearness.

The questions regarding the interactions with the electronic guide aimed to understand its actual utility and evaluate its usability leaving to the visitors the possibility of suggesting further improvements. To analyse the answers received, it can be useful to distinguish between novice users (who used a PDA for the first time) and expert users who already had a similar experience. Analysing the utility of the electronic guide, we noticed that novice and expert provided similar rate (novices provided 6.47 with 0.62 standard deviation whereas experts provided 6.40 with 0.74 standard deviation). Regarding the easiness of use, the experts provided best rates (average rating 6.60 with 0.63 standard deviation) while novices asked for improvements (average 6.28 with 1.23 standard deviation). Similar ratings were provided for the user interface, experts users found the interface rich of possibilities and clear to use, while novice users provided similar ratings with higher standard deviation and suggestions such as "the possibility of adding arrows to go forward and backward" or "improve the correspondence between the real objects in the room and the icons in the application", thus showing that some problems can arise when users interacting with the application have no previous experience with PDAs.

Regarding the interaction with the infrareds, the questions addressed issues such as their utility to support orientation, the ease with which users interact with them and localize the section where they are.

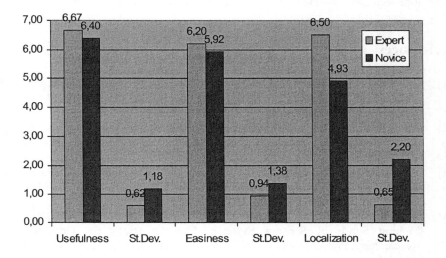

Fig. 4. User feedback on interaction with infrareds

The bar chart in Figure 4 shows that also in this case there are differences between experts and novice users. The former provided high ratings in a consistent manner, while the ratings provided by the novice users show that they found some difficulties in orienting themselves and identifying the current section. However, despite such difficulties they did not provide any particular suggestions. Some visitors provided comments regarding the location of the artworks in the rooms. One said "it would useful to have maps that change the orientation according to the user movements".

From the analysis of the data it is possible to understand that the most appreciated part of the application is the quality of the information, for example foreign visitors particularly appreciated the videos showing dynamic information related to the artworks in the museum. Novice users had some problems, both in the interaction and in the orientation but in this case it seems that the lack of familiarity with palmtop systems was a major cause and the use of infrareds added a further level of difficulty.

8   Conclusions

We have discussed criteria for designing location-aware, indoor applications. After analysing benefits and drawbacks of various technologies we have discussed our experience in developing a museum application in this field. We also report first results of the evaluation of such application and we identify a number of design criteria that can be adopted for other applications that share similar requirements.

Future work will be dedicated to the possibility of providing location-dependent support that takes into account also the preferences of the current user and apply an evaluation tool based on the intelligent analysis of the logs of the user interactions.

References

[1]   Abowd, G.D., Atkeson, C.G., Hong, J., Long, S., Kooper, R., Pinkerton, M.: Cyberguide: A Mobile Context-Aware Tour Guide. Baltzer/ACM Wireless Networks, Vol. 3. 1997.

[2]   Aoki, P.M., Woodruff, A.: Improving Electronic Guidebook Interfaces Using a Task-Oriented Design Approach. Designing Interactive Systems, 2000, pp.319-325, ACM Press.

[3]   Bahland P. and Padmanabhan, V.N.: RADAR: An InBuilding RF-Based User Location and Tracking System, Proc. IEEE Infocom 2000, IEEE Press, Piscataway, N.J., 2000, pp. 775-784.

[4]   Bellotti, V., Back, M., Edwards, K., Grinter, R.E., Henderson, A., Lopes, C.: Making Sense of Sensing Systems: Five Questions for Designers and Researchers. Proceedings of CHI 2002, Minneapolis, USA, 2002, pp. 415-422, ACM Press.

[5]   Butz, A., Baus, J., Kruger, A.: Augmenting buildings with infrared information. In Proceedings of the International Symposium on Augmented Reality ISAR 2000, 2000, IEEE Computer Society Press.

[6]   Cheverst, K., Davies, N., Mitchell, K., Friday, A., Efstratiou, C.: Developing a Context - aware Electronic Tourist Guide: Some Issues and Experiences. Proceedings of CHI 2000, The Hague, Netherlands, 2000, pp 17-24, ACM Press.

[7]   Ciavarella, C., Paternò, F.: Design of Handheld Interactive Support, Proceedings DSV-IS 2002, Rostock, Germany.

[8]   Davies, A.C.: "An overview of Bluetooth Wireless TechnologyTM and some competing LAN Standards", Invited Plenary Lecture, Proc. of 1st IEEE International Conference on Circuits and Systems for Communications, St Petersberg, Russia, 26-28 June 2002. pp 206-211.

[9]   Mori G., Paterno` F., Santoro C. : Tool Support for Designing Nomadic Applications. Proceedings ACM IUI'03, pp.141-148, January 2003, Miami, USA.

[10]   Oppermann, R., Specht, M.: A Context-Sensitive Nomadic Exhibition Guide. In the Proceedings of Symposium on Handheld and Ubiquitous Computing, pp. 127 -142, LNCS 1927, 2000, Springer Verlag.

[11]   Woodings, R., Joos, D., Clifton, T., Knutson, C.D.: "Rapid Heterogeneous Ad Hoc Connection Establishment: Accelerating Bluetooth Inquiry Using IrDA." Proceedings of the Third Annual IEEE Wireless Communications and Networking Conference (WCNC '02), Orlando, Florida, March 18-21, 2002.

The Design and Evaluation of a Mobile Location-Aware Handheld Event Planner

Rachel Fithian, Giovanni Iachello, Jehan Moghazy,
Zachary Pousman, and John Stasko

College of Computing/GVU Center, Georgia Institute of Technology
801 Atlantic Dr., 30332 Atlanta, GA, USA
{rfithian,giac,jehan,zpousman,stasko}@ cc.gatech.edu

Abstract. The problem of designing and evaluating mobile computing applications is of growing concern in the HCI community, due in part to the difficulty of applying traditional design and evaluation methods to increasingly informal and unstructured usage contexts. We describe the design and evaluation of an integrated location-aware event and meeting planner built to work in a PDA form factor. We discuss the limitations and possibilities of location technology on mobile devices and how it can be used to create useful, usable, and elegant applications. We outline major design decisions, the results of qualitative formative evaluation performed with a small number of participants, and the second iteration of the design. Finally, we offer a number of general considerations on the design process and on specific issues related to mobile handheld applications, including reference metrics for design assessment, user training and cross-over effects from desktop systems.

1   Introduction

The rise of a cell-phone culture [7] [15] has substantially changed the way people plan and manage their daily activities and social interactions. People use a range of different tools and resources to organize events and meetings, to notify, manage, and track attendees and to send last minute changes to the time, place and participants.

Cell phones, wireless email, and even wireless connectivity to calendars have progressed greatly in the past ten years, though their full capabilities are still hindered by a lack of integration and cumbersome application environments. Planning events and keeping track of others remains a cumbersome and inefficient activity and a source of anxiety [4]. As mobile devices become location-aware [6] [2] [18], the ability to track and monitor users could greatly help people at keeping a hold of this increasingly frenetic lifestyle.

The project described here investigates how individuals deal with event planning and management and the related communication tasks. Using questionnaires, interviews, and discussions with potential users, we assessed the current state of mobile device acceptance and satisfaction and attempted to catalog the personal and contex-

L. Chittaro (Ed.): Mobile HCI 2003, LNCS 2795, pp. 145-160, 2003.

tually dependent ways in which people currently plan their meetings and informal events. The development and evaluation of a prototype thought us a number of interesting lessons, which we report at the end of the paper.

1.1   Related Location-Aware Mobile Applications

Location-aware applications have been one of the drivers of third-generation (3G) mobile operators' marketing efforts in the past few years [18]. To date very few such applications have actually been implemented due to a host of technical problems related to interoperability and precision.

One of the few available applications to offer more than customized web portals based on a city-level granularity is the AT&T Wireless "Find Friends" service [2], a location-based relationship management service running on mobile phones. After signing up and building a buddy list, similarly to current instant messaging systems, it is possible to locate parties with the same service in any area covered by AT&T. After locating a friend, the user can invite him/her to some meeting point chosen from businesses in the AT&T Yellow Pages.

The system is based on iMode[1], which leads to poor performance in crowded areas, or areas with bad connectivity. The spatial precision of the system is linked to the antenna network structure; in densely populated areas, a precision of less than a kilometer is achievable, while in rural areas this figure can exceed 10 kilometers, making the localization very imprecise, and thus not very useful. This service does not fully take advantage of localization in the planning and execution of social gatherings. There is no way, for example, to sort the phone book based on proximity, or to include location information in SMS messages. Key drawbacks are the inability to invite more than one other party to a meeting and the disconnect between the "Find Friends" application, which runs in a browser, and the rest of the phone functions.

Another system of note is the HandiMessenger system [8], developed for commercial purposes but never marketed. The system adds rich meta-data to voice, email, and text messages, so that the receiver of a message can see the location (including presence) and calendar information of the sender. With this information, a user can decide on an appropriate means of getting back to someone.

Finally, the Personal Navigation Tool [3] centers around way-finding, with both map-based and text-based directions to specific locations. The system does not directly assist in the planning or execution of meetings or in communication, though its design and user preferences relate to our integrated design.

2   Analysis and Design

When people want to meet, whether for formal or informal purposes, the strategies they use to accomplish this goal can be time-consuming and cumbersome. The organizer(s) must get in touch with all the participants in order to notify them of the gathering and logistics. Unforeseen situations, such as changes to the venue or time,

---

[1]   iMode is the trademark of an implementation of a subset of HTML and related browser, which runs on 2.5G and 3G cell phones, initially developed by NTT DoCoMo. [10]

require updating participants. Based on a variety of considerations, including personal preference and availability, organizers juggle the tasks of managing the logistics of the gathering, updating participants, and keeping track of people, all in the pursuit of a successful gathering.

We surveyed and interviewed individuals in our target demographic, 19- to 35-year old females and males, chosen according to market penetration, acceptance and spending forecasts [18]. We sought to understand the tasks users currently perform when forming meetings and gatherings, and the strategies and technologies they employ to accomplish these tasks, to identify problems and concerns that a new mobile location-aware system should address.

Respondents shared the feeling that the current crop of mobile tools is poorly matched to their tasks of meeting and "keeping up with" friends and acquaintances. Respondents recounted tales of woe when plans for the evening changed and notifying all participants took considerable time and effort on the part of the organizer, calling key attendees and asking them to call others. Messages, both text and voice, are constantly traded among friends in order to facilitate both working and friendly get-togethers. In particular, younger interviewees were prone to spending "the whole night" on their cell phones trying to contact each other, verify locations and plans, get directions, and make plans based on happenstance.

Interviewees expressed strong interest in how location-based technology might assist them in these tasks. Many of them were enthusiastic at the idea of offloading cumbersome and repetitive tasks to their technology artifacts, freeing them to worry about more important things. Colbert's diary study [3] uncovered analogous frustrations among a similar demographic, noting that current mobile tools lose some of their effectiveness as participants are en route.

Further analysis showed that planning tasks vary in nature and detail depending on the formal or informal nature of the event. *Formal events* (e.g. for business purposes) are generally planned in advance. The organizer and other participants are motivated to ensure that the event runs according to plan and modifications are kept to a minimum. *Informal events* are often social in nature and do not require firm commitments ahead of time. Plans are not constrained, and individuals frequently modify logistics based on a number of social and environmental factors. Events with differing levels of formality require different tasks and therefore different support.

Users were most interested in the systems that supported informal, rather than formal, gatherings. Moreover, they liked the idea of integrating an application into existing hardware to reduce the number of carry-on devices, but also liked the interactivity and map-based visualizations provided by the unique hardware with more screen-real estate. Finally, many of our respondents indicated that privacy would be a primary concern for them when using location-aware technologies.

Preliminary designs covered the entire range of computing devices from wearable items like an "intelligent keychain" (which alerts the user to the proximity of significant individuals while remaining unobtrusive[2]) to a fully integrated meeting planner, recorder and conference phone large enough to fill a briefcase. These "creative designs" allowed us to show to potential users (in a somewhat exaggerated way), and gather feedback on, the concepts which were then later incorporated in the prototype.

---

[2]   This design is similar to the Lovegetty device. See: www.lovegetty.com.

The final prototype is based on a PDA/phone combination,[3] which does not require users to carry an extra device and has a larger screen than a smartphone[4], to support map-based visualizations. The device is assumed to integrate location technology such as GPS. The prototype is built with Microsoft Embedded Visual Basic for Pocket PC and runs on a Compaq iPaq. The design aims at supporting users in their goals of getting in touch with and keeping up with friends. Task analysis led to the identification of three main conceptual entities. *People* (and groups) hold information about contacts, including their telephone number. *Events* hold all the information related to an event: time, date, location, and invited participants. *Locations* are semantic markers associated with specific geographic positions.

Fig. 1. A test participant using the system

When a user starts up the application, she is shown the Home screen (Fig. 2), which reminds her of the people on her buddy list who can currently view her location. The man icon in the top bar fills up as she selects to be visible to more buddies. The screen also provides a summary of the most immediate upcoming events; more information about these events, or any of the others she has planned, is on the Events screen, which includes details including time, place, and people invited.

The People and Places screen (Fig. 3) supports the user in locating friends and event participants. She may wish to find out where the other participants are located in order to organize an impromptu gathering or to determine whether they are likely to be late at a planned meeting. The map displays her current location in relation to the locations of the people and groups on her buddy list. If she desires to monitor the progress of participants in getting to the meeting spot, she may select an event from her list in order to view all the participants' locations in the map display. Detailed directions for getting to a friend's location are available, as well as information about the estimated time required to get there and the distance that must be traveled.

---

[3]   Like the Mindspring Treo, Audiovox Thera and the T-Mobile PocketPC Phone Edition.
[4]   Such as the Panasonic GD87 or the Nokia 7650.

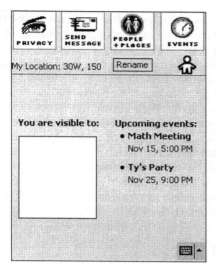

Fig. 2. Home screen

Fig. 3. People and place screen

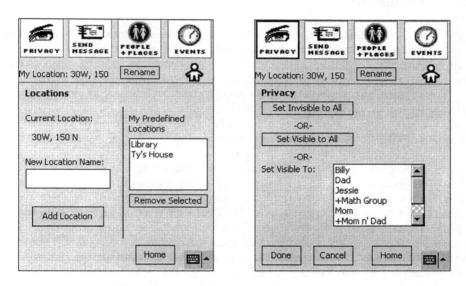

Fig. 4. Locations screen

Fig. 5. Privacy screen

A user may wish to add meaningful labels that correspond to certain GPS coordinates (e.g. turning "84.416 W, 33.75 N" into "Movie Theater"). These semantic markers can be set from the Locations screen (Fig. 4), which is accessed by clicking the "Rename" button. This label (rather than the coordinates) will be displayed thereafter as her current location whenever she is in that spot, and can also be used for scheduling future events and in writing messages.

The application allows users to organize meetings using two different methods. The more formal way is to schedule an event, which is accomplished through the Events screen (not shown). When creating a new event, the user can specify details including the time, place, and people invited and then save the event to her list and send notification to the participants. For spontaneous gatherings, she may instead rely on text messaging, by sending messages to one or more of the people on her buddy list, and automatically include her location, to help her friends locate her quickly (e.g. if she is at the coffee shop and wants them to meet her there in five minutes.)

An even simpler way for a user to assist friends in locating her is to allow them to monitor her location. This may be useful, for example, if she is running late to a meeting and wants other attendees to monitor her travel progress, reducing the need for constant calling back and forth to communicate her progress. Through the Privacy screen (Fig. 5), the user can view and make changes to her current visibility status, by allowing or disallowing select people and groups on the buddy list to view her location. To promote simple and effective actions, a single click allows or disallows everyone on the buddy to see her location.

3   Evaluation

The evaluation goal was to test the application's usefulness, appreciation, learnability and performance measures (described in detail below). Formative evaluation provided information about the prototype's qualities and shortcomings, yielding a new design and some key guidelines for the development of location-aware mobile devices.

The application was developed with enough functionality to allow for robust use during testing in an outdoors environment; the positional data for the user and the other parties (maps, locations, etc.) was hard coded in the prototype based on the location of the test. This setup was more than adequate for the purposes of our "semi-stationary" evaluation. However, in the case of evaluations involving large movements, testing would need true or Wizard-of-Oz location information.

We sought to collect qualitative data based on observation of participants' interactions with the system and post-test interviewing. In order to understand participants' mental models we adopted a talk-aloud protocol with three of the nine participants. We recorded a small number of quantitative measures, including time required to complete tasks on the remaining six tests and a satisfaction questionnaire. Because of the small number of participants, these quantitative measures are not statistically significant, but provide valuable information on the design and on timings related to interface components (e.g. the soft keyboard) and the application itself.

The average age of the nine participants was 26 (maximum 30, minimum 19, 5 females and 4 males). The average reported time for owning a cell phone was 3.9 years. All participants but one declared themselves experienced with PDAs, SMS, Instant Messaging (IM) and with stylus-based input methods. Most participants did not own a PDA and had no familiarity with GPS.

3.1   Evaluation Design

The evaluation consisted of a pre-test questionnaire to gather demographic data (including experience with mobile devices), a scenario-based evaluation, and post-test questionnaire and interview. We sought to evaluate the activities that potential users identified as important but time consuming or complicated:

- deciding on a meeting (event planning),
- inviting attendees to the event or meeting,
- making changes to the event,
- reaching the destination, and
- supporting the actual meeting (monitoring arriving participants, etc.).

We developed a set of 15 tasks covering the listed key activities and revolving around two scenarios: a typical afternoon in the life of a busy college student or young professional and his or her evening activities. Tasks included: "Locate an individual and send her a message", "View event details and attendee locations", "Make yourself invisible to all other users" and "Add a group to the buddy list". In general, each of the 15 tasks required one minute or less to complete.

One researcher carefully observed participants in order to gain understanding of their interactions with the application, including comments, errors, recovery techniques and strategies for accomplishing the tasks.

Another researcher collected task timing data[5], which we compared to pre-defined benchmarks, on six of the nine participants. Though this information is not statistically significant and is not presented here, it provided a lower bound for evaluating further design iterations. Also, users did not have canonical methods (or, in some cases, even similar methods) to accomplish the tasks of inviting and monitoring attendees, and changing venues and meeting times.

Considering the lack of benchmarks or models for assessing timings for this kind of tasks in the HCI literature, we resorted to comparing the data gathered from users with reasonable guesses at how long tasks should take, based on the same tasks accomplished using traditional means. Participants were not instructed on the specifics of the system before interacting with it, apart from a short demonstration of the soft keyboard, and were not shown how to perform the tasks beforehand; instead, they learned by trial and error to use the various features of the device. We took a cue from the current crop of mobile personal communication devices whose interfaces and system functions are all learned via use, not manuals.

All testing was performed in various environments on a university campus. Because we intend the system to support mobile and informal situations, we sought ecological validity for our evaluation, over concerns such as environmental consistency. We also attempted to simulate the integrated nature of our system inside of other personal communication devices. Users were interrupted by SMS and meeting requests while attempting to complete tasks as well as by environmental factors such as rain, friends, and traffic noise. Applications for mobile devices must be usable on-the-fly in real situations if we want them to integrate into users' lives [11].

---

[5]   The timer was paused during interruptions of various kinds (greeting a friend, receiving a phone call, etc.).

After participants interacted with the system, they were asked to fill out a questionnaire and to answer to an interview. In the questionnaire, participants rated the system (on a Likert scale) regarding usefulness, learnability, and ease of use. We also requested that participants rate their overall impressions of the system and asked whether they would use and/or purchase the application. The interview included a set of open-ended questions aimed at probing into participants' mental understandings of the system, impressions about its usefulness and usability, and suggestions for improvement.

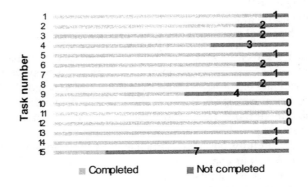

Fig. 6. Completed tasks. The numbers show how many participants did not complete the task

3.2   Evaluation Results

Generally, participants were successful in completing the tasks, especially later tasks, which may indicate that the system is in fact learnable in a relatively short time by users with no prior training (see Fig. 6). The only tasks that were consistently difficult for multiple users (including tasks 9 and 15) were those involving the "Rename location" button (see Fig. 1 through 4); these difficulties are discussed below.

The average time required to perform each task (for tasks that were completed successfully) was computed over the six participants of the timed tests and roughly corresponds to the hypothesized completion time. The exceptions fall into a few broad categories:

- performance was better on later tasks than on earlier tasks. It is difficult to derive precise data about the learning curve; however, after the fifth task, performance improved noticeably and users accomplished most tasks in consistently low times.
- Some participants performed tasks by utilizing unforeseen strategies, which met the success criteria, although requiring more time.
- Most participants had trouble locating the screen where location information could be added and edited – those who completed the tasks succeeded by activating the proper screen accidentally or gave up after stumbling for a while.

One of the reasons for the third point is to be sought in the appearance of the "Rename locations" button, which participants did not recognize as such, despite its prominent location on the top-center section of the screen next to the location label: PocketPC buttons are flat, as opposed to the usual look of desktop UI buttons.

In fact, interference between training on desktop computers and the use of handhelds was observed during the entire evaluation process. This is not surprising; however, more interesting is the way such interference happens and what the consequences are. In general, participants experienced difficulties due to unfamiliarity with the interaction syntax of the PDA: they used the UI elements like the analogous elements on desktop UIs. As a result, users had problems in identifying active elements, and missed completely parts of the interface.

Table 1. Main qualitative findings

Qualitative result	Participant comments
Did not like / understand privacy icon	Participants noticed the privacy icon but thought that it indicated proximity to someone. Others thought it was not useful, because it did not indicate *who* was watching.
Problems of understanding maps	Participants had problems in assessing distances in maps. Others did not understand the icons on the maps. Others still preferred labels on the map.
Ergonomic factors	Keyboard interaction is uncomfortable. Integrate the application with other functions (e.g. phone).
"Rename" locations is confusing	Participants did not understand the way the application manages locations.
Lack of undo or confirmations	Participants wished a confirmation before committing irrevocable actions (e.g. erasing people from contact list).

We observed a negative correlation between task completion time and participant's experience with stylus and PDAs and with IM and SMS writing: longer experience corresponded to lower times. The timing breakdown confirms that most of the task time was used in typing on the soft keyboard. Prior experience with the stylus reduced task time, but most participants found typing difficult and frustrating. Indeed, keys are tiny and close together, slowing down typing pace and increasing error rate: *the soft keyboard is not suited for on-the-move use of the PDA*.

By evaluating the prototype with participants without prior experience with the application, we gained information about how users can learn to use the application on-the-fly, and our evaluation suggests that users quickly gain familiarity with most features. However, it is unclear how a more experienced user would interact with the device. *These results suggest to separate evaluation of performance from that of learnability*, with the purpose of determining the time and effort required to learn the application and how this affects the success and satisfaction of their interactions.

Observation, questionnaires and interviews provided invaluable feedback about general design and specifics of the interface. The most interesting results of the qualitative analysis are synthesized in Table 1. Participants had problems both in understanding the iconographic meaning and the function of the privacy icon. Also, participants did not understand the significance of the asterisks in the buddy lists that indicate who can see the user's current location. This led to a complete redesign of this part of the interface (see below), in order to make the icon more informative, and by binding it to the specific function of privacy management when touched.

Maps represented a challenge for participants; the amount of information which the display can convey is very limited, and sophisticated visualizations need to be implemented to make the most of the technology. Assessing distances on a small screen map is hard, and even a scale is insufficient for providing adequate information. Instead, explicit indication of distances between places of interest would provide the users with the information they need to take decisions. Participants also asked for legends to be included in maps, a design option which was initially discarded on the grounds that it would create too much clutter – but was added to the redesigned maps.

Table 2. Results from post-questionnaire. All responses are based on a scale of 1 to 5, with 1 being most negative and 5 most positive

Query	Mean response	Std. Dev.
Rating of system as whole	3.8	0.7
Rating of usefulness of system	3.6	0.9
Easy to learn and use	4.2	0.7
Ease of privacy concepts	3.4	1.0
Ease of finding people and distances	3.9	1.1
Ease of finding event participants	4.1	0.9
Ease of creating event	4.6	1.0
Terminology	4.0	1.0
Interface pleasantness	4.0	1.0
Would you buy it?	5 Yes / 4 No	N/A

Integration with other applications and functions on the devices was mentioned by the majority of participants: being able to switch seamlessly from event planner to contact list and to phone is considered an essential feature of these designs. Integration is also a characteristic of highly successful systems like PalmOS and Symbian.

Undo was a sorely missed function. During design, undo was discarded in view of the fact that the device should be kept as simple as possible, and that interaction is structured to proceed in small, discrete steps. However, even for such simple and apparently harmless interactions steps, users need to undo or at least confirm specific actions: mobile applications are no different from desktop in this regard.

The subjective appreciation measures in the post-task questionnaire (Table 2), such as ease of learning and use and the ease of creating events, were ranked particularly positively. This confirms the choice of structuring the application around clear conceptual entities. Participants rated privacy concepts least easy to grasp; this feedback, in addition to observations and discussions with users, motivated reconsideration of privacy features in the second design iteration. The interviews aimed at gathering impressions and feedback on issues exposed during testing and unfulfilled expectations (e.g. the question: "Was there anything you wanted to do but couldn't?").

As a final comment, it should be noted that, in this early formative evaluation of a novel application, *qualitative data provided far more information than quantitative measures*.

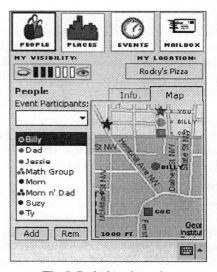

Fig. 7. Redesigned home screen   **Fig. 8.** Redesigned people screen

4   Redesign

The redesign process sought to preserve the successful portions of the interface while making it faster to use, clearer, and more consistent through extensive rework of both position and labeling of interface elements, tighter integration and an optimization of the information presentation. Improvements include reworking of the top menu bar and the privacy-options screen, improvements to maps, and redesign of the "People" screen. Updated designs were built and shown informally both to users who had seen the old product and to others who had not, with encouraging comments, but a new test would be necessary to evaluate the effectiveness of the changes.

Interaction Design. Participants had difficulties in renaming the anonymous GPS coordinates to meaningful locations, and were unable to use these "semantic locations" in their messages and meeting invitations. We sought to make these functions more intuitive, adding a full-sized "Places" button, to make the Place management more accessible. We integrated the secondary navigation bar (which contained the old "rename" button as well as a privacy indicator) into the button bar, making the privacy-level indicator more informative and the "My Location" area actionable and more understandable. (Fig. 7.)

A new incremental visibility indicator, that uses the more intuitive "watching eye" metaphor, was developed to address the shortcomings of the previous "privacy man". A button was also added on the home screen to make the user invisible, to improve user performance and decrease the anxiety about privacy.

Graphical and more representational indicators are used in the buddy list. An "open eye" is used to inform whether a given individual can see the user or not, and groups have now a graphical representation. These replace the confusing and not well liked asterisk and plus signs that were used in the original application.

Contact Management. The "People" screen, (Fig. 8) where users monitor visible buddies, view their address book and get further information like time, distance, and directions to buddy's locations, has undergone considerable redesign. A tab was added for address book data, such as street addresses, phone numbers and email. Another tab provides a map view, while buttons allow the user to send messages, get detailed directions to a friend's present location, and access a full-screen map.

Integration has also been enhanced: if a user is viewing an appointment, he or she can quickly "map the participants" to see the locations of the attendees. Similarly, it is possible to send messages and make appointments directly from the People tab because the system remembers which buddy (or buddies) is being viewed when switching modes to send messages or invite buddies to informal events.

Maps. Test participants found maps useful for identifying others' locations, especially when they were familiar with the neighborhood. A legend was one of the proposals to enhance the maps in case of unfamiliar locations, and the redesign accounts for this. *The size and detail of maps in location-aware applications is critical.* In our preliminary testing, we found that users preferred simplified, color maps of the largest size afforded by a device. The initial design was driven by this consideration, and we increased the size of the map and decreased its complexity.

However, user feedback indicated that a legend was nevertheless necessary. The last version of the design uses a transparent legend, superimposed over the corner of the image, displaying current scale and people and places (Fig. 8). Since the size of the legend is proportional to the number of people displayed in the map, the legend would cover more and more of the screen as the number of people or groups increases. This could be solved by employing dynamic visualizations which show different elements (scale, legend, distances, detail) based on threshold values of the syntactic complexity of the map. Care was taken to make sure that maps served their purpose and were suited to the target form-factor but that they would convey just enough information for users to think with the map.

5   Lessons Learned

The mobile personal communication device market is increasingly flooded with devices which are crossing the boundaries between mobile and pervasive computing [16]. In the long term, the rapid development of interoperable ubiquitous computing technologies makes it hard to predict the acceptance of services.[6] However, looking at the short term, it is possible to draw some considerations which might help in creating new and more compelling services.

While the developer community has embraced in the past couple of years a "program once, run anywhere" approach to advanced services on mobile devices, by creating automatic trans-rendering engines that format the same applications for different types of user terminals [10] [13], it is becoming apparent that a given application can be used fruitfully only on a specific hardware combination. For example, a map-based

---

[6]   The telecommunications industry history is populated by spectacular failures of supposedly successful technologies. (WAP, Videotel, DECT)

direction finder PDA might not be adopted by car drivers, due to ergonomic limitations such as bad lighting, low contrast and small screen, and the considerable attention focus required by a PDA, while it could be accepted by pedestrians, who are able to focus on the device while walking, without risk of accidents. The same service might thus be successful in dense European and Asian urban environments, and not in the United States, where people mostly need directions while moving in an automobile. *Mobile applications need to be developed for specific user, environmental and technological targets* and not as simple reduction of other applications (e.g. web-based).

In addition to the traditional usability paradigms [5] and evaluation heuristics [12], the design of resource-constrained mobile devices requires considering a broader spectrum of usability paradigms, among which *task resumability* and *integration*.

The ability of easily restarting tasks after an interruption or break is fundamental. This consideration stems from the observation of user activity on the prototype in an outdoor environment: our participants often interrupted their activity to look around, greet acquaintances, or respond to environmental stimuli, like a car passing by. This "task resumability" property is influenced by state visibility and task predictability, but also requires supporting the user in recovering the memory of system state and previous activity after a distraction. Design guidelines for supporting this include:

- stateless interaction model;
- visibility of the information needed to perform actions at any given step;
- atomic or short interaction sequences (requiring not more than a couple of steps);
- appropriate timeout on unfinished operations.

Integration also plays a fundamental role in mobile applications, because of the lack of a clipboard for temporary storage and the difficulty of taking notes to channel outputs to other applications on the device. Not only does integration ease task migration between user and system, but results in lower interaction times.[7] In the prototype, participants continuously asked for more features to be integrated in the system, such as being able to obtain navigation instructions, maps, or to call automatically a party based on location information. Mobile applications should afford this by:

- including hooks for moving from one interaction to another carrying intermediate data (e.g. when mapping a buddy's location, the selected buddy becomes the "to" line for SMS messages or event invites);
- switching among application components and resume where the user left off;
- integrating the use of data to reduce the need of accessing multiple sources (e.g. by providing location information in the buddy list).

Privacy was a major concern of almost all participants: we will not discuss this here, given the availability of dedicated studies on the matter [9]. We only would like to point out that in the case of this prototype the iconography related to privacy functions did not provide enough clues for the participants to assess their "privacy state". Usability problems of privacy enhancing technology are not new [19], and this study reiterates the need for a uniform and meaningful iconography and mixed

---

[7] Execution time is an important factor when interaction is limited to "interstitial" moments between other activities, such as walking, taking a bus, paying for coffee, etc.

iconographic/textual interfaces. Privacy is not a binary state (hidden/visible), but a range on the number of people that can see the user at a given time and here two designs were offered to represent this (the unsuccessful privacy "man" and the newer "eye bar"). Designs should also account for reflexive (where coupled partners are always either visible or invisible to each other) and non-reflexive privacy (which allows independent visibility, as in our application). *Privacy is both continuous and non-reflexive in the physical world. Location-aware designs should reflect this.*

In our system, users may label points that they visit, storing them for later use by them or their buddies. In doing this, the system implicitly draws the distinction between a location, which is any point in a given geography, and a place, which adds a meaning to a location, (which can be as simple as a label): *both abstractions are necessary in location-aware applications.*

Training has been necessary in usability tests where participants were supposed to represent a population of expert users, and reliable data needed to be unbiased by varying previous experience. As one of the aims of this study was to understand how quickly participants would be able to pick up the main concepts and functionality of the application, we did not provide any training. The drawback of this choice is that participants had problems understanding some aspects of the UI functionality: training on the specifics of the interface interaction model would have helped test participants into exposing the true learning time of the application.

Closely related to this is the problem of the *lack of quantitative historical metrics* for these new applications. While it is possible to base the comparison on the time spent in performing similar operations with 'traditional' alternative means, this is not very informative. On the one hand, with the event planner one may well communicate with a large number of acquaintances with one single operation, but the overall effect is very different from calling up each person individually: new applications elicit new behaviors and allow activities which have different mechanical and social effects.

On the other hand, basing the entire evaluation on raw timing measurements could prove to be very limiting, especially if the tasks are benchmarked in a situated action setting. Timings are important, but other performance measures such as resiliency to interruptions and interactions suspensions may be much more useful for evaluating this class of applications. Mobile and ubiquitous computing applications lend themselves well to situated action, activity theoretic or distributed cognition user models [1]; which of these are best for a particular application depends largely on the kind of application and of which aspects of the design are in the limelight.

The choice of a user model should thus be based on a critical analysis of the users and their knowledge, the tasks, and the application domain; this choice influences both the design and the evaluation of the system via a direct mapping with the system model. This evaluation design mainly used the situated action model, as we wished to examine the behavior and performance of users in real-world situations, where environmental and social factors are a source of both distraction and motivation [17]. We feel that this choice has been confirmed by the meaningful results of the evaluation.

6   Conclusions

Advancements in mobile computing have lacked the focus of blending with the everyday lives of people: it is essential not only to understand how people carry out their tasks but also to recognize how individuals use technology to build integrated applications rather than creating yet another artifact for people to worry about. User involvement is necessary especially for mobile computing – these products need to adapt to the rhythms of everyday life and the changing conditions of outdoors, leisure and informal settings. Early testing of applications in an ethnologically valid environment is vital, not only for developing better products, but also for understanding which applications will meet commercial success.

Moreover, it is necessary to test user and system models on specific mobile applications and their use in a noisy outdoor and informal environment, in order to understand which models are most appropriate. This work suggests that some common usability guidelines and evaluation metrics might not transpose from the desktop to the new breed of "disappearing hardware". While a historical base of performance measures is necessary to reliably assess future designs, recognizing the inadequacy of raw performance metrics might be even more important, to focus on people needs and expectations.

Acknowledgements

We would like to thank the anonymous reviewers, Jeremy Goecks and Duke Hutchings for providing invaluable comments and support.

References

[1]   Abowd, G., et al.: The human experience. In IEEE Pervasive Computing, 1(1), pp. 48–57, 2002.
[2]   AT&T Wireless: "Find Friends", http://www.attws.com/mmode/features/findit/FindFriends/
[3]   Chincholle, D., et al.: Lost or Found? A Usability Evaluation of a Mobile Navigation and Location-Based Service. In Proc. Mobile HCI 2002. Pisa, Italy, pp. 211–224.
[4]   Colbert, M.: A Diary Study of Rendezvousing: Group Size, Time Pressure and Connectivity. In Proc. Mobile HCI 2002. Pisa, Italy, pp. 21–35
[5]   Dix, A., et al.: Human Computer Interacion, 2nd Ed.. Prentice Hall Europe, pp.162–175.
[6]   Federal Communications Commission: Enhanced 911, http://www.fcc.gov/911/enhanced/
[7]   Geser, H.: Towards a Sociological Theory of the Mobile Phone. University of Zürich, Switzerland, August 2002   (Release 2). http://socio.ch/mobile/t_geser1.htm

[8]   Hibino, S., Mockus, A.: HandiMessenger: Awareness-Enhanced Universal Communication for Mobile Users. In Proc Mobile HCI 2002. Pisa, Italy, pp. 170–183.

[9]   Langheinrich, M.: Privacy Invasions in Ubiquitous Computing. Workshop on Socially-informed Design of Privacy-enhancing Solutions in Ubiquitous Computing. UbiComp 2002, Göteborg, Sweden.

[10]   Microsoft: Mobile Internet Toolkit 1.0 for Visual Studio .NET. http://msdn.microsoft.com

[11]   Nardi, B.: Studying Context: A Comparison of Activity Theory, Situated Action Models and Distributed Cognition. In Context and Consciousness: Activity Theory and Human-Computer Interaction, Nardi, B., Ed., 1996, MIT Press

[12]   Nielsen, J.: Enhancing the explanatory power of usability heuristics. In Proc. of CHI'94, pp. 152–158.

[13]   Nokia: Mobile Internet Toolkit 3.1. http://www.forum.nokia.com

[14]   NTT DoCoMo: Imode Information. http://www.nttdocomo.co.jp/english/p_s/imode/

[15]   Piller, C.: The Place That Tech Forgot, Los Angeles Times, October 19, 2000. http://www.technovative.com/ourpress_latimes.html

[16]   Satyanarayanan, M.: Pervasive Computing: Vision and Challenges. IEEE Personal Communications, pp. 10–17, August 2001

[17]   Taylor, A., Harper, R.: Age-old Practices in the 'New World': A study of gift-giving between teenage mobile phone users. In Proc. of CHI 2002, pp. 439–446, ACM Press

[18]   UMTS Forum, Enabling UMTS / Third Generation Services and Applications, UMTS Forum Report 11, October 2000, http://www.umts-forum.org

[19]   Whitten, A. and Tygar, J.D.: Usability of Security: A Case Study. Technical Report CMU-CS-98-155, Carnegie Mellon University, December 18, 1998

Supporting Local Mobility in Healthcare by Application Roaming Among Heterogeneous Devices

Jakob Bardram[1], Thomas A. K. Kjær[2], and Christina Nielsen[1]

[1] Center for Pervasive Healthcare
Department of Computer Science, University of Aarhus
Åbogade 34, DK-8200 Århus N.
{bardram,sorsha}@daimi.au.dk
[2] IBM Global Services, IBM Denmark
Dusager 4, DK-8200 Århus N.
thomas.kjaer@dk.ibm.com

Abstract. This paper presents results from a research project aiming at developing an architecture supporting local mobility within hospitals. The architecture is based on fieldwork and design workshops within a large Danish hospital and it has been implemented and evaluated after a pilot phase. Our fieldwork has emphasised the differences between *remote mobility*, where users travel over long distances, and *local mobility*, where users walk around within a fixed set of buildings and/or places. Based on our field studies and our design work, we conclude that local mobility puts up three requirements for computer support; (i) it should *integrate into the existing infrastructure*, (ii) it should support the use of various *heterogeneous devices*, and (iii) it should enable seamless *application roaming* between these devices. The paper describes how these requirements were realized in an architecture for local mobility, and how this architecture was implemented in the healthcare domain.

1 Introduction

Mobility and mobile computing is playing an increasing role in human-computer interaction research and design as a result of the ever-growing range of technology now supporting mobility. Mobile computers, laptops, tablet PCs, PDAs, cellular phones, and hybrids are all devices intended to support mobility of users, and the proliferation of wireless network access like WLAN, UMTS, GPRS, and GSM all support mobile computing. The increasing deployment and use of such mobile technology pose several challenges to the design of the user interaction, and we have already seen much interesting research on mobility and HCI related issues (e.g. [4, 8, 1, 7]). There is, however, a tendency to view mobility as a way to carry on working, while detached from your (physical) desk at work. For example, when users travel, attend meetings, drive a car, are in public places, etc. This is clearly the use case for laptops, but also for PDAs in many cases. The focus in that scenario is to design mobile computer support for users on

L. Chittaro (Ed.): Mobile HCI 2003, LNCS 2795, pp. 161–176, 2003.

a singular device, which can be used while away from 'the desk', where the 'real' work seems to happen. In this paper we want to draw the attention to another kind of work setting where people do not work at a desk, never move away from their work place, but yet are extremely mobile, namely work at a hospital. We found that medical work is highly mobile, but not in the sense of travelling long distances. Rather, the mobility in their work entails walking between the different sites within a hospital that a clinician needs to visit as part of her / his job. The work we have been observing thus corresponds to the local mobility, described in e.g. [3, 12, 1], where people move between buildings or rooms in a local environment. Bellotti and Bly [3] argue that we need to distinguish between local mobility and the more traditional notion of mobility which typically takes place between remotely distributed collaborating groups (remote mobility) because the needs for support vary greatly and are sometimes contradictory between the two modalities. This kind of local mobility poses new challenges for the design of computer support for mobility, and especially for the user interaction.

In our effort in designing computer support for local mobility we learned several things. First, when designing for local mobility, the *computational context* becomes relevant to consider in details. The mobile device is no longer isolated in the palm of a user sitting in an airport, or in a car driving in the streets, but is embedded within a complex infrastructure of existing computers, networks, and applications. For example, in a hospital a mobile solution needs to exist within the infrastructure set up by electronic patient records. Second, the mobile solution is now just an *option* within a range of computational devices at hand. The mobile device is no longer isolated in use either, but the user needs to be able to select from a range of devices to suit a specific task. For example, in the hospital a wide range of mobile devices (e.g. PDAs, laptops, mobile phones), as well as stationary devices (e.g. desktop PCs, projector-based PCs) that exist side by side. And third, the design for local mobility needs to recognise the *high pace in local mobility*. The mobile device is no longer something that is used for a whole journey or during a whole meeting, but can be picked up and used for maybe seconds. For example, when a nurse needs to register the measurement of blood-pressure this might take a few seconds on a PDA, after which she moves to a more comfortable desktop PC for to finish the report, using the keyboard.

The aim of this paper is twofold. On the one hand we want to draw the attention to the kind of mobility termed 'local mobility', which seems to be present in many work settings. On the other hand we want to present our design for local mobility. In the rest of this paper, we describe the hospital department we have studied and our methods. We report on our observations, discussing how mobility is key to their work and valuable for local collaboration. We then describe some of the design requirements for local mobility coming out of our studies. Then we present our design for local mobility, highlighting how we have addressed some of the thing found during our study. Finally, we conclude the paper with a discussion of related and future work.

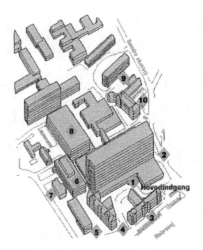

Fig. 1. Aalborg hospital. Important locations are the main building (1), the emergency room (2), and the administration building containing the offices for department T doctors and secretaries (3). Department T's operating rooms and wards are located in the main building (1) on two different floors

2   The Project

Our design for local mobility takes its departure at a surgical department at a large metropolitan hospital in Denmark (see figure 1). We studied the work within the department as a whole and with a bed ward in particular. Our mobile solution for accessing medical data was subsequently put into field trial at this ward. We start by describing the background for the project, the department involved, and our research methods.

2.1   Background – Mobile Support for Electronic Patient Records

Currently, there is an extensive focus on Electronic Patient Records (EPR) in Denmark. The current government has dictated that all hospitals in Denmark by 2005 should have total coverage for all patients in EPR systems. It is, however, up to the regional authorities (the counties) running the different hospitals to decide on the exact solution and vendor. Common for all EPR systems currently being implemented in the hospitals is that they all run on desktop PCs, and thus do not have any support for mobility. Taken the high degree of mobility within hospitals into account, there is a substantial motivation for both EPR vendors as well as the hospital administration to develop solutions for mobile access to the EPR systems. This project is made in cooperation with one large vendor of EPR systems to the Danish marked, focusing on the design of a mobile solution for clinical work building on top of an EPR system.

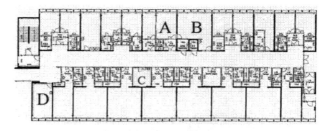

Fig. 2. Ground plan of the ward at department T. Important locations are: the ward office (A+B), the medicine room (C), and the conference room (D)

2.2 Department T

Department T specialises in surgical procedures relating to the heart, lungs and stomach – for example bypass operations and replacing heart valves. The department performs approximately 15 counts of heart surgery every week. Department T consists of one ward where the patients are initially admitted before surgery and transferred back to post-op treatment after having spent 24-48 hours at the intensive care unit immediately after surgery. The ward can carry 30 pre- and post-op patients, and department T treats approximately 1300 patients a year. The ward occupies the sixth floor in the main hospital building (no. 1 in figure 1), whereas the surgeons' and head nurse's offices are located on the second floor in the administration building (no. 3). Overall, the department employs roughly 20 surgeons, 50 nurses, 8 perfusionists and 6 secretaries.

The ground plan for the ward is illustrated in figure 2. The number of doctors and nurses present at the ward changes depending on the time of day. In a day shift, 13-15 nurses are working at the ward while 8-10 surgeons do the morning round before proceeding to operating theatres, whereas during the night shift the ward is 'guarded' by 3-5 nurses with 2 doctors on call. Department T has been using the EPR system for 2 years and is one of the departments in Denmark with most experience in using EPR systems.

2.3 Research Methods

The goal of the project is to examine the possibilities for supporting work practice at the hospital with mobile technology. It was decided to pursue this goal by (i) conducting extensive field-studies of the work at department T, especially focusing on the use of the EPR systems; (ii) initiating an iterative design process with the clinicians, focusing on the design of mobile technology, which could extend the reach of the EPR; (iii) implementing a prototype and install it in a test environment; (iv) carrying out a pilot phase where clinicians should use the mobile equipment; and (v) evaluating the design.

Field Studies. Two researchers made 80 man-hours of participant observations [14] of a mixed group of nurses and surgeons, covering different work tasks (e.g. preliminary patient examinations, different staff meetings, ward rounds, medicine dispensing and a by-pass operation), and different time slots (day, evening and night watch, week-days and week-ends).

Design Workshops. At the end of the field study, we conducted a future workshop [11] together with a group of nurses and physicians with the goal of prioritising and concretising a list of possible features in a mobile solution. During the implementation phase, three additional design workshops were held with this design group to support the collaborative design of particularly the user interface and navigation within the prototype.

Pilot Phase. The final version was installed in a test environment accessing the EPR system running at department T. The pilot phase ran for a total of 12 weeks, after which it was evaluated at an evaluation workshop and by video-recording a nurse as he was using the system for doing his daily tasks.

2.4   Local Mobility in Medical Work

A fundamental characteristic of medical work in hospitals is that clinicians of all kind are constantly moving around within their "action range". The action range of nurses is typical the ward or the outpatient clinic, and the action range of the surgeons and physicians is the hospital. Consider a typical day for a surgeon. He would start by attending the morning conference at the department's conference room located in the main doctoral building (building 3 in figure 1). This is the place for general conferences on issues related to the department as a whole. Then he would move across the parking lot and into the radiology department at the first floor of the main block (building 1), attending the radiology conference. Finally, he would take the lift to the ward (building 1) and start the ward round. The ward round is another fine example of mobility in medical work. Every morning a team of one physician and one or two nurses visit their patients at the ward. The ward rounds typically start in the ward office (see figure 2). While seated the physician and the nurse(s) go through all the patients, read the electronic and the paper-based medical patient records, and look over results from lab tests, etc. Afterwards, they take various paper-based records along together with other relevant materials (medical handbooks, medicine schemas, and small medical instruments), and visit each of the patients at their bedside. Thus, the medical team moves around the wards carrying the paper-based material. A third central mobility scenario concerns the physician on duty. The physician on duty is often responsible for a whole department, including the outpatient clinic and the ward, which are located on a different floor at the hospital. The physician on duty carries a pager and can be 'paged' by everybody at the department, in which case he often has to move around to consult patients and fellow colleagues. For the nurses, mobility is just as critical. They spend most of their working hours moving from place to place as an integral part of patient care. They constantly move between the nurses' station, the medicine room, the patients, the kitchen and various storage facilities, responding to tasks and needs as they occur as well as taking care of planned activities.

Because so many needs occur ad-hoc, they have to update patient records when other, and more important, tasks allow for it.

3   Design for Local Mobility

Based on our field studies of local mobility and the use of the EPR system at department T, we have identified three central aspects of creating computer support for local mobility. First of all, mobile computer support needs to be a natural extension of the existing infrastructure already in place in the setting, where local mobility takes place. Second, from a user interaction perspective there is a need for supporting multiple devices, each device capable of supporting specific tasks and situations. Third, there is a need for application roaming in the sense that the alternation between multiple devices can be done 'on-the-fly' by moving a task from one device to another in a fast pace. Let us consider these in turn.

3.1   Mobilising an Existing Infrastructure

Studying the use of the EPR at department T it became clear to us that there is a built-in tension between using the EPR and the mobile nature of medical work. The EPR at the ward is inherently tied to the desk because it is only running on desktop PCs. However, most clinical work takes place anywhere else but the ward office, where most PCs are located; simple things like handing out medicine to a patient is highly mobile work, including walking between the medicine room and a range of patients, carefully documenting every time medicine is poured, handed out and given to patients. In practice, the use of the EPR for this kind of documentation is impossible because it would require a nurse to walk between the medicine room, the patient's bedside, and the PCs in the office constantly, having all the trouble of logging in, finding the patient and his medicine chart every single time. The consequence of this inherent tension is that the clinicians tried to mobilise the EPR and make it a tool while moving around. Mobilisation strategies especially involves printing out various parts of the records to be carried around. For example, it has become routine to print out each patient's medicine chart on paper every morning. In this way it becomes mobile again and be carried around in the nurse's pocket. However, this eliminates all the benefits of having an electronic medicine chart because it no longer works as a central coordination mechanism. Medication given to a patient is now (as it was done prior to introducing the EPR) documented on the paper-based medical chart, and the electronic version is no longer updated until late in the afternoon. Now, for a nurse to be sure of the medication of a patient s/he will not look up this information in the EPR but rather spend a lot of time trying to locate the nurse who carry the print-out in a pocket. Hence, it is important that support for local mobility is tightly integrated with the existing infrastructure. In our case, the design of mobile support for medication should be real-time integrated with the EPR medicine chart, and cannot rely on synchronisation, which is a common strategy for PDA usage.

3.2   Supporting Multiple Devices

Another distinctive aspect of the mobile work at department T is the constant alternation between tasks. This is due to both the fact that clinicians attend many patients simultaneously as well as because there are many interruptions, partly as a result of the highly ad hoc nature of much medical work at a surgical department. This multi-tasking has resulted in a strategy for having multiple artifacts that can support the same task as well as duplicating information in several places. For example, at department T measuring blood pressure and taking the pulse frequently is important for post-op patients. Hence, everywhere at the ward there are instruments available for this kind of measurement in large numbers. As for the EPR, it has been constructed in a way so that a user can leave the PC, lock the screen, go do something else and later return to the PC, unlock it and resume his / her work as s/he left it. This feature is considered highly useful at the ward. However, problems with this feature also occurs, because it often resulted in a situation where all 8 PCs are locked, leaving them unusable for others. This is often the situation where a nurse had gone in order to make a simple measurement of e.g. blood pressure for later to return and type it in. Another interesting observation is that the use of the EPR was abandoned in the medicine room, where all medicine is poured in small containers for each patient. One would imagine that a PC here would be useful, but the UI design and layout of the medicine chart has not been made to fit the tasks in the medicine room. Furthermore, there is no room for a PC in the small room where all the table space is needed for handling medicine. Our conclusion from these observations is, that there is a need for supporting multiple devices when supporting local mobility. It is important that the nurse who is measuring blood pressure can use a small PDA type of device to input simple data, whereas the nurse typing long notes in the record needs a full-fledged keyboard and mouse, and a comfortable working setup at a desk. Correspondingly, when moving to the medicine room, the nurses' requirements for the display of medicine charts change and the technology made available to them in this situation should reflect that.

3.3   Supporting Application Roaming

The way that a task is carried along is characteristic to local mobility. At the ward round, for example, the surgeon and the nurses carry the same set of tasks around for the duration of the round. It is basic to local mobility that a task is taken to different locations. Therefore, it seems important to be able to support that a task can 'follow' the user. This can clearly be achieved by using a single mobile device, which is also the common technological strategy in contemporary mobile computing. However, if we want to take the support for multiple devices seriously, we should also provide mechanisms for transferring an ongoing task from one device to another. For example, when the nurse has finished measuring the blood pressure using a PDA, she returns to the PC and transfers the 'blood-pressure-measurement' task to a desktop PC where she can use the keyboard to add a note about the general condition of the patient due to high blood pressure. We find this last requirement for application roaming among multiple devices a central contribution from our studies of medical work.

4   An Architecture Supporting Local Mobility

Based on the requirements above, we have designed a generic architecture for supporting local mobility and we have implemented a first prototype of this architecture in the healthcare domain. This section presents this architecture and its implementation in the hospital.

4.1   A Simple Healthcare Scenario

Ms. Hansen, a nurse at department T, picks up a PDA at the beginning of her working shift. She starts by logging in and then walks around to her patients saying good morning and measures their morning temperature and other central health data. She types in the data on the PDA, which is relayed immediately to the EPR for others to see. She returns to the ward office to meet with the surgeon for the morning ward round. In front of a PC she uses the bar-code reader in the PDA to scan the bar-code strip on the PC, thereby transferring her ongoing task to the PC. The PC displays the same page as the PDA, but now accommodates the much larger screen by containing much more details than the PDA. She shows the surgeon a particular critical reading, and uses the keyboard to key in a note. The surgeon and the nurse look up the patient to be visited first on the ward round, and find his medicine chart. When ready to leave the ward office, they hit the 'Resume Session' button on the PDA, which reloads the medicine chart, adapted to this smaller screen. They now visit the patient at his bed-side.

4.2   Architecture

The overall functional architecture is shown in figure 3. There are two important components in the architecture. The *Mobile Application Server* (MAS) is responsible for the support of heterogeneous devices and the application specific logic, including integration to the existing infrastructure. The *Application Roaming Server* (ARS) is together with the JMS Server and JMS Clients, responsible for application roaming among the different devices.

The architecture of the MAS components (detailed in figure 4) implements a web-based interface to an existing infrastructure using existing access paths to databases using e.g. JDBC, Enterprise Java Beans (EJB) or application programming interfaces (APIs). The architecture is a transformation engine based on the Model-View-Control design pattern [9]. The *Controller* component is responsible for interaction control with the client, including ensuring user authentication and identifying the requesting device type. The Controller is made

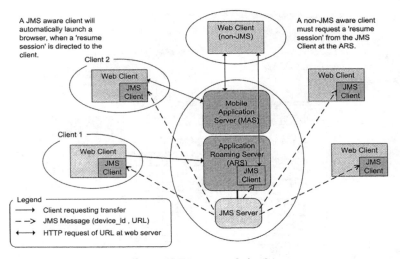

Fig. 3. Overall Functional Architecture

up of a set of servlets handling the HTTP requests from the clients. The *Application Logic* component implements the actual logic of the application by using a command pattern [9] to specify the interface for the command beans. The *View Page Construction* component is a set of Java Server Pages (JSPs), which produce the response for a particular request. In contrast to traditional web server applications, the JSP pages in our architecture do not produce HTML to be sent back to the requesting client. Here, the view is constructed in XML, and then processed by a XSLT *Transcoder Service* component, which will apply an XSL style sheet to produce the HTML content appropriate for the requesting device. By following this approach, we are able to support different devices, each having different capabilities, like network bandwidth and display size and colour. But the response is based on the same content, described by the XML produced by the JSP view pages.

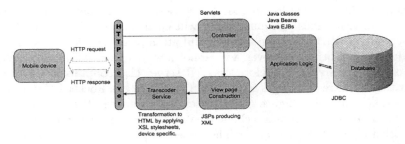

Fig. 4. relatively easy Functional Architecture of the Mobile Application Server (MAS) component

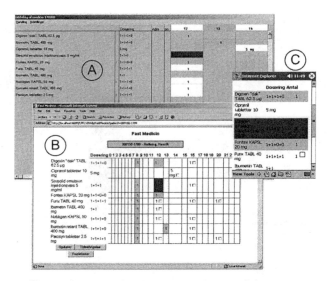

Fig. 5. Screen Shots showing the Medicine Chart. (a) from the normal EPJ system, (b) the web-based user-interface on a normal PC browser, and (c) the user-interface on a PDA

From a usability point of view, the mobile solution in many respects resembles the existing EPR systems. In figure 5 it is easy to see the resemblance between the 3 types of views on medicine; the same kind of information is listed in the same order and the same kind of colour coding is used. We have, relatively easy, been able to design, implement, and deploy new user interfaces for different situations. Figure 5 shows the two different design of the medicine chart for a PDA screen and a PC screen, respectively.

The functional architecture to support Application Roaming is shown in figure 3. We rely on Java Messaging Services (JMS) to handle the notification of application roaming events in our current implementation of the architecture. JMS is especially well-suited for this purpose, because the asynchronous communication in JMS is ideal for this kind of loosely coupled communication among devices. Asynchronous communication will ensure that neither the client nor the server will deadlock in an unsuccessful attempt to transfer the session from one device to another. However, we cannot always expect all mobile devices to support JMS natively. Therefore, the AR server also contains a 'pseudo' JMS client that manages messages to non-JMS clients (e.g. a Pocket PC device). The interaction diagram in figure 6 illustrates the sequence of events between the various components when one client (the *Producer*) tries to transfer its session to another client (the *Consumer*). The upper part of figure 6 depicts application roaming to a JMS-aware client (e.g. a PC) and the lower part depicts application roaming to a non JMS-aware client (e.g. a Pocket PC device). The basic steps

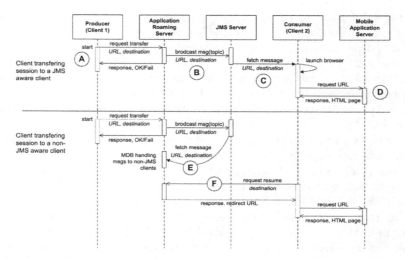

Fig. 6. Interaction Diagram showing application roaming between two clients

for client 1 to transfer its session to a JMS-aware client 2 are: Client 1 sends a transfer request to the AR server via HTTP and the ARS returns a response to the client (A in figure 6). When the transfer controller in the ARS is activated it publishes a message, containing the destination client id and URL, on a JMS topic (B). Every JMS-aware client runs a listener, always listening for messages on this topic. On the consuming client (client 2), with the corresponding device id, the JMS listener launches a browser on the client (C), and asks the browser to request the URL within the message from the MAS web server (D). If client 2 is a non JMS-aware client (the lower part of figure 6), the ARS puts the message in a JMS client (E). Client 2 can now manually ask the ARS if there is any application roaming to be activated on it (F). If there is, the url is returned and this url can be fetched from the MAS. Finally, when a user has an on-going session with the MAS, the current url is always stored in the user's session object. When a user transfer a session from e.g. a PDA to a PC, the PDA reloads with a page with a 'Resume Sesion' button on it. This page maintains a link to the on-going session object, which is used on the PC. When activating the resume button, the current url (as shown on the PC) is reloaded in the PDA's browser.

4.3   Current Implementation of the Architecture

The server-side of the architecture is implemented on an IBM WebSphere Application Server (WAS) version 4.0.4. The 'Application Logic' component in the MAS (figure 4) is ibut have to fit in time in front of the computermplemented as Java Enterprise Beans accessing the EPR server using a JDBC connection accessing a remote IBM DB2 client connection to the EPR DB2 database server. This remote DB2 connection is protected through a firewall, allowing only request from our DB2 client to access. The data accessed includes user authentication and access control lists (ACL) so that users can use their normal user names and passwords. The 'Controller' component is implemented as servlets, which each checks the user authorisation of the client trying to access the server. The 'View Page Component' is implemented using JSP pages producing XML for the 'Transcoding' component to transform to HTML using XSL style sheets. This uses the Apache Jakarta XSL Tag Library version 1.1. Identification of client devices is done by examining the client's HTTP request header. On the client side, the current prototype supports 3 types of clients. A Pocket PC based PDA with a built-in barcode scanner from Symbol Technologies, an EPOC based client from Psion, and a normal desktop PC. All of these use the built-in internet browser to display the pages. The network connection was made by Wireless LAN (IEEE 802.11b) using Symbol access points with no encryption. The application roaming (the ARS component) functionality is implemented via Java Messaging Services (JMS) using OpenJMS version 0.7.2 as the JMS provider. In our current implementation we have both JMS-aware and JMS-unaware clients (PCs and Pocket PCs, respectively), thus using both types of application roaming in our prototype. Currently, the PCs used at department T does not have bar-code readers to be used in the application roaming.

The mechanism for trickering the application roaming process illustrated in figure 6 is currently implemented via the PDA's barcode reader. Using barcodes felt natural, because it is used for other things (e.g. reading barcodes on medicine bottles and on the armband of the patients). A small barcode reader application is running on the PDA and when it scans a barcode it checks whether this is another device (typically a desktop PC) and initiates the application roaming process. Other mechanisms can, however, be deployed in our achitecture, for example using IrDA. The application roaming mechanism is independent on its trickering mechanism on the clients. Application roaming using barcode currently only works from a PDA to a PC or laptop. The 'Resume Session' button is used to roam the session back to the PDA it came from.

A current limitation in our current implementation is that the state of a user's interaction with a web page is not saved to the server, and is hence not roamed between devices. For example, if a nurse is typing in the temperature in a text field on a web page on the PDA, and tries to roam this page to a nearby PC, then the figures s/he has already entered in the temperature field is not transfered. This is mainly because we do not submit HTML forms before doing application roaming. We are currently looking into methods for handling this issue.

4.4 Evaluation

The first version of the prototype has been running in a pilot test at department T lasting 12 weeks. The setup included one WLAN base station located in the centre of the ward, 2 PDAs, and 2 laptop PCs, all with WLAN access. During this period the two PDAs were used to support mobile work. From the log we can see that approx. 50 users logged on to the mobile EPR system, and that in total approx. 200 request were made to the server, of which approx. 50 requested medical notes and approx. 100 requested medicine information. We concluded the pilot phases with an evaluation workshop where the users could brainstorm on strengths and weakness of the mobile access to the EPR. The strengths were reported to be the mobile access to the EPR, enabling limited but central functionality to be available at e.g. the patient's bed side and in the medicine room. This increased the data quality in using and reporting medical data, like medicine prescriptions. The use of of the laptops were however quite limited. It seems like either the clinicians would use a full-fledged PC on a desk or they would use the PDA that can be carried in a white coat pocket. The in-between laptop devices were not used much. The weaknesses reported was concentrated around long response time, limited screen size and lack of keyboard on the PDAs. A limitation of the pilot study was clearly the limited number of devices (4 in total), and the limited range of just one base station (the latter was also the cause of the long response times reported). It was judged that the number of PDAs should approximately match the number of clinicians in a day shift. The prototype is currently being developed into an official application supported by the vendor and is being marketed and sold to other hospitals. The next step in our project is to implement a better application roaming mechanism and to incorporate context-awareness into the prototype (see 6). This second version of the prototype will be installed at department T and a larger number of PDAs and basestation will be deployed. This new setup will accordingly be evaluated and followed during a new pilot phase. We hope in this way to learn more about local mobility as supported by technology.

5   Discussion and Related Work

Providing a range of devices (stationary, mobile, wearable) for supporting a work practice builds on the understanding of the fact that different people prefer different tools for solving similar tasks, and that a selection of tools makes nurses and surgeons better equipped to deal with the ad hoc demands they face several times a day. Carrying the context with you across devices poses challenges to the user interface design as well as the technical integration between the devices. Rist [15] proposes a technical solution to accessing a virtual meeting place through highly heterogeneous devices based on the development of device-specific user interface proxies not unlike the approach we have chosen here. Roman et al. [16] also explore the challenges of integrating a PDA in a distributed environment. They argue the importance of using PDAs as *enabling bridges* to services rather than treating the PDAs as isolated entities. Their approach to integration is technical and the consistency in their system is supported by contents alone.

Fagrell et al. [7] propose 'FieldWise' as an architecture for Mobile Knowledge Management. Like our architecture, the FieldWise architecture puts emphasis on adapting the response to a client according to its network connection and user-interface capabilities. Furthermore, the FieldWise architecture implements many other features, like support for task overviews with notification mechanisms, overview over records, and suggestions for available expertise. Our architecture does not per se support these latter features. Most of these features are a part of the EPR system and as such can be made available on the mobile devices also. There are, however, also some major differences between the FieldWise architecture and ours. These differences are based on the kind of mobility that has be the target for the two architectures. The FieldWise architecture takes its outset in studies of mobile journalists, who move around whole cities and countries. Hence, there is a major difference between this kind of remote mobility and the kind of local mobility, which we have described and designed for. As we have argued, in local mobility within the premises of e.g. a hospital, it becomes essential to make mobile support that blend seamlessly into the existing infrastructure, including the kind of application roaming we have described. Application roaming is hence not a part of the FieldWise architecture. As for application roaming among heterogeneous devices using web-based access to legacy systems we are not familiar with any related work. However, the work on Activity Based Computing [5] aims at supporting mobile work by enabling users to transfer the state of their work activities between different heterogeneous devices. Similarly, the task management architecture Prism in the Aura project [10] supports mobility by migrating application among heterogeneous computing environments. These two approaches to application roaming, however, involves the migration of whole applications on the client devices. In our work, the 'migration' only takes place on the server side, and is accessed by standard web browsers.

6   Conclusion and Future Work

In this paper we have done two things. First we have analysed mobile medical work within a large Danish hospital. Second, we have designed, implemented and evaluated an architecture supporting this kind of mobile work. Based on our field studies we have argued that there are some fundamental difference between 'remote mobility' and 'local mobility'. The former refers to the mobility of users moving *between* different working sites, e.g. between the office and home, or travelling to visit customers. Much of the literature and the technical solution for mobility concentrate on this kind of mobility. Local mobility, on the other hand, refers to users moving around – often on foot – *within* the same site. Based on our field studies and a range of design workshops with clinicians, we have argued that local mobility put forth 3 requirements, which are distinct to local mobility. First, the technological support for mobility has to *integrate seamlessly with the existing computing infrastructure* at the site. For example, in the hospital setting, the mobile support had to be tightly integrated with the existing EPR system – in function as well as in usage. In a remote mobility situation, this is less important. Here the linkage to more general-purpose infrastructures like IP over UMTS or GSM seems sufficient. Second, the technological support for mobility should support a *variety of devices*. For example, in the hospital environment, users would like to alternate continuously between using small hand-held devices and large desktop or wall-based displays. In the remote mobility situation, this is seldom a core requirement, because there is often only one device available – a laptop, a PDA, or a cell phone. Third, these multiple devices should support seamless *application roaming* among these devices. For example, if a nurse is using a PDA for documenting medicine she would be able to transfer this task, including its present state, to a PC and continue the task of documentation there. In the remote mobility scenario, there is no need for this kind of functionality, because the pace of multi-tasking is less prevalent. We have suggested an architecture that demonstrates how these three requirements can be met and a prototype for mobile access to an EPR systems has been implemented using this architecture. This prototype has been evaluated in pilot studies at the hospital and the outcome of this evaluation is currently being incorporated in a production ready version of the prototype. The architecture and the prototype were developed for mobile work within a hospital. We want to argue, however, that the architecture in general might be suitable for supporting other kinds of local mobility environments. If we look at other projects that we have been involved in (e.g supporting mobile workers at a waste water plant [13] and area managers at the county's Building and Energy Office [2]), mobile work in these settings might also be supported by our proposed general architecture. In the future we plan to take the architecture to other work domains, and apply and develop it accordingly. Another item on our list to do in the future is to make the architecture context-aware [6] in the sense that the Mobile Application Server not only adapts its response to the type of requesting device, but also according to the context of the device. For example, when the medicine chart is requested in the medicine room, the reponse is tailored to show a list of medicine for several patient to be poured now. And when the medicine chart is requested beside a patient's bed, the medicine chart shows only medicine for this patient, in a historical perspective.

Acknowledgements

This research has been funded by the Danish Center for Information Technology (CIT) and IBM. Thanks to the clinicians at department T and the employees at the IT department at Aalborg Hospital for their valuable participation in this project.

References

[1] J. E. Bardram and C. Bossen. Moving to get aHead: Local Mobility and Collaborative Work. In P. Dourish, G. Fitzpatrick, and K. Schmidtk, editors, *Proceedings of the Fifth European Conference on Computer Supported Cooperative Work*, pages xx–xx, Helsinki, Finland, Sept. 2003. Kluwer Academic Publishers.

[2] S. Bdker, J. Friis Kristensen, C. Nielsen, and W. Sperschneider. Technology for boundaries. Submitted to the 8th European Conference on Computer Supported Cooperative Work, 2003.

[3] V. Bellotti and S. Bly. Walking away from the desktop computer: Distributed collaboration and mobility in a product design team. In K. Ehrlich and C. Schmandt, editors, *Proceedings of ACM 1996 Conference on Computer Supported Cooperative Work.*, pages 209–218. ACM, ACM Press, 1996.

[4] O. Bertelsen and C. Nielsen. Dynamics in wastewater treatment: A framework for understanding formal constructs in complex techincal settings. In S. Bdker, M. Kyng, and K. Schmidt, editors, *Proceedings of the 6th European Conference on Computer Supported Cooperative Work.*, pages 277–290, Copenhagen, Sept. 1999. Kluwer Academic Publisheres, Dordrecht.

[5] H. B. Christensen and J. Bardram. Supporting human activities – exploring activity-centered computing. In G. Borriello and L. E. Holmquist, editors, *Proceedings of Ubicomp 2002: Ubiquitous Computing*, volume 2498 of *Lecture Notes in Computer Science*, pages 107–116, Gteborg, Sweden, Sept. 2002. Springer Verlag.

[6] A. Dey, G. Abowd, and D. Salber. A conceptual framework and a toolkit for supporting the rapid prototyping of context-aware applications. *Human-Computer Interaction.*, 16:97–166, 2001. Lawrence Erlbaum Associates, Inc.

[7] H. Fagrell, K. Forsberg, and J. Sanneblad. Fieldwise: A mobile knowlegde management architecture. In *Proceedings of ACM 2000 Conference on Computer Supported Cooperative Work.*, pages 211–220. ACM, ACM Press, 2000.

[8] H. Fagrell, S. Kristoffersen, and F. Ljungberg. Exploring support for knowledge management in mobile work. In S. Bdker, M. Kyng, and K. Schmidt, editors, *Proceedings of the 6th European Conference on Computer Supported Cooperative Work.*, pages 277–290, Copenhagen, Sept. 1999. Kluwer Academic Publishers, Dordrecht.

[9] E. Gamma, R. Helm, R. Johnson, and J. Vlissides. *Design Patterns: Elements of Reuseable Object-Oriented Software.* Addison-Wesley, 1994.

[10] D. Garlan, D. P. Siewiorek, A. Smailagic, and P. Steenkiste. Project aura: Toward distraction-free pervasive computing. *IEEE Pervasive Computing.*, 1(2):22–31, 2002.

[11] F. Kensing and K. Halskov Madsen. Generating visions: Future workshops and metaphorical design. In J. Greenbaum and M. Kyng, editors, *Design at Work: Cooperative Design of Computer Systems.*, pages 155–168. Lawrence Erlbaum Associates, Hillsdale, NJ, 1991.

[12] P. Luff and C. Heath. Mobility in collaboration. In S. Poltrock and J. Grudin, editors, *Proceedings of ACM 1998 Conference on Computer Supported Cooperative Work*, pages 305–314. ACM Press, 1998.

[13] C. Nielsen and A. Sndergaard. Designing for mobility: an integration approach supporting multiple technologies. In *Proceedings of the 1st Nordic Conference on Human-Computer Interaction (CD-ROM)*, 2000.

[14] M. Q. Patton. *Qualitative Evaluation and Research Methods.* Sage Publications, London, second edition, 1990.

[15] T. Rist. Using mobile communication devices to access virtual meeting places. In *Proceedings of the 2nd Workshop on Human Computer Interaction with Mobile Devices*, pages 81–86, Edinburgh, Scotland, 1999.

[16] M. e. a. Romn. Integrating PDAs into distributed systems:2k and PalmORB. In H. Gellersen, editor, *Handheld and Ubiquitous Computing. Proceedings of First International Symposium*, pages 137–149. Springer-Verlag, 1999.

Aligning Work Practices and Mobile Technologies: Groupware Design for Loosely Coupled Mobile Groups

David Pinelle, Jeff Dyck, and Carl Gutwin

HCI Lab, Department of Computer Science, University of Saskatchewan
57 Campus Drive, Saskatoon, SK, S7N 5A9, Canada
{david.pinelle,jeff.dyck,carl.gutwin}@usask.ca
http://hci.usask.ca

Abstract. Supporting mobile collaborative work over wide areas is challenging due to the limitations and unreliability of wide area wireless networks. However, variations in patterns of collaboration require different levels of timeliness and synchrony, and place different demands on groupware and its supporting technologies. In this paper, we argue that groupware supported by wide area mobile networks strongly favors loosely coupled work, where workers are autonomous and require a reduced level of communication. We examine the relationship between loosely coupled group characteristics and wide area mobile groupware by considering one particular loosely coupled group—teams of home care workers. Over a two-year period, we analyzed home care work practices, and designed and field tested Mohoc, a mobile groupware application to support home care work. From this experience, we identified four characteristics of loosely coupled groups that enable workers to accommodate the uncertainty of wide area mobile groupware: autonomy and the partitioning of work, clear ownership of data and artifacts, asynchronous awareness, and explicit asynchronous communication.

1   Introduction

In spite of ongoing advances in mobile computing, when workers are mobile over a wide area, they must rely on uncertain networks that experience disconnections and variable throughput [25]. The difficulties seen in mobile networks are particularly constraining when we consider designing groupware technologies for widely dispersed and mobile collaborators. Small group collaboration requires that members coordinate their activities, stay aware of others' activities, and explicitly communicate with each other [15]. This level of interaction is particularly challenging to support using mobile technologies when synchrony and timeliness of information is an issue.

In this paper, we will consider one particular type of mobile group—*loosely coupled mobile groups*—where workers are not strictly dependent on synchrony and up-to-date information from other group members. Churchill and Wakeford [2] have

L. Chittaro (Ed.): Mobile HCI 2003, LNCS 2795, pp. 177–192, 2003.

suggested that the level of coupling between workers is a useful design dimension when building CSCW applications for mobile groups. We expand on this work by focusing on one particular type of coupling, *loose coupling*, and by considering how this style of collaboration shapes work patterns in mobile groups and the implications these patterns have for groupware design. Pinelle and Gutwin [22] describe loosely coupled mobility as work where group members are generally autonomous and rarely synchronous, and are often able to function without ongoing interaction with others, although they still are interested in staying aware of others' activities. In this paper, we present results that suggest that these group characteristics are well suited to mobile groupware since they accommodate the uncertainties of wide area mobile technologies.

We examined the relationship between the characteristics of loose coupling and wide area mobile technologies by studying one type of loosely coupled mobile group—home care teams in Saskatoon District Health (SDH), a health district in Saskatchewan, Canada. In SDH, teams of community-based healthcare workers provide patients with services in their homes, and they carry out their work in a loosely coupled fashion. In SDH—unlike many other mobile settings (e.g. [10], [1], [21])—work is not arranged to facilitate regular synchrony. Workers do not have regular meetings, and do not see each other face-to-face very often. There is a high degree of variability in terms of schedule and location within a team and because of this, communication is difficult, and workers often carry out their work autonomously and without the benefit of regular input from others.

Over a two-year period, we analyzed the work practices of home care teams, we designed and built a mobile groupware system to support these work practices, and we evaluated the system during a 2-½ month field trial. From this process, we identified four characteristics of loosely coupled work that allow workers to cope with many of the uncertainties of wide area mobile networks, and that make workers resilient to the difficulties these uncertainties introduce in mobile groupware design:

- Workers are autonomous and partition work so that the need for ongoing coordination and planning is minimized.
- Artifacts and data are, in most cases, clearly owned by specific workers, so the need for negotiation and coordination of access is minimal.
- Workers are rarely synchronous, so they rely on asynchronous means for gathering awareness information, which allows them to tolerate delays.
- Workers carry out most of their explicit communication asynchronously, and are able to tolerate the delays inherent in these exchanges.

For each work characteristic, we will discuss how it shaped the approaches we took in implementing Mohoc, a groupware application we developed for home care clinicians in SDH. We will discuss the results of a 2-½ month field trial we carried out with the application and the influence the introduction of Mohoc had on work practices. Finally, we will consider problems associated with our approaches, and the implications these have for groupware design.

2   Related Work

Mobile work practices shape the type of groupware support that is needed by mobile collaborators. For example, Kristoffersen et al. [14] propose using real-world scenarios to guide the design of mobile CSCW applications. However, as pointed out by Dix et al. [4] the interaction offered by mobile applications is also a product of the mobile device and the underlying infrastructure used to realize the application. In this section, we review related work on loosely coupled mobile groups and on mobile computing technologies to illustrate how they shape mobile groupware designs.

2.1   Loosely Coupled Mobile Groups

In this paper, we investigate loose coupling as the primary means of organizing work and collaboration in a mobile group. Grinter et al. [12] describe loose coupling as work that occurs relatively independently of others, and that requires a reduced level of communication. Olson and Teasley [20] further elaborate on this idea: "loosely coupled work is work in which people need to be aware of others' activity and decisions, but without the need for immediate clarification or negotiation. The work can proceed in parallel." (p. 422). Loose coupling, then is a style of collaboration in which workers can function in a somewhat autonomous fashion without reliance on ongoing interaction with others. However, workers still need to stay aware of others' activities in order to manage group interdependencies.

In this research, we are interested specifically in loose coupling and mobility. Pinelle and Gutwin [22] characterize loose coupling in mobile groups by describing four work patterns that can occur. First, since workers are autonomous and communication can be difficult, workers carefully consider the effort required to share information and select communication channels that minimize effort and overhead. Second, workers utilize awareness information from shared artifacts and locations as the lowest cost means of collecting information about others. Third, workers show a preference for asynchronous communication and coordination techniques since it allows them to deal with schedule and location variability. Forth, mobility and worker autonomy makes it difficult for workers to achieve synchrony, so synchronous collaboration and back-and-forth discussions are limited, thus changing the nature of information that is shared. These findings show that managing work interdependencies is important in loosely coupled mobile groups, but that the level of effort required to stay aware of others and to explicitly communicate shapes work patterns, and has implications for design that must be dealt with by groupware developers.

2.2   Mobile Groupware Technology

The wireless networks used to support wide area mobile collaboration introduce many challenges and limitations, discussed in Satyanarayanan [25] and Edwards [9]. Mobile networks are less reliable than wired networks due to two main factors: interference and signal strength. For mobile workers who work across a wide area, both interference and signal strength change frequently due to changes in location as well as natural variability.

Variations in interference and signal strength have consequences on collaboration. Some of the direct effects are periodic disconnections, loss of data, and long delays due to congestion, retransmission, or low bandwidth. Several techniques have been offered that lessen some of these consequences under particular circumstances. Data replication (e.g. [23]) and caching increase availability of information during periods of disconnection and reduce delays. Consistency problems can be mitigated using optimistic replication schemes [24], automatically resolving conflicts when they happen (e.g. [3]), and representing conflicts to the user (e.g. [24]). Adaptive strategies (e.g. [24], [19]) allow systems to make better use of their available resources, which can also lessen delay problems and help to make smooth transitions from connected and disconnected states [9]. Although these techniques have made many mobile collaboration problems more manageable, evidence suggests that it is still difficult to mitigate, predict, and cope with wide area mobility problems at the user, application, and infrastructure levels [13].

3   Setting

We have been working with clinicians and administrators in the Home Care department at Saskatoon District Health (SDH), a health district in Saskatchewan, Canada, for the past two years as part of an ongoing project to develop group support technologies for home care workers. The functional unit for managing a community-based patient's care in SDH is a treatment team—a group of workers who separately travel to a patient's home and deliver a range of services to that patient. Treatment teams can be made of workers from several clinical disciplines, including occupational therapists, physical therapists, social workers, nurses, case managers, and home health aides. Since each worker treats multiple patients during a workday (usually 6-15 depending on the discipline), and since teams are formed around patients, each worker is a member of multiple teams.

Home care workers spend most of their time providing services to patients in their homes and driving between appointments. In addition to this, workers must spend time filling out forms that document their treatments and the interactions they have with patients. Workers have few technologies to assist them in these activities. SDH does not provide workers with mobile phones, but some workers use their personal phones while working. They have voicemail access, and nurses and home health aides carry one-way numeric pagers.

Work practices in SDH can be characterized as loosely coupled. Workers are autonomous, they are mobile and dispersed, and they communicate with each other intermittently. They autonomously set their schedules, determine their own work activities, and carry out work individually. Workers spend much of their time carrying out tasks that are not easily interrupted for communication, such as driving and delivering treatments in patients' homes, and it is difficult for them to maintain an awareness of others' locations, availabilities, and schedules. These work patterns can make collaboration difficult, and workers usually only communicate with each other intermittently, and often only when they believe the necessity of communication outweighs the effort required to communicate. When they do communicate, they usually rely on asynchronous channels such as voicemail, handwritten notes, and messages passed through office staff. In spite of the intermittent nature of collaboration, workers are still interested in others' activities, and attempt to maintain an awareness of them. But the difficulty inherent in communicating and sharing information means that this awareness is often incomplete.

4   Method

Our research activities initially focused on developing an understanding of workers, organizational structures, and work activities that are part of home care delivery in SDH. We began by carrying out three rounds of 1 to 1 ½ hour interviews, and during each round, we interviewed a member of each clinical home care discipline, for a total of seven interviews per round. In addition to the interviews, we spent approximately 60 hours carrying out field observations to develop a detailed understanding of workers' day-to-day work activities.

We analyzed audiotapes and field notes and used the findings to guide the development of early prototypes of Mohoc, a groupware system to support home care teams. We carried out ongoing prototype reviews with home care clinicians to refine our designs. Once we felt that we had adequately validated our approach, we implemented the design as a mobile groupware system.

We carried out a 2-½ month field trial of our system with a team of six home care workers from different disciplines. During the field trial, each worker carried a laptop and wireless CDPD modem. The treatment team used the application to support the treatment activities that they provided to a shared patient. Workers used the application to schedule visits, establish treatment plans, document treatments, and to explicitly communicate with each other. During the field trial, we carried out two rounds of interviews, and we met with each participant for 1 to 1 ½ hours per round. Upon completion of the field trial, we analyzed transcripts, system logs, and the private and shared workspaces that were utilized by workers during the trial.

5   Mohoc

We developed Mohoc to accommodate the loosely coupled work practices that are seen in home care in SDH. Our primary goals for the design were to support autonomous work, provide workers with information about the activities and decisions of other workers who treat shared patients (information that is currently often difficult for them to obtain), and provide workers with low-effort tools for explicit communication. Mohoc does this by giving workers private information spaces, and common information spaces that show artifacts that are created by other workers and UI representations that provide a range of information about other team members' activities. Mohoc supports common home care activities such as scheduling visits with patients, managing clinical documentation, and planning treatments.

Mohoc uses a robust client-server model with a centralized network architecture and replicated data views. During the field trial, we deployed the Mohoc client application on laptop computers connected to the Internet using the wireless CDPD network. The CDPD network in the field trial area is low bandwidth (19.2 kb/sec max; 11kb/sec max observed), and disconnections are both frequent and difficult to predict. The server was deployed on a reliable, dedicated machine with high capacity and a reliable cable network connection.

The Mohoc server maintains a master copy of all data, with replicated data views stored locally on laptops for use by each worker. All messages sent between workers are sent through the server, which reduces the effects of disconnections by allowing messages to be sent between workers even though they might not be online at the same time. When a worker's actions require a message to be sent, it cannot be assumed that a connection to the server will be available. To handle this, outgoing messages are stored in a reliable message queue on the laptop's hard drive and are not dequeued until they are confirmed as received by the server. This allows workers' laptops to maintain outgoing messages if the system is turned off or in the event of a system crash, and the queue is FIFO (first in, first out), so it guarantees that transactions are transmitted to the server in the order that they are carried out. The server uses a similar queuing method to send messages to workers' laptops.

Mohoc uses connection and data replication transparency ([8], [27]). The workers are not aware of the status of their connection or of the status of other workers' connections. They are also unaware of the messages in message queues and of how up-to-to the information is that is stored on their laptop. We decided to support transparency since most home care workers have little previous experience with computers and with client/server architectures.

6   Results

The results of our study show that four loosely coupled group characteristics are particularly significant to mobile system design: autonomy and the partitioning of work, clear ownership of data and artifacts, asynchronous awareness, and explicit asynchronous communication. For each characteristic, we consider how it shaped the design approaches that were implemented in Mohoc and the impact these approaches had on work patterns during the field trial. We discuss the implications of our findings in section 7.

6.1   Autonomy and the Partitioning of Work

In loosely coupled work, workers are autonomous and partition work so that the need for ongoing coordination and planning is minimized. This implies that the division of work is mutually understood within the group so that workers do not need regular consultation with others. This autonomy can be seen in SDH, where workers serve in well-defined and mutually understood roles within groups, and are responsible for handling issues that fall within the scope of their expertise. For example, nurses handle wound care issues and physiotherapists handle ambulation issues. This allows workers to handle problems that they identify within the domain of their expertise without first checking with others.

In loosely coupled work, the autonomy of workers and their implicit understanding of work duties frees groupware developers from some of the constraints of tightly-coupled coordination (e.g. [28]). In mobile work, this is particularly important since workers may at times need to work in a disconnected fashion without access to the most recent information from other team members. This tolerance for loose coordination and autonomy allows groupware support to be feasible using mobile computing techniques such as data replication and caching, where workers have a copy of relevant data on the mobile computing platform and can save their work locally when network access is unavailable until it can be forwarded to the server.

In Mohoc, we used a data replication technique that provides mobile clients with a local copy of all relevant data. All SDH workers who treat a given patient receive all documents, appointments, treatment plans, and awareness-related data that are pertinent to that patient's care. So, for example, if a worker adds an appointment with a given patient, that appointment is cached locally and then sent to the server as soon as a network connection is available. The server then forwards that appointment to all other workers who treat that patient as soon as a connection is available so that the appointment is viewable by all members of the treatment team.

The field trial results indicate that this data replication and caching approach was overall very successful. Since SDH work patterns are autonomous, workers liked knowing that they did not need to be concerned with the state of the network—they could continue to work regardless of the state of the connection. Workers carried out their work activities knowing that the system would exchange information with the server whenever possible. They felt that having information about other workers was a benefit, and since they are accustomed to working without up-to-date information, they were not concerned with their information being out of synch.

6.2   Clear Ownership of Data and Artifacts

In loose coupling, the partitioning of work can extend beyond the specific duties and roles of group members to the artifacts used during work activities. For example, to carry out specific duties, workers may need certain data or shared artifacts. Since collaboration occurs in a loosely coupled fashion, it is difficult to negotiate the coordination of access with others. As a means of accommodating this, workers may clearly own specific artifacts, so that the need for negotiation and coordination of access is minimal. For example, in SDH, each worker has clear ownership of his or her handwritten schedule and of the documents that they create about the care that they provide. They are the ones who are responsible for maintaining them, and are usually the only ones who are allowed to edit them.

The loosening of coordination requirements that we see in loosely coupled mobility has the potential to alleviate many of the complexities that are seen when implementing access controls in more tightly coupled groups (e.g. [16]). Since it is implicitly clear to workers which team members can access or modify a resource, and since this is often an exclusive privilege, tightly-coupled strategies such as real-time updates of a shared workspace, and locking for editing are not necessarily required.

Instead, more lightweight techniques, such as making it clear who owns what, and explicitly implementing permission policies can be sufficient to mediate access to work resources.

In Mohoc, we handle these issues by allowing clear ownership of specific data items. Even though these items are visible to all team members, only specific workers are able to edit them. For example, a given worker is the only one who is able to establish their own appointments with a patient, and the only one who is able to edit the times for that appointment. However, that appointment is clearly visible in other workers' workspaces.

We had to handle added complexity when implementing policies for clinical documents. In most cases, ownership and editing privileges of clinical documentation were clear. For example, a single nurse would treat a patient, and he or she was the only one allowed to create, edit, and delete the nursing documents. However, we also had to handle the case where two workers from a given discipline share a patient. For example, during the field trial, two home health aides treated the same patient—one during the day, and one during the evening. In this case, workers often had to edit documents that were created by a different worker of the same discipline. Our approach for handling this was to allow workers from the same discipline who share a patient to append new content to existing documents. This mirrors real-world documentation practices, and it is able to accommodate network uncertainty. We time-stamped each transaction, and when new content was appended to a document, we sorted it into the appropriate chronological order in the new version of the document.

During the field trial, these approaches were well received. As we might expect, data ownership fits existing autonomous work patterns. However, as we previously mentioned, two home health aides shared a patient across two different shifts. While this sharing took place in a loosely coupled fashion, the increased interdependencies seen in document sharing between these workers caused some minor problems for these workers.

We saw these problems in the home health aides' use of flowsheets—checklist based forms that are used to record the services provided during visits. In most cases, several days worth of services are shown on a single flowsheet, and home health aides that share a patient also share the same flowsheet. However, during the field trial, this sharing did not always take place. By analyzing system logs, we found that on several occasions, one worker would create a new flowsheet, and that flowsheet would not reach the other home health aide who shared the patient in a timely fashion. The second home health aide, unaware of the existing flowsheet, would create a new flowsheet rather than adding to the already existing one, which led to an excessive number of documents being created and frustrated the home health aides. These problems arose due to intermittent network connections and workers not staying online long enough to synchronize with the server and each other.

6.3   Asynchronous Awareness

In loosely coupled work, workers are rarely synchronous, so they rely on asynchronous means for gathering awareness information, which allows them to tolerate delays. Since workers have few direct interactions with each other, awareness information is not usually as readily available as it is in synchronous work situations. Instead, workers attempt to maintain an awareness of others not by observing them directly, but by collecting evidence of others' past activities [22]. This means that delays are inherent in retrieving awareness information; however, workers are still able to function with these limitations. For example, in SDH, workers gather information about others' activities by looking for evidence of their activities in patients' homes. This information is not available until they enter a patient's home, and given that times between visits can be up to several weeks, long delays can occur.

Unlike groupware that supports tightly-coupled groups by providing real-time and often transient awareness information (e.g. [7]), groupware for loosely coupled collaboration must account for the asynchrony of workers' interactions. This asynchrony means awareness information must be persistent and available to workers whenever they access the system. As shown by Neuwirth et al. [18], when awareness is supported asynchronously with groupware, workers should be able to view common work areas and easily develop an understanding of the state of shared work. This is particularly true since workers can be absent from the shared space for considerable time, and when they return they must be reminded of the work and how it has evolved since they last accessed the application. This concept of persistently available asynchronous awareness information is particularly valuable when designing groupware for widely distributed mobility since it is difficult to guarantee timeliness of updates, both because of work practices and technological constraints.

In Mohoc we attempted to provide workers with a range of asynchronous awareness information that was intended to help them understand the actions of others so that they could make better decisions about patient care. This information was automatically collected from each worker while they carried out autonomous work activities, passed to the server, and then routed to other treatment team members. When the information could not be pushed to a worker immediately, it was placed in a transaction queue on the server so that the sequential ordering of transactions would be preserved, and then pushed out when a connection became available The information we shared in this way included viewing histories and modification histories of mutually accessible artifacts, schedule information, and information about treatment activities.

During the field trial, workers regularly made use of awareness information. However, there was an inadvertent side effect of the approach we took in our system. We found that since some workers might be away from work for a number of days due to holidays or illness, they would not log into the system during that period, and the cached awareness information that needed to be sent to those workers would pile up in the queue on the server. This was not a problem at the architecture level (i.e. the system was able to handle large queues), but when the worker logged into the system after being away for a number of days, it could take as long as 10 minutes for them to download the large number of enqueued awareness messages from the server. If the worker accessed the system for short periods of time during the day (e.g. 2-3 minutes), it could take a prolonged period of time for the server side queue to empty, and for the worker to get the most recent updates. This was problematic since awareness information represented the clear majority of messages that were sent during the field trial.

While the delays seen in asynchronous awareness may not necessarily seem to be a problem on the surface due to the loosely coupled style of work, when a worker has already been out of touch for a number of days, they express more of a desire to "catch up" and get up to date information. However, with this queue based architectural approach, this did not happen in a timely fashion. We also observed in our system logs that many of these awareness updates that were enqueued during a prolonged period could be of questionable relevance to the workers. For example, a worker might view a given document several times. Each time the worker viewed that document, a new message was created and placed in the queue. However, workers state that they are primarily interested in the most recent viewing time, so the older messages are of lower priority.

6.4   Explicit Asynchronous Communication

In loosely coupled work, workers carry out most of their explicit communication asynchronously, and are able to tolerate the delays inherent in these exchanges. Asynchronous communication is particularly valuable in mobile loose coupling—workers may be unaware of others' locations, availabilities, and schedules, so asynchrony is a low effort way of working around this uncertainty [22]. It allows workers to retrieve messages whenever it is convenient for them rather than being forced to expend the time and effort required to negotiate common times for synchronous communication. However, the tradeoff for these benefits is that significant time may pass before a recipient receives a message. In loose coupling, workers are usually able to tolerate these delays due to the autonomy of their work practices. For example, workers in SDH use voice mail as the primary communication channel since they can leave messages with low effort, and they can retrieve them when it best suits their work schedule. Workers check their voicemail every few hours, so a significant time can pass between when a message is left and when it is retrieved.

Unlike the real-time communication that is supported in synchronous groupware (e.g. [17]), the preference for asynchronous communication that is seen in loose coupling requires that groupware messages be persistent so that they accommodate variability in availability between workers. Messages do not necessarily need to be made available to others immediately, since loose coupling implies that workers are resilient enough to work without ongoing feedback from others. This tolerance to delay in communication suits the limitations of mobile technologies that are used in a wide area and in a large number of locations. Groupware can store and forward messages to workers as connections become available.

In Mohoc, we transmit asynchronous messages like any other type of messages by using queuing, caching, and forwarding. The system supports public messages (i.e. readable by the entire treatment team) and private messages (i.e. to specified subsets of the team), and messages can be appended to specific work artifacts. Messages can be placed on a patient's chart or on clinical documents so that it is possible to have what Fitzpatrick [11] calls "conversations about the work at the point of work." These dependencies make the order of transaction and transaction guarantees important in our system design. For example, if a note is attached to a specific clinical document, it is essential that the clinical document arrive prior to the arrival of the note.

During the field trial, the asynchronous communication features were used regularly, both to pass on private (i.e. to subsets of the team) and public information to other team members. Workers liked having communication tools integrated into an application that supported their autonomous work. This allowed them to receive messages without being forced to explicitly check for them, as they do when they check voicemail or check with office staff for messages.

Overall, the time delays inherent in asynchronous messaging, and attributed to mobile networking, were not a problem. The content of most messages did not require immediate attention on the part of recipients. Most of the messages sent were informative in nature, and did not require the recipients to change their activities. However, we observed one instance where an occupational therapist (OT) needed to use asynchrony to deal with a time-sensitive issue. The OT needed to meet with a home health aide in the patient's home to train the aide on the use of a new piece of equipment. The OT sent the aide a message, but the aide had just returned from a two-day holiday. When the aide logged in to the system, she did not stay online long enough to receive the OT's message, and the system did not provide her with adequate feedback to understand that she was still not viewing the most up-to-date information that was available from the server. Therefore, a significant delay was introduced, and the meeting was delayed until a common time could be negotiated.

7   Design Implications

Most of the work practices that we have identified in loosely coupled work were well supported by the system design we deployed in Mohoc, and enabled workers to carry out their current work tasks in a flexible fashion without constraining their work activities. However, during the field trial, three unexpected problems surfaced that were not adequately addressed, and that require additional functionality to help manage the interdependencies that exist between workers. In the next sections (7.1 to 7.3), we will discuss these issues, and will suggest approaches for resolving them. These issues are: managing artifact interdependencies, managing awareness transactions, and managing explicit asynchronous communication.

7.1   Managing Artifact Interdependencies

A simple exclusive ownership policy was usually successful in managing access to data and artifacts during the field trial. However, when more than one worker from the same discipline treated a patient, editing privileges for clinical documents had to be shared between these workers. Many of the complexities inherent in shared editing (e.g. [7]) were avoided since the documents were accessed asynchronously, but we still found that more needed to be done to help ensure that workers had the latest version of the shared data before they began their work. This problem arose for two reasons. First, workers would often do their work, and then close the application before the data had been forwarded to the server, thus ensuring a local copy, but not making the data available to others in a timely fashion. Second, workers would begin their day and would make new entries into the system before receiving the latest version of the data from the server.

While the asynchrony seen in loose coupling still frees us of the need for tokens and locking for document editing, approaches need to be implemented to allow workers to successfully hand off data to each other. This is already a part of work practices in SDH—when workers from a common discipline share a common patient (e.g. shift work, or two part time workers who share the same patient) they leave the handwritten documents in a specific location so that the other worker can retrieve them. Our solutions for addressing these problems, then, should focus on making this handoff more effortless and effective for these workers by providing them with better information about the state of the data on their machines.

Our findings suggest three approaches. First, as recommended by Dix ([6], [5]), workers need to have a sense of the state of their connection with the server so that they know whether or not data can be sent and received. Second, workers need to know whether or not their work has been sent to the server, and made available to others. Third, workers need to know whether or not they have received all updates that are enqueued for them on the server.

The issues surrounding the level of detail to provide users about state of connection, replicated file systems, and caching has been discussed from a range of perspectives ([6], [5], [8], [26]). In our implementation, we avoided providing these details to workers because of their lack of understanding of computing technologies and client/server architectures. However, the work practices that emerged during the field trial indicate that these details are important to managing work within the group. However, we still need to develop representations and interaction techniques in order to allow users to interpret and make us of this information.

7.2   Managing Awareness Transactions

By providing workers with asynchronously available awareness information, they were better able to track the activities of other team members during the trial. This awareness information was valuable because it allowed workers to catch up on events that had occurred since they last accessed the application. For example, in our implementation, workers could see the activities of others replayed at the UI level as items were sequentially dequeued from the FIFO queue on the server and sent to the mobile client.

An unexpected side effect of making awareness information persistent was that when workers were away for several days (e.g. holidays, illness), a sizable queue of awareness information would accumulate on the server. These awareness transactions represented the majority of the transactions seen in our system, and when workers were away for 2-3 days, the queue could take as long as 5-10 minutes to empty, making this approach inefficient, particularly given the limitations of wide area mobile networking.

Our observations and an analysis of data from the field trial reveal that there is potential to save on the number of asynchronous awareness updates that must be sent to users. For example, in our implementation for SDH, we recorded access histories for shared messages and artifacts, so that workers could determine when others had viewed an item. However, during debriefings after the field trial, workers state that they are only interested in knowing when a worker last viewed the item (i.e. the most recent access). This implies that if a queue contains multiple access histories for a given item by the same worker, only the most recent one is relevant and the others can be discarded. Other possible methods for managing the number of asynchronous awareness transactions are by identifying a consensually agreed upon time span of relevance and pruning awareness transactions that are older than that time span, or by prioritizing specific types of awareness transactions over others.

7.3   Managing Explicit Asynchronous Communication

Our approach to asynchronous communication was generally successful during the trial—users were guaranteed to receive messages, but the delay between message composition and receipt could be substantial. In most cases, this is not a problem in loose coupling, but it is an issue that we identified as needing resolution, since the instances where timeliness of message receipt is important can be urgent for the workers who are involved. Here, we see the same bottlenecks that we discussed in section 7.1, where content can remain on the sending machine for a long period before being forwarded to the server, or content can stay on the server for a time before the user connects and gets the content. However, the implications seen in intentional asynchronous communication are somewhat different than for shared data and artifacts, since the intent of a message is that is reaches others, so more direct feedback is needed about the state of a message.

Workers need feedback about whether specific messages have been passed on to the server so that they can determine whether or not they are available for the recipient. In email communications, it is common to use an outbox metaphor to show messages that have been composed, but that have not yet been passed on to the server. This provides users with feedback about which messages have been passed on to the server. In widely distributed mobility, this type of feedback can be valuable in helping users manage their network connection. If a connection is available, the user can leave the mobile device turned on until the content is passed to the server.

Workers also pointed out the importance of knowing that specific recipients had read a message. For example, during the field trial, some workers stated that when they sent messages, they did not need a written response from the recipient, but they wanted to know that the recipient had actually received the information that they passed on in the message. In our implementation, we supported a "Viewing history" for each message left in the system. This provided all users with information about who had read a message, and most participants who sent messages reported utilizing this information regularly.

8   Conclusion

In this paper, we presented the results of interviews, fieldwork, and a field trial with home care teams in SDH, and we considered how the loosely coupled work patterns of these workers can shape system design in mobile groupware applications. Our findings show that collaboration can be effectively supported for these workers, in spite of the fact that network connections can be problematic when workers are widely distributed and work out of multiple locations. In our implementation of Mohoc, we were able to do this effectively with an architecture that supports simple policies for concurrency control and data access, and with no constraints on the timeliness of updates. The success of these approaches lies chiefly in the work patterns seen in SDH: workers are autonomous and the group's work is clearly partitioned, workers have clear policies on who can access and modify data and artifacts, workers are used to functioning with a delayed asynchronous awareness of others' activities, and workers communicate with each other asynchronously.

In the field trial, we found that even though simple system design was adequate for supporting the collaboration that occurred, workers need additional support to help them manage collaboration and information sharing. The approaches that were suggested by these findings argue for revising the information that is presented to the user, but not for a fundamental reinvention of the underlying architectural approaches. We found that even when workers are loosely coupled, they still need to manage a variety of time constraints. To handle this, workers need support for managing their network connections, for knowing whether their work and messages have been sent to the server, and for knowing whether they have the latest update that is available from the server. We also found that workers may need a reduced set of asynchronous awareness information, since this information is persistent (unlike synchronous groupware) and can become excessively long in the server side queue when workers are disconnected for a long period of time. We recommend filtering by relevance and by age of information to help manage the amount of information that must be transmitted and handled. However, there are tradeoffs inherent in this approach, and it is an open question how such filtering will work in practice.

References

[1]   Bergqvist, J., Dahlberg, P., Ljungberg, F., Kristoffersen, S. Moving out of the meeting room: Exploring support for mobile meetings, Proc. ECSCW'99, pp. 81-98.

[2]   Churchill, E.F. and Wakeford, N. 2001. Framing mobile collaboration and mobile technologies. In Wireless World: Social and Interactional Implications of Wireless Technology. Brown,B., Green, N., and Harper, R. Eds., New York, NY, Springer-Verlag.

[3]   Demers, A.J., Petersen, K., Spreitzer, M.J., Terry, D.B., Theimer, M.M., Welch, B.B. The Bayou Architecture: Support for Data Sharing among Mobile Users, Proc. Workshop on Mobile Computing Systems and Applications, IEEE, December 1994, pages 2-7.

[4]   Dix,A, Rodden,T, Davies,N, Trevor,J, Friday,A, Palfreyman,K Exploiting space and location as a design framework for interactive mobile systems, TOCHI, Sept2000, 7(3).

[5]   Dix, A., Beale, R. Information requirements of distributed workers. In Remote Cooperation: CSCW Issues for Mobile and Teleworkers, A.Dix and R.Beale, Eds. Springer, NY, 1996.

[6]   Dix, A. Cooperation without (reliable) communication: Interfaces for mobile applications. Distributed System Eng. Journal 2(3), 1995, 171-181.

[7]   Dourish, P., Bellotti, V. Awareness and coordination in shared workspaces. CSCW'92.

[8]   Ebling, M.R., John, B.E., Satyanarayanan, M. The importance of translucence in mobile computing systems, ACM TOCHI, March 2002, 9(1), pp. 42-67.

[9]   Edwards, K., Mynatt, E., Petersen, K., Spreitzer, M., Terry, D., Theimer, M. Designing and implementing asynchronous collaborative applications with Bayou. Proc UIST'97.

[10]   Fagrell, Henrik; Ljungberg, Fredrik; Kristoffersen, Steinar. Exploring support for knowledge management in mobile work. Proceedings ECSCW 1999, pp. 259-275.

[11]   Fitzpatrick, G. Understanding the Paper Health Record in Practice: Implications for EHRs. Proc. Health Informatics Conf. 2000, Adelaide, Australia. ISBN 0 9585370 5 4.

[12]   Grinter, R.E , Herbsleb, J.D., Perry, D.E. The geography of coordination: dealing with distance in R&D work. Proc. ACM SIGGROUP 1999, pp. 306-315.

[13]   Jing, J., Helal, A., Elmagarmid, A. Client-server computing in mobile environments. ACM Computing Surveys, Volume 31 Issue 2, June 1999, pp. 117-157.

[14]   Kristoffersen, S., Herstad, J., Ljungberg, F., Lobers, F., Sandbakken, J.R., Thoresen, K. Developing scenarios for mobile CSCW. Proc Wkshp HCI with Mobile Devices'98, p7.

[15]   Malone, T.W., Crowston, K. What is coordination theory and how can it help design cooperative work systems? Proc. CSCW'90, pp. 357–370.

[16]   Munson, J., Dewan, P. A concurrency control framework for collaborative systems, Proc. CSCW'96, pp. 278-287.

[17]   Neal, L. Virtual classrooms and communities, Proc. SIGGROUP'97, pp. 81-90.

[18]   Neuwirth,C, Morris,J, Harkness Regli,S,Chandhok,R,Wenger,G. Envisioning communication: task-tailorable representations of communication in asynchronous work. Proc. CSCW'98.

[19]   Noble, B., Satyanarayanan, M. A research status report on adaptation for mobile data access. ACM SIGMOD, Volume 24 Issue 4, December 1995, pp. 10-15.

[20]   Olson, J.S. and Teasley, S. Groupware in the wild: lessons learned from a year of virtual collocation. Proc. CSCW96, pp. 419-427.

[21]   Orr, Julian E. Talking About Machines: An Ethnography of a Modern Job. Cornell University Press, 1996. ISBN: 0801483905.

[22]   Pinelle, D., Gutwin, C. Designing for Loosely coupled Mobility, Department of Computer Science, HCI Technical Report, HCI-TR-2003-01, available at http://hci.usask.ca

[23] Ratner, D., Reiher, P., Popek, G., Kuenning, G. Replication requirements in mobile environments. Mobile Networks and Applications November 2001. 6(6), pp. 525-533.

[24] Satyanarayanan, M. The evolution of Coda. ACM TOCS 20(2), May 2002, pp. 85 – 124.

[25] Satyanarayanan, M. Fundamental Challenges in Mobile Computing. Fifteenth ACM Symposium on Principles of Distributed Computing, May 1996, pp. 1-7.

[26] Satyanarayanan, M., Kistler, J.J., Kumar, P., Okasaki, M.E., Siegel, E.H., Steere, D.C. Coda: A highly available file system for a distributed workstation environment. IEEE Trans. Comput. 39(4), 1990, pp. 447-459.

[27] Terry, D. B., Petersen, K., Spreitzer, M. J., Theimer, M. M. The Case for Non-transparent Replication: Examples from Bayou, IEEE Data Engineering, Dec'98, p12-20.

[28] Whittaker, S., Schwarz, H. Meetings of the board: The impact of scheduling medium on long term group coordination in software development, Computer Supported Cooperative Work, June 1999, 8(3), pp. 175-205.

Encouraging Face-to-Face Collaborative Learning through the Use of Handheld Computers in the Classroom

Gustavo Zurita[1], Miguel Nussbaum[1], and Mike Shaples[2]

[1] Pontificia Universidad Católica de Chile
Departamento de Ciencia de la Computación, Escuela de Ingeniería
Casilla 306, Vicuña Mackena 4860, Santiago de Chile, Chile
{mn, gzurita}@ing.puc.cl
http://www2.ing.puc.cl/nussbaum/
[2] University of Birmingham, Departament of Electronic
Electrical and Computer Engineering
Edgbaston, Birmingham, B15 2TT, UK
m.sharples@bham.ac.uk
http://www.eee.bham.ac.uk/sharplem/index.htm

Abstract. To achieve the maximum benefit, a collaborative learning activity in the classroom requires effective coordination, synchronization, face-to-face communication, negotiation, interactivity, and participant mobility conditions. In this paper, we perform a usability analysis on a specific collaborative learning activity and identify several problems with fulfilling these conditions. A second usability analysis shows how these problems can be solved with a Mobile Computer Supported Collaborative Learning activity, using wirelessly networked Handhelds. A controlled experiment was run to asses the learning benefit of using Handhelds to support a math-based collaborative learning exercise with seven year old children. Statistically significant results were observed showing that the experimental collaborative learning group using the Handhelds learned more than the control group which had no technological support.

1 Introduction

As early as 1900, social psychology literature discusses the social facilitation effect on learning ([1], [2]) introduced by Collaborative Learning (CL) activities in a classroom ([3], [4]). The goal of CL is to assist in the teaching of a specific educational objective to students working in groups. To do this, a CL activity must provide the following *essential conditions of effective CL activities*: the interactivity required to achieve shared goals; the enablement of discussions about the goals; the support of both individual and group outcome achievement; the coordination of participant roles

L. Chittaro (Ed.): Mobile HCI 2003, LNCS 2795, pp. 193–208, 2003.
© Springer-Verlag Berlin Heidelberg 2003

and rules; and the synchronization and sharing of tasks ([5], [6], [7]). All this can be done by means of face-to-face social interactions of the group members.

Face-to-face social interactions are crucial to achieving the desired learning and collaborative skills, through a continuous attempt to construct and sustain a shared and open point of view of the problem ([2], [5], [7]). Research has shown that under the *essential conditions of effective CL activities* listed above, working together collaboratively to achieve a common goal is more productive than working alone and produces greater social and learning advancements in participants ([6], [7], [8]). Therefore, achieving the essential conditions is critical to the success of a collaborative learning activity.

Computer Supported Collaborative Learning (CSCL), where the learning experience is extended to include communication and computing capabilities, fosters new possibilities for achieving these conditions ([8], [9], [10]). However, today's CSCL applications for children limit their collaborative interactions [11] since they are developed with the underlying assumption that they will be used by students sitting behind a PC at a desk. Most of today's CSCL applications support collaboration only when children "take turns" using the mouse when they collaborate on one machine, or when they collaborate from different locations over the Internet ([11], [12]).

Recent investigations ([13], [14], [15]) study the potential properties of mobility and portability offered by wirelessly networked Handhelds used in face-to-face CSCL activities. Handhelds allow a natural mobile collaboration environment with face-to-face social interactions ([14], [15], [16]). Each participant also has physical control over the hardware, which helps to provide the necessary synchronization and interactivity in their collaborative activities.

In this paper, we examine the extent to which wirelessly networked Handhelds do effectively support the CL process. To do this, we first study the usability of a given CL activity to evaluate how well the *essential conditions* are established and the pedagogical aims of the activity are achieved. We identify key aspects for usability improvement by viewing the activity from the user's perspective ([17]).

The CL activity chosen covers a basic math skill: ordering numbers. In our analysis, we identify several key usability problems in this CL activity, including: activity coordination problems; within-group communication problems; the difficulty of properly organizing individual work with joint group activities; negotiation problems; lack of group synchronization; lack of interaction with other group members; and lack of the necessary mobility for group members to carry out their social interactions. These usability problems can be solved by implementing a CSCL activity using wirelessly networked Handhelds.

In this article, we first describe a basic math CL activity (Sect. 2). In Sect. 3, we perform a usability study on this CL activity with 11 children to identify problems in achieving the goals of the activity. We then attempt to solve these problems with a face-to-face Mobile CSCL activity (Sect. 4, Sect. 5). A second usability analysis with another 11 children and an heuristic evaluation by experts was then performed on this new Mobile CSCL activity to evaluate if the usability problems identified before were, in fact, solved (Sect. 6). In Sect. 7, we report the statistically significant results of an experiment comparing the impact on learning of the Mobile CSCL activity with the original non-computer based CL activity. Finally, we report our conclusions in Sect. 8.

2   Description of a Simple Math CL Activity

We describe a simple CL activity for ordering numbers that we will call Ord-CL.

2.1   Description

The Ord-CL activity for ordering numbers is described as follows:

Objective: The main purpose of the CL activity is to practice number ordering skills. By working collaboratively, groups of three to five participants of both genders order seven series of three to five numbers (from 1 to 100) in either an ascendant or descendent way.

Materials: Each group is given seven envelopes, each containing a set of instructions and either three or five numbers (depending on the group size) written on small squares of laminated paper (tokens). Each group is also given a board made of laminated cardboard with seven rows to which they are instructed to affix, in order, each of the seven sets of numbers. The board is constructed in such a manner that it is easy to affix and remove the tokens as many times as necessary.

Individual and Group Task: One participant is to take the envelope and read the instructions out loud for the rest of the group. The instructions indicate the numbers to be ordered and the ordering direction (ascending or descending). The participant with the envelope then distributes one number each to the other children. Each child is to read aloud his/her number to the others. Then, each group is to work together to affix their numbers in the proper order to the board.

Individual and Group Rules and Roles: Children should rotate who takes the envelope and distributes the numbers. All participants should take one number. The participants should work together to order their numbers, using their social skills to interact with one another and negotiate any differences of opinion that arise. Each participant should attach his/her number to the board in the correct order, as defined by the directions contained in the envelope.

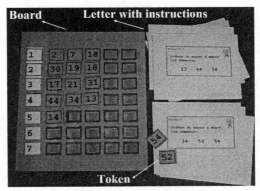

Fig. 1. The Ord-CL activity materials for ordering seven sets of three numbers in a three participant group

3   Usability Methodology and Results

In this section we describe the usability methodology for evaluating the Ord-CL activity and the results obtained.

3.1   Usability Methodology for Evaluating the Ord-CL Activity

Universe and Sample. The experimental universe was comprised of first grade children of both genders. For our sample size, we used 11 children. Some researchers have recommended five children as the appropriate sample size, because after the fifth child, most issues simply tend to repeat themselves ([17], [19]). However, neither [17] nor [20] would advocate rigid sample size limits. In our study, we were confident that 11 children was a sufficiently large sample size because we did observe the repetition of many usability problems. We chose our sample size at random from all first grade children at the school. The children had been in school for three months at the time of the experiment.

Measuring Instruments. To measure the usability of the collaborative activity, we used a technique called Discount Usability Engineering, as described by [17]. Interviews were the primary method of data gathering, backed up by observations. The interviews and observations were recorded in specially designed forms, using the *essential conditions of effective CL activities* as *usability heuristics*. To verify the data collected, interview and observation forms were subjected to reliability and validity criteria. One data-validation technique used was triangulation ([21]) by which data gathered in interviews were compared to data from classroom observations. At any points where the data did not coincide, further research was performed to clear up the inconsistency.

We also took into account research that recommends slight methodology modifications when studying the usability of a computer application from a child's perspective, as opposed to that of an adult ([22]).

Data Analysis Technique. As discussed above, the qualitative interview and observation data were first categorized according to the usability components listed in the *usability heuristics of CL activities*. These categories included ease to learn, efficiency of use, ease to remember, error rates, and user satisfaction. Once categorized into these usability components, the data was then mapped to the categories listed in the *essential conditions of effective CL activities*. When this mapping was complete, we had a relatively clear picture of how well the observed collaborative learning activity fulfilled each of the *essential conditions* required.

Procedure. The instruments described above were applied to two groups of three children and one group of five children all working on the Ord-CL activity oulined in Sect. 2. This activity was carried out during regular class time. The children were asked to sit in their assigned groups at a desk. Basic instructions on the Ord-CL activity were given (e.g. rules, roles, individual activities, and the global objective). For a period of 25 to 30 minutes, the children's activities were closely observed and only interrupted when help was needed. Once the observation period was finished, each group was interviewed for 10 to 15 minutes. The interviewer first asked questions from a defined form, but then opened up the discussion to the children's unprompted comments. To test the reliability of the data, the experiment was repeated three weeks later under the same conditions.

3.2   Usability Results of the Ord-CL Activity

The results of the usability analysis led us to find the following CL activity problems:

- *Coordination.* Some group members took control of the activity while others were left aside, even when decisions had to be made at a group level (Fig. 2). Some children were unsure of how to proceed with the activity or did not follow the established rules and roles of the activity.

Fig. 2. Screenshots of the Ord-CL activity with a group of five participants (left side), and a of three participants (right side)

- *Communication.* There were communication problems that considerably hindered social interaction between the group members (in the left of Fig. 2, the boy with his hand on his face is trying to say something to the rest). These communication problems were caused by several factors, including time pressure created by the need to administer the materials (envelopes, boards, and numbers), negative personal affinity, and physical distance (left of Fig. 2). The children did not follow the activity rules to regulate their social interactions and negotiate their differences.
- *Organization.* All participants had to manage and organize a considerable amount of material in the collaborative activity (as shown on the left of Fig. 2). This turned out to be uncomfortable for the participants and delayed their activities due to the effort it took to organize their work.
- *Negotiation.* Some participants tended to impose their point of view, hindering constructive social interaction. The nature of the activity made the children responsible for creating their own mediation and negotiation space. The lack of an enforced negotiation space in the interactions led to some participants carrying out the goals by themselves, while leaving others aside. The exercise was turned into a personal learning activity, instead of a collaborative one (on the right of Fig. 2, a boy is left aside and does not participate in the negotiation between the other two children).

- *Synchronization.* The tasks in the CL activity had to be performed in a synchronized manner by the children (setting up the board, placing their numbers one at a time in the correct order). However, some participants did not respond to this requirement due to a lack of organization, attention, or motivation. The lack of synchronization produced inefficiency in the learning activity progress and caused some members participate while others were left out.
- *Interactivity.* A lack of interactivity was observed among some members, as they did not respond to their partners' requests due to social differences, lack of motivation (left of Fig. 2), or attention problems. The other members of the group were then forced to look for other, non-collaborative, ways to reach their goal.
- *Mobility.* In many cases, the social interactions among the children required them to be physically close. The children's mobility was frequently hindered by the quantity of material they had to take with them.

4   Solutions to the Usability Problems

The above problems were solved by introducing technology into the CL activity.

4.1   A Model of Mobile CSCL Activities

The CL activity outlined in Sect. 2 can be generalized by the model described in [4], supporting face-to-face communication and high levels of social interaction between three to five participants (see the *face-to-face CL model* in Fig. 3). The model was extended by giving each participant a wirelessly networked Handheld (*Mobile CSCL* in Fig. 3), allowing participants to move freely with their portable computers. A key feature of the extended model is that the Handhelds do not get in the way of the participants' normal social interactions. On the contrary, the Handhelds' wireless network makes information available to the participants that fosters their social interactions and helps to provide the conditions necessary for successful CL activities by solving common usability problems.

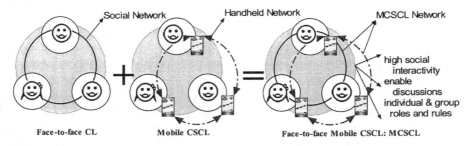

Fig. 3. An extended model of a face-to-face CL activity that combines a Social Network with a Handheld Network to form a Mobile CSCL (MCSCL) activity

A *face-to-face Mobile CSCL (MCSCL)* activity, as modeled in Fig. 3, can be easily introduced into any classroom. The classroom does not need to go to a Computer

Room. On the contrary, the Handhelds can go anywhere needed within the school. In an MCSCL activity, each participant has a Handheld wirelessly networked to the other Handhelds. The Handheld becomes the only required material, and contains the tasks, rules, and roles required for the collaborative activity. The Handheld can be moved to any part of the classroom.

In an MCSCL environment it is possible to create both a technological and a social network. While the users communicate face-to-face in a social network, they support their work with the technological network created by the Handhelds. It is of critical importance to transfer information from the technological network to the social network in an effective way. Therefore, the Human Computer Interface (HCI) design must transparently show each user the information s/he individually needs, as well as the information the group needs. Furthermore, the interface design at each stage should be simple so as to facilitate each participant achieving their individual goal, each group achieving its group goal, and each individual and group adhering to the appropriate rules and roles of the activity.

4.2   MCSCL Solutions to Usability Problems Encountered

Table 1 summarizes how an MCSCL activity can be used to solve each of the usability problems encountered in Ord-CL.

5   Description of the Ord-MCSCL Activity

Below, we describe an ordering MCSCL activity named Ord-MCSCL, and we use an example to illustrate how the software works.

Objective: The objective is the same as that of the non-technological CL activity described in Sect. 2.

Materials: Each member is given a Handheld: Pocket PC, Compaq iPAQ H3700 with a 240x320 pixel resolution touch screen display and upgraded with an IEEE 802.11b WI-FI communication card.

Individual and Group Task: Each participant's number is written on the cloud that appears on his/her interface. In the example in Fig. 4, Miguel has number 54 (Fig. 4a), Gustavo has number 78 (Fig. 4b), and Rodrigo has number 15 (Fig. 4c). Each participant should read this number out loud to the rest of the group. The arrows pointed up in Fig. 4 indicate that the numbers are to be ordered in ascending order, whereas arrows pointing down would indicate descending order.

Next, the group is to order the numbers by having one member at a time press the cloud on which his/her number appears. In the example, Rodrigo selects his number first and it appears on the first cloud on the ascending scale (Fig. 4f). This same image also appears on Gustavo's and Miguel's screens (Figs. 4d and 4e, respectively). Gustavo and Rodrigo should then continue by selecting their numbers in sequence to arrive at a screen like that shown in Fig. 5a (for Miguel) with the entire sequence of numbers in order. When the numbers have all been ordered, all participants must agree that this is the correct order before continuing on to the next sequence. To do this, they must select one of the two buttons that appear on the bottom of their screen (Fig. 5a). If not all participants select the same button (i.e. Miguel elects the check mark in Fig. 5b, and Gustavo elects the "X" in Fig. 5c), a text message and voice command is displayed to all users telling them to reach an agreement (i.e. Fig. 5f, as shown for Rodrigo).

Table 1. Outline of MCSCL solutions to usability problems found in Ord-CL

CL usability problems	Mobile Technology solutions to the CL usability problems
Coordination	The HCI design of the MCSCL activity should force each participant to do one task at a time. Each participant's interface should force him/her to carry out his/her actions in a specific sequence, allowing for the coordination of activities.
Communication	Messages that appear on one user's machine (activity status, data, error, or results) should appear on all other users' machines as well. This simplifies communication among users since no information is hidden.
Organization	Each participant's Handheld should provide all material and information that s/he needs. It should not be necessary to give the children any additional material to run the collaborative learning activity.
Negotiation	The interface should provide a negotiation space for all participants. The Handheld requires that all users must agree on an answer to proceed.
Synchronization	Each Handheld waits for the action of the other Handhelds before moving on to the next stage of the activity. As such, the participation of each member of the group is required. This synchronization is facilitated by the machines' mobility, as it is sometimes efficient for participants to physically show each other the message on their Handheld in order to come to agreement and move on to the next stage.
Interactivity	The MCSCL activity requires group interaction in order to come to an agreement and move on to the next stage of the exercise. Furthermore, the portable nature of the machines facilitates face-to-face interaction.
Mobility	The use of Handhelds allows the members of the group to take the technology anywhere and allows for natural social interactions.

If Gustavo and Rodrigo are in agreement with Miguel's answer (Fig. 5b), and the answer is correct, the group obtains a point, backed up by a congratulatory text message and an applause sound from the Handheld. In Fig. 5d, Miguel now has two points, since this was the second sequence of numbers to be ordered. Next, a text and voice message asks if the children would like to continue playing (Fig. 6b). If all respond "YES", another set of numbers to be ordered is displayed. If all respond "NO", the activity ends. If the children's answers are not in agreement, the screen shown in Fig. 6b reappears.

Fig. 4. Screen shots of the Ord-MCSCL activity for three participants. Each participant is assigned one number

If all group members are in agreement on the order of the numbers, but their response is incorrect, the score remains as it was before (Fig. 5e for Gustavo). All children are then shown a text and voice message that asks if they would like to try again, and "YES" and "NO" buttons appear at the bottom of the screen (Fig. 6a). If all respond "YES", their screens return to the state shown in Figs. 4a, 4b, and 4c. If all respond "NO", a new sequence of numbers is displayed. And, if the group members can not reach a consensus, the question shown in Fig. 6a is displayed once again.

Individual and Group Rules and Roles: The participants should work together to order the sequence of numbers they are given according to the direction indicated on their Handhelds (as explained in the example above). Each participant is responsible for giving his/her own answer reflecting his/her agreement with the final answer and his/her decision to continue playing or not.

The rules the participants must follow and the roles they must play are supported by the technology. The interfaces have been designed to take into account the principles of simplicity, familiarity, clarity, user satisfaction, and user affinity.

Fig. 5. Interfaces of the Ord-MCSCL activity that ask for decisions or show information

6   Usability Study of the Ord-MCSCL Activity

First, we describe the two methodologies used for evaluating the usability of Ord-MCSCL. Then, we explain the results obtained.

6.1   Usability Methodologies Used on the Ord-MCSCL Activity

Two methods were used to evaluate the usability of the Ord-MCSCL Activity. First, usability experts performed an heuristic evaluation of the Ord-MCSCL activity on Handhelds and suggested design improvements. Once the suggested changes were made, the revised Ord-MCSCL program was subjected to a usability study with children, similar to that performed on the paper-based Ord-CL activity.

Methodology of the Heuristic Evaluation with Experts. Three experts on CSCL and software usability performed the heuristic evaluation ([17], [18]) of the user interface design. They followed the procedure established by Nielsen ([17]), taking into account the goal and description of Ord-MCSCL (Sect. 5), as well as the *usability heuristics of CL activities* (Sect. 3). They used the rating system established by Nielsen to grade the usability problems that they found. Each expert was given a wirelessly networked Handheld running the Ord-MCSCL activity described in Sect. 5. The evaluation was completed in approximately two hours.

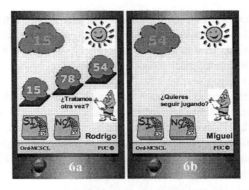

Fig. 6. Interfaces of the Ord-MCSCL activity that ask participants for their decisions

Methodology of the Usability Evaluation with Children. The usability evaluation methodology used for Ord-MCSCL was very similar to that used for Ord-CL (Sect. 3). The universe was the same, but the sample was composed of a different randomly selected 11 children of both genders. All children in the sample were seven years old and had been in school for seven months at the time of the usability analysis. The Ord-MCSCL activity described in Sect. 5 was carried out during class time by two groups of three children and one group of five children. The measuring instruments and data analysis technique used were the same as in Sect. 3.

The main difference from the methodology described in Sect. 3 was the procedure. The children were invited to work in groups anywhere in the classroom. Basic instructions on the Ord-MCSCL activity were given, including the rules, roles, individual activities, and global objective (Sect. 5). The children were observed and interviewed with the goal of analyzing their behavior both with one another and in relation to the software and hardware.

6.2   Results of the Usability Analysis of the Ord-MCSCL Activity

Results of the Heuristic Evaluation with Experts. Several small usability problems were identified: color-coding of buttons was not obvious, voice messages should have been the same as the text messages, and the wording of several text and voice messages could have been improved. All of these usability problems were easily fixed in a revised version of Ord-MCSCL. The experts indicated that the activity offers a scaffold for synchronization and coordination; additionally, they emphasized that the communication necessary to achieve the objective was produced in a natural way.

Results of the Usability Evaluation with Children. The usability analysis applied to the Ord-MCSCL activity showed that the problems of coordination, communication, organization, negotiation, synchronization, interactivity and mobility found in the Ord-CL activity, had been solved by using the Handhelds. The portable and mobile nature of the Handhelds, combined with the HCI design of Ord-MCSCL had solved the problems in the following ways:

- For the *coordination* and *synchronization* problems between children, the Handhelds were used as mediation elements to coordinate their activities and to assure that all of the group members participated (in both photos in Fig. 7, all the participants are working together to coordinate and synchronize their individual and group tasks of ordering numbers in a sequence).
- The *communication* problems between the children due to information management and personal affinity in Ord-CL were easily solved by Ord-MCSCL. The Handheld interfaces gave the children complete information, showing them all of the numbers that had been ordered and the remaining numbers to be ordered.
- Handhelds regulated social interactions because children needed to read information off of their Handhelds in order to tell their number to the other children. The handhelds mediate the collaborative work and act as a referee to regulate behavior, leaving the children to interact socially, make decisions, and negotiate their differences of opinion.
- Handhelds minimized the effort required to *organize and manage the material* of the activity by providing all of the information needed at each stage (Fig. 7).
- Ord-MCSCL supported a *negotiation* space by requiring that all children vote in agreement before continuing on to the next stage of the activity (agreeing with the numbers ordered, trying again if incorrect, or finishing the activity). In Ord-CL, this negotiation and agreement had to be guaranteed by a rigid adherence to the roles and rules of the activity. Frequently, however, the children did not obey these roles and rules.
- To provide an *interactive* environment, children could easily take the Handhelds with them anywhere in the classroom. This encouraged face-to-face social interactions.
- Finally, the mobility restrictions of Ord-CL were clearly eliminated by the portable nature of the Handhelds used in Ord-MCSCL, facilitating social interactions as discussed above.

One usability problem was discovered through testing with the children, though it only occurred on the first day. A few children had difficulty pressing a button on the touch screen because it triggered an action only when the finger was removed from the display. Many children were expecting immediate feedback, and this was not a natural way to operate a button. However, this problem was easily solved by self-training.

Finally, we observed that a voice synthesis in the Handhelds highly reinforced the visual text messages. We also observed differences in behavior by gender, though these observations fall outside of our current research scope.

Fig. 7. Screenshots of the Ord-MCSCL activity with a group of five participants (left side), and a group of three participants (right side)

7   Experimental Results: Ord-CL vs. Ord-MCSCL

A controlled experiment was run to test the impact on learning of Ord-MCSCL vs. Ord-CL for first grade students. The experimental group, who performed the Ord-MCSCL activity, was composed of 24 children (12 boys and 12 girls). The control group, who performed the Ord-CL activity, was also composed of 24 children (11 boys and 13 girls). All children in the experiment were seven years old.

In both classrooms, three groups of three members were formed for ordering three numbers (right of Fig. 7), and three groups of five members were formed for ordering five numbers (left of Fig. 7). These groups were maintained throughout the experiment. The children were students at a low-income public school in Santiago de Chile (Villa Macul). They all had basic knowledge of ordering numbers, and they had been in school for eight and a half months at the time of the experiment.

A pretest was taken at the beginning of the experiment by both the control and experimental groups. It was a 35-minute individual assessment to measure the children's previous knowledge of ordering numbers. It used the standard Chilean grading scale from 1 (no correct answer) to 7 (all answers correct).

Table 2. Mean and Standard Deviation (SD) for the control and experimental groups

	Pretest Results		Posttest Results	
	Control Group	Exp. Group	Control Group	Exp. Group
Mean	3,53	3,88	3,91	5,77
SD	2,68	2,74	2,64	1,82

The experiment lasted for four weeks with 20 daily sessions of 25 minutes each in the Ord-CL group and 15 minutes each in the Ord-MCSCL group. Both groups were given the same set of activities and daily goal, but it was discovered that the Ord-MCSCL group needed 40% less time on average to complete this goal. The first two sessions were slightly longer (30 min. for Ord-CL and 20 min. for Ord-MCSCL) to allow the children to get used to the activity and technology. By the 12th session, some Ord-CL groups were achieving their goal in 20 minutes, and some Ord-MCSCL groups were achieving their goal in 10 minutes. In both groups, the children occasionally required assistance, primarily with problems of arithmetic origin.

On the first day, the aim of the activity was explained to the children, and the rules and roles were outlined (see Sect. 2 and Sect. 5). In the Ord-CL group, children were also assigned to groups by the teacher and asked to sit at a specific table. In the Ord-

MCSCL group, the children's partners were listed on their screens, allowing them to move freely throughout the classroom to find their other group members and sit where they wished.

Table 3. Analysis of Variance for posttest, with pretest as a covariate (using the software package SPSS) between the Control (N = 24) and Experimental Groups (N = 24)

Tests of Between-Subjects Effects Dependent Variable: posttest					
Source	Type III Sum of Squares	df	Mean Square	F	Sig.
Corrected Model	169,143(a)	2	84,571	34,981	,000
Intercept	107,610	1	107,610	44,511	,000
pre-posttest	127,423	1	127,423	52,706	,000
Group	32,549	1	32,549	13,463	,001
Error	108,794	45	2,418		
Total	1401,688	48			
Corrected Total	277,936	47			
a R Squared = ,609 (Adjusted R Squared = ,591)					

Each day, the students had to order seven sets of numbers, with increasing complexity. The first sets were made up of small numbers, but the latter sets used numbers up to 100. At the beginning of the experiment, the numbers were relatively easy to order and the children spent a high percentage of their time learning to use the technology (Ord-MCSCL) or materials (Ord-CL). Later, when the children had the more difficult task of ordering bigger numbers, they were already familiar with the technology and materials, and so were still able to complete the activity in the same amount of time. In both Ord-MCSCL and Ord-CL, the children were given assistence by the teacher each time they could not arrive at a correct answer. At the end of the 20-day experiment a posttest was performed using the same test that was administered as pretest. As in the pretest, each child was given 35 minutes to complete the test. The means and standard deviations of the pretest and posttest data for the control and experimental groups are showed in Table 2.

Analysis of variance for the posttest score, with the pretest score as a covariate between Control and Experimental Groups was run to test the effect of the intervention on number ordering ability. Pretest scores on the specific subject tested were introduced as covariates in order to control for initial levels of ability. As can be seen in Table 3, the type of intervention had a significant effect on posttest ordering scores, controlling for pretest ability. The comparison showed that there was a significant difference between means for participants in the experimental vs. control groups.

8   Conclusions

A number of problems were observed to reduce the effectiveness of Ord-CL, a traditional collaborative learning activity. However, the incorporation of wirelessly networked handheld computers into the collaborative learning process helped to solve many of those problems. In the Ord-MCSCL activity presented, the handheld computers were observed to support and enhance the collaborative work by:

- Organizing the materials and information
- Providing a negotiation space
- Encouraging coordination between the activity states
- Mediating the synchronization of activities
- Providing a communication channel between the technological, wireless network and the social, face-to-face network
- Mediating the social interaction of the participants
- Allowing the participants to be mobile

Furthermore, the last three points mark an important difference in how collaboration is supported by MCSCL activities in comparison to traditional CSCL.

This paper also demonstrated the learning benefits of MCSCL when compared to traditional CL for a number ordering activity. In a month-long controlled experiment, subjects performing the Ord-MCSCL activity were observed to have significantly higher number ordering test score improvements than subjects performing the Ord-CL activity. This result controlled for ability through the introduction of pretest results as a covariate and was statistically significant at the 99% level. We conclude, therefore, that the introduction of mobile computing technology into a collaborative learning activity focused on ordering numbers can have significant learning benefits.

Our future research includes the design of a framework to conceptualize the MCSCL activities that can be supported by Handhelds. We are also investigating the impact on learning and social skills of frequently changing group partners during an MCSCL activity.

Acknowledgments

This paper was partially funded by FONDEF, Microsoft Research, Compaq Chile, and DIPUC. Special thanks to Camila Cortez, Carlos Torres, Francisco Jofree, Rodrigo Salinas, Tony Chan, and Mary Ulicsak.

References

[1]   Slavin, R. E.: Research on cooperative learning and achievement: What we know, what we need to know. Contemporary Educational Psychology, Vol. 21 (1996) 43-69

[2]   Vygotsky, L.: Mind in society: The development of higher psychological processes. Cambridge, Harvard University Press (1978)

[3]   Cohen, E.G.: Restructuring the classroom: Conditions for productive small groups. Review of Educational Research, Vol. 64 No. 1 (1994) 1-35

[4]   Davidson, N., Worsham, T.: Enhancing Thinking Cooperative Learning. Published by Teachers College Press (1992)

[5]   Davidson, N.: Small-group learning and teaching in mathematics: A selective review of the research. In R. E. Slavin, S. Sharan, S. Kagan, R. Hertz-Lazarowitz, C. Webb, & R. Schmuck (Eds.). Learning to cooperate, cooperating to learn, NY: Plenum. (1985) 211-230

[6]   Dillenbourg, P.: Collaborative Learning: Cognitive and Computational Approaches. Edited by Pierre Dillenbourg. Pergamon, Elsevier Science Ltd (1999)

[7]   Johnson, D., Johnson, R.: Learning Together and Alone. Ed. Allyn and Bacon. 5a. ed. (1999)

[8]   Lou, Y., Abrami, P. C., d'Apollonia, S.: Small group and individual learning with technology: A meta-analysis. Review of Educational Research, Vol. 71 No. 3 (2001) 449-521

[9]   Roschelle, J., Teasley, S.: The construction of shared knowledge in collaborative problem solving. In C. O'Malley (Ed.), Computer-Supported Collaborative Learning, New York: Springer-Verlag (1995) 79-77

[10]   Silverman, B.: Computer Supported Collaborative Learning (CSCL). Computers & Education, Vol. 25 No. 3 (1995) 81-91

[11]   Inkpen, K. M., Ho-Ching, W., Kuederle, O., Scott, S. D., Shoemaker, G.: This is fun! We're all best friends and we're all playing: Supporting children's synchronous collaboration. Proceedings of Computer Supported Collaborative Learning (CSCL) '99, Stanford, CA December (1999)

[12]   Wang, X. C., Hinn, D. M., Kaufer, A. G.: Potential of computer-supported collaborative learning for learners with different learning styles. Journal of Research on Technology in Education, Vol. 34 No. 1 (2001) 75-85

[13]   Danesh, A., Inkpen, K.M., Lau, F., Shu, K., Booth, K.S.: Geney: Designing a collaborative activity for the Palm handheld computer. In Proceedings of CHI, Conference on Human Factors in Computing Systems. Seattle, USA, April (2001)

[14]   Inkpen, Kori M.: Designing Handheld Technologies for Kids. Personal Technologies Journal, Vol. 3 (1&2), (1999) 81-89

[15]   Mandryk, R.L., Inkpen, K.M., Bilezikjian, M., Klemmer, S.R., Landay, J.A. Supporting children's collaboration across handheld computers. In Extended Abstracts of CHI, Conference on Human Factors in Computing Systems. Seattle, USA, April (2001)

[16]   Imielinsky, T., Badrinath, B.R.: Mobile Wireless Computing. Communications of the ACM, Vol. 37 No. 10 (1994)

[17]   Nielsen, J.: Usability Engineering. New York, Academic Press Professional (1993)

[18]   Shneiderman, B.: Designing the User Interface. Strategies for effective Human-Computer Interaction. (3rd. Editon). New York, Addison Wesley (1998)

[19]   Lewis, J.R.: Sample Sizes for Usability Studies: Additional Considerations. Human Factors, Vol. 36 (1994) 368 – 378

[20]   Virzi, R.: Refining the Test Phase of Usability Evaluation: How Many Subjects is Enough?. Human Factors, Vol. 34 No. 4 (1992) 457-468.

[21]   Norman, D., Yvonna, L.: Handbook of Qualitative Research. USA, Sage Publications (1994)

[22]   Hanna, L., Risden, K., Alexander, K.: Guidelines for Usability Testing with Children. Interactions Vol. 4 No. 5 (1997) 9–14.

Human Pacman: A Mobile Entertainment System with Ubiquitous Computing and Tangible Interaction over a Wide Outdoor Area

Adrian David Cheok, Siew Wan Fong, Kok Hwee Goh, Xubo Yang, Wei Liu, Farzam Farzbiz, and Yu Li

National University of Singapore
{adriancheok,engp1620,g0202687,eleyxb,eleliuw,eleff,elely}@nus.edu.sg

Abstract. Human Pacman is an interactive role-playing game that envisions to bring the computer gaming experience to a new level of emotional and sensory gratification by setting the real world as a playground. This is a physical fantasy game integrated with human-social and mobile-gaming that emphasizes on collaboration and competition between players. By setting the game in a wide outdoor area, natural human-physical movements have become an integral part of the game. Pacmen and Ghosts are now human players in the real world experiencing mixed reality visualization from the wearable computers on them. Virtual cookies and actual physical objects are incorporated to provide novel experiences of seamless transitions between real and virtual worlds and tangible human computer interface respectively. We believe Human Pacman is pioneering a new form of gaming that anchors on physicality, mobility, social interaction, and ubiquitous computing.

1 Introduction

Human Pacman is a real-world-physical, social, and wide area mobile entertainment system that is built upon the concepts of ubiquitous computing, tangible human-computer interaction, and wide-area entertainment networks. The game has several novel aspects: Firstly, the players immersively role-play the characters of the Pacmen and Ghosts in the real physical world. Secondly, users enjoy unrestricted movement outdoor and indoor while maintaining their social contacts. Thirdly, Human Pacman also explores novel tangible aspects of human physical movement and perception, both on the player's environment and on the interaction with the digital world.

In this system the users are provided with custom-built wearable computers; and they interact both directly with other players when in physical proximity, or indirectly via the Wireless LAN network. Virtual fantasy and imaginative play activity elements, which have made computer game popular [1], are incorporated using augmented reality techniques. The players also experience seamless transitions between real and virtual worlds as they swap between immersive first person augmented reality view and full virtual reality view of the Pac-world throughout the game.

L. Chittaro (Ed.): Mobile HCI 2003, LNCS 2795, pp. 209–223, 2003.

Employing the philosophy of ubiquitous computing [2], we have implemented a system that embeds everyday physical objects with digital fantasy meanings. For example, we have attached Bluetooth devices to sugar jars which when being picked up, will automatically communicate with the wearable computer by adding the corresponding virtual ingredient to the inventory list of the player.

Each of the novel interactions of Human Pacman mentioned is summarized in Table 1. We will proceed by firstly giving a research background to this system and previous works that have motivated us. Then we go on to clarify the actual game play designed. More importantly in the section that follows, the system is analyzed in the context of addressing various Human Computer Interaction issues. Lastly we conclude with our reflections on the future impacts of the system on everyday life.

2   Background

Entertainment with interactivity [3] and sociality [4] are becoming important as reflected in the growing popularity of online games [4]. These computer games provides unrivalled richness of human interaction [5] between players despite of geographical separation. Nevertheless, social interaction between players is limited with no behavioural engagement and cognitive exchange. Human Pacman aims to merge interactive aspects of networked gaming with the real physical world, while maintaining social contact in reality and virtuality.

Human Pacman has aspects derived from pioneering work on ubiquitous gaming. Multi-players mobile gaming is demonstrated in 'Pirates!' [6] which is a game on PDAs with proximity sensing technology. However, it provides little immersive experience since there is no Augmented Reality and Virtual Reality support. The E3 project [7] examines the essential elements of free play, and multi-user social interaction. However it does not explore large-scale configuration where users walk around.

Augmented reality techniques are used as part of Human Pacman's interface. Previous works done on using augmented reality in entertainment include AR2 Hockey [8] and AquaGaunlet [9]. However, these games are played in a small area, with limited movement and little interaction with physical space. Another important mobile game is known as ARQuake [10], which is an AR extension of the popular computer game Quake. Using Wearable Computer equipped with global positioning system, ARQuake can be played indoor and outdoor. However it is a single player game with practically no social interaction.

Lastly, the transition between the real and physical world in Human Pacman is derived from research that has been done on continual transversal along the Reality-Virtuality continuum [11]. The Magic Book [12] uses a book metaphor to demonstrate the seamless transitions between augmented and virtual reality. Nevertheless collaboration is carried out only in a small-scale and closed-up configuration. Touch-Space [13] is an embodied computing based mixed reality game space with free movement between the real world and virtual world. However they are constrained by small game space and limited physical movement.

Table 1. Detail descriptions of each novel features of Human Pacman.

Feature	Details
Physical Gaming	Players are physically role-playing the characters of Pacmen and Ghost; with Wearable Computers donned, they use free bodily movements as part of interaction between each person, and among objects in the real wide area landscapes and virtual environments.
Social Gaming	Players interact both directly with other players when they are in physical proximity, or indirectly via the Wireless LAN network by instant messaging. All Internet users can participate in the game by viewing and collaborating with real Human Pacmen and Ghosts.
Mobile Gaming	Players are free to move about in the indoor\outdoor space without being constrained to the 2D\3D screen of desktop computers.
Ubiquitous Computing	Everyday objects throughout the environment seamlessly have a real-time fantasy digital world link and meaning. There is automatic communication between Wearable Computers and Bluetooth devices embedded in certain physical objects used in game play.
Tangible Interaction	Throughout the game people interact in a touch and tangible manner. For example, Players need to physically pick up objects and tap on the shoulder of other players to devour them.
Outdoor Wide-Area Gaming Arena	Large outdoor areas can be set up for the game whereby players carry out their respective missions for the role they play.
Seamless Transition between real and virtual worlds	Players swap freely between immersive first person augmented reality view and full virtual reality view of the Pac-world in the game.

In Human Pacman, the interface and transition between the real world and virtual world is achieved in real time throughout the spacious indoor and outdoor physical world.

3   System Design and Game Play

Human Pacman features a centralized architecture that is made up of four main entities, namely the central server, wearable computers, laptops, and Bluetooth embedded objects. An overview of the system is shown in the Fig. 1.

The underlying program is built on a client server architecture with wearable computers and helper laptops as clients, and the desktop computer as a cen-

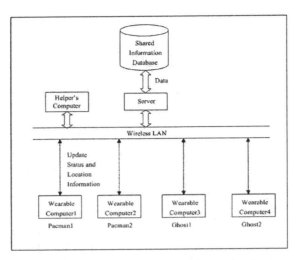

Fig. 1. Complete top level system design overview of Human Pacman.

tral server communicating via Wireless LAN. Physical location and players' status updates are done between the client wearable computers and the server on a regular basis. The server maintains up-to-the-minute players' information, and presides over any communication between Bluetooth objects and the wearable computers. Detail configuration of the wearable computers as seen in Fig. 2 is described as follows.

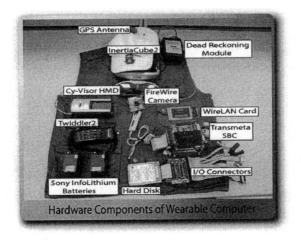

Fig. 2. Detail configuration of wearable computer

The main components of the wearable computers are Transmeta Single Board Computer (PC104 plus compliant motherboard running on Crusoe processor), Twiddler2 (handheld keyboard and mouse), Cy-Visor Head Mounted Display (video see-through HMD) with FireWire camera attached, two Sony F960 InfoLithium batteries, InertiaCube2 (inertia sensor from Intersense [14]), DR-MIII module (GPS and Dead-Reckoning device from Point Research Corporation [15]), and JVC Bluetooth device. Position tracking is done using DRM which measures the displacement of the user from an initialization point by measuring the direction (with data obtained from the compass), and distance traveled (using accelerometer data) with each footstep taken. Although the DRM is a self-contained navigation unit, in-built GPS receiver can be used to collect data for the correction of both the distance and direction calculations. InertiaCube2, which is used for head tracking for the implementation of augmented reality display, is an inertial three degree-of-freedom orientation tracking system of high accuracy.

With the software architecture mentioned as the backbone of the game engine and the hardware as enabling tools, we proceed to describe the game play of Human Pacman and then discuss some of the problems we have encountered.

3.1 Main Concepts: Team Collaboration, Ultimate Game Objectives and the Nature of Pac-World

The players are assigned to two opposing teams, namely the Pacman team and the Ghost team. Each Pacman\Ghost is in coalition with one Helper who is an Internet online player.

Human Pacman has similar game objectives as the original Pacman. Basically the goal of the Pacman team is to collect all virtual plain cookies in Pac-World while avoiding the Ghosts. Meanwhile, the aim of the Ghost team is to devour all Pacmen. For excitement of game play, after 'eating' special ingredients, a Pacman gains Ghost-devouring capability and henceforth can attack her enemy for a limited period of time.

Pac-World is a fantasy world existing dualistically in both Augmented Reality (AR) and Virtual Reality (VR) mode. Pacmen and Ghosts are allowed to switch between the two viewing modes; whereas Helpers can only view in VR mode. Most importantly there is a real time link between the wide-area physical world and the virtual Pac-World, thus providing the users with a marriage of fantasy digital world and realistic physical world. As seen in Fig. 3 where the 2D map of the selected game play area in our university campus and the 3D map of Pac-World are shown side-by-side, we have converted the real world to a fantasy virtual playground by ingraining the latter with direct physical correspondences.

3.2 Pacman, Ghost, and Helper

Pacman has to physically move about collecting virtual cookies in AR mode where the real world is being overlaid with them as shown in Fig. 4. In addition

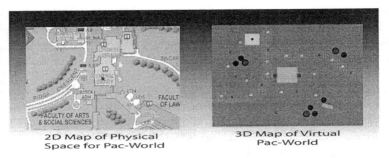

2D Map of Physical
Space for Pac-World

3D Map of Virtual
Pac-World

Fig. 3. 2D map of game play area and its corresponding 3D map of Pac-world

to the virtual cookies, she has to find and collect physical ingredients as shown in Fig. 5. Besides, the Pacman should avoid the Ghost, i.e. not letting Ghost tapping on her shoulder capacitive sensor pad. This physical touch interaction exemplifies tangible physical interaction between humans, which is commonly found in traditional games such as hide-and-seek, but is now being revived in computer gaming arena. The role of a Ghost is simply to track down all Pacmen and devour them. Nevertheless, she has to shun of Pacmen with Ghost-devouring power. Helper is a new character in Human Pacman who acts as an advisor to her partner(a Ghost or Pacman), informing her the positions of enemy mobile units and ingredients which are not labelled in AR mode. Therefore the Helper messages important information to her partner as shown in Fig. 6 and thus this promotes collaboration and interaction between human.

Fig. 4. First person view as presented in HMD display of Pacman

Fig. 5. Bluetooth embedded object

Fig. 6. Close collaboration between the outdoor Pacman and her Helper

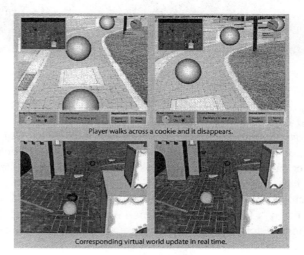

Fig. 7. Pacman collecting cookies

3.3   Actual Game Play

Starting the Game: Pacmen and Ghosts start from two different physical locations called Pac-castle and Ghost-house in Pac-world (physical game area).

Collection of Plain Cookies: When Pacman collects a cookie by walking through it, this action is reflected visually in Pac-World through the disappearing of the cookie in both the AR and VR mode as shown in Fig. 7.

Fig. 8. Sequence of pictures showing the collection of an ingredient

Collection of Ingredients: In the game, Pacman collects ingredients including flour, butter, sugar, and special ingredients (e.g. Chocolate Chip, Almond) to make special cookies. There are two types of them: a butter cookie is made up of flour, butter, and sugar; a super cookie is made up of butter cookie and a special ingredient.

When Pacman eats a butter cookie, she achieves 1 minute immunity from being consumed by a Ghost. When Pacman eats a super cookie, it takes a time lag of 30 seconds before she achieves 3 minutes of ghost-devouring power. (30 seconds is for the Ghost to run or devour the Pacman).

In the game, real Bluetooth-embedded objects are scattered in the game area to be collected as shown in Fig. 8. When the Pacman is within 10 meters of the Bluetooth object, communication takes place between the wearable computer and the Bluetooth device. After being alerted, she hunts for it in the surrounding physical area. Having found the object, collection is done simply by physically holding the object in her hands. Technically charge transfer sensing on the object (designed using QT161 IC chip from Quantum Research Group [16]) detects the player's touch and sends a message to the wearable computer which will send an corresponding message to the server to update the event. The collection of the ingredient will be kept in a virtual inventory list as seen in the figure as an icon.

Collaboration between Players: There is an essential element of collaboration in the game play between a Pacman\Ghost with her Helper, and between any allied Pacmen.

(i) *Pacman\Ghost and Helper Collaboration–* The Helper always has a complete view of Pac-world, including the positions of all players and ingredients. Mobile players can also do so in VR mode, but AR mode is more advantageous for mobility. Furthermore Helpers collaborate among themselves to work out a strategy to achieve the team's goal. In this way, social interaction and collaboration is significant between Helpers, as well as between Helpers and her partner.

(ii) *Pacman and Pacman Collaboration–* Pacman players can collaborate through exchanging ingredients between them. For example Pacman A can initiates request for the list of unused ingredients Pacman B has. Upon approval, A can request for transfer of ingredient from B, subjected to approval by B. However, Pacman are not allowed to transfer special cookies so as not to disadvantage the Ghosts.

Use Special Cookie: All special cookies can only be used once. When a Pacman consumes a special cookie, an alert message is shown to her, and at the same time her Pacman avatar in the VR mode is labelled. This serves to inform all Helpers, including those from the Ghost-team, of her ability.

Devouring Enemy Player: To devour a Pacman, a Ghost must physically touch the Pacman's capacitive sensor pads on her shoulders as seen in Fig. 9. The same applies when a Pacman with Ghost-devouring capability devours a Ghost. When a Pacman player is the prey, her agility determines the "life-and-death" of her virtual Pacman role. Thus this computer game provides the benefits of natural wide area free bodily movements as part of humanistic interaction between each person.

Ending the Game: The game ends when either team meets their goal or when a time limit of ten minutes has been reached.

3.4   Problems in Implementation

From a broader perspective, the game of Human Pacman is a type of user adaptive application that is built upon the infrastructure of wearable and mobile computing, as well as the wireless multimedia communication. It aims to utilize the mentioned technology to provide nomadic players with personalized location based entertainment. However there are numerous problems associated with the actualization of these concepts.

We have identified three main problems in deploying the wireless communication network, in this case, the Wireless LAN of IEEE 802.11b. Firstly disconnections in communication often interrupt the flow of the game. Secondly limitation in bandwidth sets constraints on the type of multimedia data that can be sent between players and between the players and the server. For example we have to limit ourselves to simple text files for the frequent location, perspective, and status updates between the player's wearable computer and the server; and forego with the initial intention of sending live video streams between players. Thirdly unstable outdoor conditions often resulting in high error rate of the network. These three factors in turn increase communication latency which is due to retransmission, retransmission on time-out delays, error control processing, and short disconnections. We try to minimize the problems by carefully selecting the area for game play in the vicinity of the University campus in Singapore where network connectivity is good. Also, when designing the software for the game, we have embedded components that enable continual processing based on local data on the wearable computer so that when short disconnections occur, the game can still proceed without much disruptions.

Besides communication problems, we have to bear with constraints on the wearable computers too. Maintaining power for the computing device is essential in this system. Since Human Pacman is a game with short duration of play (recommended ten minutes), the wearable computer that is powered by two Sony Infolithium batteries lasting about three hours can adequately manage the task. Also, in designing for the user interface, we have considered the disadvantages of using HMD as mentioned by Duchamp at el [17] such as the hassle of the head gear, low-resolution, eye fatigue, and the requirement for dim lighting conditions. The problems mention also exist in Human Pacman since we are also using HMD for Augmented Reality outdoor gaming. Nevertheless as mentioned previously about the short duration of play in Human Pacman, the problem is so acute as to becoming unbearable to the players.

Scene of Ghost catching PacMan

Fig. 9. A Ghost player tapping on the shoulder of Pacman player

4   Human Computer Interface Issues in Human Pacman

Human Pacman envisions applying the concept of calm technology as described by Weiser [18] into computer gaming by experimenting with two of the interaction themes in Ubicomp, namely tangible interfaces and context-awareness. Details about them are discussed in the following subsection. After that, we will discuss Human Computer Interaction design issues in Human Pacman.

4.1   Tangible Interface

Even though Graphical User Interface (GUI) is still the dominant paradigm for interactions with computers, we are increasingly encountering computation that moves beyond the traditional confines of the desk and attempts to incorporate itself more richly into our daily experience of the physical and social world. Work on physical interaction started with the introduction of Computer-Augmented Environments [19] that have visioned the merging of electronic systems into the physical world.

Over the years, a number of projects have explored this new paradigm of interaction termed tangible computing. Early attempts include Bishop's Marble Answering Machine [20], "Brick" by Fitzmaurice [21], "Tangible Bits" and "mediaBlocks" from MIT media lab [22]. Nevertheless in all of these implementations of tangible computing, computer interaction remains passive with human initiating communication, and is confined between humans and virtual objects.

However, in Human Pacman, active communication and graspable interactions are explored with the use of embedded Bluetooth devices and capacitive sensors. Bluetooth is incorporated into the system where there is already Wireless LAN support because firstly it provides paired communication with security which is essential for one-to-one communication between the 'Ingredient' and the player; secondly Bluetooth devices support automatic device discovery and connection setup when they are within range therefore provide the backbone for reasoning by close physical proximity (Pacman has to search nearby area for 'Ingredient' once being alerted of it). Besides, tangible interaction between the Bluetooth embedded object and the player is made possible by using capacitive sensor for detecting the action of touch. Another important aspect is the clever exploitation of the affordances of the object's physical properties whereby players can intuitively associate the action of picking up the 'Ingredient' object with the collection of it in their virtual inventory.

The use of capacitive sensor shoulder pads of wearable computer for the detection of 'Devouring' action in game play, serves the purpose of demonstrating how computation can be used in concert with naturalistic activities. Also, by making the distinction between "interface" and "action" very much reduced, i.e. physical action of tapping versus a mouse-click for interaction, Human Pacman allows the players to experience transparent interchange between human and computer as never before in computer gaming.

4.2   Context Awareness in Outdoor Environment

Researchers at Olivetti Research Ltd. (ORL) and Xerox PARC Laboratory pioneered the context-aware computing area with the introduction of Active Badge System and PARCTab [23][24]. However, these systems were expensive, and were confined to an indoor room. With the introduction of GPS and emergence of cheap but accurate sensors, a number of context-aware systems for outdoor applications were built. Notable systems include Georgia Tech Cyberguide project [25], and context-aware fieldwork tools at the University of Canterbury (an archeological assistant tool [26], a giraffe observation tool [27], and a rhino identification tool [28]). Unlike Human Pacman that uses augmented reality techniques as its main computer human interface, these systems have only primitive 2D maps and text presented on palmtops.

Another tourist assistant called Smart Sight was developed at the Carnegie Mellon University [29], which has an audio interface and aid navigational around the campus. Nevertheless since laptops were used as part of the mobile computer system, their weight and bulkiness have reduced user's mobility and comfort of use. In Human Pacman, players are provided with custom-built wearable computers.

There are three ways in which the idea of context awareness is being applied to in Human Pacman. Firstly, with the use of GPS and DRM, location awareness of players is made possible. Although GPS suffers from accuracy and selective availability, the problems are compensated through sensorfusion with DRM. The system's behavior is adapted to the player's current location for augmented reality (AR) placing of virtual cookies, and for calculating the relative positions of allied players.

Another important component in realizing AR elements in Human Pacman is the inertia sensor which provides the system with the current perspective of the player. Besides, Human Pacman also experiment with information context with the Helper player having information access to other players via Wireless LAN and providing them with necessary and timely information.

4.3   Human Computer Interaction Design in Human Pacman

In Human Pacman, we tried to combine materials from cognitive psychology and sociology with that from computer science. However the vast amount of issues encountered have exceeded the scope of this paper. Therefore we will concentrate on discussing issues with respect to Human Computer Interface design. According to Bellotti [30], there are five questions posing human-computer communication challenges for interaction design. In Table 2, we summarize the sensing approaches to interaction in Human Pacman with respect to the five questions raised.

5   Conclusion

The continual propagation of digital communication and entertainment in recent years forces many changes in societal psyche and lifestyle, i.e. how we think,

Table 2. Five questions and answers posing human-computer communication challenges for interaction design in the case of Human Pacman

Basic Question	Human Pacman Interface Answers
Address: How do I address one (or more) of many possible devices?	With the implementation of Ubiquitous Computing, the system constitutes a more amorphous concept with automated interactions between sensors and computer. The existence of unique address for each Bluetooth device disambiguates the Bluetooth embedded objects. Furthermore, centralized control of the server prevents ambiguity of intended target system even when there are more than one players are near the Bluetooth device. Keyboard and mouse are used for messaging and selection of the 'Ingredients' to be exchanged between Pacmen.
Attention: How do I know the system is ready and attending to my actions?	Graphical feedback is used extensively from providing alert message in popped up window, to refreshing virtual inventory after Pacman picked up Bluetooth embedded object. Also, since this graphical information is provided in the HMD directly in the zone of the user's attention, they are highly effective.
Action: How do I effect a meaningful action, control its extent and possibly specify a target or targets for my action?	The Pacman\Ghost click on preset messages to be sent to Helpers. Pacmen click on graphical representation of 'Ingredient' to be exchanged. Clearly labeled Bluetooth embedded objects are to be found in physical space where interaction is intuitive. According to Norman's Theory of Action [31], this form of tangible interface bridges the 'Gulf of Execution'.
Alignment: how do I know the system is doing (has done) the right thing?	Real time graphical feedback presents distinctive and timely graphical elements establishing the context of the system.
Accident: How do I avoid mistakes?	Pacman right-click on virtual ingredient in order to dump the ingredient.

work and play. With physical and mobile gaming gaining popularity, traditional paradigms of entertainment will irrevocably shake from the stale television-set inertia. We believe that Human Pacman heralds the conjuration and growth of a new genre of computer game that is built on mobility, physical actions and the real world as a playground. Reality, in this case, is becoming more exotic than fantasy because of the mixed reality element in the game play. On the other hand, emphasis on physical actions might even bring forth the evolvement of professional physical gaming as competitive sport of the future, for example 'PacMan International League'.

Element of social gaming in Human PacMan symbolizes the nas-cence of humanity in future digital entertainment. People are looking forward to widening their circle of friends and colleagues through social collaboration in game play. A new form of interactive entertainment is evolved.

Another important area of impact is the field of education. The technology presented in Human PacMan can be exported to applications in educational training that stresses on "learn by experience". Students are immersed in real site of action, and are given instructions visually through head mounted display or verbally through speaker\earphone. This technology serves as a powerful instrument of cognition since it can enhance both experimenting and reflective thoughts through mixed reality and interactive experience.

In conclusion, we believe Human PacMan is a pioneer in the new hybrid of physical, social, and mobile gaming that is built on ubiquitous computing and networking technology. The players are able to experience seamless transition between real and virtual world and therefore a higher than ever level of sensory gratification are obtained.

References

[1] Myers, D.: Computer game semiotics, Play and Culture. 1991, 4, 334–345.

[2] Weiser, M.: The computer for the 21st century. Scientific American 1991, 265(3), 94–100.

[3] Interactive Digital Software Association: State of the Industry - Report 2000-2001. [online document] 2001, Available at http://www.idsa.com.

[4] Interactive Digital Software Association: Essential Facts About the Computer and Video Game Industry. [online document] 2002, Available at http://www.idsa.com.

[5] Crawford, C.: Live: What a Concept!àNetworked Games. Digital Illusion, Dodsworth, C. Jr, ACM Press, 241–248.

[6] Björk, S., Falk, J., Hansson, R.,and Ljungstrand, P.: Pirates! - Using the physical world as a game board. Interact 2001, IFIP TC. 13 Conference on Human-Computer Interaction, Tokyo, Japan 2001.

[7] Mandryk, R. L.,and Inkpen, K. M.: Supporting free play in ubiquitous computer games. Workshop on Designing Ubiquitous Computer Games, UbiComp 2001, Atlanta, GA 2001.

[8] Oshima, T., Satoh, K., Yamamoto, H.,and Tamura, H.: AR2 Hockey system: A collaboration mixed reality system. Trans VRSJ 1998; 3(2); 55–60.

[9] Tamura, H., Yamamoto, H.,and Katayama, A.: Mixed Reality: Future Dreams Seen at the Border between Real and Virtual Worlds. Computer Graphics and Applications, vol. 21, no. 6 pp. 64–70, 2001.

[10] Thomas, B., Close, B., Donoghue, J., Squires, J., Bondi, P. D.,and Piekarski, W.: First Person Indoor\Outdoor Augmented Reality Application: ARQuake. Personal and Ubiquitous Computing, vol. 6, no. 1, pp 75–86, 2002.

[11] Milgram, P.,and Kishino, F.: A Taxanomy of Mixed Reality Visual Displays. IECE Trans on Information and Systems (Special Issue on Networked Reality), vol E77-D, no. 12, 1321–1329, 1994.

[12] Billinghurst, M., Campbell, S., Hendrickson, D., Chinthammit, W., Poupyrev, I., Takahashi, K.,and Kato, H.: Magic Book: Exploring Transitions in Collaborative AR Interfaces. SIGGRAPH 2000, 2000.

[13] Cheok, A. D., Yang, X., Zhou, Z. Y., Billinghurst, M.,and Kato, H.: Touch-Space: Mixed Reality Game Space Based on Ubiquitous, Tangible, and Social Computing. Personal and Ubiquitous Computing, vol. 6, no. 2, 430–442, 2002.

[14] InterSense Inc: Inertia Cube2 Bringing 3D To Life - Manual for Serial Port Model, 2001.

[15] Point Grey Research Corporation, http://www.ptgrey.com.

[16] Quantum Research Group Ltd, [online document] 2002. Available at http://www.qprox.com.

[17] Duchamp, D., Steven, K. F., and Gerald Jr. Q. M., "Software Technology for Wireless Mobile Computing", IEEE Network Magazine, 12-18, Nov 1991.

[18] Weiser, M.: Some computer science issues in ubiquitous computing. Communications of ACM, 36, 7: Special issue on computer augmented environments: back to the real world.

[19] Computer Augmented Environments: Back to the Real World. Communications of the ACM, July 1993, 36, 7.

[20] Smith, C. G.: The Hand That Rocks the Cradle. I. D., May/June 1995, 60–65.

[21] Fitzmaurice, G., et al.: Bricks: Laying the Foundations for Graspable User Interfaces. Proceedings of the Conference on Human Factors in Computing Systems (CHI '95), ACM, Denver, May 1995, 442–449.

[22] Ishii, H.,and Ullmer, B.: Tangible Bits: Towards Seamless Interfaces between People, Bits, and Atoms. Proceedings of the Conference on Human Factors in Computing Systems (CHI '97), March 22-27, 1997.

[23] Want, R., Hopper, A., Falco, V.,and Gibbons, J.: The Active Badge location system. ACM Transactions on Information Systems, 10(1):91–102, January 1992.

[24] Schilit, B. N., Theimer, M. M.,and Welch, B. B.: Customizing mobile applications. In Proceedings of USENIX Mobile & Location-Independent Computing Symposium, Cambridge, Massachusetts, August 1993. USENIX Association, 129–138.

[25] Long, S., et al: Rapid Prototyping of Mobile Context-aware Applications: The Cyberguide Case Study. 2nd ACM International Conference on Mobile Computing and Networking (MobiCom'96) 1996 November 10-12, 1996.

[26] Ryan, N., Pascoe, J.,and Morse, D.: Enhanced Reality Fieldwork: the Context-Aware Archaeological Assistant. Gaffney, V., Van Leusen, M., Exxon, S., Eds. Computer Applications in Archaeology. http://www.cs.ukc.ac.uk/pubs/1998/616/content.html.

[27] Pascoe, J., Ryan, N. S.,and Morse, D. R.: Human Computer Giraffe Interaction - HCI in the Field. Workshop on Human Computer Interaction with Mobile Devices. http://www.dcs.gla.ac.uk/ johnson/papers/mobile/HCIMD1.html.

[28] Pascoe, J., Ryan, N. S.,and Morse, D. R.: Issues in Developing Context-Aware Computing. Proceedings of the International Symposium on Handheld and Ubiquitous Computing, Karlsruhe, Germany, September 1999, Springer-Verlag, 208–221.

[29] Yang, J., Yang, W., Denecke, M.,and Waibel, A.: Smart sight: a tourist assistant system. 3rd International Symposium on Wearable Computers, San Francisco, California, 18-19 October, 1999, 73–78.

[30] Bellotti, V. M. E., Back, M. J., Edwards, W. K., Grinter, R. E., Lopes, C. V.,and Henderson, A.: Making sense of sensing systems: Five questions for designers and researchers. Proc. CHI 2002, 415–422. ACM.

[31] Norman, D. A.: The Design of Everyday Things. Doubleday: New York, New York.

OpenTrek: A Platform for Developing Interactive Networked Games on Mobile Devices

Johan Sanneblad and Lars Erik Holmquist

Future Applications Lab, Viktoria Institute
Box 620, SE-405 30 Göteborg, Sweden
{johans,leh}@viktoria.se
www.viktoria.se/fal

Abstract. Programming interactive networking applications for mobile devices is currently a laborious process, due to the lack of standardized development support. We introduce a new software platform, *OpenTrek,* primarily intended to assist the development of multiplayer networked games on Pocket PC devices. OpenTrek is similar to game development environments on stationary PCs, such as DirectX, but is fully optimized to work with mobile devices. It is a freely downloadable package with a fast learning curve, which includes support for ad hoc networking and efficient graphics. We successfully deployed OpenTrek in a course at a local university. 28 students with no previous experience in Pocket PC programming were able to create 12 different advanced multiplayer networked games in only five weeks (which included introduction to the platform). By easing the development of advanced interactive applications on Pocket PC, OpenTrek can lower the hurdle for researchers who wish to prototype and test novel user interfaces for mobile devices.

1   Introduction

In many ways, *games* are at the forefront of mobile HCI. A successful game must provide instant and intuitive interaction to novice users, while at the same time pushing the latest mobile technology to its limits. Previously, mobile gaming has primarily been the domain of specialized devices, such as Nintendo's *Gameboy.* Although most mobile phones also have a few built-in games, these have been fairly primitive. Recently, however, the capabilities of handheld computers and mobile phones have been increasing. A typical Pocket PC such as the *Toshiba e330* has a screen with 64.000 colors and a resolution of 240 x 320 pixels, a processor running at 300 megahertz, and built-in wireless networking. The *Nokia N-Gage* mobile phone is specifically developed to run games, and includes a 4096 color display with a resolution of 176 x 208 pixels, a 104 MHz ARM processor, plus Bluetooth and Java support. With devices such as these in the pockets of general consumers, we are likely to see an increase in full-color, networked interactive applications – many of which will be games.

L. Chittaro (Ed.): Mobile HCI 2003, LNCS 2795, pp. 224-240, 2003.

Fig. 1. *Spaceball* is one of 12 interactive networked multi-player games created by students using the OpenTrek platform

But in our opinion, faster processors and colorful graphics is only part of what will make the future of mobile applications so interesting. What makes the next generation of mobile gaming devices different, be they Pocket PC, mobile phones or something else, is the inherent support for wireless networking. This will come in the form of the new generation of mobile phone networks, such as GPRS (2.5G) and broadband (3G) nets. It will also come in the form of wireless local-area networks such as Wi-Fi, and personal-area networks such as Bluetooth. All of these networking capabilities open up new possibilities for interactive entertainment and collaboration, which so far remain mostly untapped. The only gaming device that is currently designed primarily with wireless networking games in mind is the *Cybiko* [4] but more are certain to follow as the technology matures.

However, the initial hurdle that needs to be overcome to develop applications for mobile devices is currently much greater than the equivalent for desktop computer. There are several game middleware platforms that support Windows PCs, such as DirectX [6], SDL [11] and ClanLib [3]. These platforms offer a standardized way of accessing advanced hardware features, such as graphics acceleration; they also provide a level of abstraction that makes the development of networking functions much easier. Although they are primarily intended for commercial development they have successfully been used in research projects, for instance to develop virtual reality applications [2] and videoconference systems [8]. But whereas for instance Microsoft's Pocket PC platform has become a widespread standard for handheld computing systems, there is yet no equivalent development support for such devices.

We have developed *OpenTrek,* a software platform for mobile devices, in particular those based on the Pocket PC standard. It includes middleware layers that aid in the development of interactive graphics and ad hoc networking, and a set of helper applications and APIs to ease development. The platform was designed primarily for prototyping multiplayer networked games, but can equally well be used for other demanding interactive applications. The design of OpenTrek was based on a game middleware platform for stationary computers, which will make it possible to transfer existing interfaces and prototypes from stationary to mobile devices.

In the following we will first briefly discuss some problems in designing software for mobile devices, after which the OpenTrek platform and its components will be described in depth. Following this we account our experience of the first practical deployment of OpenTrek during a university course, and exemplify with two games developed by students. Finally we conclude and discuss some future work.

2   The Need for a Development Platform for Mobile Devices

Handheld computers and mobile phones provide many new challenges for application developers and interface designers. A handheld computer is not simply a scaled-down desktop PC. Input methods differ radically, and interaction techniques that work well with a mouse and a keyboard may very well be completely inappropriate for the capabilities provided on a handheld. The usage situation differs too: whereas developers can count on desktop users to be in a situation where they can give the application more or less their undivided attention, mobile users may be walking, riding the bus, or engaging in social interaction while using an application. Thus it is extremely important to develop and test mobile HCI techniques on *actual mobile devices,* rather than running them in a simulated environment on a desktop workstation, or evaluating them in limited lab settings. This puts a high demand on researchers to make their applications run as efficiently as possible on mobile devices, to be able to correctly evaluate new applications and interaction concepts.

Whereas standardization has made it possible to run the same graphics-intensive code with virtually no performance loss across desktop computers from a wide range of manufacturers, this is not yet the case for handheld computer. Although Microsoft's Pocket PC standard is widely accepted, hardware details vary extensively between manufacturers. In particular, the way in which graphics is stored in memory can be quite different – a Casio Pocket PC does not use the same internal representation as for instance an IPAQ. If a developer wants to access the display on a Pocket PC without using middleware it is necessary to write directly to a specific memory area. But since displays are represented differently in memory on different devices, this makes it necessary to write several versions of the code to update the display efficiently on different devices.

On stationary computers, applications typically send messages over the network using insecure UDP packets. To move such an application to a Pocket PC device without using middleware would in practice require a complete re-design of its network communications. This is because of the limited network resources on mobile devices, where the incoming network buffer by default is only capable of storing a single large network packet at a time. Unlike stationary computers, the size of the incoming packet buffer cannot be changed. A networked application targeting Pocket PCs must therefore include at least a multithreaded incoming queue system, to avoid incoming network sockets from being recycled by the network interface. Other networking features such as service discovery, guaranteed transfer of messages, message priorities and automatic multicast are standard on game middleware platforms for stationary computers but are not available for mobile devices. To provide the same functionality for a mobile device, the developer would not only have to design protocols to support these features, but must also design a software architecture to integrate the networking features with the rest of the application.

3   OpenTrek

In our previous work we created several networked applications for handheld computers, where issues like those mentioned above had to be considered in every new project (such as ProxyLady [5] and Fieldwise [7]). What eventually became OpenTrek began as several thin class libraries created for these applications, targeting graphics, network connections and network communications. Using these class libraries required extensive knowledge, and preliminary feedback from students who used them was that the learning threshold was considered too high for use in most time-limited academic settings (such as courses and thesis work). Thus, work begun on an integrated solution, a platform based on the class libraries we had created but with a much shorter learning time.

OpenTrek is the common name for our collection of helper applications, class libraries, and run-time modules to aid in the creation of networked games for handheld computers. The platform is "open" in that it is modularized, enabling developers to add, change or remove features from the platform while it is running. The name OpenTrek originated in the project where the platform was first used, in which students used their handheld computers to "Trek" different physical areas using ad hoc network connections.

Choosing a hardware platform for OpenTrek, our requirement was that the handheld computer should support Wireless LAN for network communication. When work begun on OpenTrek, the only handheld computer platform capable of WLAN communication was the Pocket PC platform by Microsoft. Choosing the Pocket PC platform also meant that a version of OpenTrek for stationary computers could be developed in parallel using the same code base. The stationary version supports high resolution and hardware accelerated graphics and can be used for development and demonstrational purposes.

We will now describe the OpenTrek platform and motivate its design, illustrate its components and highlight how OpenTrek supports the creation of networked games and other applications for mobile devices.

3.1   Platform

The most widespread platform for creating networked games on stationary computers is the Microsoft DirectX platform [6]. The DirectX platform is a collection of thin class libraries, targeting graphics, sound, input, and network communication. The DirectX platform is similar to the class libraries we created in our previous projects, but requires extensive knowledge to use. When developing the OpenTrek platform, it was designed to be as similar to the graphics and network class libraries of DirectX as possible, so that students familiar with OpenTrek also would feel proficient with the DirectX platform, and vice versa. Helper applications and "wrapper classes" that simplify the use of the class libraries in OpenTrek make it easier to use and improves the learning time for new users.

Microsoft has recently ported part of their DirectX platform (DirectPlay for network communication) to handheld computers. Since it is similar to the version for stationary computers, it still requires a significant learning time and experience to use in actual projects. This makes it unsuitable for student work in academic settings.

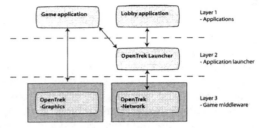

Fig. 2. The OpenTrek platform

Fig. 3. A typical Lobby application, showing online users and their activities

The OpenTrek platform is shown in Figure 2 above. Hardware access is controlled with a graphics and networking middleware, and applications created using the platform can take advantage of several thin class libraries and "wrapper classes". An OpenTrek application can itself not be started separately, but has to be initiated by a helper application called the *OpenTrek Launcher*. The OpenTrek Launcher can start several applications in parallel on the same handheld device, all of which may use the same graphics and networking middleware. The OpenTrek Launcher monitors the performance of each application so that the applications can cooperate using the same limited amount of graphics and networking hardware. The OpenTrek launcher has by itself no user interface. The user interface is started from the OpenTrek Launcher as an application called a *Lobby*, enabling the end user to customize its use and function. A typical function of a Lobby is to show what users have their devices switched on and what their activities are, as seen in Figure 3.

3.2   Using OpenTrek

There are already many software platforms assisting with the development of networked games (such as DirectX [6], SDL [11] and ClanLib [3]). OpenTrek differs from these in that it provides a combination of high abstraction "wrapper classes" and helper applications that are specifically designed for networked games development for handheld devices. Both the wrapper classes and helper applications simplify the development process and shorten learning time. We will now describe the development process for a minimal whiteboard application to highlight how OpenTrek can be used in practice.

Fig. 4. The BlueBoard application

The BlueBoard Application. BlueBoard (as seen in Figure 4) is a simple whiteboard application that captures stylus strokes on a handheld computer and sends them to other devices on the same network. People should be able to initiate, join and leave whiteboard sessions at any time. Multiple whiteboard sessions should be able to run on the same network. BlueBoard should support ad hoc networking, so that it can be used in places where no Wireless LAN infrastructure is available.

The BlueBoard Implementation. There are three steps involved in creating BlueBoard. First an application wrapper class is used to create a new application shell. The wrapper class is then extended to handle coordinates received from the stylus input, and to pass them on to the OpenTrek Launcher as messages to be sent over the network. Finally the wrapper class is extended to handle coordinates received from other users over the network and draw them on the display.

Many of the features in BlueBoard are provided by the OpenTrek helper applications. The OpenTrek Lobby application provides a way for people to initiate, join and leave sessions such as whiteboard and game sessions on the current network. The networking middleware of OpenTrek includes support for ad hoc networks. The graphics middleware provides a toolkit to draw double-buffered brush strokes on the display.

The application wrapper class in OpenTrek encapsulates device dependent logic such as messaging events, stylus input and button presses. It also contains logic for linking the application and the OpenTrek Launcher together. This link enables the OpenTrek Launcher to start and close applications as needed. One such example is when a person uses a Lobby to start a new BlueBoard session (as seen in Figure 5): the OpenTrek Launcher automatically starts BlueBoard on all devices simultaneously.

Fig. 5. Using a Lobby to start the BlueBoard application

The BlueBoard application starts out as a subclass to the application wrapper class. Extending the application wrapper class, code has to be added so that coordinates received from stylus input are encapsulated as coordinate objects inside network message objects. The network message object has fields such as ID, destination user, delivery mode, and timeout. Leaving the destination user field empty sends the message to all current users in the session. Code has to be added to pass the coordinate network messages to the OpenTrek Launcher, which places them in an outgoing network queue for immediate delivery. The code necessary to capture stylus coordinates and send them to all other users in the same session is listed below. Coordinate objects and network message objects are all a part of the OpenTrek class library, which is Open Source.

The program code to send stylus coordinates to all other users in the same session

```
HRESULT CMyApplication::OnStylusMove(POINT p)
{
 CDataPoint point(p);      // Create a coordinate object
 CDataMessage msg(MSGID_COORD);// Create message object
 msg.SetData(point);           // Store the coordinate
 m_pLauncher->SendMessage(msg); // Send the message
 return S_OK;
}
```

Again extending the wrapper class, the BlueBoard application is notified when messages arrive from other users (via the OpenTrek Launcher), and extract the coordinate objects contained within them. Using a list of previous coordinates received from each user, a line is drawn on the display. The code required to store the incoming coordinates received over the network is shown below.

The program code to receive coordinates from other devices in the same session and store them in a list

```
void CMyApplication::OnMessageReceived(const
CDataMessage& message)
{
 switch (message.GetID())  // The ID is set when the
 {                         // network message object is
 case MSGID_COORD:         // created
   {
    CDataPoint point;         // Create empty coordinate
    message.GetData(point); // Retrieve values
    m_incomingcoordlist.AddTail(point); // Store in list
   }
   break;
 }
}
```

The application wrapper class contains a display thread that is called several times each second, in which the lines are drawn to the display.

3.3   OpenTrek Helper Applications

In the following we will describe the two helper applications that are part of the OpenTrek platform: *OpenTrek Launcher* and *OpenTrek Lobby*.

OpenTrek Launcher. The OpenTrek Launcher is used to start applications built on the OpenTrek platform. Internally, the OpenTrek Launcher is the runtime engine that connects OpenTrek applications with the graphics and network middleware. The OpenTrek Launcher operates as a message router, to which modules can be added dynamically while it is running. Examples of modules that can be added are Lobby applications that provide a user interface, and network modules that provide support for application sessions running on the local network.

All network communication for OpenTrek applications pass through the Launcher. The rationale for this is to allow seamless communication across multiple network interfaces (such as Bluetooth and Wireless LAN), and also to provide transparent session initiation and session management for ad hoc networks (the OpenTrek Launcher is responsible for creating a session on the network when needed). The layered approach makes it possible to send network messages to a specific application instead of a device, enabling multiple applications to run in parallel on the same device and network interface.

Another reason for using the launcher is that software running on a typical handheld computer never closes. When a Pocket PC device is "shut off", it is actually frozen in its current state, and applications continue running as normal when the device is switched on. The feature where modules such as applications can be linked to the OpenTrek Launcher while it is running was required, since the user otherwise would sometimes be forced to reset the entire state of the device, shutting down all programs.

OpenTrek Lobby. An OpenTrek Lobby is an application whose primary purpose is to enable users to initiate, join and leave application sessions on the local network. A Lobby application contains the interface that is presented to the user when the OpenTrek Launcher is started, showing what people have their devices switched on and what they are doing. The user can switch between different Lobby applications, and it is also possible for a Lobby application to start other Lobby applications locally.

Lobbies are used in most networked computer games, and are typically located on a remote computer and accessed over the Internet (e.g. DirectPlay [6]). In OpenTrek, each network interface module is responsible for automatically joining and managing a "lobby" for the user. If the OpenTrek Launcher is run on an ad hoc network, all devices physically located nearby automatically join the lobby. If the OpenTrek Launcher is run using a module for mobile phones, lobbies are stored on specific devices running as servers (similar to "chat rooms").

3.4   OpenTrek Middleware

The OpenTrek platform comprises two middleware components: networking and graphics.

OpenTrek Network. The OpenTrek Launcher has an Application Programming Interface (API) to which it is possible to plug in network modules. The API defines commands and requests sent by the OpenTrek Launcher to the network module, and callback operations that the network module can use to notify or request information from the Launcher. Examples of commands sent from the OpenTrek Launcher to the network module include: *go online; get a list of online users; get a list of running sessions; create session; join session;* and *send message.*

The interface for the network modules was designed so that it would suit most types of network hardware, from infrared connections, to server-based connections over mobile phone connections, to ad hoc wireless network connections over WLAN. To test the interface specification in practice we implemented network modules for infrared, mobile phone and WLAN networks. The features that should be implemented by the networking module were defined by compiling a feature list from the Microsoft DirectPlay documentation [6]. Some of these features are: reliable and unreliable delivery of messages, sequential and non-sequential delivery of messages, automatic multicast delivery if applicable, automatic message fragmentation and reassembly, congestion control, and message timeouts using multiple outgoing queues.

Peer-to-peer. OpenTrek network modules are strictly peer-to-peer, meaning that there is no central host controlling the sessions on the network. Each network module is responsible for sending out online status information to all other devices, and to collect information on other devices and report back to the OpenTrek Launcher. The network module in OpenTrek that supports mobile phone connections sends and retrieves online status information from a central device that has been configured as server, and can be placed anywhere on the network. The approach where no specific device is used as a host enables ad hoc networking, where people can join and leave network sessions immediately as the device is switched on and off.

Server Mode. The OpenTrek Launcher can be configured to run as a "server". This does not alter the functionality of the launcher, but it may change the functionality of the modules plugged into it. If for example a networking module designed for mobile network connections is running in server mode, it will change mode from send and retrieve information about online status to collect and distribute. Examples of OpenTrek applications using server mode are file servers, where the application changes from downloading files to distributing files to users in the proximity. A Lobby application running in server mode might be used to start an advertisement application on a user's device as soon as the person comes within the proximity of the server node. The server mode of the launcher is typically used on devices with no user input, such as service-providing nodes in proximity-based and context aware service networks.

Session Initiation. The network modules in OpenTrek do not assign a host for each session. However, in some situations applications created on the OpenTrek platform need to assign one of the devices in the session as a controller, deciding who should be able to join the session and when. This controlling device could also be used to generate data that should be available before the session is initiated (such as map data for a game).

The OpenTrek Launcher initiates sessions on the network by starting the application on the first two devices synchronously, where the rest are allowed to join asynchronously. Applications can check during startup how many users are already participating in the session, meaning that one device will have only one user in the session (the local user) and another device will have two users. The motivation for starting the first two devices synchronously is so that one device can be assigned as a backup host, in case the primary host should choose to leave the session. The Session Initiation Protocol used by the OpenTrek Launcher can be seen in Figure 6.

Network Protocol. Networking modules in OpenTrek use the built-in IP stack for communication. Messages are sent as UDP packets, enabling multicast when used on local networks. Multicast improves performance scaling when the number of users joining a session increases. Networked games often send time-critical redundant data repeatedly, using UDP guarantees that the network hardware will not try to resend packages lost due to high packet-loss wireless networks.

One of the features in the network modules is the ability to send guaranteed messages. Guaranteed messages are sent using the Trivial File Transfer Protocol [13], TFTP. Messages are sent as small packets that are each acknowledged by the receiver. OpenTrek implements TFTP extensions such as the TFTP Blocksize option [12], to enable a variable packet size based on measured packet loss.

Information about online status is broadcast continuously in the current network Lobby as a small UDP packet. The online status information comprises information such as user id, device id, what sessions the user participates in, and the ID of every application participating in each session.

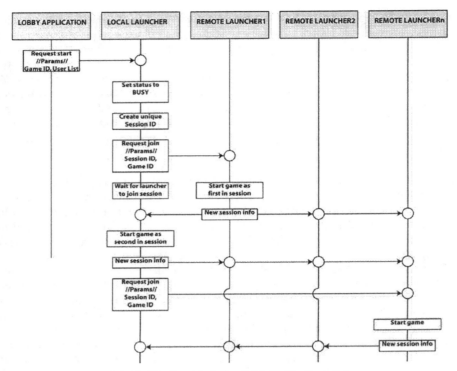

Fig. 6. The OpenTrek Session Initiation Protocol

Fig. 7. *Pocket EverQuest* by Sony Online Entertainment was created using our graphics middleware *GapiDraw*

OpenTrek Graphics. The graphics middleware in OpenTrek is a toolkit we have created for fast graphics on handheld computers, called *GapiDraw*. GapiDraw is not accessed through the OpenTrek Launcher, but is called directly by the OpenTrek applications using a class library. The OpenTrek Launcher is however responsible for starting the middleware and sharing it to the applications. The OpenTrek Launcher also determines when a specific application can draw to the display, in case several applications are started in parallel.

The interface to using GapiDraw is nearly identical to using DirectDraw in the Microsoft DirectX platform. The motivation for creating GapiDraw came from the lack of available platforms to create fast graphics on handheld devices. Commonly available platforms for stationary computers such as DirectX [6], SDL [11] and ClanLib [3] are not optimized for and will not work on handheld computers. Handheld computer platforms such as Overloaded [9] and PocketFrog [10] have all been abandoned by their authors and are no longer being supported or updated. As of current, the only graphics toolkit available for Pocket PCs still being maintained, updated and supported is our GapiDraw toolkit.

GapiDraw has been separately released on the Internet and input from game development companies have resulted in a feature set comprising most 2D operations necessary for games development. Some of these features are alpha blends, rotation, zoom, bitmapped fonts, collision masks and sprite intersections. An example of a GapiDraw game, *Pocket Everquest,* is shown in Figure 7.

4   Implementation

The OpenTrek platform is implemented in C++ and runs on Pocket PCs and stationary computers. For a Pocket PC device to use the OpenTrek platform it must be equipped with a network interface, such as Wireless LAN or GPRS. An internal test version of OpenTrek for the Symbian operating system was created to verify that the class libraries and APIs would work on devices other than the Pocket PC.

Applications created for the OpenTrek platform will automatically run on both Pocket PCs and stationary PCs, simply by recompiling them for the correct system. When OpenTrek runs on a stationary computer, the built-in video card will accelerate all graphics operations. Video hardware acceleration enables high-resolution stationary applications that communicate with their Pocket PC counterparts.

The modular design of the platform has made it possible for third party developers to expand the platform with additional features. Extensions currently available are 3D graphics, streaming video and sound support. All of these extensions build on our middleware and extends it with new functionality.

OpenTrek has been tested to run on stationary operating systems such as Windows 95/98/ME/2000/XP and most 12-bit and 16-bit color Pocket PCs.

5   Experience: OpenTrek in Education

OpenTrek was developed to allow rapid prototyping of interactive networked applications on handheld computers, primarily games. An important requirement of the platform was that it should be so easy to use that even developers with little or no experience could quickly get up to speed and develop new applications. In particular, we intended OpenTrek to be used in an educational setting.

The first practical use of the OpenTrek platform was in a course at the local university, attended by 28 students. The students were at the graduate level, with approximately three years of studies in computer science or equivalent. Each student was equipped with all the necessary development tools for targeting both stationary computers and handheld devices, including a personal laptop and a WLAN-equipped Pocket PC (Compaq IPAQ H3630). The goal with the course was to develop a game from scratch in five weeks.

All students had at least two weeks of C++ programming experience, but none had previous experience of game development. The first week of the course we introduced the students to the OpenTrek platform. We also taught the students some fundamental principles in game development, and supplied them with various design patterns suitable for real time networked games development. After the initial week, the students were divided into 12 groups, ranging from 1-3 people. The groups were then allowed an additional four weeks to develop their games.

The major requirement to pass on the course was to produce a fully working multiplayer networked game within the time given for the course. The game should be responsive in real-time, fully interactive and preferably multithreaded. To pass with distinction, the game should use advanced visually responsive graphics. Ideally, the game should also define some new and innovative uses of mobile ad hoc networks for gaming.

After the four weeks were up, each group was required to present not only their game concept and design, but also demonstrate their game live using two or more actual handheld devices. At this time, all students sent us the latest version of their source code so we could perform a thorough code review to search for problems and provide feedback for improvements.

5.1   The Games

All of the student groups managed to develop and demonstrate a fully working game during the five-week course. The twelve games ranged from simple card games to advanced real time action games. Eight of the game used what we would term visually responsive graphics, i.e. they were full-fledged arcade-style action games. Two of the games supported more than two players.

Several groups introduced innovative ways to use networking to support new types of games. For instance, one group created a form of meta-game where players would move between different "islands" where they could buy and sell various items, that could then be used in other games. Each island was in fact a Pocket PC, and the size of the island was defined by the range of the devices' wireless network range. In other words, to be able to trade with an island, the player would have to be within physical range of it, or rather the device which represented it. This is a way of promoting players to move around and socialize, much in the way of context-aware social game s like *Pirates!* [1].

In the following we will highlight two of the more advanced games. More information about all games developed during the course can be found at:

http://www.cafetrek.com/

Fig. 8. *TrekFighter*, a variation of the classic game *Snake*, supporting up to four players playing over a wireless network

TrekFighter. *TrekFighter* (Figure 8) is an updated version of the classic multiplayer game *Snake,* often found in mobile phones (e.g. Nokia 6110). In the game each player controls a small figure on the display – the "snake". The player must take charge of his or her snake so that it does not run into the wall or into another player – or it's own tail! During the course of the game, the length of the snake increases, making it more and more difficult to maneuver. The winner of the game is the player who is the last to run into a wall or the tail of the other persons snake.

The students' game is a significant advance on the traditional version. It supports up to four players over the network; when the game starts, the players' snakes are distributed over the corners of the playing area. The students added many features such as "pick up bonuses" that give the ships a speed-up or slow them down. The application even supports game maps that are larger than the actual display area; the graphics will scroll smoothly to focus on the player's own snake. An external artist was called in to design the game's graphics.

The network communication was implemented using unreliable peer-to-peer model. The first device to start a session is automatically assigned server status, whereas the second device is assigned as a backup server. All devices in a game session continuously send their ship coordinates and ship rotations to the server device. This device in turn continuously broadcasts all ship coordinates using automatic multicast to all the other devices in the current session. This model does lead to some problems, since if the server device leaves the game, all clients will be forced to leave the game as well.

TetTrek. *TetTrek* (Figure 9) is based on the classic game *Tetris,* where the player controls falling bricks. If the bricks can form a solid horizontal line, that line is removed from the screen. The goal is to keep playing for as long time as possible, and points are awarded as lines are removed. This multi-player version of Tetris allows two opponents to play over the wireless network. Each player can see both his or her own map and that of the opponent.

Fig. 9. *TetTrek* is a two-player networking version of Tetris

The students added some additional features to spice up the game. In particular, "bombs" can be earned by successfully clearing rows of bricks in a certain pattern. These can then be set off on the opponents map to cause various types of mischief, such as creating walls, adding bricks, etc. All graphics for the game was developed by the students themselves. The network communication in TetTrek is based on a model with guaranteed message transfers. The local game area is continuously sent to the other device in the current session. Other commands, such as bomb transfers, are also sent in a secure way.

6   Conclusions and Future Work

We have presented OpenTrek, a software platform that allows developers with little or no previous experience of software development for handheld computers to quickly create advanced interactive networked applications. Based on the results from the use of OpenTrek in an educational setting, we argue that the platform provides an efficient way to quickly develop new games as well as other interactive applications. By giving developers and researchers the ability to make efficient interactive prototypes that can be run on a variety of Pocket PC devices, OpenTrek makes development and testing of mobile interfaces much easier. This means that it can be an important contribution towards enhancing the usability of mobile applications.

Future work involves adapting the OpenTrek platform to work on mobile phones. Mobile phones introduce use situations that differ from handheld computers, situations that can be explored with the help of new OpenTrek applications. Work is also planned to create interfaces to programming languages other than C++. For example using a managed wrapper for the Microsoft .NET platform, OpenTrek applications can be created with programming languages such as Visual Basic, C# and Java.

7   Download

The OpenTrek platform can be downloaded freely from the web using the following URL:

http://www.opentrek.com/

GrapiDraw, the graphics component of OpenTrek, can be downloaded from:

http://www.gapidraw.com/

Acknowledgements

This research was funded by the Swedish Research Institute for Information Technology (SITI), and the Mobile Services project financed by the Foundation for Strategic Research (SSF). Special thanks go to all our students who worked very hard to create some amazing games!

References

[1]   Björk, S., Falk, J., Hansson, R., Ljungstrand, P.: Pirates! - Using the Physical World as a Game Board, Proc. Interact 2001, IFIP TC.13 Conference on Human-Computer Interaction, July 9-13, Tokyo, Japan.

[2]   Chiang, C.C., Huang, A., Wang, T.S., Huang, M., Chen, Y.Y., Hsieh, J.W., Chen, J.W., Cheng, T.: PanoVR SDK—a software development kit for integrating photo-realistic panoramic images and 3-D graphical objects into virtual worlds," In Proceedings of the ACM symposium on Virtual reality software and technology, 1997, Lausanne, Switzerland, pp. 147–154.

[3]   ClanLib, http:// http://www.clanlib.org/ Last visited Feb. 18, 2003

[4]   Cybiko, http://www.cybiko.com/ Last visited Feb. 18, 2003

[5]   Dahlberg, P., Ljungberg, F., Sanneblad, J.: Proxy Lady: Mobile Support for Opportunistic Interaction, Scandinavian Journal of Information Systems volume 14, 2002, Gothenburg, Sweden.

[6]   Fagrell, H, Forsberg, K., Sanneblad, J.: FieldWise: A Mobile Knowledge Management Architecture, In Proceedings of the 2000 ACM conference on Computer supported cooperative work, 2000, Philadelphia, Pennsylvania, United States, pp 211-220.

[7]   DirectX, http://www.microsoft.com/directx/ Last visited Feb. 18, 2003

[8]   Lin, C.S.: On design of network scheduling in parallel video-on-demand systems, In Proceedings of the seventh ACM international conference on Multimedia, 1999, Orlando, Florida, United States, pp 211-212.

[9]   Overloaded, http://overloaded.pocketmatrix.com/ Last visited Feb. 18, 2003

[10]   PocketFrog, http://pocketfrog.droneship.com/ Last visited Feb. 18, 2003

[11]   The Simple DirectMedia Layer (SDL), http://www.libsdl.org Last visited Feb. 18, 2003

[12] The TFTP Blocksize Option, http://www.faqs.org/rfcs/rfc2348.html Last visited Feb. 18, 2003
[13] The TFTP Protocol, http://www.faqs.org/rfcs/std/std33.html Last visited Feb. 18, 2003

Supporting Efficient Design of Mobile HCI

Francesco Bellotti, Riccardo Berta, Alessandro De Gloria,
and Massimiliano Margarone

DIBE – Department of Electronics and Biophysical Engineering,
University of Genoa
Via Opera Pia 11/a, 16145 Genova Italy
Tel: +39-010-3532780, Fax: +39-010-3532795
{franz,berta,adg,marga}@dibe.unige.it
http://www.elios.dibe.unige.it

Abstract. Recent advances in mobile computing and communication technologies have spurred nomadic use of computers. In order to support HCI design for new mobile services, we have developed the MADE (Mobile Applications Development Environment) software development kit. MADE includes M^{3}P (MicroMultiMedia Player), a network-enabled multimedia player easily programmable through the Micromultimedia Services Language (MSL). MSL provides high-level components encapsulating advanced services (e.g. positioning, database query, path search, games, etc.), that can be easily integrated in multimedia presentations. This allows building modular applications that provide information-rich services to the general public through a coherent and homogeneous multimedia HCI, that can be learned with low mental workload. On the other hand, MADE hides the low-level aspects of multimedia and service management, allowing designers to focus on the modalities of presentation of information and on user interaction. The paper describes MADE and briefly sketches some tour guide applications we developed using the tool.

1   Introduction

Recent advances in mobile communications and computing technologies are spurring the diffusion of network-enabled nomadic devices providing information and entertainment services for mobile users. This will let a great computing power always available to millions of people in their daily life activities. But a full exploitation of such a potential, which can offer location-aware services, positioning, e-ticketing, etc., requires study and implementation of Human-Computer Interaction (HCI) modalities that support usability of the new mobile tools by the general public. Putting it in Johnson's words: "The case remains that functionality does not exist for the user if that functionality is not usable" [1]. This aspect is particularly critical for mobile devices featuring limited hardware resources of mobile devices (e.g. CPU speed,

L. Chittaro (Ed.): Mobile HCI 2003, LNCS 2795, pp. 241-255, 2003.
© Springer-Verlag Berlin Heidelberg 2003

battery life, screen size and memory availability) [2, 3]. Thus, new, ad-hoc solutions in HCI have to be found to guarantee usability of applications by the general public.

We have explored design and implementation of new mobile services in the context of the E-Tour, IST (Information Society Technologies) European project [4]. E-Tour is aimed at developing information-rich, multimedia guides on mobile devices for tourists. In particular, the focus is on edutainment, that is: providing cultural and tourist information and services in a pleasant and appealing fashion through high-quality interactive programs.

The contribution presented in this paper does not concern new HCI theories for mobile computing platforms. Rather, we present a new tool aimed at supporting efficient development of mobile tour guide applications. The tool has been designed to meet the requirements, coming from both end-users and tourist sites' management, captured in field-tests of early prototypes and from analysis of tourist information needs in environments such as museums, parks and urban and mountainous areas [4]. The E-Tour project adopted an user-centric design methodology, including participatory design [5], contextual design [6] and usability specifications [7], in order to support wide usability by the general public. This analysis highlighted in particular the need for integrating several different services, such as interactive maps, database querying, positioning and tour planning, within a single, highly usable interface.

We could not make extensive use of standard desktop HCI solutions to face these issues, since end-users, usage patterns, sensors and computational tools of our tourist applications are significantly different from the ones typical of the desktop-computing environment. Thus, it was very important for us to use dedicated tools supporting efficient exploration of HCI solutions. In particular, the user needs analysis revealed that usability of applications requires provision of advanced contents and functions through a pleasant multimedia interface.

While a lot of research work has been done in the single fields off multimedia presentations and advanced functions for mobile users [e.g. 3, 8, 9], little has been done concerning tools able to support integration of advanced functions in appealing multimedia interfaces usable by the general public. Our work aims at bridging this gap, developing a software development toolkit (namely: MADE, Mobile Applications Development Environment) that supports integration, at programming-language level.

MADE includes the Micromultimedia Services Language (MSL) and the MicroMultiMedia Player (M^3P). MSL provides components encapsulating advanced services and multimedia features, while M^3P manages communication among the objects, with the system, and with the user. Such language-level integration allows the developer to focus on a single development tool (MSL), which should reduce learning, development and maintenance time.

2   Related Work: Mobile Guides for Tourists

Design of electronic mobile guides for tourists is a well-explored research area in ubiquitous computing [10]. We briefly present here just two large projects in this area.

The GUIDE project at the University of Lancaster has explored issues concerning development and user acceptability of a mobile context-aware (especially location-aware) interactive assistant to city visitors. The project focuses on positioning technology and wireless communications [11], on generation of tours customized according to contextual triggers and user preferences [12] and on sharing of contextual information between members of groups of mobile users [13]. HCI aspects have been investigated in depth, for example in the implementation of a friendly approach to novice users [11] and of a wizard-based interface to enable users to specify constraints on the way their personal context is shared with other visitors [13]. The User Interface (UI) relies on HTML pages shown by a customized web-browser.

The Hewlett-Packard's CoolTown project has studied infrastructure and applications for ubiquitous systems in which people move about while using portable devices to access services and applications integrated in the physical world [14, 15]. The project has developed also an electronic mobile guidebook which has been tested at the Exploratorium Museum of San Francisco to support museum visitors with web resources [16]. The UI relies on Pocket Internet Explorer and on standard WinCE Graphical User Interface (GUI) components.

While a lot of work has been done to make these applications powerful from the functional point of view, their interfaces use standard GUI components, such as buttons and other controls, with the typical look-and-feel of the underlying operating system. These components are suitable for people familiar with computer systems, but may be awkward for the general public. For wide usability, it is important also to consider graphics interfaces that use elements immediately appealing to the public.

Our research is similar, but the approach slightly different. We do not use experimental sensing technology, which may not be suitable at present for usage by the general public [10]. Instead, we are more interested in improving the end-user's experience by providing high-quality multimedia customized UIs integrating various kinds of services (e.g. databases, games, automatic positioning).

3   Enhancing Efficiency in Development of Multimedia Mobile HCI

A crucial factor to developing interfaces usable by the general public is the possibility of using design tools that support HCI designers in their research for new interaction solutions [7]. MSL supports development of interactive multimedia programs able to integrate added-value services for mobile users. A typical MSL presentation consists of a set of pages (*CARD*s, in MSL terminology) containing multimedia and service objects. The MSL script specifies pages' layout and objects' appearance, synchronization and user-interaction modalities. MSL scripts are interpreted at runtime by an OO multimedia player, MicroMultiMedia Player (M^3P), that manages presentation of contents and user interaction according to the instructions specified in the input MSL script.

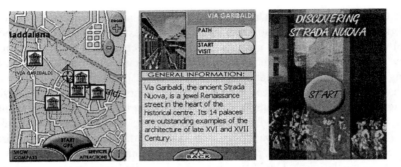

Fig. 1. Selecting a museum guide from the city-guide application (the tour guide for the Genoa's historical center)

Such a high-level, integrated approach to building multimedia and service-rich mobile applications provides significant advantages to end-users and developers.

Users benefit from interacting with a single HCI framework and from exploiting synergies between the integrated services. For instance, a tourist using a city-guide application featuring a GPS-enabled interactive map with layered information on commercial and leisure activities can select a museum area to enter the museum's multimedia guide (Fig. 1). These services are part of a single application, with a consistent and homogeneous HCI, to which the tourist can get accustomed in limited learning time. That is, the tourist does not have to acquaint to different programs' interfaces in order to access to different services.

On the other hand, developers can leverage a single and simple script language to implement highly usable applications. Using such a high-level tool allows designers to concentrate on the analysis of HCI methodologies, exploring several solutions, without caring for the low-level aspects of writing code for event handling and multimedia/service management. Moreover, MSL enhances design productivity by employing the O.O. technology, supporting code-reuse and program extensibility.

4 M^3P Architecture

M^3P is the software engine that interprets at runtime the MSL script specifying the behavior of the multimedia application.

Since the mobile devices' market, including Internet-enabled phones, is fragmented in a number of different, still incompatible hardware/software platforms [17], cross-platform portability is a key-factor for the multimedia player. In order to support portability, the M^3P's core relies on a two layer architecture as depicted in fig. 2, involving a high-level, platform independent, director and a low-level driver. The director is the responsible for creating, initializing and managing the objects that implement the multimedia presentations. Moreover, it conveys to the target objects events coming from user and system.

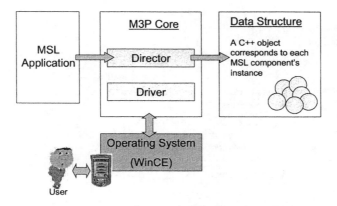

Fig. 2. M³P architecture. The core of M³P involves a platform independent director and a platform dependent driver. The director manages the multimedia objects of the presentation. Objects are organized in hierarchical structures. For instance, a CARD (i.e. a multimedia page) may include several images, buttons and mpeg players. The driver implements the access to the hardware, while the director deals with the logic of the multimedia presentation

In order to support incremental development of the player, we have developed M³P as a set of modules. In particular, the *Director* has been designed to be independent of the components it manages. According to the instructions specified by the MSL developer in the script, events (either from the system or from user interaction) are conveyed to the director, which simply redirects them to the target components.

Events are implemented as messages, which are interpreted by the target objects. Thus, the director's code is independent of the components and the components are independent of each other. The basic assumption of this schema is that each component exports a well-defined interface (i.e. a set of messages to which it is able to react) and implements this interface (i.e. implements the reaction to such messages).

Thus, components can be seamlessly added and interchanged (in this last case, as long as they comply with the same interface). Adding a new component (i.e. a new functionality) does not involve any change neither in the director's code, nor in the other components' code.

Such a design choice supports easy incremental development, allowing seamless integration of services within a single application framework. This implies that a homogeneous HCI can be applied to an application that hosts several different services that have been developed independent of each other (e.g. intelligent tour planning, interactive maps, positioning, database access). The *Director*'s code is platform independent, while the *Driver*, implementing the multimedia I/O functions, is strictly platform dependent. The *Driver* extends a platform-independent abstract superclass providing to the director all the I/O functions. This simplifies porting M³P across platforms. The driver includes functions such as compressed format decoding (e.g. mp3, mpeg and jpeg), audio and video playing and graphics memory management.

M³P has been developed in C++, using the Microsoft eMbedded Tools 3.0. The UML (Unified Modelling Language) [18] diagram of fig. 3 synthesizes the software architecture.

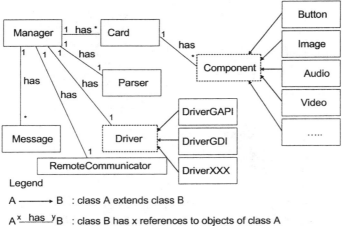

Fig. 3. M³P's UML diagram

The platform-independent module (*Director*), which manages the logic of the mobile applications, consits of six main classes: *Card, Parser, Message, Component* (and its subclasses), *RemoteCommunicator* and *Manager*.

Card containis multimedia and service objects (e.g. buttons, videos, maps)

Parser reads the MSL files, checking the syntax and instantiating the components.

Message is used to implement the exchange of messages between the objects and with the Operating System. For instance, if the user touches the screen a Message is delivered by the Manager to the active objects, specifying the point touched on the screen. In this way, touch-sensitive objects - like buttons - can take the relevant actions specified in the MSL file.

Component is an abstract class that defines the features shared by all the hypermedia objects of a presentation – such as name, messages handling method. This class is extended by a set of subclasses (e.g. *Button, Image, ImageList, Audio* and *Video*), that represent every specific hypermedia component's type.

RemoteCommunicator manages the M³P network connection. All resource files (e.g. videos, sound-clips) are addressed through a string, which can point to a local file or a URL, to dynamically load resources from a local network or the Internet. M³P uses the currently available remote-connection hardware (we have implemented interfaces for GSM/GPRS, Bluetooth, Ethernet and 802.11b), to get connected with the external world, overcoming the limitations of the palmtop computers' memories.

Manager manages the runtime system: it instantiates a Parser object for every MSL file, keeps the references to every Card, delivers messages to objects, manages the context change when control is transferred from one Card object to another.

The M³P platform dependent module (the *Driver* abstract class) defines the interfaces to access the low-level device functions. In this way the Director is independent of the actual Driver implementation, which is platform-dependent. The Driver class is extended by subclasses, which implement its interface's methods using a specific technology. We have realized three subclasses, at present: DriverGDI (that implements the code on PocketPC using the Windows GDI API), DriverGAPI (that optimizes the previous implementation using the low-level GAPI library), and Driver-WIN32 (that implements the code on Windows 98, 2000 and XP). Next steps of our work will imply implementing drivers also for other platforms such as palm devices and cellular phones.

5   MSL: Micromultimedia Services Language

The MSL file is given as input to the M^3P multimedia engine. The file specifies the objects involved in the presentation, their appearance, relationships and reaction to user interaction. The M^3P *Parser* reads the MSL instructions, specifying to the *Manager* what components to instantiate and how to manage their runtime operations.

We initially chose to design MSL as a new Object Oriented (OO) scripting language. The OO approach allows modeling the application domain in terms of objects, which is generally closer to human intuition and experience. The object model allows developers and multimedia designers to formalize specifications and easily agree on terminology, facilitating communication and code's inspection, correction and improvement during the whole life cycle of software. Moreover, this also allows using OO tools to support development (e.g. UML specifications [18]).

However, given the ever more widespread diffusion of XML, we decided to implement also an additional XML parser - which is simply an alternative front-end to support development of MSL applications in XML -, providing the same functionalities as the first parser. In this paper we focus on this XML interface (section 5.2), while in a companion paper we described the original MSL syntax [19].

5.1   MSL Components

MSL relies on a component-based data structure. An MSL file specifies creation of components, attributes of components and their reaction to the user interaction. Components are organized in three main libraries: multimedia, synchronization and services. The first library involves multimedia components (e.g. AUDIO, BUTTON, IMAGE). The second includes utilities, such as TIMER and POSINTERPOLATOR, that can be used to synchronize and schedule of the contents. The third category includes objects that encapsulate services such as positioning, shortest path search, database query, games, etc.

Since it is important to develop the components efficiently (i.e. exploiting code reuse) and with flexibility, according to the feedback coming form the user needs analysis and field tests, the M^3P's engine is independent of the components it manages. This allows an iterative and incremental development of the components' libraries.

First, we implemented basic modules, such as buttons, images, videos and audioclips. Our early guide's prototypes were built just on these simple components. Then, we added new functionalities and built more complex objects. For instance, we built a VIRTUALKEYBOARD high-level component in order to improve development of data-entry modules (Fig. 4a). As another example, the ANIMATEDASSISTANT (Fig. 4b) exports a simple interface through which the MSL developer specifies the frames' timeline and the commands to be performed on user's interaction. The component hides the low-level aspects of managing overlapping with the scene, correct sequencing of the frames and communication with other components.

(a)   (b)

Fig. 4. Sample instances of MSL components: a VIRTUALKEYBOARD (a) and an ANIMATEDASSISTANT (the Venetian Lion on the upper right corner) (b)

5.2   Structure of an MSL File

The structure of an MSL file is defined in the *msl.dtd* Document Type Definition. The file includes an *Application* route element, with several children nodes: the *CARD* elements representing the multimedia pages of the presentation (Fig. 5). Every card has children nodes that represent the MSL components (e.g. *BUTTONs*, *VIDEOs*, *MAPs*, *VIRTUALKEYBOARDs*, *PUZZLEs*, etc.) belonging to that card.

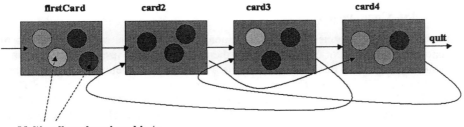

Fig. 5. An MSL application consists a set of cards containing multimedia and services objects. Arrows indicate possible transitions from one card (page) to another

For each component, the MSL developer has to specify information about: attributes, childrenComponents, triggerEvents, and receivable dynamic messages.

ChildrenComponents. A component may contain other components. For instance, an IMAGEZOOMPAN can contain one or more AREABUTTON objects, which are touch-sensitive areas a user can push (e.g. to get specific information about those areas – which is useful, for instance, for building interactive maps).

```
<CARD name="cName">
  <IMAGEZOOMPAN name="izpName">
    <areaButtons>
      <AREABUTTON name="ab1"></AREABUTTON>
      <AREABUTTON name="ab2"></AREABUTTON>
    </areaButtons>
  </IMAGEZOOMPAN>
</CARD>
```

Trigger Events. These are special children of a node. They specify the possible events to which the component has to react (e.g. *onMouseUp*, *onEntry*, *onExit*) and the actions to be performed (i.e. the messages to be sent to other components) when such events occur. The types of events to which a component can react is specified in the *dtd*. More than one action can be specified for a given event. For instance, a BUTTON has to react to a *mouseUp* event.

```
<BUTTON name="button " position="53 179"
        imageUpFile= "relativePath\up.gif"
        imageDownFile="relativePath\down.gif">
  <events>
    <onMouseUp>
      sendMessageLocal imageList.nextImage 1;
      sendMessageLocal button2.visible 0
    </onMouseUp>
  </events>
</BUTTON>
```

Receivable Dynamic Messages. This information specifies the various messages that a component can receive at runtime. For instance, the visible attribute of an IMAGE can be modified at runtime (i.e. an IMAGE can receive a visible message). Messages are sent through sendMessage commands, that we describe in the next subsection.

```
FireEvent myImage.visible 1
```

On receiving the *visible* message, an myImage becomes visible.

5.3   MSL Commands

Dynamic exchange of messages is implemented through 2 main commands: *sendMessageLocal* and *sendMessageGlobal*.

sendMessageLocal. Send a dynamic message to a component contained in the same CARD as the sender (e.g. a BUTTON pushed by an user makes an image visible, as shown in the code sample concerning the events child).

sendMessageGlobal. As above, but the message's target component may be contained in any CARD.

A second kind of commands involves setting the current CARD.

setActiveCard. Specifies what card to display.

```
<BUTTON name=" myButton" position="53 179"
        imageUpFile="images\demo1startup.gif"
        imageDownFile="images\demo1startdown.gif">
  <events>
    <onMouseUp>setActiveCard aCard </onMouseUp>
  </events>
</BUTTON>
```

setPreviousCard. This command shows the CARD shown before the current one.

```
<BUTTON name=" myButton" position="53 179" ...>
  <events>
    <onMouseUp>setPreviousCard </onMouseUp>
  </events>
</BUTTON>
```

Fig. 6 shows a simple example of the code for a CARD.

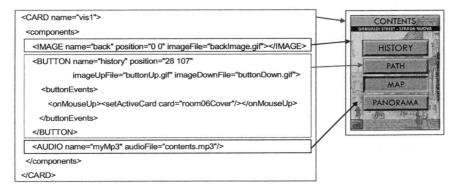

Fig. 6 An MSL sample from the "Strada Nuova" tour guide

6   Integration of Hardware and Software Subsystems

A major feature of MADE consists in the possibility of incrementally adding new hardware and software modules, that are integrated in the HCI framework with no need for modifying the M^3P core, since every component's class is responsible for interpreting its receivable messages, independent of the others.

M^3P Driver's classes, that have to be developed to integrate every new hardware subsystem, manage the low level aspects of the hardware modules, while the MSL interface to the application developer abstracts the services at high level (ideally: at user-interaction level). This implies that (i) a homogeneous HCI can be applied to an application that hosts several different services that have been developed independent of each other (e.g. automatic positioning, intelligent tour planning, and database access can be integrated in an interactive map) and (ii) the MSL developer can exploit the service modules focusing on the integration of the HCI.

For instance, an MSL developer can exploit information from a positioning system by using the MSL's Positioning and Orientation Module (POM) component. POM manages the NMEA string (the standard format for Global Positioning Systems) and, as came out from the user needs analysis of the E-Tour project, also an extension for receiving orientation information from an electronic compass, which has been as-hoc developed in E-Tour. The information received from the POM can then be dispatched to other components - such as maps - for a full integration in a multimedia presentation (Fig. 7a).

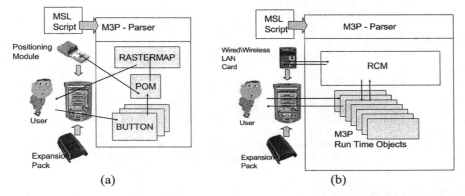

Fig. 7. Integration within MADE of (a) the Positioning and Orientation Module and (b) the Reomte Communication Module

In order to integrate the Remote Communication Module (RCM), which is able to exploit the hardware available for connection with the external world (e.g. wired and/or wireless Local Area Network LAN, Bluetooth, GSM/GPRS), the M^3P software has a C++ class that manages the procedures to establish a connection. Whenever a MSL component references a files (such as an image, a sound, a movie, a link to an HTML page or to another MSL file) M^3P checks if such file is available on the mobile device. If it is not available, the M^3P automatically uses the established connection to download the file from the network (see fig. 7b). This mechanism – which implements a virtual file system spread over the whole web - is transparent to the MSL developer, who has simply to specify one or more hosts for eventual retrieval of remote contents.

Integration involves also software modules, such as games, search algorithms, database access, etc. As an example, the RightPlace game involves dragging some objects - the details, represented by small icons - in their right position on a map (Fig. 10c). The following code example (Fig. 8) is taken from the "VeGame" ubiquitous game we have developed for the city of Venice in collaboration with the Future Center of Telecom Italia Lab. The example shows that the MSL developer has to specify few simple configuration items, such as position and names of the detail icons, targets' right positions, parameters for computing the score, and actions to be taken at the end of the game.

```
<!-- RightPlace game at stage 2, Santa Maria Formosa -->
<RIGHTPLACE name="RightPlaceS02" position="0 0"
```

```
        mapFile="mapRightPlaceS02.gif"
        okIcon="ok.gif" errorIcon= "error.gif"
        maxScore="100" bonus="10" penalty="5">

           <detailIcons>
        icon1.gif; …; icon5.gif;
   </detailIcons>
           <detailIconInitialPositions>
        28 34; … ; 28 86
   </detailIconInitialPositions>
           <detailIconSizes>
        86 20; … ; 86 20
   </detailIconSizes>
           <detailRightPositions>
        206 247; … ; 87 184
   </detailRightPositions>

           <events>
   <!—events to be triggered at the end of the game-->
           <onSolved>
        sendMessageLocal button04MenuS02.visible 0
        setActiveCard cardRightPlaceSolvedS02
      </onSolved>
         </events>
   </RIGHTPLACE>
```

Fig. 8. A fragment of the MSL code to implement a RightPlace's game instance

7   Conclusions

Using MADE we have developed innovative educational and entertainment services for tourism, which is a very promising application domain for mobile services. In the context of E-Tour, we have implemented a Tourist Digital Assistant (TDA) [4], which is a commercial hand-held computer loaded with a MADE-based tourist application to enhance fruition of the cultural and environmental heritage. Some versions of the TDA are already available for rent to the public, in the Spanish region of Castellon, at the Costa Aquarium of Genoa [6], in the Renaissance street "Strada Nuova" of Genoa (see fig. 9).

Moreover, we have recently developed "VeGame" an ubiquitous game distributed in the city of Venice. Through VeGame the players can learn history and art of the city by interacting in a pleasant and challenging fashion with the surrounding urban environment (including monuments, churches and palaces, local people and other players).

By developing these applications, analyzing feedback from end-users, and coping with logistic issues concerning deployment and operation of the tour-guide service, we learned several lessons, that we have partly published in [6]. A major finding of that research was a high degree of user acceptance, which we found to be statistically correlated with high quality of multimedia and interface elements.

Fig. 9. The TDA of the Aquarium of Genoa

Fig. 10. Snapshot from VeGame: (a) the path through the city, (b) the game-access menu, and (c) a RightPlace game: drag the name of the product to the right place in the map from where it was imported by the XIII century's Venetian merchants

Other important factors include: (i) all controls available at a given moment should be immediately visible, (ii) well known metaphors (e.g. the interface of common electronic appliances such as radios) should be adopted in order to reduce the cognitive effort to learn the interface, (iii) graphics designers should use large size software buttons, that can be pressed with fingers, avoiding using the stylus, which is more difficult to use and may be easily get lost, (iv) presentation of contents should be synergistic with the direct experience of the visitor, helping to understand what she/he is looking at, without distracting her/him [6].

MADE has been very useful in developing these applications according to a user-centric design methodology in an iterative development process aimed at supporting wide usability by the general public. As sketched in Fig. 11, MADE supports a flow of design which allows technicians, managers, graphics designers and cultural experts to collaborate on a common ground to develop the tourist application.

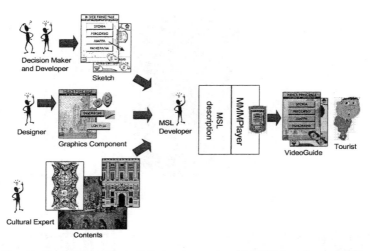

Fig. 11. The "flow of design" for implementing a MADE-based tour guide

The HCI designer, in collaboration with the tourist site managers, prepares a graphical sketch of the application aspect, of the multimedia contents and of the user-interaction modalities. On the basis of the sketch, a multimedia designer develops the graphic and audio components of the interface (for example, the buttons, the background images, the animated assistant, etc.). In parallel, cultural experts prepare the multimedia contents (images, texts and videos), possibly using already available information. When contents and interface elements are ready, the developer describes the sketch in MSL language. Thanks to the availability of the MSL high-level objects, translation from the paper sketch into code is quite simple. Moreover, in the case of specific requirements not yet implemented in MADE, the MSL library can be extended so that the new functionalities can be accessed directly at language-level (as shown for the RightPlace game, for instance).

We are now conducting experiments in order to qualitatively and quantitatively assess the contribution of MADE to support collaborative and participatory design.

Next steps of our work will involve integration of other modules (e.g. interactive 3D graphics) and development of drivers for other platforms, such as cellular phones.

References

[1]   Johnson C., Rebuilding the Babel Tower, Proceedings of the First Workshop on Human Computer Interaction for Mobile Devices, 21-23 May 1998.
[2]   Chittaro L., Dal Cin P., Evaluating Interface Design Choices on WAP Phones: Navigation and Selection, Personal and Ubiquitous Computing, Vol.6 , Issue 4, September 2002.
[3]   Rist T., Bradmeier P., Customizing graphics for tiny displays of mobile devices, Vol 6, Issue 4, September 2002

[4]   Bellotti F., Berta R., De Gloria A., Gabrieli A. and Margarone M., E-Tour: Multimedia Mobile Guides to Enhance Fruition of the Heritage, in E-work and E-commerce, ed. Brian Stanford-Smith and Enrica Chiozza, IOS Press, 2001.

[5]   A. Beck, User Participation in System Design: Results of a Field Study, Human-Computer Interaction: Applications and Case Studies, M. J. Smith and G. Salvendy, eds., Elsevier, Amsterdam, 1993, pp. 534–539.

[6]   Bellotti F., Berta R., De Gloria A., and Margarone M., User Testing a Hypermedia Tour Guide, IEEE Pervasive Computing, Volume 1, Issue 2, April-June 2002.

[7]   J.M. Carroll, Human-Computer Interaction: Psychology as a Science of Design, Int'l J. Human-Computer Studies, vol. 46, no. 4, Apr. 1997, pp. 501–522.

[8]   Schilit B. N., Trevor J., Hilbert D. M., Koh T. K., Web Interaction Using Very Small Internet Devices, IEEE Computer, Vol. 35, No. 10, October 2002.

[9]   Hinckley K., Pierce J., Sinclair M., Horvitz E., Sensing Techniques for Mobile Interaction, Symposium on User Interface Software and Technology, CHI Letters, Vol. 2, No. 2, pp 91-100.

[10]   Abowd G. D., Mynatt E. D., Charting Past, Present, and Future Research in Ubiquitous Computing, ACM Transaction on Computer-Human Interaction, Vol. 7, No. 1, March 2000, pp. 29-58.

[11]   Cheverst K, Davies N, Mitchell K, Friday A, Efstratiou C. Developing a Context-aware Electronic Tourist Guide: Some Issues and Experiences. Proceedings of the ACM CHI 2000, The Hague Netherlands, April 1-6 2000, pp. 17-24.

[12]   Davies N., Cheverst K., Mitchell K., Efrat A., Using and Determining Location in a Context-Sensitive Tour Guide, IEEE Computer, August 2001, pp. 35-41.

[13]   Cheverst K., Smith G., Mitchell K., Friday A., Davies N., The role of a shared context in supporting cooperation between city visitors, Computer & Graphics, August 2001, Vol 25, No. 4, pp.555-562.

[14]   Pradhan S., Brignone C., Cui J., McReynolds A., Smith M. T., Websigns: Hyperlinking Physical Locations to the Web, IEEE Computer, August 2001, pp. 42-47.

[15]   Kindberg T. and Barton J., A Web-based Nomadic Computing System, Computer Networks, vol. 35, no. 4, Mar. 2001, pp. 443–456.

[16]   Fleck M. et al., From Informing to Remembering: Deploying a Ubiquitous System in an Interactive Science Museum, IEEE Pervasive Computing, vol. 1, no. 2, Apr.–Jun. 2002, pp. 13–21.

[17]   Krikke J., Graphics Applications over the Wireless Web: Japan sets the Pace. IEEE Computer Graphics and Applications, May-June 2001, pp. 9-15.

[18]   Unified Modeling Language UML Resource Page. http://www.omg.org/uml/

[19]   Bellotti F., Berta R., De Gloria A., Margarone M., MADE: Developing Edutainment Applications on Mobile Computers, August 2003, Vol. 27, No. 4.

Dygimes: Dynamically Generating Interfaces for Mobile Computing Devices and Embedded Systems

Karin Coninx, Kris Luyten, Chris Vandervelpen,
Jan Van den Bergh, and Bert Creemers

Limburgs Universitair Centrum, Expertise Center for Digital Media
Universitaire Campus, B-3590 Diepenbeek, Belgium
{karin.coninx,kris.luyten,chris.vandervelpen,
jan.vandenbergh,bert.creemers}@luc.ac.be
http://www.edm.luc.ac.be

Abstract. Constructing multi-device interfaces still presents major challenges, despite all efforts of the industry and several academic initiatives to develop usable solutions. One approach which is finding its way into general use, is XML-based User Interface descriptions to generate suitable User Interfaces for embedded systems and mobile computing devices. Another important solution is Model-based User Interface design, which evolved into a very suitable but academic approach for designing multi-device interfaces. We introduce a framework, Dygimes, which uses XML-based User Interface descriptions in combination with selected models, to generate User Interfaces for different kinds of devices at runtime. With this framework task specifications are combined with XML-based User Interface building blocks to generate User Interfaces that can adapt to the context of use. The design of the User Interface and the implementation of the application code can be separated, while smooth integration of the functionality and the User Interface is supported. The resulting interface is location independent: it can migrate over devices while invoking functionality using standard protocols.

1 Introduction

A variety of new techniques for creating User Interfaces (UIs) for deployment on several different devices are emerging. Model-Based User Interface (MBUI) design is evolving from an academic solution into a practical software engineering methodology for designing multi-device interfaces. XML-based UI descriptions have matured and several toolkits allow building extensive interfaces based on XML documents.

This paper presents a framework for dynamically generating User Interfaces for embedded systems and mobile computing devices. The main purpose of the framework is to ease the work of the mobile and embedded UI designer and implementor. Often the software implementor of an embedded system or mobile computing device also takes care of the design and implementation of the UI for

L. Chittaro (Ed.): Mobile HCI 2003, LNCS 2795, pp. 256–270, 2003.

the system. This is mainly due to the device specific constraints that have to be taken into account: a thorough knowledge of the device is necessary. The Dygimes framework is conceived to ease the creation of the UI without the need for specific knowledge of the hardware or software platform. Runtime transformations of UIs for adaptation to the target device are also supported.

The next section introduces the UI creation process, and discusses the required components to build multi-device UIs for embedded systems and mobile computing devices. These components are discussed into detail in the following sections. First, XML-based UI descriptions are introduced in section 3 as the basic building blocks for the process. Continuing with section 4, the use of a task specification will be explained, and its relation to the XML-based UI descriptions. Section 5 shows how the created UI can be attached (or "glued") to the interfaced functionality it presents in a location-independent manner. Section 6 and 7 show respectively how the system can ensure consistent UIs and how the resulting (concrete) UI can be tailored for a more appealing result. Finally, section 9 discusses the applicability of the system and the obtained results, followed by an overview of the future work.

2   Dygimes Process

As stated in the introduction, the main purpose of the framework is to ease the work of the UI designer as well as the work of the application implementor. At the same time a clear separation between the work of the designer and the work of the implementor is supported. This is desirable because of the pitfalls involved in implementing UIs for embedded systems and mobile computing devices, which require specific knowledge about the device and the software platform available for that device.

Throughout this paper we will use a case study, managing a simple publication database, to show how the framework helps the UI designers and system implementors. The database requires the user to login before using the system. The system offers roughly two different kinds of tasks: adding a paper to the database or searching for a paper in the database. Both require some information to complete the tasks successfully. We kept the example intentionally simple for illustration purposes. The next sections explain how we can develop a multi-device UI for this task using the Dygimes framework.

A task specification for this task is developed, enriched with the UI building blocks. This will be sufficient to generate prototype UIs useful in a user-centered design process. The necessary time to create these prototypes is extremely short because many of the steps the designer had to do manually with traditional GUI building toolkits are now automated by the framework. For example; the transformation from the task specification to the resulting functional UIs built by the UI designer is done automatically. A micro-runtime environment offers support for rendering the created UIs independent of the chosen widget toolkit. Section 4 will show how all UIs stay consistent with regard to the task specification. A graphical overview of the UI construction and rendering process is

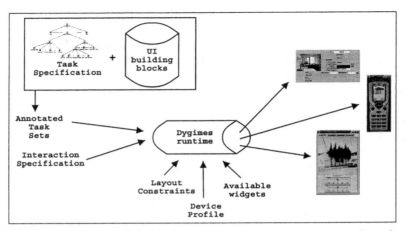

Fig. 1. The process for creating mobile and multi-device User Interfaces

shown in Fig. 1, all parts (including how the actual communication with the functionality takes place) will be explained in the following sections.

3   XML-Based User Interface Descriptions

In accordance with the recent growth in mobile computing devices usage, the demand for more suitable multi-device UI building toolkits also increases. The reuse of existing UI designs for new devices is problematic: new devices have other or less constraints making the reuse difficult. In contrast consistent look-and-feel is very important, as it contributes to creating a "brand" for the products and makes it easier for customers to use the new device. To enable flexible reusability of existing designs, we need to abstract the way the UI is created for a device in a way it becomes less dependent on device-specific properties.

One way of doing this is the use of high-level XML[1]-based UI descriptions. There are already several propositions and real world examples of the usage of XML to describe UIs for multiple devices: [1, 7, 12, 13, 14]. To give the reader an idea of which kind of XML-based UI descriptions are used in our system, listing 1.1 shows the specification of a simple login-dialog. For simplicity, the interaction glue and spatial constraints are omitted from the description. Section 5 discusses how generated events are handled and section 6 discusses the spatial layout constraints. When the renderer (the runtime environment) processes the description shown in listing 1.1, it can produce concrete UIs for different target platforms (shown in Fig. 2) *without* any human intervention.

---

[1] eXtensible Markup Language, http://www.w3.org/XML/

Listing 1.1. The login dialog UI description

```
<ui>
  <group name="login">
   <group name="userinfo">
     <interactor>
      <textfield name="login">
        <info>login</info><text size="10"/>
      </textfield>
     </interactor>
     <interactor>
      <textfield name="passwd">
        <info>password</info><text size="10"/>
      </textfield>
     </interactor>
   </group>
   <group name="control">
     <interactor>
      <button name="in"><info>Log In</info></button>
     </interactor>
     <interactor>
      <button name="reset"><info>Reset</info></button>
     </interactor>
   </group>
  </group>
</ui>
```

Notice the XML description allows to hierarchically group widgets using the "group" tag: this way all groups of widgets that logically belong together are put in the same physical space (e.g. in the same panel or window). At the lowest level, all widgets in a group should always be presented to the user together. The hierarchical structure of the UI description allows to recursively group parts of the UI, i.e. groups can contain other groups, which on their turn can contain other groups themselves.

4   Task Model

The design of a consistent interface starts at the task level. There are several advantages of using a task specification: better requirements capturing, consistent and detailed interface design and better integration with real-life situations [6]. Nevertheless, software developers seldom use task specifications to develop UIs for embedded systems and mobile computing devices. One of the main reasons is the wide gap between the implementation of the UI with its specific device-dependent constraints, and the task specification. To make task modeling more attractive there should be a glue to overcome the gap between the technical challenge of realizing the concrete UI and designing it with help from a task model. The framework presented here will offer such functionality.

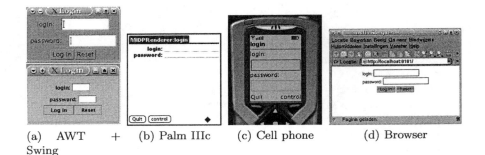

(a)   AWT   +   (b) Palm IIIc   (c) Cell phone   (d) Browser
Swing

Fig. 2. The login dialog, rendered for several devices

The framework discussed in this paper uses the ConcurTaskTree task model (CTT) proposed by Fabio Paternò [15]. This notation offers a graphical syntax, an hierarchical structure and a notation to specify the temporal relation between activities. For illustration purpose, a simple CTT of the paper-database example is shown in Fig. 3. A lot of current research extends the ConcurTaskTrees notation for multi-device task specifications. For a good understanding of this paper, it suffices for the reader to know that siblings in the tree can be connected with a temporal relation, such as a disabling operator, independent concurrency between two tasks or an enabling operator.

To convert the task specification into a concrete UI, the *Enabled Task Sets* (ETS) have to be calculated. An Enabled Task Set is defined in [15] as:

> a set of tasks that are logically enabled to start their performance during the same period of time.

The ETS generation is used as a glue between the realization of the UI and the task specification. This approach has also been described in [11, 16] where the

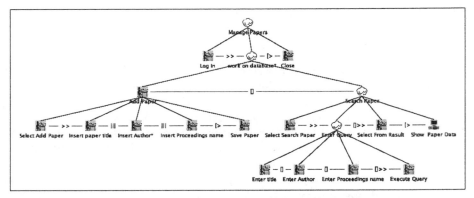

Fig. 3. Managing a simple publication database

focus is on the design of UIs, whereas we concentrate on runtime support for creating the UIs dynamically using widget toolkits as well as markup languages for the resulting UI.

For this purpose we implemented a tool chain for preparing the UI starting from a ConcurTaskTree task specification. The first graphical tool in the tool chain allows to attach the XML-based UI descriptions to leafs in the CTT tree. Next, a tool is offered to describe spatial layout constraints, so the designer can make sure the interface is rendered in a visually consistent manner. Section 6 elaborates on the use of the layout constraints. The last tool is the runtime library: it reads the constructed UI specification (including the task specification), adapts it to the target platform and renders it. The library will stay in memory where it captures events from the UI and handles these in a location transparent way (see Sect. 5). An algorithm for calculating the ETS is included in the framework; the different task sets are generated by the runtime environment. Although the task models can be made with the ConcurTaskTrees tool[15], we can not use their ETS calculation algorithm: the CTT model is annotated with extra information to work with our system. The designer does not have to check whether every possible UI is created for covering each aspect modeled in the task specification: this is done automatically at runtime by the framework through the use of the ETS[10].

The paper database example illustrates this: its CTT specification is saved as an XML file and loaded in the annotation tool where the specification can be decorated with XML-based UI descriptions. Fig. 4 shows the appropriate building block linked to the "Log In" task.

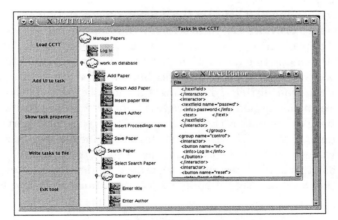

Fig. 4. The CTT annotation tool

5   The System Glue: An Interaction Model

Once the designer is satisfied with the UI, the next step is to "attach the UI to the application". More particulary we need to provide a mechanism in which the user can interact with application logic through the generated UI. An important property for this interaction mechanism is the support for *location transparency*: when a mobile device is used, the implementation of the functionality does not have to be on the same device as the UI presenting this functionality. Section 2 also emphasized that we intend to enable the separation of the UI design and system implementation of embedded systems and mobile computing devices. This means we also need to support several ways to exchange interactive messages between the UI and the application logic, which could be local or remote.

To overcome these problems, the framework offers an extensible "action-handling" mechanism [19]. This mechanism is the glue between the UI and the functionality that will be invoked by the UI. Because a clear separation between the UI and the application logic is needed, Dygimes only needs to know which functionality can be invoked on behalf of the logic and which interactors can be used to execute interactions. It does not need to know how the logic implements the functionality (code encapsulation) or where the implementation resides (location transparency). Even the used technique to invoke the functionality needs to be adaptable. To accomplish these goals, we use interaction descriptions that represent the functionality offered by the application.

In Dygimes, an interaction description is based on the Web Services Description Language (WSDL)[2]. This technology allows the application logic implementor to describe the operations, messages and data types that are supported by the application while existing WSDL editing tools can be used. However, Dygimes also needs a binding between the interaction description and the abstract UI. This binding provides Dygimes with the information needed to determine what must happen when a particular event occurs. For this reason we added a section to the interaction description that describes in what way the generated UI will be bound to the application logic. Suppose, for example, a user pushes the "in" button from listing 1.1. Listing 1.2 then shows what should happen as a response to this action. In this case the loginProcedure operation is sent to the service. This operation is defined in the "paperDBport" portType of the WSDL document. The <uib:parameter> tags describe the parameters. In this case, their values will be extracted from the "login" and "passwd" interactors. It is clear that this kind of description separates the development of the UI and the application logic and that it supports location-transparent late binding.

---

[2] http://www.w3.org/TR/wsdl

Listing 1.2. The binding between an abstract UI and the application logic

```
<uib:uibinding name="actionbinding" type="paperDBport">
  <uib:interactorbinding name="in">
     <uib:operationlink name="loginProcedure">
        <uib:parameter name="login"/>
        <uib:parameter name="passwd"/>
     </uib:operationlink>
  </uib:interactorbinding>
</uib:uibinding>
```

Dygimes supports different methods to carry out the specified interactions. First, Direct Method Invocation (DMI) can be used to invoke functionality on the application. DMI has the benifit of being fast. However, the drawback with this technique is that DMI can only be used for local invocation with applications implemented in a programming language supporting a reflection mechanism (such as Java). To overcome this problem and to enable location transparency, we make use of web service messaging protocols. These protocols enable us to deploy Remote Procedure Calls (RPC) in an XML-syntax to invoke application functionality. An example of such a technology is the Simple Object Access Protocol (SOAP)[3]. This protocol uses an XML-syntax to describe which method needs to be invoked upon a web service, together with the method's actual parameters. Those parameters are marshalled from language constructs to XML by using particular serializers. Dygimes also supports XML-RPC[4], which is a more efficient implementation of XML-based RPC. Figure 5 shows the extensible architecture of Dygimes enhanced with an interaction model.

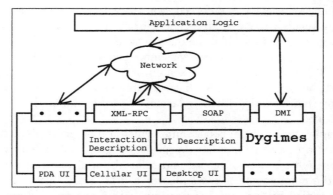

Fig. 5. The location-transparent action handling glue

---

[3] http://www.w3.org/TR/SOAP/

[4] http://www.xml-rpc.com

A WSDL-based interaction description together with XML-based messaging protocols offer the following benefits:

- Applications become web services-aware through the SOAP implementation. This will be an important advantage in the near future;
- The used approach is device and programming language independent. Java Remote Method Invocation (RMI) for example would restrict the use to Java implemented applications only;
- Interaction with remote logic that runs behind company firewalls is supported;
- Common standards for handling interaction are used, namely XML and web services;
- The automatic generation of functional UIs for remote applications in a location transparent manner is supported.

6 Automatic Layout Management

Abstract UI descriptions and a constraint-based layout management system are combined in our Dygimes framework for developing adaptive UIs for a wide range of devices. When developing a UI description language that enables us to render the UI presentation on several different devices, a more flexible approach for laying out concrete widgets than the traditional layout management techniques offer is necessary. We focus on screen size constraints because this is the most stringent device constraint in this matter. For example, when a graphical UI designed for a desktop system has to be rendered for use on a very small screen space (like on a mobile phone) most techniques fail to present a usable interface. The usage of spatial layout constraints can help the designer in these situations: the consistency of the UI is enforced, yet the UI is flexible enough for large differences in available screen size. There exist several other constraint-based layout management systems like the ones presented in [2, 8, 17], but none really focus on providing a flexible layout for embedded systems and mobile computing devices. The layout manager presented here does not guarantee a "visually pleasing" UI, but makes sure the UI is suitable and consistent on different devices. Adding (platform dependent) placement strategies, like the ones presented in [4], is planned.

Four simple linear spatial constraints, which are described in a simple XML based syntax, are used to express the positioning of components with respect to each other: *left-of*, *right-of*, *above* and *below*. In addition, the available space to lay out the components is divided over a grid. Each bucket in the grid is uniquely identified by its x and y position within the grid. Notice the linear constraints can be expressed in a mathematical form: assume the constraint *widget A right-of widget B* for example. This means widget A is put in a bucket X with coordinates (x_1, y_1) and widget B is placed in a bucket Y with coordinates (x_2, y_2): the constraint can be expressed as $x_1 > x_2$. A simple constraint solving algorithm can be used to solve these constraints, we refer to [9] for a survey of several methodologies used for information presentation.

Only constraints between siblings[5] are allowed in our framework: each component of the group will be associated with a unique bucket in the grid. Our layout system will initially solve the x coordinates of the components (coordinates indicate the position in the grid, not the absolute coordinates on the screen). A graph will be composed where each node represents a component with his x coordinate and each edge represents a constraint between the two components connected by the edge. As mentioned before, each edge with the label *right* can be expressed as $x_1 > x_2$. A possible solution for the x coordinates will be calculated. The same strategy will be applied for the y coordinates. The results of the two previous steps will be combined in a general solution. The possibility exists however that cycles or multiple edges occur in the graph which imply the presence of conflicting constraints. For handling this kind of inconsistencies, priorities are introduced into our system. The conflicting constraints with the highest priorities will survive. Necessary tool support for specifying constraints is provided in the framework, by means of a specialised constraint editing tool (Fig. 6).

After the presentation structure is calculated, the possibility exists that the layout does not fit on the screen. A layout adapter is imposed to resolve this problem by rearranging and adapting the presentation structure to the screen size of the target device. One of the strategies employed by the adapter consists of placing the components of a splittable group behind each other in a card layout or with tabbed panes. However, sometimes it is impossible to shrink the layout to the size of the screen of the target device. An appropriate warning will be shown to the UI designer at design time.

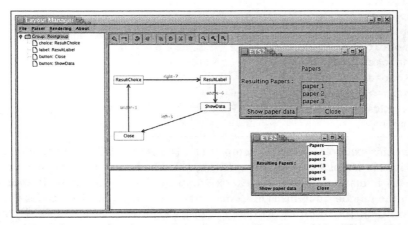

Fig. 6. Tool for managing spatial constraints. Preview of the UI is supported

---

[5] The UI descriptions are XML-based: they can be structured as a tree.

7   Customization and Templating

The previous sections explained that the framework uses abstract User Interface (AUI) descriptions with constraints to render the user interface. The translation from the abstract interaction objects (AIO) into concrete interaction objects (CIO)[18] can be done fully automatically, however this can give unexpected results. For this reason, the Dygimes framework allows the designer to have more control over the rendering of the UI by allowing them to specify which CIO is used to render an AIO [5]. Mapping rules can specify mappings for one AIO in one specific interface or they can specify mappings for a range of AIOs. This way, the designer can define a template, in the form of a set of mapping rules for a certain platform, that can be refined and adapted for specific user interfaces.

The mapping rules are intentionally kept simple because they are to be used at runtime on devices that can have very limited resources. The CIO that will be used to render a certain AIO depends on the type of the AIO and the name that identifies the AIO. Mapping rules can specify part of the name of an AIO, the complete name of an AIO or no name in order to define their applicability. We will illustrate this with the example of the paper database.

Listing 1.3. Two of the specified mapping rules

```
<mapping>
  <aio2cio>
    <aio>choice</aio>
    <cio>awt.CheckboxGroup</cio>
  </aio2cio>
</mapping>
<mapping>
  <aio2cio>
    <aio>choice</aio>
    <cio>awt.List</cio>
    <name>large</name>
  </aio2cio>
</mapping>
```

For this example, we used a template for the Java AWT platform. Two of the rules in this template are shown in listing 1.3. The first rule shows that the AIO "choice" is mapped onto a CheckboxGroup by default (no name is specified). When the number of items is large or varies over time, as is the case for the AIO that contains the result of the query, a List widget is a better choice. By giving the AIOs a name that contains "large", the second rule in listing 1.3 is used which gives the wanted result (figure 7(a)). If the designer prefers a Java AWT Choice for rendering the query result, this can be indicated by adding a rule that contains the full name of the AIO (Fig. 7(c)).

A feature of the templating system, which is not shown in this example, is that it allows to specify a "null" CIO for AIO's that should not or cannot be

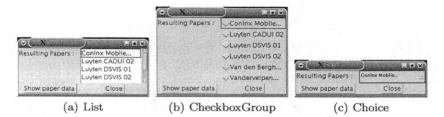

(a) List   (b) CheckboxGroup   (c) Choice

Fig. 7. Three possible mappings for the query result on the AWT platform

represented on a certain platform. This generates a lot of flexibility but can introduce problems as well: when the AIO that cannot be represented is crucial in a certain task, it can render a whole part of the user interface useless. A way to deal with this situation in an effective way, without loosing the flexibility of the system, is being worked on. Currently, the designer is still being forced to deal with this situation explicitly, by providing an adapted task model for the specific device, as needs to be done in the approach taken by Calvary et al[3].

8   The Paper Database Example: Resulting User Interfaces

Now that all the different parts are discussed, these techniques can be applied to a simple but illustrative example: the paper database (see Fig. 3). This task specification is annotated by high-level XML-based UI descriptions, depicted in Fig. 4.

Next, a set of (optional) spatial constraints can be defined to ensure consistent presentation of the UI on different devices (see Fig. 6). The annotation tool does its job by reading the XML-document which can be saved by the ConcurTaskTree tool, and inserting the UI building blocks into the XML-document. The result is a new XML document containing all the necessary information. The inserted UI building blocks can have spatial layout constraints defined.

These are the three things the designer should provide:

1. The task specification
2. The UI building blocks and their layout constraints
3. The relation between the UI building blocks and the different tasks in the task specification

This information is saved in an XML document. From this point the Dygimes runtime will handle everything automatically.

The XML document (describing the annotated task models and the constraints) produced by the tool can be fed directly to the runtime environment. First, it calculates the Enabled Task Sets. For the example it finds the following sets:

$$ETS_1 = \{LogIn\}$$
$$ETS_2 = \{Close, SelectAddPaper, SelectSearchPaper\}$$
$$ETS_3 = \{Close, SavePaper, Insertpapertitle, InsertAuthor,$$
$$InsertProceedingsname\}$$
$$ETS_4 = \{Close, SelectFromResult, ShowPaperData\}$$
$$ETS_5 = \{Close, Entertitle, EnterAuthor, EnterProceedingsname\}$$
$$ETS_6 = \{ExecuteQuery, Close\}$$

When these sets are calculated, it is known which UI building blocks should be presented at the same time. For example, ETS_3 contains a UI for adding information about a paper into the database. The UI building blocks attached to the different tasks of ETS_3 are extracted and merged into a single XML-based UI description (see Fig. 8). The resulting description is rendered by the framework, according to the mapping rules and layout constraints. Depending on the device an appropriate UI is generated: Fig. 9 shows how Java Swing or a Java-enabled Mobile Phone can be used.

Until now all the UIs are generated automatically out of the annotated task specification. Using the runtime environment, this can also be done dynamically (at runtime). Following this methodology, we get a set of User Interfaces which are perfectly fit to perform the task described by the task specification. This is one of the advantages of this approach.

Switching from an ETS to another requires a dialog model: an activity chain diagram is generated out of the task specification to indicate in which order the dialogs appear for the user. A detailed description of the dialog generation algorithm can be found in [10]. The activity chain describes the transitions of an ETS to another ETS. A State Transition Network for the dialog model is built by inspecting the temporal relations to solve this problem.

9   Conclusion and Future Work

We presented a framework for creating UIs for embedded systems and mobile computing devices. It incorporates several techniques from model-based UI de-

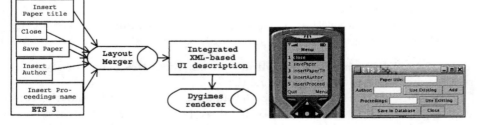

Fig. 8. Merging the UI building blocks of ETS_3

Fig. 9. ETS_3 automatically generated

sign, XML-based UI descriptions, automatic layout management and location-transparent event handling. The main purpose is to ease the creation of consistent, reusable and easy migratable UIs. The UIs can automatically adapt to new devices, offering the same functionality, without being redesigned. If one wants a better adaptation to a particular device, the designer can choose to provide a set of mapping rules and/or a set of better spatial constraints to embellish the presentation of the UI for that device. Notice the actual UI does not need to be rebuilt from scratch here.

The Dygimes framework is already successfully used in the SEESCOA[6]-project. Most developers in this project had no prior experience in UI design, but were able to use the tool within a few hours for creating simple UIs. This practical experience allowed us to use real-life experience to add tools and other techniques necessary to create suitable UIs.

We are looking to extend the framework not only to support multiple devices, but also to support multiple and mixed modalities. The final goal is to make the tool suitable for the usage in pervasive and ubiquitous environments, where the UI is loosely-coupled to the devices and can migrate from one device to another device. An important aspect here is to take the human factors in account (e.g usability of the interface in certain situation).

The Dygimes process can be described using the reference framework for platicity of Calvary et al. [3]. We plan to do this, so the properties of our system can be compared with other systems. Using the framework to describe Dygimes will allow a better localization of important shortcomings. For now, we focused on building a framework to generate multi-device UIs at runtime provided an annotated task model is given as input.

Acknowledgments

The research at the Expertise Center for Digital Media (EDM/LUC) is partly funded by the Flemish government and EFRO (European Fund for Regional Development). The SEESCOA project IWT 980374 is directly funded by the IWT[7]. The authors would like to thank Jos Segers, Tim Clerckx, the SEESCOA partners and the reviewers of this paper for their contributions.

References

[1] Marc Abrams, Constantinos Phanouriou, Alan L. Batongbacal, Stephen M. Williams, and Jonathan E. Shuster. *UIML: An Appliance-Independent XML User Interface Language*. World Wide Web, http://www8.org/w8-papers/5b-hypertext-media/uiml/uiml.html, 1998.

---

[6] Software Engineering for Embedded Systems Using a Component Oriented Approach, http://www.cs.kuleuven.ac.be/cwis/research/distrinet/projects/SEESCOA/
[7] Flemish subsidy organization

[2] Alan Borning. ThingLab – A Constraint-Oriented Simulation Laboratory. Technical report, XEROX PARC, 1979. report SSL-79-3.

[3] Gaëlle Calvary, Joëlle Coutaz, David Thevenin, Quentin Limbourg, Nathalie Souchon, Laurent Bouillon, and Jean Vanderdonckt. Plasticity of user interfaces: A revised reference framework. In *Task Models and Diagrams for User Interface Design*, pages 127–134, Bucharest, Romania, July 18-19 2002. TAMODIA 2002.

[4] François Bodart, Anne-Marie Hennebert, Jean-Marie Leheureux, and Jean Vanderdonckt. Towards a dynamic strategy for computer-aided visual placement. In *Workshop on Advanced visual interfaces*, pages 78–87. ACM press, 1994.

[5] Jan Van den Bergh, Kris Luyten, and Karin Coninx. A Run-time System for Context-Aware Multi-Device User Interfaces. In *HCI International*, June 2003. Accepted for publication.

[6] Alan Dix, Janet Finlay, Gregory Abowd, and Russel Beale. *Human-Computer Interaction (second edition)*. Prentice Hall, 1998.

[7] Jacob Eisenstein, Jean Vanderdonckt, and Angel Puerta. Applying Model-Based Techniques to the Development of UIs for Mobile Computers. In *IUI 2001 International Conference on Intelligent User Interfaces*, pages 69–76, 2001.

[8] Maloney J, Boming A, and Freeman-Benson BN. Constraint Technology for User Interface Construction in ThingLab II. In *OOPSLA*, 1989.

[9] Simon Lok and Steven Feiner. A Survey of Automated Layout Techniques for Information Presentations. In *Proceedings of SmartGraphics 2001*, March 2001.

[10] Kris Luyten, Tim Clerckx, Karin Coninx, and Jean Vanderdonckt. Derivation of a Dialog Model for a Task Model by Activity Chain Extraction. In *Interactive Systems: Design, Specification, and Verification*, 2003.

[11] Giullio Mori, Fabio Paternò, and Carmen Santoro. Tool Support for Designing Nomadic Applications. In *Intelligent User Interfaces*, 2003.

[12] Andreas Muelller, Peter Forbrig, and Clemens Cap. Model-Based User Interface Design Using Markup Concepts. In *Interactive Systems: Design, Specification, and Verification*, pages 30–39, 2001.

[13] Jeffrey Nichols, Brad A. Myers, Michael Higgins, Joseph Hughes, Thomas K. Harris, Roni Rosenfeld, and Mathilde Pignol. Generating remote control interfaces for complex appliances. In *User Interface Software and Technology*, 2002.

[14] Dan R. Olsen, Sean Jefferies, Travis Nielsen, William Moyes, and Paul Fredrickson. Cross-modal interaction using XWeb. In *Proceedings of the 13th Annual Symposium on User Interface Software and Technology (UIST-00)*, pages 191–200, N.Y., November 5–8 2000. ACM Press.

[15] Fabio Paternò. *Model-Based Design and Evaluation of Interactive Applications*. Springer, 2000.

[16] Fabio Paternò and Carmen Santoro. One model, many interfaces. In Christophe Kolski and Jean Vanderdonckt, editors, *CADUI 2002*, volume 3, pages 143–154. Kluwer Academic, 2002.

[17] Michael Sannella, John Maloney, Bjorn Freeman-Benson, and Alan Borning. Multi-way versus One-way Constraints in User Interfaces: Experience with the DeltaBlue Algorithm. *Software - Practice and Experience*, 23(5):529–566, 1993.

[18] Jean Vanderdonckt and François Bodart. Encapsulating knowledge for intelligent automatic interaction objects selection. In *ACM Conference on Human Aspects in Computing Systems InterCHI'93*, pages 424–429. Addison Wesley, 1993.

[19] Chris Vandervelpen, Kris Luyten, and Karin Coninx. Location Transparant User Interaction for Heterogeneous Environments . In *HCI International*, June 2003. Accepted for publication.

Online Transcoding of Web Pages for Mobile Devices

Somnath Banerjee[1], Arobinda Gupta[1,2], and Anupam Basu[1]

[1] Department of Computer Science and Engineering
[2] School of Information Technology
Indian Institute of Technology, Kharagpur – 721302, India
{somnath,agupta,anupam}@cse.iitkgp.ernet.in

Abstract. Accessing Internet from mobile devices such as PDAs and cell phones is becoming widespread. Since these devices do not have the same rendering capabilities as desktop computers, it is necessary for web contents to be transcoded for proper presentation on these types of devices. In this paper we propose an architecture for online transcoding of web documents. In the proposed system, a proxy fetches web pages on the client's behalf, categorizes the contents into predefined domain-specific categories, and dynamically generates a hierarchical summary view of the relevant topics of the page based on domain specific knowledge. This hierarchical summary of information is then transmitted to the client. The architecture uses domain specific knowledge, but allows easy adaptation to different domains by plugging in rule sets specific to the domain. The system does not expect any adjustment in the existing WWW contents. Results for one test domain, News, are shown. The results indicate that the system can produce high precision transcoded pages online using domain specific knowledge with very little performance penalty.

1   Introduction

Information access from mobile devices such as PDAs and cell phones is becoming common practice. In U.S alone, ten million users are accessing Internet from their PDAs or cell phones [11]. It has been projected that by the year 2005 mobile Internet users will be 48% of the total Internet users [12]. Although other limitations of mobile devices such as memory capacity, CPU speed, bandwidth, display resolution etc. are likely to improve, but the mobile terminals will remain small and will have a small or no display. It has been reported [8] that browsing a document from a small screen is approximately 50% more difficult than browsing it from a large screen. Large page area increases searching and scrolling complexity in a device with small display. As most of the web documents are designed for desktop computers, which are and will remain the primary access device for Internet, we need some sort of re-authoring of WWW contents to have a better presentation in a small display area.

It is expected that palm sized devices on the Internet will not be used primarily for recreational, undirected browsing, but rather for extracting particular bits of

L. Chittaro (Ed.): Mobile HCI 2003, LNCS 2795, pp. 271–285, 2003.

information relevant to a current task [2]. So users may not be interested in all the information available on a webpage. It is convenient to them to have only the information of interest displayed on their small screen device. Presenting only the relevant information on small display area will also lessen the task of scrolling and searching. Moreover, wireless transmission is expensive. In future users may get enough bandwidth but the billing is often done on the basis of transmitted data. Irrelevant information will only increase the volume and hence the cost of data transmission.

This paper describes an architecture using online transcoding to improve WWW navigation from mobile devices. The system acts as an intermediary between a client and a server. It uses domain specific information in the form of a rule set that is applied on an input page to transcode it. For every requested page the transcoding module extracts the relevant information from the page, categorizes it, and re-authors the page based on the available information specific to the domain of the requested page. A hierarchical summarization technique is also applied on the relevant objects. The client gets the hierarchical summary view of only the relevant objects of the requested document. The hierarchical presentation strategy is adopted as several earlier works [3, 9] have concluded in favor of this type of presentation in case of displaying in small display terminals. Though the system uses domain-specific knowledge, the architecture is general enough to handle any domain. Different domains can be handled by updating a set of plug-in files relevant to each domain of interest. We can also plug in a domain-independent rule set based only on HTML syntax to completely ignore domain knowledge if so desired. We have implemented the transcoding architecture and tested it for News domain. News sites contain several other sub-domains like Politics, Sports, Business etc. and therefore our system is inherently tested for these domains too. A comparative usability study shows that our system works very well when compared to commercially popular news sites that have manually re-authored pages for mobile devices. The time taken to transcode a page is also very little with no discernible effect on the browsing.

The rest of this paper is organized as follows. Section 2 discusses related works. Section 3 describes the architecture of the system. Section 4 discusses the working of the system when applied to the News domain. Section 5 and 6 describes the client application and discusses results of our experiments respectively. Section 7 presents some concluding remarks and discusses scope for future works.

2   Related Works

There are broadly two approaches of re-authoring a webpage. The first approach is manual re-authoring of the page. In this technique, the information content is manually formatted explicitly for small screens. Avantgo [13] and I-mode [14] of NTT DoCoMo relies on this approach. Another example is the Wireless Access Protocol (WAP) [15], which includes its own mark up language to replace HTML on small display devices. Manually prepared pages are optimized for small screens and therefore have the best transcoding precision. This transcoding technique is also commercially successful. But the problems of this approach are increased cost of creation and maintenance of different copies of the same document. Also a vast number of HTML pages remain inaccessible to the mobile user since they are not re-authored.

The other approach to re-authoring a web page is automatic re-authoring. There are several research projects and commercial applications based on this transcoding technique [1, 2, 5, 6, 7, 16]. Microsoft's Pocket Internet Explorer [16] implements compression technology which shrinks a page and associated font to fit into small displays. However, for a page to be readable, font size cannot be reduced beyond a threshold. Therefore scrolling is required for most of the pages which makes searching for a piece of information on a page cumbersome [17]. HANd [6] and ProxyWeb [5] tries to miniaturize standard Web pages with a zooming facility. Pocket Internet Explorer [16], HANd [6] and ProxyWeb [5] each tries to transcode all the information in a page whereas Power Browser [2] does some sort of relevance calculation on the duplicate links (links on the same page pointing to the same URL). But to a mobile user there are several other irrelevant elements other than the duplicate links. None of them uses any other knowledge about the document except general HTML syntax. In particular, none of them use any knowledge about the domain of the page. While this makes the tools quite general, transcoding precision can be improved significantly by using domain knowledge along with the HTML syntax.

There are other transcoding techniques which assume some server side content adjustment. For example, IBM's transcoding proxy [7] uses an annotation file associated with a document. It determines the relevance of different portions of a document based on the annotation file associated with it. Although the presence of an annotation file improves the precision of transcoding, all sites are not expected to provide such file.

In our system we have used automatic re-authoring along with knowledge associated with the domain of the page to improve the transcoding precision. No external annotation file associated with every page is expected and no server side content adjustment is assumed.

3   System Architecture

The system works as an intermediary between a client and a server. It can be physically located anywhere. In order to handle the limitations of client devices and make the server free from any adjustment, a proxy based system is adopted. Every communication between a client and a server is routed through the proxy. We require an application to be installed at the client side. This constrain is put to optimize the presentation and to reduce data transfer between the proxy and the client. The application is integrated with a simple user interface which hierarchically displays a transcoded page. A special protocol is used to reduce data transmission between the client and the proxy. For example, all HTML tags are removed and URL of every link is replaced by just a number.

The browsing process is initiated by typing a URL. At the browsing initiation the client application sends a request along with the URL to the proxy. The proxy starts a session for that client, downloads the required page from the corresponding server, re-authors it and then sends it to the client. The re-authoring technique calculates the relevance of the information on a page based on the available rules for the domain of the page. The relevant information is categorized into predefined domain-specific categories or sub-categories by applying the rule set relevant to the current page. A hierarchical summary tree of this relevant, categorized information is created and transmitted to the client. In subsequent navigations, the client application sends the link number of the link clicked. The proxy maintains a database of information for each session of each client, from which it gets the URL of the clicked link.

The transcoding proxy consists of five modules, *communicator*, *page retrieval process*, *fragmentation process*, *punctuation process*, and *category profile manager*. The *communicator* handles all the communications between the proxy and the client. The *page retrieval process* downloads the requested page from the corresponding WWW server. The *fragmentation process* parses the retrieved page and fragments it based on HTML syntax. A fragment consists of one or more elements. An element can be either a block of text or an image. The *punctuation process* does all the relevance calculation, categorization, and hierarchical summary tree generation tasks. The *category profile manager* updates the category profile of the current page as a client navigates. The category profile is a pointer to a set of possible categories of information in the page being viewed.

The second, third, and fourth processes run in parallel. The first two processes are simple, therefore only the last three processes are discussed in details in this paper.

3.1   Fragmentation Algorithm

The fragmentation algorithm is primarily based on HTML syntax. A page is fragmented at every occurrence of <table>, </td>, </table> and <hr> tags. But fragmenting on every occurrence of these tags splits a page into several unnecessary fragments and often a fragment contains only one element. So we have included a merging policy to merge the fragments if necessary. A fragment is merged with another fragment if they are in the same column and in subsequent rows of the same table, having same column span and not separated by <hr> tag. The aim of the fragmentation algorithm is to split a page into several semantic units, i.e., units with closely related information.

Based on extensive empirical study of web pages of different domains, we have taken a syntax-driven approach towards identifying the semantic units. This approach works very well for web pages of structured or semi-structured domain. However, for domains whose pages follow no specific structure, more complex interpretation of the web page is necessary for semantic splitting.

The fragmentation algorithm also determines the crude position of each fragment in a page. Some amount of pruning is also done by this process. For example, among the duplicate links, the links containing fewer words are considered as less informative and pruned. Images with less than 10 pixels in height or width are also pruned as most of the times they are bullets or white spaces or simply thin lines. It also prunes any fragment that was already encountered in any pages along the user navigation path so far. For example, the navigation bar is repeated among several pages of a site and will be pruned from navigation depth 2. Each fragment is searched in the space of all previously encountered fragments and pruned if found.

This process outputs three arrays, array of *Links*, *Elements*, and *Fragments*. For each link on the page, an entry is created in the array of *Links*. A *Link* entry contains the URL and the anchor text of the link. This is done so that subsequently we can refer to a link by its array index only. An *Element* is the basic unit of a fragment. For every continuous text or image, an entry is created in the array of *Elements*. An *Element* is marked by a 5-tuple *<string, link_id, emphasizer, category_no, nonterminal >*. The *string* field contains the text string for a text block or the entire <IMG> tag for an image. If the element is a link then *link_id* contains the index of the corresponding *Link* entry in the array of *Links*, otherwise it is set to −1. The *emphasizer* value is a measure of how prominently a text appears in the document. It is set to −1 for an image. For a text element it is calculated from the font size of the text and other attributes that affect the size of a text. Typically the other attributes that affect the size of a text are tags such as <b>, <strong>, <h1>, <h2> etc. The *category_no* and the *nonterminal* fields, indicate the type of an element as defined in the plug-in files. The following paragraphs discuss these two fields in more details.

Each domain is broken up into a hierarchical structure of categories and subcategories. Each page of a particular domain belongs to any of the category or subcategory and contains information on some subcategories (categories and subcategories are treated essentially in the same manner and we will use the name interchangeably). For example, the Business page and the Sports page of News domain belong to the categories *Business* and *Sports* respectively. The Business page contains information on subcategories like *Stock Quotes, Business News* etc. and the Sports page contains information on subcategories like *Football, Cricket, Baseball* etc. In a page containing information of multiple categories, some elements are the name of a category itself and mark the beginning of information belonging to that category. For example, the heading *Publications* in a faculty's home page marks the beginning of the list of publications. These elements need not to be categorized any further during the punctuation process, but its relative location with respect to other elements can be used to classify those elements under this category. For example, in a faculty's homepage the elements placed under the heading *Publications* should be categorized under the *Publications* category. The fragmentation algorithm determines whether an element is a category name or not using hints from a domain specific xml configuration file called *Categories.xml*. The xml file contains the important category-subcategory tree for the entire domain. The xml file encodes the tree using nesting of xml tags. For each important category or subcategory name of a domain there is an xml tag in the xml file with proper nesting of subcategory tags under corresponding category tags. Each node (i.e. xml tag or element) for a category name also includes some other types of child nodes providing hints to identify that category name. The hints are basically keywords and the context in which the keywords should occur. The xml file contains a special type of tag called *<Forbidden>* which lists a set of keywords that should not be taken as a valid category name for that domain.

The category names, mentioned in the xml file for the current page are kept in an array. If an element is identified as any of these category names its *category_no* field gets the corresponding index value. If an element is not a known category name, does not contain any forbidden word that cannot be a category name, but otherwise looks like a category name (e.g. it has relatively higher *emphasizer* value and has two or less words), its *category_no* field gets the value *OTHERCATEGORY*. If the element cannot be identified as a valid category name (known or otherwise), its *category_no* field gets the value *NOTCATEGORY*. In short the *category_no* field indicates whether an element is a category name (listed or other) or not.

The fragmentation process also checks whether an element is any of the *Nonterminals* defined in the *Rules.xml* file. The *Rules.xml* file contains a set of *Nontermials* definition and their identifying parameters such as number of words, *emphasizer* value etc. The *Nonterminals* define certain basic types of element such as *story text* or *story link* in a news page. The *nonterminal* field of an element gets a positive integer if that element matches any of the *Nonterminals* defined in *Rules.xml*. The mapping from *Nonterminals* to integers is done in the order in which they appear in the *Rules.xml* file.

The third array output by the fragmentation process is the array of *Fragments*. A *Fragment* is a set of elements and is marked by 4-tuple <*start_index, end_index, location, fragment_type*>. The *start_index* and the *end_index* is the index of the first and the last element of this fragment. The *location* is any feasible combination of *Top-most, Bottom-most, Left-most, Right-most,* and *Middle*. The *fragment_type* indicates the content type of the fragment (advertisement, category links etc.). If 90% of the elements of a fragment are of type image or external link then its *fragment_type* is set to *ADVERTISEMENT*; else if 90% of the elements of the fragment have *category_no* ≠*NOTCATEGORY* then its *fragment_type* is set to *CATEGORYNAMES*. Otherwise the *fragment_type* is set to *GENERAL*.

The fragmentation process is executed while the page is being downloaded using a single pass algorithm. Certain other optimizations are done to speed up the algorithm.

3.2   Punctuation Process

The punctuation process uses the output of the fragmentation process and computes the relevance of elements that are not a category names (i.e. elements with *category_no = NOTCATEGORY*). It tries to identify the category of each element. As the category of an element is determined as any of the listed categories the element is selected as relevant. The punctuation process also organizes the relevant elements in a hierarchical summary tree for better presentation in the client device.

The process applies the categorization algorithm on all the elements of a fragment only if the *fragment_type* of the fragment is equal to *GENERAL*. An *ADVERTISEMENT* fragment is not considered to be relevant; a *CATEGORYNAMES* fragment contains only the names of categories, and not the elements that need to be classified under a category. The punctuation process only picks up the available URLs corresponding to the important category names from the *CATEGORYNAMES* fragments. These URLs will support navigation to the pages containing information about that category. For fragments with *fragment_type* equal to *GENERAL*, it applies the categorization algorithm on a set of elements belonging to the fragment. The boundary of each set within the fragment is determined either by an element with *category_no* ≠ *NOTCATEGORY* or by the fragment boundary.

For categorization of elements the punctuation process uses a default technique and rules from the domain specific *Rules.xml* file. The default technique tries to identify the pre-categorized elements. In web documents many information is already categorized by the author of the document. For example, in a faculty's homepage, publication list, research interest, courses taken etc. are often categorized under the category names like *Publications, Research Interest, Courses* respectively. Here we assume a set of elements is pre-categorized if they are preceded by an element having *category_no* $\neq$ *NOTCATEGORY*. The punctuation process maintains a list of known categories and selects the set of elements preceded by any of these known category name. Note that reaching an element with the *category_no* value *OTHERCATEGORY* can be used to signify the end of a list of elements belonging to a known category, and start of an unknown category. If a set of element cannot be classified under either a known or an unknown category by the default technique because they are not preceded by any category name (i.e. they are not pre-categorized), the rule set of the *Rules.xml* file is applied to it. For example, in a faculty's home page the person's name and designation is often placed at the top of the page in an uncategorized way. The *Rules.xml* file for this domain can specify the possible attributes such as *location, emphasizer* value, keywords (e.g. "professor", "associate professor") etc. to identify and categorize these elements.

A rule is basically a regular expression over some *Nonterminals* defined under a Grammar tag. Each category name listed in *Categories.xml* at any nested depth can have zero or one rule nested under the *Grammar* tag. Each *Nonterminal* definition contains a DNF (disjunctive normal form) rule. Every clause of the DNF rule can specify some attributes of an element, for example, whether it is a link or not, number of words contained, *emphasizer* value, keywords etc. In the fragmentation phase every element is checked against these definitions and a positive integer corresponding to the matched *Nonterminal* is preserved in the *nonterminal* field of that element. Basically the *Nonterminal* definitions help to identify a single element with certain characteristics. Sometimes the sequence among these elements serves as an important identification attribute. For example, in a news paper front page a block of text containing the word "*football*" with *emphasizer* value greater than 3 and followed by a "*full story*" link can be categorized under *Sports Stories*. Our rule specification captures this sequence through a regular expression over the *Nonterminals*. Regular expressions with flexible *Nonterminal* definitions make the rule set powerful enough to specify almost any certain characteristics of a set of elements. The punctuation process applies these rules on a set of uncategorized elements and the matched sequence is inserted under the corresponding category.

At the end of this phase, an element can fall into one of two classes. If the element is classified under a known category, it is considered as relevant and its category information is preserved. If it is classified under an unknown category (not a listed category name for the domain), the element is not considered to be relevant and is dropped. Note that it is easy to change the behavior of the system so that all elements that are either not classified or are classified under an unknown category are not dropped, but are gathered under a separate *Others* link. It is then up to the client application to decide whether to show this link or to drop it.

As and when each element is categorized under a known category, it is inserted in a hierarchical summary tree whose root is the corresponding category name. The tree is built with the aid of the *emphasizer* values. Each node of the tree contains a pointer to the corresponding element. Consecutive elements are inserted in the tree in such a fashion so that an element with higher *emphasizer* value will be the parent of its subsequent element with lower *emphasizer* value. The idea is that a text with higher *emphasizer* value (i.e. bold/strong text or text with bigger font size) is the heading or title of subsequent text. The summarization algorithm and building the hierarchical summary tree is similar to the accordion summarization techniques used in Stanford's Power Browser [3], and the details are omitted here. We just present an outline of the algorithm to form the summary tree for a single category out of the selected consecutive elements.

```
//curr_node is the node under which it will try to
//insert the next element. Root node is a node
//corresponding to the category name having infinite
//emphasizer value.
        curr_node = node(category_name);
    for every Element E  in the matched set of Elements
        while (curr_node.emphasizer<=E.emphasizer)
                curr_node = curr_node.parent;
        curr_node.insertChild(node(E));
        curr_node = curr_node.childNode(E);
```

The trees for the different categories are then combined to get a single hierarchical summary tree. The combined tree preserves the category-subcategory hierarchy as well as the summary trees formed for selected elements in each category.

3.3   Category Profile Manager

Category profile is a pointer to the set of possible categories that can appear in the page being viewed. As a client navigates from a category to any of its subcategories we need to update this pointer. The information in each page may be classified under different categories. Once a link belonging to any of these categories is followed, the information in the new page already belongs to that category, which may then be classified under further subcategories. Keeping a pointer to the current set of valid categories serves two important purposes. Firstly, it helps the system to identify the valid set of categories in the current page. *Categories.xml* encodes the category-subcategory tree for the entire domain. Moreover, the same subcategory may appear under several different categories. For example, the subcategory *Sports* may appear in the front page, the International page, and the Regional page of a news paper. Therefore the category-subcategory tree can have multiple nodes with same name having a single rule enlisted in the *Rules.xml* file. This pointer determines which one is the valid node in the current context, i.e. under which category to place an element when the single rule for that category is satisfied. Secondly, there can be same rules for multiple categories. So applying all rules for all categories on every page may sometimes categorize an element into a less appropriate category. Maintaining a pointer to the current set of valid categories narrows down the subset of the rules that are applicable to a page. In particular, only rules specified for the current set of valid categories are applied. A category-subcategory tree is created by the server on startup from the *Categories.xml* file. As a client requests for a page, the category profile manager checks the anchor text of the link being clicked. If the anchor text is the name of any subcategory then it adjusts the pointer accordingly to point to that sub-tree.

4   Application to News Domain

The architecture described above has been implemented. Configuration files and rule sets are plugged in for the News domain to transcode news pages online. In this section we describe and show examples of some of the concepts mentioned above with respect to the News domain.

We have determined some common attributes of News domain based on an empirical study [10] of 85 popular English news sites of different countries. Firstly we have determined the typical categories and subcategories present in the entire News domain. For example, *Headlines, Politics, Sports, World* etc. are some of the typical, categories present in a news paper's front page. Similarly *Football, Cricket, Basketball* etc. are the common categories found in the Sports page of a news site. The identifying keywords of these category names are then determined. For example, the category name *International* can be identified by the word "International", "World" or "Foreign". The other common structural attributes for relevant information is also determined. For example, the *Headlines* are often placed in the *middle* (according to the fragment *location* terminology) of the page with large enough *emphasizer* value to make it clearly visible. These common attributes are found to be very consistent across most of the news sites. Another work [4] regarding news pages also substantiates this claim. These attributes are then captured formally in the files *Categories.xml* and *Rules.xml*. Fig. 1a and Fig. 1b shows parts of typical *Categories.xml* and *Rules.xml* files respectively for News domain.

In the *Categories.xml* file the *keyword* tag for each category specifies the necessary keywords for identifying a text as that category name. A text is selected as a category name if it matches any of the keywords specified under the corresponding category tag. The length attribute of a keyword element specifies the maximum number of words a text can contain to be selected as that category name. For example, to be selected as category name *Cricket,* an element identified by the fragmentation algorithm must contain the keyword "Cricket" and can be at most two words long. For example, "Cricket", "Cricket News", "Cricket Stories" are all going to be qualified as the category name *Cricket*. The category name specification thus gives the flexibility of capturing a wide variety of texts by relatively less number of specifications. Note that only the categories and subcategories of interest are needed to be specified in the *Categories.xml* file. Information belongs to unspecified categories and subcategories are automatically detected and categorized under a separate *Others* link.

In the *Rules.xml* file, each *Nonterminal* is in DNF and each clause of DNF is defined under a <cl> tag. Each clause can have conditional statements and/or keywords, for example, the clauses under *Cricket_Headlines* and *Story_Link*. In a conditional statement, the keywords *anchorWords* and *plainTextWords* are used to distinguish between link and plain text. For example, "*anchorWords* > 2" means that the accepted element must be a link with anchor text of at least 2 words in length. An element can match to multiple *Nonterminals*. In that case the *Nonterminal* containing maximum number of clauses is accepted. A rule for a listed category is placed under the tag having the name of the category. These tags are further nested under the *Grammar* tag.

```
<Categories>
<Sports>
 <keyword length="2">Sports
 </keyword>
 ...

 <Stories>
  <keyword length="2">Top Stories
  </keyword>
  <keyword length="2">Top News
  </keyword>
 </Stories>
 <Cricket>
  <keyword length="2">Cricket
  </keyword>
  <Stories>
   <keyword length="2">Top Stories
   </keyword>
   <keyword length="2">Top News
   </keyword>
  </Stories>
 </Cricket>
 ...
</Sports>
...
<Forbidden>
 <keyword> full story </keyword>
 <keyword> More </keyword>
 ...
</Forbidden>
</Categories>
```

Fig. 1a. A part of the *Categories.xml* file

```
<Rules>
 <NonTerminals>
  <Cricket_Headlines>
   <cl emphasizer="3">
    anchorWords > 2 ^"Cricket"
   </cl>
  </Cricket_Headlines>

  <Story_Text>
   <cl emphasizer="3">
    PlainTextWords>5 </cl>
  </Story_Text>

  <Story_Link>
   <cl emphasizer="2">
    anchorWords <3 ^"full story"
   </cl>
  </Story_Link>
 </NonTerminals>

<Grammar>
.<Cricket>
 (Cricket_Headlines • Story_Text) |
 (Cricket_Headlines • Story_Text
              • Story_Link)
</Cricket>
<Stories>
 ...
</Stories>
</Grammar>
</Rules>
```

Fig. 1b. A part of the *Rules.xml* file

We next show an example output of the punctuation process using a typical news page fragment where the information is not pre-categorized. In Fig. 2a the image and the texts, "Hussain sulks: Indira works damaged.", "full story", "Govt braces for attack in House on Gujarat, drought", and "full story" are links. Fig. 2b shows the hierarchical summary tree for the page fragment output by the punctuation process. Note that the image and the "full story" links are pruned as they were duplicate links. The elements are selected as relevant by applying rules from the *Rules.xml* file. The elements are organized in the tree according to their *emphasizer* values. The root node of the tree is the category name under which the elements are selected and it has infinite *emphasizer* value. The first and the third elements of Fig. 2a are bold and have a font size equal to 3; thus their *emphasizer* values are 4. They are inserted as direct children of the root node. Other elements have font size equal to 2, therefore their *emphasizer* values are 2. These elements have relatively lower *emphasizer* value and therefore they are inserted as child node of the first and the third element.

Husain sulks: Indira works 'damaged'

 "The paintings had been thrown somewhere. They had been torn and damaged... How would you feel if you donated your works to someone and they were treated like this?" The question, coming as it does from artist M.F. Husain, is not to be taken lightly. [full story]

Govt braces for attack in House on Gujarat, drought

The developments in Gujarat, where the Vishwa Hindu Parishad has already set the pace for the assembly elections next month, and drought hold the key to the functioning of the month-long winter session of Parliament which gets underway on Monday. [full story]

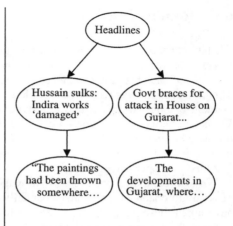

Fig. 2a. Front page of "Indian Express" news paper

Fig. 2b. Hierarchical summary tree for the page fragment of Fig. 2a

Trees of the different categories are then combined to get a single hierarchical summary tree of the entire page, which is then transmitted to the client according to the protocol running between the server and the client application.

Note that although the application is designed for News domain, a client has full navigation facility either to any of the domains like Sports, Cricket, Business, Politics etc. or to just the full story page. The navigation facility to these domains inherently enables our system to work for those domains.

5   Client Application

In order to use the system, a special application compatible with our transcoding proxy needs to be installed on a client device. This restriction is kept to optimize the presentation and to reduce the data transfer between the proxy and a client. This restriction can be easily removed by adjusting the proxy to output HTML files. In that case a user can browse using any HTML browser in lieu of all the optimization.

The client application is a simple browser that runs on a Compaq iPAQ PDA. The server is written in Java and can run on any platform. Normal browsing begins with typing the URL. After the user has tapped the **"Go"** button to initiate browsing, the Pocket PC client sends an appropriate request to the Proxy server. If it is a valid URL of any known domain, the server sends back the page after all the aforementioned processing. If the request is for a page from an unknown domain, the server presents just a hierarchical summary view of the entire page without applying the categorization algorithm at the punctuation phase. The client browser receives a tree from the proxy server. Each node of the tree is an element. The tree is displayed as a conventional tree widget using plus and minus signs. Each node can be expanded or collapsed using left to right gesture on the corresponding node. To follow a link a user need to tap on the link. Figures in Appendix show two typical navigation patterns using our client application.

6   Results

We have tested our system on almost 80 pages of 30 news sites spanning all over the world. For the purpose of testing, a human agent determined the relevance and category of each text and we checked the recall and precision of our system against it. The human agent was restricted to underscore an element as relevant if and only if the element belongs to any of the important categories listed in the *Categories.xml* file. We have obtained a very good recall, that is almost all the underscored elements were presented in the client device. The precision was also good. It was seen that very little irrelevant elements were present at the end of the transcoding and elements were included in proper categories.

We also compared our system with pages in Avantgo [13] channels. As the pages of Avantgo channels are created manually and they are commercially successful, we have taken these pages as the reference for one of the best small screen presentation of the desktop versions of the pages. Our system was targeted to bring a look and feel of Avantgo. But Avantgo displays many other links that are not in the desktop version of the page in question and only available after following some links in the desktop version. Avantgo pages are transcoded manually and it is optimized in such a way so that it is a microcosm of the entire site, not of just a page. We never intended to achieve this and we have done only a page by page transcoding. However, the entire site can be surfed by following the links from the top level pages. Moreover, our system allows the user to surf more number of news sites as the transcoding is online and no manual re-authoring is needed.

There is hardly any performance penalty for transcoding. As all the processing is done in a powerful proxy and in parallel with page retrieval from the WWW server, transcoding time has no discernible effect on the page download time on client device. High page retrieval time always subsumes the processing time and therefore it always achieves nearly the same performance as compared to any other browser.

7   Conclusions and Future Work

In this paper, we have presented an architecture for online transcoding of web pages using domain knowledge. The architecture is general enough to handle different domains by just plugging in two files for each domain. The files capture the domain-specific knowledge. The developed system requires no server side content adjustment, and no manual re-authoring of pages. The transcoding process attempts to filter out only the relevant information from a page and presents it to enable easy searching and browsing. The developed system also categorizes and summarizes the information presented to further improve on the time and effort to browse for specific information. We have tested our system extensively on the News domain and the results obtained are very good.

We are currently working on extending the system in different ways. Firstly, we are implementing rule sets for other domains.   Secondly, we are working on incorporating client profile in the transcoding process to have a better, user-specific presentation. The client profile can either be specified or can be inferred by watching the browsing pattern of the client at the proxy. The current version cannot handle HTML forms and scripts properly. Transcoding of pages with HTML forms and scripts are also being investigated.

References

[1]   Bickmore, W., Timothy, Schilit, N., Bill, "Digestor: Device-independent Access to the WWW", *Proc. of the 6th WWW Conference, 1997.*
[2]   Buyukkokten, O., Garcia-Molina, H., Paepcke, A., Winograd, T., "Power Browser: Efficient Web Browsing for PDAs ", *Proc. of the CHI'2000.*
[3]   Buyukkokten, O., Garcia-Molina, H., Paepcke, A., "Accordion Summarization for End-Game Browsing on PDAs and Cellular Phones", *Proc. of the Conf. on Human Factors in Computing Systems, CHI'01, 2001.*
[4]   Dey, L., Raghu, B., Sharma, H., Sharma, A., "Bringing Internet Services to Wireless Devices", *IETF Technical Review volume 18, No. 4, July-August 2001, pp295-305.*
[5]   Fox, A., Goldberg I., Gribble, S. D., Lee, D. C., Polito, A., Brewe, E., A., "Experience With Top Gun Wingman: A Proxy-Based Graphical Web Browser for the 3Com PalmPilot", *Proc of Middleware, 1998.*
[6]   Gonz_alez-Casta~no, F. J., Rif_on, L. A., Costa-Montenegro. E., "A new transcoding technique for PDA browsers, based on content hierarchy", *Proc. of the Mobile HCI'2002.*
[7]   Hori, M., Kondoh, G., Ono, K., Hirose, S., Singhai, S., "Annotation-based web content transcoding", *Proc. of the 9th Int. WWW Conference. Amsterdam, The Netherlands. May 2000.*
[8]   Jones, M., Mardesen, G., Mohd-Nasir, N., Boone, K., Buchanan, G., "Improving Web Interaction on small displays", *Proc. of the 8th Int. WWW Conference.Toronto, Canada. May 1999.*
[9]   Jones, M., Mohd-Nasir, N., Buchanon, G., "An Evaluation of WebTwig - a Site Outliner for Handheld Web Access", *Proc. of the International Symposium on Handheld and Ubiquitous Computing, Karlsrhue, Germany, September 1999. Gellerson, H-W (Ed.), LNCS 1707, pp 343-345. Springer.*
[10]   Shekhar, S., "Extraction of Transcoding Metadata from Web Pages" *BTech thesis, 2001 CSE Dept. IIT Kharagpur.*
[11]   "Ten Million Internet Users Go Online Via A Cell Phone Or PDA, Reports *comScore Media Metrix" Press Release, August 27, 2002, comSocre Networks.* http://www.comscore.com/news/cell_pda_082802.htm
[12]   "Internet Users Will Top 1 Billion in 2005. Wireless Internet Users Will Reach 48% in 2005", Press Release, March 21, 2002, Computer Industry Almanac Inc. http://www.c-i-a.com/pr032102.htm
[13]   Avantgo, http://www.avantgo.com
[14]   NTT DoCoMo, http://www.nttdocomo.com
[15]   Wireless Application Protocol (WAP), http://www.wapforum.com
[16]   Microsoft Pocket Internet Explorer, http://www.microsoft.com/mobile/pocketpc/software/features/internetexplorer.asp

[17] Bernard, M. "Criteria for optimal web designing (design for usability)" http://psychology.wichita.edu/optimalweb/position.htm

Appendix

In a client application the hierarchical summary tree is displayed as a conventional tree widget using plus ('+') and minus ('−') signs. For displaying a node i.e. an element it shows only the *string* field of it. In case of displaying a non-leaf node the application adds a preceding plus or minus sign. A preceding plus sign signifies that it can be expanded to see its child nodes. A preceding minus implies that it is an expanded node and can be collapsed. The HTML convention for displaying a link is preserved, i.e. blue colored and underlined text is a link and can be followed. So in the displayed page a user can do two types of actions, to expand/collapse a node and to follow a link. To expand/collapse a node a user needs to do a left to right gesture on the corresponding text. To follow a link a pen tap is required on the link. In the next series of figures we will show two typical browsing patterns in the news site http://www.independent.co.uk. Fig. 3a to Fig. 3d shows a browsing pattern starting from the front page to a full story under the category *Headline* and Fig. 4a to Fig. 4b shows a browsing in another direction through the *Sports* page.

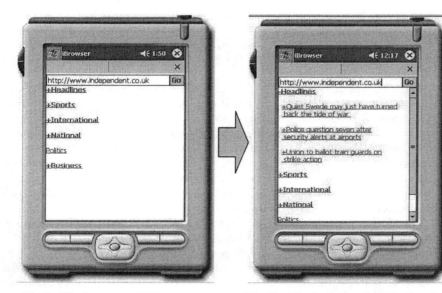

Fig. 3a. The front page of "The Independent" news paper

Fig. 3b. After Expanding the "*Headlines*"

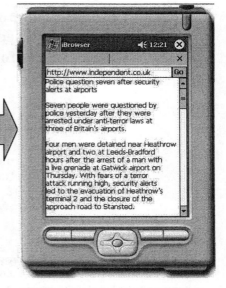

Fig. 3c. After Expanding *"Police question seven..."* A short story is available under it.

Fig. 3d. After following the link *"Police question seven..."*. Entire story is visible.

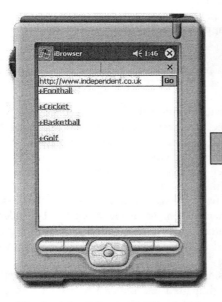
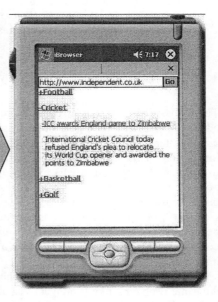

Fig. 4a. After following the *Sports* link from the front page.

Fig. 4b. After expanding the *Cricket* and the story link under it.

Multi-modal Framework to Support Users with Special Needs in Interaction with Public Information Systems

Kai Richter[1] and Marita Enge[2]

[1] Zentrum für Graphische Datenverarbeitung e. V.
Fraunhoferstr. 5, 64283 Darmstadt, Germany
`kai.richter@zgdv.de`
[2] Humboldt Universität zu Berlin
Oranienburger Str. 18, 10178 Berlin, Germany
`marita.enge@rz.hu-berlin.de`

Abstract. A framework that provides means for users with special needs to interact with otherwise not accessible public kiosk systems is being introduced. On terminals extended by this framework users can interact with kiosk systems through their own mobile device permitting them customized means for interaction. Additionally personal information stored on the mobile device can be used to provide further assistance to the user. Several psychological studies have been conducted in order to evaluate this approach.

1   Introduction

The EMBASSI project is a research projected co-funded by the German ministry of education (BMBF). The goal of this project to develop solutions for supporting the user in interacting with tomorrow's technical systems. One focus was the multi-modal interaction. This article describes a framework, which has been developed and implemented within the EMBASSI project [3]. This framework provides access to public information systems like e-kiosks (ticket machine, ATM) for everyone. As at present disabled users are often excluded from the use of public kiosk systems they were the principal target user group of the system to be developed. Also elderly people and people that are not used to interaction with information systems are often not supported so that the demand for a „design for all" has gained increasingly in importance.

Because of growing perceptive and physical restrictions elderly people have almost the same problems like (younger) visually impaired and physically disabled people, i.e. elderly with respect to their needs in accessibility (slower perception, memory access and actions) could be counted to the group of disabled people. Finally it is obvious that average users with no disabilities also could profit from an increase in accessibility and assistance in interaction with public kiosk systems.

L. Chittaro (Ed.): Mobile HCI 2003, LNCS 2795, pp. 286-301, 2003.

Equipping public kiosk systems with all the input and output devices, which would be necessary to make them accessible for every user's needs is hardly possible as handicaps are as diverse as mankind itself. The idea developed within the EMBASSI project was it to provide an additional interface to public kiosk systems allow users to access such systems through their own personal interaction agents. Those agents could be private mobile devices configured to the needs of the individual user. So visually impaired could use a device with audio in- and output and an additional Braille-line while the user with motor impairments could use a single-button device. Terminals should provide an interface for such devices to control the terminal application without using the terminals user interface. This could be an addition to the common touch screen and button interfaces which could still be used.

Additionally to the individually configured devices further personalization could improve accessibility by using user preferences and device profiles for scaling and pre-configuration of user interfaces and services and for persistent storage of relevant information. The mobile device could become a real personal assistant in interaction with real world services [17].

The following chapters are organized as follows. The first chapter will give a short introduction to related work followed by an overview of the psychological and technical requirements that have been identified. In the subsequent chapter of the framework we will give an overview of the framework followed by a more detailed description of the multi-modal interface framework and the service concept. The description of an example implementation will give more information on how this concept can be realized. We will report the results of first evaluations of the framework and we will then conclude this article with a summary of open questions that will be subject of future research.

2   Related Work

There are several projects addressing problem of making public information systems accessible for people with special needs, as there is the Trace Center [22, 24] or the Archimedes project [20].

Apart from terminal-sided improvements of accessibility like EZ access [9] the Trace Center takes part in the V2 Universal Remote Console Specification (see [24] for further information) addressing a standard for remote access to terminal systems. Other approaches for remote controlling complex applications are for example the "Personal Universal Controller" (PUC) by the Pittsburgh Pebbles PDA project [12] or XWeb [13] which defines an architecture for multimodal interaction with applications based on extended Web protocols (HTTP mainly). Another approach focusing on ad hoc network of devices allowing interaction by exchanging user interfaces is described by Newman et al. [11].

While V2 and PUC are focused on defining access and interaction protocols EMBASSI intends to provide a complete assistance environment rather than a mere multimodal remote control platform.

Archimedes is another well known project that focuses on alternative access to information systems like standard desktop computers through special interfaces. It differs from the EMBASSI project in the aspect that Archimedes intends to define the protocol between special I/O components and standard computer platforms rather than access to information systems in the public.

Another approach for improving accessibility to kiosk systems by providing multimodal interfaces is developed by the Tivis project that employs XML technologies to generate different versions of a user interface [21].

An overview of current developments in mobile devices and public kiosk systems has been given by Reimann [16].

3   Analysis of Requirements

Previous Research has revealed two principal requirements for all users of public kiosk systems, no matter if disabled or not. For all these people there are the same two requirements: to recognize the functions of the terminal and to use them for task managing. The following requirements are common to all kinds of user groups:

- Temporal restrictions: people want to use the terminal at their own pace, without the thread of early time-outs.
- Mental support: people don't want to remember data like e.g. PIN and would therefore appreciate support in remembering this kind of data.

Generally: People's wishes are greater than the opportunities for their fulfilment [23]. For example: When using a cash dispenser (also handicapped and visual impaired) people want to have the possibility to save (e.g. via CD or another media) or to print data from the terminal, or to telephone or to use internet or e-mail [4]. Nevertheless there have been identified some improvements that would lead to more user-friendly terminals for all user groups, as there are:

- Biometric method for identification (e.g. fingerprint, iris-scanning)
- Alternative multimodal access to the terminal.
- A standard layout for keypads is essential for blind people.
- Buttons on the Interface should be adaptable in size
- There should be high contrasts between touch areas, text and background colour.
- If user passes with a fingertip over the screen, he should get speech output describing the active area his fingers are touching at the time.
- Consistency in command language during the program.
- Graphics, captions, animations, symbols as well as pictures or tables should be replaced by meaningful verbal descriptions for the screen reader.
- For a better orientation Gorski & Kempke [5] advice multi-speech output: first voice for screen information; second voice for information about the task-procedure and third voice for special signs, numbers, symbols, abbreviations.

Some requirements are specific to certain handicapped user groups due to their specific limitations, those requirements are being listed in the following chapters grouped by requirements of visually impaired and physically handicapped users.

3.1   Special Requirements for Visually Impaired People

- Location and self-description of terminals: Where are terminals and if there are several, which one to choose? What are the services a terminal offers?
- Graphical terminal interfaces have to be adaptable in font size, contrast and complexity otherwise no autonomous usage possible.
- Braille as only alternative output has severe drawbacks: At outdoor terminals tactual sensitivity is dramatically reduced with decreasing temperature. The estimated number of Braille readers in Europe is less than 0.02% of the population.
- Standardized structures for public terminal interfaces would be very helpful for blind persons to allow transfer of experience between different applications.
- Physical interactions like inserting cards or money should be reduced as card or money slots are difficult to be located.

More than non-disabled or handicapped people the visually impaired want to have/get

- A preview what will happen after pressing a key.
- Information step by step.
- Information for orientation in the terminal area.
- A connection to other terminals/or services while using one of them in order to get more specific information, e.g. like internet.
- Speech recognition and voice output favoured before Braille edition or the relief through an Avatar (aid through a like a human being figure on the screen).

3.2   Special Requirements for Physically Handicapped People

Physically impaired people are often excluded from the use of public kiosk systems because interaction components are positioned out of reach or the interface is a touch screen display, which is operated with fingertips. Physically impaired people often are limited to minimal movements with eyelid or mouth. If only a forward approach in a wheelchair is possible, then the maximum height of any interactive element on the terminal should not exceed 1.2 metres. The lowest height of any operable part of the user interface should not be less than 0.7 metres. Further physically impaired people are hindered by early time outs by the machine and they have difficulties to access the card reader or other physical slots of the machine.

4   Assistance

Assistance gives access to functions assigned to machines. This means functions that are not accessible because they are unknown to the user or their use requires too much sensory, cognitive or motor effort from the user. Assistance systems include all the components of a user interface that support the user in solving a task. According to [23] assistance by technical components could be necessary for six steps in human action:

1. Motivation, activation and goal setting
2. Perception
3. Information integration, generating situation awareness
4. Decision making, action selection
5. Action execution
6. Processing feedback of action results.

To support the use of public terminals for elderly, visually impaired and physically handicapped people requires assistance in perception, information integration, generation of situational awareness, decision making and action selection as well as action execution.

A survey conducted during the initial phase of the EMBASSI project (2000) inquiring which kinds of technical assistance were desired by the different user groups revealed that all the three user groups (visually and physically impaired and non-impaired) preferred a pocket-sized portable assistance system with long stand by time and visual display a configuration similar to today's palmtops or smart phones. All users preferred adaptable assistance which could be configured at any time by the user himself.

Mainly visually impaired users preferred additional means to access terminal systems going beyond the standard configuration which seems clear as common touch screens or buttons are hardly usable for them. As shown below handicapped persons compared to others would in general accept a greater degree of automatic assistance.

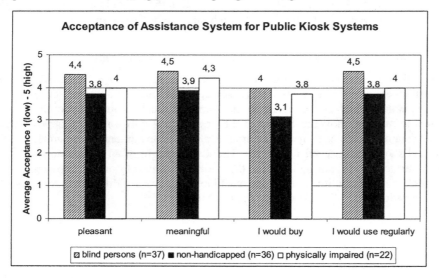

Fig. 1. Distribution of the acceptance data between handicapped and not handicapped persons while operation of terminals with a future assistance system

5   Framework Overview

In the EMBASSI framework a mobile device serves as personal assistant in interaction with public terminal systems and other information systems. The personal device serves as holder of personalized input and output components, as platform for personal assistive software and as storage for personal information that can support the user during interaction.

All software modules implemented in this framework are realized as software agents, independent modules communicating over TCP/IP and a special protocol an extended version of the Knowledge Query and Manipulation Language (KQML)[8]. Agents are connected to a router and each router forms an own agent platform. Agents can dynamically connect to platforms and platforms can be connected dynamically to.

In order to provide access to an existing e-kiosk application with minimal modification of the original application a narrow interface had to be defined, allowing the exchange of information of the application state (dynamic contents, interface presently visible) between application and framework [19]. Application user interfaces had to be rebuild in a generic user interface description language (XUI, see below) allowing the delivery of the interfaces to a remote device. On the terminal a complete autonomous agent platform is installed. There can be different assistant components on a platform advertising their services.

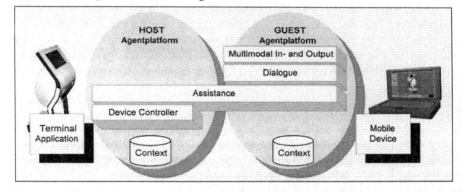

Fig. 2. Overview of the framework architecture. The terminal application is connected to his local agent platform through a device controller. Assistance or Service components can be found on both platforms while only on the client side user interface controllers are located. A mobile platform (left) can connected to a terminal platform (right) and create a new session in which all services are available to all components

A mobile device also has a complete agent platform running. One specialized agent is responsible to control user interaction. It receives abstract user interface descriptions and hands them on to suitable input and output devices to generate the interface.

How does the mobile device discover the terminal? Over a network the terminal sends broadcasts advertising its services by sending an XML document containing the description. When the user chooses to connect to a terminal a TCP-connection is established and the host-router (the terminal located router) sets up a new session allowing communication between mobile device and terminal.

This framework represents a location-aware and dynamic ad-hoc infrastructure that can be used for any kind of interaction between devices in a continuously changing environment.

6   The Multimodal Framework

Integration of different multi-modal interaction devices requires several layers of abstraction as described in the EMBASSI framework [6, 7]. In order to combine and synchronize input from various sources a central instance receives abstract notifications of user events. Those event notifications are generated by so called input filters translating platform and device specific signals into generic events and sometimes performing low-level fusion of predefined sensor or input device arrays. System output is distributed by the polymodal output to a set of output components, so called rendering components, which are responsible for generation and update of the user interface. While the polymodal output is responsible for the concrete instances of modality-dependent interfaces the management of the abstract interfaces is performed by the dialog manager, controlling focus, zoom state and other parameters. One abstract interface may have several presentations generated by different rendering components. As part of the framework presented here a dialog manager, a poly-modal in- and output manager and a prototypical renderer and filter component for Java Swing® and HTML have been developed and implemented. Also an abstract description for the user interface the extensible User Interface Language (XUI) has been developed [18]. The following chapters will give a short overview of the components and XUI.

6.1   eXtensible User Interface Language

Providing access to existing applications requires a means to create a true representation of the original applications user interface. Further the presentation on different devices in different modalities requires a high level of abstraction that allows convergence between the different platforms. A variety of approaches for a abstract description of user interface were developed in the past years, as for example the User Interface Mark-up Language (UIML)[1, 14] or the Mozilla project's Cross Platform Front End (XPFE) described in the XML-based User Interface Language (XUL) [10] integrated in their browser. While XUL is designed mainly for graphical user interfaces UIML claims to provide means for describing user interfaces in an amodal and platform independent way. Unfortunately present version only provides a syntax to describe such structures but no set of amodal controls to be applied. Another promising solution is the model-based eXtensible Interface Markup Language (XIML) [15] which allows interface definitions on base of user and task models. This approach is still new and evolving (see [18] for a more detailed discussion).

The eXtensible User Interface language (XUI) is an adaptation of the W3C XForms specification [2] providing an abstract definition of user interfaces in XML syntax. W3C XForms defines the next generation web forms standard. W3C XForms defines a set of abstract user interface components representing an extension to today's HTML form components. One of the most powerful concepts of the W3C XForms addresses the processing of data. The data to be collected from the user or the state of the user interface is represented and handled in an own structure, which is called the data model. This model includes a data typing and validation mechanism which can be used for client side evaluation of user input and which is based on the W3C schema definitions.

6.2   Control Elements

XUI adapts a subset of user interface elements from XForms, which were considered to be sufficiently abstract for presentation on any device and in any modality. User interface elements are defined mainly by the type of data accepted (e.g. "input" can be used to collect string input, "selectBoolean" allows the choice between two alternatives). Unlike XForms, where controls are handled as part of a form, which is submitted as a whole, XUI focuses on the abstraction of an application front-end allowing direct interaction with an application. Hence every XUI control holds a separate data model that is submitted directly on user interaction.

XUI also specifies a mechanism for defining events and actions within a user interface (e.g. enabling or setting visible controls by selecting or unselecting a choice) that also consists on a subset of XForms events and actions.

6.3   Accessibility

Every XUI control has to hold a caption describing the control. This seems trivial but in fact many of today's toolkits handle caption and control separately. In Java Swing for instance a label has to be assigned to a control explicitly. This is often ignored or forgotten by programmers leading to interfaces where both elements are separate items related only by their spatial position unperceivable for e.g. a blind user. In XUI a caption is an integral part of a control describing the control to the user as depicted in figure. In cooperation with providers of supportive technology for visually and physically disabled the control set was evaluated and improved in order to achieve a maximum of accessibility for such users.

6.4   Polymodal In- and Output

The framework as mentioned above is designed to support simultaneous input from and output to several modalities. The polymodal in- and output (PMIO) is the central component, which distributes user amodal interface-descriptions to different modality-specific presentation components and on the other hand integrates input from several input components.

A new user interface before being distributed to different renderers has to pass a pipeline of different processing modules, as there are the analysis (e.g. how many elements; how many items in a selection list; e.g. to change input mode); the extraction of data model and instance date (e.g. the initial content of fields); adaptation (e.g. reordering, changing layout, reducing number of controls) and distribution to the different presentation and input components.

Due to the modular architecture different modules can be plugged into the pipeline. User input on the other hand is sent by the input components to the PMIO, which has to solve competitive inputs and merge additive information. This can be realized e.g. by tracking temporal relations. After integration of the user input the data is validated against the control's schema that has been extracted before. On validation success instance data in the PMIO is updated and send to all registered components and also to the underlying application core.

6.5   Rendering and Input Components

Rendering components are needed to generate a user side representation of the application interface. This presentation can be realized in different modalities at the same time. In the present system there exist renderers for visual output (Java Swing®, HTML), aural output (IBM Via Voice®), and tactile output. The visual renderers allow the presentation of XUI interfaces in a common visual way in input with mouse, keyboard or pen either as Java Swing Interface or as HTML page on a mobile device (Compaq iPAQ). The aural renderer is optimised for the use in combination with visual output addressing the elderly user, users with motor problems or just those preferring voice commands. The aural renderer reads the caption of the control, which has the present focus. On a "help" command the hint text is read to the user with another voice. Navigation can be realized in different ways: by reading the caption of a control, focus is set to this control; another commands allows, "tabbing" through the interface. The tactile renderer controls a hardware extension to a common Braille-line allowing visually impaired to get a low-resolution impression of graphic information. In interaction with interface controls, certain standard elements like "next", "ok" or "abort" can be emphasized by presenting a key symbol on the tactile display.

7   The Service Framework

Within the framework described here a service is represented by the single assistant-agents rather than the terminal itself (which can serve as host for a variety of applications. Those agents are publishing their services to the platform they are registered to. If another platform (e.g. the mobile user's device) connects to this platform, registered assistants are published to the guest platform and hence are made available to the user.

Due to the classification of services that is based o standards users and applications can, without having visited a location or a terminal before, inquire for services available and then request an offer from the ones that are fitting. Such a general classification is a necessary precondition for integrating and discovering services in a heterogeneous and dynamic environment.

7.1   Power of Personalization

Together with the general service concept depicted above individual services or assistants can be combined in order to obtain the possibility of personalization in a dynamic and "stateless" environment. As services may not only be located on the terminal but also on the mobile device those services can be used to store and apply persistent and individual data, like e.g. preferences, personal data, etc. This information then is not revealed to a terminal that is visited but stays local, to be processed on the mobile device.

If for instance a user accesses a ticket machine in order to get a ticket back home the ticket machine itself is not aware of the user personal data, and of course it should not be so. On the other hand storing personal information like home address on a mobile device is common practice, either in an address book or in the "owner info sheet". So why not using this information in interaction with the ticket machine? In the framework described here a local assistant could be used to fill in this information automatically into a request for a ticket. Of course this could be extended further, that the calendar application on the mobile device could be checked if there is any meeting that could be missed if choosing the wrong connection, etc.

This is only possible either if there is only a limited amount of static services knowing each other and implementing clearly defined protocols in order to exchange data or if there is a general classification and an open protocol that makes it possible to exchange such requests in a common format.

Each service can offer a user interface that allows the user to interact with the application directly on his own device by means of the XUI user interface definition. But there is also a programmatic interface defining a protocol on base of article data which can be used for inter-assistant communication.

7.2   An Example Implementation: Shopping List Assistant

As a proof of concept an example application of a shopping list assistant has been implemented. The shopping list assistant is an assistant agent running on the mobile device allowing the user to keep a local list of goods to be bought. This can be done offline, for instance at home where no terminal is available. Later, when the user is on his way downtown by passing by a shopping terminal he can submit this list and in return receives a priced offer. He now can either edit this offer for new submission or buy the items on the list. The user can do this by interacting with the local shopping list assistant providing always the same interface. So no matter where he is or on which terminal he executes his order, the user does not have to get used to a new interface every time.

After submitting the order to the terminal the user is forwarded to the terminal application and can either continue browsing the shop for further articles of follow the final steps to complete the order (payment, delivery, etc.).

Personalization is realized through a history function, where every article that is bought is being stored and rated by relevance (frequency, amount, last purchase). So the user always has a list of articles to choose from and that is ordered by relevance to him stored persistently on the device. Another personalization function is the possibility to store shopping lists on the mobile device allowing the user to reuse them as often as wanted.

Together with a prototypical terminal application an example platform has been implemented and deployed on several platforms in combination with additional supportive I/O components (see above).

8   Evaluation

Several evaluation studies have been carried out during this project. The example implementation of a shopping terminal (serving as prototype for a arbitrary kiosk system) and a variety mobile devices equipped with the EMBASSI platform were used as test bed for a set of psychological evaluations. The multi-modal assistant on the mobile device should support the user in browsing and interacting with the terminal-interface.

1. At first, different kinds of multimodal access for visually impaired and handicapped disabled people were evaluated by usability experts and real users assessing if disabled and non-disabled people were able to use supply and functions of the shopping-terminal with a first version of the special multimodal technical devices (without any help by another person).
2. What kind of assistance under which conditions were be the best support for visually impaired or non-disabled users and how special assistance functions should be implemented were inquired in a Wizard of Oz-Simulation.
3. At last the shopping assistance in the second version of the mobile multimodal systems has been tested and evaluated by usability experts and possible users, e.g. non-handicapped and physically handicapped people (e. g. with paraplegia at the neck).

8.1   Results of the First Study

When interacting with the terminal by means of the first version of the personal assistant visually impaired persons were not able to recognize the user interface or concept of use without additional social assistance. Only technical aid (screen reader scanned the screen step by step for speech output, Braille-wave and tactile display) was not sufficient for solving the shopping task. Most problems resulted in the synthetic speech output because blind users did not comprehend the given information. So they did not understand the concept of use, i.e. what and how to do it. Additional explanations by the researcher were necessary which had negative effects on the operational time. As a summary blind people wish an adaptable speech output referring to sound volume, gender of voice and speech pace. They also wish a natural speech output, e.g. English words should be translated adequately into proper German.

Physically handicapped test subjects were offered a special system (with max. 3 sensors to navigate or scan the screen step by step) as well as a mobile touch screen to solve the shopping task wireless. Most problems occurred by presenting screen contents because of an unexpected order, e.g. information were not given in the expected way: from left to right or up to down.

Due to the results of this study the personal assistant devices have undergone a complete revision addressing the interaction devices, user interfaces and communication protocols. A second version of those devices has been implemented.

8.2   Results of the Study with Wizard of Oz-Method
to Simulate Shopping-Assistance

In this study the shopping-terminal system has always been the same but it was expanded by natural voices (pre-recorded speech snippets) and different kinds of speech assistance. The speech output was realized by natural male and female speaking assistants. While the screen contents remained the same, screen information without relevant button-activity and different kinds of assistive speech were given by a female voice and information with relevant button-activity were presented by a male voice. Making the navigation or orientation easier additional higher categories for the lists of articles were named by a female voice. E.g. the interface showed 12 different articles of milk but the female voice distinguished between only two categories: long-life milk and full-cream milk. In each of these categories were less options to choose from. All these improvements were realized for blind users in order to achieve mental support, better orientation and saving of time.

Three kinds of speech assistance were realized and could be described according to [23] as the following:

1. Assistance through information: given information by female speech was more than just perception of a button-labelling. User was informed about the consequences on a pragmatic level, e.g. like tool-tips.
2. Assistance through delegation: assistance does not only support action selection but also execution. One option is offered. But the user does not have to execute this alternative by him- or herself. The system does this automatically if the user agrees. If the user does not agree, the system may recommend another option or it will wait for further user actions or changes in the progress of solving the task.
3. Assistance through informative execution: the entire action is executed by the system. The user cannot directly control the operation. He is in a supervisory role and may switch off this assistance completely, but as long as it is 'on', it controls the process autonomously.

Because of the growing perceptive restrictions of elderly people as we have discussed above we focussed in our study on comparable user groups of similar age (36 visually impaired people and 40 non-handicapped people older than 50 years). Additionally a group of 10 sighted persons older than 50 had to solve the tasks only with speech output. In this way we wanted to control that the tasks could be solved in a speech-only manner. All of them solved four shopping tasks under four different conditions (with / without time pressure or limit of money). All of them were able to solve the shopping task on their own with the improved natural speech output and without social assistance. The best results were achieved with assistance through informative execution. Different voices were recommended in order to present different kinds of information: one for global information, one for action-possibilities and one for help like tool-tips.

8.3   Results of the Evaluation by User Tests

Two mobile multimodal systems have been tested by potential users (non-disabled and physically handicapped people). Non-disabled persons were divided in two groups, one that had to solve the tasks without assistance and the other that could use the personal assistance device. Each person had to solve various shopping tasks.

The effect of assistance has been evaluated by comparing non-handicapped users with and without assistance. Further performance of non-handicapped and handicapped persons has been compared trying to answer the question whether these personal assistance would allow handicapped to interact as efficiently with the terminal as the others. In fact results proved that this concept could provide more independence to handicapped users in interaction with public information systems:

- Even persons with heavy physical impairments were able to use the shopping terminal by means of the assistance system without additional aid by other persons. Their performance was almost as precise and complete as performance of non-handicapped users.
- Even though introducing new interaction concepts when using the personal assistants the mental load was comparably small in all groups. However persons without assistance perceive more mental load if they have to memorize things.
- Users of the assistance systems feel smaller physical load when repeating tasks.
- The usability of the assistance systems has been judged well to very well. However willingness of non-handicapped persons to use this system in their real life turned out to be limited.
- A major drawback were the long durations mainly physically handicapped users took to complete the tasks with the assistance system. However through learn- and assistance effects this duration decreases significantly. Also the number of interaction steps was greater with than without assistance. But also here the tendency was decreasing.

In order to reduce required time and effort it would be reasonable to offer additional assistance to interactions; e.g. in the case of text entries (context sensitive word forecast); the navigation over the screen (task oriented presets, jump functions); or paging functions (aid during the selection of stored data).

Willingness of non-handicapped persons to use this system could be increased by improving the quality of speech in- and output. But it seems a general shortcoming of this interaction method that reliability and speed still is not at an acceptable level yet. Adaptable contexts and dictionaries are being developed in order to improve recognition performance.

9   Conclusion and Outlook

It has been shown that a multi-modal framework for remote access to public information systems can alleviate user interaction, above all for users with special needs. The concept of allowing the user to access kiosk systems by means of their own mobile device has the advantage of not causing huge additional cost for the service provider if using a pre-existing framework which allows to integrate existing applications while providing a maximum of customizable and scalable access for the user. The ubiquitous availability of personal data as basis for personalized services and interaction to service independent of provider or location seems a promising possibility for the future and could be extended to other applications than kiosk systems, e.g. administrative and municipal infrastructures or alike.

XUI as an amodal and platform independent user interface description language has proved to allow remote interaction between mobile users and applications through different modalities and I/O components. Still there is need for improvements considering the set of available controls and style definitions which are still limited. Abstraction of local interaction (coded within the interface) should be extended according to the efforts made in the W3C XForms. Serialization and segmentation of interaction paths or complex interfaces still is a problem if the client is not aware of the underlying application logic. Providing abstractions of the task as proposed by model-based approaches like XIML could serve as basis for further improvements.

When thinking of platform independent application interfaces in most cases the focus is on providing the same functionality to different platforms through an equivalent interface. What to our knowledge has not yet been defined is the term of equivalence of such multi-platform presentations. Does the user perceive different presentations of the same application as instances of the same interface. Does the user profit from experience with other presentations of the same interface or does he have to learn it all new from the start? Are two users interacting on the same application but on different presentations able to work cooperatively? Do they work on equivalent interfaces? In other words: what is the measure of equivalence? Equivalence should be defined as equivalence from the user's point of view or in terms of the user's mental model of an application. Future research will try address the point of defining and measuring equivalence of different interface presentations.

The service concept introduced here is presently limited to interaction with public kiosk systems. In the context of a multi channel information and service infrastructure such kiosk systems could serve as one alternative channel providing access to real-world goods. As supplementary to internet shops kiosk systems have the advantage of immediateness. Goods are available immediately and not only after the order-and-delivery delay of some days. Such mobile kiosks (mKiosks) could then combine location aware services, kiosk specific services and traditional internet services perhaps in combination with so-called WLAN hotspots. The framework presented here has made a first step into that direction and future research will address integration of this approach into a multi-channel service infrastructure.

References

[1]   Abrams, M., Phanouriou, C., Batongbacal, A.L., Williams, S.M. and Shuster, J.E., UIML: Appliance-independent XML User Interface Language. in *8th International World Wide Web Conference*, (Toronto, 1999), 1695-1708.

[2]   Dubinko, M., Dietl, J., Merrick, R., Raggett, D., Raman, T.V. and Welsh, L.B. XForms 1.0 - W3C Working Draft, W3C, 2001.

[3]   Webpage: EMBASSI - Elektronische Multimediale Bedien- und Service-Assistenz, (1999), Available at: http://www.embassi.de

[4]   Enge, M. and Massow, S. Needs for assistance of visually and physically disabled and non-disabled persons when using money-/cash dispensers. *Human-System Interaction: Education, Research and Application in the 21st Century.* 263 - 266.

[5]   Gorski, H. and Kempke, G., Software-ergonomische Gestaltung von Computerarbeitsplätzen für Blinde und Sehbehinderte. in *Software-Ergonomie '93*, (Bremen, Germany, 1993), 2 ff.

[6]   Kirste, T. An experimental communication framework for EMBASSI supporting data-flow based distributed agent systems, 2002.

[7]   Kirste, T. and Rapp, S., Architecture for Multimodal Interactive Assistant Systems. in *Statustagung der Leitprojekte "Mensch-Technik-Interaktion"*, (Saarbrücken, Germany, 2001), 111-115.

[8]   Labrou, Y. and Finin, T. A Proposal for a new KQML Specification, 1997.

[9]   Law, C.M. and Vanderheiden, G.C., The development of a Simple, Low Cost Set of Universal Access Features for Electronic Devices. in *ACM CUU 2000 (The Association of Computer Machinery Conference on Universal Usability)*, (Washington D.C., USA, 2000).

[10]   Mozilla.org. XPToolkit Project, Mozilla.org, 1999.

[11]   Newman, M.W., Izadi, S., Edwards, W.K., Sedivy, J.Z. and Smith, T.F., User interfaces when and where they are needed: an infrastructure for recombinant computing. in *15th annual ACM Symposium on User Interface Software and Technology*, (Paris, France, 2002), ACM Press, 171-180.

[12]   Nichols, J. and Myers, B.A., Studying the use of handhelds to control smart appliances. in *International Workshop on Smart Appliances and Wearable Computers. IWSAWC 2003*, (Providence, USA, 2003).

[13]   Webpage: XWeb Project, (2000), Available at: http://icie.cs.byu.edu/ICE/XWeb

[14]   Phanouriou, C. UIML: A Device-Independent User Interface Markup Language *Computer Science and Applications*, Virginia Polytechnic Institute and State University, Blacksburg, Virginia, 2000, 158.

[15]   Puerta, A. and Eisenstein, J. XIML: A universal language for User Interfaces, RedWhale Software, Palo Alto, CA, USA, 2002.

[16]   Reimann, E., Neue Einsatzszenarien für den Handel - Kiosks als Communication Stations für mobile Anwendungen. in *P.O.S. MarketingCongress 2002*, (Düsseldorf, Germany, 2002).

[17]   Richter, K., An advanced concept of assistance for mobile customers of POS. in *E2002*, (Prague, Czech Republic, 2002).

[18]   Richter, K., Generic Interface Descriptions using XML. in *CADUI*, (Valenciennes, France, 2002).

[19]   Richter, K., Remote Access to Public Kiosk Systems. in *1st International Conference on Universal Access in Human - Computer Interaction*, (New Orleans, USA, 2001).

[20]   Webpage: The Archimedes Project, (2003), Available at: http://archimedes.stanford.edu/

[21]   Webpage: Tivis: Accessible Kiosks an Assistive Technologies, (2003), Available at: http://www.tivis.net.au/

[22] Webpage: Trace Research and Development Center, (2001), Available at: http://trace.wisc.edu

[23] Wandke, H. Assistance in human-machine interaction: a conceptual framework and a proposal for a taxonomy., Humboldt-Universität, Berlin, Germany, 2003.

[24] Zimmermann, G., Vanderheiden, G. and Gilman, A., Universal Remote Console - Prototyping for the Alternate Interface Access Standard. in *7th ERCIM Workshop "User interfaces for All"*, (Paris, France, 2002).

Usability Evaluations
for Multi-device Application Development
Three Example Studies

Verena Giller, Rudolf Melcher, Johann Schrammel,
Reinhard Sefelin, and Manfred Tscheligi

CURE Center for Usability Research & Engineering
Hauffgasse 3-5, 1110 Vienna, Austria
cure@cure.at

Abstract. This paper discusses three example studies, that informed user interface guidelines, developed for a set of different classes of mobile devices. The results of these studies show answers to typical design problems arising during the development of mobile applications. Furthermore the studies are meant to be examples showing which kind of studies are required in order to develop a sufficient pool of user interface guidelines covering almost all sorts of mobile devices.

1   Introduction

This paper presents the results of three example studies, which compare different ways of navigation, selection and interaction implemented on five classes of mobile devices. These studies were part of an EU funded project (CONSENSUS [3]). CONSENSUS develops a mark-up language supporting the automatic adaptation of user interfaces for mobile devices. The mark-up language development process, however, will not be discussed in this paper. The studies discussed in our paper are three examples of a large number of empirical studies, which informed the development of user interface guidelines on which the adaptation process is based.

As one important prerequisite of these studies a device classification was developed, which enabled us to draw generic conclusions from our studies. The classification of the devices was based on an analysis focusing on those device characteristics that have an influence on users' behaviour and on their perception of the user interface. This analysis led to three main dimensions defining the eight device classes, which we finally developed. These dimensions are: presentation structure, supported input modality, mark-up language. Van Welie and de Groot [11], who also developed a device classification, used a very similar approach, which was also based on these three dimensions.

The classification on which we based our empirical studies included eight classes. The classes ranged from class 0 (speech input and output only) to class 7 (laptop-PC). Speech interfaces were included because in a lot of mobile contexts (take for example

L. Chittaro (Ed.): Mobile HCI 2003, LNCS 2795, pp. 302–316, 2003.
© Springer-Verlag Berlin Heidelberg 2003

car driving) hands-free interaction is required. In this paper only studies with devices of the classes 0 to 4 will be discussed.

The first study, which we discuss in this paper compares different ways of text presentation. The second study investigated the optimal depth and breadth of trees enabling users to navigate through content structures. Finally the third study discusses how we defined optimal and maximal numbers of list entries for two different kinds of speech-lists. The studies were conducted with one device of class 1 (typical mobile WAP-phones; representative: SIEMENS, ME45), one of class 2 (mobile phones with large colour displays; representative: NOKIA, 7650) two different devices of device class 3 (a COMPAQ: iPAQ Pocket PC (browser type: Konqueror) and a handspring treo-Communicator (browser type: Blazer) and one of class 4 (clamshell devices; representative: NOKIA, Communicator 9210i). Our third study dealt with speech interaction via fixed line telephones or mobile phones (class 0).

2   Optimising Text Presentations for Reading Tasks

2.1   Motivation

Today's web guidelines, which are dealing with text reading come to the conclusion that texts should be as short as possible but that users will scroll content pages if they expect further information which is relevant to their tasks (see e.g. [6], page 115 and [9], page 77). The splitting of texts into chunks of two or more pages should be avoided.

Screens of mobile devices, however, are much smaller than the screens for which "ordinary" web pages are designed. These differences may lead to different rules regarding the optimal lengths of pages for these devices. Since the handling of screen elements like scroll bars displayed on mobile devices cause more effort compared to the handling of such elements on a computer screen, users might tend to prefer a pagination mechanism. Therefore our hypotheses was that mobile devices are closer to the book than to the desktop computer and need therefore a metaphor of turning pages rather than the one of a paper roll.

These and other considerations led us to the set up of this study. We wanted to answer the question, whether users prefer a pagination mechanism or a scrolling mechanism to read longer texts. Furthermore we wanted to investigate whether these preferences are device class dependent.

The study was necessary because at the moment there is no empirical data available, dealing with these questions. Although Buchanan et al. [1] compare different possibilities to scroll though lists of headlines, these tests are of small relevance for our questions. Firstly this study is not dealing with longer texts and secondly it is using interaction techniques, which are not supported by today's state of the art wap-browsers.

Another goal of this study was to see whether line breaks inside words displayed on devices of device class 1 and 2 can increase users' reading speed and whether they are reducing their subjective reading satisfaction.

2.2   Methodology

Devices of device class 1 to 4 were used for this study. The representative of class 3 was a "COMPAQ: iPAQ Pocket PC". The test sessions started with a briefing phase where demographic variables as well as variables concerning users' experiences with the four device classes were gathered. Subjects who were not familiar with device class 2 and 4 got a special introduction of the handling of these two device classes. All subjects were familiar with device classes 1 and 3.

The test of each device class started with the reading of a sample text. This sample text gave users the possibility to get used to the devices and to the task of reading a text with it. After that we started the test phase during which users' reading speed, their comprehension of the text and their reading satisfaction were measured. With the devices of device class 1 and 2 we compared pagination with scrolling and we compared also texts, which included line breaks inside words, with texts, which did not include such line breaks.

After subjects had completed a reading task (the reading time was measured in seconds), we asked them three questions concerning the content of the text. This enabled us to measure whether they had understood the text and, more important, we forced our subjects to read carefully and to make sure that they get the text's main messages.

The alternative display method was presented to the subjects directly afterwards. That means that a subject who was first confronted with a text, which he/she had to scroll, was then confronted with another text, which had to be paged through. A special index (see [4]) made sure that the complexity and readability as well as the number of words of both texts was almost equal. Texts used for tests with mobile phones included less words and characters than those used for tests with PDAs (mobile phones: approximately 400 words, PDAs: approximately 550 words). The texts were in German. We used modified articles of an Austrian newspaper about economical topics. The texts were slightly changed in order to make sure that they are fulfilling our requirements.

After the user had finished this alternative text (again the reading time was measured) the same procedure as described above was repeated. Finally we asked users to draw a line for each of the two possibilities. The length of the line should express their reading comfort. Users who were satisfied with the pagination method but not with the scrolling method drew a longer pagination-line compared to the scrolling-line and vice versa. The sheet on which users should draw the line included a clear marker for the starting point of the line that users should draw. These lines enabled us to measure the exact proportion of users' assessments of both methods.

This procedure was repeated for all the six alternative text displays on our four devices. The test design made sure that order and learning effects could not occur. Therefore the orders of devices and of text presentation styles were randomised. A short qualitative interview was conducted at the end of each session.

The pagination was implemented in the following way: At the end of the last line of the page/card three dots were displayed. Users then had to use a next button to go to the next page/card. Breaks inside of sentences only occurred once per text when the texts were displayed on devices of classes 3 and 4. The chunks of text displayed on devices of class 1 and 2 were implemented as single cards rather than as a whole deck. This decision was based on the assumption that users prefer to wait relatively short periods of time for each chunk and that loading the whole deck at once would lead to a too long waiting period.

The line breaks inside the words did not include hyphenation because this feature currently is not supported by state of the art WAP-browsers.

2.3   Results

10 subjects participated in our test sessions. 4 of them were female and 6 male. Their average age was 27.5 years (Std. Dev.: 7 years). All subjects were experienced users of device class 1 and 3.

Figure 1 shows a comparison of users' reading speed with the four device classes. On the left diagram scrolling is compared with pagination. The figure shows that big differences occur only when devices of device class 1 were used.

For the statistical analysis we used a two-way ANOVA with device class and presentation style (scrolling vs. paging) as within-subjects factors. Both main effects as well as their interaction were significant (Device classes: $F(3.27)=7.03$, $p=0.001$; Presentation styles: $F(1.9)=21.78$, $p=0.001$; Interaction: $F(3.27)=30.77$, $p<0.0005$). Due to the different text lengths the main effect of the device classes cannot be interpreted unambiguously. Post hoc analysis of the simple main effects showed that the time-difference between scrolling and paginating are only significant for device class 1 $(F(1.9)=108,4$, $p<0.0005$. The reason for this might be that users who were confronted with devices of device class 1 and who had to page through the texts had to deal with relatively high total loading times. Since one card only displayed a rather small number of characters (approximately 45) a relatively high number of cards had to be loaded in order to read the whole text.

Figure 2 shows the subjects' reading comfort expressed in line lengths.

Again a two-way ANOVA was used to analyse the data. The main effect of the presentation styles $(F(3.27)=15.12$, $p=0.004)$ and the interaction effect $(F(1.9)=7.42$, $p=0.001)$ were significant, whereas the main effect of the device classes was not $(F(3,27)=2.64$, $p=0.07)$. A post hoc analysis of the simple main effects showed, that similar to the time results the difference between scrolling and pagination is only significant for device class 1 $(F(1.9)=30.69$, $p<0.0005)$.

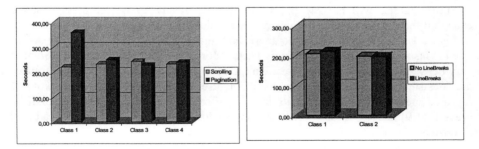

Fig. 1. Mean reading speed in seconds: left: Comparison of pagination and scrolling for device classes 1-4; right: Comparison of line breaks inside words and no such line breaks for device classes 1 and 2

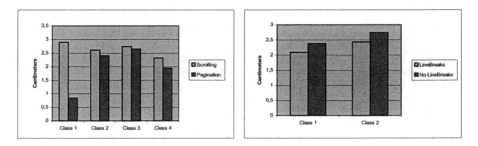

Fig. 2. Mean reading comfort in centimeters: left: Comparison of pagination and scrolling for device classes 1-4; right: Comparison of line breaks inside words and no such line breaks for device classes 1 and 2 (the longer the line the higher the expressed satisfaction)

The results of this study lead to the conclusion that in general a designer should have good reasons to use a pagination mechanism instead of a scrolling one. This is especially true when he/she is designing for devices of class 1.

The tests were conducted with typical content pages, which did not contain interaction elements. Our hypothesis was that possibly users prefer to page through the text displayed on mobile devices because the handling of elements that are supporting scrolling may be more difficult than the handling of these elements with a typical desktop PC. Another advantage of pagination might have been that scrolling easily can lead to a loss of orientation between the lines and that, on the other hand, the pagination mechanism provides users with pages whose content does not move.

However, the empirical data gathered could not prove that these two possible advantages outperform the disadvantages of long loading times and of an interaction mechanism, which is not consistent with today's web sites. That means that as long as loading times are at today's level there seem to be no clear reasons for pagination. Some user statements collected during our tests also support this. So a lot of users complained that the loading times are too long and that they are often loosing the plot of the texts. Another advantage of the scrolling concept, which was often mentioned by our subjects, was that scrolling gives them more control over the text. So one user said, "When I am scrolling I can control the speed. On the other hand the pagination thing gives me the feeling that the computer controls how fast I am allowed to read."

Future studies will have to prove whether the results of device class 1 and 2 change if the chunks of text are implemented as decks rather than as single cards.

Figure 1 and Figure 2 (right pictures) show that the differences, which are due to line breaks inside words, are relatively small. Moreover the reading speed differences vary between the two device classes. On the other hand we see that these differences are consistent over both measurements of the users' reading satisfaction. A two-way repeated measures ANOVA results in a significant main effect for the factor linebreak ($F(1.9)=5.98$, $p=0.037$). That means that line breaks inside of words lead to a lower reading satisfaction.

3   Content Structures: Depth versus Breadth

3.1   Motivation

Navigation is one of the most critical factors of user interface design. A very important aspect of navigation is its structure, which is determined by the number of levels (depth) and by the number of items per level (breadth). In this context the question arises, whether it is better to offer a deep structure with few items per level or a broad one with many items per level. In the literature there are several recommendations available concerning this issue, but they mainly refer to desktop systems (see e.g. [6]).

This study aimed at estimating the influence of navigation structures on the searching performance and on the subjective satisfaction of users.

Our hypothesis was that all items on the same level should be perceptible at a glance, without forcing users to scroll. Therefore the optimal breadth would be determined by the screen size. We estimated the optimal depth of the navigation structure of device class 1 and 2 on the basis of available WAP-guidelines (see e.g. [10]). Regarding device class 3 and 4 we assumed that the structure should not be more than four levels deep. Starting from the premises mentioned above we defined an assumed optimal structure for each device class (see the grey coloured fields in Table 1).

Tabel 1. Tested structures per device class. Variations in breadth and depth (ST1, ST2, ST3). The grey fields indicate the assumed optimal structures

	Depth	Breadth		Depth	Breadth
Class 1 ST1	4	3	Class 3 ST1	4	12
Class 1 ST2	2	6	Class 3 ST2	2	24
Class 1 ST3	3	4	Class 3 ST3	8	6
Class 2 ST1	3	8	Class 4 ST1	4	12
Class 2 ST2	2	12	Class 4 ST2	2	24
Class 2 ST3	6	4	Class 4 ST3	8	6

3.2   Methodology

The goal of this study was to compare the assumed optimal structure with two alternative structures differing in depth and breadth. We measured users' searching performance and their subjective satisfaction.

Most of the items used for the different structures were terms of yahoo's content classification. To get reliable data, users had to perform three different search tasks per structure. Subjects were asked to find different items at the deepest levels of the structure. Two target items where located in the same main path and one in a second main path. That means that to reach the second target item users had only to go back to the middle of the first path, before they could enter the correct sub-path leading to this second item.

After each task users had been asked to estimate the complexity of the navigation on a 5 point rating scale. After each device users had to compare the three different structures in terms of their navigation- and selection-comfort. Again we asked the subjects to draw a line for each structure. In this case the sheet given to the subjects included a clearly defined starting point and a line representing users' subjective threshold of pain. Users should express their comfort relative to this threshold. (This threshold-line is also represented in the right hand picture of Figure 3.) Therefore, in contrast to the first study, in this case, a shorter line meant higher comfort and vice versa. Additionally we conducted a short qualitative interview where we asked users to explain their preferences. Again, the tests started with a briefing session.

Devices of device class 1 to 4 were used for our tests. The representative of class 3 was a "handspring treo-Communicator". Devices and structures had been randomised between subjects to avoid order and learning effects. Note that the items of the structure "ST1" on class 4 were displayed side by side in order to use the whole screen real estate.

3.3   Results

10 subjects participated in these sessions. 5 of them were female and 5 male. Their average age was 26 years (Std. Dev.: 5 years). Figure 3 (left picture) shows the average satisfaction ratings of the different types of structures per device class. The higher the rating the higher was the user satisfaction. As expected, with the exception of device class 3, there is a small trend towards a preference of the structure "ST1".

The right picture of Figure 3 shows users' relative ratings expressed in line lengths. The shorter the line, the higher was the users' satisfaction. Here the differences of users' preferences are stronger. Statistical analysis showed significant main effects for both, device classes ($F_{(3.27)}=3.16$, $p=0.041$) and used structure ($F_{(2.18)}=4.52$, $p=0.026$). The interaction effect did not show a significant result ($F_{(6.54)}=0.069$ $p=0.662$).

To explore these results in detail we performed post hoc comparisons of the main effects of the three structures. We observed a significant difference between the structures "ST1" and "ST2" ($F_{(1.9)}=21.38$, $p=0.001$). No significant difference could be observed between "ST2" and "ST3" ($F_{(1.9)}=0.90$, $p=0.367$) and between "ST1" and "ST3" ($F_{(1.9)}=2.80$, $p=0.129$).

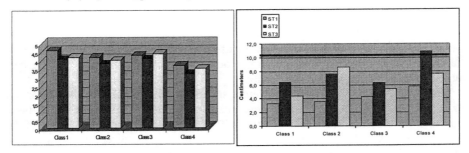

Fig. 3. Left: Average user satisfaction per device. (1=uncomfortable; 5=comfortable); right: User satisfaction expressed in line lengths (the shorter the line the higher the user satisfaction

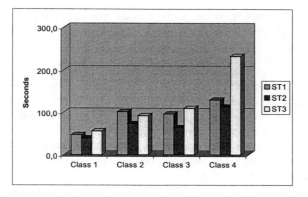

Fig. 4. Averaged search performance per device and structure (in seconds)

Finally we calculated the mean search performance per device and structure (see Figure 4). In all the cases with the exception of device class 2 the most time consuming structure was "ST3". The outlier (device class 2) was due to a semantic problem (most of the subjects initially searched in the wrong category). The big differences of the search performances of device class 4 can be attributed to the deep structure and also to some semantic problems. Note that the total number of items differed between the structures presented to our users. Therefore, the search performances can only be interpreted as possible explanations of users' preferences but not as a source of recommendations of the optimal structure.

Quantitative as well as qualitative data confirm our assumption that all items on the same level should be perceptible at a glance. Although the structure "ST2" was faster in terms of task performance (see Figure 4), subjects preferred the structure "ST1" (see Figure 3).

Averaged user's preferences of structures "ST2" (broad) and "ST3 (deep) are not that clear and consistent. Figure 3 shows, that over all device classes, with the exception of class 2, users preferred "ST3". The deviation of device class 2 can be attributed to the specific navigation functionality of the used representative of device class 2. In comparison to the other devices it was hard for the users to navigate back to the superior levels. The subjects in particular experienced this problem when they had to navigate through the structure "ST3". In this structure (6 levels x 4 items) they had to navigate six levels deep. For this reason and because of the rather small sample the post hoc analysis of the line lengths delivered only significant differences between "ST1" and "ST2".

In sum the data show at least the tendency that users prefer deep structures to broad ones although broad ones lead to faster search performances. The most striking reason is the more concise arrangement of items. This tendency is also reflected in the user statements gathered during the qualitative interviews.

4   Maximal and Optimal Lengths of Speech Lists

4.1   Motivation

Speech applications are like conversations between the user and the computer. Conversations are characterized by turn-taking, shifts in initiative, and verbal and non-verbal feedback to indicate understanding.

There are only a few elements, which a designer of voice applications can use to enable the user to interact with a system. These elements are (1) direct speech input and (2) the selection from lists of n items. Often these two possibilities have to be combined. So, for example, a system may first ask the user to utter a certain item and presents then a list with those items, which match best with the user's speech input.

We distinguish between two kinds of list selection: (1) selections, where the user knows which item he/she wants to select (known target item) and (2) selections, where the system presents a list of available items from which the user has to choose (unknown target item).

Although the adaptability of Miller's [5] well known magic number 7±2 for the design of visual displays certainly is debatable, it is still well known and accepted when it comes to the design of telephone systems. Nevertheless, systems which allow both speech input and output require less memory load than systems which are operated with the telephone keypad because the user does not have to remember a number associated with the item she/he wants to choose.

The goal of this study was to investigate how many items can be presented to users without annoying and overloading them. Both kinds of the lists, which we discussed above, were tested.

4.2   Methodology

The test was divided into two parts: The first part defined the maximal number of items, which can be presented in a list when the target item is unknown. The second test also defined a maximum number of listed items, but in this case the user already knew which item he/she wanted to select.

The tests were realised with a wizard of oz prototype (see e.g. [8], page 541). During the tests one person was sitting in another room and was simulating the system. She did that by operating a computer on which all the system's commands were saved as wav-files. The wizard, used a special software to start the wav-files, which the system presented according to the user's speech inputs. This wav-file then was transmitted to the user via a telephone line. This approach enabled us to avoid biases due to voice recognition problems. Note that the only interaction device of our subjects was the telephone receiver. There was no additional display and subjects could not use the keypad of the telephone to make their selections.

After a briefing session and before the actual test was started users had to go through a sample test, where they had first to select their favourite season from a list. Then they should name one number out of ten. After that we started with the first part of the test.

First Test (Unknown Target Item)

Subjects were confronted with four lists. These lists contained a selection of 4, 8, 15, 20 convenience foods. (The items included three to nine syllables.) The facilitator explained the background of this task to the subjects. They should imagine that they are performing a part of a larger product-ordering task.

First users were confronted with the following text, which the system spoke in German:

Step1: "Please select one product from the following list. The list contains 4 [8,15,20] products. After you have heard all list entries, please repeat the product which you want to order."

The subjects were instructed that they should really choose the product, which they would like to have for dinner or for lunch. The four list lengths were presented in different orders to the subjects to avoid order effects.

If the user then repeated one of the products which was part of the list that was presented to him/her the system answered:

Step2: "You have selected the product XY? Is that correct?"

If the user then answered yes, the task was finished. If the user gave an answer that was not part of the list, which was presented to him/her, or if the user asked the system to repeat or if the user did not say anything, the system answered:

Step3: "I am sorry, I could not [understand, hear] you. I will repeat the list. When I mention the product that you want to order, please repeat the product name immediately."

After the user had uttered the correct product name the system went to "step 2" and finished this task.

After each list we asked users to rate the subjective complexity of the task on a five-point scale. After the subject went through the four lists we encouraged him/her to express how close the selection process was to the subject's subjective threshold of pain. Again we made subjects draw lines to express this closeness. On the sheet, which we gave to our users, the line, marking users' subjective threshold, was 9,5cm from the starting point of the lines drawn by our subjects. The starting point of the lines was marked on the sheets that we gave to our subjects. Therefore, the line-lengths indicated not only the selection comfort but also whether the particular list length exceeded the user's subjective threshold. Finally we conducted a short qualitative interview and asked users to explain their ratings. Furthermore we asked them to define the maximum number of list items, which is acceptable for this kind of list selection.

Second Test (Known Target Item)

In this case we asked users to imagine that they want to edit customer details from a database. In order to do this they had to select a customer. After this selection we abandoned the task.

Users got the following instruction from the system in German:

Step 1: "Please say the name of the customer that you want to edit."

In the second step the system presented lists of different lengths to the users. These lists contained the items, which the system associated with the user's input. Four lists were presented to the users. The lists contained 4, 8, 15 and 20 items. (The items included one to three syllables.) Again the lists were presented in different orders to our subjects. The correct name was always two entries before the end of the list. The system's instruction were as follows:

Step 2: "I could not understand you. I will now read a list with the names, which you possibly uttered. When I mention the name that you have said, please repeat the name immediately."

Then the system presented the lists to the user. After the user has uttered the correct name the system replied as follows:

Step 3: "You have selected the name XY? Is that correct?"

The user then answered yes, which was the end of the task.

After each task and after the four lists again the same procedure as described above was repeated.

4.3   Results

The tests were conducted with ten subjects (7 males and 3 females). Their average age was 28 years (Std. Dev.: 13 years). Figure 5 shows users' ratings of the complexity of the list selection tasks. On the left hand side the figure shows the results of the selection with unknown target items (convenience foods), on the right hand side it shows the results of the selection with known target items (names). The next figure (Figure 6) shows the users' comfort of the selection expressed in line lengths. A length of more than 9.5cm means that at this point users would prefer another kind of selection (for example a list, which is divided into sub-lists). Both figures show that when users know the target item 15 items still seems to be OK, whereas on the other hand this number is too high for a selection of an unknown target item.

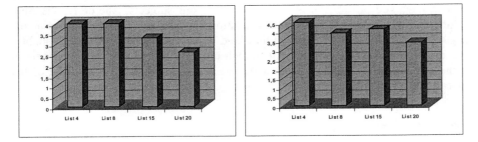

Fig. 5. Mean complexity and comfort of selection expressed in ratings from 1 to 5 (1: uncomfortable, 5 comfortable) left: Selection of unknown items, right: Selection of known items

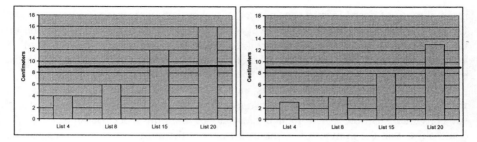

Fig. 6. Mean complexity and comfort of selection expressed in line lengths (centimetres) left: Selection of unknown items, right: Selection of known items (The shorter the line the higher the user satisfaction

Figure 5 and 6 show that if the target item is unknown, there is a clear border, which lies between list lengths of 8 and of 15 items. For lists where the user knows the item he/she wants to select, there does not exist such a clear borderline. This can also be seen when we have a look at the "thresholds of pain", which were defined by our subjects during the qualitative interviews and at their confidence intervals. The mean values of these thresholds can be seen in Figure 7. The 95% confidence interval for a selection with an unknown target item lies between 8.4 and 13.2 items, whereas the 95% confidence interval for a selection with a known target item lies between 8.2 and 18 items.

These results show that the optimal number of list entries of lists with unknown target items should lie around 8. Lists longer than eight are possible but should not exceed approximately 13 items. This absolute maximum is derived from the confidence interval of users' thresholds of pain and from the fact that there is a clear borderline between lists of 8 and lists of 15 items in terms of selection comfort. Two users said also that after the 15th item they forgot to listen because then the task was too demanding for them.

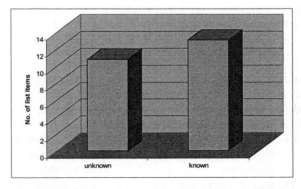

Fig. 7. Mean "thresholds of pain" as defined by our subjects

The results of the second type of list were slightly different. Again, 8 items seem to be the optimum. So we can say that this number of list entries is optimal independent form the type of list, which is presented to the user. However, in this case the maximum number of possible entries seems to lie higher than in the case discussed above. On the one hand the confidence interval of users' thresholds is much broader and on the other hand there are two equal steps (see Figure 6) from lists of eight to lists of 15 and from lists of 15 to lists of 20. Therefore the maximum number of possible list entries should lie around 18.

Note that all the items of our lists included different numbers of syllables and words. Future studies will have to investigate the influence of these numbers on users' subjective satisfaction. An influence seems to be possible since Baddely et al. [2] could show that the number of syllables influences the number of words that can be stored in humans' working memory (word length effect).

5   Conclusions

In the last chapters only three of our studies were reported. We discussed a study on text reading, where we saw that for content pages/cards scrolling seems to be more appropriate than pagination. In the second study we proved the hypothesis that in a tree structure all items on the same level should be perceptible at a glance. Finally we defined optimal and maximal numbers of list entries for two different kinds of speech-lists.

Our overall approach was to develop a mosaic of empirical tests, which are well fitting together. In synergy with the already available empirical and qualitative data they led to a picture of do's and don't's included in our user interface guidelines.

Examples of other research questions, which we answered by empirical studies and whose answers were fed into our guidelines are listed below:

- Task efficiency of direct text input tasks
- Thresholds of pain of unsorted WAP- and html-lists
- Thresholds of pain of sorted WAP- and html-lists
- Navigation through forms (scrolling vs. pagination)
- Comparison between navigation by search entries and by tree-navigation
- Comparison of speech feedback mechanisms of number input
- Definition of mean viewing distances per device class

The three examples presented in this paper show how empirical studies informing the development of user interface guidelines can be conducted and to which kind of results they lead. They also show that studies like these can only answer very detailed questions and that there is an almost infinite number of further open questions. You cannot assume to cover a broader range of questions with one study because studies like these include a lot of devices and require carefully chosen set ups.

We want also to emphasise that because of differences inside the device classes the results have to be analysed very carefully. Often these differences are not obvious before the actual study has been conducted. Therefore it is important that appropriate conclusions are drawn from these data.

An example of such a problem was given in chapter 3 (second example study). There we saw that some users had difficulties to navigate backwards with one of the representatives of our device classes and some users experienced also other hardware related difficulties. That means that users' performance with two devices of one and the same device class may differ because of hardware- or browser-specific differences, which are not part of the device class specification.

Future research should focus on the definition of classes, which are minimising these problems. As long as this concerns the browser capabilities the number of differences, which have to be considered, may be manageable. However, when it comes to hardware differences the number of differences is almost infinite and steadily growing.

So the challenge of the future development of device classes will be to include such differences and to define them and their effects on the efficiency and user satisfaction of each task. Furthermore new classes will have to be developed because of new products and types of interface designs that are entering the market. Therefore the three dimensions, which currently are used for the definition of device classes, will have to be evaluated on a current basis to ensure that they fulfil the requirements of a device classification including the latest developments.

Acknowledgements

The empirical studies and the guideline development were conducted as a part of the CONSENSUS project, which is funded by the European Commission. We would like to thank all our partners for their inputs and for their comments.

References

[1]   Buchanan, G., Farrant, S., Jones, M., Thimbleby, H., Marsden, G., Pazzani, M. (2001). Improving mobile internet usability. WWW10, May 1-5, 2001, Hong Kong, China

[2]   Baddely, A.D., Thompson, N., Buchanan, M. (1975). Word length and the structure of short term memory. Journal of Verbal Learning and Verbal Behavior, 14, 575-589

[3]   CONSENSUS: IST PROGRAMM/KA4/AL:IST-2001-4.3.2/CONSENSUS/ CN:IST-2001-32407 3G Mobile Context Sensitive Adaptability User Friendly Mobile Work Place for Seamless Enterprise Applications. (www.consensus-online.org)

[4]   Dickes, P. and Steiwer, L. (1977). Ausarbeitung von Lesbarkeitsformeln für die deutsche Sprache. In Zeitschrift für Entwicklungspsychologie and Pädagogische Psychologie. Band IX, 1/1977, 20-28 (in German)

[5]   Miller, G.A.. (1956). The magic number seven plus or minus two: Some limits of our capacity for information processing. Psychological Review, 63(2), 81-87

[6]   Nielsen, J. (2000). Designing web usability. New Riders Publishing, Indianapolis, Indiana USA

[7]   Paap, K.R. and Cooke, N.J. (1997). Design of Menus. In Helander, M.G, Landauer, T.K., Prabhu, P.V. Handbook of Human-Computer Interaction (second edition)

[8]   Preece, J., Roger, Y., Sharp, H., Benyon, D., Holland, S., Carey, T. (1994). Human-Computer Interaction. Addison-Wesley

[9]   Spool; J.M., Scanlon, T., Schroeder, W., Snyder, C., DeAngelo, T. (1999). Web site usability: A designer's guide. Morgan Kaufmann Publishers, Inc.

[10]   Telenor Mobile Communications (2000). User Interface design guidelines for WAP applications. Version 1.4

[11]   Van Welie, M. and de Groot, B. (2002). Consistent multi-device design using device categories. In Proceedings of the 4th International Symposium, Mobile HCI 2002, Pisa, Italy

A Review of Mobile HCI Research Methods

Jesper Kjeldskov and Connor Graham

Department of Information Systems, University of Melbourne
Parkville, Victoria 3010, Australia
jesper@cs.auc.dk, cgraham@unimelb.edu.au

Abstract. This paper examines and reviews research methods applied within the field of mobile human-computer interaction. The purpose is to provide a snapshot of current practice for studying mobile HCI to identify shortcomings in the way research is conducted and to propose opportunities for future approaches. 102 publications on mobile human-computer interaction research were categorized in a matrix relating their research methods and purpose. The matrix revealed a number of significant trends with a clear bias towards building systems and evaluating them only in laboratory settings, if at all. Also, gaps in the distribution of research approaches and purposes were identified; action research, case studies, field studies and basic research being applied very infrequently. Consequently, we argue that the bias towards building systems and a lack of research for understanding design and use limits the development of cumulative knowledge on mobile human computer interaction. This in turn inhibits future development of the research field as a whole.

1   Introduction

The study of human computer interaction for mobile devices is a relatively young research field in which commercially successful devices have only been available for less than a decade and leading conferences have only a few years of history. In young research fields there is often a tendency to be highly opportunity and technology driven and to focus primarily on producing *solutions* while reflecting less on methodology. This characterized early computer research and can also be seen in relation to emerging research areas such as virtual and augmented reality. As a research field matures, examining how the research is being conducted and reflecting on the impact of this on the knowledge being produced is necessary in order to be able to understand and influence the future direction of the field. So far, this has not been done consistently within the community of mobile HCI and consequently little knowledge on a methodological level exists about the research field. This analysis and discussion will be borne out by this paper.

Inspired by related studies within the field of Information Systems (IS), we aim at evoking more discussion of research methodology in mobile HCI by presenting a

L. Chittaro (Ed.): Mobile HCI 2003, LNCS 2795, pp. 317–335, 2003.
© Springer-Verlag Berlin Heidelberg 2003

snapshot of current research practice within our field, identifying and discussing shortcomings in present research and opportunities for future approaches.

Focus and reflection on research methodology has been a key subject within information system research for decades (see e.g. [1, 3, 5, 8, 11]). Facilitating this discussion, a number of frameworks for describing and categorizing IS-research methods have been developed (see e.g. [5]), which could also be relevant in relation to discussions of mobile HCI research. Specifically, we find that the classification of computer-aided software engineering (CASE) research by Wynekoop and Conger [11] demonstrate a generally usable (and relatively simple) approach to informing the discussion of research methods applied within a given area. Wynekoop and Conger [11] reviewed and classified 40 IS-research papers in a two-dimensional matrix relating research methods and research purpose, providing a picture of the research field facilitating discussion of current research practice. In this paper we replicate elements from this study by applying its overall approach to the field of mobile HCI. In section 2 and 3 we present the categories of research methods and research purposes used in our classification. In section 4 we describe the conducted review of Mobile HCI research papers and present a matrix describing the resulting classification. Trends highlighted by this matrix are then discussed in section 5 and in sections 6 and 7 we indicate limitations, conclude our study and point out paths for further work.

2   Research Methods

Defining and especially differentiating research methods can be a challenge. Definitions are sometimes vague and often different aspects of different methods overlap. As the purpose of this paper is not to discuss definitions of research methods as such, we have chosen to apply eight definitions extracted from Wynekoop and Conger [11] with supplementary input from general references on research methodology in information systems [7, 8, 9, 12]. Knowing that these definitions may themselves be objects for disagreement, we refer to [11, 5] for further discussion of the definitions.

Table 1. Summary of research methods (extracted from Wynekoop and Conger [11])

	Method	Strengths	Weaknesses	Use
Natural setting	Case studies	Natural settings Rich data	Time demanding Limited generalizability	Descriptions, explanations, developing hypothesis
	Field studies	Natural Settings Replicable	Difficult data collection Unknown sample bias	Studying current practice Evaluating new practices
	Action research	First hand experience Applying theory to practice	Ethics, bias, time Unknown generalizability	Generate hypothesis/theory Testing theories/hypothesis
Artificial setting	Laboratory experiments	Control of variables Replicable	Limited realism Unknown generalizability	Controlled experiments Theory/product testing
Environment independent setting	Survey research	Easy, low cost Can reduce sample bias	Context insensitive No variable manipulation	Collecting descriptive data from large samples
	Applied research	The goal is a product which may be evaluated	May need further design to make product general	Product development, testing hypothesis/concepts
	Basic research	No restrictions on solutions Solve new problems	Costly, time demanding May produce no solution	Theory building
	Normative writings	Insight into firsthand experience	Opinions may influence outcome	Descriptions of practice, building frameworks

In this section, we present and review the eight research methods used in our classification of mobile HCI research. For each method, strengths and weaknesses are identified as well as primary uses and possible application in mobile HCI research. This discussion is summarized in table 1. As an overall categorization, we group the eight research methods according to Benbasat's [2] categories of *natural, artificial* and *environment independent* settings.

2.1 Case Studies

Yin [12] defines a case study as "an empirical enquiry that investigates a contemporary phenomenon within its real-life context, especially when the boundaries between phenomenon and context are not clearly evident". Thus case studies are often intensive empirical studies of small size entities such as groups, organizations, individuals, systems or tools with the researcher distinct from the phenomena being studied [11]. When conducting case studies, data is typically collected by a combination of various qualitative and quantitative means such as observations, interviews and questionnaires etc. with little experimental or statistical control enforced. The data collected is grounded in natural settings, typically very rich and sometimes contradictory or inconsistent, thus often resulting in complicated analysis. Case studies are particularly well suited for research focusing on describing and explaining a specific phenomenon and for developing hypothesis or theory through, for example, applying grounded-theory approaches. However, case studies are very time demanding and generalizing findings can be difficult.

Since mobile HCI is a relatively young research area, case studies could be used to provide rich data explaining phenomena involving mobility or the use of mobile devices in context.

2.2 Field Studies

Generally, field studies are characterized by taking place in "the real world" as opposed to in a laboratory setting. Field studies cover a range of qualitative and quantitative approaches from *ethnographic* studies of phenomena in their social and cultural context inspired by the discipline of social and cultural anthropology [7] to field *experiments* in which a number of independent variables are manipulated [11].

Ethnographic field studies are characterized by researchers spending significant amounts of time in the field and, to some extent, immersing themselves into the environment they study. Typically, data is gathered through observations and/or interviews and the phenomena studied are placed in a social and cultural context. The major advantage of ethnographic field studies is the generation of large amounts of rich and grounded data in relatively short time. The major disadvantages are unknown biases and no guarantee of collected data being representative.

While ethnographic field studies are non-experimental, field experiments are characterized by manipulation of a number of independent variables to observe the influence on dependant variables in a natural setting. The major advantages of field experiments are increased realism and increased control in comparison to ethnographic field studies and support for studying complex situated interactions and processes.

Disadvantages include limited control of experiments and complicated data collection compared to, for example, experiments in laboratory settings. Furthermore, as experimental manipulation increases, realism typically decreases.

In relation to mobile HCI research, field studies could be applied for either informing design for or understanding of mobility by ethnographic studies of current practice or for evaluating design or theory by conducting experiments in realistic use settings.

2.3   Action Research

Originating from the social sciences, action research is a well-established research method through which researchers not only apply scientific knowledge to an object of study, but also add to the body of scientific knowledge through that study, thus differentiating action research from applied science or research [8]. Conducting action research, the researcher participates in the intervention of the activity or phenomenon being studied while at the same time evaluating the results [11]. More specifically, Rapoport [9] defines action research as aiming "to contribute both to the practical concerns of people in an immediate problematic situation and to the goals of social science by joint collaboration within a mutually acceptable ethical framework".

The advantage of action research is the very close relationship between researchers and the phenomena of interest. This facilitates first-hand insight, limits researcher influence on subjects being studied and supports a prosperous way of applying theory to practice and evaluating its outcome. However, action research is very time consuming, and since the researcher takes part in the phenomena studied remaining objective can be difficult. Also, when participating in the intervention of an activity or phenomenon, considerations emerge concerning if it is ethically acceptable for a researcher, for example, to conceal knowledge of particular approaches having better effects than others. Finally, the outcome of this research can be difficult to generalize.

In relation to mobile HCI research, action research could be used for extending field or case studies by researchers participating actively in real world activities involving mobility, introducing different solutions or theories "on-the-fly" as well as evaluating their effects and/or validity.

2.4   Laboratory Experiments

In contrast to field studies, laboratory studies are characterized by taking place in a controlled environment created for the purpose of research. Thus laboratory experiments do not necessarily have to take place in dedicated "laboratories" as such but can be conducted in various controlled environments such as in an office [10], in a hallway [4] or in a simulator [6]. Laboratory experiments facilitate various types of data being collected using different experimental methods depending on the style of subsequent analysis desired. While traditional quantitative measurements of factors such as error rate and task completion times collected through, for example, cognitive walkthrough methods are suitable for statistical methods of analysis, using more qualitative approaches such as heuristic evaluation or think-aloud protocols during the conduct of experimental tasks also produces results suitable for analysis.

The major advantages of laboratory studies are the opportunity to focus on specific phenomena of interest and a large degree of experimental control in terms of manipulation of variables before and during the experiment through for example assignment of test subjects and exposure to different treatment variables [11]. Also, laboratory experiments are typically highly replicable and facilitate good data collection. Disadvantages include limited relation to the real world and an unknown level of generalizability of results outside laboratory settings.

In mobile HCI research, laboratory experiments are suitable for evaluating design ideas, specific products or theories about design and user interaction in controlled environments with little or no interference from the real world.

2.5   Survey Research

Surveys usually inform research by providing information from a known sample of people gathered through various systematic techniques such as questionnaires and interviews. Using surveys, data is gathered directly from selected respondents and it is assumed that these are independent of their environment [11]. Typically, data from questionnaire surveys is collected without researcher intervention and is analyzed quantitatively while data from interview surveys are analyzed qualitatively.

The major advantages of surveys are that they facilitate large amounts of data to be gathered with relatively little effort, supporting broad generalization of results. Also a high level of control regarding sample subjects makes reduction of bias possible thus increasing validity. However, surveys suffer from providing only snapshots of studied phenomena and rely highly on the subjective views of respondents.

In mobile HCI research, surveys could, for example, facilitate generalizable information being gathered about user needs and requirements for understanding a phenomenon, building theory or developing systems. Also, surveys could be used for gathering data about the user experience of specific products or designs for evaluation purposes.

2.6   Applied Research

According to [11] applied research, builds on trial and error on the basis of the researchers capabilities of reasoning through *intuition, experience, deduction* and *induction*. Typically the desired goal or outcome of the research process is known in terms of requirements on some level of abstraction, but methods or techniques for accomplishing this outcome are unknown and thus sought through applying potentially relevant research. The advantages of applied research is that it is very goal directed and (typically) results in some kind of product being produced, which can be evaluated against the initial goals. The major disadvantages of applied research are that initial solutions may be very limited and not generalizable and that appropriate solutions for accomplishing the desired outcome may not be produced at all.

In mobile HCI research, applied research is relevant in relation to design and implementation of systems, interfaces and techniques, which meet certain requirements for performance, user interaction, user satisfaction etc.

2.7   Basic Research

Doing basic research, researchers develop new theories or study well-known problems to which neither specific solutions nor methods for accomplishing solutions are known [11]. Like applied research, the approach of basic research is trial and error based relying on the competences of the researcher. The major advantage of basic research is the openness of the research facilitated both in terms of approaches and time, allowing a high level of creativity in the search for methods and solutions. However, basic research, like applied research, can be very time consuming and there is no guarantee of any solution eventually being produced.

In relation to mobile HCI, basic research may be applied to the development of theoretical frameworks for, for example, understanding basic issues of mobility or for identifying new problems and possible solutions related to human-computer interaction while being mobile.

2.8   Normative Writings

In order to include the significant body of so-called "non-research" writings about phenomena of interests in their classification of research methods, Wynekoop and Conger [11] suggests the category of *normative writings,* covering concept development writings, presentation of "truth" and Benbasat's [3] category of "application descriptions". While concept development writings organize ideas in order to stimulate and indicate directions for future research, such as the case of this paper, normative writings belonging to the "truth" category present ideas, concepts and suggestions, which seem intuitively correct but are not based on theory or research. Application descriptions are defined as "narratives written by practitioners" [11], describing subjective views on a situation and what worked for them in that particular situation. The primary advantage of normative writings is that they require little effort to produce compared to presenting complex theoretical concepts. Disadvantages include limited theoretical and methodological reflection and limited generalizability.

In mobile HCI, normative writings describing designs and processes that worked well or did not prove successful may be useful for inspiring future research or design.

3   Research Purpose

Research methods as discussed above and research *purpose* are typically closely related but not necessarily determined by one another. Like Wynekoop and Conger [11] we thus use the second dimension of our matrix for classifying mobile HCI research to describe research purpose. Populating the categories this dimension we borrow the categories and definitions of research purposes originally proposed in [1] and also used in [11]. These are briefly defined below.

Understanding is the purpose of research focusing on finding the meaning of studied phenomena through e.g. frameworks or theories developed from collected data.

Engineering is defined as the purpose of research focused towards developing new systems or parts of systems such as e.g. an interaction technique for mobile phones.

Re-engineering describes the purpose of research focusing on improving existing systems by redeveloping them such as e.g. adapting a web browser to a small display.

Evaluating is the purpose of research assessing or validating products, theories or methods e.g. the usability of a specific mobile device design or a theory of interaction.

Describing finally refers to research focusing on defining desirable properties of products e.g. a mobile system.

4   Classification of Mobile HCI Research

In this section we present a classification of selected mobile human-computer interaction research papers in relation to the research methods and purposes discussed above.

A total of 102 conference and journal papers were classified in relation to the described categories of research purpose and research methods applied. These papers constitute all publications related to mobile human-computer interaction between 2000 and 2002 in the following top-level conference proceeding series and journals:

- Conference on Computer-Human Interaction, CHI, ACM
- Conference on Advanced Visual Interfaces, AVI, ACM
- Conference on User Interface Software and Technology, UIST, ACM
- Conference on Computer-Supported Cooperative Work, CSCW, ACM
- Symposium on Human-Computer Interaction with Mobile Devices, Mobile HCI
- Symposium on Designing Interactive Systems, DIS, ACM
- Transactions on Computer-Human Interaction, TOCHI, ACM
- Journal of Personal and Ubiquitous Computing, Springer-Verlag

While other conferences and journals exist, presenting interesting research on mobile human-computer interaction, we found that the listed conferences and journals provided a solid and adequately representative base for this study given the number of publications on the topic and the general level of the reviewing processes for these conferences and journals.

The 102 papers specifically focusing on mobile human-computer interaction were identified by thoroughly reading through abstracts (and sometimes introductions) of all publications between 2000 and 2002 in the listed conference proceeding series and journals. A paper was selected for the study if it was in any way related to mobile devices and human-computer interaction. Thus a paper would be omitted if it focused only on mobile network protocol design or did not involve any aspect of mobility of users or systems. All papers were printed, numbered, read through and classified over a period of two weeks by the first author of this paper with particular focus on identifying the purpose of the presented work and the research methods applied in achieving this. The classification is shown in table 2 below.

Table 2. Classification of mobile human-computer interaction research. Numbers refer to indexes in the appendix of reviewed mobile HCI research papers bibliography

Research Method

		Case studies	Field studies	Action research	Lab experiment	Survey research	Applied research	Basic research	Normative writings
Research purpose	Understand	10, 11, 51	67, 68, 69, 101		91	14, 25, 53, 72	43	1, 21, 32	16, 20
	Engineer	24, 49	3, 65, 71, 85, 94				2, 4, 9, 12, 17, 18, 19, 23, 27, 28, 29, 33, 34, 36, 38, 39, 41, 45, 46, 48, 50, 52, 57, 58, 59, 60, 64, 70, 73, 74, 76, 77, 78, 79, 81, 83, 84, 86, 89, 90, 92, 93, 95, 97, 98		
	Re-engineer	22					7, 8, 31, 55, 63, 75, 80, 100, 102		
	Evaluate		6, 9, 41, 63, 71, 81, 85, 89		4, 5, 6, 7, 8, 9, 12, 13, 18, 22, 30, 40, 42, 44, 49, 50, 55, 56, 58, 60, 61, 66, 75, 77, 82, 90, 94, 97, 98, 99	26, 33, 64, 93			
	Describe		47, 62, 96		47		35		15, 37, 54, 87, 88

To ensure consistency, the initial classification of the papers was evaluated by scanning through all the papers a second time on a single day. To ensure validity, the second author of this paper subsequently evaluated the classification by blindly classifying 20 randomly selected papers. As this resulted in a number of disparities, all 102 papers were discussed and classified one by one through the collaboration of the two authors.

While in the review presented in Wynekoop and Conger [11] each paper is only attributed to one research method and purpose, this was not possible with all of the papers on mobile human-computer interaction. Some of the reviewed papers clearly employed more than one research method and had multiple purposes. A common example of this would be papers presenting a system engineered by applying research and subsequently evaluated in a laboratory. Consequently, such papers were given multiple classifications and appear more than once in table 2 above. As a consequence of multiple research methods and purposes in the same paper, aggregate percentages will sometimes amount to more than 100%.

Table 2 shows that 55% of mobile HCI research falls within the applied category (56 of 102 papers). The secondly most used method is laboratory experiments being applied in 31% of the research (32 of 102 papers). 20% of the papers report from field studies and 8% report from survey studies while 7% are normative writings and 6% report from case studies. Only 3 papers were classified as basic research and no entries were found for action research. This distribution shows a clear bias towards environment independent and artificial setting research in the form of applied and laboratory based approaches at the expense of natural setting research focusing on real use and basic and action research generating theory and refining it in practice.

Looking at the research purpose, 51% of mobile HCI research is done for engineering with additional 10% done for re-engineering. Thus in total, 61% of the research reported involves building systems. 41% of the papers involve evaluation, of which 71% is done through laboratory experiments 19% through field experiments and the remaining 10% through surveys. Research for understanding mobile HCI accounts for 18% of the papers, of which 22% reports from the use of surveys and 22% from field studies. Describing different aspects of mobile HCI accounts for 10% of the research, of which 50% are in the form of normative writings. Thus within mobile HCI research there is a clear tendency towards building systems and if evaluating them, doing so in laboratory settings. Understanding and learning from the design and real use of systems is less prioritized, limiting the generation of a cumulative body of knowledge on mobile human-computer interaction.

Of the 56 papers applying research, 96% do so for the purpose of engineering or re-engineering. Thus in total, these two cells in the matrix account for more than 50% of the mobile HCI research classified. Of the 32 papers in the laboratory experiment category, 94% use this method for evaluation purposes. Of the 20 papers reporting from field studies, 40% use this method for evaluation purpose while 25% use it for engineering. 20% (4 papers) report from field studies for the purpose of understanding. Thus when building systems within mobile HCI research, there is a clear tendency to do so primarily by trial and error and a lesser tendency to do so based on actual user studies. Also, controlled environments are used primarily for product evaluation purposes. Field studies are only applied to inform the design of new systems to a limited extend.

Of the 45 papers reporting applied research with the purpose of engineering systems, only 37% (17 papers) *also* report evaluating the produced solutions. 61% of these evaluations are done through laboratory experiments, 22% through field studies and the remaining 17% by surveys. Of the 9 papers reporting the *re-engineering* of systems, 56% also report evaluations of these systems. 80% of these are through laboratory experiments and 20% through field studies. Thus when building new systems, there is a tendency towards *not* evaluating them while when subsequently *rebuilding* them, evaluation is more prevalent. When evaluating engineered or re-engineered systems, there is a large bias towards applying laboratory-based approaches.

5   Discussion

Table 2 reveals a lack of focus on real use contexts in relation to engineering and evaluating mobile systems as well as limited construction and use of theory. While field studies *are* being done, natural setting research is not prevalent. One reason for this may be that applied research and laboratory experiments are simply easier to conduct and manage than field studies, case studies and action research. Another reason may be that mobile HCI has strong roots in computer science and human-computer interaction. These fields collectively have a strong bias towards engineering and evaluating systems, with input from fields such as ethnography only recently emerging.

Reflecting further on table 2, a number of features seem to characterize the field of mobile human-computer interaction. Firstly, given the prevalent applied approach to engineering it seems assumed that we already know what to build and which specific problems to overcome such as limited screen real estate, limited means for interaction, dynamic use-contexts and limited network bandwidth. As only a little research actually addresses the question of what is useful and what is perceived problematic from a user-perspective and as a qualitative review of the classified papers reveal that evaluations are often focused on functionality rather than contextual issues, it is difficult to set aside this assumption and identify and face more fundamental challenges to mobile human-computer interaction. Secondly, given the limited focus on real-world studies it seems that the real contexts are not actually important for the mobile system we build and use and that mobile computer systems are a generically applicable solution. The view that building and evaluating systems by trial and error is better than grounding engineering, evaluation and theory in user-based studies weakens research in mobile HCI. Thirdly, given the fact that only few studies are based on a methodological foundation, it seems assumed that methodology matters very little in mobile HCI research. This supposition is problematic as the choice of methods clearly has influence on the results subsequently produced [8]. From a cognitive psychology perspective, for example, problem solving by applied research is viewed as a rather poor method as it demands huge efforts by researchers that often "translate into poor performance because they require search of a large space of possibilities" [11].

The distribution of research methods and purposes shown in table 2 offers a number of opportunities in the area of mobile HCI. Firstly, the fact that field studies are mostly being used for the purpose of evaluation presents the opportunity to use this method to explore use context and user needs to promote understanding. Field studies could assist with the translation of needs into new designs and the re-engineering of existing designs. Mobility is very difficult to emulate in a laboratory setting, as is the dynamism of changing context. Field studies offer the ideal opportunity for the study of rich real-world use cases. Learning from other disciplines that have struggled with the study of similar "slippery" phenomena, such as ethnography in this regard could provide important insight. The lack of survey and case study research also presents an opportunity. Information Systems uses these approaches widely, with the former research method often being used to collect large amounts of data from, for example, actual end-users of a system. In addition this approach offers a good opportunity to study the use of systems in the hands of a large segment of the population, enabling wider reaching generalizations. Case studies within mobile HCI could increase learning from existing implemented systems within real-world contexts, for example mobile systems and infrastructure within organizations. Such case studies would enable the close scrutiny of pre-defined phenomena in fixed contexts, which could then be used to enrich the collective knowledge in the discipline and to enable key issues to be described and understood. The issues generated could then be used to generate hypotheses to propagate further research. The limited use of action research points to both the lack of a well-established body of theoretical research within the discipline and the unwillingness to implement mobile systems which are uncertain to succeed and take a long time to evaluate and implement. This is perhaps not surprising, given the current cost of such technology and the associated implementation overhead. Nonetheless, this is, again, an opportunity to develop knowledge in the discipline through practice and evaluation. Finally, the lack of basic research means that opportunities exist for the development of theoretical frameworks to promote description and understanding. In addition, the applicability of theories from other disciplines to mobile HCI can be examined through basic and action research.

6   Limitations

The presented review of research methods has a number of limitations. First of all, the categories of research methods can be criticized for being vague and overlapping. Thus for example, case studies are often done in the field but it is unclear how this method differs from field studies. If a case study were, on the other hand, conduced in a controlled environment, how would it be different from a laboratory experiment? Furthermore, it can be discussed whether the eight categories of methods belong to the same level of abstraction or if some categories could be subordinated others. Combined with the fact that many research papers provide only little information about method, it can be difficult to decide which category a specific paper belongs to. Thus the presented study relies on the researchers comprehension of the categories and ability to make a qualified judgment on the basis of sometimes scarce information. Also, it can, of course, be questioned if the selected papers are representative and to what extent activities within a given area are actually reflected through publications.

7   Conclusions

In this paper we have examined and reviewed research methods within the field of mobile HCI through classifying 102 research papers. We have identified a number of significant trends in research purpose and methods with a clear bias towards engineering systems using applied approaches and, if evaluating them, doing so in laboratory settings. In addition we have found that research methods examining phenomena in context such as case studies are not widely used. These findings present a number of opportunities for further research suggesting the need for a change of emphasis within the field of mobile HCI.

References

[1]   Basili, V.R., Selby, R.W. and Hutchins, D.H.: Experimentation in software engineering. IEEE Transactions on Software Engineering, SE-12 (1986) 733-743

[2]   Benbasat, I.: An analysis of research methodologies. In MacFarlan, F.W. (Ed.) The Information System Research Challenge. Boston, Harvard Business School Press (1985) 47-85

[3]   Benbasat, I., Goldstein, D.R. and Mead, M.: The case research strategy in studies of information systems. MIS Quarterly, Vol. 7(3) (1987) 369-386.

[4]   Bohnenberger, T., Jameson, A., Kruger, A. and Butz, A.: Location-Aware Shopping Assistance: Evaluation of a Decision-Theoretic Approach. In Proceedings of Mobile HCI 2002, Pisa, Italy, Springer-Verlag, Berlin (2002)

[5]   Galliers, R.D.: Choosing Appropriate Information Systems Research Approaches: A Revised Taxonomy. In Proceedings of the IFIP TC8 WG 8.2 Working Conference on The Information Systems Research Arena of The 90's, Copenhagen, Denmark (1990)

[6]   Kjeldskov J. and Skov M. B. (2003) Evaluating the Usability of a Mobile Collaborative System: Exploring Two Different Laboratory Approaches. In Proceedings of the 4th International Symposium on Collaborative Technologies and Systems 2003. Orlando, Florida.

[7]   Lewis, I.M.: Social Anthropology in Perspective. Cambridge University Press (1985)

[8]   Myers, M.D.: Qualitative Research in Information Systems. MIS Quarterly, Vol. 21(2) (1997) 241-242

[9]   Rapoport, R.N.: Three Dilemmas in Action Research. Human Relations, Vol. 23(4) (1970) 499-513

[10]   Tang, J., Yankelovich, N., Begole, B., Van Kleek, M., Li, F. and Bhalodia, J.: ConNexus to Awarenex: Extending awareness to mobile users. In proceedings of CHI2001, Seattle, WA, USA, ACM (2001)

[11]   Wynekoop, J.L. and Conger, S.A.: A Review of Computer Aided Software Engineering Research Methods. In Proceedings of the IFIP TC8 WG 8.2 Working Conference on The Information Systems Research Arena of The 90's, Copenhagen, Denmark (1990)

[12]   Yin, R. K.: Case Study Research, Design and Methods, 2nd ed. Newbury Park, Sage Publications (1994)

Appendix: Reviewed Mobile HCI Research Papers, 2000-2002

[1] Abowd, G.D. and Mynatt, E.D.: Charting Past, Present and Future Research in Ubiquitous Computing". ACM Transactions on Computer-Human Interaction, Vol. 7, No. 1 (2000) 29-58

[2] Beigl, M.: MemoClip: A Location-Based Remembrance Appliance. Personal and Ubiquitous Computing, Vol. 4. Springer-Verlag, London (2000) 230-233

[3] Bertelsen, O. and Nielsen, C.: Augmented Reality as a Design Tool for Mobile Devices. In proceedings of DIS 2000, ACM (2000)

[4] Bohnenberger, T., Jameson, A., Kruger, A. and Butz, A.: Location-Aware Shopping Assistance: Evaluation of a Decision-Theoretic Approach. In Proceedings of Mobile HCI 2002, Pisa, Italy, Springer-Verlag, Berlin (2002)

[5] Brewster, S. and Murray, R.: Presenting Dynamic Information on Mobile Computers. Personal and Ubiquitous Computing, Vol. 4. Springer-Verlag, London (2000) 209-212

[6] Brewster, S.: Overcoming the Lack of Screen Space on Mobile Computers. Personal and Ubiquitous Computing, Vol. 6. Springer-Verlag, London (2002) 188-205

[7] Buyukkokten, O., Garcia-Molina, H., Paepcke, A. and Winograd, T.: Power Browser: Efficient Web Browsing for PDAs. In Proceedings of CHI2000, The Hague, Amsterdam, ACM (2000)

[8] Buyukkokten, O., Garcia-Molina, H., Paepcke, A.: Accordion Summarization for End-Game Browsing on PDAs and Cellular Phones. In proceedings of CHI2001, Seattle, WA, USA, ACM (2001)

[9] Cheverst, K., Davies, N., Mitchell, K., Friday, A. and Efstratiou, C.: Developing a Context-aware Electronic Tourist Guide: Some Issues and Experiences. In Proceedings of CHI2000, The Hague, Amsterdam, ACM (2000)

[10] Cheverst, K., Mitchell, K. and Davies, N.: Investigating Context-aware Information Push vs. Information Pull to Tourists. In Proceedings of Mobile HCI 2001, Lille, France (2001)

[11] Cheverst, K., Davies, N., Mitchell, K. and Efstratiou, C.: Using Context as a Crystal Ball: rewards and Pitfalls. Personal and Ubiquitous Computing, Vol. 5. Springer-Verlag, London (2001) 8-11

[12] Chincholle, D., Goldstein, M., Nyberg, M. and Eriksson, M.: Lost or Found? A Usability Evaluation of a Mobile Navigation and Location-Based Service. In Proceedings of Mobile HCI 2002, Pisa, Italy, Springer-Verlag, Berlin (2002)

[13] Chittaro, L. and Cin, P.D.: Evaluating Interface Design Choices on WAP Phones: Single-choice List Selection and Navigation among Cards. In Proceedings of Mobile HCI 2001, Lille, France (2001)

[14] Colbert, M.: A Diary Study of Rendezvousing: Group Size, Time, Pressure and Connectivity. In Proceedings of Mobile HCI 2002, Pisa, Italy, Springer-Verlag, Berlin (2002)

[15] Constas, I. and Papadopoulos, D.: Interface-Me: Pursuing Sociability Through Personal Devices. Personal and Ubiquitous Computing, Vol. 5. Springer-Verlag, London (2001) 195-200

[16] Coschurba, P., Baumann, J., Kubach, U. and Leonhardi, A.: Metaphors and Context-Aware Information Access. Personal and Ubiquitous Computing, Vol. 5. Springer-Verlag, London (2001) 16-19

[17] Danesh, A., Inkpen, K., Lau, F., Shu, K. and Booth, K.: Geney: Designing a Collaborative Activity for the Palm Handheld Computer. In proceedings of CHI2001, Seattle, WA, USA, ACM (2001)

[18] De Bruijn, O,, Spence, R. and Chong, M.Y.: RSVP Browser: Web Browsing on Small Screen Devices. In Proceedings of Mobile HCI 2001, Lille, France (2001)

[19] Dey, A.K.:Understanding and Using Context. Personal and Ubiquitous Computing, Vol. 5. Springer-Verlag, London (2001) 4-7

[20] Dix, A., Rodden, T., Davies, N., Trevor, J., Friday, A. and Palfreyman, K.: Exploiting Space and Location as a Design Framework for Interactive Mobile Systems. Transactions on Computer-Human Interaction, Vol. 7, No. 3. ACM (2000) 285-321

[21] Dubois, E., Gray, P., and Nigay, L.: ASUR++: A Design Notation for Mobile Mixed Systems. In Proceedings of Mobile HCI 2002, Pisa, Italy, Springer-Verlag, Berlin (2002)

[22] Ebling, M.R., John, B.E. and Satyanarayanan, S.: The Importance of Transludence in Mobile Computing Systems. ACM Transactions on Computer-Human Interaction, Vol. 9, No. 1 (2002) 42-67

[23] Fano, A.: What are a Location's File and Edit Menus? Personal and Ubiquitous Computing, Vol. 5. Springer-Verlag, London (2001) 12-15

[24] Forlizzi, J. and McCormack, M.: Case Study: User Research to Inform the Design and Development of Integrated Wearable Computers and Web-Based Services. In proceedings of DIS 2000, ACM (2000)

[25] Fortunati, L.: The Mobile Phone: An Identity on the move. Personal and Ubiquitous Computing, Vol. 5. Springer-Verlag, London (2001) 85-98

[26] Frohlich, D. and Murphy, R.: The Memory Box. Personal and Ubiquitous Computing, Vol. 4. Springer-Verlag, London (2000) 238-240

[27] Geldof, S. and Terken, J.: Talking Wearables Exploit Context. Personal and Ubiquitous Computing, Vol. 5. Springer-Verlag, London (2001) 62-65

[28] Gelgon, M. and Tilhou, K. Automated Multimedia Diaries of Mobile Device Users Need Summarization. In Proceedings of Mobile HCI 2002, Pisa, Italy, Springer-Verlag, Berlin (2002)

[29] Goldstein, M., Oqvist, G., Bayat-M, M., Ljungstrand, P. and Bjork, S.: Enhancing the Reading Experience: Using Adaptive and Sonified RSVP for Reading on Small Displays. In Proceedings of Mobile HCI 2001, Lille, France (2001)

[30] Goldstein, M., Alsio, G. and Werdenhoff, J.: The Media Equation Does Not Always Apply: People are not Polite Towards Small Computers. Personal and Ubiquitous Computing, Vol. 6, Springer-Verlag, London (2002) 87-96

[31] Gonzalez-Castano, F.J., Anido-Rifon, L. and Costa-Montenegro, E.: A New Transcoding Technique for PDA Browsers, Based on Context Hierarchy. In Proceedings of Mobile HCI 2002, Pisa, Italy, Springer-Verlag, Berlin (2002)

[32] Green, N., Harper, R.H.R. and Cooper, G.: Configuring the Mobile User: So-
      ciological and Industry Views. Personal and Ubiquitous Computing, Vol. 5.
      Springer-Verlag, London (2001) 146-156
[33] Hibino, S. and Mockus, A.: handiMessenger: Awareness-Enhanced Universal
      Communication for Mobile Users. In Proceedings of Mobile HCI 2002, Pisa,
      Italy, Springer-Verlag, Berlin (2002)
[34] Hinckley, K., Pierce, J., Sinclair, M. and Horvitz, E.: Sensing Techniques for
      Mobile Interaction. In proceedings of UIST2000, San Diego, CA, USA, ACM
      (2000)
[35] Hinckley, K. and Horvitz, E.: Toward More Sensitive Mobile Phones. In pro-
      ceedings of UIST2001, Orlando, Florida, USA, ACM (2001)
[36] Holland, S. and Morse, D.R.: AudioGPS: spatial audio in a minimal attention
      interface. In Proceedings of Mobile HCI 2001, Lille, France (2001)
[37] Holland, S., Morse, D. and Gedenryd, H.: Direct Combination: A New User
      Interaction Principle for Mobile and Ubiquitous HCI. In Proceedings of Mobile
      HCI 2002, Pisa, Italy, Springer-Verlag, Berlin (2002)
[38] Huang, E.M., Terry, M., Mynatt, E., Lyons, K. and Chen, A.: Distributing
      Event Information by Simulating Word-of-Mouth Exchanges. In Proceedings
      of Mobile HCI 2002, Pisa, Italy, Springer-Verlag, Berlin (2002)
[39] Huttenrauch, H. and Norman, M.: PocketCERO – mobile interfaces for service
      robots. In Proceedings of Mobile HCI 2001, Lille, France (2001)
[40] Isokoski, P. and Raisamo, R.: Device Independent Text Input: A Rationale and
      an Example. In Proceedings of AVI2000, Palermo, Italy, ACM (2000)
[41] Izadi, S., Fraser, M., Benford, S., Flintham, M,, Greenhalgh, C., Rodden, T.
      and Schnadelbach, H.: Citywide: supporting interactive digital experiences
      across physical space. In Proceedings of Mobile HCI 2001, Lille, France
      (2001)
[42] James, C.L. and Reischel, K.: Text Input for Mobile Devices: Comparing
      Model Prediction to Actual Performance. In proceedings of CHI2001, Seattle,
      WA, USA, ACM (2001)
[43] Jameson, A.: Modeling both the Context and the User. Personal and Ubiquitous
      Computing, Vol. 5. Springer-Verlag, London (2001) 29-33
[44] Jones, M., Buchanan, G. and Thimbleby, H.: Sorting Out Searching on Small
      Screen Devices. In Proceedings of Mobile HCI 2002, Pisa, Italy, Springer-
      Verlag, Berlin (2002)
[45] Kehr, R. and Zeidler, A.: Look, Ma, My Homepage is Mobile! Personal and
      Ubiquitous Computing, Vol. 4. Springer-Verlag, London (2000) 217-220
[46] Kohtake, N., Rekimoto, J. and Anzai, Y.: InfoPoint: A Device that Provides a
      Uniform User Interface to Allow Appliances to Work Together over a Net-
      work. Personal and Ubiquitous Computing, Vol. 5. Springer-Verlag, London
      (2001) 264-274
[47] Lacucci, G., Kuutti, K. and Ranta, M.: On the Move with a Magic Thing: Role
      Playing in Concept Design of Mobile Services and Devices. In proceedings of
      DIS 2000, ACM (2000)
[48] Laerhoven, K.V. and Aidoo, K.: Teaching Context to Applications. Personal
      and Ubiquitous Computing, Vol. 5. Springer-Verlag, London (2001) 46-49

[49] Lamming, M., Eldridge, M., Flynn, M., Jones, C. and Pendlebury, D.: Satchel: Providing Access to Any Document, Any Time, Anywhere. Transactions on Computer-Human Interaction, Vol. 7, No. 3. ACM (2000) 322-352

[50] Lehikoinen, J. and Salminen, I.: An Empirical and Theoretical Evaluation of BinScroll: A Rapid Selection Technique for Alphanumeric Lists. Personal and Ubiquitous Computing, Vol. 6. Springer-Verlag, London (2002) 141-150

[51] Licoppe, C. and Heurtin, J.P.: Managing One's Availability to Telephone Communication Through Mobile Phones: A French Case Study of the Development of Dynamics of Mobile Phone Use. Personal and Ubiquitous Computing, Vol. 5. Springer-Verlag, London (2001) 99-108

[52] Lin, J., Laddaga, R. and Naito, H.: Personal Location Agent for Communicating Entities (PLACE). In Proceedings of Mobile HCI 2002, Pisa, Italy, Springer-Verlag, Berlin (2002)

[53] Ling, R.: We Release Them Little by Little: Maturation and Gender Identity as Seen in the Use of Mobile Telephony. Personal and Ubiquitous Computing, Vol. 5. Springer-Verlag, London (2001) 123-136

[54] Ljungstrand, P.: Context Awareness and Mobile Phones. Personal and Ubiquitous Computing, Vol. 5. Springer-Verlag, London (2001) 58-61

[55] MacKenzie, I.S., Kober, H., Smith, D., Jones, T. and Skepner, E.: LetterWise: Prefix-Based Disambiguation for Mobile Text Input. In proceedings of UIST2001, Orlando, Florida, USA, ACM (2001)

[56] MacKenzie, S.: KSPC (Keystrokes per Character) as a Characteristic of Text Entry Techniques. In Proceedings of Mobile HCI 2002, Pisa, Italy, Springer-Verlag, Berlin (2002)

[57] Mantyjarvi, J. and Seppanen, T.: Adapting Applications in Mobile Terminals Using Fuzzy Context Information. In Proceedings of Mobile HCI 2002, Pisa, Italy, Springer-Verlag, Berlin (2002)

[58] Marsden, G., Thimbleby, H., Jones, M. and Gillary, P.: Data Structures in the Design of Interfaces. Personal and Ubiquitous Computing, Vol. 6. Springer-Verlag, London (2002) 132-140

[59] Matsushita, N., Ayatsuka, Y. and Rekimoto, J.: Dual Touch: A Two-Handed Interface for Pen-Based PDAs. In proceedings of UIST2000, San Diego, CA, USA, ACM (2000)

[60] Mayol, W.W., Tordoff, B.J. and Murray, D.W.: Wearable Visual Robots. Personal and Ubiquitous Computing (2002), Vol. 6. Springer-Verlag, London (2002) 37-48

[61] Mizobuchi, S., Mori, K., Ren, X. and Michiaki, Y.: An Empirical Study of the Minimum Required Size and the Minimum Number of Targets for Pen Input on the Small Display. In Proceedings of Mobile HCI 2002, Pisa, Italy, Springer-Verlag, Berlin (2002)

[62] Mikkonen, M., Vayrynen, S., Ikonen, V. and Heikkila, O.: User and Concept Studies as Tools in Developing Mobile Communication Services for the Elderly. Personal and Ubiquitous Computing (2002), Vol. 6. Springer-Verlag, London (2002) 113-124

[63] Milewski, A. and Smith, T.M.: Providing Presence Cues to Telephone Users. In Proceedings of CSCW2000, Philadelphia, PA, USA, ACM (2000)

[64] Nakanishi, Y., Tsuji, T., Ohyama, M. and Hakozaki, K.: Context Aware Messaging Service: A Dynamical Messaging Delivery using Location Information and Schedule Information. Personal and Ubiquitous Computing (2000), Vol. 4. Springer-Verlag, London (2000) 221-224

[65] Nigay, L., Salembier, P., Marchand, T., Renevier, P. and Pasqualetti, L.: Mobile and Collaborative Augmented Reality: A Scenario Based Design Approach. In Proceedings of Mobile HCI 2002, Pisa, Italy, Springer-Verlag, Berlin (2000)

[66] Oquist, G. and Goldstein, M.: Towards an Improved Readability on Mobile Devices: Evaluating Adaptive Rapid Serial Visual Presentation. In Proceedings of Mobile HCI 2002, Pisa, Italy, Springer-Verlag, Berlin (2002)

[67] Palen, L., Salzman, M. and Youngs, E.: Going Wireless: Behavior & Practice of New Mobile Phone Users. In Proceedings of CSCW2000, Philadelphia, PA, USA, ACM (2000)

[68] Palen, L., Salzman, M. and Youngs, E.: Discovery and integration of Mobile Communications in Everyday Life. Personal and Ubiquitous Computing, Vol. 5. Springer-Verlag, London (2001) 109-122

[69] Palen, L. and Salzman, M.: Beyond the Handset: Designing for Wireless Communication Devices. Transactions on Computer-Human Interaction, Vol. 9, No. 2. ACM (2002) 125-151

[70] Partridge, K., Chatterjee, S. and Want, R.: TiltType: Accelerometer-Supported Text Entry for Very Small Devices. In proceedings of UIST2002, Paris, France, ACM (2002)

[71] Pascoe, J., Ryan, N. and Morse, D.: Using While Moving: HCI Issues in Fieldwork Environments. Transactions on Computer-Human Interaction, Vol. 7, No. 3. ACM (2000) 417-437

[72] Perry, M., O'Hara, K., Sellen, A., Brown, B. and Harper, R.: Dealing with Mobility: Understanding Access Anytime, Anywhere. Transactions on Computer-Human Interaction, Vol. 8, No. 4. ACM (2001) 323-347

[73] Petrelli, D., Not, E., Zancanaro, M., Strapparava, C. and Stock, O.: Modeling and Adapting to Context. Personal and Ubiquitous Computing, Vol. 5. Springer-Verlag, London (2001) 20-24

[74] Pham, T., Schneider, G., Goose, S. and Pizano, A.: Composite Device Computing Environment: A Framework for Situated Interaction Using Small Screen Devices. Personal and Ubiquitous Computing, Vol. 5. Springer-Verlag, London (2001) 25-28

[75] Pirhonen, A., Brewster, S. and Holguin, C.: Gestural and Audio Methaphors as a Means of Control for Mobile Devices. In Proceedings of CHI2002, Minneapolis, Minnesota, USA, ACM (2002)

[76] Pospischil, G., Umlauft, M. and Michlmayr, E.: Designing LoL@, a Mobile Tourist Guide for UMTS. In Proceedings of Mobile HCI 2002, Pisa, Italy, Springer-Verlag, Berlin (2002)

[77] Poupyrev, I., Maruyama, S. and Rekimoto, J.: Ambient Touch: Designing Tactile Interfaces for Handheld Devices. In proceedings of UIST2002, Paris, France, ACM (2002)

[78] Raghunath, M.T., Narayanaswami, C.: User Interfaces for Application s on a Wrist Watch. Personal and Ubiquitous Computing, Vol. 6. Springer-Verlag, London (2002) 17-30

[79] Randell, C. and Muller, H.: The Shopping Jacket: Wearable Computing for the Consumer. Personal and Ubiquitous Computing, Vol. 4. Springer-Verlag, London (2000) 241-244

[80] Randell, C. and Muller, H.L.: The Well Mannered Wearable Computer. Personal and Ubiquitous Computing, Vol. 6. Springer-Verlag, London (2002) 31-36

[81] Rantanen, J., Impio, J., Karinsalo, T., Reho, A., Tasanen, M. and Vanhala, J.: Smart Clothing Prototype for the Artic Environment. Personal and Ubiquitous Computing, Vol. 6. Springer-Verlag, London (2002) 3-16

[82] Ren, X., Moriya, S.: Improved Selection Performance on Pen-Based Systems: A Study of Pen-Based Interaction for Selection tasks. Transactions on Computer-Human Interaction, Vol. 7, No. 3. ACM (2000) 384-416

[83] Rist, T., Brandmeier, P., Herzog, G. and Andre, E.: Getting the Mobile Users in: Three Systems that Support Collaboration in an Environment with Heterogeneous Communication Devices. In Proceedings of AVI2000, Palermo, Italy, ACM (2000)

[84] Rist, T., and Brandmeier, P.: Customizing Graphics for Tiny Displays of Mobile Devices. In Proceedings of Mobile HCI 2001, Lille, France (2001)

[85] Ross, D.A. and Blasch, B.B.: Development of a wearable Computer Orientation System. Personal and Ubiquitous Computing, Vol. 6. Springer-Verlag, London (2002) 49-63

[86] Roth, J. and Unger, C.: Using Handheld Devices in Synchronous Collaborative Scenarios. Personal and Ubiquitous Computing, Vol. 5. Springer-Verlag, London (2001) 243-252

[87] Roth, J.: Patterns of Mobile Interaction. In Proceedings of Mobile HCI 2001, Lille, France (2001)

[88] Ruuska-Kalliokulja, S., Schneider-Hufschmidt, M., Vaananen-Vainio-Mattila, K. and Von Niman, B.: Shaping the future of Mobile Devices – Results of the CHI2000 Workshop on Future Mobile Device User Interfaces. In Proceedings of Mobile HCI 2001, Lille, France (2001)

[89] Sawhney, N. and Schmandt, C.: Nomadic Radio: Speech and Audio Interaction for Contextual Messaging in Nomadic Environments". Transactions on Computer-Human Interaction, Vol. 7, No. 3. ACM (2000) 353-383

[90] Sazawal, V., Want, R. and Boriello, G.: The Unigesture Approach: One-Handed Text Entry for Small Devices. In Proceedings of Mobile HCI 2002, Pisa, Italy, Springer-Verlag, Berlin (2002)

[91] Schenkman, B.N.: Perceived Similarities and Preferences for Consumer Electronics Products. Personal and Ubiquitous Computing, Vol. 6. Springer-Verlag, London (2002) 125-131

[92] Schmidt, A., Takaluoma, A. and Mantyjarvi, K.: Context-Aware Telephony Over WAP. Personal and Ubiquitous Computing, Vol. 4. Springer-Verlag, London (2000) 225-229

[93] Schmidt, A., Stuhr, T. and Gellersen, H.: Context-Phonebook – Extending Mobile Phone Applications with Context. In Proceedings of Mobile HCI 2001, Lille, France (2001)

[94] Sharples, M., Corlett, D. and Westmancott, O.: The Design and Implementation of a Mobile Learning Resource. Personal and Ubiquitous Computing (2002) Vol. 6. Springer-Verlag, London (2002) 220-234

[95] Silfverberg, M., Mackanzie, I.S. and Korhonen, P.: Predicting Text Entry Speed on Mobile Phones. In Proceedings of CHI2000, The Hague, Amsterdam, ACM (2000)

[96] Strom, G.: Mobile Devices as Props in Daily Role Playing. In Proceedings of Mobile HCI 2001, Lille, France (2001)

[97] Swindells, C., Inkpen, K.M., Dill, J.C. and Tory, M.: That one There! Pointing to establish device identity. In proceedings of UIST2002, Paris, France, ACM (2002)

[98] Tang, J., Yankelovich, N., Begole, B., Van Kleek, M., Li, F. and Bhalodia, J.: ConNexus to Awarenex: Extending awareness to mobile users. In proceedings of CHI2001, Seattle, WA, USA, ACM (2001)

[99] Thomas, B., Grimmer, K., Zucco, J. and Milanese, S.: Where Does the Mouse Go? An Investigation into the Placement of a Body-Attached TouchPad Mouse for Wearable Computers. Personal and Ubiquitous Computing, Vol. 6. Springer-Verlag, London (2002) 97-112

[100] Trevor, J., Hilbert, D.M., Schilit, B.N. and Koh, T.K.: From Desktop to Phonetop: A UI For Web Interaction On Very Small Devices. In proceedings of UIST2001, Orlando, Florida, USA, ACM (2001)

[101] Weilenmann, A.: Negotiating Use: Making Sense of Mobile Technology. Personal and Ubiquitous Computing, Vol. 5. Springer-Verlag, London (2001) 137-145

[102] Wobbrock, J.O., Forlizzi, J., Hudson S.E. and Myers, B.A.: WebThumb: Interaction Techniques for Small-Screen Browsers. In proceedings of UIST2002, Paris, France, ACM (2002)

Exploring the Utility of Remote Messaging
and Situated Office Door Displays

Keith Cheverst, Alan Dix, Dan Fitton, Adrian Friday, and Mark Rouncefield

Department of Computing, Lancaster University
Lancaster, LA1 4YR.
kc,dixa,df,adrian@comp.lancs.ac.uk
m.rouncefield@lancaster.ac.uk

Abstract. In recent years, the proliferation in use of the GSM short message service (or SMS) has prompted numerous studies into person to person messaging via mobile devices. However, to date, there has been relatively little exploration of systems that enable mobile messaging to (potentially ubiquitous) situated displays rather than the mobile devices of particular individuals. In this paper, we describe the results of an ongoing trial to explore the utility of a system that enables lecturers in a computing department to use their mobile phones to send messages to digital displays situated outside their offices.

1   Introduction

Perhaps one of the most surprising phenomena to have occurred within the field of mobile computing within recent years has been the uptake of SMS (or Short Message Service) text messaging. For example, according to the Mobile Data Association (MDA), the total number of chargeable person-to-person SMS text messages sent across the four U.K. GSM network operators during the day between midnight on 31st December 2002 and midnight on 1st January 2003, was 102 million, a 59% increase compared to figures over the same period in 2002 [3].

One use of SMS that has received little investigation to date is to enable a (potentially mobile) user to message a display in a particular place rather than a mobile device owned by a particular individual. O'Hara *et al* [4] discuss situated displays as being "situated at particular locations within our environment" and yet which, paradoxically, "allow information to be more easily updated dynamically and remotely". Although the origins of our work pre-date this quote, it is exactly this potential for updating situated displays remotely that forms the focus of this paper.

The Hermes system [2] was designed to explore the issues that arise when office owners are provided with a digital 'office door display'. One issue we wished to explore was whether the traditional way of posting messages on post-it notes in 'semi-private' places could be enhanced with such a digital equivalent. One of the major gains of an electronic system is that it supports remote interaction. This includes a web-based interface, email and, most significantly for this paper, SMS.

L. Chittaro (Ed.): Mobile HCI 2003, LNCS 2795, pp. 336–341, 2003.
© Springer-Verlag Berlin Heidelberg 2003

There are numerous examples of office door display systems and a full overview of these and related systems can be found in [2]. However, none of these currently provide (much less evaluate) an explicit facility for mobile messaging. One interesting example of a system that utilises SMS messaging in conjunction with situated display involves a U.K. police force. This police force has developed a system that enables appropriate personnel to use SMS in order to post road warnings to displays situated on the roadside [1]. In common with Hermes, the system is designed to supplement existing approaches. In this case, the existing approach for alerting anonymous drivers of hazardous road conditions is local radio.

2   A Brief Overview of the HERMES System

Work on developing the Hermes system started in October 2001 and the first unit was installed outside one of the offices in the computing department in March 2002. Currently ten Hermes displays are deployed around the department outside the offices of lecturers, research assistants, PhD students and department secretaries. Figure 1 illustrates a Hermes display and one of the department's corridors containing a concentration of Hermes displays.

Fig. 1. Picture of an early Hermes display (left) and deployed displays (right)

The functionality supported by the system can be considered from two main perspectives, namely: the perspective of the *owner* of the Hermes display and the perspective of a *visitor* to the Hermes display.

Owners can create messages to appear on their own Hermes displays. Messages (which can take the form of text or graphics) can be created on the display itself, via the Hermes web page, an e-mail client or by sending an SMS text message. This message is then visible on the door display.

One important aspect of a Calm technology is that it "...engages both the *center* and the *periphery* of our attention, and in fact moves back and forth between the two" [5]. The Hermes display has just these properties: for a passer-by it does not grab attention, but for someone visiting the office it is immediately obvious. The situated nature gives us this flexibility of attention 'for free'.

Visitors can also leave messages on an owner's display. However, once entered, messages left by visitors are not visible to passers-by. There are two main reasons for controlling this aspect of visibility. Firstly, because of the limited display space, Hermes must give priority to the owner's message. Secondly, we wanted to encourage owners to feel in control of the personal space represented by their individual Hermes displays. The owner can read left messages via a web portal, email or using his or her Hermes display directly. Owners can also request notification via SMS when a new message is left on their Hermes display.

A sketch illustrating the basic system architecture of Hermes is shown in figure 2. A detailed explanation of the architecture is beyond the scope of this paper, but more details of the approach can be found in [2]. Briefly, at the heart of the system is a single central server application that stores messages and user profile information, hosts the Hermes web portal and supports communication with the SMS Gateway.

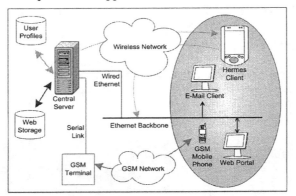

Fig. 2. The System Architecture of Hermes

3   Motivation for Enabling "Texting" to Hermes Displays

From an early design stage we realized the potential importance of providing the owners of Hermes displays with the ability to send a message to the display situated outside their office using their mobile phone. Our reason for providing this facility was based on personal experiences in the past where we have felt the need to post messages on our door from some remote location and so have had to phone through to a secretary or colleague and ask him or her to stick an appropriate post-it note message on our door. The typical message that a lecturer might ask to be posted would be something like "Sorry, car problems, away this A.M.", or "Sorry, running 30 mins late". Clearly such an approach disturbs the person being asked to write the post-it note and requires the person to be contactable (often not the case with very busy secretaries) and free to perform the task.

Sometimes, the message posted may also be posted to the computing department's mailing list, e.g. if the person has been taken ill and is likely to be off the entire day. However, for messages of slightly less importance (or less wide appeal) it is very unlikely that such an e-mail would be sent. During a typical office day, lecturers have a series of fixed appointments with students and also maintain a 'drop-in' period for students to discuss problems. A message such as "Running 30 mins late" is therefore extremely useful for supporting dynamic rescheduling and for reaching students that may not read their e-mail in time if an accompanying e-mail was actually sent.

4   Experience and Analysis

As Hermes has been deployed on a substantial scale and for a prolonged period we have been able to obtain significant feedback, both to enable evolutionary improvements and to give us a rich understanding of real use.

The remote messaging facility in Hermes (though not the overall Hermes system) was primarily envisioned as a feature to support lecturers in the department. Currently, six of the ten Hermes display owners are lecturers. Here are views of three of these lecturers (A, B and C) towards the remote messaging facility who have been long term Hermes users.

Lecturer A attempted to use the remote messaging feature on a small number of occasions when the remote messaging feature was first introduced and unfortunately the reliability of the system was poor. He had found that the messages which he had sent using SMS had was not appeared on his Hermes display. This early experience damaged his trust of this aspect of the system and so he has subsequently not used this feature (although he very frequently posts messages on his Hermes display using the other approaches available). This lecturer is keen for the system to reassure him that a message has actually been displayed by providing him with improved feedback.

Lecturer B has used the feature on several occasions. In common with lecturer A this lecturer started using the feature when it was first introduced and encountered some reliability problems. However, he has used the remote messaging feature successfully on several occasions and is prepared to trust the feature. In common with lecturer A, this lecturer is also keen for a greater level of feedback to be provided to increase his confidence that a sent message has successfully been displayed.

Lecturer C was issued with a Hermes display several months later than lecturers A and B at a time when the reliability of the remote messaging feature was very high. Indeed, this lecturer has used the remote messaging feature fairly frequently for approximately six months and has not experienced any reliability problems with the SMS feature. Indeed, he has expressed a strong level of trust in the reliability of the remote messaging facility. Examples of his messages include "am running 20 mins late", "On bus 2.15 - in soon", "On bus - in shortly", "Gone to the gym", "Derek - in ww burger joint" and "In big q at post office.. Will be a bit late. C"

As can be seen, Lecturer C's messages include both temporal and location elements. Also, most messages are not targeted to a specific individual, with the exception of the message directed to Derek. We specifically asked the lecturer about his reasons for posting this targeted message and he revealed some interesting points.

It transpired that when the message was sent, lecturer C had an appointment with Derek in lecturer C's office but was delayed at a working lunch. He did not have Derek's mobile phone number, but, interestingly, he said he doubted whether he would have tried to contact Derek by mobile phone anyway (he suspected that Derek did not regularly carry a mobile phone). Also, by the time he realized he would be late, he doubted that Derek would have received an e-mail in time. Lecturer C also commented on the situated and "multipurpose" nature of his message, it provided not only the right notification to Derek but also informed those passing his office that he was currently delayed and likely to be running late. On this occasion situation, the SMS to his office door display was his primary means for communication.

5   Discussion and Future Work

In this paper, we have described the results of our initial exploration into a novel messaging paradigm, which focuses on enabling users to remotely update their (situated) office door displays. This has shown that:

Trust and reliability are key issues for this use of messaging. Appropriate feedback is essential in order to establish confidence that the message has really been displayed and thus encourage continued use.

This approach supplements existing email, voice and paper systems, but in some circumstances can become the primary means of communication.

Traditionally, a lecturer might phone a secretary or colleague in order to ask him or her to place a post-it note message. As envisaged, Hermes has reduced this and so reduced disturbance, but in addition has encouraged messages such "In big q at post office.. Will be a bit late" would probably not have warranted a special phone call to the secretary.

Our current development effort is focused on extending the current level of feedback provided by the Hermes system, answering one of the key problems highlighted above. The sender of a message will be provided with an acknowledgement when his or her SMS message is actually received by the door display as opposed to simply received by the SMS gateway (see figure 2).

One area of future work will be to explore the potential use of the Multimedia Messaging Service (MMS). This will allow the owner of a Hermes display to receive messages left on his or her door via an MMS capable mobile phone and also to enable the owner to send multimedia messages to display on the door display.

We also intend to trial the use of situated displays and remote messaging in the family home. One can envisage a situated display placed in the kitchen with other, more private, displays situated in other locations around the house, such as outside bedrooms. Family members would then be able to send messages to situated displays in addition to, the mobile phones of individual family members.

In summary, we believe that our initial studies suggest the significant potential of messaging to situated displays, as providing a simple, lightweight and flexible mechanism for displaying informal notifications to an appropriate location.

References

[1]   BBC News item: http://news.bbc.co.uk/1/hi/england/2784425.stm
[2]   Cheverst, K., D. Fitton, and A. Dix. "Exploring The Evolution Of Office Door Displays", In K. O'Hara, M. Perry, E. Churchill, D. Russell (ed) Public and Situated Displays: Social and Interactional aspects of shared display technologies. To appear.

[3]   Mobile Data Association, http://www.mda-mobiledata.org/resource/ hottopics/sms.asp

[4]   O'Hara, K. et al, Public, Community and Situated Displays: Design, use and interaction around shared information displays, Call for papers, available at: http://www.appliancestudio.com/cscw/cscwdisplayworkshopcall.htm (2002)

[5]   Weiser, M. and J. Seely Brown, "Designing Calm Technology," Chaper 6 "The Coming Age of Calm Technogy" in "Beyond Calculation – The Next Fifty Years of Computing" by P. J. Denning and R. M. Metcalfe, Copernicus/An Imprint of Springer-Verlag.

TimeMachine Oulu – Dynamic Creation of Cultural-Spatio-Temporal Models as a Mobile Service

Jaakko Peltonen[1], Mark Ollila[2], and Timo Ojala[1]

[1] MediaTeam, University of Oulu
P.O.BOX 4500, FIN-90014 University of Oulu, Finland
{jaakko.peltonen,timo.ojala}@oulu.fi
http://www.mediateam.oulu.fi/
[2] Norrköping Visualization and Interaction Studio, Linköping University,
60 174 Norrköping, Sweden
marol@itn.liu.se
http://nvis.itn.liu.se/

Abstract. The use of architectural and historical information in a mobile environment is investigated in this paper. We have created a system for dynamic creation of spatio-temporal VRML-models for context aware clients in a mobile cultural setting. The user can interact and query objects using standard web interfaces as well interaction in the 3D environment. We perform a preliminary user evaluation for iterative design of future versions of the mobile service.

1 Introduction

Recent advances in wireless communication and portable terminals have engendered a new paradigm of computing, called mobile computing. Users are able to carry portable devices and have access to data and information services regardless of their physical location or movement behavior. In the meantime, research addressing information access and human computer interaction in mobile environments has proliferated. The Virtual Reality Modeling Language (VRML) and the World Wide Web (WWW) offer new opportunities to communicate temporal-spatial architectural information across the desktop. When mobile devices are added, the client-server paradigm is enhanced [1]. In this short paper, we have investigated the use of VRML to display historical records of buildings on both desktops, as well as mobile devices, with location information (positioning) available. We discuss the dynamic creation process of the historical architectural visualizations (aka cultural-spatial-temporal), and the human computer interactions issues that were encountered in a small test group in a mobile setting. The system is know as "TimeMachine" and shall be referred to as such.

There exists previous research in the reconstruction of a city from historical knowledge and for on-site visualization [2]. Augmented reality has also been used in various arhaeological projects where location is achieved by tracking

L. Chittaro (Ed.): Mobile HCI 2003, LNCS 2795, pp. 342–346, 2003.
© Springer-Verlag Berlin Heidelberg 2003

with reference images [3] [4]. In other areas, generation of VRML city models for focus based tour animation, with the integration of geo-data sources is becoming popular [5]. As mobile devices become more advanced, the development of 3D information systems for mobile users is a growing research area [6].

2 Implementation

The material for the database was obtained from fire-insurance registry of the Tarmo Insurance Company. They insured most of the buildings in Oulu, and had documented material covering approximately 80% of the city. The insurance documents have been verified to be accurate by local researchers [7]. The characteristics for the city of Oulu in 18th and 19th century are quite unique for the region. The city was fairly large and a major part of the houses were built from timber logs. The city consisted of a vast number of small wooden one and one and half story height buildings. The current database covers the years between two devastating fires in Oulu, 1822-1882. Previous research in this area which is similar is the reconstruction of 3D virtual buildings from 2D architectural floor plans [8].

2.1 Creating a Dynamic Model

There are several implementations of VRML as a user interface for databases. VirtuAL Project is such implementation with case study of the Cathedral of Wells [9]. Unlike TimeMachine, their system uses a database mainly to store the multimedia underlying the spatial model. A typical time-model is often using static VRML files that have been created for a certain moment in time.

In TimeMachine, we have overcome this limitation by using dynamic VRML-creation that is generated directly from the database that was created from the insurance documents. The material and the data for each building is in a database and a model of the city is dynamically created from SQL queries that the user might have. The implementation uses standard internet components, such as VRML for the 3D model representation, with a backend architecture of Apache, mySQL, PHP4 and Java-servlets. The composition of the user interface is formed on the clientside with standard HTML, VRML and javascript. User actions and input are posted and prosessed on server-side PHP-scripts. TimeMachine also provides storage for various user definable historic events or models. The secondary goal of TimeMachine is to study and define object models for cultural data, which we have labelled Cultural Objects, CObs'. It should be noted that TimeMachine is not a GIS (Geographic Information System) nor SIS (Spatial Information System) system, but has common relations to them [10].

The 3D model represents merely dimensions of building, location, slot, block, colour as material and shoreline. Acheiving photorealistic visual representations requires significant rendering power, network bandwidth and storage. As such, the following factors are used to outline the visual characteristics of the spatial view in TimeMachine. These include the limited knowledge of the appearance and details of the buildings; the large dataset growing towards present day; limited power and rendering capabilities on mobile clients; storage, network and bandwidth limitations on mobile clients; limitations of using VRML (simple lighting model).

Sharing the database to the Internet is somewhat straightforward procedure, allowing desktop and mobile access. However, using VRML makes the site more dependent on the client connections, browser software, and ability to handle different constraints demanded by the client. Parameters include level of detail in the model, textures, other model features such as animations, client operating system, client hardware type, network throughput and user settings. VRML-generation for each various client is different, with all optimization performed on the server-side. This set of continuous transparent flexible optimizations perform a key role in providing viable contents on a mixture of clients such as mobile devices.

2.2 TimeMachine as SmartRotuaari Service

TimeMachine is provided as a mobile service in SmartRotuaari, which is a research environment developed in the University of Oulu's Rotuaari project [11]. It aims at prototyping and empirical evaluation of future context-aware mobile multimedia services in real end user environment at downtown Oulu. TimeMachine can be launched from location-aware WLAN operated PDA. TimeMachine receives call with parameters of user identity and position. These are processed and a rendered VRML model is sent to client from referring point (users' present location). The user is able to perform keyword searches, move around the 3D world, query about specific objects by performing picking operations and so forth. An example screen shot is found in Figure 1.

3   User Evaluation of TimeMachine in a Mobile Setting

Usability of the service and user experience was assessed with a user evaluation in real operating situation (see Figure 1). The test users were first given a short introduction of the service, and then they were asked to carry out four tasks: T1: to go to year 1826, T2: to move around the church, T3: to find any red, yellow or green building and name its owner and insurance number, and T4: to find out the width and length of mayor Appelgren's house by keyword-based search. After completing the tasks the test users completed a questionnaire addressing various aspects of the perceived usability and user experience. The questionnaire contained two types of questions, of which some were answered on scale 1-5 and the other with yes/no answer.

The evaluation involved 10 test users, 6 males and 4 females, of which 9 lived in Oulu. Although all test users reported at least average (3 on scale 1-5) skills and experience in using computers, only two of them had significant prior experience in using a PDA. None of the test users had used any location-based services before. For brevity we just summarize some of the main results: all users

Fig. 1. Two test users with the system, one standing up, and another sitting down to the right of the photo. The old church from 1826 is still standing in the immediate background. The building in front of it is only "recently" constructed

were able to complete tasks T1, T2 and T3 successfully; 7 users completed task T4 successfully; 7 users thought that TimeMachine was slow; 6 users found the visual quality of TimeMachine sufficient ; 8 users concluded that they would have been able to use TimeMachine independently; 9 users would like to use TimeMachine in the future, as well; 9 users would recommend TimeMachine to their friends.

4   Conclusions and Future Work

Time Machine Oulu does not seek high-end visualizations, but to give views to a historic database on various clients, and be able to interact with that data in 3D. The limitations are acceptable since there are no photographs available during the time period represented in the dataset. TimeMachine Oulu has been developed to allow various types of multimedia to be distributed to various devices, such as PC's and PDA's. As the database of original data becomes larger, there will more and more CObs' available to be linked into the system, as the intention now is to increase the richness of the spatio-temporal-cultural information with the years 1882 to 1939. In addition to the preliminarly user-test evaluation, we will have a further, more thorough field trial in mid 2003 with over 100 users to gather specific design related feedback which will be evaluated and used to iterate the next version. Technically, future work includes more advanced mobile specific interfaces, utilizing location information more thoroughly and based on feedback from the field trials. As the database expands, we are particularly looking at what photographic material will be available and how this can be combined with Image Based Rendering techniques and various multimedia adaption methods that have been recently become available. We will also be investigating the use of smart phones (such as the Symbian based Series

60 phones), and examining non-pen based input methods with a goal to be able
to interact and navigate the system with one hand.

Acknowledgements

We would like to acknowledge Urban Research Group at the University of Oulu
for allowing us access to the raw data.

References

[1] Jin Jing, Abdelsalam Sumi Helal, and Ahmed Elmagarmid. Client-server computing in mobile environments. *ACM Computing Surveys (CSUR)*, 31(2):117–157,
1999.

[2] V. Vlahakis, J. Karigiannis, N. Ioannidis, M. Tsotros, M. Gounaris, D. Sticker,
P. Daehne, and L. Almeida. 3D interactive, on-site visualization of ancient
Olympia. In *3D Data Processing Visualization and Transmission, 2002.*, pages
337–345, 2002.

[3] Marc Pollefeys, Luc Van Gool, Ive Akkermans, Dirk De Becker, and Kris De-
muynck. A Guided Tour to Virtual Sagalassos. In *Proceedings of the 2001 conference on Virtual reality, archeology, and cultural heritage*, pages 213–218. ACM
Press, 2001.

[4] Vassilios Vlahakis, John Karigiannis, Manolis Tsotros, Michael Gounaris, Luis
Almeida, Didier Stricker, Tim Gleue, Ioannis T. Christou, Renzo Carlucci, and
Nikos Ioannidis. ARCHEOGUIDE: First Results of an Augmented Reality, Mo-
bile Computing System in Cultural Heritage Sites. In *Proceedings of the 2001
conference on Virtual reality, archeology, and cultural heritage*, pages 131–140.
ACM Press, 2001.

[5] Arne Schilling and Alexander Zipf. Generation of VRML city models for focus
based tour animations: integration, modeling and presentation of heterogeneous
geo-data sources. In *Proceeding of the eighth international conference on 3D web
technology*, pages 39–47. ACM Press, 2003.

[6] Teija Vainio and Outi Kotala. Developing 3D information systems for mobile
users: some usability issues. In *Proceedings of the second Nordic conference on
Human-computer interaction*, pages 231–234. ACM Press, 2002.

[7] P. Kovalainen and P. Vuojala. Aspect on the Building History of Oulu 1822-1882.
In *Proceedings of Historical European Towns Identity and Change.*, pages 166–171,
2000.

[8] Clifford So, George Baciu, and Hanqiu Sun. Reconstruction of 3D Virtual Buildings from 2D Architectural Floor Plans. In *Proceedings of the ACM symposium
on Virtual reality software and technology 1998*, pages 17–23. ACM Press, 1998.

[9] Bates-Brkljac. Virtual Project - A Prototype for Virtual Archive and Library for
Cathedrals. In *Proceedings of EVA 2002,*, page 279. ACM Press, 2002.

[10] T. Abraham and J. Rodding. Survey of spatio-temporal databases. *GeoInformat-
ica,*, 3(1):62–99, 1999.

[11] Smart Rotuaari, http://www.rotuaari.net, 2002.

Awase-E: Image-Based Authentication for Mobile Phones Using User's Favorite Images

Tetsuji Takada[1] and Hideki Koike[2]

[1] SONY Computer Science Laboratories
Muse Bldg. 3-14-13 Higashigotanda, Shinagawa-ku, Tokyo 141-0022, Japan
zetaka@computer.org
[2] Graduate School of Information Systems, University of Electro-Communications
1-5-1 Chofugaoka, Chofu, Tokyo 182-8585, Japan
koike@acm.org

Abstract. There is a trade-off between security and usability in user authentication for mobile phones. Since such devices have a poor input interfaces, 4-digit number passwords are widely used at present. Therefore, a more secure and user friendly authentication is needed. This paper proposes a novel authentication method called "Awase-E". The system uses image passwords. It, moreover, integrates image registration and notification interfaces. Image registration enables users to use their favorite image instead of a text password. Notification gives users a trigger to take action against a threat when it happens. Awase-E is implemented so that it has a higher usability even when it is used through a mobile phone.

1 Introduction

As mobile phones become widely used in various situations, a suitable method for user authentication is strongly required because they are often used as a user terminal for e-commerce and mobile banking. We currently, however, only have the option of using text-based authentication, such as user ID and password. This, however, is undesirable because of the trade-off problem between security and usability. It is better to use a longer password to ensure security. This, however, brings about usability issues such as the difficulty of remembering, recalling and inputting passwords. In particular, the difficulty of inputting passwords is critical in mobile phones because of the tedious input interface. In my mobile phone, for example, string "zetaka" requires 11 times of key typing. A simplified password, therefore, has been used such as a 4-digit number. However, we think that this type of authentication does not qualified enough to meet security requirements for e-commerce and mobile banking.

This paper proposes a novel authentication method for a mobile phone called "Awase-E". We assume that it will be used with a mobile phone with a digital camera. It uses photographic images taken by the users instead of text-based passwords. We also integrate two kinds of user interfaces into current authentication frameworks so that it not only improves usability but also enhances its security.

L. Chittaro (Ed.): Mobile HCI 2003, LNCS 2795, pp. 347–351, 2003.

2   Awase-E: Image-Based Authentication with Image Registration and Notification Interfaces

Awase-E is an authentication system using photographs instead of passwords. It, moreover, integrates image registration and notification interfaces into current authentication frameworks (Fig. 1).

The image registration interface enables users to add their favorite images to the authentication system. As a result, this makes it possible for users to use their favorite image as a "pass-image". Almost 20 million users currently have mobile phones with digital cameras in Japan. Most of them send photos by E-mail with a few key clicks on the spot. The image registration interface is implemented using this function. It is implemented separately from a pass-image setting in order to ensure the security against impersonation attempts. This function simply enables users to add a photo to the system and a registered photo does not automatically become a pass-image. In other words, not all registered images become a pass-image. A user must set at least one pass-image before authenticating oneself using Awase-E.

The notification interface gives users a trigger to handle a threat practically. It notifies users of the occurrence of all kinds of events related to the authentication process. For example, Awase-E sends an E-mail to the user who has registered a photo. The E-mail has a URL. The web page that is linked by that URL contains the photo that a user has just registered. A user can thus confirm the registered photo immediately through a web page. If a user receives such an E-mail even though the user had not registered the photo, it means that someone has registered it masquerading as a legitimate user. A legitimate user, therefore, quickly knows when an intrusive attempt has been made. From these scenarios, we would strongly recommend using Awase-E with mobile phones to ensure a user's prompt awareness of a security breach.

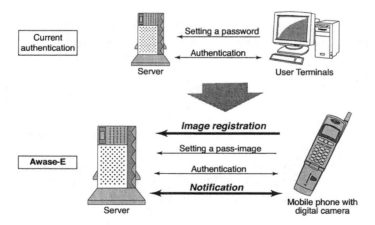

Fig. 1. Transition between Current and Proposed Authentication Framework

Verification stage

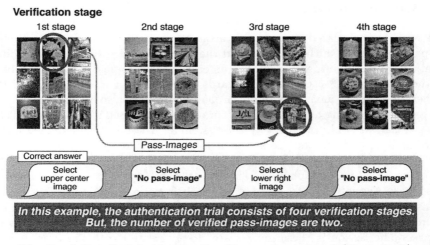

Fig. 2. A Detailed Authentication Process in Awase-E(N=4, P=9)

Awase-E keeps an event history of past usage for certain periods for the purpose of auditing the user's authentication usage. A user can investigate the history through a web page. It enables users to check the authentication usage even if a user has lost their mobile phone.

Awase-E is implemented through both E-mail and Web. Prerequisite requirements for a user terminal is that it has access to the above two network service types. This means that it is also possible to use Awase-E from computers.

The detail of the authentication process is shown in Fig. 2.

One authentication trial consists of **N** times of verification stages. Awase-E, of course, authorizes a user as a legitimate user only if all verifications are successful. In each verification stage, Awase-E shows **P** pieces of images on the screen, a user must select a pass-image correctly from them. Only one pass-image is included in each verification image set. The reason for this is to reduce the possibility that a randomly selected attacker's answer would be a correct answer. We call an image that is not a pass-image as a "decoy image". The location of each image in the image set is randomly determined. This means that the location of both pass-image and decoy images can change each time. It is also possible that there is no pass-image in an image set. In this case, the user must answer "no pass-image".

Awase-E is an easier method for users to complete the authentication process than before, even when using a mobile phone. The numerical keys on a mobile phone are uniquely correspond to each of the images on the screen at any given stage. This enables users to choose any image in the screen with one click. In using Awase-E, it is possible to authenticate oneself by just **N** + 1 times of key types. Moreover, Awase-E does not need to input any text in authenticating oneself because it uses an E-mail address as a user ID.

3 Considerations

There are some related works which make an attempt to improve the problem of password-based authentication and the experimental results clearly indicate that image-based authentication has an advantage over password or PIN-based authentication[1, 2] especially in regards to the human interface aspect. It is easier for a user to memorize an image than a text. It is also easier to identify an image than recalling a text. However, previously proposed systems make use of images that are only provided by the system[3]. These system-assigned images have little relation to the users, and it is possible that a user will forget it as time goes on, even though it is an image.

Awase-E, then, uses photographs that are taken by users for authentication. Moreover, Awase-E enables users to add their favorite images to the system and to use them as pass-image in an easy way. This feature greatly reduces the load of memorizing and recalling the secret information over using system provided images. The reason is these images are closely related with the user's experience. This means that the user tends to remember the images subconsciously when the user looks at it. Using photographs also make it easier to generate and select a pass-image. We think that these advantages result in motivating users to change their pass-image more frequently. This is a feature that has not been realized in any current authentication methods. Another benefit of image registration is that it increases the number of total images in the authentication database. An image-based authentication, theoretically, has a vast information space for secret information. It is, however, practically limited by the number of total images that the system has in its database[1, 2]. In Awase-E, the database for images continues to expand as time passes.

Awase-E also introduces the case that there is no pass-image in generating a verification image set. This feature has two merits. One is that it reduces the number of pass-images that a user must remember. and therefore reduces the memory load on users. Of course, the case of a user selecting all "no pass-image" is not allowed for security reasons. The other advantage is that it also enhances the security level against "Intersection Attack"[1] which is a specialized attack method to this kind of image-based authentication. The reason is that this kind of attack can only occur when a pass-image is included in the image set in all verification stages.

The notification interface gives users the information of an occurrence of an attack through E-mail and the web. In other words, it gives a trigger to users to take a response against it. If a user is aware of an attempt that an attacker impersonates yourself, a user should add a new photo and change their pass-image to a new one. Current security assessments of existing authentications are evaluated by statistical methods only. It is clear that Awase-E has the same security level of N-digit number passwords. We think, however, the evaluation method ignores the aspect of users in authentication. It is difficult to rectify the well-known problem that "a user is the weakest link in the security chain". Awase-E provides a notification interface to address this issue. We expect that this type of alerting mechanism has a positive effect on changing the user's view against computer security. The reason is that every user will probably encounter a malicious attempt in the near future. We believe that notification will become important in order to ensure the security level in any authentication system, and mobile terminals will become an essential device that can receive these notifications immediately on the spot.

The number of verification stages in Awase-E is variable. Awase-E, therefore, provides a flexible authentication framework that can handle various situations. For example, to emphasize security over usability, you could configure Awase-E such that a user must verifies 5 sets and must select a pass-image in 4 of the sets. On the contrary, if you put weight on usability over security, you can configure the process such that the user verifies only 3 sets and must select a pass-image in 1 of the sets.

From these considerations, we believe that Awase-E provides a better authentication framework that addresses both security and usability issues. In other words, Awase-E satisfies both security and usability issues at higher level than existing authentication methods.

4   Conclusion

In this paper, we proposed a novel authentication method called "Awase-E" that is used with mobile phones with digital cameras. We integrate image registration and notification interfaces into image-based authentication. Image registration enables users to use their favorite pictures as pass-images. And the notification interface gives users a trigger to take appropriate action against malicious attempts.

Awase-E is easily operable even when used through a mobile phone. Using a favorite picture as a pass-image reduces the memory load on users regarding secure information and is less memory-intensive than simply using system-assigned images. The notification function enables users to take appropriate action by themselves. In other words, it provides users with a method of ensuring the security of their own right. This feature is important in order to keep the user from being the weakest link in the security chain. We think that Awase-E realizes a higher level of coexistence in both security and usability than previous user authentication methods.

References

[1] R. Dhamija and A. Perrig: Deja Vu: A User Study Using Images for Authentication, 9th Usenix Security Symposium, pp. 45–58, Aug (2000).

[2] A. D.Angeli, M.Coutts, L.Coventry and G. I.Johnson: VIP: a visual approach to user authentication, Proc. of the Working Conference on Advanced Visual Interface (AVI2002), pp. 316–323, May (2002).

[3] A. Perrig and D. Song: Hash Visualization: a New Technique to improve Real-World Security, In International Workshop on Cryptographic Techniques and E-Commerce (CrypTEC), (1999).

Older Users' Requirements
for Location Based Services and Mobile Phones

Zaheer Osman, Martin Maguire and Mikko Tarkiainen

Ergonomics and Safety Research Institute, Loughborough University
Holywell Building, Holywell Way, Loughborough, UK LE11 3UZ
Tel: +44 01509 283 300
{z.osman, m.c.maguire}@lboro.ac.uk
mikko.tarkiainen@vtt.fi

Abstract. It is important that studies are carried out to enable developers of new products and services to take into consideration the requirements of the older population and work towards an inclusive design. This paper presents two studies carried out to determine the attitudes and requirements of older users towards location based services and their needs for mobile phone functions and features. The resulting implications and benefits for the developers of future products and services are briefly discussed.

Technological advances are occurring at a more rapid pace than ever before and have allowed the development of evermore sophisticated and ubiquitous products and services. In order for technology and services to be successful, they need to be embraced by the population. An example of this is the mobile phone which is now a commonly owned device. Location based services (LBS) are services in which the location of a person or an object is used to shape or focus the application or service (Duri 2001). According to a new report from ARC Group[1], LBS will account for over 40% of operators' mobile data services revenues in 2007,

It is apparent that people in modern day society are living longer compared to their predecessors. This is leading to an increased number of "Third Agers" (people 55 years and over). Coleman (2001) estimated that by the year 2020 almost half the adult population in the UK would be over 50 years of age. If products and services do not include this age group in their development processes then market exploitation will be adversely affected. Meeting the requirements of the older and younger age groups can be achieved by taking an inclusive design approach. Hardie and Plaice (1991) defined inclusive design as "an approach to creating environments and products that are usable by all people to the greatest extent possible". A question that needs answering is whether the developers of products and services are taking the

---

[1]   ARC Group Press Release, LONDON, 19 August 2002
http://www.arcgroup.com/index.html.

L. Chittaro (Ed.): Mobile HCI 2003, LNCS 2795, pp. 352–357, 2003.

rapidly growing older population into consideration. This paper is an initial attempt to address this need for LBS and mobile phones.

1   A Study on User Requirements and Attitudes for LBS

LBS have yet to penetrate the mainstream consumer market and are still being developed.   One might say that until recently they were driven primarily by technological developments therefore a user centered approach has scarcely been taken. This short study aimed to explore views, thoughts and attitudes of potential users towards LBS.   Requirements, preferred applications, advantages and disadvantages for LBS were identified from the future user's perspective.

1.1   Scenario Development

In order to present a practical example of the use of LBS to the participants, short scenarios were constructed. The scenarios were based on the current and possible future applications of LBS.   The scenarios were constructed after attending an industry seminar organized by HELIOS Technology UK[2] that included delegates from the major stakeholders in LBS. In total five future scenarios were constructed. These are summarized below:

- Scenario 1: "Finding your nearest" – traveling to another city and using LBS to locate a cash point to pay for the taxi fare and using LBS to locate a taxi rank.
- Scenario 2: "Traveling to a destination" – Organizing a trip to a theme park. Finding out train times and alternative transport using LBS. Also identifying a route to the theme park using LBS.
- Scenario 3: "Meeting up" – Locating the whereabouts of a friend using LBS on a night out. Finding a route to get to them also using LBS.
- Scenario 4: "Virtual Messaging" – Leaving and receiving spatially tagged messages to and from friends.
- Scenario 5: "Shopping" – Using LBS to locate products. Receiving a special promotional offer through LBS.

1.2   Focus Groups

The participants were split into four groups: "younger males" and "younger females" (20 –25 yrs old), "older males" and "older females" (55 yrs and above). In total four focus groups were conducted with six participants in each focus group.   The participants voted for the discussion of three out of the possible five scenarios to explore in each focus group session.

---

[2] Seminar titled "Migrating from Ideas to Income" organized by HELIOS Technology in London, UK. (November 2001)

1.3   User Requirements

Requirements for LBS were extracted from the discussions within each of the scenarios. They were categorized into primary, secondary or tertiary requirements according to their importance displayed within the discussions that was indicated by the level of group consensus. The general requirements of the older participants are displayed in table 1. Scenarios 1, 2, 3 and 5 were discussed.

Table 1. Summary of older users' requirements for LBS categorized into primary secondary and tertiary requirements. (Numbers indicate which scenarios the requirements were discussed in)

Primary	Secondary	Tertiary
Reliability of information [1,2,3,5]	Alternative routes/options [1,2]	Flight Bookings [2]
Personalization of LBS services[5]	Zoom in/out of display [1,3,5]	Receipt printing facility [2]
Integration into mobile phone [1,2,3,5]	Large Screen [1,2,3,5]	Color Screen [1,2,3,5]
Accuracy of information [1,2,3,5]	Usable abroad [2,5]	Guide book facility abroad[2]
Low cost of LBS service [1,2,3,5]	Information about charges for use of LBS service [1,2,3,5]	Specific information about facilities [1,2,5]
Ease of use of LBS device & LBS service [1,2,3,5]	Translation facility [2,5]	
Up to date information [1,2,3,5]	Comparison of different prices of external services [2]	
Maps for routes [1,3]	Check Stock in shops [5]	
Landmarks for places [1,2,3]	Print Facility [1,2,3,5]	
Directions to places [1,2,3]	Ability to locate lost people [3]	
Access of location information for police [2]	Reserve products in shops [5]	
Location inside building [5]	Security of different places [1,2]	

It is important to note that the requirements from both the older and younger age group had similarities (i.e. LBS should be reliable, integrated into mobile phones and up to date) and differences (i.e. older users required the text on the screens to be clear and easier to read whilst the younger age group wanted a more interactive service). This may be due to the difference in prior experience with new services between older and younger users. Younger users' were more technologically aware and therefore had more experience regarding the possible advantages and disadvantages of new services.

1.4   Group Attitude Ratings

A group attitude rating (GAR) was given by each of the focus groups for each of the scenarios discussed. The averages of the attitude ratings allow comparison of the acceptance levels of different groups for using LBS within different scenarios. It is interesting to note the contrasting attitudes towards LBS between the older and younger females within the shopping scenario discussion. The older females viewed LBS as a service that would facilitate and enhance their shopping activities whereas the younger females viewed LBS as a hindrance to their social interaction. Overall the older age groups (male and female) had a more positive attitude towards LBS compared to their younger counterparts (male and female). This is an assuring result for the developers of LBS and adds to the case of including the older age groups in the development of new services and products. The older users were comparing LBS to mobile phones and strongly suggested that LBS access should be integrated into the mobile phone. Therefore considering the mobile phone needs of older users was thought to be important.

2   Older Users and Mobile Phones

Interviews were carried out with a group of 17 users between the ages of 47 and 79 including 10 males and 7 females. They were generally inexperienced with mobile phones. Users were asked consider the situation where they were purchasing a new mobile phone. They were asked to choose from, and rank, a range of 12 features (printed on cards) divided into 3 categories: usability/ergonomic features, phone functions, and advanced services. The mean rank of each factor is shown below (12=high, 1=low):

Table 2. Mean rankings of required phone features

Feature required	Category	Mean rank
Easy menus	Usability/ergonomics	10.2
Large screen text	Usability/ergonomics	8.6
Small/compact	Usability/ergonomics	7.9
Large buttons	Usability/ergonomics	7.7
Information services	Advanced services	5.4
Voice dialing	Functions	5.1
Photo messaging	Advanced services	4.7
Handling calls intelligently	Advanced services	4.3
Radio	Functions	2.3
Phone shopping	Advanced services	2.2
Ring tones	Functions	1.7
Play games	Functions	1

Interestingly the four usability/ergonomic factors occupy the top four positions in the list. The list shows that there is significant interest in an information service through the phone. There was also some interest in photo-messaging and handling calls in helpful ways. However the idea of shopping through the phone received limited support.   Many preferred to view the real products before buying and also enjoyed the social aspects of going to shop for, say, groceries on a weekly basis.

The results show that the users were prepared to accept the integration of a range of services into the mobile phone, provided those services meet their needs and are of interest to them. Location-based services through the phone might thus be accepted by older users provided those services meet their needs.

Participants were asked which were the most important factors in learning how to use their mobile phone. Being shown by a friend or relative was the most important factor closely followed by use of the handbook. Exploring on one's own was fairly important. Only one person stated that a shop demonstration had been useful, and no one had received telephone support from the supplier. It will be important then for future location-based services to be very intuitive and additional support may be required for the users especially the older age groups.

Regarding method of payment, 14 out of the 17 users wanted their phone on a 'pay as you go' basis, only 2 wanted a contract. It is thus in the interest of phone companies to make the 'pay as you go' option attractive in terms of cost and services available, as this seems the preferred basis for the older user group in the UK.

3   Implications of Older Users on Design

The Mobile industry is moving into a new phase as 3G networks are emerging in many countries. The new terminals have many features and learning how to use them may prove to be difficult for many users especially the older age group. Furthermore, if older people cannot perceive the benefits or added value of the device and new mobile services provided, they would not be willing to invest in them.

The requirements and needs of older users need to be clarified in order to develop mobile services that are adopted by all possible users. However, the acceptance of mobile services (and new technology in general) is a gradual process, where users must understand the value added by services before they are readily accepted and integrated into everyday life. Simple and easy-to-use access methods with services provided by mature technology and with straight forward billing may be the key to the familiarization of LBS and mobile services for the older age groups.

Many people may have the perception that older users' have more demanding requirements that conflict with the requirements of their younger counterparts (i.e. large screen compared to small compact phone). This may be true to an extent for both LBS and mobile phones but as displayed by the first study there are many similarities that should be exploited. In addition to this, including the older age groups at a development stage of a new product or service will help identify minor alterations that may make the product or service more usable not only by the older age group but the population in general.

References

[1]   Coleman, R.: Designing for our Future Selves. Universal Design Handbook, McGraw Hill USA (2001)
[2]   Duri, S., Cole, A., Munson, J. and Christensen, J.: An Approach to Providing a Seamless End-User Experience for Location-Aware Applications. In Proceedings of 1st international workshop on mobile commerce, (2001) Vol. 86(4), 20-25
[3]   Hardie, G., Plaice, J. and Mace, R.: Accessible Environments towards Universal Design, In: Design Interventions: Towards more Humane Architecture. Van Nosk and Reinhold, New York, (1991)
[4]   Maguire, M. and Osman, Z., Designing for older and inexperienced mobile phone users, Paper to be presented at the HCI International Conference, June 23-27, Crete, (2003) www.http://www.hcii2003.gr/

GentleGuide: An Exploration of Haptic Output for Indoors Pedestrian Guidance

S. Bosman, B. Groenendaal, J.W. Findlater, T. Visser,
M. de Graaf, and P. Markopoulos

Industrial Design, Eindhoven University of Technology
postbus 513, 5600 MB Eindhoven, The Netherlands
{S.J.Bosman,B.Groenendaal,J.W.Findlater,T.Visser,
M.J.d.Graaf, P.Markopoulos}@tue.nl

This paper describes an investigation into how haptic output can be used to deliver guidance to pedestrians, who do not have any particular disability, to find their way to a particular destination indoors, e.g., a room in a hospital. A prototype device called GentleGuide was designed iteratively, resolving several design issues for the use of haptic output. GentleGuide has been assessed experimentally. Our conclusion is that haptic output offers significant promise both in improving performance and in reducing the disruptiveness of technology. A negative aspect of exclusively relying on a device like GentleGuide is the reduced location and orientation awareness by some participants.

1   Introduction

The haptic modality is relatively unexplored in the domain of mobile human computer interaction. Existing work often focuses on people with a severe visual impairment, e.g., the wearable navigation system by Ertan et al. [2]. This paper presents an application of haptic output to provide guidance to people without any particular disability walking inside buildings, e.g., to help first time visitors and patients find their way through large hospital or office complexes. Contrary to drivers or pilots, pedestrians can travel in jagged trajectories, can make shortcuts, can pause and turn back to easily to correct errors. Way finding is the task of determining how to get to a destination and directing the activities needed to get there [3]. Way finding requires simultaneous processing of several sources of information: monitoring the environment, architectural patterns, other people, obstacles, etc. The visual modality is often used to display maps or text instructions. However, graphical visual displays usually require users to operate the device 'head down', thus disrupting their primary tasks. As a recent evaluation showed, the limited screen space of mobile devices, make maps and text instructions difficult to use on the move [1].

Three output techniques for providing guidance to blind pedestrians outdoors are compared in [5]: binaural audio beacons, speech advice and haptic guidance in the form of shoulder tapping. Their empirical results show a clear advantage of the haptic

L. Chittaro (Ed.): Mobile HCI 2003, LNCS 2795, pp. 358-362, 2003.
© Springer-Verlag Berlin Heidelberg 2003

modality, both in objective performance and subjective preference. Notably, some of their subjects commented that it didn't compete for their attention, as audio information does. A prototype of a haptic device for way finding in complex indoor complexes is described in [6]. The advantage of their device is that it can easily be ignored or consulted at will.

A range of design options that must be addressed for designing haptic output are discussed in section 2, in the context of the iterative development of GentleGuide. We then describe the implementation of the prototype, its experimental assessment and conclude with some preliminary conclusions from this research.

Although this work focuses on pedestrian navigation, in essence the Gentle Guide adds an extra modality to navigation feedback in a broader sense.

2   The Design of GentleGuide

The original concept for the GentleGuide was of a wearable haptic device that would provide the analogue of a little nudge one gives to a disoriented companion to gently guide them in the correct direction. Pressure seems the obvious way of realizing the concept of the friendly nudge (see, e.g., [5]). However, mild pressure, tends to be ignored after the initial stimulus, is hard to convey through clothing and may be confounded by forces from the environment. Vibration output was eventually selected, not least because it easy to produce, as tiny vibration alarms are commercially available (e.g., those used inside mobile telephones). GentleGuide was developed iteratively, by several prototype and test cycles, which concluded on the following points:

- Using a single output device on one wrist is confusing. Two devices, one on each wrist is more appropriate.
- Vibrations are interpreted by users as a beacon to follow, rather than as a corrective nudge for one's direction.
- Direction is better encoded in the duration of pulse trains rather than in intensity.
- Vibrations should simply indicate left, right and stop, rather than more refined directions, e.g., 45 degrees to the left or proportional to the change of direction.
- A signal on both wrists, proved very intuitive as a stop signal.

We note that the first two design decisions, contrast the design of [5] for a very important reasons: contrary to their target users, our users are not visually impaired and are able to maintain straight line trajectories; i.e., even when lost, the non visually impaired users will not have the problem of veering.

Eventually, after repeated trials, we settled on the following conventions: 0,7 sec. right (left) receiver: go to your right (left), 0,7 seconds on both receivers: destination reached and 1,5 sec. both receivers: wrong direction. The final GentleGuide prototype is shown in fig. 1. The central box generates the navigation signals. The wrist devices contain a receiver, a decoder used to identify the signal and a battery fed vibration alarm. If the received pulse train is coded for the wrist device, the vibration alarm will be switched on as long as the pulse train is received. The prototype devices are housed in a plastic box. This box serves as a resonator for the vibration alarm. The prototypes are typically technical prototypes: focus was on functionality. Currently we are working on miniaturizing the devices and to improve their aesthetic appeal.

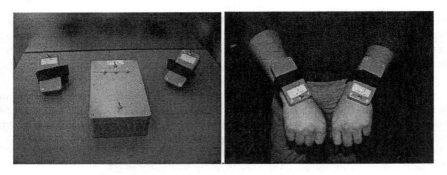

Fig. 1. (a) GentleGuide control unit and wrist devices (b) GentleGuide worn by a participant

3   Evaluation of GentleGuide

An experiment was conducted to assess the potential of GentleGuide for supporting way finding by pedestrians indoors. GentleGuide was compared to signage, which is how way finding inside buildings is currently supported. Because of familiarity with signage, this puts novel systems at a disadvantage, but improvements upon this 'benchmark' are necessary for providing added value to the non-blind user who can read. The experiment was conducted inside campus buildings that have a complexity in layout not uncommon for large buildings.

Participants. 16 paid persons (9 male and 7 female) without any disabilities took part in this study. All subjects are undergraduate students, who were screened so that they would not be familiar with the buildings where the experiment took place and would not be involved or familiar in any way with the experiment. They were all familiar with the signage conventions of the test environment to make the benchmark harder to match.

Design of the Experiment. A mixed design was followed. The within subjects condition was the use of GentleGuide or signage. The between subjects condition was the specific route concerned. Each subject had to walk 4 different routes, 2 with the GentleGuide and 2 with signage in mixed order. 8 subjects using the GentleGuide and 8 different subjects using signage attempted each of our 4 routes. The actual locations had been selected with pilot testing to ensure that the signage was adequate.

Independent Variables. The use of signage or GentleGuide.

Procedure. All way-finding tasks involved finding a room in an office building, without walking out of the building or going up or down a floor. Subjects were instructed to walk at their normal pace; they were introduced to GentleGuide by a brief written explanation and a 30 sec practice session. The experimenters would walk 5-6m behind the subjects issuing guidance instructions from the remote control console. Through pilot testing the appropriate position for issuing the instruction for the turn had been set to 2 meters before the turn. If subjects would take the wrong turn, they would be issued a command to stop. If they would ignore this command for more than 5 sec, the task would be declared a failure. Subjects were instructed to follow instructions, until they would be given a signal that they have arrived. In the visual condition, the subjects were allowed to find their way freely. They were stopped if they walked out of the building. The task then was declared a failure.

Dependent Variables. By counting how many of the tasks were completed successfully the effectiveness of GentleGuide was assessed. The time G it takes to get to the destination was measured. As a baseline measure, subjects were asked to return to the starting point at the same pace as they had just walked to get to the destination. This time, the evaluators would walk 1m behind the participant, telling them well in advance of approaching turns which way to go. We assume the time back B approximates the time needed by someone who knows the way. We added these measures for the two routes where a subject used GentleGuide and the two where signage was used. The dependent variable relative delay of getting to somewhere unknown was calculated as follows $\tau = (G-B)/B$.

The number of errors was counted for the two conditions. An error was simply defined as a subject not making the right decision at a junction point (a point where they have to turn). In order to distinguish from a momentary hesitation/confusion, a margin distance of 2 meters at the wrong direction was allowed. When subjects without GentleGuide would make an error they had to rectify it with help of signage (as is normally the case when no advice is sought by passers by). No new errors were counted till the subject would get back on the right track. Following the tests, subjects answered several questions to help us assess their subjective experience of the system.

Results. All GentleGuide users got to their destination on all occasions. One subject got lost when relying on signage. Only on one occasion did a subject make an error following the GentleGuide while 4 errors were made following the signage.

The average relative delay was 0.08 for the GentleGuide (i.e., subjects were 8% slower with GentleGuide than when walking back) and 0.40 with the signage. A one-tailed related t-Test, showed the difference to be significant (a=0.05). As not all test-trajectories consisted of 90 degrees turns to the left or right or binary choices, but more complex patterns were involved, this result suggests that participants easily interpret haptic guidance in combination with their perception of the space around them, their destination and their trajectory.

The experience of using GentleGuide was reported as positive. Interpretation was found intuitive and no further training was needed than the 30 seconds. Following signage seemed to help subjects feel they knew where they were more than when they used GentleGuide (a 2-tailed Wilkoxon signed ranks test showed this to be significant at a=0.05). This is partly because in the haptic condition subjects were not told their destination to avoid contamination of the haptic experiments with visual input. Further, continuous, turn-by-turn instructions make it unnecessary for users to actively plan their path and orientate themselves. In contrast, signage supports subjects to build a mental map of their path. Ratings of subjects on 5-point Likert scales, as to whether they felt confident they were walking the right way, showed a significant preference for Gentle Guide over signage, (2-tailed Wilkoxon signed ranks test at a=0.01). Further, the subjective reports by participants seem, in large, to support our belief that GentleGuide is understandable, pleasant, discrete, efficient, easy to use and easy to get used to. Mostly it was found helpful. Most ambivalent responses concerned the intuitiveness of the system, with one subject feeling and acting like a robot following instructions.

4   Conclusion

Vibration pulses delivered by two wrist-mounted devices are a practical way to deliver guidance information for pedestrians indoors. This approach works quite efficiently and reliably. Low-resolution guidance was reliably and effectively interpreted from the duration of pulses (just 4 types of directions). Vibrations are more intuitive when they indicate the direction where the person should go to at junction points, rather than corrective advice. A device like the GentleGuide is arguably a non-disruptive, easily learnable means to support way finding in complex indoors environments. We plan to extend this study to include more complex routes, e.g., including multiple floors and open spaces, as well as outdoors tasks where guidance information is more commonly needed and signage more often absent. Particularly where outdoor applications are concerned, an important limitation of continuous guidance seems to be the loss of orientation by the user. The combination of haptic output with graphical displays seems to be a promising approach to address this problem.

Acknowledgements

The authors wish to thank T. van de Graft and P .Peters for assistance with the electronics, B.Eggen for discussions on the experimental evaluation, J.B.Martens and J.Terken for advice upon the statistical analysis of evaluation results.

References

[1]   Chincholle, D., Goldstein, M., Nyberg, M., Eriksson, M. (2002) Lost or Found? A usability evaluation of a mobile navigation and location based service. In Paternó, F., (Ed.) Proceedings Mobile HCI, Lecture Notes in Computer Science 2411, 211-224.

[2]   Ertan, S., Lee, C., Willets, A., Tan, H. Z., Pentland, A. (1998): A Wearable Haptic Navigation Guidance System, Digest of the Second International Symposium on Wearable Computers, 164-165.

[3]   Jul, S., (2002) A framework for locomotional design: toward a generative design theory, CHI '02 Extended Abstracts on Human factors in Computer Systems, ACM Press, 862-863.

[4]   Muller, C., Wasinger, R., (2002) Adapting Multimodal Dialog for the Elderly, Proceedings of the ABIS-Workshop 2002 on Personalization for the Mobile World. Hannover, Germany, Oct. 9-11, 2002.

[5]   Ross, D.A., Blasch, B.B., (2000) Wearable interfaces for orientation and wayfinding, ASSETS'00, ACM Press, 193-200.

[6]   Sokoler, T., Nelson, L. and Pedersen, E.R. (2002) Low-Resolution Supplementary Tactile Cues for Navigational Assistance. In Paternó, F., (Ed.) Proceedings Mobile HCI, Lecture Notes in Computer Science 2411, 369-372.

Sound Visualization and Retrieval Technique for Assisting Hearing Memory of Patrol Worker

Fujio Tsutsumi

Communication and Information Research Laboratory
Central Research Institute of Electric Power Industry
2-11-1, Iwado Kita, Komae-shi, TOKYO, 201-8511, Japan
tutumi@criepi.denken.or.jp

Abstract. In this paper, we propose a system to support equipment check patrol. One of the most difficult tasks for patrol worker is discriminating the difference of equipment sound in the check spot. The main purpose of our system is to support human hearing by automatic segmentation, visualization and retrieval of equipment sound. Automatic segmentation function is realized using a new video shot segmentation method. The method uses fluctuating thresholds according to time transition of visual changes, and performs automatic segmentation of recorded sound according to the step of check work. The visualization and the retrieval functions are based on the spectrum subtraction method and analyzing technology of the temporal frequency map. This paper shows the evaluation result of the segmentation method using equipment check video. And it also shows the effectiveness of the proposed visualizing and retrieval method through an example of electric discharge sound.

1 Introduction

Recently personal visual assistants (PVAs) with wearable micro video camera which support the human's memory are widely studied[2, 5]. The main purpose of these PVAs is support of daily life activities and field works. Our objective is to develop a mobile PVA for the maintenance worker in the field of electric power industries. In this paper we propose a system supporting human's hearing capability of equipment sound by automatic segmentation, visualization and retrieval of the sound.

2 Segmentation of Equipment Sound

In order to realize segmentation of sound data corresponding to check work, we propose a simple and robust video segmentation method. The basic idea is automatic segmentation of acoustic data by observing the visual change of video stream captured by a mobile / head-mounted camera. The segmentation method is based on the idea of classifying the transition of video data statistically. Our method divides the video stream into stationary shots ("stationary") and

L. Chittaro (Ed.): Mobile HCI 2003, LNCS 2795, pp. 363–367, 2003.

transitive shots ("active" and "depressive"). First the sum of frame differences (d_k) is computed by the following equation:

$$d_k = \sum_{x,y} q(dist(c(k,x,y), c(k-1,x,y))), \tag{1}$$

where $c(k,x,y)$ is the color value of the location x,y in the k-th video frame. The function $dist()$ returns the Euclidean distance of two color values in a standard RGB color space $(0 < R, G, B < 255)$. The function $q()$ is a step function to reduce the influence of noise. In the next step, the average (μ) and the standard deviation (σ) of the past n values of differences $(d_{k-n+1}, ..., d_k)$ is computed. The state of **frames** ("active", "depressive" or "stationary") are determined by the following condition:

$$\begin{aligned}
&\textbf{if } d_k > \mu + \alpha\sigma \textbf{ then } \textit{"active"} \\
&\textbf{elseif } d_k < \mu - \beta\sigma \textbf{ then } \textit{"depressive"} \\
&\textbf{otherwise } \textit{"stationary"},
\end{aligned} \tag{2}$$

where α and β are parameters controlling the range of the stationary state $(\alpha > 1, \beta > 1)$. The states of **shots** are derived by the state of frames. When the states of continuous m frames are different from the state of a current shot, the state of the shot is updated to the same state of the current frame. The parameters (n, m) influence the constancy of state change.

3   Visualization and Retrieval of Equipment Sound

After the segmentation the audio clips are processed and visualized by a signal processing technique which is based on the classical spectral subtraction(SS)[1].

At first, the acoustic spectrum distribution of two or more sound information in the past at the same place is equalized for every frequency band, and let it be a "base spectrum" in each check place. Let all the base spectrum be expressed as an m-dimensional vector. The i-th element bs_i of a base spectrum bs is computed from spectrums corresponding to registered sound data as follows,

$$bs_i = \sum_{\forall s_j \in S} s_{j,i}/n, \tag{3}$$

where S is the set of all the spectrums about a check point, the number of spectrums in S is n, $s_{j,i}$ is the i-th element of the spectrum s_j. This base spectrum expresses the sound feature peculiar to the equipment. Furthermore, the base spectrum of the check place is removed from a spectrum distribution of the sound data in each check time, and it considers as the characteristic spectrum distribution in each check time (it is called the temporary spectrum feature). The i-th element $ts_{j,i}$ of a "temporal spectrum" feature ts_j is computed as follows,

$$ts_{j,i} = |s_{j,i} - bs_i|. \tag{4}$$

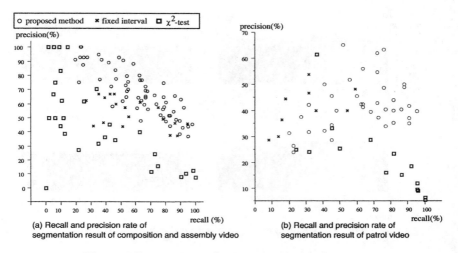

Fig. 1. Comparison of segmentation performance

The temporary spectrum feature will express the feature of the sound in a certain check time, and the unusual sound observed at the time of check will be expressed. The spectrum information visualized on the user interface is the result of filtering this temporary spectrum feature by a fixed sound pressure.

Next, for index creation and retrieval of the equipment sound data, the statistical partial feature of time-frequency space of the temporal spectrums is extracted. We use a high dimensional characteristics in the temporal frequency map as partial feature. We call them L triangle sound patterns. The L triangle sound pattern is a vector expressed as $(v_{t-1,i}, v_{t,i}, v_{t,i+1})$, where $v_{t,i}$ is the vector $(i, ts_{t,i})$ that expresses both frequency and amplitude information of the temporal spectrum at a sampling time t. The method computes the histogram H_L of all the L triangle sound patterns in the temporal frequency map. The retrieved feature includes both the direction of time, and the frequency direction. And the totaled histogram H_L is indexed and retrieval is performed using the index. Similarity is judged by the histogram intersection [6] between the histograms.

4 Evaluation

Our segmentation method has been evaluated for two types of video corresponding to two types of maintenance work style(with/without moving). Three human subjects did the two types of work. The total length of video recorded by the wearable camera is 55 minutes (decomposition: total 26 min, 8min30sec per subject , assembly: total 22min, 7min20sec per subject, patrol: total 7min, 2min15sec per subject). Three methods including our method, χ^2-test [4] method and fixed interval method[3] were compared. The recall and precision rates are used for the evaluation ($recall = C/(C+I), precision = C/(C+O)$), where C denotes the

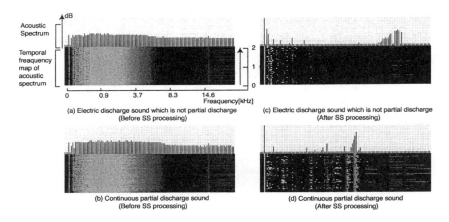

Fig. 2. Visualization of electric discharge sound

total number of correct divisions, I denotes the insufficient number of divisions and O denotes the overflow number of divisions by each method).

Figure 1 plots results on the coordination of the recall and precision axes. The figures have many points, since we changed the parameters of the methods and observed the results. The result plots of our method are distributed in the upper right area (meaning high recall and precision rate) of figure 1. It shows that the segmentation result of our method is similar to the regular segmentation that we inspected from the video.

We evaluate our sound processing methods using the video data recorded, in order to observe the electric discharge phenomenon of electric power equipment. We selected 87 samples of sound data from the video. The samples include 27 samples (group C) about the partial discharge which is the target phenomenon, 9 samples (group B) which are unrelated to electric discharge phenomena, and 51 samples (group A) about ordinary discharge which are not partial discharge. Visualization examples by our method are shown in figure 2. It was difficult to discriminate the change of electric discharge sound in a standard spectrogram((a) and (b)). The visualization result of the proposal technique ((c) and (d)) clearly shows the difference in electric discharge sound. We conducted the retrieval experiment using the 87 sound samples. The figure 3 visualizes all the retrieval results. Each rectangle in the figure expresses each sound sample in a retrieval result. By the figure we can get the new observation that group A includes the samples (from No. 9 to No.18) which are similar to the samples of the group C. This shows that the sound retrieval function is effective in detection of unusual sound.

We evaluate the actual registration and retrieval speed of L triangle patterns[1]. The average registration speed of 1,000 patterns was 17.7 msec, and the

---

[1] Apple PowerMac G4/733MHz was used.

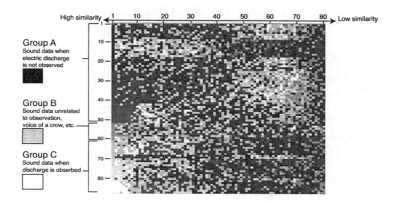

Fig. 3. Retrieval result of electric discharge sound

standard deviation was 44.9 msec to register 780,000 pieces of L patterns (It corresponds to the sound sample for 1400 seconds.).

5 Conclusion

In this paper, we proposed a system which supports the hearing of a check member with automatic segmentation, visualization and reference technology of equipment sound. Usability evaluation of the whole system is a future subject.

References

[1] Steven F. Ball. Suppression of acoustic noise in speech using spectral subtraction. *IEEE Trans. Acoust. Speech & Signal Process.*, ASSP-27(2):113–120, April 1979.

[2] Steve Mann. WearCam' (the wearable camera): Personal imaging systems for long–term use in wearable tetherless computer–mediated reality and personal photo/videographic memory prosthesis. In *Proc. of the IEEE 2ND. International Symposium on Wearable Computers*, pages 124–131, October 1998.

[3] Michael Mills, Jonathan Cohen, and Yin Yin Wong. A magnifier tool for video data. In *Proceedings of ACM CHI '92*, pages 93–98, 1992.

[4] Akio Nagasaka and Yuzuru Tanaka. Automatic video indexing and full-video search for object appearances. In *Visual Database Systems, II, IFIP, Eleesevier Science Publishers*, pages 113–127, 1990.

[5] Bernt Schiele, Nuria Oliver, Tony Jebara, and Alex Pentland. An interactive computer vision system - DyPERS: Dynamic personal enhanced reality system. In *Proc. of International Conference on Vision Systems*, pages 51–65, 1999.

[6] Michael J. Swain and Dana H. Ballard. Color indexing. *International Journal of Computer Vision*, 7(1):11–32, 1991.

Constructing Public Discourse with Ethnographic/SMS "Texts"

Mike Ananny[1], Kathleen Biddick[2], and Carol Strohecker[1]

[1] Everyday Learning, Media Lab Europe
Sugar House Lane, Bellevue Dublin 8, Ireland
{ananny,stro}@medialabeurope.org
[2] Department of History, University of Notre Dame
Notre Dame IN 46556, USA
biddick.1@nd.edu

Abstract. We are interested in how individuals and communities develop opinions as they design and use new mobile, public-sphere technologies. We situate our work among new considerations of ethnography, mobile technologies and rhetoric and describe the design and pilot installation of a new technology called *TexTales* designed to support mobile public discourse.

Mobility in the end may supply the means by which the spoils of remote and indirect interaction and independence flow back into local life, keeping it flexible, preventing the stagnancy which has attended stability in the past, and furnishing with it the elements of a variegated and many-hued experience.
– John Dewey, The Public and Its Problems.

1 Introduction

How do individuals construct, share and revise opinions about themselves and their communities and how can new technological tools and ethnographic techniques reflect and support these processes?

We investigate this question through longitudinal, participatory design where our goal is to learn how public discourse spheres can be created by building with people new kinds of communications tools (not just observing and analyzing current community communication). In the tradition of Constructionist design [15] and within an evolving "Citizen Journalism" framework [2], we aim to support the reflexive creation of two kinds of artifacts: technological tools for public discourse; and dynamic, "intermodal texts" created as people use the tools. We consider building these artifacts to be complementary activities. In our framework, it is equally valid for opinions to manifest themselves in technologies, in discussions during their design and in conversations during their use. Our assertion is that we can best learn how individuals develop opinions by creating new public spheres in which people construct and critique both digital and political representations.

Designing for this pluralism brings technological and analytic challenges. To address the technological challenge we focus on how newly ubiquitous mobile tech-

L. Chittaro (Ed.): Mobile HCI 2003, LNCS 2795, pp. 368-373, 2003.

nologies can create public spheres that are fixed neither in time nor space. To address the analytic challenge, we propose a new kind of "participatory ethnography" in which distinctions between participant and observer are purposefully blurred, and in which those who are usually portrayed in ethnographic texts become their authors and critics. We are not designing *using* ethnography (as is usual in HCI) but are, instead, designing to help people *do* their own ethnography. This necessitates a shift not only in how we think about ethnography but also in how we think about certain kinds of discourse technologies. The nomadic communications of mobile technologies may constitute new discourse spheres in which public opinions are constructed, shared and revised across both time and space in new ways.

An extensive review of the emerging synergies among ethnography, mobile technology, HCI and rhetoric is beyond the scope of this paper. However, we can see that *ethnographers* are beginning to develop techniques that emphasize "following the people/thing/metaphor/story/biography/conflict", are reconsidering definitions of "field" and "subject" [12] and are articulating new relationships between ethnographic and digital representations [10]. *Mobile technologists* are focusing on how hybrid virtual-physical spaces support different kinds of design contexts [7], "socially translucent systems" [9] and distributed, "everyday computing" [1]. *HCI designers* are practicing new methodologies for "unpacking" tensions between public and private spaces [14], for applying ethnography to both system design and critique [8, 13] and – of specific relevance to this project – for helping physical communities establish on-line presences [5] and visual archives [18]. Finally, *rhetoricians* are developing new, but historically based, models of multiple, permeable public spheres [3], relating them to everyday actions [17] and new technologies [4] and asking what kinds of representations [11, 16] best support public discourse.

We situate our work at the intersection of these domains. Our goal is to create with people new exemplars that enrich these synergies and that advance the notion of dynamic, technologically-supported public spheres. Here we describe the development and initial use of one such system – *TexTales*, a large-scale, public publishing tool in which individuals create captions for community photos with SMS texts.

2   Designing *TexTales*

To investigate the notion of technologically supported public spheres, we engaged in a longitudinal, participatory design relationship with Fatima Mansions, an urban flat complex near our lab in Dublin, Ireland. We worked with them over 6 months to take photos, design interfaces and install *TexTales*. The community consists of approximately 700 residents living in 14 4-story apartment blocks built in 1951 and has undergone considerable social and economic change. Of immediate concern is an upcoming "regeneration" in which all buildings are to be demolished and replaced. The residents are focused on creating their own ways to understand and manage this change and are considering the redesign of the physical architecture but also more abstract notions of community and culture. In short, Fatima is eager to experiment with constructing new public spheres. Our principal contact in Fatima is the Fatima History Project, a group that meets weekly to discuss the community's history and, increasingly, to debate its future. In an early meeting, the group expressed frustration with relating their current archiving projects (primarily newsletters and public photo exhibits) to the community at large. This dissatisfaction, combined with our goal of researching-by-building new interactive public spheres, served as a starting point for creating *TexTales*, a new kind of contemporary, discursive archive.

We first distributed 50 disposable cameras among the residents, asking them questions like "show me something in your community you love", "show me something you hate" and "show me something you'd like someone standing here 100 years from now to see"[1]. With these loose guidelines (very few people answered the questions explicitly), residents began to gather pictures for the new archive. They took over 700 photos and our challenge became finding ways to use these images to spark dialogue within and about Fatima. Over the course of several weeks, approximately 10 women from the Fatima History Project surveyed all images, selecting and arranging 90 photos for the first *TexTales* installation. Concurrently, at Media Lab Europe, we developed a technical architecture for large-scale public display and annotation of digital images. This necessitated selecting a display mechanism (public projection) and supporting a commonly used ubiquitous technology (mobile phones)[2].

TexTales has 3 components: custom software interfacing with a Nokia Card Phone to receive and parse standard SMS text messages; a custom tcl/HTML script to create the image-text combinations; and a web server to display the interface. Users contribute a photo caption by sending a text in the form `<picture number> <caption>` to the system (*e.g.* `4 who's that?`) and, approximately 20 seconds later, the caption appears anonymously under the image. Earlier captions appear progressively smaller and all captions are stored in log files. In designing this interface, we were inspired by the provocative public projection installations Krystof Wodiczko embeds in social and architectural spaces [19] as well as the City of Leeds's *CityPoems* project [6].

3   Pilot Installation

In preparation for a larger launch, we recently conducted a pilot installation of *Tex-Tales* in one of Fatima's public squares. The installation began at approximately 9pm and lasted for about an hour. Approximately 40 people of various ages (the youngest participant was 8 years old) participated and observed, creating 20 SMS text captions for 3 different sets of images (27 images in total).

---

[1] Thanks to Frank O'Connor, Jeff Cooper and Loyalist College Canada's photojournalism editing class for initiating this process and asking these questions. Thanks to Kodak Canada for donating the cameras.

[2] An informal survey confirmed that most Fatima residents have mobile phones and that SMS texting is a common way of communicating.

Fig. 1. Clockwise from top left: women of the Fatima History Project editing more than 700 images taken by residents and selecting sets of 9 images for use with *TexTales*; one of 12 interfaces prepared by the women and used by residents; residents with *TexTales*. (For technical reasons, we projected onto the ground; subsequent installations are designed for the community center's wall)

4　Discussion and Conclusions

Several compromises and decisions emerged during the design and process and pilot and, while still early, some helpful observations were made.

First, we decided that there would be no filtering of texts sent to the system. Although this risks displaying "inappropriate" texts, we decided that text filters are imperfect, easily subverted and do not reflect the language often used in casual conversation. The participants commented that, since the system only displays the latest 3 texts for each image, offensive texts could quickly be deleted from the display (but not the log file) by sending further texts to the picture. Also although texts were displayed anonymously, the crowd immediately asked who sent all texts, each caption demanding attribution and inviting conversation. Although authors remain anonymous in the digital archive, during the installation, their captions were starting points for public discourse. Thus, the "censorship" and anonymity that existed in the *TexTales* pilot installation did not involve blocking content or tracking users but was instead distributed more subtlety among social, design and technological considerations. *TexTales* also attracted interest among a range of residents, with many young children, young adults and older people observing and participating. The system seemed to support people easily transitioning between being participants and observers, supporting simultaneous contributions from multiple sources and leaving most regulation of the interaction to the social space surrounding the interface.

TexTales seems to support a new kind of public sphere: it attracts diverse interest, supporting people as both participants and observers; participation is through mobile technology that is accessible, appropriate and socially situated; and, *TexTales* results in public and publicly-constructed ethnographic "texts" that are available for further analysis. These observations suggest that ubiquitous mobile technologies offer a new opportunity to create dynamic discourse spaces in which people and groups can experiment with creating, sharing and revising personal and public opinions.

Acknowledgements

Thanks to the Fatima History Project, Kieron Doyle O'Brien, Niall O'Boille and residents of Fatima Mansions. Thanks also to Media Lab Europe's Everyday Learning group, especially Brendan Donovan and Jamie Rasmussen for help implementing *TexTales* and Niall Winters for help during the pilot. Thanks to Frank O'Connor, Jeff Cooper, Loyalist College and Kodak Canada for collaboration and support.

References

[1]   Abowd, G.D. & E.D. Mynatt. (2000). Charting past, present, and future research in ubiquitous computing. *Transactions on Computer-Human Interaction*, 7(1):29-58.

[2]   Ananny, M. & C. Strohecker (2002). Sustained, Open Dialogue with Citizen Photojournalism. *Proceedings of Development by Design Conference*. Bangalore, India.

[3]   Asen, R. (2003). The Multiple Mr. Dewey: Multiple publics and permeable borders in John Dewey's theory of the public sphere. *Argumentation and Advocacy*. 39:174-188.

[4]   Bimber, B. (2000). The study of information technology and civic engagement. *Political Communication*, 17:329-333.

[5]   Carroll, J.M., Rosson, M.B., Van Metre, C., Kengeri, R.R., Kelso, J. & M. Darshani. (1999). Blacksburg Nostalgia: A Community History Archive. *Proceedings of Interact*. IOS Press.

[6]   Centrifugalforces. (2003). *City Poems*. http://www.centrifugalforces.co.uk/citypoems/ (June 4, 2003).

[7]   Dix, A., Rodden, T., Davies, N., Trevor, J. Friday, A. Palfreyman, K. (2000). Exploiting space and location as a design framework for interactive mobile systems. *Transactions on Computer-Human Interaction*, 7(3):285-321.

[8]   Dourish, P. & G. Button. (1998). On "Technomethodology": Foundational Relationships between Ethnomethodology and System Design. *Human Computer Interaction*, 13(4):395-432.

[9]   Erickson, T. & W.A. Kellogg. (2000). Social translucence: an approach to designing systems that support social processes. *Transactions on Computer-Human Interaction*. 7(1):59-83.

[10]   Fischer, MMJ. (1999). Emergent forms of life: Anthropologies of Late or Postmodernites. *Annual Review of Anthropology*, 28:455-78.

[11]   Gastil, J. (2000). Is Face-to-Face Citizen Deliberation a Luxury or a Necessity? *Political Communication*, 17:357-361.

[12] Marcus, G.E. (1995). Ethnography In/Of The World System: The Emergence of Multi-Sited Ethnography. *Annual Review of Anthropology*, 24:95-117.
[13] Millen, DR. (2000). Rapid ethnography: Time deepening strategies for HCI field research. *Proceedings of Designing Interactive Systems*.
[14] Palen, L. & P. Dourish. (2003). Unpacking "Privacy" for a Networked World. *Proceedings Computer Human Interaction Conference*. Pp. 129-136.
[15] Papert, S. & I. Harel (1991). Situating Constructionism.   In Papert, S. & I. Harel (Eds.) *Constructionism*. Ablex Publishing.
[16] Peters, J.D. (2001). "The Only Proper Scale of Representation": The Politics of Statistics and Stories. *Political Communication*. 18:433-449.
[17] Schudson, M. (2001). Politics as cultural practice. *Political Communication*, 18:421-431.
[18] Shen, C., Lesh, N.B., Vernier, F., Forlines, C. & J. Frost (2002). Sharing and building digital group histories. *Proceedings of Computer Supported Cooperative Work*. Pp. 324-333.
[19] Wodiczko, K. & MIT Committee on the Visual Arts. (1987). *Counter-Monuments: Krzysztof Wodiczko's Public Projections*. Catalogue by MIT List Visual Arts Center (ISBN 0-938437-18-6).

A Customer Satisfaction Evaluation Model for Mobile Internet Services

Hee-Sok Park[1] and Seung J. Noh[2]

[1]School of Information and Computer Engineering
Hongik University, Seoul, Korea
[2]Department of Business Administration
Myongji University, Seoul, Korea

Abstract. This study established a mobile Internet customer satisfaction (CS) evaluation model using the structural equation model. The factors affecting the CS were identified, and grouped into three constructs. Field experts participated in a brainstorming process to extract the factors affecting the CS. Through experiments, it was shown that CS of the mobile Internet service was influenced by information quality, system quality, along with interface quality. For each construct, major factors were again extracted with their importance. The results would be of help for strategic improvement of mobile Internet services and user interface.

1 Introduction

Over the past few years, enormous changes have been made in the information and telecommunication environment. One of the notable changes is the emergence of the mobile Internet, and it is now becoming more and more popular. Specifically in Korea, one of the leading countries in information infrastructure, over 23 millions used mobile Internet services as of 2001, which is 81% of the total mobile phone users [1]. Along with the rapid growth of the mobile Internet business, more attention is being paid to the customer satisfaction (CS). There has been a number of research work on the CS of wired Internet. To our knowledge, however, scant research has been reported on the CS of mobile Internet since it is a relatively young research area.

Our study aims to identify the factors affecting the CS, with their relative importance, and propose a quantitative model that establishes the relationship between the factors and CS of the mobile Internet services. We adopted the structural equation model (SEM) technique. SEM is an extension of multivariate statistical analysis that examines a series of dependence relationships among variables simultaneously and comprehensively [2]. SEM has been used in many fields including marketing, human-computer interaction, and in some studies on the wired Internet [3, 4]. Our results will be directly beneficial to the design of systems and services in the life cycle of the mobile Internet services.

L. Chittaro (Ed.): Mobile HCI 2003, LNCS 2795, pp. 374-377, 2003.
© Springer-Verlag Berlin Heidelberg 2003

2   Modeling

2.1   Contents Categorization

Various types of contents are available in current mobile Internet services. A focus group interview (FGI) was done to classify those contents into several categories based on their characteristics. Five experts have participated in the FGI who are working in one of major mobile Internet service carriers. All the contents were classified into five categories: entertainment, communication, information/data base, decoration, and business transaction. NTT DoCoMo's classification scheme of mobile Internet services was also taken into account.

2.2   Model Building

The five field experts participated in a brainstorming process to extract the factors affecting the CS. Those factors were finally reduced to 16 relevant ones after removing redundant and irrelevant factors. Then thirty sample users from applications' target audience were asked to assess the factors' importance to the CS on a 7-point Likert-type scale. Statistical factor analysis was carried out to reduce the factors into several groups. As a result, 16 most important factors were grouped into three constructs (groups) as shown in Table 1.

Information quality is a function of the value of the output produced by a system as perceived by the user. System quality is a measure of the information processing system itself. Interface quality reflects the usability of service and terminal. It is noted that the first two constructs are consistent with those from previous studies [4]. The structure of our model for entertainment content is shown in Fig. 1. The model structure for other representative contents is set to be the same in the study.

2.3   Model Fitting

For model fitting, the sample users were again asked to use the five representative mobile Internet services. The sample users then rated the factors for each of contents on a 7 point Likert-type scale. Resultant data was tested for fit with a statistical package. Fig. 1 shows the results with path coefficients. The model fulfilled the common test criteria [2], including root mean square error, a ratio of chi-square statistics to degrees of freedom, and goodness of fit indices. This implies that the established model is well acceptable with the appropriate factors.

Table 1. Constructs and factors for the Model

Constructs	Factors
Information quality	Responsiveness and feedback, Currency, Accuracy, Structure and format, Diversity, Timeliness, Completeness, Uniqueness
System quality	Reliability, Security, Response time, Accessibility
Interface quality	Ease of navigation, Readability, Aesthetic, Ease of terminal use

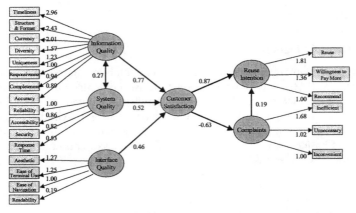

Fig. 1. The model with path coefficients (Entertainment service)

3   Interpretation

In Fig. 1, the factor loading values can be interpreted as follows. If information quality increases by one unit, CS can then increases by 0.77 units. It is also seen in the figure that information quality is the most critical factor for the CS of the entertainment service, followed by system quality and interface quality. And it is also shown that there exists an interrelationship between information quality and system quality. For the information quality, the relative importance of timeliness is 2.96 times of that of responsiveness. If CS increases by one unit, the customer's intention to reuse this service increases by 0.87 units, while the complaints decrease by 0.63 units. Once the customer is satisfied with the content and has reuse intention, the chances to keep using it and to pay more are 1.81 and 1.36 times, respectively, higher than the chance to recommend this content to friends or acquaintances.

Table 2. Relative importance of constructs for the five representative contents

Entertainment	Communication	Information/DB	Decoration	Transaction
Information (100%)	Information (100%)	Information (100%)	Information (100%)	Information (100%)
System (68%)	Interface (15%)	Interface (56%)	Interface (74%)	Interface (43%)
Interface (60%)	System (3%)	System (5%)	System (2%)	System (29%)

The results for the five contents are summarized in Table 2. In the table, the degree of relative importance was normalized. The largest factor loading value was set to 100%. In other contents than entertainment, information quality and interface quality were the most critical factors.

4   Remarks

This study established a mobile Internet CS evaluation model using SEM. We identified the factors affecting the CS, with their relative importance, and proposed a quantitative model that establishes the relationship between the factors and CS of the mobile Internet services. It was shown that CS of the mobile Internet service is determined by information quality, system quality, along with interface quality. The results would be of help for strategic improvement of mobile Internet services and user interface. This modeling methodology can also be applied to other problems of human-computer interaction, for example, the usability of mobile device.

Our analysis relied on the data from five experts. To provide more reliable results, additional data from a large number of experts is needed. In addition, the model can be expanded model by introducing some business-related factors such as brand image, price policy, and customer service into the model.

References

[1]   National Computerization Agency: 2002 Korea Internet White Paper (2002)
[2]   Hair, J.F., Anderson, R.E., Tatham, R.L., Black, W.C.: Multivariate Data Analysis. 5th edn. Prentice-Hall, New Jersey (1998)
[3]   Bauer, H.H, Grether, M., Leach, M.: Building customer relations over the Internet. Industrial Marketing Management 31(2002) 155-163
[4]   Negash, S., Ryan, T., Igbaria, M. Quality and effectiveness in web based customer support systems. Information & Management 2029 (2002) 1-12

Designing Adaptive Mobile Applications:
Abstract Components and Composite Behaviors

Manuel Prieto[1,2] and Miguel A. Sicilia[2]

[1] Telefónica I+D
C/. Emilio Vargas, 6 – 28043 Madrid, Spain
mjpm@tid.es
[2] Computer Science Department. Carlos III University
Avda. de la Universidad, 30. – 28911 Leganés, Madrid, Spain
{mprieto,msicilia}@inf.uc3m.es

Abstract. Current commercial software frameworks for the development of mobile applications targeted at heterogeneous devices are based on a paradigm of *abstract* user interface components (or 'controls') that change its rendering depending on device characteristics. In this paper, we approach the problem of extending that paradigm to handle adaptiveness to user models for the purpose of improving usability. A generic approach along with its concrete realization on `ASP.NET` technology is described. The approach is centered on the notion of componentized adaptive *behaviors*, that can be easily added to user controls by designers. These components can also be chained to come up with more complex behaviors. In addition, some experiences on the automatic, rule-based dynamic addition of such behaviors to concrete controls based on usage data are described.

Keywords: Heterogeneous mobile devices, abstract user interface components, adaptive hypermedia.

1 Introduction

The design of applications for mobile clients poses significant problems derived from two essential constraints [1]. On the one hand, these devices usually provide limited display and interaction capabilities and, on the other hand, their characteristics are widely diverse. Limitations and heterogeneity entail that the tasks that should be analyzed for such systems are different from those found in desktop computers [3], and, as a consequence, the design of the interface must follow different priorities. In this context, adaptiveness becomes an important feature in mobile applications, since it increases navigation efficiency, as has been addressed in previous studies like [6]. In an effort to cope with heterogeneity in limited devices, some industrial user interface development frameworks have been crafted recently. Most notably, Microsoft's Mobile Internet Toolkit (MIT)[1]

---

[1] http://www.gotdotnet.com/team/mit/

L. Chittaro (Ed.): Mobile HCI 2003, LNCS 2795, pp. 378–383, 2003.
© Springer-Verlag Berlin Heidelberg 2003

and Java Micro Edition[2] provide a programming paradigm based on what may be called 'abstract user interface components' (AUIC), which in essence are common interface components (e.g. lists, labels) that are prepared to be rendered — and even reshaped — in different ways depending on the characteristics of the device interacting with them. In this paper, a model for the development of adaptive interfaces for heterogeneous and limited devices is described, explicitly targeted towards AUIC-based frameworks. A concrete instantiation of the model on the MIT framework is also described — both the model and the implementation are based on previous work described in [4]. The most salient feature of our approach is that adaptiveness is associated to abstract components, easing the design of personalized interfaces by means of the possibility of selecting and arranging some generic adaptive behaviors for specific component instances. In addition, an initial exploration on the automatic selection of adaptive behaviors based on usage data has been approached. The rest of this paper is structured as follows. In Section 2, the principal elements of our model are described in abstract terms. Section 3 sketches the concrete realization of the model on top of the MIT framework, along with a brief description of some concrete automatic adaptation functionality. Finally, conclusions and future research directions are provided in Section 4.

2   A Model of Composable Adaptive Behaviors

An abstract model of AUIC for personalized mobile applications must provide modelling constructs for describing devices, interface components and users. In addition, it must provide a paradigm for expressing adaptations. Devices can be described by device profiles in the form $\wp_x = \{(p_i, v_i)|p_i \in P \land v_i \in type(p_i)\}$, where P denotes a set of device parameters (capabilities) defined in a pre-existing ontology — as the FIPA device ontology[3]— and $type(p)$ denotes the type of the parameter (e.g. integer, string, set, sequence). Parameters may describe software (e.g. operating system), hardware (e.g. memory, screen height, resolution) or network (e.g. quality of service) characteristics. A generic attribute-based user model can be specified by considering in a similar way a set $U = \{u_m\}$ where $al(u_j)$ denotes the collection of attribute–value pairs describing the concrete user. Our model of the structure of the application is limited to describing the AUIC components in set C that contains, in the form $\mathcal{A} = \{c_k|c_k \in t_x\}$, where $t_x \in \mathcal{T}$ denotes an specific *component type* in the set of types $\mathcal{T}$. As usual in component frameworks, each component type is described by a set of predefined attributes denoted by $at(t_x)$. Types and subtypes may be interrelated in a generalization–specialization hierarchy so that if type b specializes type a, denoted by $a \succ b$, then $at(a) \subset at(b)$. Following the above definitions, our AUIC–centric paradigm

---

[2] http://java.sun.com/j2me/
[3] FIPA Device Ontology Specification, doc. number XC00091C, available at http://www.fipa.org.

describes adaptation in terms of an ordered sequence of behaviors attached to each specific component:

$$b(c) = b_1, \ldots b_l, \quad l \geq 0, \; c \in t, \; t_i \in \mathcal{T} \tag{1}$$

Each b_i in expression (1) represents a software entity that transforms the state of component c by changing some of the values of the attributes in $at(t)$. Behaviors are also typed, so that each b_i has a type $h \in \mathcal{B}$. In addition, each type of behavior h is associated to exactly one type of component in $c(h) \in \mathcal{T}$. By virtue of this association, behaviors of type h can only be applied to components of that type. Composability can be easily introduced as simple rewriting, so that a sequence of behaviors $b_r \ldots b_s$ can be labelled as b_q, so that the new label functions as a higher-level, more complex behavior that sequentially applies its contained elements. It should also be noted that order is important in (1) since the order of processing b_i, b_j need not produce the same final result than the order b_j, b_i. In general, behaviors produce a change in its associated control dependant on device characteristics and the characteristics of the current user (or characteristics of one of the groups to which he/she belongs), which can be denoted abstractly as $b : 2^U \times C \times \wp \rightarrow C'$. All the definitions given above can be easily recognized in current commercial mobile development frameworks, and in consequence, they provide a basis for extending them in a straightforward way, as will be demonstrated in what follows.

3   MIT Implementation of Adaptive Behaviors

Microsoft's Mobile Internet Toolkit (MIT) provides a server runtime that allows the automatic adaptive presentation of Web contents to a number of supported devices. Adaptation is based on a set of mobile server controls, which are an abstraction of the rendering and interaction features of specific languages like WML and cHTML (the approach is similar to that of [2] although their scope is different). In our extension of the MIT, application designers can add personalization behaviors by simply typing it in the control's definition. For example, the following code fragment shows the declaration of an abstract component ($p \in C$, with $b(p) = f_2, f_5$) that specializes a list, called PersonalizedList. Note that two behaviors f5 and f2 are specified in one of the attributes.

```
<mobile:Form id="Form1" runat="server"> <shadow:PersonalizedList
id="p" runat="server" NAME="p_1" behaviours="f2;f5">
    <Item Text="Palacio de la Prensa" Value="http://www.pmc.es/" />
    <Item Text="Benlliure" Value="http://www.benlliurecines.es/" />
    ...
</shadow:PersonalizedList> </mobile:Form>
```

Behaviors (in $\mathcal{T}$) are defined in a separate XML file with the following appearance:

```
<behaviors-def> <behavior>
  <name>f1</name>    <desc> Discard visited links. </desc>
  <class>MobilePrb1.DeleteVisitedBehavior</class>
  <file>C:\\Inetpub\\wwwroot\\M1\\MobilePrb1.dll</file>
  <type>PersonalizedList</type>
</behavior> <behavior>    <name>f2</name>   ...
```

Each behavior definition contains its name and description, the class that realizes the personalization, the physical file in which the code is located and the abstract control class it can adapt. This programming model also allows to customize the behaviors without recompilation. Customized mobile server controls can be defined by simply subclassing them. For example, the component called System.Web.UI.MobileControls.List can be subclassed to carry out the adaptation of lists. The following C# code fragment illustrates it.

```
public class PersonalizedList: System.Web.UI.MobileControls.List {
private void Page_Load(object sender, System.EventArgs e) {
  GeneralPage page = (GeneralPage) this.Page;
  ListPersonalization persEngine = new ListPersonalization();
  MobileListItemCollection result =
        persEngine.getPersonalizedList( this.Items,  page.userId,
                       page.Request.Path, behaviours,  restr_disp);
  while (this.Items.Count > 0){ this.Items.RemoveAt(0); }
  foreach (MobileListItem it in result){
    it.Value="ListRedirect.aspx?dest=" + it.Value +
         "&page=" + page.Request.Path + "&user=" + page.userId;
       this.Items.Add(it);
  }
   this.ItemsAsLinks = true; }
```

Basically, the ListPersonalization class encapsulates the behaviors that depend on the model of the user, which is identified by the userId attribute. The collection of behaviours is extracted from the declaration of the control (like the one showed before). The collection called restr_disp of device capabilities is obtained from the run-time information provided by ASP.NET. Note also that the items in the list are changed to ListRedirect.aspx so that the navigation of the user is recorded. Behaviors can be aggregated according to the *Composite Filter* pattern [7]. The pattern is embedded in the call to getPersonalizedList, and the reflective capabilities of the .NET framework are used to dynamically instantiate and invoke the filters.

```
public MobileListItemCollection getPersonalizedList (
          MobileListItemCollection items, string userid, string page,
          string behaviours, MobileCapabilities capabilities)
{  ArrayList b = behaviorsParser(behaviours);
   foreach (string be in b) {
       items = doFilter(items, userid, page, be, capabilities);}
   return items; }
```

Access to the user model server (or a wrapper to existing ones) is implemented as a standard-based Web Service, allowing for the federation of user model servers (details are not covered here).

Behaviors can be selected by designers to improve user experience according to their knowledge of the context of each specific control instance. But in some cases, the system may be able to automatically set (or rearrange) behaviors. Currently, we have formalized some of these updates through rules of two types: (a) oriented towards performance, e.g. given that o is a sorting behavior and d is a behavior that removes items in a list: $\{o_i, d_j\} \subseteq b(c) \Rightarrow i \geq j$ to avoid unnecessary sorting processing time, and (b) based on usage patterns. The second category aims at direct improvements of usability and require heuristic approaches. For example, some lists show highly volatile information (like soccer scores), so that once consulted by the user, they're rarely re-visited, and they also change frequently. This usage pattern may be detected whenever periodical variations are detected, and most users do not consult the list more than once, resulting in chaining a 'remove once visited' behavior to the list. Sorting behaviors are another case of automatic behavior chaining. Given a static list control $l \in C$, sorting can be activated if the following rule holds: $\exists l.item_i, \ most \ visits(l.item_i)$ or $\exists l.item_i, l.item_j, \ visits(l.item_i) \ mgt \ visits(l.item_j)$ signifying that there exist items that receive most of the visits or there are large differences in usage for different items. Quantifier *most* and the expression 'much greater than' (mgt) are implemented as described in [5] through fuzzy sets.

4   Conclusions and Future Work

A component-based model has been described for extending AUIC frameworks with control-oriented adaptation. The model can be easily implemented in existing commercial frameworks, and a case study of a MIT-based implementation has been sketched. Future work should deal with the automatic selection of behaviors and also with adaptations involving more than one control.

References

[1] Billsus, D., Brunk, C. A., Evans, C., Gladish, B and Pazzani, M: Adaptive Interfaces for Ubiquitous Web Access. Communications of the ACM 45(5) (2002):34–38

[2] Gaedke, M., Segor, C. Gellersen, H. W.: WCML: Paving the Way for Reuse in Object-Oriented Web Engineering. In: Proceedings of the 2000 ACM Symposium on Applied Computing (SAC 2000), (2000):19-21

[3] Landay, J. A. and Kaufmann, T. R.: User Interface Issues in Mobile Computing. In: Proceedings of the 4th Workshop on Workstation Operating Systems (1993):40–47

[4] Prieto, M. and Sicilia, M. A.: Designing Agent-Based Personalized Filtering Behaviors for Heterogeneous Mobile Internet Devices. In Proceedings of the 1st International Workshop on Practical Applications of Agents and Multiagent Systems (2002):125–134

[5] Sicilia, M. A., Díaz, P., Aedo, I. and García, E.: Fuzzy Linguistic Summaries in Rule-Based Adaptive Hypermedia Systems. In: Proceedings of the 2nd International Conference on Adaptive Hypermedia and Adaptive Web Based Systems (2002):317–327

[6] Smyth, B. and Cotter, P.: Personalized Adaptive Navigation for Mobile Portals. In: Proceedings of the 15th European Conference on Artificial Intelligence – Prestigious Applications of Intelligent Systems (2002)
[7] Yacoub, S. M.: A Versatile Filter Pattern. In: Proceedings of the EuroPLoP 2001 Conference, Irsee, Germany, 4-8 July (2001)

Cinematic Techniques for Mobile Presentations[*]

M. Zancanaro, O. Stock, and I. Alfaro

ITC-irst
38050 Povo,Trento, Italy
{zancana,stock,alfaro}@itc.it

Abstract. This work is about the use of dynamically produced video clips to present information on the small screen of a PDA. These video clips are part of a museum guide and are built as sequences of pictures synchronized with a dynamic audio commentary. The transitions among the pictures are planned according to cinematic techniques. The theoretical background is presented, discussing the language of cinematography and the Rhetorical Structure Theory to analyze dependency relationships inside a text. The results of a preliminary evaluation are also presented and discussed.

1 Introduction

In a museum setting a mobile assistant must provide information in an engaging way, while helping to focus the visitor's attention on specific exhibits and details. Our work is about the use of dynamically produced video clips to present information on the small screen of a PDA. Starting from a dynamically assembled audio presentation of a complex exhibit (Not and Zancanaro, 2000), a sequence of pictures is displayed in combination with an audio commentary where the transitions among them are planned according to cinematic techniques. Our hypothesis is that the use of this type of animation to present an exhibit allows the visitor to better identify the details introduced by the audio counterpart of the presentation. The language of cinematography (Metz, 1974) is employed in order to plan the animation and to synchronize the visual and the verbal parts of the presentation. At present, we have completed a first prototype of a multimedia guide that employs cinematic techniques in presenting information for a fresco at Torre Aquila in Trento, Italy.

Many research projects are exploring the new possibilities offered by Personal Digital Assistants (PDAs) in a museum setting (for example, see Grinter et al, 2002, and Not et al., 1998). Usually, these multimedia guides use static images, while others employ pre-recorded short video clips about museum exhibits.

---

[*] This work has been supported by the PEACH and TICCA projects, funded by the Autonomous Province of Trento.

L. Chittaro (Ed.): Mobile HCI 2003, LNCS 2795, pp. 384–389, 2003.

2   The Prototype at Torre Aquila

We have applied the idea of using cinematic techniques for presenting details of artworks in a prototype of a multimedia guide for Torre Aquila; a frescoed tower at the Buonconsiglio Castle in Trento, Italy. Our multimedia guide detects the position of the visitor by means of infrared emitters placed in front of each panel. Interaction with the system is both proposed by the system itself and accepted by the user, thus sharing the responsibility of information access (see figure 1, left).

Fig. 1. Snapshots of the multimedia guide

The multimedia presentation is composed of an audio commentary accompanied by a sequence of images that appear on the PDA screen and that help the visitor quickly identify the fresco's details mentioned in the commentary. For instance, when a specific detail of the panel is explained by the audio, the PDA may display or highlight that detail, thus quickly calling the attention of the user to the area in question. During the presentation, the PDA displays a VCR-style control panel and a slide bar to signal the length of the video clip and its actual position (see figure 1, right). In this manner, the visitor is able to control the delivery of the information as well as the information that most interests her, while also revisiting sections that called her attention.

3   The Language of Cinematography

According to (Metz, 1974), cinematic representation is not like a human language, defined by a set of grammatical rules, yet it is guided by a set of generally accepted conventions. These guidelines may be used for developing multimedia presentations that can be best perceived by the viewer.

The shot is the basic unit of a video sequence. In the field of cinematography a shot is defined as a continuous view from single camera without interruption. Since we only deal with still images, we define a shot as a sequence of camera movements applied to the same image. The basic camera movements are pan, from "panorama", a rotation of the camera along the x-axis, tilt, a rotation along the y-axis, and dolly, a rotation along the z-axis.

Transitions among shots are considered the punctuation symbols of cinematography; they affect the rhythm of the discourse and the message conveyed by the video. A cut occurs when the last frame of a shot is immediately replaced by the first frame of the following shot. A fade occurs when one shot gradually replaces another one either by disappearing (fade out) or by being replaced by the new shot (fade in). A cross fade (also called dissolve) occurs when two shots are gradually superimposed during the moment when one is faded out while the other is faded in.

4   Rhetorical Structure Theory

Rhetorical Structure Theory (Mann and Thompson 1987) analyses discourse structure in terms of dependency trees, with each node of the tree being a segment of text. Each branch of the tree represents the relationship between two nodes, where one node is called the nucleus and the other is called the satellite. The information in the satellite relates to that found in the nucleus in that it expresses an idea related to what was said in the nucleus. This rhetorical relation specifies the coherence relation that exists between the two portions of text contained in the nodes. For example, a Cause rhetorical relation holds when the satellite describes the event that caused what is contained in the nucleus. Figure 2, shows an example of a rhetorical tree. Here the second paragraph provides background information with respect to the content expressed in the first paragraph. This additional information acts as a sort of reinforcement for what was previously said in the first paragraph and consequently facilitates the absorption of information.

RST was originally developed as part of work carried out in the computer-based text generation field. In a previous work (Not and Zancanaro, 2001), we described a set of techniques to dynamically compose adaptive presentations of artworks from a repository of multimedia data annotated with rhetorical relations. These techniques have been exploited in an audio-based, location-aware adaptive audio guide described in (Not et al., 1998).

5   Video Clips on Still Images

In our system, video clips are built by first searching for the sequence of details mentioned in the audio commentary, deciding the segmentation in shots and then planning the camera movements in order to smoothly focus on each detail in synchrony with the verbal part.

In building a video clip, a set of strategies similar to those used in documentaries are employed. Two broad classes of strategies have been identified. The first class encompasses constraints, imposed by the grammar of cinematography, while the second deals with conventions normally used in guiding camera movements in the production of documentaries.

While the constraints are just sequence of forbidden camera movements, the conventions are expressed in terms of rhetorical structures found in the audio commentary. The verbal part of the documentary always drives the visual part (see also Rocchi and Zancanaro 2003).

In order to assure a pleasant presentation, constraints on camera movements have to be imposed. For example, a pan from right to left forbids a subsequent pan from left to right. In general, applying any given movement (pan, tilt and zoom) and then immediately reapplying it on the reverse direction is discouraged because this action renders the video uncomfortable to watch.

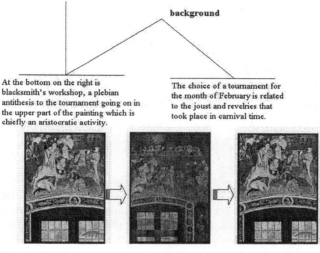

Fig. 2. The "Tournament" example: from the text to the video clip

While constraints on camera movements alone are sufficient to ensure a pleasant presentation, they do not impact the effectiveness of the video clip. In order to have a more engaging presentation, the visual part should not only focus on the right detail at the right time, but it should also support the presentation of new audio information by illustrating its relation to information that has been already given. In this manner, continuity between the information is built, which in turn facilitates the viewing of the video clip while stimulating the absorption of new information.

The text in figure 2 can be visually represented with two shots of the same image (in our example, the tournament) linked by a long cross fade. First, the image is presented while the first paragraph is heard over the audio. Then, when the audio switches to the background information the image is cross-faded with itself. The purpose being that of emphasizing the difference between the types of information provided in the two paragraphs; that is, factual and background information respectively.

A rhetorical strategy suggests, on the basis of a rhetorical tree configuration, what shot segmentation and which transition effect should be applied. The strategies employed in the Torre Aquila multimedia guide were elicited by a focus group activity with a documentary director.

6   Preliminary Evaluation

A formal evaluation of the prototype will start next March at Torre Aquila. Preliminary studies and pilot tests show encouraging results and interesting effects.

All users became acquainted with the system very quickly. Most of them used the PDA as a "3D mouse", pointing directly to the infrared emitters to speed up the localization. Future investigations will evaluate how users can be more directly involved in the process of localization.

Most of the users complained before actually using the system that a video sequence on a PDA would distract their attention from the real artwork. After a short interaction with the system, however, they appreciated the possibility of quickly localizing small details on the fresco. This demonstrates that use of cinematic techniques in a multimedia guide can be effective particularly when explaining complex painting. The different effects that the verbal and the visual parts of the presentation have on the user's attention are yet to be investigated.

7   Conclusions

This paper has discussed how cinematic techniques can be used in a multimedia museum guide to have a more pleasant and effective presentation of information. Video clips are built by first searching for the sequence of details mentioned in the audio commentary, deciding the segmentation in shots and then planning the camera movements in order to smoothly focus on each detail in synchrony with the verbal counterpart. In our approach, the verbal part always drives the visual part. Future work will investigate the introduction of a more interactive structure to the video sequences.

References

[1]   Metz, C. (1974). *Film Language: a Semiotics of the Cinema*. Oxford University Press, NY.

[2]   Grinter, R. E., Aoki, P. M., Hurst, A., Szymanski, M. H., Thornton, J. D. and Woodruff, A. (2002). Revisiting the Visit: Understanding How Technology Can Shape the Museum Visit. In Proc. *ACM Conf. on Computer Supported Cooperative Work*, New Orleans, LA.

[3]   Mann, W.C. and Thompson, S. (1987). Rhetorical Structure Theory: A Theory of Text Organization, In L. Polanyi (ed.), *The Structure of Discourse*, Ablex Publishing Corp.

[4]   Not E., Petrelli D., Sarini M., Stock O., Strapparava C., Zancanaro M. (1998) *Hypernavigation in the Physical Space: Adapting Presentations to the User and the Situational Context*. In New Review of Hypermedia and Multimedia, vol. 4.

[5]   Not E. and Zancanaro M. (2001). Building Adaptive Information Presentations from Existing Information Repositories. In Bernsen N.O., Stock O. (eds.), Proceedings of the *Int'l Workshop on Information Presentation and Multimodal Dialogue*, Verona, Italy.

[6]   Rocchi, C., and Zancanaro, M. (2003). Generation of Video Documentaries from Discourse Structures. In Procs. of 9th *European workshop on Natural Language Generation*. Budapest.

[7]   Stock, O., Zancanaro, M. (2002). Intelligent Interactive Information Presentation for Cultural Tourism. *Int'l Workshop on Natural, Intelligent and Effective Interaction in Multimodal Dialogue Systems*. Copenhagen, Denmark.

Using a Mobile Device to Vary the Pace of Search

Matt Jones[1], Preeti Jain[1], George Buchanan[1] and Gary Marsden[2]

[1]Department of Computer Science, University of Waikato, New Zealand
always@acm.org
[2]Department of Computer Science, University of Cape Town, South Africa
gaz@cs.uct.ac.za

Abstract. Although online, handheld, mobile computers offer new possibilities in searching and retrieving information on-the-go, the fast-paced, "sit-forward" style of interaction may not be appropriate for all user search needs. In this paper, we explore how a handheld computer can be used to enable interactive search experiences that vary in pace from fast and immediate through to reflective and delayed. We describe a system that asynchronously combines an offline handheld computer and an online desktop Personal Computer, and discuss some results of an initial user evaluation.

1   Introduction

Almost all web searches are carried out while the user is sitting at a conventional, desktop Personal Computer (PC) connected to the Internet. It is likely, though, that search needs take shape away from the desktop, stimulated by activities a user is involved in, such as attending a meeting or listening to a presentation or lecture.

Mobile, handheld devices are beginning to be used to provide online search access. Clearly, these services will be useful, especially to meet specific, focused and urgent information needs. However, these approaches ask much of the user who has to engage in a cognitively demanding, "sit-forward", foreground information seeking process [3].

For some use-contexts and information needs, this burden is unhelpful and inappropriate. Sometimes search is a background user activity – the information need does not have to be satisfied immediately and the process of satisfying the need is not the user's main focus. For example, a seminar participant might be interested in discovering more about something mentioned by the speaker; however, if they began to search online immediately, they would quickly lose track of the rest of the talk.

In this paper, we present a prototype system that aims to support background information seeking while still enabling more engaged, focused searching. The work explores how a mobile device can be combined asynchronously with a desktop PC to permit such shifts in the user's interactive pace.

L. Chittaro (Ed.): Mobile HCI 2003, LNCS 2795, pp. 390-394, 2003.
© Springer-Verlag Berlin Heidelberg 2003

2   The Laid-Back Search Tool

The laid-back tool enables users to capture background information needs *in situ* over time. It also provides them with facilities to use search results, later, in a number of ways and at varying paces of interaction. The approach asynchronously combines a handheld computer with a desktop PC. Myers and his group have combined these two types of device, in synchronous ways, for other sorts of user needs [6].

The user enters search terms on an offline handheld computer. They can record simple keyword searches and use the "advanced search" interface to restrict the scope of the search to a particular web site etc. (Fig. 1). The handheld application checks for duplicate entries and allows the complete set of queries to be viewed and edited.

The handheld, then, gives the user greater support for query noting than when they simply use paper and pen; but, as with paper and pen, the user's main focus – such as listening to a talk – is not disrupted greatly while their search need is captured.

When the handheld is reconnected to the PC, the queries are automatically sent to a search engine (Google ™). For each query, the search engine returns a result set and this, along with the web pages associated with each result, is copied to the handheld. In this way, the user's searches are guaranteed to be performed, even if the user has forgotten about the notes they made, or has no time to do the searches manually.

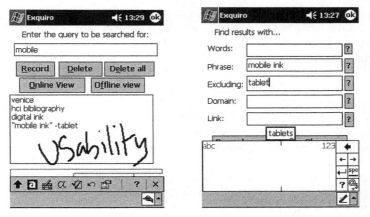

Fig. 1: Handheld application for query capture. In the left-hand screenshot, the user is entering a new query ("mobile usability"), using handwriting recognition input, and a list of all previously entered queries is shown. One of the queries ("mobile ink" –tablet) was entered using the "Advanced Search" interface (see screenshot to the right)

Later, the user can browse the search results on the handheld *offline*, wherever they are. They can view a list of all the queries recorded – along with the date and time each was input – and access the downloaded result sets and associated web pages (see Fig. 2). Millions of handheld users are already using services such as Avantgo (www.avantgo.com) to read web pages offline; our approach extends this popular activity to search.

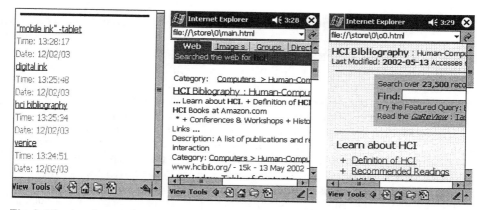

Fig. 2. Viewing the search results, offline, on a handheld computer. User views a list of queries captured over time (left). After selecting a query, e.g., "hci bibliography", a search result list is then available (centre). For each result, a set of web pages (to a depth specified by the user) are accessible offline: the screenshot on the right shows the top-level page for the first search engine result; clicking on further links (e.g. "Definition of HCI") will retrieve further cached pages

As well as accessing queries and results on the handheld, this information is also available on the desktop PC via a specially built browser tool. This tool also allows the user to carry out further searches online, thereby interactively refining the results of the initial, handheld captured queries.

To explore an alternative, further use of the handheld gathered queries, we are adapting the Collage Machine [4], developed by Kerne. The approach involves extracting images and key text from each search result web page. As the analysis proceeds, for each handheld captured query, a composite collage of this information is built (Fig. 3). The aim is to investigate the benefits of a calmer approach to information discovery. The Collage can be displayed on a desktop and much larger displays. We are also investigating the use of the technique on the handheld screen.

Google™ has recently begun to offer a search result "viewer"[1]: this displays results for a *single* query as a continuously scrolling slide show. The user can "lean-back" and watch as the results are automatically presented. We are investigating how *sets* of search queries captured by the handheld, over time, could be presented using this sort of viewer to further provide a "relaxed" form of search.

The prototype, then, allows the user to vary the pace of their search activities. They can use the conventional, fast-paced, "sit-forward" approach to follow-up results of recorded queries online. At the other end of the pace spectrum, they can "lean-back" and simply observe a collage or slide-show of results. Half-way between the "sit-forward" and "lean-back" is, what could be called, the "laid-back" pace that is seen when terms are captured and a user browses results offline on the handheld. Here, the interaction is not as fast, time pressured and transient as the "sit-forward" mode but also it is not as slow, passive or minimally engaging as "lean-back".

---

[1] http://labs.google.com/gviewer.html

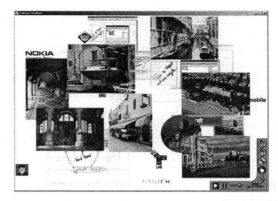

Fig. 3. Collage created by the Collage Machine [4] given search queries captured by the handheld device. This collage is made up of images extracted from web pages that match the query terms shown in Figure 2 – for example, there are graphics from Nokia (the logo is on the "mobile hci" website), Venice tourist sites and digital ink screenshots from Microsoft

3   Related Approaches

Aridor *et al* [1], have demonstrated a related offline/online search system. Their scheme "pushes" information from a PC-based intelligent agent to a handheld device. The laid-back system, in contrast, is a "pull" technology, with the user directly requesting searches that arise in their everyday contexts.

Other researchers have looked at linking physical contexts while mobile with later online information access. The InfoPoint [5], for instance, is a hand-held device that allows users to capture information from objects tagged with a visual code. One of the applications discussed by the researchers, is a conference aid that allows users to grab web URLs from research posters. On return from the conference, the data is transferred from the InfoPoint and the associated information viewed on a web browser.

4   User Evaluation

Three experienced handheld computer users were given the prototype system for a two-week initial user study. We asked them to record observations about the system each day in a diary. At the end of the trial, we interviewed each user individually.

An analysis of their diaries and the interview transcripts showed that the subjects used the handheld system in a range of contexts: e.g., while watching television; during meetings; while on the telephone; and, at their desk when planning their daily tasks. Although they all noted the potential benefits of the system, they also encountered three interesting problems.

Firstly, the users saw their handheld device as a medium to make "rough" notes. For example, they said they paid less attention to spelling when they used their device. For the search application, such "inaccuracies" caused problems.

Secondly, all three users regularly used other handheld applications like the notepad during meetings. They indicated a preference for a search capture tool that integrated better with these other applications. The XLibris digital library appliance [7] illustrates a possible approach. It is a handheld device that enables users to read and manipulate documents. Readers can highlight terms and make annotations. The system generates hypertext links to related documents based on these user interactions.

Finally, in common with many other systems, they also reported frustrations in trying to read web pages designed for the large screen on the handheld device [2].

5   Conclusions

In this paper we have challenged the notion of the fully connected "eager" mobile computer user whom many mobile HCI researchers focus on. We wish to put forward the notion that this type of interaction is not always appropriate and that mobile users have a range of tasks with varying degrees of urgency. The design goal for our system was to present a tool which supports a variety of urgencies (sit-forward, laid-back & lean-back) for a common task (searching). Our hope is that other interaction designers will not become lured into supporting only sit-forward tasks, simply because the technology now allows it, but will remember that being laid-back is also a noble goal.

References

[1]   Aridor, Y., Carmel. D., Maarek, Y. S., Soffer, A. & Lempel, R. (2001). Knowledge encapsulation for focused search from pervasive devices. *ACM Transactions on Information Systems*, **20**(1) pp 25-46.

[2]   Jones, M. Marsden, G., Mohd-Nasir, N & Boone, K (1999). Improving Web Interaction in Small Screen Displays. *Computer Networks* 31 (1999) pp 1129-1137. Elsevier.

[3]   Jones M., Buchanan, G. & Thimbleby, H. (2002). Sorting out searching on small screen devices. In Paterno, F. (Ed.), *Proceedings of the 4th International Symposium on Mobile HCI*, Pisa, Italy, September 2002, LNCS 2411, pp 81-94. Springer.

[4]   Kerne, A. (2000) "CollageMachine: an interactive agent of Web recombination." *Leonardo*, Vol. 33, No. 5, pp. 347–350.

[5]   Kohtake, N., Rekimoto, J. & Yuichiro, A. (2001). Infopoint: a device that provides a uniform user interface to allow appliances to work together over a network. *Personal & Ubiquitous Computing* 5: 264-274.

[6]   Myers, B. (2002). Mobile Devices for Control. *Proceedings of the 4th International Symposium on Mobile HCI*, Pisa, Italy, September 2002, LNCS 2411, pp 1-8. Springer.

[7]   Shilit, B. N., Price, M. N. & Golovchinsky, G. (1998). Digital library information appliances. *Proceedings Digital Libraries '98*, Pittsburgh, 217-225.

Designing Advanced Mobile Applications
Examples of UMTS Trial Applications

Fritjof Kaiser[1], Volker Gruhn[2], and Heinz Bergmeier[1]

[1] Siemens AG
{fritjof.kaiser,heinz.bergmeier}@siemens.com
[2] Universität Dortmund
Gruhn@ls10.cs.uni-dortmund.de

Abstract. This paper shows applied usability rules and guidelines by means of a UMTS trial application. The application was designed for the PocketPC environment, running within its own full screen user interface. All user interface elements were designed completely new to provide the necessary added value for the end user that 3G is promising.

1   Introduction

During the last years PDAs (Personal Digital Assistants) were getting very popular among users, enabling them to look up information such as appointments, notes, addresses and even emails anytime and anywhere. With the launch of UMTS the possibilities for mobile applications will greatly expand. New services using instant connectivity to provide push / pull capability of data, localization and personalization will emerge. In the future we can communicate in a much richer way than just by voice as we are doing it today with our mobile phones.

The chasm between availability and execution of transactions is going to vanish, making it possible to spend our time in a much more efficient and effective way.

UMTS provides the necessary technology, but its success is profoundly dependent on the offered mobile applications and their mobile quality.

1.1   How to Define Mobile Quality?

The quality of a mobile application or service is rated by the user according to the offered added value. Key questions that arise are:

- Which tasks can I do on the fly?
- How valuable or needful is the application / service for me?
- Is it easy to access and use the application / service?
- What is the price for it?

Each of these questions encompasses further sub-questions. Of course not all questions can be measured with concrete answers and some sub-questions may affect the

L. Chittaro (Ed.): Mobile HCI 2003, LNCS 2795, pp. 395–399, 2003.

evaluation of other questions. Except for the costs, all questions are direct related to the mobile device, the user and his or her possible tasks.

2   Application Example

The following application was created as a Siemens UMTS trial to promote UMTS. During the development phase it was very important that the application meets the promised expectations of 3G as well as offers a very high usability to the user. The application shows that it's possible to create complex usable applications on mobile devices despite all the given limitations.

Again consider that the application is developed for the PocketPC environment. All user interactions will be conducted over pen input.

2.1   '3G Chat On Air'

'3G Chat on Air' is a mobile chat application with avatars which enables its users to communicate with each other. As such '3G Chat on Air' can be classified as community application since the members of a chat session will establish a temporary companionship.

Basically the whole application is a normal chat application, but only on the first sight.

The main idea is that users are not only represented over their text messages to the other participants but also over one specific avatar. The user can choose between eleven different avatars. Another important aspect of chat applications is the usage of so called emoticons, like :-) or :-<.

In '3G Chat on Air' the user can also express and change their personal mood over an easy to use slider. Each time the slider is set to a different mood level the expression of the avatar is changing in a funny animation. This animation is then shown on each of the participants' devices. But users can take actions on each other too. For example it is possible to kiss or slab another participant as well as scream or whisper to each other. Other features that are available: supports up to twenty participants, synthetic speech output and compatible with IRC (Internet Relay Chat).

2.1.1   Applied Design Decisions and Usability Rules

Target Users

The target user group for the chat application is determined by the younger generation and all those who are addicted to messaging (e.g. SMS). The goal was to create an application that delivers the expectations of these users as much as possible. Furthermore the application should deliver outstanding fun and excitement. Therefore we decided to exclude the look of the PocketPC operating system as far as it was possible from the application because it does not meet our demands to create a visual attractive environment for the user. This makes it necessary to create a new user interface with its own look and feel.

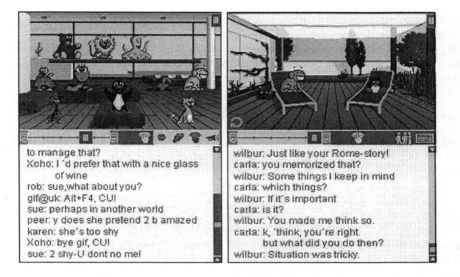

Fig. 1. Screenshots from 3G Chat on Air, collective chat (left) and private chat (right)

Application Layout (Main Use Case)

We have taken the whole screen size of 240x320 pixels as application area, thus maximizing the available area for information for the user. Figure 1 shows the state of an active chat session between participants. The taskbar in the middle of the screen solves two problems. First it contains the available functions that can be executed by the user. Second it also separates the screen into two areas. The lower area shows the usual text messages whereas the upper area is defined to display the chat avatars. Thus greatly improves the self-descriptiveness of the chat.

Ease of Use, Readability, Controls and Behavior

Emoticons are very difficult to enter over the embedded virtual software keyboard. We invented an emotion-slider that facilitates and substitutes the input of textual emoticons. The user can adjust the emotional expression of his or her avatar just by moving the emotion-slider to one of its five positions. The selected text fonts, size, colors and contrasts ensuring good readability and recognizability even if the application is used in bright daylight. The text area provides sufficient space for 10 messages before vertical scrolling within the text area gets active. We disallowed horizontal scrolling in the application, because usability tests with news portals showed that horizontal scrolling leads to bad readability for longer texts. The user can also replay a complete or partial history of chat contributions. Although the taskbar contains four different control sections and over twenty possible user actions it stays within its own boundaries. Thus it will never conceal important information inside the avatar section or inside the text section. Different from desktop applications the screen area for mobile applications is underlying a higher complexity (measured in number of different user interface elements according to screen size). To create a steady and neat flow of events on the user interface is very important because it reduces the subjectively sensed screen complexity of the user. The solution for the taskbar was a little bit tricky but at the end it worked fine. We defined an easy to understand menu-expand-select-shrink mechanism. It is able to expand temporarily to the right, concealing two other controls that are not within the same use-case branch which means that there exists no interaction violence.

Feedback of User Actions

Since we have not used the available widget set and behavior of the underlying programming language we had to ensure that appropriate interaction feedback is available to the user. Each selectable icon on the screen is designed to be available in two states: unselected (normal state) and selected (action state). Some actions of the taskbar (e.g. kissing or slapping) require the further selection of another avatar in order to get transacted. The question was how to transmit the need for this second selection to the user. First we had the idea to place a simple request message on the screen. We discarded this solution because we wanted to have a fluent flow of events when an action of the taskbar is triggered. Now the second needed selection is visually demanded from the user by highlighting the other avatars with blinking rectangles around them, inducing the user to make a selection. Anyway, what happens if the user makes no selection? The whole action will be discontinued if there is no detected selection within a timeframe of 2 seconds.

To support appropriate feedback regarding the origin of text contributions we decided to place the responsible avatar on a pedestal for a certain amount of time or until the next contribution takes place. To raise the attention of the user we decided that each avatar that is placed on the pedestal is shown larger than the other avatars around.

Concurrent Events and Interaction Violation

Due to the high level of possible concurrent events in this application (remember the many connected users) we have inspected each condition of the chat for possible interaction violation. For example interaction violation occurs by presenting more than one message-window at the same time to the user. In this case the second message conceals the first one leaving a possible bad impression of message handling to the user (violation of controllability). Such violations can be found by extensive application testing after the coding. A more reliable method is to generate and analyze a non-deterministic finite automat (NFA) or state transition diagram for all major use cases. The latter ones can help you detecting interaction violation early during the design phase. The found interaction violations can than be considered in the usage concept before coding has even started.

Hiding Menus

In order to reduce screen complexity and maximizing user experience we used the concept of hiding menus for functions that are only used casually or once during the application session (e.g. close application, change background image, profile information). The hiding menu is located at the top right corner of the screen.

3   Summary

New and adapted user interface design strategies which are overcoming the limitations of today's mobile devices are indispensable to design usable mobile applications. With the upcoming of UMTS and WLan we need smart user interface metaphors and concepts which are taking into account the characteristics of mobile restrictions. Visual design greatly helps to convey and express information efficient and elegant to the user. As stated before mobile applications will change the way we communicate and live. The key factor remains the user. Therefore always remember: It's not the device that's mobile – it's the user.

Reference

[1]   Weiss, S.: Handheld Usability, John Wiley & Sons, (2002)

iCAMS2: Developing a Mobile Communication Tool Using Location Information and Schedule Information with J2ME

Yasuto Nakanishi, Shouichi Kumazawa, Takayuki Tsuji, and Katsuya Hakozaki

Graduate School of Information Systems, Univ. of Electro-Communications
1-5-1 Chofugaoka, Chofu-City, Tokyo 182-8585, Japan
{naka,kumazawa,taka,hako}@hako.is.uec.ac.jp

Abstract. In this paper, we introduce a mobile communication tool which uses location and schedule information. From the lessons learned by conducting user studies on our previous system, we made improvements by implementing the use of mobile phones equipped with a GPS and a J2ME. We conducted user studies for this new system, and the results showed that differences in the size of the area in which users move about as they conduct their daily activities might account for their different preferences.

1   Introduction

The spread of cellular phones, email, and mobile computers have freed human beings from the restrictions of time and place. Although human beings use these tools daily and appreciate the advantages they offer, their use has spurred new problems. In a mobile environment, it is particularly difficult to find out where a person is located at any one time, and what media he or she is using or can be contacted by, since this can quickly change. Many researchers have explored how to provide awareness information to help distributed collaborators communicate smoothly. Especially with the increasingly widespread use of mobile phones, researchers have been studying how to provide meaningful awareness information to anyone, anywhere, in order to facilitate communication among persons in a mobile environment [1-5].

We have developed and tested a mobile communication tool called "iCAMS," which uses location and schedule information to connect callers with callees [6]. The iCAMS which is designed to be used with cellular phones, is a dynamic address book on the WWW. It is a client/server system designed to make CHTML (Compact HTML) enabled mobile phones an integrated part of the communication network of companies. With the lessons provided from trials using the iCAMS system, we developed a new mobile communication tool with the J2ME (Java 2 Micro Edition) called "iCAMS2," and have conducted user studies to test its effectiveness. Our aim with the iCAMS2, which uses J2ME and GPS, is to improve user interfaces and location information precision. In this paper, we introduce our new system, and present the results of the user studies conducted on the user interface of this system.

L. Chittaro (Ed.): Mobile HCI 2003, LNCS 2795, pp. 400-404, 2003.

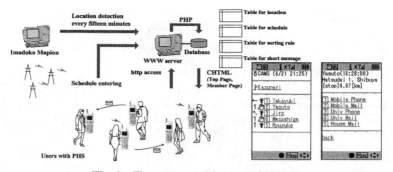

Fig. 1. The system architecture of iCAMS

2   System Implementation

2.1   iCAMS

The intended users of the iCAMS would be friends willing to share their location or other sensitive information with each other. Each user carries a PHS, a type of cellular phone that contains an email client and a WWW browser, which also works as a location sensor. To obtain location information, our system utilizes a location detection service provided by NTT DoCoMo, which performs localization through the cell phone network, with a precision of about 100m. The location information for each user is detected every fifteen minutes, and users input schedule information with a WWW browser in a PHS. Whenever a user accesses our WWW server, a PHP script queries the database and returns a CHTML file called "Top Page." Using the latest location information, the file sorts other users in their nearest order of position. It also shows whether they are moving or not, and in which direction they are located in relation to the user. When clicking an entry in the Top Page, another PHP script queries the database and returns a CHTML file called "Member Page". This file contains more detailed location information on the user, as well as a list of telephone numbers and email addresses for the selected user, which are sorted by registered rules concerning locations and schedules. For example, if a person is in his/her house, the phone number of the house might be listed first. If that person is in a meeting in his/her office, that person's office email address would be listed first. The caller can find out which channel is the best for the callee by looking in the Member page. Even if the mobile phone number is listed second in the list, the caller can make a call to the callee in case contact is urgently required.

We previously conducted user studies in Tokyo on the iCAMS for eight weeks with a group of students and another group of small-office workers [6]. These problems were found: 1) Because the system performs location detection with a precision of about 100m, users couldn't find out if the user they were trying to contact was in the same building or in an adjacent building. 2) Using PHP scripts slowed down the server response, and users were bothered by the fact that in order to get some of the member pages, they needed to use the same frequency to access the server. 3) The list sorted using the nearest order of position didn't show who and who were together.

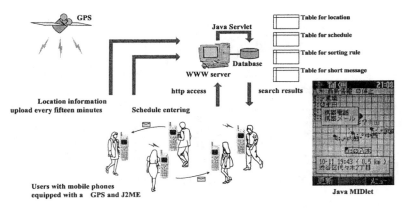

Fig. 2. The system architecture of iCAMS2

2.2   iCAMS2

In response to these comments, we developed a new mobile communication tool, the "iCAMS2," for cellular phones that have a GPS and J2ME built in (Fig. 2). The precision of location information detected with a GPS in a mobile phone is about 10m-50m, and therefore the location information precision problem is alleviated. In the iCAMS2, location information is detected in the client program every fifteen minutes (and only when activated by the user). The client program in the mobile phone is a Java MIDlet which communicates with a Java Servlet in the WWW server. The Servlet keeps a connection pool to the database, which improves the speed of the server response. The Servlet transmits queries to the database, and the information requested is then returned via the http connection according to a request from the client program, which enables the transmission of all of the information needed on the other users in one connection. By developing the client as a MIDlet, it is possible to visualize the relationship between each user's location, and therefore it might be possible to detect who and who are together.

We conducted user studies on the iCAMS2 for seven weeks in Tokyo with a group of students and another group of small-office workers. The group of small-office workers consisted of the same persons who had participated in the user study on the iCAMS. Because the same group participated, it would be possible to make a valid comparison between the iCAMS and iCAMS2. We changed the interfaces every week during the first five weeks, and the users evaluated them following the user studies (in the remaining two weeks, the interface was the same as that used in the fifth week).

In the first week of the study, the list of users was sorted in the nearest order of position of each user. In the second week, the location name was shown under each name in the list of users. Users could estimate, from viewing the names of these locations, who and who were together. After the third week, location information was shown on a grid. A user's location was shown as a black circle, and the name was shown beside the circle. Users could change the scale of the grid (100m, 1km, 5km, 10km, 25km), and when the distance between users was under the selected scale, the users' names were shown in a list next to a circle, which showed who and who were together. In the fourth and fifth week, the location information of the selected user was shown at the bottom of the grid. From the first to the fourth weeks, selecting one user resulted in another panel being shown, which showed the location information of the person selected or the communication channels list. In the fifth week, the communication channels list were shown in a popup panel. We analyzed the logs in the server and administered questionnaires and interviews to all of the users at the end of the study. We would especially like to present the results we obtained on the user interface.

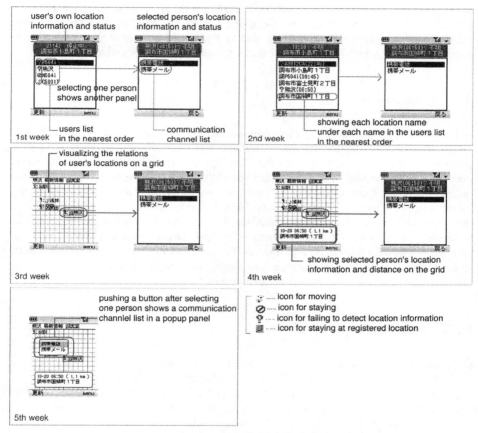

Fig. 3. Changes of user interfaces in the user studies

Our user interfaces were roughly classified into methods which showed the relations of user's locations in a sorted list in their nearest order of position or mapping, and methods which showed detailed location information and sorted communication channels which showed another panel or a popup panel. We presented four combinations, all of which the users evaluated. All persons in the group of students (five persons) gave the combination of the mapping and the popup panel the highest rating. However, four persons in the group of small-office workers liked this combination, but the remaining five persons gave the combination of the sorted list and popup panel the highest rating. These differences seemed to be due to the size of the space in which the users moved about. Because the students spent most of their time on campus (an area of about 1km), they found the 100m-grid easy to use, and were able to grasp their position relation at one glance without changing the scale of the map. However, the small-office workers moved around within an area of about 10km, and therefore sometimes had to change the scale of the map in order to determine their position in relation to others. They had to reduce the scale in order to see where other persons with whom they might have a chance to meet were, but had to magnify the scale to see their location relation with all members for knowing the context of the group. Those who liked the sorted list told us that reducing and magnifying the scale was bothersome, and that it would be best if they were able to view a sorted list which visually presented who and who were together.

3   Conclusions

In this paper, we introduced a mobile communication tool using location and schedule information, and evaluated its user interface. Because different models of mobile phones contain Java virtual machines that operate at different speeds, it wasn't possible to determine differences between the users' responses based on the differences in the types of mobile phones they owned. We utilized a GPS in detecting location information, however, the users weren't able to find out if another user was in the same building or in an adjacent building. In order to solve this problem, it will be necessary to integrate an indoor location system. However, there were merits to develop our system with Java, and it would be advantageous among the user interface in the client program to visualize the relationship between each user's location and to show the communication channels list in a popup panel.

References

[1]   Bergqvist, J. and Ljungberg, ComCenter: a Person Oriented Approach to Mobile Communication, CHI2000 Extended Abstract, pp.123-124 (2000).

[2]   Schmidt, A., Takaluoma, A. and Mantyjarvi, J., Contex-Aware Telephony Over WAP, Journal of Personal Technologies, Vol.4, No.4, pp.225-229 (2000).

[3]   Pedersen, E.R., Calls.calm: Enabling Caller and Callee to Collaborate, CHI2001 Extended Abstract, pp.235-236 (2001).

[4]   Tang, J., Yankelovich, N., Begole, J., Van Kleek, M., Li, F. and Bhalodia, J., ConNexus to Awarenex: Extending awareness to mobile users, Proc. on CHI2001, pp.221-228 (2001).

[5]   Milewski, E, A and Smith, M, T, Providing Presence Cues to Telephone Users, Proceedings of CSCW2000 (2000).

[6]   Nakanishi, Y., Takahashi, K., Tsuji, T., Hakozaki, K.: iCAMS : a Mobile Communication Tool using Location Information and Schedule Information, Proceedings of First International Conference on Pervasive Computing, pp. 239-252, Springer (2002).

Understanding and Modeling Physical Environments for Mobile Location Aware Information Services

Jeni Paay

Department of Information Systems and Faculty of Architecture
Building and Planning, University of Melbourne
Parkville, Victoria 3010, Australia
jpaay@unimelb.edu.au

Abstract. This paper describes ongoing research into the understanding and modeling of physical environments for the development of mobile location aware information services. The value of a location aware information service relies fundamentally on the relations to its physical surroundings within the context of the social settings of its users. Based on methods developed within architecture proposing the use of ethnographic field studies for acquiring insight into people's use of physical environments, a research design is proposed for describing and analyzing the relations between architectural, social and informational space of the recently built Federation Square in Melbourne, Australia. Preliminary outcomes of this study indicate that the proposed research design assists in understanding and modeling a physical environment and identifying a number of shortcomings valuable for the development of location aware information services for such environments.

1   Introduction

The value of a mobile location aware information service relies fundamentally on the relations to its immediate surroundings within the context of the social settings of its users. Whereas many location based information services such as mobile tourist guides deliver information based entirely on their user's x, y coordinates in physical space [13] other factors such as existing information in our surroundings, the built environment itself and the use of that environment by other people also have an impact on our perception of specific locations – our „locatedness". Locatedness is derived from the synchronicity of three overlapping layers: the social world [12] that we currently belong to; the physical space or built environment we are inhabiting; and the informational space augmenting that environment, telling us where we are, where we can go [5] and what individual actions and collective activities are supported [8]. This information layer can be implemented in various forms ranging from static signposts, dynamic digital maps through to mobile information devices providing „just-in-place" [7] information to support the activities of visitors. Consequentially, architectural, social and informational space all affect the requirements for mobile

L. Chittaro (Ed.): Mobile HCI 2003, LNCS 2795, pp. 405–410, 2003.

location based information services and hence need to be understood and modeled in order to support design. Within the field of architecture the importance of context in the design of built environments has long been understood [2]. With interest growing in the field of HCI into the importance of context for improving the usability and usefulness of digitally enhanced environments and mobile information systems [1, 4, 6, 11, 13] there is a case for applying architectural methods to inform design of such systems. For the purpose of supporting the generation of insight into the design of mobile location aware information services, this paper takes architectural methods used retrospectively to analyze and proactively to inform the design of built environments and applies them to the challenge of identifying, understanding and modeling properties of architectural, informational and social aspects of an environment that contributes to a persons sense of locatedness.

2   Analyzing Physical Environments

Architectural design has a history of incorporation of social theories and user needs into design decisions. Thus the issue of *usability* has implicitly been a key issue in the design of spaces for human habitation for centuries. In a study of the legibility of cities, Kevin Lynch [9] developed a method for visual analysis of city precincts, diagramming the interplay of visible elements in the environment that contribute to peoples environmental image of a place through descriptions of key aspects of the space held by people as they navigate and orient themselves within city precincts. To establish the imageability of the precincts being studied, Lynch carried out two basic analyses. Firstly, a field reconnaissance was done by an architecturally trained observer mapping the presence of elements in the physical environment and making subjective judgments about their visible contribution to the image of the city. Secondly, interviews were conducted with people who either lived or worked in that area, which included asking participants to describe features of the city from memory, draw sketches of the city, and making imaginary trips to destinations within the city precinct. Similar to Lynch, Christopher Alexander [3] empirically investigated the interplay between architectural space and its inhabitants, identifying a „checklist" of plausible solutions for the design of towns, buildings and constructions in the form of „design patterns". Design patterns describe solutions to design problems within a given context and come with empirical evidence for their validity. Similar to the diagrams and descriptions produced by Lynch, Alexandrian patterns form a sort of „rich picture" of context and form including photographs, sketches and text. While these methods have proved valuable within architecture, they may also prove useful for analyzing the interplay between architectural, social and informational space for the purpose of location aware mobile information service design.

3   The Study: Federation Square

Federation Square, opened in October 2002, is a collection of buildings and public spaces designed to provide a civic focus for the city, which through architectural excellence and incorporation of digital technologies aims to be „Between the Virtual and the Real". However, public acceptance is low. Although one architectural critic described the visitor experience as „liberating bewilderment" [10], in reality most people just find this frustrating.   Thus visitors to the square are still asking the questions: What is the purpose of this space? What kinds of facilities and activities are available here? How do I find my way around this space? etc.

Inspired by Lynch and Alexander a three-step study was designed to investigate relations between informational, physical and social space at Federation Square.

1.   Qualitative observations of informational space in terms of static and dynamic signposts and people's use of the information provided, leading to the description of elements in informational space in terms of properties such as visibility of signage, legibility, and content of the signs classified into categories such as way finding, advertising and general information. The informational space is documented through photographs annotated to plan views of the square (fig. 1).

2.   Qualitative observations of physical space identifying architectural surfaces and features (e.g. paths, sitting surfaces etc.) in terms of their contribution to the legibility of the public square where form is indicating function, and classifying them in accordance with Alexander's class of design patterns defining „individual buildings and the space between buildings". Like informational space, architectural space is documented through annotated plan views of the square.

3.   Observations and contextual interviews focusing on social space in terms of human groupings, activities and flow within the physical space focusing on the social activities facilitated by the space and the emergent social patterns which evolve from use of it. Social space is documented through annotated plan views of the square illustrating flow, groupings, scenarios etc. (fig. 2).

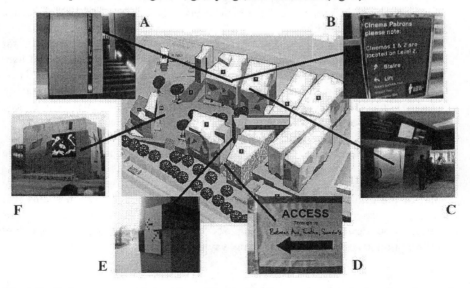

Fig. 1. Preliminary annotated plan view of Federation Square showing the location of a number of static and dynamic signposts

Fig. 2. Preliminary observations of flow and grouping of people

Following the empirical observations and interviews, the annotated plan views recording the results of each of the three field audits, including sketches, photographs and written notes are overlaid in such a way that features from all layers are visible concurrently. This is done in order to look for emergent relationships between the layers such as architectural space supporting (or not supporting) flow of people, or social space being supported (or not supported) by informational space, informing the requirements for an information system to enhance legibility of the environment.

Although Federation Square was designed to represent excellence in relating architectural space and state-of-the-art digital displays, a number of limitations in the relation between informational, physical and social space were identified:

1. Poorly designed static signposts: many of the signposts around the site are located on divergent surfaces, which means that arrows and related labels are often not both visible when approaching them, so the full contextual meaning of the sign is lost. It appears that aesthetic design choices have taken precedence over usefulness (fig. 1E).

2. Poorly designed dynamic displays: most dynamic displays are not being used for contextual information dissemination, but rather display „mood" video and text, such as old movies and famous quotations. The problem here is that there is no other provision of the information needed to support activity within this space (a cinema), and therefore people need to queue at the service counter to ask basic questions such as „What films are showing?" and „What does it cost to go to the cinema?" (fig. 1C).

3. Vertical scrolling dynamic displays unreadable: vertical displays whose purpose it is to support flow and navigation between different levels of this building are completely unreadable, and in an attempt to compensate for that, only display part of the information needed to move around the space. Again it seems that aesthetic design considerations were primary (fig. 1A). To support poor information design temporary signposts have had to be put up displaying information necessary to support basic way finding (fig. 1B, 1D).

4   Conclusions and Future Work

The research design proposed is based on architectural methods for representing and analyzing components of the built environment. Based on preliminary findings, this also seems to be an appropriate methodology for auditing social space and informational space and their relationship to physical space, and will assist in understanding and modeling the layered complexity of that environment. By making diagrammatic representations of factors influencing a person's locatedness within a physical space, it will be possible to make visual connections between these factors and from there advise design of effective mobile information services.

Future work includes completion of a full audit of social space, information space and architectural space of Federation Square, and representation of the findings in a form supporting analysis of interacting factors that traverse virtual, social and physical boundaries. The aim is to develop and evaluate a representation for this knowledge to inform the design of a mobile location aware information system, and to position these findings within an HCI approach for understanding context.

References

[1]   Agre, P. (2001) „Changing Places: Contexts of Awareness in Computing". *Human Computer Interaction*, Vol. 16, pp. 177-192.

[2]   Alexander, C. (1964) *Notes on the Synthesis of Form*, Harvard University Press, London.

[3]   Alexander, C., Ishikawa, S., and Silverstein, M. (1977) *A Pattern Lang*uage, Oxford University Press, New York.

[4]   Bradley, N. and Dunlop, M. (2002) „Understanding Contextual Interactions". Proceedings of MobileHCI 2002. Berlin, Springer-Verlag, pp. 349-353.

[5]   Dillon, A., McKnight, C. and Richardson, J. (1993) „Space – the final chapter: Or why physical representations are not semantic intentions". In C. McKnight and J. Richardson (eds.), *Hypertext: A psychological perspective*, Ellis Horwood, New York, pp. 169-171.

[6]   Graham, C. and Kjeldskov, J. (2003) „Indexical Representations for Context-Aware Mobile Devices".   Proceedings of IADIS e-Society 2003, Lisbon, Portugal.

[7]   Kjeldskov, J. (2002) „Just-In-Place Information for Mobile Device Interfaces". Proceedings of MobileHCI 2002. Berlin, Springer-Verlag, pp. 271-275.

[8]   Kuutti, K. (1996) „Activity Theory as a Potential Framework for Human-Computer Interaction Research". In B. Nardi (ed.) *Context and Consciousness: Activity Theory and Human-Computer Interaction*, The MIT Press, Cambridge, MA, pp. 17-44.

[9]   Lynch, K. (1960) *The Image of the City*, MIT Press, Cambridge, MA.

[10]   Macarthur, J. (2003) „The Aesthetics of Public Space". Architecture Australia, March/April 2003, Vol. 92, No. 2, pp. 44-49.

[11]   Nardi, B. (1996) „Studying Context: A Comparison of Activity Theory, Situated Action Models, and Distributed Cognition". In B. Nardi (ed.) *Context and Consciousness: Activity Theory and Human-Computer Interaction*, The MIT Press, Cambridge, MA, pp. 69-102.

[12]   Strauss, Anselm L. (1976)„Life Styles and Urban Space" In H. Proshansky (ed.) *Environmental Psychology: People and Their Physical Settings,* Holt, Rinehart and Winston, New York, pp. 528-537.

[13]   Vainio, T., Kotala, O., Rakkolainen, I., and Kupila H. (2002) „Towards Scalable User Interfaces in 3D City Information Systems". Proceedings of MobileHCI 2002. Berlin, Springer-Verlag, pp. 354-358.

SmartLibrary –
Location-Aware Mobile Library Service

Markus Aittola[1], Tapio Ryhänen[2], and Timo Ojala[1]

[1]MediaTeam Oulu, University of Oulu
P.O.Box 4500, FIN-90014 University of Oulu, Finland
http://www.mediateam.oulu.fi
2Oulu University Main Library
P.O. Box 7500, FIN-90014 University of Oulu, Finland
http://www.library.oulu.fi
{markus.aittola,tapio.ryhanen,timo.ojala}@oulu.fi

Abstract. Searching books in large libraries can be a difficult task for novice library users. This paper presents SmartLibrary, a location-aware mobile library service demonstrated in the main library of the University of Oulu. The service provides map-based guidance to books and collections on a PDA. SmartLibrary is a completely software-based solution, which can be provisioned atop a WLAN installed for wireless Internet access, without any additional hardware. In a user evaluation conducted with over 30 patrons SmartLibrary was preferred over traditional shelf classification for finding books. After user evaluation the main library added SmartLibrary into their standard customer service.

1   Introduction

Many location-aware mobile services have been proposed for public spaces such as museums and exhibition areas. Costa Aquarium in Genoa, Italy [1], and Exploratorium in San Fransisco, US [2], are examples of exhibition areas enhancing the visitor experience with mobile multimedia guides. User tests have also been conducted on those guides to find out usability issues and user acceptance.

In museum multimedia systems, location information is typically used in one hand to aid navigation, and in other hand to show user information of the exhibits nearby. In libraries, the user needs are different. Library patrons are typically searching for a particular book, or books concerning a certain topic. The problem is how to locate the target material from the numerous shelves of the library. The traditional solution is to classify the books into holdings and shelf classes. The solution works well if the user is familiar with the shelf classification. For larger libraries, however, there can be tens of holdings, hundreds of classes and thousands of shelves. This results in especially novice library users consulting the library personnel for personal guidance, which consumes the library's resources.

L. Chittaro (Ed.): Mobile HCI 2003, LNCS 2795, pp. 411–416, 2003.
© Springer-Verlag Berlin Heidelberg 2003

This paper describes SmartLibrary, a location-aware mobile library service, which helps users to find books and other material from the library. The help is provided in form of map-based guidance to the target bookshelf on a PDA. The guidance is integrated to the online catalog of library, so that books retrieved from the catalog can be located. Using a mobile device, the patrons of the library can access the online resources anywhere within the library, not only from the public stationary terminals available in the library. Wireless connectivity is provided in form of WLAN (IEEE 802.11b). The devices can also be positioned, which enables dynamic guidance from user's location to the books. The service is a completely software-based solution, which can be provisioned atop a WLAN installed for wireless Internet access, without any additional hardware. We demonstrate the service in the main library of University of Oulu. We also present a user evaluation of the service with real patrons of the library.

To our best knowledge, there are not many proposals for location-aware services for libraries. Jones et al. [3] conducted a scenario-based user survey to find out what kind of mobile library services the patrons would prefer to use. The survey included a scenario where a user is provided with mobile access to the on-line catalogs of the library. The scenario was evaluated with a service prototype, which included static map-based guidance functionality in a small library. The test users were enthusiastic about the ability to access on-line catalogs from all locations in the library building. The users suggested, however, that the map-based guidance might be more useful within larger libraries.

Reitmayr & Schmalstieg [4] and Nagao & Rekimoto [5] have proposed mobile augmented reality applications for locating books from library bookshelves. Their systems, used with wearable computers, locate users and books using visual tracking of markers or barcodes attached to the shelves and books. The required equipment and changes to physical shelves, however, make it difficult and expensive to employ those systems in large public libraries.

2   SmartLibrary

We illustrate the use of SmartLibrary with a following scenario: "A user is visiting the library the first time. He is intended to find a certain novel by Tolkien. The user takes his mobile client and opens the library web pages. He inputs the name of the novel as search parameter. He is returned the result entry of the book. The location code of the book is "P L 820/89engl Tolkien J. R. R.", pointing to the publicly available holding of English books. The user does not know where the holding is located in the library, so he asks SmartLibrary for guidance. The shelf containing the book is shown on a library map, as well as the shortest path from the user's current location to the shelf. The user follows the guidance to the shelf and finds the book easily."

SmartLibrary service is built on top of two existing systems, namely OULA and SmartWare [6]. OULA is the online catalog of the library of University of Oulu. SmartWare is a prototype system architecture built in University of Oulu for providing context-aware mobile multimedia services.

We demonstrate SmartLibrary in the main library of University of Oulu. Fig. 1(a) shows the locations of the WLAN access points installed in the first floor of the library for wireless Internet access. We used six access points to ensure more accurate WLAN positioning of the mobile device. Positioning is implemented with Ekahau's positioning technology [7], based on WLAN signal strength measurements.

Fig. 1(b) shows the run-time view of the architecture of SmartLibrary. There are three executables in the client domain: Ekahau client, SmartServices software and a web browser. Ekahau client measures the WLAN signal properties on the client device and sends them to Ekahau Positioning Engine, which calculates the location estimate for the client. Web browser is used to browse the OULA-pda user interface. OULA-pda is a web application tailored for small devices such as PDA's, providing a simple yet powerful access to the OULA database. User invokes the guidance service in SmartServices software by clicking a hyperlink. SmartServices communicates with SmartWare server in order to locate the user and the shelves. The locations of the bookshelves are stored in the SmartWare database. The location information of the user and the shelves are transferred to the guidance service user interface via the SmartWare server.

Fig. 1(c) illustrates the definition of a query for a book authored by Tolkien. Fig. 1(d) shows the presentation of the entries matching the query. By clicking the "Locate"- link of the book of interest the user gets access to the map-based guidance visualized in Fig. 1(e). In the map view the red dot denotes the location of the user, while the rectangular icon shows the shelf where the requested book resides.

3   Evaluation

A user test was conducted to find out if SmartLibrary really helps the library users in finding books. The goal was also to get feedback on usability and user experience.

In the test, the supervisor first gave the user a brief description of the SmartLibrary service and taught her how to use it by showing an example. The user was then given two tasks: first, to find a certain book by Tolkien, and second, any issue of a certain economic science periodical. Half of the users completed the first task using public desktop library terminals providing shelf classification, and the other half using SmartLibrary providing map-based guidance. The terminal was changed between the tasks. The supervisor followed the user and he was the only one the user was allowed to ask for help. After the tasks were completed, the users were asked to fill in a questionnaire containing multiple-choice questions and space for feedback.

Total 32 users, 14 females and 18 males, participated in the evaluation. The users were randomly selected among the library customers. The age of the participants varied between 19 and 49 years with median of 24, and most of them were university students. 66 % of the subjects had been customers of the library over two years. 46 % used OULA every week, while 9 % had never used OULA before. 25 % of the users had used a PDA device before the test. The users were also asked to estimate their experience in using the shelf classification system on a four-level scale (1 = low, 4 = high), most of them grading their experience to level 2.

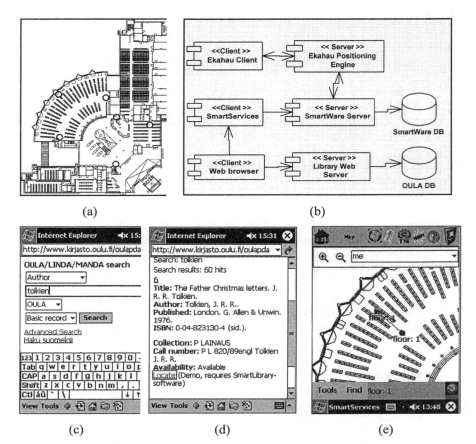

Fig. 1. (a) The locations of WLAN base stations in the first floor of the main library of University of Oulu. (b) The run-time architecture diagram of SmartLibrary. (c) The query definition UI of OULA-pda. (d) The results of the query. (e) Visualization of the map-based guidance to the shelf containing the book searched for

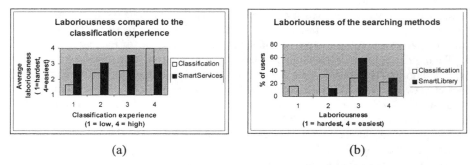

Fig. 2. Laboriousness of the book searching methods

After completing the two tasks, the users were asked which of the two methods they would prefer for finding books in the library and why. All males and 64 % of females chose map-based guidance. The users were also asked to judge how laborious it was to find a book from the library using shelf classification or map-based guidance, on a four-level scale (1 = very laborious, 4 = very easy). Fig. 2(a) shows that the laboriousness of shelf classification correlated heavily with the users' experience in using the shelf classification system. The average laboriousness value for the shelf classification was 2.53, while the corresponding value for map-based guidance was somewhat better 3.16. Fig. 2(b) shows the distribution of the laboriousness estimates of the two searching methods. 16 % of the users considered the shelf classification as 'very laborious', and 22 % 'very easy'. None of the users regarded map-based guidance as 'very laborious'. The figures show that finding books with map-based guidance of SmartLibrary was considered generally easier in comparison to shelf classification.

4   Conclusions and Future Work

We presented SmartLibrary, location-aware mobile library service. User evaluation conducted in the main library of University of Oulu showed that SmartLibrary helps the library users to find books easier in comparison to conventional shelf classification. After evaluation the library added SmartLibrary into their standard customer service. To promote the use of the service the library loans out PDA's to its customers. As the customers use the service, we continue collecting user feedback for further improvements of the user interface.

We consider adding textual instructions and landmarks into the guidance information. As there are collections also in other floors of the main library, we are developing solutions for guiding the customers between floors, as well. We are also building support for mobile phones, especially for the new smart phones equipped with a web browser.

Acknowledgements

The financial support of the National Technology Agency of Finland and the Academy of Finland is gratefully acknowledged.

References

[1]   Bellotti F., Riccardo B., de Gloria A., Margarone M.: User Testing a Hypermedia Tour Guide. Pervasive Computing 1 (2002) 33-41.
[2]   Fleck M., Frid M., Kindberg T., O'Brien-Strain E., Rajani R., Spasojevic M.: From Informing to Remembering: Ubiquitous Systems in Interactive Museums. Pervasive Computing 1 (2002) 13-21.

[3]   Jones L.W., Rieger R.H. Treadwell P., Gay G.K.: Live from the Stacks: User Feedback on Mobile Computers and Wireless Tools for Library Patrons. Proc. 5th ACM Conference on Digital Libraries, San Antonio, TX (2000) 95-102.

[4]   Reitmayr G., Schmalstieg D.: Location Based Applications for Mobile Augmented Reality. Proc. 4th Australasian User Interface Conference, Adelaide, Australia (2003) 65-73.

[5]   Nagao K., Rekimoto J.: Ubiquitous Talker: Spoken Language Interaction with Real World Objects. Proc. 14th International Joint Conference on Artificial Intelligence, Montreal, Canada (1995) 2:1284-1291.

[6]   Ojala T., Korhonen J., Aittola M., Kostamo N., Ollila M., Koivumäki T.: SmartRotuaari - Context-aware Mobile Multimedia Services, submitted. http://www.rotuaari.net.

[7]   Ekahau Positioning Engine. (2003) http://www.ekahau.com/products/positioningengine/.

The Human Interface in Mobile Applications

Lynne Baillie and Oliver Jorns

ftw.
Donau-City-Strasse 1, 1220 Vienna, Austria
{baillie,jorns}@ftw.at
http://www.ftw.at

Abstract. This paper describes a new type of application, which we foresee will be available on mobile devices in the future. In this paper we describe how we designed the application. The application is a parking ticket application (V-Ticket) for use on mobile devices. The application tries to match the needs of the user whilst taking into account the problems inherent in small wireless handheld devices such as limited network bandwidth, limited processing power and display dimensions.

1 Introduction

We wished to build a practical application for use on a mobile device. We brainstormed various possible concepts and this resulted in the scenario of a user wishing to buy a parking ticket. Scenarios have been used in the past to aid designers in building applications which take into account users needs[1, 2]. We first of all used a conceptual scenario to aid us in our discussions with users and to help us collect user stories. ISO13407[3] recommends that we should understand the specific context of use and try to understand and specify the users' requirements. By collecting user stories and incorporating these into our conceptual scenarios we hoped that we were fulfilling part of the ISO13407 remit. Some of the issues raised by users were common place and recognisable to all of us who have undertaken the task of purchasing a parking ticket e.g. not having enough change for the ticket machine, paying for time not used, having to locate the nearest ticket machine and having to dispose of the ticket after use. We further learned that users have only a very limited time span in which to carry out the task of ordering a ticket. After collating the user stories we began to move away from a very conceptual scenario to a more concrete one. For each of the user stories in the corpus we worked through the descriptions identify the various objects and the actions that are performed. From this we constructed a concrete scenario that contained more detail and more precise information about the application and how the user would interact with it. We then moved onto the third part of our user centred design process: production of possible design solutions.

In the first part of the paper we describe the application and how it is anticipated the user will interact with it. In the second and third parts we describe the underlying architecture. In the final part of the paper we look to the future and describe the user trials we will undertake.

L. Chittaro (Ed.): Mobile HCI 2003, LNCS 2795, pp. 417–421, 2003.

2 Application

2.1 The Application (User View)

The application enables a user to order a parking ticket via their handheld device if it has a GPRS connection. The following steps are carried out by the user in order for them to be able to download the application and access the service:

1. Apply for the service via a website.
2. Fill in an electronic application form (this requests the following information from the user: name, car registration, phone number, two security questions and email address.
3. Download the application to their mobile device (this only takes a few seconds and only needs to be done once).

In our discussions with users they raised the point that they may share one or more cars, therefore the system enables the user to registration more than one car. We realised that this was an important addition to the application as a car can play an important role in a user's family and company life. Figure 1 shows the three screens that a user would have to navigate to order a ticket. The screen on the left hand side is the first screen the user will see. The interface offers the following menu options: order a new ticket, cancel a ticket, or view a ticket. If the user decides to order a ticket they merely have to scroll down to 'Order Ticket' and press 'Submit'. Once they have done this the next interface appears which has a list of the vehicle licence plates they have registered. The user in Figure 1 has registered three licence plates and has decided to choose the first licence plate. The user merely scrolls (using the 'up and down' cursor buttons) to the appropriate licence number to select it and then presses 'Send'. Pressing the 'Send' button initiates the ticket ordering process. After the ticket is registered in the database, the server sends information back to the user which indicates that the ticket ordering process was successful (how the confirmation looks to the user is shown in the right most screen).

The user stories had alerted us to the fact that the users would like to know how long they have been parked for; therefore we included this possibility in the design of the application. This option allows the user transparent control and interaction at any time. Figure 2 depicts the three step sequence to view

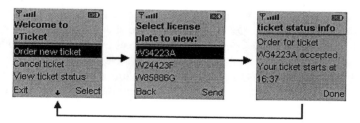

Fig. 1. Ordering Interfaces

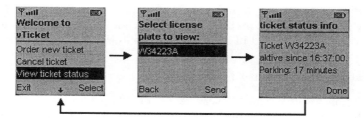

Fig. 2. View Ticket Status

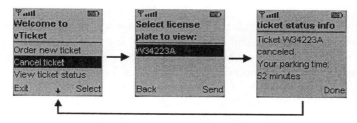

Fig. 3. Menu sequence for cancelling tickets

a current ticket for a licence plate. The user can easily and quickly view the current ticket and know how long it is since they ordered it, in this case 17 minutes. The user can then either return to the main menu or exit the program. By selecting the second item on the main menu as it is depicted in Figure 3 the ticket cancelling process is initiated. The display shows the active ticket.

Again it can clearly be seen how easy it is for the user to navigate the system and complete the task.

2.2   The Application (System View)

We now explain, the same operations from the systems point of view, this includes a concise explanation of the underlying database. Once the user has registered on the website the user's details are captured and a password is automatically generated and emailed or sent via SMS to the user. This password must be used the first time the user activates the application or when the user's details change i.e. when the user wants to add a new vehicle license plate or change their personal details. We realize that this does not provide an adequate level of security and would, therefore propose that the password could be used for signing device dependent information using asymmetric encryption techniques. After the validation of a user (e.g. checks to ensure authenticity of phone number etc) and system checks (e.g. the person is not already registered) have taken place each user's registration information is stored in the systems database. The database stores information about the cars, which are uniquely identified by the license plate number. The concept of user groups (families or businesses) implies that each car may be shared by several users and each user may have access

to more than one car, a separate table in the database defines the relationship
between the user and the cars they have registered. Once all information about
user and their cars is stored in the database the user can start to order tickets.

2.3   System Architecture Overview

In this section we give a brief overview of how data and instructions are exchanged between the mobile device and the server. The components and technologies used in order to produce this prototype application are also explained.

During registration the user has to select at least one service, e.g. the V-
Ticket application. As figure 4 depicts, the V-Ticket application may be one of
many services offered by a provider. The user can add or delete an application
via the internet or directly from their mobile. If the user wishes to add a new,
or delete, an old application the the management software checks whether the
new or existing service is available and initiates either a cancellation or a setup
operation.

We used Java 2 Micro Edition software to help us write the code for the
mobile application (API[4]). The communication between the mobile clients and
the server is realized by using an open source implementation called kXML-
RPC[6] of the XML-RPC[9] protocol which was preferred over kSOAP[5] because
of its simplicity. Basically, XML-RPC allows remote procedure calls between
a mobile device and a server in a straight forward manner using XML. On
the server side XML-RPC is integrated into a Servlet based environment which
connects to a MySQL[10] database.

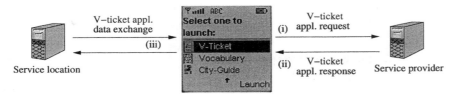

Fig. 4.   System Architecture Overview

3   Discussion and Future Work

We found that we had many problems in realizing the application. The first
problem we encountered in building the application was how complex should it
be? For example should we include in our conceptual scenario the possibility of
businesses registering their whole fleet of cars? Should the order of the menu
change once the user has ordered a ticket with view ticket coming first? What
words should we use to confirm the ticket status? We found that discussing the
parking ticket scenario with users helped us to concretize the main functions that

the application should have. It also helped us to decide that the first prototype application would not take into account the company concept as we could not, as yet, deal with the security issues. On the wording and ordering of the menus we tried to make the interaction as quick and as straightforward as possible. When we were in doubt as to whether we were making the correct choices we would go back to the users who had worked through the original parking scenario with us and ask them their opinion. We did this by sending them the screen shots of the application and a short explanation of the envisioned interaction.

We think that this application shows the future possibilities for such applications and is an improvement on the existing SMS system which allows a user to pay for parking via SMS, as that system setup requires the user to pay in advance for their parking or via credit card. This application gives the user the freedom to order tickets whenever they want, for as many different cars as they want and to pay for the parking at their normal billing time. We expect that in the next few months we will undertake some live trials of the application (we have already conducted some mock trials) in Vienna. We would like to add that this is only one possible use for an application of this type and in fact this type of application could be used quickly and easily to pay for all sorts of services.

References

[1] Carroll, J. M. (1996) Becoming Social: Expanding Scenario-based Approaches in HCI. Behavior and Information Technology, 15(4), 266-275.
[2] Carroll, J. M., Rosson, M. B., Chin, G. & Koenemann, J. (1998) Requirements Develop-ment in scenario-based design. IEEE Transactions on Software Engineering, 24(12), 1156-1170.
[3] ISO13407 (1999) Human-Centered Design Processes for Interactive Systems.
[4] Java 2 Platform, Micro Edition (J2ME), (2003) URL: http://java.sun.com/j2me/.
[5] kSOAP Project. (2003) URL: http://ksoap.enhydra.org/.
[6] kXML-RPC Project. (2003) URL: http://kxmlrpc.enhydra.org/.
[7] Legion of the Bouncy Castle, (2003) URL: http://www.bouncycastle.org/.
[8] Lipp, P., Bratko, D., Farmer J., Platzer W. & Strebenz A. (2000) Sicherheit und Kryptographie in Java. Addison-Wesley.
[9] XML-RPC.com. (2003) URL: http://www.xmlrpc.org/.
[10] MySQL.com. (2003) URL: http://www.mysql.org/.

I'm Here!: A Wearable Object Remembrance Support System

Takahiro Ueoka, Tatsuyuki Kawamura, Yasuyuki Kono, and Masatsugu Kidode

Graduate School of Information Science, Nara Institute of Science and Technology
8916-5 Takayama, Ikoma, Nara 630-0192 Japan
{taka-ue,tatsu-k,kono,kidode}@is.aist-nara.ac.jp

Abstract. In this paper we propose a wearable vision interface system named "I'm Here!" to support a user's remembrance of object location in everyday life. The system enables users to retrieve certain information from a video database that has recorded a set of the latest scenes of target objects which were held by the user and were observed from the users' viewpoint. We propose the object recognition method to associate the video database with the name of objects observed in the video. The offline experiments demonstrate that the system is useful enough to recognize the objects.

1 Introduction

We propose a wearable vision system to help the user remember where portable, rigid objects are placed in his/her everyday circumstances. This system retrieves the last recorded video of a user's viewpoint including the target object from a video database termed "video memory".

In the field of wearable computing for memory-aid, a Video Albuming system [1] is proposed to support a user's memory retrieval. The Video Albuming system always records a video of the user's viewpoint in his/her video memory, and analyses context information included in the video memory. The "I'm Here!" system follows the concept of the Video Albuming system, and focuses on the idea that users forget where they placed objects. DyPERS [2] assists users by reminding them of information about an object. This is accomplished by replaying a video explicitly associated with a snapshot of the object. In contrast, our system can retrieve the video without a user's explicit association, because the "I'm Here!" system automatically associates the video memory with the previously registered objects. The registration of an object is done by simply holding the object and gazing at it. Hide and Seek [3] is a system that navigates with the frequency of sound how far an object is placed from the user. The small devices attached to the target objects are each assigned a unique ID. In the "I'm Here!" system, a user simply has to wear some devices and there is no need to place such devices in the real world.

L. Chittaro (Ed.): Mobile HCI 2003, LNCS 2795, pp. 422–427, 2003.

2   Design Concepts of the System

The "I'm Here!" system shows a user the latest video recorded when he/she lastly held a target object through a head-mounted display. Viewing the video that was observed by his/her head-mounted camera, he/she can remember where and when he/she placed the object. Ultimately we expect that the system will act as if the object itself sends a message, such as "I'm Here!" to the user.

As depicted in figure 1(a), the user registers an object by holding and rotating it in view of his/her head-mounted camera. The system extracts visual information of the object from the video and records its features with the object's name as assigned by the user.

In the user's everyday life, the system continuously records a video of the user's viewpoint in a video memory. Simultaneously, the system identifies an observed object, held by the user, as the registered one. Using the result of identification, the system then associates the name of the identified object with the video and automatically constructs an index of video memory, which is named "augmented memory."

Figure 1(b) shows a scene of object retrieval. The user, via the selective list of registered objects, assigns a name to the object so as to remember where it is placed. The retrieved video is displayed as shown in figure 1 (b).

3   System Implementation

We have developed a prototype of the "I'm Here!" system. The hardware mainly consists of a head-mounted camera called "ObjectCam", a wearable PC, and a head-mounted display (HMD). The ObjectCam captures the user's viewpoint image. The PC executes the processes of the system. The HMD shows the user system information and the retrieved video.

(a) A video of user's viewpoint at object registration

(b) The system interface and a displayed video at object retrieval

Fig. 1. Support for object remembrance using video memory

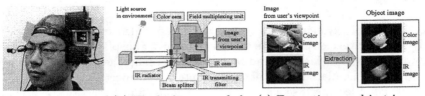

(a)   Head-mounted (b) Block diagram of the (c) Extracting an object image
devices   ObjectCam

Fig. 2. Newly developed camera and display device

3.1   Camera and Display Devices

Figure 2(a) denotes head-mounted camera and display devices. We have newly
developed an "ObjectCam," which is a head-mounted combined camera device,
to extract an object image from a user's viewpoint image. A frame of the image
consists of a color and an infra-red (IR) image for each field (figure 2(b)). An
IR image displays the reflected IR luminance caused by the IR light source on
the devices [4]. The system obtains the object image by eliminating background
regions from the viewpoint image with the luminance of the IR image, and hand
regions by using skin color (figure 2(c)).

3.2   System Functions

Figure 3 shows both the system function provided to the user and the process diagram of each function. In "object registration" (figure 3(A)) the system records
a video of the object held and manipulated by the user. The object is observed
in several appearances from the user's viewpoint in everyday life. The system
thus extracts the images of the object in several appearances from the video
memory. The image groups are made from the extracted object images, based
on the appearances of the objects. The system constructs the feature values from
representative images of each group.

In "object observation" (figure 3(B)) the system abstracts the object feature
values from the user's viewpoint images just as in the case of figure 3(A). Com-

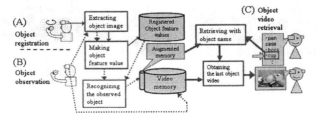

Fig. 3. System functional diagram

paring the target object with registered objects, the system makes a decision based on their feature values. The system records the user's viewpoint image, and labels the image with the registered object name if the target object is recognized as one of the registered objects.

When the user wants to remember where one of registered object is, he/she selects the target object from the list of registered objects (figure 3(C)). The system retrieves the name of the target object from the augmented memory, and obtains the last recorded video of the target object. Lastly, the system displays the retrieved video to users through the HMD.

3.3   Object Recognition

A $\{H\text{-}Z\text{-}C\}$ feature value of an object image consists of $\{H, Z, C\}$ elements. These elements are obtained from each pixel of the image. $\{H\}$ is a hue value. $\{Z\}$ is an IR luminance value. $\{C\}$ is a group of pixels divided by the distance from the median point of the silhouette of the object image. The $\{H\text{-}Z\text{-}C\}$ feature value denotes a 3D distribution. The equation 1 and 2 show the $\{H\text{-}Z\text{-}C\}$ feature value expressed by Integrated Probabilistic Histogram value (IPH) in the case of $j \in H, k \in Z,$ and $l \in C$.

$$IPH(j,k,l) = \sum_i N\big(j - H_i, \sigma_H(S_i)\big) \times N\big(k - Z_i, \sigma_Z(S_i)\big) \times C_{il} \qquad (1)$$

$$C_{il} = \begin{cases} 1 : l = \left[\dfrac{L_i}{L}\right] \\[2ex] 0 : l \neq \left[\dfrac{L_i}{L}\right] \end{cases} \qquad L : const. \qquad (2)$$

When $\{H_i, Z_i, S_i\}$ means a value of the ith pixel, $N(j - H_i, \sigma_H)$ and $N(k - Z_i, \sigma_Z)$ are normal distribution functions. $\sigma_H(S_i)$ and $\sigma_Z(S_i)$ denote dispersion values of distribution based on the exponential decreasing function including S_i in the exponent part. The element L_i denotes the distance between the median point of the silhouette of the object image and the ith pixel.

The similarity between two $\{H\text{-}Z\text{-}C\}$ feature values is calculated by the Sum of Absolute Difference (SAD) method. The system compares a feature value of an observed object with feature values of registered objects to identify the observed object. The system then selects the most similar object from the entire group of registered objects when the similarity shows higher than the preset threshold.

4   Experimental Results

We have estimated the recognition performance of the system through an offline experiment. The test images were recorded under fluorescent lights. As depicted in Figure 4, Test group (a) consists of the images of ten objects, and test group (b) consists of twenty objects including the objects in (a), and an additional

(a) 10 objects

(b) 20 objects

Fig. 4. Test objects

Table 1. Recognition rate

	Object feature value			
	H	H-C	H-Z	H-Z-C
(a) 10 objects (%)	99.2	99.2	91.7	96.7
(b) 20 objects (%)	81.7	88.8	87.5	94.1

ten objects. The images of an object consist of twenty different configurations of distance and perspective.

We compared the $\{H\text{-}Z\text{-}C\}$ method with the $\{H\}$, $\{H\text{-}C\}$ or $\{H\text{-}Z\}$ method in terms of recognition rate. The result of recognition allows a matching between patterns in the same object. Table 1 shows results of the experiment. The recognition rate using the $\{H\text{-}Z\text{-}C\}$ method is the highest among the methods. Furthermore, the decrease in the recognition rate caused by the increase of the number of test objects is shown, but the decrease using the $\{H\text{-}Z\text{-}C\}$ method is significantly smaller than other methods.

From the result, we found that the $\{H\text{-}Z\text{-}C\}$ method is more robust when the number of registered objects increases. We believe that the proposed $\{H\text{-}Z\text{-}C\}$ method is appropriate for object recognition in "I'm Here!"

5 Concluding Remarks

In this paper we proposed the "I'm Here!" system, which is a wearable interface system for remembering where an object used in everyday life was placed. The performance of object recognition directly affects the performance of the system in its adequacy of support.

The proposed "I'm Here!" system supports retrieving only the objects placed by the user himself/herself. We are planning to apply the system to support the case where the objects have been moved and placed by others. In everyday life, a human sequentially handles objects to perform a task. For instance, when he/she wants to have a cup of coffee, he/she prepares his/her cup, boils water in a kettle, and stirs the coffee with a spoon. We are also extending the "I'm Here!" system to recognize the sequence of accesses to objects in a task to suggest to the user what objects should be used and where they are placed.

Acknowledgements

This research is supported by Core Research for the Evolutional Science and Technology (CREST) Program "Advanced Media Technology for Everyday Living" of the Japan Science and Technology Corporation (JST).

References

[1] Tatsuyuki Kawamura, Yasuyuki Kono, Masatsugu Kidode: Wearable Interfaces for a Video Diary: towards Memory Retrieval, Exchange, and Transportation. In Sixth International Symposium on Wearable Computers, Seattle, Washington (2002).

[2] Tony jebara, Bernt Schiele, Nuria Oliver, Alex Pentland: DyPERS: Dynamic Personal Enhanced Reality System. In Proceedings of the 1998 Image Understanding Workshop, Monterrey CA, November 1998. Also appears as Vision and Modeling Technical Report #463.

[3] M. Shinnishi, S. Iga, F. Higuchi, M. Yasumura: Hide and Seek: Physical Real Artifacts which Responds to the User. In Proc. of World Multiconference on Systemics, Cybernetics and Informatics (SCI'99/ISAS'99) Vol.4, pp.84-88 (1999).

[4] Cameron M. Lee, Konrad E. Schroder, Eric J. Seibel: Efficient image segmentation of walking hazards using IR illumination in wearable low vision aids. In Sixth International Symposium on Wearable Computers, Seattle, Washington (2002).

Towards a Framework to Develop Plastic User Interfaces

Montserrat Sendín[1], Jesús Lorés[1], Francisco Montero[2], and Víctor López[2]

[1] Computer Science and Industrial Engineering Department
University of Lleida, Spain
{msendin,jesus}@eup.udl.es
[2] Higher Polytechnic School of Albacete
University of Castilla-La Mancha, Spain
{fmontero,victor}@info-ab.uclm.es

Abstract. In previous works we have been developing a tourism support prototype that offers a proven solution for aspects of multi-platform, personalization and spatial-awareness. The aim of this paper is to analyze its drawbacks and to propose a framework and the underlying architecture, inspired by the model-based approach, to solve those relying on the principle of abstraction. It consists of a reflexive architecture that allows specifying a generic user interface (UI) independently of the rest of the implementation, fulfilling the *plasticity* property. Developers only have to focus on modelling the functionality of the application –residing at a base level-, leaving the interface to a meta level, constructing thereby *interfaces "on the fly"*. The generation of the UI is not carried out until run-time, translating automatically abstract interaction components to concrete ones according to the device, the user's features and the current context, accordingly reusable in other applications.

1   Introduction

Mobile computing offers the possibility of dramatically expanding the versatility of computers, by bringing them off the desktop and into new and unique contexts. As it grows, it offers a wider variety of devices suitable for multiple and varied *contexts of use*[1]. However, to take advantage of all these new possibilities, UI designers are forced to accommodate a growing variety of devices and contexts of use, as well as to solve any contextual or environmental changes, in order to satisfy all the demanded features: adaptivity, context-awareness, multi-platform, while preserving usability.

In this line, what we intend is to exploit the possibilities of mobile computing in the tourism sector. Our specific aim is to develop a generic tourism support tool that gets together all of the mentioned features, applicable to any tourist enclave. This is the same purpose that in the PALIO project [1].

---

[1]   It includes a set of environment parameters (values of variables) that describe a particular context where the interaction takes place by a determined user [12].

L. Chittaro (Ed.): Mobile HCI 2003, LNCS 2795, pp. 428-433, 2003.

The previous prototype we developed –tested and published in [2]- already solved the adaptation to the device and to the user's profile, by providing a specific template in XSL (eXtensible Style Language) adapted to each context of use. However, that solution had strong limitations because it requires as many versions as contexts of use. Because of the increasing availability of diverse devices, this will grow quickly and cause great problems for maintenance and coherence.

These considerations motivate the development of a more generic methodology that allows specifying a unique, generic and *abstract UI*[2], flexible enough to serve multiple sources of physical variations. The goal is to guarantee usability continuity under any variation, while minimizing development and maintenance costs. This capacity of adaptation from a same generic UI to different contexts of use, without reducing usability, is called *plasticity* property, a concept defined in [3].

Model-based (MB) approach provides methods for supporting the systematic development of application interfaces formalizing and exploiting all of the relevant aspects of the UI in declarative models that get together all the different requirements of each context of use, and store the conceptual representation of the interface [4]. See [5] to look up a complete overview of some of the best-known MB techniques.

The current MB-IDEs are criticized because they mostly support the generation of form-based UIs only [6], leaving the problem of content adaptation flexibility and coherence unsolved [7]. Task models need to be improved for addressing the problem of plasticity. In our opinion, on one hand the set of models taken into account is quite limited, and on the other hand, the resulting MB systems are in general substantially static, leaving without solving the anticipation to contextual changes, as it occurs, for example, in ARTStudio (Adaptation by Reification and Translation) [8]. Another aspect that we miss is the lack of semantic information inside the models.

Particularly we have revised in depth the MB techniques developed for three members of the RedWhale: Eisenstein, Vanderdonckt and Puerta [9], the method for *Universal Design of UIs* in [10], as well as a framework for supporting plasticity [3]. This last recaptures the notion of *Presentation Unit* presented in TRIDENT [11] to set the foundations of a canonical representation for the abstract UI. ARTStudio provides a concrete, although incomplete, application of the design time aspect of this framework. On the contrary, Probe [12] deals with the run time aspect for the detection of context changes, although not formalized yet as an environmental model.

It is also worthy to mention other alternatives to MB techniques, like UMLi [13] or UIML [14], although there is no language that are completely device independent and integrates all the aspects of content adaptability [7].

The design and implementation base proposed in this paper consist of the provision of as many concrete components of interface as necessary, adaptable to different contexts and formalised through models, such as it is advocated by the *component-oriented paradigm*. The suitable component will be automatically selected according to the user's technology (device) and preferences, using some concepts and heuristics. In this line, we are thinking of JavaBeans components -portable, platform-independent, event-support (mechanism to relay and react to changes of state),

---

[2] Canonical expression of abstract domain concepts and functions to be translated to diverse concrete objects, prevailing the functionality in any case. Thus, it is interactor independent (Thevenin, 1999).

resusable software-, which provide support to adaptivity. JavaBeans will make up our concrete interaction objects, called *basewidgets*. The abstract interaction objects, the *metawidgets,* provide a high abstraction level at which design decisions are made. The rest of the application will work making use of the abstract interface components. The translation of abstract to concrete components, and the relation between functionality and interface are situated at a meta level of a typical *reflexive architecture.*

2   Our Proposal

2.1   Environment Recognition

As a tourism support tool, our system has to solve all kind of spatial consultations, providing the *spatial-awareness* property. In order to offer environment recognition, a detailed spatial model from the real world is required, which has to be built and integrated into the architecture. The modelling is solved using an object-oriented approach –making so the adaptation to each particular case easier, following the *ontology* concept-, in an XML-based language. We call this model *Augmented World model* (AW-m). It provides an integrated and homogeneous view of the data.

The automatic extraction of the objects in the model that may interest the user – according to his profile and current state- with regard to position, is being delegated to a spatial data managing module: the *Nexus platform* [15]. It consists of a global and open infrastructure, sufficiently versatile to contact to any spatial-awareness application –independently of its functionality-, provided that the application works with XML-based languages to define the AW-m, and also with XML-based query languages to formulate the queries. It is currently being developed at the University of Stuttgart. For more details about how to join our prototype, consult [2].

The essential components of the AW-m are the static geographical objects –places of interest to be visited-, the location information of some mobile objects, and also virtual objects that provide additional information or services to Nexus users. The answer to a query consists of a list of matching objects in a particular zone. For example, a list of the nearest restaurants with their respective attributes -address and menu-, if it is lunchtime, or a list of the castles that can be visited in the zone, according to attributes such as historical period and visiting timetable. This would be suitable if our user had a certain preference for History. There are a lot of parameters related to the user that also take part in the adaptation. See [2].

2.2   The Reflexive Architecture

Under an object-oriented reflexive architecture view [16], a system is considered to be integrated by two parts: the application part and the reflexive part, which reside at two different levels: the base level and the meta level, respectively. The application is represented at the base level and is manipulated by the meta level. Both levels are connected causally, so that changes in the base level are reflected in the meta level. The meta level is formed by objects that carry out computation about a system materialized by objects at the base level. The base level contains program objects that solve a problem in a platform and return information about the application domain.

Our objective consists of developing a system where the part destined to contemplate the interface and the part destined to the functionality are independent. At the base level, following the abstraction principle, there is no conception of interface. The interface will be taken on at the meta level, at run-time, fixing which concrete interface components will represent the functionality described by the abstract ones, depending on the device and the user's profile. Other responsibilities of the meta level will be the interaction validation, the aid to the user in his actions, etc, in a transparent way. The base level can be formed, independently of its functionality, by a control structure similar to a *states machine* –or state-transition diagram-, where each state is associated with a dialogue which is at the same time associated to a task, all of them identified in the design phase. Fig. 1 represents the whole idea.

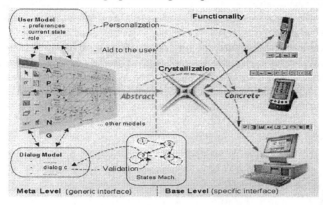

Fig. 1. Reflexive architecture and distribution of responsibilities

The models that we consider relevant for our purpose are the next ones: user model, task model, dialogue model, presentation model, platform model –explicit expression of the target platforms in terms of quantified physical resources-, and finally a contextual model -to take into account daily aspects like the time, the day of the week, weather condition, etc, which also can influence in the adaptation.

We don't have devised yet a framework for the development of plastic UIs, but until now, the ideas we can bring forward are the following ones:

- the connections between the platform and the presentation model acquire crucial importance because they lead in a great deal the transition from abstract components to concrete ones
- in the presentation model, interactors should specify the abstract data types they are able to handle. Complementarily, abstract data type description should provide the information necessary to perform the mapping between a domain concept and a set of candidate interactors
- we think that not necessarily all models should be involved all the time. According to that, we can distinguish two phases in the generation of the concrete UI. In the first phase they will act the context, user, task and AW-m models. And in the second one the presentation, platform and dialogue models

- domain objects should be ranked according to their level of importance in the task domain involved, and particularized to each user's profile, covering so the semantic aspect. This will help the rendering process, using suitable heuristics

3   Conclusions

This paper presents the preliminary ideas to devise a framework and the underlying architecture to develop plastic –highly adaptable- UIs "on the fly" -where interaction and domain components are independent, i.e., based on the Model-View-Controller pattern. These ideas need to be elaborated, completed and formalized with a more thorough analysis to devise an operative framework. That will be our future work.

Reflection is proposed as the mechanism to carry out the crystallization from abstract to concrete components, taking into consideration as many contextual aspects as necessary, trying to overcome the challenges posed by mobile computing. Another advantage of this mechanism is that the developer only has to focus on modelling the functionality of the application, leaving the interface to a meta level.

References

[1]   Zampi, P.: Personalized Access to Local Information and services for tourists. Information Society Technologies (2001)
[2]   Sendín, M., Lorés, J., Solà, J.: Making our Multi-device Architecture Applied to the Montsec Area Heritage Adaptive and Anticipating. Proc. Workshop on HCI in Mobile Tourism Support (Mobile HCI 2002) Pisa, Italy (2002) 51-56
[3]   Thevenin, D., Coutaz, J.: Plasticity of User Interfaces: Framework and Research Agenda. Proc. of Interact'99, Edinburgh (1999) 110-117
[4]   Paternò, F.: Model-Based Design and Evaluation of Interactive Applications. Springer-Verlag, London (2000)
[5]   Pinheiro, P.: The Unified Modeling Language for Interactive Applications. (2002) http://www.cs.man.ac.uk/img/umli/links.html
[6]   Schlungbaum, E.: Model-Based User Interface Software Tools. Current state of Declarative Models, GIT-GVU-96-30 (1996)
[7]   Lemlouma, T., Layaïda, N.: Device Independent Principles for Adapted Content Delivery. INRIA (2002)
[8]   Thevenin, D.: Adaptation en Interaction Homme-Machine: Le cas de la Plasticité. PH.D. thesis, Joseph Fourier University, Grenoble (2001)
[9]   Eisenstein, J., Vanderdonckt, J., Puerta, A.: Adapting to Mobile Context with User-Interface Modeling. Workshop on Mobile Computing Systems and Application. Monterey (2000)
[10]   Furtado, E., Vasco, J., Bezerra, W., William, D., da Silva, L., Limbourg, Q., Vanderdonckt, J.: An Ontology-Based Method for Universal Design of User Interfaces. Workshop on Multiple User Interfaces over the Internet: Engineering and Applications Trends (2001)

[11] Vanderdonckt. J.: Knowledge-Based Systems for Automated User Interface Generation; The TRIDENT Experience. Technical Report RP-95-010, University of N.D. de la Paix (1995)

[12] Calvary, G., Coutaz, J., Thevenin, D.: Supporting Context Changes for Plastic User Interfaces: a Process and a Mechanism. Proc. IHM-HCI'2001 (2001) 349-363

[13] Pinheiro, P.: UMLi: Integrating User Interface and Application Design. Proc. of Workshop on Towards a UML Profile for Interactive Systems Development. TUPIS2000 (2000)

[14] Abrams, M., Phanouriou, C., Batongbacal, A, Williams, S., Shuster, J.: UIML: an Appliance-Independent XML User Interface Language. Proc. of WWW'8 (1999)

[15] Grossmann, M., Leonhardi, A., Mitschang, B., Rothermel, K.: A World Model for Location-Aware Systems. Published on behalf of CEPIS by Novática and Informatik/Informatique http://www.upgrade-cepis.org., Vol.II, Issue, 5. Ubiquitous Computing (2001) 32-35

[16] Zimmerman, C.: Advances in Object-Oriented Metalevel Architectures and Reflection. CRC Press, Inc., Boca Raton, Florida 33431 (1996)

Context-Aware Interaction in a Mobile Environment

Daniela Fogli[1], Fabio Pittarello[2], Augusto Celentano[2], and Piero Mussio[1]

[1] Università degli Studi di Brescia, Dipartimento di Elettronica per l'Automazione
Via Branze 38, 25123 Brescia, Italia
{fogli,mussio}@ing.unibs.it
[2] Università Ca' Foscari di Venezia, Dipartimento di Informatica
Via Torino 155, 30172 Mestre (Ve), Italia
{pitt,auce}@dsi.unive.it

Abstract. This paper addresses context awareness of user interaction in real spaces where a number of places devoted to interaction are defined, following a concept called *interaction locus* (IL). In the IL a coordinated set of information notifies the user about the specific nature of the place he/she has currently entered. The interaction takes place through mobile devices which manage the context of the user, and is mediated by two agents that are called the *genius loci* and the *numen* of the user. Context awareness is achieved by cooperation between the two agents, which interact according to the user history and the place interaction opportunities. An implementation architecture is described, suited for mixed reality environments. A case study related to cultural heritage is presented.

1 Introduction

In this paper we elaborate on a novel approach to interaction in *lightweight* mixed reality environments, i.e., mixed reality environments [5] where humans interact with small portable devices, which has been presented and discussed in earlier papers [1,3]. Here we present an architecture for implementing *Experiential Interaction Paradigms* (EIP) in a context-aware mobile environment [2]. EIPs extend the *Positional Interaction Paradigms*, where humans participate to the interaction with their body, whose position is tracked by some input device and considered as one of the main data for interaction. In EIPs the experience of a user interacting with a system becomes an important source of knowledge. To deal with such knowledge we propose a methodology and a system architecture for the observation of the interaction and for the recognition of recurrent user behaviors. The approach aims at supporting the user during navigation and interaction, and also at supporting the designer in the discovery of usability problems and in the consequent improvement of system design.

The approach is based on a set of cooperating *agents* [4], which act keeping track of the initial background of the human involved in the experience and of the relevant interaction in order to facilitate further interaction. Agents become *aware of the context* and able to adapt their behavior to it.

L. Chittaro (Ed.): Mobile HCI 2003, LNCS 2795, pp. 434–439, 2003.

The approach is based also on the *interaction locus (IL)* concept, introduced in the context of a research that aimed at resolving current weaknesses for interaction inside 3D environments [6]. In the context of this paper an *interaction locus* is a connected portion of space characterized by the presence of an underlying base world, the possibility of perceiving when a user enters and exits the IL, and the presence of identifiable interaction devices which support the exchange of information between the user and the world. In a mixed reality environment an interaction *locus* is the part of the world to which experiences are attached, i.e., the part of the world in which the user can interact with the embedded computing devices.

Different types of interaction devices receive user input and provide information to the user: *interactive objects*, on which the user operates directly, which change their state or their appearance as a consequence of the user interaction; *artifacts*, mediators of the interaction between the user and the world, which make evident to the user interaction opportunities that would otherwise be unknown; *dynamic information objects*, which modify their state or appearance, e.g., show up or hide, as a consequence of the user interaction on other devices in the environment.

2   Agent-Mediated Interaction

The interaction between a user and the objects of an *interaction locus* is observed and mediated by two agents, one associated to the *locus*, and the other associated to the user. The agent bound to the IL knows the information opportunities of the specific place and the interaction possibilities, therefore is able to assist the user in exploring the place. Borrowing the terminology from ancient roman religion we call such an agent a *genius loci*, a kind of local divinity who takes care of the place by giving the visitors the opportunity to get most benefit from its exploration. The agent can perceive the user behavior and actions such as entering and exiting the IL, moving freely or along paths, interacting with artifacts and interactive objects, etc. It is of course limited in perception to what the user is able to manifest about him/herself. Therefore, the agent is bound to the presence of a number of "sensors" in the scene, that are the devices which sense the user actions.

Also the user has his/her own genius, that we call *numen*, a kind of *guardian angel* who follows the user during navigation by accumulating and managing knowledge about him/her. The *numen* knows the user character (the profile), can accumulate the exploration history across several places, and is able to interact with the *genii* of the different places in order to give them information about how to help the user in his/her visit. The two agents mediate the interaction between a user and a rich and differentiated environment accumulating, maintaining and exchanging knowledge about the user and the interaction place. Figure 1 pictorially describes this scenario in a virtual exhibition application; the *genius loci* is represented by a snake.

The communication protocol between a user *numen* and a *genius loci* is activated when the user enters an IL and is defined by four steps. (1) The *genius loci* reacts to the user presence and starts a dialog with the user *numen*, by asking information about the user. (2) The *numen* gives the *genius* the information requested. In particular, the *numen* knows two kinds of information: a user profile, which is a static collection of properties and data about the user, and a user history, which is a set of data about previous user actions collected during exploration, transmitted by the *genii* of the other *loci* visited. (3) On the basis of the information provided by the *numen*, the *genius* is able to modify, if needed, the properties of interaction in that *locus* [1]. (4) On exiting the interaction locus, the *genius loci* returns to the *numen* the result of its observations, i.e., the discovered patterns of interactions for that *locus*. The *numen* decides, according to its own knowledge base (i.e., the user profile and the accumulated knowledge about other *genii* observations), how to consider the received information, which is processed according to the *numen* rules. More details can be found in [1]. Both types of agents are context-aware. The context of the *numen* is constituted by the user and by the *genius loci*; the *numen* adapts its knowledge according to the data received by the *genius loci* and to the current state of the user. The context of the *genius loci* is constituted by the user and by the *numen*; the *genius loci* determines its own behavior according to the data on the user obtained by the *numen*, to its current perception of the user and to its knowledge of the IL itself.

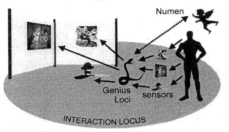

Fig. 1. The *genius loci* mediating the user actions

3   An Implementation Architecture

Figure 2 describes an architecture targeted towards distributed context-aware interaction in mixed-reality environments, implementing the concepts described above. The monitoring of the user position in the real world requires a special attention, because of the errors that occur in determining it using, e.g., GPS technology.

For diminishing the impact of errors, we split the components for monitoring the user position from the representational and proactive part of the system. Two different 3D representations of the real 3D scene where the user interaction will take place are modeled: the *3D base world* with the associated *experience layer* containing a 3D model of the scene to display on the PDA and a set of ILs mapped over this model with their genii loci, and the *3D internal representation* of the real scene. The latter representation is not meant for visualization purposes and contains only a georeferenced set of volumetric sensors that have the same geometric limits of the set of ILs used for the experience layer. The positional parameters of the user received by the GPS are compared with the limits of these volumetric sensors. The result of the monitoring activity is passed to the *filter component* that interprets data.

For example, if the user stays in a certain position for some time, the filter may infer that the user doesn't move because he/she's looking to something interesting and therefore he/she's probably inside an interaction locus, even if the raw GPS data communicates that the user is on an 'empty' area. The filtered information is then passed in the form of updated positional data for the current camera of the 3D experience layer, i.e., the viewpoint in the 3D scene as seen by the user on the PDA screen. The filter may be programmed for sending a continuous correction of the raw data or for sending the coordinates of a significant stable point of view on a certain IL, once it has inferred that the user is inside the IL. The software simulator discussed below uses the second approach.

Concerning the user input, we can distinguish two different categories of data: *user profile*, that is made of data collected from the user at the beginning of the interaction, and *usage data*, that are generated by the user during the interaction. Besides, there is a third category of *data coming from the environment* (time, weather, light, etc.) that can be meaningful for the interaction and therefore may be monitored from the system.

A specific component of the architecture, the *experience selector*, composes the mixed reality experience, selecting the experience layer and the associated 3D internal representation. The experience selection is guided by the user, through the choice of his/her profile at the beginning of the interaction. The experience selector will compose the experience according to the mapping between experiences and user profiles, determined in the authoring phase [6]. The user is enabled to change the profile during the interaction. In that case, the experience selector will be responsible for coordinating the actions necessary to conclude the current experience in a consistent way and to load the experience layer related to the new choice.

The filtered user position and the user interaction with the mobile device are caught by a set of sensors embedded in the experience layer. Activation and changes of their significant parameters are communicated to the *script components* of the world. These script components are embedded into the experience layer and implement the *genii loci*. Their function is to collect the user actions perceived through the sensors in specific areas of the environment (the ILs) and to mediate the action of the associated interactive objects. Each script component runs a separate computation process. The state of the computation is maintained consistent by a different component, the *experience handler*, external to the 3D world; it implements the *numen* entity discussed above. The experience handler receives information from the script components concerning the usage data; besides, it accesses the user profile and environmental data as input for its coordination activity. The accumulated knowledge is filtered and passed to the script components that will pilot the interaction objects.

A software simulator of the architecture described in Figure 2 has been built. The main components, a GPS simulator for streaming user position data and a prototypical user interface have been implemented. We used VRML, the language for describing geometry and interaction primitives related to a 3D environment, for building the experience layer and all the components embedded inside of it. GeoVRML [7], an extension of the VRML language that allows to represent accurately georeferenced data, has been used for building the 3D internal representation of the environment.

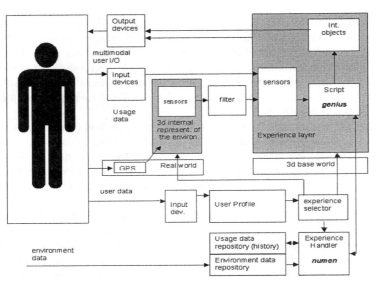

Fig. 2. An architecture for interaction in mixed reality environments

4   A Case Study

In order to test the potentialities of the system in a real case study, we started a collaboration with the National Archaeological Museum of Altino, located near to a roman archeological site nearby Venice, Italy. We used three different sets of interaction loci to map the archaeological area, corresponding to three different user profiles: the student, the average visitor and the expert. We are currently working on the implementation of different proactive behaviors. In the experimental scenario, visitors are free to wander through the open area. Each time the user enters a locus that was never visited by him/her, a 3D representation of the IL is visualized on the lower part of the PDA interface, an auditory description of the locus starts and a portion of a roman coin is added on the right upper part of the interface. When the user enters the last locus left to visit, an additional message informs him/her that there are no other interesting places in the archeological area. Besides, if the user enters a locus already visited, no portion of coin is added and an alternative text or audio message advises him/her of this condition. This behavior results from the interaction between the *numen* and the *genius loci*. Each time the user enters an IL, the *genius loci* notifies the *numen* the event. The *numen* passes to the *genius loci* the accumulated patterns of interaction related with previous user actions, which include the information that the current locus has already been visited. The *genius loci* uses this information to activate the standard behavior (add a new portion to the coin and start standard description of the location) or to start the alternative messages discussed above.

References

[1]   Celentano, A., Fogli, D., Mussio, P., Pittarello, F.: Agents for distributed con-
       text-aware interaction, Proc. Workshop Artificial Intelligence in Mobile Sys-
       tems (AIMS 2002), ECAI Conference, Lyon, France, July 2002, pp. 29-36.
[2]   Chen, G., Kotz, D.: A Survey of Context-Aware Mobile Computing, Technical
       Report TR2000-381, Dartmouth College, Department of Computer Science,
       2000.
[3]   Fogli, D., Mussio, P., Celentano, A., Pittarello, F.: Toward a Model-Based
       Approach to the Specification of Virtual Reality Environments, Proc. Multime-
       dia Software Engineering (MSE'2002), Newport Beach (CA), USA, December
       2002, pp. 148-155.
[4]   Jennings, N. R.: An Agent Based Approach for Building Complex Software
       Systems, Communications of the ACM, 44(4) (2001) 35-41.
[5]   Milgram, P., Kishino, F.: A Taxonomy of Mixed Reality Visual Displays,
       IEICE Transactions on Information Systems, Vol. E77-D No. 12 (1994) 1321-
       1329.
[6]   Pittarello, F.: Accessing Information Through Multimodal 3D Environments:
       Towards Universal Access, Universal Access in the Information Society Jour-
       nal, 2(2) (2003) 1-16
[7]   Reddy, M., Iverson, L.: GeoVRML 1.1. Specification, Web 3D Consortium,
       (2002) http://www.geovrml.org/1.1/doc/index.html.

Platform Awareness
in Dynamic Web User Interfaces Migration

Renata Bandelloni and Fabio Paternò

ISTI-CNR
Via G.Moruzzi 1, 56100 Pisa, Italy
{r.bandelloni,f.paterno}@isti.cnr.it

Abstract. The goal of this work is the design of an environment for supporting run time migration of Web applications among different platforms. This allows users interacting with a Web application to change device and continue their interaction from the same point. The migration takes into account the runtime state of the interactive application and the different features of the devices involved. We consider Web applications developed through a multiple-level approach using: the definition of the tasks to support, the abstract description of the user interface, and the actual code. The runtime migration engine exploits information regarding the application runtime state and higher level information on the available target platforms. Runtime application data are used to achieve interaction continuity, while information on the different platform types involved are deployed to adapt the application's appearance and behaviour to the specific device.

1   Introduction

A wide variety of devices is now available on the market, and people are more and more likely to operate in a multiplatform environment where different platforms have different interaction capabilities. Many efforts are currently aimed at allowing users to interact through multiple devices. A framework discussing the issues associated with applications that can be spread over different surface areas, each supporting diverse user interaction techniques, is discussed in [1]. In our work we focus on Web-enabled platforms. For example, a user browsing the net with a PDA touch screen or a mobile phone keypad would be more comfortable using the mouse and keyboard of a stationary PC. Conversely, a user may be entering private data through a stationary PC and wish for the greater privacy afforded by a PDA. In both cases, a multiplatform migration service would be necessary, by which the user could interact with web applications while changing devices and still maintaining interaction continuity. There are two main issues concerning this kind of service. Firstly, the diversity in features of the platforms involved in migration, like different screen size, interaction facilities, processing power and energy supply, can make a Web application developed for a desktop, unsuitable for a PDA and vice versa. Thus, an application cannot

L. Chittaro (Ed.): Mobile HCI 2003, LNCS 2795, pp. 440–445, 2003.

migrate as it is from one device to another, and must be adapted at runtime, taking into account the diversity of the devices involved [2]. The second issue concerns interaction continuity. Users who want the application to migrate, do not want to have to restart the application on the new device; they want to continue their interaction from the same point where they left off, without having to re-enter the same data and going through the same long series of links to get to the page they were visiting on the previous device [3]. Two main kinds of information are relevant in performing migration: static information refers to the features of the devices, whereas runtime information refers to the state of the migrating application that can be summarised by the history of user interactions with the application, including visited pages, submitted data and results of previous data processing. There are several techniques for migrating user interfaces to different devices, in particular to small screens, and most of them rely on size reduction and data summarisation [4], with the risk of making the application unusable because objects on the page are difficult to recognise. Herein we focus on interaction continuity and device adaptation at runtime that takes into account usability principles. We consider different platform-specific versions of the same application, starting with a general task model [5] from which we generate the actual application by means of the TERESA tool [6]. We take into account the migration of TERESA-generated applications, for which a description of the pages and the interactions that they support, are produced by the tool itself, at different abstraction levels. Runtime data on the state of the application for which migration is required will be collected locally from the platform requesting migration. This information is transmitted to the server in order to recreate the corresponding state in the application for the target device.

2   Generating Device Aware Web Applications

We consider Web applications developed through a multiple-level approach able to obtain versions suitable for different kinds of devices and platforms. The starting point is the task model of a nomadic application that can be accessed through different platforms. The general model is refined for each of the specific platform that must be supported by the application and by means of the TERESA tool, different implementations are generated fitting different platform features and according to usability principles. The main levels involved in the generation process are:

1. *Task Model (TM)*: describes the logical activities that must be performed by users in order to reach their goals. A set of attributes is defined for each task and tasks are composed by semantic and temporal relations.
2. *Abstract User Interface (AUI)*: defines the main characteristics of the interaction objects supporting task performance, abstracting from low level details. AUIs are defined in terms of presentations identifying the set of user interface elements perceivable at the same time. These elements are represented as interactors being Abstract Interaction Objects (AIO) described in terms of their main semantic effects.

3. Concrete User Interface (CUI): this is the implementation level, the actual user interface produced for a specific device in a given implementation language as Java, XHTML and so on.

3   Runtime Migration Cases

Different types of runtime migration can be identified, along with different levels of complexity for each one of them:

- *Total Migration*: the client application migrates totally from a device to the other.
- *Control Migration*: the client application is divided into two parts, one for user interaction (control part) and one for information presentation (presentation part). The control part remains on one device, while the presentation one migrates to the other device, or vice versa [7].
- *Mixed Migration*: the client application is split into several parts, concerning both control and presentation and different parts are distributed over two or more devices.

In our work, we focus on *Total Migration*, with the goal to support a runtime migration that takes into account the differences between the two platforms involved. TERESA structures an interactive application into presentations and transitions among them. When we migrate a presentation from a platform to another one the runtime support first identifies the closest presentation in the target platform. The difference between presentations in different platforms is calculated in terms of the number of logical tasks supported. A task can be supported through different interaction techniques. However, the logical meaning of the task is still the same. Taking into account interactive applications developed by means of TERESA we can identify the following situations concerning the runtime migration of a presentations between two platforms:

- The migrating presentation corresponds to one target presentation supporting:
  - Same number of tasks.
  - Lower number of tasks.
  - Higher number of tasks
- The migrating presentation corresponds to multiple target presentations that make an exact partition of the task set associated with it.
- Multiple presentations in the source platform correspond to one presentation in the target platform.

4   Our Migration Solution

Information concerning the platform asking for migration, and the state of the application running over it, is collected and elaborated in order to activate the application on the target platform without losing interaction continuity. Since the presentation number and the tasks supported by the various platforms can be different, it is not possible to create a one-to-one correspondence between presentations for different platforms. Source and target platform versions are generated by TERESA separately, using the information contained in the two corresponding task models. One important issue is how to identify the presentation for the target platform corresponding to the one active on the platform requesting migration while maintaining the state of its interaction objects. The run-time state, consisting of the visualized page and the state of its objects, is mapped first onto the corresponding abstract presentation and then onto the corresponding set of tasks. The page to be visualized on the target device will be identified using the inverse process: from the set of tasks to support the tool identifies the most similar abstract presentation and then the corresponding page in the application version for the target platform. Similarity is calculated in terms of tasks supported, the more the tasks associated to the two presentations are similar, the more the presentations are similar. Presentation similarity is the basic criterion to be considered, but under particular conditions it cannot be enough. When the migrating presentation supports a task set that is associated with multiple presentations in the target version, each of them supporting the same number of tasks, similarity degree will be the same for each potential target presentation. Thus, a further criterion should be used to decide which target presentation to activate. To this end, we use the identification of the target presentation supporting the task associated with the interaction object last modified by the user, since it is more bound to continue interaction from that point.

Once the corresponding presentation has been identified, it is necessary to calculate the state of the objects contained in the page that will be sent to the target device. For this purpose, runtime data referring to the runtime state of the application will be associated to the corresponding AIOs and adapted to the object implementation for the target device.

5   Migration Service Architecture

We aim at supporting Web application migration for a wide variety of devices like desktops, laptops, PDAs, cellular phones and generally any device able to access the Internet through a browser. Our migration service relies on a server machine working both as a Web server storing the platform specific implementations of the application, making them accessible to client platforms, as well as a migration server, managing context information to support migration requests. Client platforms use the migration client loaded from the server in order to enabling or disabling the possibility of receiving incoming applications and migrating Web applications. References to all platforms, which enabled the reception of incoming applications, are stored in the server. When a platform asks for migration, the request sent by the locally running migration client, reaches the migration server, which will deploy both runtime and static context data to perform the presentation mapping process as described in Section 4. The corresponding page and its runtime context for the target device will be finally sent to the migration client that will open locally a browser window allowing the user to continue its interaction (the sequence of functionalities to perform is indicated in Figure 1).

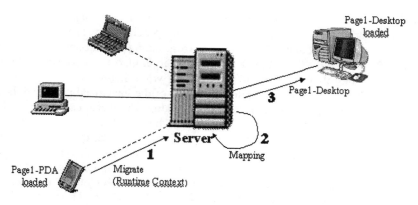

Fig. 1. The Migration Process

6   Conclusions and Future Work

We have discussed an architecture to support migratory Web interfaces. A first prototype for total migration of applications obtained through the TERESA tool has been developed. We are now improving the collection of run-time state data in order to make it more complete and improve the support of interaction continuity. Future work will be dedicated to extending this approach in order to address other types of user interface migrations.

This work has been supported by the CAMELEON project (http://giove.cnuce.cnr.it/cameleon.html). We thank colleagues for useful discussions.

References

[1]   J. Coutaz, C. Lachenal, S. Dupuy-Chessa. Ontology for Multisurface Interaction. Proceedings INTERACT 2003. IOS Press. Zurich, September 2003.

[2]   A. Kaikkonen and V.Roto. Navigating in a Mobile XHTML application. In Proceedings of CHI 2003. Ft. Lauderdale, Florida, April 5-10, 2003. Vol.5, pp. 329-336.

[3]   H. Song, H. Chu, S. Kurakake. Browser Session Preservation and Migration. In Poster Session of WWW 2002, Hawai, USA. 7-11. May, 2002. pp. 2.

[4]   B. MacKey. The gateway: A Navigation Technique for Migrating to Small Screens. Doctoral Consortium, CHI 2003. Ft. Lauderdale, Florida, April 5-10, 2003. pp. 684-685.

[5]   F. Paternò, C. Santoro, A Unified Method for Designing Interactive Systems Adaptable to Mobile and Stationary Platforms, Interacting with Computers, Vol. 15, N.3, pp 347-364, Elsevier, 2003.

[6]   G. Mori, F. Paternò, and C. Santoro. Tool support for designing nomadic applications. In Proceedings of IUI 2003 . ACM Press, 2003. pp. 141–148.

[7]   J. Nichols, B. A. Myers, M. Higgins, J. Hughes, T. K. Harris, R. Rosenfeld, M. Pignol. Generating remote control interfaces for complex appliances. Proceedings ACM UIST'02. October 27 – 30. Paris, France. Vol.4, pp.161-170.

User Needs for Development
of Context Dependent Devices in Mobile Home Care

I. Scandurra[1], M. Hägglund[1], N. Johansson[2], B. Sandblad[2], and S. Koch[1]

1. Department of Medical Sciences, Medical Informatics and Engineering
{isabella.scandurra,maria.hagglund,sabine.koch}@medsci.uu.se
http://www.medsci.uu.se
2. Department of Information Technology, Human Computer Interaction
{niklas.johansson,bengt.sandblad}@it.uu.se
http://www.hci.uu.se

Abstract. Mobile work situations within home care of the elderly require immediate and ubiquitous access to patient-oriented data. We intend to develop a mobile information system that provides *correct information in a proper way to the right person in the appropriate occasion of care*. This requires a thorough user needs analysis that so far often has been neglected during systems development in health care. We conducted the user needs analysis in interdisciplinary working groups in order to achieve a holistic view of the entire work process. This allows for the development of not only patient-oriented but care process oriented systems. In this paper, we describe how the user needs analysis was conducted, the impact of this work on the user group and some of the requirements found to be specific for mobile IT-support for home care of the elderly.

1   Introduction

Ageing of population, growing mobility in society and growing shortage of staff resources in the health care sector require new models for information handling and communication in order to guarantee quality-oriented health care of the elderly.

Home care of the elderly today is performed by different types of care providers: medical personnel such as general practitioners or district nurses, and community service personnel in charge of non-medical services as e.g. the patient's daily hygiene.

Even though these care providers, especially the community service personnel, have a mobile work situation, they very rarely have any mobile IT tools supporting their work. Most mobile access to information is today paper based, which is not only inflexible, but also a risk when it comes to documenting new information and sharing information within the working group. Important information is often not documented correctly due to the fact that it has to be remembered until the care providers reach their office. As a consequence, it is often not communicated to other personnel that need the information in order to be able to provide high quality care.

L. Chittaro (Ed.): Mobile HCI 2003, LNCS 2795, pp. 446–450, 2003.

IT-systems available in health care today have very rarely taken the end user's needs into account when developed, but have traditionally been the tools of administrators rather than clinicians. Especially the community service personnel have rarely been in focus for user-centred systems development. The user needs have subsequently not been sufficiently described and analysed, making a thorough user needs analysis necessary before developing a new IT-support in this area. A user group with very little experience when it comes to IT and often insufficient consciousness of the entire work process makes it difficult to identify the care providers needs and requirements. Health care professionals have their primary focus on the quality of health care they provide for their patients and therefore the IT-system must be developed to be as transparent as possible to let the users keep the focus on the patient and to support and not hamper clinical work processes. Usage of existing and modified HCI-methods and techniques during user needs and requirements analysis is therefore of great value.

2   Method

In order to identify and describe the different care provider's needs when it comes to a mobile work situation, a user-centred system development approach is followed [1]. In iterative seminars, interdisciplinary working groups define future user-oriented work scenarios and develop prototypes. During seminar work, methods like brainstorming, scenario building and in depth interviews are used. The iterative seminar process aims at analyzing and improving the practical and organizational work as well as identifying the user needs and requirements of the forthcoming information technology in different work situations.

The importance of having a process oriented view of the work, that takes different care provider's needs into account requires that the analysis is done in interdisciplinary working groups. The general practitioners (GPs), district nurses and community service personnel work together with researchers in medical informatics and human-computer interaction in order to detail the specific work scenarios. The use of observation and participation according to the Master-Apprentice approach described by Lave and Wenger [2], together with interview techniques for work analysis in interdisciplinary seminars has resulted in a user needs analysis.

3   Results

The approach described above has been used for the user needs analysis in one research project and will be used in a second project shortly, both focusing on mobile home care for the elderly. The first project OLD@HOME (Technical Support for Mobile CloseCare) [3] focuses on providing a seamless and consistent information flow between different care providers involved in the home care of elderly people, using different mobile information technologies. By improving the tools for the personnel in their mobile work situations the project aims at providing elderly people with better and improved health care in their homes and in the primary health care.

The VIHO-project (Efficient computer support in care for the elderly) will focus on the development of both organisation and technology. Mobile tools for the home care personnel will be developed together with the end users to fully support their mobile work with mobile technology.

While working in interdisciplinary seminar sessions the conclusion has been made that different care providers have similar yet distinct needs. The different users all need to access information in their mobile work situation, but the kind of information and the optimal way of presenting it differs.

3.1   The Care Process – A Team Work

The shift from user-centred care towards patient-centred care demands new requirements in the development and integration of mobile IT-support for home care. It is becoming increasingly more important to consider the care process as a team effort, rather than isolated events performed by a single profession. IT-support has traditionally been developed for one care provider or specialist, but the entire care process is performed by several care providers who communicate and share information. Therefore, new systems should not only be patient-oriented but care process oriented.

When analyzing the care providers different mobile work situations in the interdisciplinary working groups a holistic view of the care process is achieved. This has given the members of the working groups a deeper insight in each others work and an understanding of the different needs and how they can support each other in the specified work situations.

3.2   Shared Information

The requirements from the personnel working together around one patient, but with different specialities, are specified in the interdisciplinary seminar sessions. In order to provide good quality care, the health care professionals need access to both their own clinical documentation about the patient as well as the other professionals' documentation. Any relevant information about the patient has to be collected and presented in a comprehensive way to the personnel while taking care of the patient at home.

3.3   Avoiding Information Overload

When introducing a new mobile tool that gives the users access to all available information, there is a risk that they cannot make optimal use of this tool due to "information overload". Therefore the amount of information has to be reduced, carefully selected and presented in a user friendly way. Different categories of care providers need different views on a common set of data, depending on both their respective needs and the limitations of the mobile device they are using.

3.4   Different Interfaces and Devices

Devices such as today's personal digital assistants (PDA's), Tablet PC's and laptops can be used as supporting tools for the personnel working in the home care of the elderly. The choice of device is made depending on the different care providers work situation and requirements. It is extremely important that the device is designed for the needs originated in a specific work situation and suited to the environment in which it will be used. Portable devices often have small displays and less memory than an ordinary PC, which demands optimization of the information presented on the screen. Today's mobile devices also suffer from inadequate access time and transfer limitations. The information selected to be displayed must therefore be relevant, not just to avoid cognitive information overload but also to optimize the graphical user interfaces for correct information presentation and to attain good usability [4].

4   Conclusions

In order to develop a mobile health care system that provides *correct information in a proper way to the right person in the appropriate occasion of care* a thorough user needs analysis is necessary. By conducting this in interdisciplinary working groups a holistic view of the work process can be achieved and systems developed from this basis will be not only patient-oriented but care process oriented.

The health care professionals need information both from their own information system, e.g. specified parts from the patient's records, and the other professionals' systems independently if they belong to community health service, primary care, secondary care or a private care giver.

When the users are given access to all available information, there is a risk that they cannot make optimal use of it due to "information overload". Therefore, the amount of information has to be reduced, carefully selected and presented in a user friendly way.

Immediate and ubiquitous access to patient-oriented data will be needed in specific work situations for different kinds of care providers. The different users will use different tools or techniques to access various types of medical information.

4.1   Future Work

New methods for information visualization and interaction, which adapt to new mobile environments, are called for. Prototypes for mobile visualisation of, and interaction with, medical information for some specific clinical work situations in order to support the process of clinical decision-making in an optimal way will be developed. This work aims to confirm and substantiate the requirements identified so far, and within this research work, the graphical user interface for the different views of the prototypes as well as the modes of user interaction will be developed.

Acknowledgement

The project "OLD@HOME – Technical Support for Mobile CloseCare" is sponsored by VINNOVA - Swedish Agency for Innovation Systems (P23037-1 A), August 2002 - July 2005 and Trygghetsfonden.

The project "VIHO - Efficient computer support in care for the elderly" is sponsored by VINNOVA - Swedish Agency for Innovation Systems (2001-05296).

References

[1]   ISO 13407:1999: Human-Centred Design Processes for Interactive Systems. International Organization for Standardization, Geneva (1999)
[2]   Lave, J. and Wenger, E.: Situated Learning: Legitimate Peripheral Participation. Cambridge University Press, Cambridge, UK (1991)
[3]   Koch, S., Hägglund, M., Scandurra, S: Enhanced health care of the elderly - the OLD@HOME project, to be submitted
[4]   Sandblad, B., Lind, M., Nygren, E.: Design of human-computer interfaces in health care, based on task analysis and theories of human cognition. In: Proceedings of MEDINFO 92, Lun et al. (eds.) Elsevier Science Publishers B.V. North-Holland (1992)

Context Information in Mobile Telephony

Louise Barkhuus

The IT University of Copenhagen
Glentevej 67, DK-2400 Copenhagen, Denmark
barkhuus@it.edu

Abstract. Most research in context-aware computing offers definitions
of context that consist solely of measurable information. Using mobile
telephony as an example of a computing area, we provide a set of context
information relevant to the area drawn from a qualitative case study:
identity, location, time and present activity. After arguing that these
context measures are not the same for other areas of computing, three
guidelines for designing context-aware features for mobile telephony are
provided. We conclude that context information should be defined for the
area in which the researcher is present instead of attempting to provide
an overall definition of context.

1 Introduction

Context-aware computing describes the applications or devices that adapt according to situational variables [1]. Since it was coined in 1994 [4], numerous
definitions of *context* have been provided, both in relation to the development
of context-aware applications and in relation to theoretical contributions to the
area. The first studies defined context as environmental measures, where more
recent definitions acknowledge that context is more than that; for example they
also include features such as the individual's internal state. However, until now,
no common view or definition has been dominant.

To counteract this search for a broad ranging definition of context, the goal of
this paper is to analyze and rank-order context information for a specific domain:
Mobile telephony. The purpose of this is to provide the area with guidelines about
which context information should be supported in context-aware applications.
The domain is chosen as an example of an area that is likely to benefit from
context-aware features. The context information is found through a case study
exploring the use of mobile telephony and its communication facilities.

First related work in the field of context-aware computing is reviewed, and
second, the case study of mobile phone use is presented. Third, the findings of
context information are presented and we provide three guidelines for designing
context-aware applications for mobile communication. Finally, we conclude and
suggest further research.

L. Chittaro (Ed.): Mobile HCI 2003, LNCS 2795, pp. 451–455, 2003.

2   Context-Aware Computing

Context-aware computing is a recent area of research and through the last decade, many context-aware applications have been developed. Context-aware applications include the Olivetti Active Badge system [7] and the Conference Guide [2]. The first application is a stationary service, rerouting phone calls to the phone closest to the individual and the latter is a handheld guide for conference attendants.

The early work often only defined *context* in terms of measurable information. Schilit and Theimer defined it as location, nearby people and objects and changes to those objects [4] and many researchers just added new sensor information to the list in their definition of context [2, 5]. Other, more theoretical approaches, claim that context is a fluid notion, not possible to describe in terms of measurable variables and that a definition should comprise such vague measures as the individuals previous experience [3]. The difference between the two approaches is that application oriented research defines context in relation to their application, where theoretically oriented research attempts to provide a broad definition of context that can be used in the general area of context-aware computing.

Unlike general context-aware applications, only a few applications focus on mobile telephony and even fewer are actually employed in real consumer devices. An example of a context enabled application is the context-call application by Schmidt et al. [5]. It enables the user to preset his/her context, for example, to settings like 'meeting', 'working' or 'at home' and have the information available to potential callers. Context-aware applications actually used in mobile telephony today include location tracking features offered by some phone service providers [6].

3   Case Study and Research Method

The context measure study was designed as an exploratory case study of context measures in mobile telephony. By interviewing high-level users of mobile telephony, the users' contextual cues of the communication situation are traced. The study consists of eight qualitative interviews carried out in the participants' own environment. It was structured into six parts with questions regarding demographics, three measures of context, general use of mobile phones and a scenario. The purpose of the study is to trace the context information in play in mobile communication and to obtain results that can help in providing guidelines for designing context-aware applications.

3.1   Participants

The participants were selected among heavy users of mobile telephony, to get the most thorough insight into their use; their age range is therefore fairly young. People with a variety of occupations were chosen to get broad range of mobile phone use among the participants. The details are listed in table 1.

Table 1. Participant description

Participant	Age and gender	Occupation	Had a mobile phone for
p1	21, female	Service assistant	7 years
p2	21, female	Retail assistant	3 years
p3	25, male	Graduate student	7 years
p4	26, female	Graduate student	6 1/2 years
p5	21, male	Military service	6 years
p6	27, female	Freelance consultant	7 years
p7	19, male	Unemployed	4 years
p8	29, female	Research assistant	6 years

4 Four Pieces of Context Information

The participants all express that their reactions and behavior within their use of mobile phones depend on the overall situation. When elaborating on the more specific situational cues, the information that they exchange and rely on in their communication is fairly consistent. A surprisingly few number of specific measures are in play; the participants mainly mention four. Some other measures are also mentioned but have, according to the participants, limited influence on the overall situation. These secondary measures include whom the person is together with as well as time of day. The specific context information that the participants consider as part of the overall situation is ranked by importance according to the participants:

- Identity of the other person
- Location of both communicators
- Relative time of the receiver of the call
- Present activity of both communicators

Identity is the major factor in communication situations; the participants all agree that how they act and react depends highly on who they are communicating with. This information is technically supported by caller id, meaning that the information is (usually) available immediately in the conversation.

Location is ranked as the second most important context measure that users rely on, which supports the development of location tracking applications in mobile telephony, such as location tracking service mentioned in section 2. Location, however, is a complex piece of information because participants refer to it at several levels of detail, such as in a specific building or office, or 'on the bus'. These nuances are difficult to support technically.

Although time seems to be a simple piece of context information, the finding was that actual time did not matter very much to the users; relative time, defined as the communicator's time limit before a new activity, on the other hand, was important. Many of the participants inferred, as one of the first things, if the receiver had 'time to talk'. This piece of context information is fairly complex and important to support by technological means, however, because it is a fairly important part of the context in mobile telephony, the information should not be ignored in the design of context-aware applications.

The finding that present activity is an important context measure supports the applications that facilitate the display of activity information [5]. However since it is ranked last, these types of applications might not be as relevant as claimed and a more simple version of this function could be a profile tracker based solely on location information.

One relevant observation is that users seem to be satisfied with how the context is already communicated verbally. The exchange of context information is in many cases even seen as a positive part of the conversation, which opens up the question if context-aware functions are appropriate to mobile telephony. The findings of the case study resulted in a set of guidelines that should be observed in designing context-aware functionality for applications in the area.

5   Guidelines for Context-Aware Mobile Services

The case study illustrates that the context information relevant in the mobile communication situation is very different from other areas of computing. For example, the use of stationary work stations where location information is less dominant if not unimportant. Based on the findings of the case study, the following guidelines for designing context-aware applications for mobile telephony are proposed:

1. Provide context information at the time of the users' need
2. Make sure that it is not more desirable for the user to obtain the facilitated context information in another way, e.g. verbally
3. When context information is too complex to support technically it can be broken down to sub-information for the user to interpret

Each guideline is exemplified by context information from the case study: Considering guideline 1, for example, the context information of 'present activity' is not relevant to anyone at anytime; it should be displayed only to potential callers, for example after the number is dialed, but before the call has been put through. The second guideline is derived from the result that users often *want* to infer context information verbally. Context information such as location of the receiver is also difficult to acquire technologically; displaying the position of the user's closest GSM antenna will in many cases only give a fragmented notion of where the person is. Therefore this information is more easy communicated verbally at the moment of communication. An example of applying the third guideline relates to the participants' need for relative time information. This is a complex piece of information not measurable by technology; it is likely that breaking the information down to display the next scheduled appointment provides at least a partial notion of relative time.

From these guidelines it should now be evident that it is not appropriate to use an overall definition of context to develop context-aware applications; the context information differs according to the domain of interest. It is our belief that researchers should analyze context information for their domain in order to facilitate the design of context-aware applications, instead of attempting to provide an overall definition of context as a concept.

6   Conclusions and Further Research

We have stated how defining context in relation to context-aware computing can lead to confusion about how context information should be handled in research. We suggested limiting the definition to a special area, mobile telephony and after reviewing work in context-aware computing, we presented the case study, which provides the foundation for context information that comprise the communication situation in mobile telephony. Finally, we provided three design guidelines for developing context-aware computing in the area of mobile telephony. We concluded that a wide-ranging definition of context is not useful for for designing actual applications, but that each specific area needs to find which context measures are relevant to support.

Because of the study's qualitative nature, the suggested guidelines could benefit from quantitative research. It should also be considered how people perceive actual context-aware features in mobile telephony, to evaluate the actual need for these interactive features and the provided guidelines.

Acknowledgements

Thanks to all the participants of the case study for their active collaboration. Also thanks to Anind Dey for initial comments on the paper and Paul Dourish for inspiration and comments.

References

[1] L. Barkhuus. Context information vs. sensor information: A model for categorizing context in context-aware mobile computing. In *Symposium on Collaborative Technologies and Systems*, pages 127–133, San Diego, CA, 2003.

[2] A. K. Dey, D. Salber, G. D. Abowd, and M. Futakawa. The conference assistant: Combining context-awareness with wearable computing. In *Proceedings of the 3rd International Symposium on Wearable Computers*, pages 21–28, Los Alamitos, CA: IEEE, 1999.

[3] S. Greenberg. Context as a dynamic construct. *Human-Computer Interaction*, 16(2–4):257–269, 2001.

[4] B. Schilit, N. Adams, and R. Want. Context-aware computing applications. In *Proceedings of the 1st International Workshop on Mobile Computing Systems and Applications*, 1994.

[5] A. Schmidt and H.W. Gellersen. Context-aware mobile telephony. *SIGGROUP Bulletin*, 22(1):19–21, April 2001.

[6] Telia. Friendfinder, hitta dina vanner med mobilen. www.teliamobile.se, October 2002.

[7] R. Want, A. Hopper, V. Falco, and J. Gibbons. The active badge location system. *ACM Transactions on Information Systems (TOIS)*, 10(1):91–102, 1992.

Component Model and Programming: A First Step to Manage Human Computer Interaction Adaptation

Anne-Marie Dery-Pinna, Jérémy Fierstone, and Emmanuel Picard

Rainbow project, I3S
930, route des Colles, 06903 Sophia-Antipolis cedex, France
{pinna,fierston,picard}@essi.fr
http://rainbow.essi.fr

Abstract. In this paper we present our component architecture considering HCI as a technical service of a business component just like security or persistence. The dialog between UI and business components is managed by an interaction/coordination service that allows the reconfiguration of components without modifying them. Such a service has proved its interest in software engineering and we will show that it is well adapted to handle adaptation of HCI.

1 Introduction

This paper deals with Human Computer Interaction (HCI) adaptation. Its motivation comes from new requirements from ubiquitous computing where the desktop PC is being progressively replaced or extended by new devices such as graphic tablets, PDAs and mobile phones whose User Interfaces (UI) cannot be identical. Current practices in HCI engineering still consist in developing one interface per target platform. This case-by-case method entails extremely high development and maintenance costs. Another requirement specific to a mobile application is to be dynamically adaptable to the mobile users' requirements (for example to be able to dynamically load/unload new functional tasks). In the field of software engineering, components and reconfiguration mechanisms exist, but these results have never been applied to HCI. The originality of our component architecture[1] is to consider HCI as technical services of a business component (which contains only the application logical part) just like security or persistence. So, we can manage the dialog between UI and business components by an interaction/coordination service that allows the reconfiguration of components without modifying their source code. Such a service has proved its interest in software engineering and seems to be well adapted to handle HCI adaptation.

In the first section, we briefly present the kind of applications and adaptations we target. The second section describes through examples our component model that allows adaptation. Finally we conclude with our perspectives.

---

[1] This work is financially supported by the "*Réseau National en Technologie du Logiciel*".

L. Chittaro (Ed.): Mobile HCI 2003, LNCS 2795, pp. 456-460, 2003.
© Springer-Verlag Berlin Heidelberg 2003

2   Which Kind of Application? Which Kind of Adaptation?

We mainly target applications following Application Service Provider constraints. An illustrative scenario is the case of a management firm building customized applications specifically for each client. Applications are built from an existing library of components such as *Customer, Salesperson, Bill, and Stock*. These components can be specialized and statically or dynamically assembled. We focus on two main goals.

The first goal is to allow a user to get a homogeneous and coherent HCI whatever the device is. *HCI must be adaptable to the device:* a *salesperson* must be able to transfer the application from PC to PDA and PDA to PC. UI components have to be remodelled to follow screen constraints or device limitations. Many research works on multi platform UI covers this problematic. Solutions are often built around markup languages [7,8] that can be translated into concrete interface languages. Most of them are too systematic and do not take into account plasticity of UI except recent works such as [9,12]. Nevertheless, no solution is well designed for component specification.

The second goal is to fill the gap between the components assembly construction of the application's business side, and the classical single-component construction of the application UI, which makes the HCI development and maintenance difficult. We should be able to merge/unmerge UI components according to the business components assembly. At design time, an application can be built from two components statically assembled together (*Customer* and *Bill* in order to invoice the firm customers). But, sometimes, the assembly should be dynamic (at runtime). E.g., in order to facilitate interactivity between the customer and the salesperson, the salesperson must be able to dynamically load a *Stock* business component on his PDA and confirm whether an article is still available or not. The new HCI has to integrate the *Stock* UI components. In the following we will say that *HCI must be adaptable to business constraints*. In HCI research, no work directly addresses the problematic of merging/unmerging components at HCI level. Although classical component-based models (EJB, CCM, .Net) generally propose a static components assembly in the components integration step, only research works [2,3,4] allow dynamically adding or removing a new component. Our solution is based on the independent language ISL and on the interactions service Noah[2] [1] which reifies interactions between components and allows to dynamically changing the behaviour of components linked by an interaction.

3   Adaptation of UI Components

Our component architecture is based on three main parts: (a) the interaction service which prepares components for interacting together and its associated interaction server which stores interaction patterns and binds/unbinds components with interactions (cf. [1] for details on this part), (b) the UI components associated with their business components (cf. 3.1), (c) the merging service for UI components (cf. 3.2).

---

[2] Noah is currently available for the Java RMI and Java EJB platforms. Other implementations of this interaction model have proved its generalization.

3.1   A Component Architecture Integrating UI Components

The originality of our component architecture is to consider HCI as an orthogonal property of a business component. So we split UI in standalone components. In this architecture, a business component can be connected to its UI components by means of software interactions. In this case, these interactions represent the communication controller (as in the Arch model [6]). For example, the *Customer* business component can have two kinds of HCI: one for the customer and another one for the staff service. In the component architecture, the interaction server allows to register and use interaction/coordination schema to assemble business components and to interact with their technical components[3]. In Fig. 1, the interaction *Controller* between a component *Customer* and its graphical representation contains a rule that implies updating the *Customer*'s logical name when the widget *Name* is modified. When the *Customer* and its UI component are unbound, the *Customer* is no longer visualized.

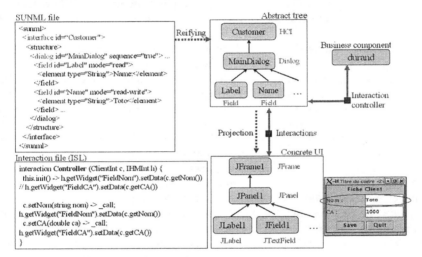

Fig. 1. UI and Business Components

In our model, the UI component contains two parts described by a UI specification: the abstract UI and one or several concrete UI (cf. Fig. 1). The UI specification is described with a small platform independent language, SUNML (for Simple Unified Natural Mark up Language) similar to other multiplatform mark-up languages. SUNML has the particularity to be simple and adapted to structural assembly. The few available abstract widgets of this language (Interface, Dialog, List, Element and Link) can be assembled in order to represent a larger range of abstract widgets (like menu and matrix). The abstract UI is the SUNML object reification (abstract tree). Renderers project the abstract representation into concrete UI in specific platform languages (for instance Swing, VXML and HTML renderers).

---

[3] The interaction model enforces the commutability and associability of integration i.e. these components can be merged in any order without changing the integration consistency.

3.2   A Component Architecture Helping UI Components Merging

The software interactions maintain the consistency between business components and their potential HCI. To manage dynamic adaptation, this solution allows to dynamically changing the UI representation of the business components and its corresponding interactions, depending on the context. This aspect needs a set of predefined interactions patterns and SUNML specifications for this application. The structural assembly of a UI component can be expressed statically in a SUNML file or dynamically computed using the abstract UI. The structural merging/unmerging service manages dynamic assembly using a specific UI merging language based on merging rules (union, intersection, selection): e.g. the union operator is used when the merged UI should correspond to the union of each set of widgets, and the substitution operator when a widget common for each merged UI should be unified (Fig. 2). The resulting assembly becomes a new UI component, which can be assembled or rendered as the other UI components.

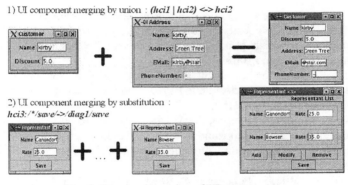

Fig. 2. Structural merging of UI components

4   Conclusion

In this paper, we have briefly presented the specificity of our component-based architecture. One of the main advantages of SUNML is that it provides a HCI component-based construction which allows reusing existing HCI components. SUNML is simple but this could be considered as a disadvantage due to the limited usability of the generated UI. Moreover the renderers do not integrate the checking of interface plasticity. The main difficulties will be to solve plasticity problems of component merging. Our objective is to propose a programming environment integrating HCI adaptation. The first implementation of this environment already contains a SUNML editor and parser, Swing and VoiceXML renderers, a merging service, the Noah server and the Noah service. The programming environment is under development. We will improve its facilities to change one of the basic components (e.g. SUNML parser) and to add new components (e.g. a renderer). So we are optimistic on the integration of HCI research results such as user interface plasticity [10] and context specification tool [11]. In the future, we aim to deal with distributed HCI. In this case, the abstract part could be located on the server side and the concrete parts on several devices. For this purpose, we intend to use the Noah server, which allows the components to run on different devices at the same time. Finally, the HCI could be migrable, thanks to the user interface abstract reification, which can maintain HCI data.

References

[1]   A-M. Pinna-Dery, M. Blay-Fornarino, B. Arcier, L. Mule, and S. Moisan. Distributed access knowledge-based system: Reified interaction service for trace and control. IProc. of DOA 2001, Rome, Italy, pages 76-84, September 17-20 2001.

[2]   M.T. Segarra, F. André. A Framework for Dynamic Adaptation in Wireless Environments. Proc. of TOOLS Europe 2000, June 2000, Mont St. Michel, St. Malo, France.

[3]   Eric Bruneton, Thierry Coupaye and Jean-Bernard Stefani. Recursive and Dynamic Software Composition with Sharing. In Proceedings of the 7th ECOOP International Workshop on Component-Oriented Programming (WCOP'02), Malaga (Spain), June 10th-14th, 2002.

[4]   Pawlak R., Seinturier L., Duchien L., Florin G., « JAC : A Flexible and Efficient Solution for Aspect-Oriented Programming in Java », A.Y.,S.M., Eds., Reflection 01, v. LNCS 2192,

[5]   O. Nano, M. Blay-Fornarino, A-M. Dery, and M. Riveill. An abstract model for integrating and composing services in component platforms. In Seventh International Workshop on Component-Oriented Programming ECOOP'2002, Malaga, June 10, 2002.

[6]   L. Bass, R. Little, R. Pellegrino, S. Reed, R. Seacord, S. Sheppard, The Arch Model: Seeheim Revisited (version 1.0). « The UIMS Tool Developers Workshop » (April 1991) in ACM SIGCHI Bulletin Vol. 24, No. 1, January 1992.

[7]   C. Phanariou. « UIML: a Device-Independent User Interface Markup Language ». PhD Software Ingeneering, faculty of Virginia Polytechnic Institute and State University Blacksburg, Virginia, September, 2000.

[8]   A. Puerta, J. Eisenstein, XIML: a common representation for interaction data, In procs of IUI'02, pp 214-215 (see also http://www.ximl.org)

[9]   Calvary, G., Coutaz, J., Thevenin, D., Limbourg, Q., Souchon, N., Bouillon, L. Vanderdonckt, Plasticity of User Interfaces: A Revised Reference Framework, First International in Proc. TAMODIA'2002, Bucarest, 18-19 July 2002

[10] G. Calvary, J. Coutaz, D. Thevenin. A Unifying Reference Framework for the Development of Plastic User Interfaces. IFIP WG2.7 (13.2) Working Conference, EHCI01,Toronto, May 2001, Springer Verlag Publ., LNCS 2254, M. Reed Little, L. Nigay Eds, pp.173-192.

[11] Dey, A.K., Salber, D. Abowd, G.D. A Conceptual Framework and a Toolkit for Supporting the Rapid Prototyping of Context-Aware Applications in Human-Computer Interaction (HCI) Journal, Vol. 16(2-4), 2001, pp. 97-166.

[12] Paternò, F., Santoro, C. Teresa. One Model, Many Interfaces. Proceedings of CADUI 2002, Valenciennes, France, May 2002.

Mobile Tele-instruction
Using Interactive Augmented Reality

Jun Park

Computer Engineering Department, Hong-ik University
Sangsu-dong 72-1 Mapo-Gu, Seoul 121-791, Korea
jpark@cs.hongik.ac.kr

Abstract. Augmented Reality technologies, which enable virtual object overlay on real images, are useful for interactive tele-instruction. Current advances in mobile computing and imaging technologies enabled image capture on small mobile devices (e.g., PDA's) using micro cameras. However, this imaging capability is not being efficiently leveraged, not yielding many useful applications. In this paper, an interactive mobile tele-instruction technology is described where an on-site non-expert can be instructed using graphics and text annotations created by an off-site expert. For tracking and 3D visualization, augmented reality technologies are applied.

1 Introduction

Augmented Reality (AR) is a human computer interaction technology used to enhance the user's perception of and interaction with the real and the virtual environments [1]. Using AR technologies, users can perceive computer-generated virtual objects as well as the real environment. Applications of AR include assembly [2], architecture [3], medicine [4], and collaboration [5]. AR technologies can be also applied to tele-instruction and tele-manipulation through superimposed graphical and text annotations composed by remote experts. On-site users, instructed by virtual information, are able to interact with the user's real environment, and successfully perform given tasks. This tele-instruction system, if implemented on mobile device, is a mobile and collaborative AR system [8].

Recent advances in mobile technologies allow for applications that require higher computation than before. Wireless communication services also become easily accessible in wide range of area. For example, Korean government, in cooperation with Intel Korea and LG-IBM, started "Mobile Jeju" project to provide wireless LAN services over Jeju island. In addition, micro cameras are available for PDA's and mobile phones. Therefore, mobile technologies combined with wireless communication services form basis for AR-based tele-instruction systems.

There are several issues for mobile tele-instruction system design: mobile computing power, device categories, image analysis & pose computation, and interactive AR authoring. n this paper, these design issues are discussed. Interactive AR tech-

L. Chittaro (Ed.): Mobile HCI 2003, LNCS 2795, pp. 461–465, 2003.

nologies are also introduced including pose computation, 3D feature calibration, graphics overlay, and AR authoring. Lastly, implementation methods of marker-detection and pose computation are described.

2   System Architecture

For mobile tele-instruction, two types of sensory information can be provided to the on-site users: visual and aural information. Aural communication is convenient for general information exchange including questioning and answering. Visual information is effective when the text information is spatially linked to a specific part of the real environment or when the information takes graphical form. AR technologies are used to maintain spatial linkage between the real environment and virtual text or graphical information.

The scenario of our tele-instruction system is as follows. The on-site user posts questions with two or more snap shots of the user's real environment. The remote expert provides answers with relevant text and graphical information (instruction) that are spatially linked to the real environment. Three-dimensional positions of certain points are computed to build spatial linkage between the virtual and the real objects. The provided visual information remains visually linked to the real environment images as the on-site user pans or zooms in the environment while practicing the instructions (Fig. 1).

For AR-based mobile tele-instruction system, several tasks are required: interactive AR authoring, 3D feature calibration, image analysis and pose computation, and virtual information visualization. AR authoring is performed by a remote expert on the remote server, while pose computation and visualization are generally computed on the mobile client. These components are depicted in Fig. 1.

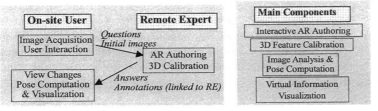

Fig. 1. Mobile Tele-instruction System: Scenario (left) and Main Components (right)

3   Design Issues

In this section, mobile tele-instruction system design issues are introduced and discussed. The issues include mobile computation, mobile device categories, image analysis & pose computation, and interactive AR authoring.

3.1   Mobile Computation

On desktop, notebook, or wearable computers, AR systems are performed in real-time: in most cases, frame rates are above 10 fps. However, despite of recent advances in mobile technologies, real-time image processing, and hence, real-time AR tracking and visualization are not feasible for small mobile devices such as PDA's and mobile phones.

Alternatively, still images can be used to provide instructions and virtual annotations on user's hand-held mobile units periodically (e.g., every one second) or on user's request. Because augmented images are displayed on user's hand-held devices, non-continuous display would not much reduce user's perception of the environment.

3.2   Mobile Device Categories

Small mobile devices can be categorized mainly into PDA's and mobile phones. PDA's provide stylus and touch-screen that are useful for user interaction, especially in AR-based tele-instruction. Graphics capabilities of PDA's have been also advanced. As an example, 3D graphics libraries are available for Windows CE based PDA's [7]. Owing to technology availability, image analysis, camera pose computation, and 3D virtual information visualization can be performed on PDA's (Fig. 2).

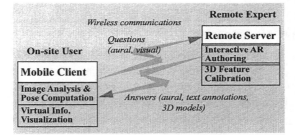

Fig. 2. Tele-instruction System for PDA's

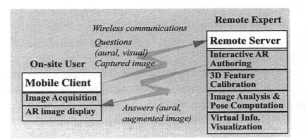

Fig. 3. Tele-instruction System for Mobile Phones

On the contrary, user-interaction and graphics capabilities of mobile phones do not meet the requirements of AR-based tele-instruction. The computational capabilities are also below the requirements of image processing and other computations. For tele-instruction on mobile phones, arrow keys can be used, in place of stylus, to select a region from the sub-areas (grids) of the captured image. Image processing, pose computation, and graphics overlay can be performed on the remote server based on the images sent to the server. The resulting augmented images can be transferred back to the on-site client (Fig. 3). The Role of mobile phones is to send acquired images to the remote server, and display the received augmented images.

3.3   Image Analysis & Pose Computation

Images produced by micro cameras of mobile devices are of low quality, and may be involved in high degrees of lens distortion and lots of noise. Lens distortion can be recovered by off-line calibration. Use of Gaussian filters can reduce noise in the image. In order to reduce computation for image analysis, simple artificially-designed markers can be used. Three or more of these markers (with their known 3D positions and detected 2D image space positions) can be used for camera pose computation.

Low computational pose computation methods can be also employed. Instead of optimization methods or iterative methods, which require initial estimates, closed-form methods can be used for marker-based pose computation. Multiple solution problems of closed-form methods can be solved by switching between solutions based on user's selection.

3.4   Interactive AR Authoring

Virtual annotations can be interactively created by remote experts. To build spatial linkage between the real environment and the virtual information, 3D positions of certain features need to be calculated. With two or more images, 3D positions can be recursively calculated [6].

Fig. 4. An Example of 2D Graphical Annotations

Given 3D positions of certain points, virtual information can be rendered in the forms of text, 2D graphics, and 3D graphics. Text can be used to add explanation to certain parts of the environment. In most cases, 2D graphics is enough to provide assembly or maintenance instructions. For example, frequently-used instructions such as rotation and push / pull can be denoted using 2D graphical primitives (Fig. 4). For rendering 3D objects (e.g., CAD models), 3D graphics libraries [7] can be used.

4   Implementation and Conclusion

Major parts of the AR-based tele-instruction system have been implemented targeting a PDA-based tele-instruction applied to copy machine maintenance. In this application, an on-site non-expert asks for remote expert's instruction in case of copy machine mal-function. The image analysis, pose computation, and 2D / 3D visualization are performed on the PDA, while interactive AR authoring and 3D feature calibration are performed on the remote server.

To reduce computation, low computational methods were employed. For image analysis, a simple blob search algorithm was used to search for dark markers under favorable illumination conditions. When marker detection algorithm fails, users can use stylus to manually point on the markers. These markers are used for camera pose computation. For pose computation, classical three-point method was used [9].

In this paper, a low computational AR-based tele-instruction method was introduced. Using this method, dynamically created virtual information can be rendered on user's mobile device periodically or on user's request. The virtual information provides step-by-step instruction to the on-site user.

References

[1]   Ron Azuma, "A survey of augmented reality", Presense, Vol.6, No.4, August 1997, pp 355-386

[2]   D. Curtis, D. Mizell, P. Gruenbaum, and A. Janin, "Several Devils in the Details: Making an AR Application Work in the Airplane Factory", Proc Int'l Workshop Augmented Reality ,98 (IWAR'98). San Francisco, 1 Nov. 1998, pp. 47-60, 1999.

[3]   Webster, Feiner, MacIntyre, Massie, Krueger, "Augmented Reality in Architectural Construction, Inspection, and Renovation", Proceedings of Computing in Civil Engi-neering, ASCE, (1996) 913-919

[4]   W.E.L. Grimson, T. Lozano-Perez, W.M. Wells III, G.J. Ettinger, S.J. White, and R. Kikinis, "An Automatic Registration Method for Frameless Stereotaxy, Image Guided Surgery, and Enhanced Reality Visualization", In Transactions on Medical Imaging, 1996

[5]   M. Billinghurst, H. Kato, "Collaborative Mixed Reality", Proc. Int'l Symp. Mixed Reality (ISMR '99). Mixed Reality - Merging Real and Virtual Worlds, Yokohama, Japan, 9-11 Mar. 1999, pp. 261-284.

[6]   Ulrich Neumann and Jun Park, "Extendible Object Centric Tracking for Augmented Reality", Proceedings of IEEE VRAIS (Virtual Reality Annual International Symposium)'98, March 1998

[7]   http://ekkla.free.fr/versengl/pgopengl_uk.htm

[8]   P. Renevier, L. Nigay, "Mobile Collaborative Augmented Reality: the Augmented Stroll", Proceedings of EHCI'01, IFIP WG2.7 (13.2) Conference, Toronto, May 2001, LNCS 2254, Spinger-Verlag, pp. 315-334.

[9]   Fischler, M. A. and Bolles, R. "Random sample consensus:- a paradigm for model fitting with applications to image analysis and automated cartography", Communications of the ACM, 24(6), 1981, pp.381–395.

A Study on the Predicate Prediction Using Symbols in Augmentative and Alternative Communication System

Eun-sil Lee[1], Ein-jeong Hwang[1], Tai-sung Hur[2], Yo-seop Woo[1], and Hong-ki Min[1]

[1] Dept. of Inf. & Telecomm. Eng., Univ. of Incheon, Korea
les@incheon.ac.kr
[2] Dept. of CIS., Inha Technical College, Incheon, Korea

Abstract. This study generally is purposed to develop a mobile augmentative and alternative communication system (hereinafter referred to as "a mobile AAC system"). Also the device is aimed as a mobile AAC system for HCI, allowing a handicapped person to make a general communication with others in a free and convenient manner. This study specifically presents a method of predicting predictions, which contributes to reducing the size of the mobile system. This method includes selecting vocabulary and classifying it by domains so as to meet the characteristics of the mobile AAC communication, using a noun thesaurus for semantic analysis, and building a sub-category dictionary. Predicting predicates by selecting symbols in accordance with this method is tested and the utility thereof is confirmed.

1   Introduction

Our society rapidly changes as information communication technology develops, and our daily life greatly becomes convenient. The progress in technology allows us to easily get data in a desired format in a desired place. However, the technology of processing language mostly depends upon inputting words by using a keyboard. Handicapped people, who have problems in using a keyboard to input words, are left isolated from various information. Although systems utilizing the voice-recognition technology are developed, such is never helpful to auditorily handicapped persons who can talk only with finger language.

So they have to be assisted by other devices. A variety of a mobile AAC devices and techniques are now existing. One of them is the sentence generation system which should be adaptable to mobile AAC(augmentative and alternative communication). It should be made as easy for the users as possible. So we use pre-stored messages and message prediction techniques(1). Both methods are called acceleration techniques because their purpose is to increase the speed of communication. Most of the word-based techniques use a frequency of use for word prediction. The software presents word choices based on previously written words(1). Sometimes they also use abbreviation expansion system, but users must memorize a

L. Chittaro (Ed.): Mobile HCI 2003, LNCS 2795, pp. 466–470, 2003.

lot of encoded words(2). Recently it has been developed by selecting semantic symbol by users and lexical sense analysis for prediction(3).

This study presents a method for predicting predicates, thereby allowing the size of the system to be reduced. The method includes building a noun thesaurus based on concepts used to browser information in a natural-language process and building a sub-category dictionary.

2   Classification of Vocabulary

Since the device is aimed as a mobile AAC system, situations of conversation and type of handicaps should be considered, and vocabulary is required to be collected and classified in accordance with ages. Domains are classified into restaurant, home, transportation, shopping and hospital etc. Vocabulary frequently used regardless of place is classified into a main vocabulary section.

The purpose of classifying vocabulary is to provide users with mostly frequently used terms or vocabulary in a specific place so that the users can easily select desired vocabulary. If the vocabulary is classified in accordance with domains, prediction reliability will increase.

Each domain is provided with the vocabulary found in finger-language related sites or general conversation texts and the vocabulary selected by those who are engaged in the special education. The vocabulary is classified into words/expressions for the input part and words/expressions for the predicate prediction part. The input part mainly includes nouns, each of which has a corresponding semantic symbol, and the predicate prediction part includes verbs, adjective-form verbs and application form of verbs. The domain of place is divided into regions such as home, restaurant, transportation and hospital. The vocabulary is classified in accordance with regions. Greeting expressions and auxiliary words are classified to belong to the main vocabulary section.

3   Method for Predicting Predicates

The Korean language is called as a "situation-centered language", since situation, meaning and context play a more important role rather than syntactic characteristics. Predicts are modified by complements to specifically express a situation. The use of complements are restricted depending upon the situation expressed by predicts, which is called "sub-categorization." Thesaurus refers to a dictionary that shows a hierarchy of the vocabulary including predicts and words meaningfully related thereto. The vocabulary is arranged by separating a sentence into an input part and a predicate prediction part. A semantic symbol corresponding to a noun is formed by morphemes. As for nouns, a semantic symbol for each noun is provided, thereby building up database based on concepts.

In order to predict predicates, required is a step of deriving what is desired to be expressed by matching the meanings of the vocabulary, as represented in a noun thesaurus, and the situations expressed by predicates, as contained in a pattern dictionary, with the semantic dependency. This is referred to as a "limited selection, " and predicates are predicted by the limited selection. Predicate application forms are classified by domains. Field for predicate application enables making various sentences and changing basic predicate forms to desired application forms.

A sub-categorization dictionary is build up based on the thesaurus, sentence pattern and predicate application forms. The sub-categorization dictionary includes basic forms of predicates, application form, and nouns related to predicates, and postpositional words, together with the meanings thereof. The sub-categorization dictionary is based on the reference numbers of sentences, application forms of predicates, and postpositional words to be added to nouns that are inputted. Thesaurus dictionary of nouns and sub-categorization dictionary are build-up and predicates for an inputted semantic symbol are presented by the limited selection. The mostly often-used predicates are located on the very top of the pop menu.

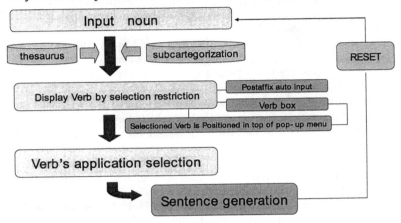

Fig. 1. Flow of Formation of Sentence

4   Results

The transportation domain is taken as an example for explaining the structure in accordance with the a mobile AAC system. Main vocabulary that is often used regardless of place, including greeting words, is provided on the right side. The vocabulary for each branch is provided at the center, together with their semantic symbols. The semantic symbols for the same branch are located near one another, so that those related semantic symbols are easily accessible. The semantic symbols belong to the identical branch are colored with the identical color so that symbols for a branch can be clearly distinguished from those for another branch. The semantic symbols are pictures associated with the meaning of the vocabulary, which are provided together with words so that a user can easily recognize what the symbols mean. However, since semantic symbols specifically used for the mobile AAC system have not yet been developed, the images, as included in the clip art, are instead employed.

When a user selects a semantic symbol, the message, "the selected word," appears before the word corresponding to the symbol is displayed. If the right side of the mouse is clicked the semantic analysis and the limited selection for the word are made on the basis of the noun thesaurus and the sub-categorization dictionary. Fig. 2 shows how the corresponding phrase is outputted and possible predicates are presented by the limited selection on a pop-up menu, when "train ticket for Pusan" is inputted by the corresponding semantic symbol. The predicates are presented in basic forms thereof and also provided with the marks such as . ? ! , which are required when the type of sentence is changed. If a user selects the basic form of predicate, the predicate is converted to a desired application form. Postpositional words are properly added before a complete sentence is produced at the top of the right side.

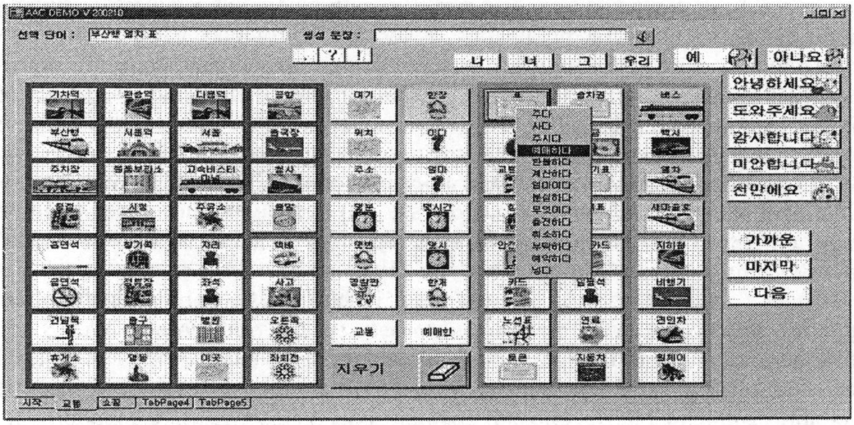

Fig. 2. Structure I in accordance with mobile AAC System (Predicted Predicates)

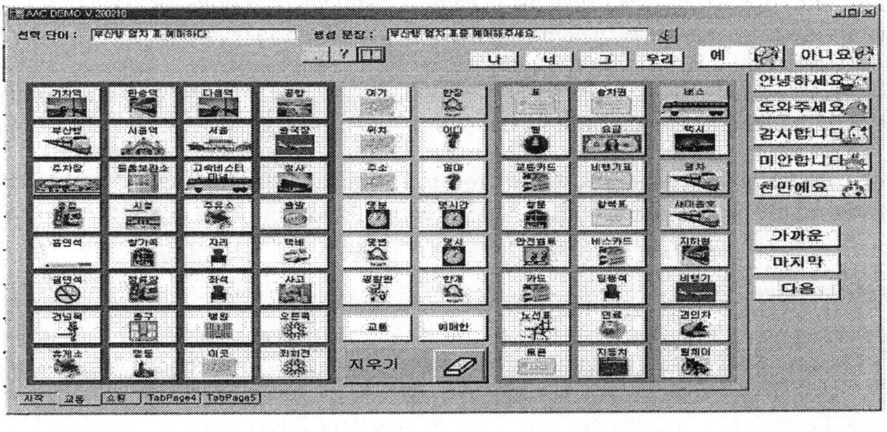

Fig. 3. Structure II in accordance with mobile ACC system (Completion of Sentence after Predicate Selection)

Figure 3 shows the process for producing a complete sentence, which includes selecting a semantic symbol, selecting a desired predicate on a pop-menu, selecting a desired application form of the predicate, and adding proper postpositional words.

Further, in order to increase the accuracy in predicting predicates, predicates once selected by a user may be seen on the very top of the pop-menu, when the next predicate is selected. As a result, frequently used predicates are located on the upper part of the pop-menu.

5   Conclusion

The mobile AAC system is a kind of communication device for handicapped people. In the system, a method for predicating predicates is provided, thereby reducing the size of device. Noun thesaurus and the sub-categorization dictionary are build up, which enables predicting predicates. Application forms of predicates are presented to provide sentences more suited to a conversation. According to the system, postpositional words are properly added to nouns, thereby helping a user having a limited knowledge of grammar to make a perfect sentence. It is not easy to symbolize all the vocabulary in a limited-sized device. In particular, it is more difficult to symbolize predicates than nouns, because specifying states or actions meant by predicates into symbols is not simple work. Thus, an attempt to predict predicates by the semantic symbolization is so desirable. The system, in combination with a synthetic voice system, will be developed to be a conversation system.

Our country is yet in the infant stage in developing a mobile AAC system, while other advanced countries have seen some progress in studying the related field, while developing various models. The currently developed a mobile AAC system does not apply to all types of handicapped. The present study is purposed to develop terminals for handicapped people in terms of intellectual human interface, which will contribute to upgrade the level of the existing terminals. Accordingly, in order to realize more substantial a mobile AAC system, a complex study on various fields including a mobile AAC system's size, weight, design and electronics is required.

Acknowledgments

This work was partially supported by research fund from University of Incheon and Multimedia Research Center of the KOSEF.

References

[1]   David R. Beukelman, Pat Mirenda,   *"Augmentative and Alternative Communication,* Management of Severe Communication Disorders in Children and Adults." Paul .H. Brookes publishing Co. 1995

[2]   Sharon L. Glennen, DeCote, Ed.D, *"The Handbook of Augmentative and Alternative Communication."* Singular Publishing Group, Inc. 1996

[3]   Gittins, D. Icon-based Human-Computer Interaction, International Journal of Man-Machine Studies, 24, 519, 543, 1986

Electronic Navigation – Some Design Issues

Corina Sas, Michael O'Grady and Gregory O'Hare

Practice & Research in Intelligent Systems & Media (PRISM),
Department of Computer Science, University College Dublin (UCD),
Belfield, Dublin 4, Ireland
{corina.sas,michael.j.ogrady,gregory.ohare}@ucd.ie

Abstract. Navigation support will form a critical component of future mobile computing systems. However, the ability of people to navigate in unfamiliar environments can vary substantially. In this paper, it is argued that the current generation of mobile devices and associated software does not adequately support the navigational requirements of a broad segment of users and that alternative strategies and design criteria need to be considered.

1 Introduction

Mobile computing is likely to be the next major computer-usage paradigm. As such, the area remains the focus of much research as advances in pervasive computing, wearable computing and location-aware computing testifies. One service that is considered fundamental in future mobile computing environments is that of navigation support. Such support could encompass an electronic map with the user's position highlighted in real-time or, perhaps, route planning and direction giving.

Researchers have known for some time that males and females adopt different strategies when navigating in the real world [1]. The reason for this difference, possible routed in anthropology, is still unclear but indications are that males have a somewhat higher spatial ability than females. Though navigation aids are starting to proliferate under various guises, there are no indications that the differing spatial abilities of their target population are being considered and addressed. In short, the female population is currently at a disadvantage when using current navigation tools; a disadvantage that may have serious ramifications when carrying out their everyday work. A critical challenge for researchers in mobile HCI is to identify design principles that can compensate for and ultimately eliminate this disadvantage.

In the following sections, the current state-of-the-art in electronic navigation is briefly outlined. After this, Gulliver's Genie, a mobile electronic tourist guide is introduced. The results of evaluations conducted on it are then analysed and discussed in terms of the gender differences that emerged.

L. Chittaro (Ed.): Mobile HCI 2003, LNCS 2795, pp. 471–475, 2003.

2   Advances in Electronic Navigation

Though there exists quite a number of technologies that can be used to determine position, techniques using satellites are by far the most prevalent The Global Positioning System (GPS) is the most popular system at present and is being used in many diverse areas. Reasons for its success include among others, reliability and worldwide coverage. GLONASS, deployed by the Russian Federation, offers similar features to GPS. It is important to remember that both GPS and GLONASS were designed with military applications in mind and remain under the control of their respective defence ministries. More recently, the EU have launched the Galileo initiative, a system oriented towards the needs of civilians and includes safeguards regarding the status and reliability of the positioning signal. Galileo is scheduled to be fully operational by 2008. In the meantime, significant effort is being expended in the area of Satellite Based Augmentation Systems (SBASs) which seek to augment the original GPS signal with addition data leading to more accurate position readings.

An alternative to satellite techniques includes approaches based on the topologies of cellular telecommunication networks. The impetus for research into such techniques came from the FCC's E-911 directive, which stipulates that network operators must be able to pinpoint an emergency call to within 100 meters on average. Technically, deploying networks that utilise these techniques has proved somewhat difficult. However, the next generation or Third Generation (3G) of cellular networks will actively support a number of such techniques.

3   A Mobile Electronic Tourist Guide

A portable electronic guide that tourists could carry around with them while exploring a city is regarded by some as an archetypal mobile computing application. A number of prototypes of such systems have been developed in the laboratory, for example, CRUMPET [2] and GUIDE [3]. Likewise, a number of commercial products have also been developed including Vindigo [4] and Port@ble Guide [5].

3.1   Gulliver's Genie

Gulliver's Genie [6] was developed to provide navigation and location-aware services to tourists. An additional benefit that it can offer is a better understanding of how tourists act when exploring an outdoor environment. The system is hosted on a PDA which is connected to a set of back-end servers via a wireless data connection. GPS is used for determining position and a suite of intelligent agents has been developed for anticipating the tourist's requirements. Adaptivity is a key principal underpinning the Genie so all information presented to the tourist has been adapted to their location, orientation and interest profile.

Navigation support is delivered via a geocoded electronic map. In essence, this is an electronic image of an appropriately scaled map that has been tagged with such information as facilitates the swift resolution of a GPS position into its corresponding point on the electronic map. The map itself, supplied by the local municipal authority, shows routes and buildings. However, any item that is of likely to be of interest to tourists has been highlighted and labelled (Fig. 1). As the tourist explores their environment, their position and orientation on the map is highlighted and continuously updated. In this way, they can see their position relative to the various attractions at a glance. The option of explicitly scrolling the map is also available.

Fig. 1. The Genie's navigation screen. In this case the tourist is approaching a church

3.2   Evaluation

A thorough user evaluation of the Genie has been carried out here on the campus of University College Dublin. Though relatively modern, the campus contains a number of historical building as well as being adorned with various works of art. Participants were invited to take a tour of the campus with the Genie for about 40 minutes. On completion, a questionnaire was filled in which, amongst other things, tried to ascertain how they rated the Genie as an aid when navigating. The sample group consisted of 40 subjects of which less than half were female (46%). Though most of the participants had some experience of computing, a small majority (56%) did not have any prior experience of PDAs. Initial reaction to the Genie was favourable with over 85% of participants indicating satisfaction with the system. From a navigational perspective, just over half (51%) identified navigation support as the Genie's most important feature. It also emerged that females were significantly more dependant on external aids such as maps ($t(35) = 2.03$, $p < 0.05$) and guides ($t(35) = 2.65$, $p < 0.05$). To identify differences when using the Genie and to formulate solutions for a better design that would address the specific needs of female users, we investigated both sense of direction and the manner of using the Genie. Without identifying statistically significant differences, the males' sense of direction surpasses the females' sense of direction. In fact, twice as many females (40%) consider their sense of direction as poor or average, against 21% of males who gave the same estimation (Fig. 2). With respect to the manner of using the system, we identified a difference regarding the rotation of the device. When asked about the Genie's support for orientation, female users admitted to rotating the PDA so that the map coincided with their own immediate heading significantly more often than males ($t(35) = 2.09$, $p < 0.05$).

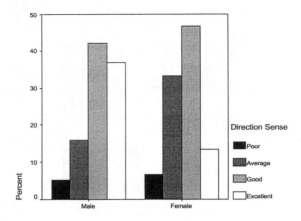

Fig. 2. Users' sense of direction

3.3   Implications for Navigation

Results of the evaluations clearly indicate that users see navigation support as a useful and desirable feature. Findings suggest not only the necessity but also the means for improving system usability to specifically address the needs of female subjects, a significant segment of potential users. The option of being able to ascertain their position at all times was an attractive feature and helped in maintaining good position and orientation awareness. Naturally this provided a comfort and reassurance to some thus facilitating a more proactive and adventurous approach to exploration.

3.4   Some Possible Solutions

Some clues as to how the navigation issue might be addressed have been gleaned from further analysis of the evaluation feedback.

- Automatic map rotation which would match the user's heading: This solution is suggested by the previously presented findings, as well as being mentioned in the users' answers regarding system improvements. This (optional) facility would enable users gain a better spatial awareness and orientation. The position on the map and its corresponding position in the real world would be easily identified thus reducing the cognitive overload associated with the manual rotation of the device.
- Improved Position: While GPS enables position readings to within 20 meters on average, this can make the association between one''s actual position and that on the electronic map somewhat difficult. If an SBAS can be used, readings of up to

five meters in accuracy can be obtained thus improving the situation dramatically.

- 3D Interface: Augmenting the electronic map with its 3D equivalent was another suggestion as to how the interface might be improved. In this case, the user would have the option of selecting their preferred mode. When using a 3D interface, the user would have the 3D equivalent of the real world in front of them. However, the success of such an approach is closely related to the availability of more accurate position readings as any divergence between the 3D scene and its geographic equivalent would be even more pronounced than when using a normal 2D map.

4   Future Work

An immediate priority is to improve the accuracy of the position readings available to the Genie by using an SBAS, probably the European Geostationary Navigation Overlay Service (EGNOS). Different applications involving 3D representations of real or virtual environments have been developed with the purpose of improving user's navigation. However, few attempts have been concerned with the usability of PDA devices supporting navigational tasks. Tourist attractions could be emphasised by presenting them in a 3D form at the user's request, in the context of a 2D map. This would enable the users to maintain their orientation due to the bird's eye view afforded by the 2D map, as well as providing additional information on landmarks of interest. Therefore, the development of a mixed 3D landmark representation in the context of 2D maps, is another direction which should be tested by further studies.

References

[1]   Halpern, D. F.: Sex Differences in Cognitive Abilities. 3rd edition. Lawrence Erlbaum Associates, Inc. Mahwah, NJ 07430–2262 (2000)
[2]   Poslad, S., Laamanen, H., Malaka, R., Nick, A., Buckle, P., Zipf, A., "CRUMPET: Creation of User-friendly Mobile Services Personalised For Tourism", In: Second International Conference on 3G Mobile Communication Technologies, London, UK, March 2001.
[3]   Cheverst, K., Mitchell, K., Davies, N.: The Role of Adaptive Hypermedia in a Context-Aware Tourist Guide. Communications of the ACM, Vol. 45 (5) (2002) 47-51.
[4]   Vindigo, Inc. New York. http://www.vindigo.com
[5]   Port@ble Internet, Inc. New Jersey, http://www.portableinternet.com/frommers
[6]   O'Hare, G., O'Grady, M..: Gulliver's Genie: A Multi-Agent System for Ubiquitous and Intelligent Content Delivery. Computer Communications, Vol. 26 (11) (2003), 1177-1187.

The Use of Statistically Derived Personas in Modelling Mobile User Populations

John Greaney and Mark Riordan

Centre for Creative Technologies and Applications
School of Science and Technology
Dun Laoghaire Institute of Art, Design and Technology
Kill Avenue, Dun Laoghaire, Co. Dublin, Ireland
John.Greaney@iadt.ie

Abstract. The successful and effective mobile services of the future will be those that meet the needs of users. Therefore, any mobile service design project must have the needs of users paramount in its thinking. In order to keep the characteristics and needs of a user population to the fore throughout design and development, the technique of Personas is examined. This technique involves creating a set of composite characters to represent a target population. An obvious challenge is the choice of the set of Personas to represent a given population. This paper discusses how this choice might be made on the basis of a statistical analysis of a user population.

1   Rationale

People vary in their needs and therefore HCI professionals need valid ways of capturing this diversity. Too often, these individual differences can be overlooked and talk of "the user" may focus on qualities or attributes that are not grounded in data. Further, when data has been collected it is important that it is communicated in ways that are easy-to-understand and memorable. To address these points we explore the use of "Principal Components Analysis" and "Personas". We argue that these techniques have a place in the toolkit of HCI professionals.

2   Background:
Can Technology Enable Community Interaction?

The examination of the techniques presented here comes from the work of the NOMAD project. This project, begun in 2002, is a collaboration between the Irish Institutes of Technology at Dun Laoghaire, Dundalk and Waterford. The overall aim of this three year project is to study what technical, process or HCI design techniques work best when designing for the mobile environment. In furthering this work NOMAD is using a demonstrator application focused on enhancing the community life of academic institutions with particular focus on student life.

L. Chittaro (Ed.): Mobile HCI 2003, LNCS 2795, pp. 476-480, 2003.

The campus environment contains a diverse user base ideally suited to experimental deployment of innovative services. Full time and part time students, support staff, academic staff, administration and visitors all interact with the campus environment in many different ways, with differing objectives and utilizing both manual and automated process.

The data here are designed to measure "Social Capital". Whereas Physical Capital refers to physical objects and Human Capital refers to properties of individuals, Social Capital refers to connections among individuals – social networks and the norms of reciprocity and trustworthiness that arise from them [1]. Technology may have a role in enhancing social relations and Resnick [2] has coined the term "SocioTechnicalCapital" to refer to productive technology-mediated social relations.

Given the goal of the demonstrator application it was felt that a study to measure Social Capital in the student community would provide the basis for extracting relevant Personas for the population. In our research we adapted an existing measure of Social Capital [3] as a tool for understanding key user characteristics with respect to the community of students. The target population were students in a particular third level college. The on-line questionnaire was completed anonymously by students in class.

3   Characterising the Mobile User with Personas

A Persona can be defined as a composite character that is used to convey key characteristics of a population in a memorable fashion. For example, *"Kate is a 30 year old school teacher who uses her mobile mainly for social purposes, she values security etc."* By constructing a set of such Personas the key aspects of the population's attitudes and behaviours can be captured. Although Personas originated in field of marketing, Cooper [4] has presented a case for their use in design.

Personas act as a medium for communication. How many design team members will read or remember detailed market research and usability reports? Personas take advantage of the mind's ability to extrapolate from partial knowledge of people to create coherent characters and project them into new situations [5]. For instance, in attempting to answer questions like. "Why are we building this feature?" we can instead ask "Would Kate use this feature?" The team may well develop a sense of "Kate's" attitude to the feature by extrapolating their knowledge of "Kate" but in the absence of specific knowledge of a single real user's attitude to the feature.

It is important to remember that this technique is not necessarily meant to replace primary sources of user data but rather to complement it. In any case, Cooper [4] argues that designing for any one external person is better that trying to design vaguely for everyone or, worse still, specifically for oneself.

A key question in using this technique is how to choose a set of Personas for a given user population. This can be carried out in a semi-intuitive fashion. Recently, Grudin and Pruitt [5] have argued that Cooper appeals to intuition rather than data. Instead they emphasize Personas constructed on the basis on empirical data. This paper outlines an attempt by the authors to create a set of Personas from a statistical analysis of a user population.

4   Characterising the Mobile User Using Principal Components Analysis (PCA)

Principal Components Analysis (PCA) is a multivariate technique enabling a large data set to be simplified. When research reports contain only single variable statistics about a population this does not tell you how the information is inter-related. For example, if 50% of users want feature X and 50% of users what feature Y, this does not tell you whether the same people want both or everyone wants either X or Y. The truth is likely to be somewhere in between. When the list of questions expands we can see that we need techniques for capturing the inter-relationships between data and communicating these findings in ways that people find easy to grasp. In PCA, variables that are correlated with one another and which are also largely independent of other subsets of variables are combined. These factors are thought to represent underlying processes that have created the correlations among variables.

Table 1. Principal Components derived from the data showing the questions with the highest factor loadings

Principal Component 1 (High Social Capital)	Factor Loadings
Most people can be trusted	0.68
People in college can be trusted	0.56
All things considered I would say I am happy	0.55
There are several people at college with whom I can discuss difficulties	0.58

Principal Component 2 (College/Neighbourhood Focus)	
Inadequate transport is a barrier to being involved in college life	0.59
Distance from home to college is a barrier to being involved in college life	0.56
People in the neighbourhood where I live can be trusted	0.56

From a randomly selected set of eight classes across a range of subject disciplines, 85 students were asked to complete the questionnaire and 79 questionnaires were completed. The responses to the questionnaire were coded numerically (i.e. Strongly Agree=1, Agree=2, Neutral=3, Disagree=4, Strongly Disagree 5) and entered into an SPSS spreadsheet for analysis.

Principal Component Analysis (PCA) was applied to the responses to the questionnaire in order to help explain some of the relationships between variables. The aim was to uncover patterns of responses that might be usefully represented in Personas. In PCA, the linear combination of variables that accounts for the largest amount of variance in the sample is the first Principal Component. The second Principal Component is the linear combination of the variables, uncorrelated with the first Component, that accounts for the maximum amount of the remaining variation in the data, and so on. There are statistical considerations to how many Components should be extracted but here we focus on generating two Components – since that would yield four Personas (any more Personas being unwieldy).

In order to assist the interpretation of the factors, they were rotated using the Equamax method (a combination of orthogonal and oblique rotation methods). Table 1 shows the questions that were highly associated with the first two Principal Components. These groups of questions were examined in order to identify the common underlying themes. These were defined as being "High Social Capital" and "College/Neighbourhood Focussed".

Therefore, all the individuals in the study can be said to vary along these two dimensions and Figure 1 shows preliminary Personas derived from these dimensions. The horizontal axis in Figure 1 shows increasing Social Capital; the vertical axis shows increasing college versus neighbourhood focus.

5   Discussion

Principal Component Analysis is a powerful tool for data reduction that aims to capture the underlying patterns in complex data. We have applied this method to the problem of representing characteristics of the mobile user. The resulting profiles summarize the characteristics that tend to go together measured by people's answers to a questionnaire. These descriptions lead to particular Personas that would certainly not have emerged from sifting through the questionnaires in an unsystematic way. We would expect that the long term value is that the Personas built upon this data have greater validity than those derived from a partial reading of the data or worse, from imagination of researchers and software developers.

The results must be interpreted bearing in mind one aspect of human thinking that is both a strength and a weakness: the ability to make projections based upon partial data. This means that people will tend to infer characteristics of someone based upon partial information. It is better to base this on data.

One question that emerges is whether Personas should have characteristics that are more "central" or more "extreme". On the one hand "extreme" characteristics may be more memorable on the other hand they are less realistic.

One question differentiating people in the analysis is the existing degree of affiliation (trust) they feel towards their college community. Can technology alone be used to enhance or develop interaction between people who are already alienated? This seems unlikely. However, if mobile information services are linked to existing contacts (e.g. fellow students who are already known), there may be potential for enhancing Social Capital.

So an advantage of these techniques may be to help a design team focus on a Persona (section of the population) with the most potential for making use of a service idea – in this context, it might be students who are focused more towards their neighbourhood due to considerations such as distance e.g. "Hometown Harry". The eventual outcome is to allow developers to imagine "Hometown Harry" in a mobile context and ask the question "would Harry use this feature?" and then to derive useful answers.

Finally, the authors would like to thank their colleagues Aisling Hickey, Cyril Connolly along with the anonymous reviewers for their help in preparing this paper.

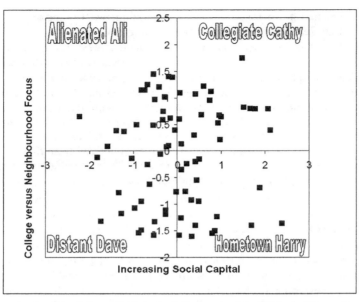

Fig. 1. Personas developed from the Principal Components in Table 1. The scatterplot shows individuals in the study in relation to the two Principal Components

References

[1]   Putman, R. D. (1999). *Bowling Alone*. NY: Simon and Schuster
[2]   Resnick, P. (2002). Beyond Bowling Together: SocioTechnicalCapital. In J. M. Carroll (Ed). *HCI in the New Millenium*. . Addison-Wesley. (pages 247-272)
[3]   Kennedy School of Government, Harvard University (2000) The Social Capital Community Benchmark Saguaro Seminar: Civil Engagement in America
[4]   Cooper (1999) The inmates are running the asylum. Macmillan
[5]   Grudin, J. and Pruitt, J.(2002) : Personas, participatory design and product development: An infrastructure for engagement. Proc. PDC (Participatory Design Conference).144-161

M3I in a Pedestrian Navigation & Exploration System

Rainer Wasinger, Christoph Stahl, and Antonio Krüger

DFKI GmbH,
66123 Saarbrücken, Germany
{rainer.wasinger,christoph.stahl,antonio.krueger}@dfki.de

Abstract. In this paper, we describe a near-complete Pocket PC implementation of a Mobile Multi-Modal Interaction (M3I) platform for pedestrian navigation. The platform is designed to easily support indoor and outdoor navigation tasks, and uses the combination of several modalities for presentation output and user input. Whereas 2D/3D-graphics and synthesized speech are used to present useful information on routes and places, fused input from embedded speech and gesture recognition engines allow for situated user interaction.

1 Introduction

Mobile navigation services are becoming one of the more successful applications of 3G mobile communication. However, the use of a navigation and exploration system on the go, poses special requirements on the design of appropriate presentation and interaction techniques. This paper presents our M3I-platform, which incorporates different presentation and interaction techniques to provide flexible and robust levels of user interaction in an indoor and outdoor environment. Our M3I-platform is unique in that it combines mobile 2D/3D graphics with synthesized speech generation, and the fusion of both speech and gesture input through the use of multiple recognizers. All of this functionality is embedded on a predominantly off-the-shelf mobile device.

Different approaches to mobile navigation and exploration services have been investigated in the past. Whereas first versions ran on laptops [1,2] with limited interaction possibilities, more recent approaches use PDAs [3] that are equipped with touch-screens and therefore allow for at least simple stylus gestures. Some of the newer approaches combine 2D and 3D representations of the environment [4]. A strong focus on distributed multi-modal interaction is demonstrated in [5]. Whereas all these systems focus on single aspects of mobile multi-modal user interactions, the M3I-platform presented here aims at combining all of these features on one mobile device to support users in navigating and exploring the real world.

2 Design Requirements

The navigation system allows a user to download predefined routes onto a PDA, and then select a route for *indoor* and *outdoor* pedestrian navigation and exploration. The

L. Chittaro (Ed.): Mobile HCI 2003, LNCS 2795, pp. 481–485, 2003.

navigation mode directs a user from start to destination through combined speech and graphics output, as shown in Fig.1. The *exploration* mode relaxes the direction information presented through speech and graphics, and instead allows the user to freely roam or explore a place. The navigation mode is best suited when a user is either under a high *cognitive load* (e.g. business people), or simply uninterested with their immediate surroundings, while the exploration mode is best suited to people with more time (e.g. travelers). For natural and flexible use, such a system must also be *multi-modal*. Route descriptions may be presented via 2D/3D graphic visualizations and an audio headset, and user input can take the form of combined speech and stylus requests, incorporating objects on the PDA's display, or objects in the real world around them (see Fig. 2). Possible user inputs are for example "what is that [gesture]?", or "describe this [gesture] church". The language and objects that the user refers to on the map, such as parks, churches, museums, and other buildings, must also be known to the system. This requires the incorporation of *dynamic speech grammars* and *graphics* that can adapt to a changing environment. Other features of the system include the ability to zoom and to rotate the map (reduces the user's cognitive load in associating the map with the environment [6]), a birdseye and egocentric view (egocentric shown in Fig.1 and 2), and a feature to record memos to geographical locations on the map.

3   The M3I Navigation Platform

The pedestrian navigation system comprises a navigation server and a Pocket PC. The Pocket PC component developed in C/C++, incorporates the IBM Embedded ViaVoice formant-based speech synthesizer and dynamic rule grammar based recognizer. The 2D- and 3D-graphics are generated via the embedded Cortona VRML[1]-browser. A magnetic compass provides the user's (i.e. the PDA's) current facing direction used in determining gestures. GPS provides further sensor information such as velocity and direction, and is also required to locate the user when outside. Infrared beacons are used to locate a user when inside. PDA communication with the server is via a standard HTTP connection, for example through a bluetooth capable GPRS/UMTS mobile phone, WLAN, or a USB desktop connection.

3.1   GIS Server

The only part of this system that is not embedded on the Pocket PC is a custom made GIS server, based on the open source GRASS[2] project. It generates the graphic and text-based route descriptions for a particular trip, and contains street names and very limited landmark information. This is not currently being processed on the PDA due to performance issues. Outdoor navigation is based on commercially available material from NavTech, but data on indoor floor plans and detailed landmark information (e.g. opening hours, cost and description) have to be modeled by hand. All informa-

---

[1]   Virtual Reality Markup Language
[2]   More information on the grass project can be found at http://grass.baylor.edu

tion that is necessary for the presentation and interaction is collected into a set of XML files and passed to the embedded components of the M3I-platform.

3.2   Speech

The speech synthesizer receives navigational data such as street names, distance, turning angle and landmark information from the XML files, from which it then generates appropriate route descriptions. Long, middle and short phrases are created for each segment and presented to the user in combination with graphics.

The recognizer currently implements the use of static rule grammars that cover command-and-control functionality (e.g. zoom in), trip queries (e.g. where is my start?), and simple multi-modal interaction (e.g. what is *that* [gesture]). It is now intended to extend this functionality by incorporating dynamic rule grammars that can more closely model objects on the map such as landmarks and streets. These objects are generally difficult to manage because they change when a new map is loaded. Aside from the base functionality provided by our static pre-compiled grammars, three sets of dynamic grammars (see Fig. 1) provide extended interaction for the user.

The first dynamic grammar will allow for interaction with landmark types, while the second will allow for interaction with specific street and landmark names. These grammars will be created each time a map is loaded, but due to the large amount of specific street and landmark information, the latter will only be activated upon request. A third grammar analogous to information found in tourist pamphlets (e.g. description, opening hours, cost) will allow for detailed interaction with the individual landmarks. This interaction is landmark dependent as the different landmarks including parks, churches and museums all display significantly different characteristics. The above strategy, in combination with our relatively small map sizes, and acoustic models designed for hand-held devices will allow for robust rates of user-recognition.

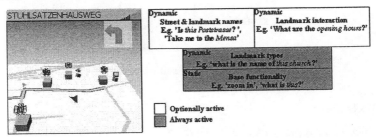

Fig.1. Static and dynamic speech grammars, and a PDA screen-shot of a route containing landmark interaction objects

3.3   Gesture and Sensor Fusion

The fusion of speech with gesture increases the flexibility and naturalness of a user's interaction. It also supports a more robust level of interaction in that non-conflicting but overlapped verbal and gesture segments (e.g. describe this [gesture] church') can reduce the recognition search space. This also gives rise to the need to unify results, as described in [7]. We use a blackboard architecture to capture the results of gesture, speech and sensor input, and a media fusion module to combine these inputs based on timestamps. Gesture input can be either *intra*, in that the user points to an object on the display through the use of a stylus, or it can be *extra* in that the PDA is used as a pointing stick to point at an object in the real world. Intra gestures are currently limited to 'point-like' gestures that can be used to query landmarks, but we plan to extend this to include 'line-like' gestures that will enable the querying of street names. Intra and extra gestures are both illustrated in Fig. 2.

Extra gestures are currently detected with the help of a magnetic compass/GPS CF-Card from Pointstar that is inserted into the PDA. Based on the movement and the position of the PDA, the system is able to answer requests on the landmarks that a user is currently looking at. These sensors can also provide information on the user's velocity (e.g. stopped, walking, running), and whether the device is being looked at by the user. This allows for better adaptation of the presentation, for example by placing higher importance on either the graphical or speech modality. Sensor fusion is also used to improve localization by combining information from infrared beacons, GPS and the magnetic compass. A further improvement is achieved through map-matching, i.e. snapping the user to the closest point on a route segment of their current path.

Fig. 2. Intra and extra gestures respectively

3.4   3D Graphics

The graphics architecture of the M3I-platform is based on the Cortona VRML 3D component, which consists of three layers. The bottom layer deals with the loading and rendering of the 3D-VRML scene. All visible objects are represented as nodes in a scene graph, and interaction through gesture is provided by adding touch-sensors to geometry nodes. The middle layer provides a generic C++ class that implements the functionality to model interactive 3D objects as a complex collection of basic VRML nodes, and provides simple methods for creation and localization. On the upper layer, the application derives classes to represent landmarks, users and media-icons from the generic 3D object class. These classes store all symbolic information about the object such as name and description, and also define the individual 3D geometry in VRML code. The consistent object-oriented representation of all localized objects in the application, allows for the handling of both data and graphics by a single object reference. This simplifies the unification of object references in the media fusion module, based on timestamps.

4   Conclusions

In this paper we have described the design issues arising in the implementation of our M3I-platform for pedestrian navigation and exploration. The platform combines 2D/3D-graphics and synthesized route descriptions, with combined speech and gesture recognition. It is unique in embedding all of this functionality on a mobile device. The system is near completion and has been demonstrated in the German cities of Saarbrücken and Munich for both indoor and outdoor use. Future work will take the form of user studies, and we plan to make parts of the M3I platform publicly available on completion.

References

[1]   K. Cheverst, N. Davies, K. Mitchell, A. Friday, and C. Efstratiou. Developing a context-aware electronic tourist guide: Some issues and experiences. ,CHI 2000, Amsterdam, 2000.

[2]   J. Baus, A. Krüger, and W. Wahlster. A Resource-Adaptive Mobile Navigation System. In: IUI2002: International Conference on Intelligent User, ACM Press, 2002.

[3]   G. Popischil, M. Umlauft, E. Michlmayr: Designing Lol@, a mobile tourist navigation guide, In: Proceedings of HCI with mobile devices 02, Springer LCNS 2411, 2002.

[4]   C. Kray, K. Laakso, C. Elting, V. Coors: Presenting Route Instructions on mobile devices, In: Proceedings of IUI 03:Intelligent User Interfaces, ACM Press, 2003.

[5]   Cohen, P., Johnston, M., McGee, M., Oviatt, S., Pittman, J., Smith, I.,Chen, L., Clow, J.: Quickset: Multimodal interaction for distributed applications, In: Proceedings of the Fifth ACM International Multimedia Conference, 1997, pp 31-40.

[6]   2. Hunt, E., Walter, D.: Orientation and wayfinding: A Review (Tech. Rep. Nr.N00014-96-0380, Arlington: Office of Naval Research, 1999.

[7]   Alexandersson, J., Becker, T.: Overlay as the Basic Operation for Discourse Processing in a Multimodal Dialogue System, Proceedings of the IJCAI Workshop Knowledge and Reasoning in Practical Dialogue Systems, 2001.

Mobile Devices:
Opportunities for Users with Special Needs*

Enrico Bertini and Stephen Kimani

Università di Roma "La Sapienza", Dipartimento di Informatica e Sistemistica
Via Salaria 113, 00198 Roma, Italy
{bertini,kimani}@dis.uniroma1.it

Abstract. Breakthroughs in mobile and wireless technologies have rev-
olutionized the world in virtually every aspect. While much work has
been and is being done regarding the opportunities and challenges arising from these technologies, much less exists on the unique opportunities
and implications the same devices present and raise to users with special
needs. Furthermore, the existing little work is normally specific to only
a certain type of disability or device. While addressing a specific type of
disability or mobile device has its place, it is also significant to ensure
that one is operating based on a holistic perspective/framework of the
entire audience of the disabled mobile device users.

1 Introduction

Advances in mobile and wireless technologies have, to a great extent, revolu-
tionized the world. A user carrying out one or many parallel activities, from
virtually anywhere at anytime while at the same time interacting with other
user(s) has become commonplace. While the opportunities, challenges and benefits stemming from mobile device usage are clearly evident and widely published,
much less exists about the unique opportunities and requirements mobile devices
present and pose to users who have special needs. There have been and are various efforts pertaining to mobile devices and users with special needs. Most of
the efforts have addressed the two arenas as two independent or separate aspects. Surprisingly enough, the few research efforts that cover both arenas are
normally specific to only a certain type of disability (or even device). We should
quickly point out that we do commend such efforts as they venture to ensure
that a certain type of disability (or device) is addressed to reasonable depth.
While we acknowledge that addressing only a particular type of disability (or
mobile device) has its place, we do however find it also worth to operate based
on a rather comprehensive or holistic framework of the entire audience of the
disabled mobile device users. A few related efforts are discussed in the sequel.

* The work presented in this paper is funded by the Italian Ministry for Education, University and Research (MIUR) through the MAIS (Multichannel
Adaptive Information Systems) project. More information can be found at
http://black.elet.polimi.it/mais.

L. Chittaro (Ed.): Mobile HCI 2003, LNCS 2795, pp. 486–491, 2003.

Fellbaum's enlightening work on general speech and hearing technology [1] has some hints on the same technology with respect to the deaf and the speech impaired. Although Freitas et al [2] focus on mobile phones, their work does partially propose various ideas that can be helpful toward meeting the special needs of the disabled and the elderly. Abascal et al [3] explore various implications on the elderly, emanating from the use of mobile phones. The research effort [4] presents display techniques to aid visually impaired users by the enhancement of the screen objects whereas [5] focuses on the use of haptic interfaces for motion-impaired users. Though existing accessibility standards e.g. the ones proposed by ETSI [1] often pertain to the wide arena of Information and Communications Technologies (ICTs), they have resourceful information that can be exploited in mobile computing to support users with special needs.

The primary purpose of this paper is to describe the unique opportunities that mobile devices present to users with special needs such as the disabled/impaired, the elderly, and the sick. Rather than focusing on a certain type of disability or mobile device, the paper presents the discussion based on a more holistic perspective of this type of user audience.

2   Opportunities for Users with Special Needs

This section starts by presenting an analysis of the unique opportunities for users with special needs that are offered by mobile devices. It should be pointed out that such users do have special requirements. Toward ensuring that their special needs are catered for, this section later describes various approaches that can be used to address the special challenges facing such users in the context of mobile computing.

2.1   What the Mobile Devices Offer to the Disabled

The core benefit concerning the use of mobile devices for disabled users is that the devices' mobility and connectivity can assure the users a constant "companion". The applications of mobile devices for disabled users fall in the following three classes:

Mobiles as an Aid to Carry Out Functions: Mobile devices can host applications that permit the users to be actively involved in everyday activities, as though they were not disabled e.g. the physically impaired can use the devices to remotely instruct PCs [6] or even lifts, doors, ATMs, etc.

Mobiles as a Means to Communicate: Since the devices are mobile and can be connected, the disabled users can always carry them and communicate with them. Communication from virtually anywhere is hence rendered easier. In fact, the devices can function even when the user's inherent communication functionalities are impaired [7].

---

[1] http://www.etsi.org

Mobiles as Assistants: Mobile devices can exploit the context which is in itself a great opportunity for the disabled e.g. advising the users of particular dangers, acting as guides, etc.

Besides the foregoing direct opportunities deriving from the increase in availability, there are also some indirect opportunities arising from the use of mobile devices including:

Non-conventional Interactions: Many of the standard settings are no longer applicable in mobile computing. The foregoing challenge is indeed an opportunity to carry out corresponding studies. For instance, investigating relevant interaction paradigms that take into account users with special needs. (Section 2.2 has more information on such aspects.)

Democratization: Through mobile devices, computing technology is no longer a territory of a selected few. In part, the extended user audience stems from the declining cost of mobile and wireless technologies, and the type of operations/work mobile devices are designed to support. Consequently, more disabled users have managed to access or acquire the devices. (Section 2.2 has more information on the economic aspect.)

2.2   Toward Fulfilling the Users' Special Needs

As it was observed in Section 2.1, mobile devices present many opportunities for the elderly, the impaired/disabled, and the sick. Nonetheless, the users have special needs/requirements. In the sequel, is a discussion of various approaches that can be adopted toward fulfilling the special needs of these users while interacting with mobile devices.

Alerting Techniques: Mobile devices should use alerting techniques that can be comprehended by users with special needs. Alerts are often signaled in an audible (sound), visible (flashing light) and felt (vibrating transducer) form. The alert is also coupled with some message/cue (e.g. audio, graphical/icon, text) pointing out what the alert is for.

Wearability: The market of mobile devices and wireless technologies offers a lot toward rendering mobile devices wearable. With wearability, the disabled user need not worry about physically reaching or misplacing the device. An interesting example is the wearable PDA for the blind [2].

---

[2] http:// www.freedomscientific.com

Non-conventional Input and Output Paradigms *Auditory Services and Interfaces:* Despite the challenges that come with auditory interfaces [1], they still can be very useful to the disabled especially the physically impaired and/or the visually impaired. It is important to ensure that the voice interface has a volume control that is easily accessible. Speech input and output devices (hearing aids) for mobile devices do exist and some can actually be worn. There are also various services that go together with voice interfaces. For any audio output/input, it is highly desirable, though non-trivial, that the system be able to make available the corresponding textual output/input and vice versa, if the situation demands so. On the whole, it might be worth exploring the relevance of enabling mobile devices to support/handle input and output in various data formats and being able to interpret from any of the formats and convert to any of the formats.

Visual Interfaces: The small screen size of mobile devices has been a major challenge in ubiquitous computing. It would be interesting to see how existing proposals could be useful in addressing problems that the disabled experience when using the small screens. It might be worth investigating the effectiveness of developing customized/personalized visual output devices for users with special needs. Using pictorial representations to represent functionalities offered by the mobile device can be helpful especially to the cognitively impaired. On another note, the mobile device could offer an optional and special character set with fewer characters and that of a larger size than the standard set.

Keyboards/keypads: As far as the keyboard/keypad is concerned, special keyboards/keypads may be considered. The keyboards/keypads could still offer the traditional 5-key dot/cue. It could be important to providing tactile, audio, and visual cues on the keyboard/keypad. Moreover a strong contrast of the keys and the labels should be adopted; in fact contrasting should be effectively applied to the whole device. Further, disabled users might find a simple keyboard/keypad having only a few (and slightly bigger) key buttons reasonably sufficient. Such a keyboard/keypad would enable the users (including the cognitively impaired) to easily/quickly perform operations.

Simple and Shallow Menu/Command System: The mobile device should enable the user to access certain functionality without having to go through a lot of steps. The menu/command system should be easy to understand, simple and direct, with help (described in the next discussion on Multilevel assistance) whenever necessary.

Multilevel Assistance: This assistance/help facility may comprise two layers for instance local/device-based help and remote/service center-based help. On the whole, help should be directly/easily accessible, interactive and easy to understand/interpret. Some circumstances would necessitate the automatic activation of help (e.g. connectivity status, battery status). Consider in some detail the latter example of battery status. If the device's battery needs recharging, the device could use the aforementioned alerting techniques. If the user does not respond to the alert (local help), the device could activate service center-based help by notifying the center about the situation.

User Interface Considerations: The user interface could be designed in a manner such that it adapts its interaction mechanism(s) and presentation style(s) in order to meet the specific needs of a particular disabled user. Such a feature essentially requires that various aspects of the particular user be modeled. Such aspects include: the user, the information, and the context. Moreover, it is worth embracing the *design for all* or *universal design* approach [8, 9].

Economic Aspects: It is gratifying to observe that the prices of mobile devices and wireless technologies are decreasing. However, the prices are still fairly high for the disabled users who normally are financially disadvantaged. Various stakeholders regarding matters pertaining to pricing and social welfare e.g. government(s), organizations, etc should help to make the mobile devices affordable to users with special needs (e.g. subsidized prices, donations). It is interesting to realize that, though *design for all* may be costly in the short-term, it is ultimately beneficial not only to the users but also to businesses.

3   Conclusions

In this paper we have addressed the question of the unique opportunities mobile devices offer to the disabled. We have also presented various approaches that can be used toward meeting the special needs of the disabled. A lot of work is yet to be done and the success of the next generation of user interfaces and devices depends in part on our understanding of how disabled users can benefit from these new technologies and in part on the evolution of markets and political/sociological directions. There is still much to be done, novel and otherwise, toward supporting the exploitation of this great opportunity and addressing respective challenges.

References

[1] K. Fellbaum: Speech and Hearing Technology: A Critical Review. In: Proceedings of COST 219 Seminar on Speech and Hearing Technology. (2000)
[2] D. Freitas and J. Gjöderum and G. Hellström and M. Soede: Mobile Telephony. In: Telecommunications for All. (1995)
[3] J. Abascal and A. Civit: Mobile Communication for Older People: New Opportunities for Autonomous Life. In: Proceedings of EC/NSF Workshop on Universal Accessibility of Ubiquitous Computing: Providing for the Elderly. (2001)
[4] Jacko, J.A., Scott, I.U., Sainfort, F., Barnard, L., Edwards, P.J., Emery, V.K., Kongnakorn, T., Moloney, K.P., Zorich, B.S.: Older adults and visual impairment: What do exposure times and accuracy tell us about performance gains associated with multimodal feedback? In: Proceedings of Conference on Human Factors in Computing Systems, ACM Press (2003)

[5] Hwang, F., Keates, S., Langdon, P., Clarkson, P.J.: Multiple haptic targets for motion-impaired computer users. In: Proceedings of Conference on Human Factors in Computing Systems, ACM Press (2003)

[6] Myers, B.A., Wobbrock, J.O., Yang, S., Yeung, B., Nichols, J., Miller, R.: Using handhelds to help people with motor impairments. In: Proceedings of Conference on Assistive technologies, ACM Press (2002)

[7] Ashraf, S., Judson, A., Ricketts, I.W., Waller, A., Alm, N., Gordon, B., MacAulay, F., Brodie, J.K., Etchels, M., Warden, A., Shearer, A.J.: Capturing phrases for icu-talk, a communication aid for intubated intensive care patients. In: Proceedings of Conference on Assistive Technologies, ACM Press (2002)

[8] Story, M.F.: Maximising usability: The principles of universal design. Assistive Technology Journal 10 (1998) 4–12

[9] Stephanidis, C., Salvendy, G., Akoumianakis, D., Bevan, N., Brewer, J., Emiliani, P.L., Galetsas, A., Haataja, S., Iakovidis, I., Jacko, J., Jenkins, P., Karshmer, A., Korn, P., Marcus, A., Murphy, H., Stary, C., Vanderheiden, G., Weber, G., Ziegler, J.: Towards an information society for all. International Journal of Human-Computer Interaction 10 (1998) 107–134

Author Index

Lecture Notes in Computer Science

For information about Vols. 1–2704
please contact your bookseller or Springer-Verlag

Vol. 2739: R. Traunmüller (Ed.), Electronic Government. Proceedings, 2003. XVIII, 511 pages. 2003.

Vol. 2740: E. Burke, P. De Causmaecker (Eds.), Practice and Theory of Automated Timetabling IV. Proceedings, 2002. XII, 361 pages. 2003.

Vol. 2741: F. Baader (Ed.), Automated Deduction – CADE-19. Proceedings, 2003. XII, 503 pages. 2003. (Subseries LNAI).

Vol. 2742: R. N. Wright (Ed.), Financial Cryptography. Proceedings, 2003. VIII, 321 pages. 2003.

Vol. 2743: L. Cardelli (Ed.), ECOOP 2003 – Object-Oriented Programming. Proceedings, 2003. X, 501 pages. 2003.

Vol. 2744: V. Mařík, D. McFarlane, P. Valckenaers (Eds.), Holonic and Multi-Agent Systems for Manufacturing. Proceedings, 2003. XI, 322 pages. 2003. (Subseries LNAI).

Vol. 2745: M. Guo, L.T. Yang (Eds.), Parallel and Distributed Processing and Applications. Proceedings, 2003. XII, 450 pages. 2003.

Vol. 2746: A. de Moor, W. Lex, B. Ganter (Eds.), Conceptual Structures for Knowledge Creation and Communication. Proceedings, 2003. XI, 405 pages. 2003. (Subseries LNAI).

Vol. 2747: B. Rovan, P. Vojtáš (Eds.), Mathematical Foundations of Computer Science 2003. Proceedings, 2003. XIII, 692 pages. 2003.

Vol. 2748: F. Dehne, J.-R. Sack, M. Smid (Eds.), Algorithms and Data Structures. Proceedings, 2003. XII, 522 pages. 2003.

Vol. 2749: J. Bigun, T. Gustavsson (Eds.), Image Analysis. Proceedings, 2003. XXII, 1174 pages. 2003.

Vol. 2750: T. Hadzilacos, Y. Manolopoulos, J.F. Roddick, Y. Theodoridis (Eds.), Advances in Spatial and Temporal Databases. Proceedings, 2003. XIII, 525 pages. 2003.

Vol. 2751: A. Lingas, B.J. Nilsson (Eds.), Fundamentals of Computation Theory. Proceedings, 2003. XII, 433 pages. 2003.

Vol. 2752: G.A. Kaminka, P.U. Lima, R. Rojas (Eds.), RoboCup 2002: Robot Soccer World Cup VI. XVI, 498 pages. 2003. (Subseries LNAI).

Vol. 2753: F. Maurer, D. Wells (Eds.), Extreme Programming and Agile Methods – XP/Agile Universe 2003. Proceedings, 2003. XI, 215 pages. 2003.

Vol. 2754: M. Schumacher, Security Engineering with Patterns. XIV, 208 pages. 2003.

Vol. 2756: N. Petkov, M.A. Westenberg (Eds.), Computer Analysis of Images and Patterns. Proceedings, 2003. XVIII, 781 pages. 2003.

Vol. 2758: D. Basin, B. Wolff (Eds.), Theorem Proving in Higher Order Logics. Proceedings, 2003. X, 367 pages. 2003.

Vol. 2759: O.H. Ibarra, Z. Dang (Eds.), Implementation and Application of Automata. Proceedings, 2003. XI, 312 pages. 2003.

Vol. 2761: R. Amadio, D. Lugiez (Eds.), CONCUR 2003 - Concurrency Theory. Proceedings, 2003. XI, 524 pages. 2003.

Vol. 2762: G. Dong, C. Tang, W. Wang (Eds.), Advances in Web-Age Information Management. Proceedings, 2003. XIII, 512 pages. 2003.

Vol. 2763: V. Malyshkin (Ed.), Parallel Computing Technologies. Proceedings, 2003. XIII, 570 pages. 2003.

Vol. 2764: S. Arora, K. Jansen, J.D.P. Rolim, A. Sahai (Eds.), Approximation, Randomization, and Combinatorial Optimization. Proceedings, 2003. IX, 409 pages. 2003.

Vol. 2765: R. Conradi, A.I. Wang (Eds.), Empirical Methods and Studies in Software Engineering. VIII, 279 pages. 2003.

Vol. 2766: S. Behnke, Hierarchical Neural Networks for Image Interpretation. XII, 224 pages. 2003.

Vol. 2769: T. Koch, I. T. Sølvberg (Eds.), Research and Advanced Technology for Digital Libraries. Proceedings, 2003. XV, 536 pages. 2003.

Vol. 2776: V. Gorodetsky, L. Popyack, V. Skormin (Eds.), Computer Network Security. Proceedings, 2003. XIV, 470 pages. 2003.

Vol. 2777: B. Schölkopf, M.K. Warmuth (Eds.), Learning Theory and Kernel Machines. Proceedings, 2003. XIV, 746 pages. 2003. (Subseries LNAI).

Vol. 2779: C.D. Walter, Ç.K. Koç, C. Paar (Eds.), Cryptographic Hardware and Embedded Systems – CHES 2003. Proceedings, 2003. XIII, 441 pages. 2003.

Vol. 2782: M. Klusch, A. Omicini, S. Ossowski, H. Laamanen (Eds.), Cooperative Information Agents VII. Proceedings, 2003. XI, 345 pages. 2003. (Subseries LNAI).

Vol. 2783: W. Zhou, P. Nicholson, B. Corbitt, J. Fong (Eds.), Advances in Web-Based Learning – ICWL 2003. Proceedings, 2003. XV, 552 pages. 2003.

Vol. 2786: F. Oquendo (Ed.), Software Process Technology. Proceedings, 2003. X, 173 pages. 2003.

Vol. 2787: J. Timmis, P. Bentley, E. Hart (Eds.), Artificial Immune Systems. Proceedings, 2003. XI, 299 pages. 2003.

Vol. 2789: L. Böszörményi, P. Schojer (Eds.), Modular Programming Languages. Proceedings, 2003. XIII, 271 pages. 2003.

Vol. 2790: H. Kosch, L. Böszörményi, H. Hellwagner (Eds.), Euro-Par 2003 Parallel Processing. Proceedings, 2003. XXXV, 1320 pages. 2003.

Vol. 2794: P. Kemper, W. H. Sanders (Eds.), Computer Performance Evaluation. Proceedings, 2003. X, 309 pages. 2003.

Vol. 2795: L. Chittaro (Ed.), Human-Computer Interaction with Mobile Devices and Services. Proceedings, 2003. XV, 494 pages. 2003.

Vol. 2796: M. Cialdea Mayer, F. Pirri (Eds.), Automated Reasoning with Analytic Tableaux and Related Methods. Proceedings, 2003. X, 271 pages. 2003. (Subseries LNAI).

Vol. 2803: M. Baaz, J.A. Makowsky (Eds.), Computer Science Logic. Proceedings, 2003. XII, 589 pages. 2003.

Vol. 2805: K. Araki, S. Gnesi, D. Mandrioli (Eds.), FME 2003: Formal Methods. Proceedings, 2003. XVII, 942 pages. 2003.

Vol. 2810: M.R. Berthold, H.-J. Lenz, E. Bradley, R. Kruse, C. Borgelt (Eds.), Advances in Intelligent Data Analysis V. Proceedings, 2003. XV, 624 pages. 2003.

Vol. 2817: D. Konstantas, M. Leonard, Y. Pigneur, S. Patel (Eds.), Object-Oriented Information Systems. Proceedings, 2003. XII, 426 pages. 2003.